JOURNEY TO THE JONES ACT

U.S. Merchant Marine Policy

1776-1920

Charlie Papavizas

JOURNEY TO THE JONES ACT

U.S. Merchant Marine Policy
1776-1920

Charlie Papavizas

JOURNEY TO THE JONES ACT
U.S. MERCHANT MARINE POLICY 1776-1920

COPYRIGHT © 2024 CONSTANTINE G. PAPAVIZAS

All rights reserved. No part of this publication may be reproduced or transmitted in any form or by any means, electronic or mechanical, including photocopying, recording, or any information storage and retrieval system now known or to be invented, without permission from the author.

ISBN 978-1-962729-04-8 (PAPERBACK)

PUBLISHED IN THE UNITED STATES OF AMERICA BY FORTIS, AN ADDUCENT NONFICTION IMPRINT.

ADDUCENT, INC.
JACKSONVILLE, FLORIDA
ADDUCENTCREATIVE.COM

TITLE PAGE BACKGROUND PHOTO: HOG ISLAND, NATIONAL ARCHIVES.

Contents

Foreword i
Preface iv
Dramatis Personae vii
Chapter 1—Introduction 1
Chapter 2—English Origins 14
    Back to Discriminating Duties 15
    Charta Maritima 17
Chapter 3—Setting the American Maritime Policy Stage 26
    The Sloop Liberty 26
    The Plan of Treaties 30
    Silas Deane and Lord Sheffield 33
Chapter 4—Early American Navigation Policy 48
    Articles of Confederation Policy Failure 48
    Constitutional Convention—Slavery and Navigation 50
    The Second and Third Acts of the Republic 54
Chapter 5—Era of Free Trade Reciprocity 67
    1815 U.S.—Great Britain Commercial Convention 67
    March 1, 1817, Navigation Act 69
Chapter 6—First Government Subsidies 80
    The Unlucky Collins Line 81
    The Pacific Mail Steamship Company 87
Chapter 7—American Civil War 95
    C.S.S. Alabama 96
    The American Claims—Treaty of Washington 99
    The Great Flag Exodus 101
Chapter 8—Lynch Committee 109
    Lynch Committee Report 110
    John Codman ("Captain Ringbolt") 112
    Lynch Committee Proposed Legislation 115

Chapter 9—Subsidies vs. Free Ships 123
   The Three Mainers 124
   1882 Dingley Committee 129
   1884 Dingley Act 130
   1891 Ocean Mail Act 133
   1893-1895 Free Ship Legislation 138
Chapter 10—Discriminating Duties Return 147
   Eugene Tyler Chamberlain 148
   1894 Tariff 154
   1897 Dingley Tariff 155
   1913 Underwood Tariff 157
Chapter 11—The Spanish-American War 165
   A Mongrel Fleet 167
   Nanshan and Zafiro 171
Chapter 12—The Great Subsidy Stalemate 181
   The Delaware River—the American Clyde 182
   Hanna-Payne-Frye Bounty Bills 188
   The Merchant Marine (Gallinger) Commission 194
Chapter 13—Coastwise Trade 211
   Passengers and Dredging 211
   Philippines and Hawaii 213
   Coastwise Whack-A-Mole 221
Chapter 14—Cargo Preferences, Tolls, and Free Ships ... 236
   1904 Cargo Preference Act 237
   Voyage of the Great White Fleet 239
   Panama Canal Act 244
Chapter 15—Combinations and Conferences 260
   The American Peril 261
   Royal Commission on Shipping Rings 268
   Alexander Committee Report 270
Chapter 16—Seamen's Rights 279
   Special Status of Seamen 280

  Land-Sharks, Land-Rats, and Other Vermin 284
  Andrew Furuseth.. 288
  1915 Seamen's Act 294
Chapter 17—Wesley Livsey Jones 319
  Yakima Jones 319
  The Five-And-Ten Senator 326
Chapter 18—1916 Shipping Act 337
  William Gibbs McAdoo, Jr.. 338
  Ship Registry Act and War Risk Insurance 344
  Ship Purchase Bill 351
Chapter 19—Shipping Board 378
  The Wooden Ship Controversy 378
  The Board Chairmen 389
Chapter 20—Shipping Board at War and in Peace 410
  Mobilization.. 410
  Hog Island 420
  Virginia Shipbuilding Corporation................................. 429
  Demobilization and the Paris Peace Talks 436
  Ghost Fleet at Mallows Bay... 444
Chapter 21—Framing the 1920 Merchant Marine Act........ 466
  Shipping Board Proposals... 467
  1919 Senate Hearings and Jones's Proposals 471
  The Greene Bill... 474
  1920 Senate Hearings... 478
  Origin of the "Jones Act"... 487
  Commerce Committee Bill... 492
Chapter 22—1920 Merchant Marine Act Enactment.......... 506
  Senate Consideration.. 506
  End Game 513
  Aftermath 519

Chapter 23—Conclusion 540
Acknowledgments 544
Appendix 546
    World War II Liberty Ships Named for Dramatis Personae 546
    Timeline of Significant U.S. Merchant Marine Legislation 1789–1920 548
Selected Bibliography 559
    Original Sources and Government Publications 559
    Books, Dissertations, and Authored Web Sites 567
    Periodicals and Journals 573
Index 577

Foreword

When I was the seventy-fifth U.S. secretary of the Navy, the U.S. merchant marine was always in my peripheral vision–omnipresent, important, but not seen as central to the Navy's core missions. The U.S.-flag vessel *Maersk Alabama* had a moment shortly before I was confirmed in May 2009, and the U.S. Navy and Navy SEALs performed extraordinary service in saving Captain Richard Phillips and the vessel. But that was the exception and the U.S. merchant marine, although valuable to the Nation, remained generally outside the public eye.

The relationship with U.S. merchant marine policy became more direct in the aftermath of the *Deepwater Horizon* oil spill. President Obama asked me to develop the recovery and restoration plan for the Gulf Coast. One of the key operational issues was whether the president should waive something called the "Jones Act" to aid in the spill response. It was obvious to me then that the "Jones Act" animated strong feelings, although it was not clear how a maritime policy could do that. And it was not even obvious that those opinions were grounded in anything other than impressions of the Act rather than a real understanding of where the Jones Act came from and why the United States had adopted it in the first place.

It was about that time that I met Charlie Papavizas, who was a law partner of my roommate at the University of Mississippi and a lifelong friend. Charlie had no trouble explaining the history, the context, and the present-day politics of the Jones Act because that is what he dealt with in his daily practice. He was incredibly enthusiastic about what to many people would seem to be an obscure and complex maritime policy. I appreciated that enthusiasm even if I did not always completely comprehend what he was saying.

It was not until I read Charlie's manuscript that I fully realized what Charlie was talking about. The "Jones Act" is U.S. maritime policy history, and not because of how it is framed today, but because it was the culmination of a long history of English and then American merchant marine ideas. The "Jones Act" teaches us what was tried, what worked, and what did not work.

That history as told in this book is filled with interesting people and events not usually recounted in U.S. history books generally or maritime history books in particular. Senator Wesley Livsey Jones, for whom the "Jones Act" is named, is a good example of someone who should get a better account than has been accorded him to date. Few people know, for example, how influential Jones was on maritime policy long before 1920, saying in 1902 as Congressman, "You may vote for the foreign ship; I will vote for the American ship, and I have no fears of the verdict of the American people on such a proposition."

The connection between my former job, as secretary of the Navy, and the Jones Act became very close during the term of Josephus Daniels, the longest serving secretary in history. Daniels oversaw the creation of the office of Chief of Naval Operations, the top uniformed officer in the Navy. In 1915 he picked Captain William S. Benson as the first CNO. After Benson's retirement from the Navy in 1919 he became the fourth chairman of the United States Shipping Board, a crucial post he held during the debate, passage, and signing of the "Jones Act" in June 1920.

As a complete aside, Josephus Daniels gave rise to an expression in common use today. An ardent prohibitionist, he removed alcohol from Navy ships, a practice which continues to this day. The alcohol was replaced with coffee, about which sailors would very sarcastically say "let's get a cup of Joe."

What Charlie recounts in the long and winding journey to 1920 and the "Jones Act" is not ancient history. The U.S. merchant marine today is at a low ebb, arguably too low to support U.S. national strategic objectives. But as Charlie explains, that was also the case at the outset of the Spanish-American War and at the outset of World War I and at many other points in time in U.S. history. The United States succeeded in obtaining the vessels it needed on each occasion—but both these wars could easily have turned out differently if there had been insufficient cargo vessels to support the U.S. war effort.

Maritime policy no longer commands the level of attention it did during the first 130 years of the country's history recounted in this book. The lessons are nevertheless there to be learned today. In his famous 1890 work, *The Influence of Sea Power Upon History, 1660-1783*, Alfred Thayer Mahan doubted that the United States could have a navy without a merchant marine. Today we act as though that is not true. But the Nation proceeds at its peril if it focuses solely on its armed forces and neglects the supply chain needed by those armed forces including, and especially, the U.S. merchant marine.

Mahan went on to write that "how such a merchant shipping should be built up, whether by subsidies or by free trade, by constant administration of tonics or by free movement in the open air, it is not a military but an economical question." It is an "economical" question, indeed, but also a strategic one and one that should come out of our peripheral vision to be a central consideration. This is an excellent and important book, which frames the history, the context, the characters, and the issues of this overlooked but crucial subject.

—Ray Mabus, 75TH UNITED STATES SECRETARY OF THE NAVY (2009-2017)

Preface

The "Jones Act" is the most widely known American maritime policy law. That is not saying much since maritime policy, critical at the founding of the United States and through much of its early history, has faded from public view.

The Jones Act nevertheless pops up in national affairs often enough, usually in connection with some disaster like a hurricane or an oil spill. In between, the Jones Act tends to be a political football. Some treat it as a hero in the national story, others treat it as a villain.

Those who treat it as a hero argue that the United States cannot defend itself without the Jones Act, and the longevity of the Act is confirmation that the Act is good policy. For those who see villain, the Jones Act inhibits U.S. domestic commercial prosperity and has outlived its usefulness.

The "Jones Act" is, in fact, neither a hero nor a villain. If it were a character in a story, it would be an ill-defined one because the one thing that is undeniable about the popular use of the term "Jones Act" is that it is a flawed label.

The "Jones Act" is not even one "Act." The term is used as a proxy for several U.S. laws that reserve U.S. domestic maritime trade—such as a voyage from Houston to Tampa—to qualified "U.S.-flag" vessels. Such vessels are entitled to fly the U.S. flag by virtue of being registered with the U.S. Coast Guard, much like an automobile is registered in a state. Other laws referred to as the "Jones Act" cover transportation of passengers, towing, dredging, and fishing.

The term "Jones Act" also used to mean something else. It was originally used to refer to the whole of the 1920 Merchant Marine Act. The portion of that Act that deals with the U.S. domestic trade reservation is only a section in the whole law, which mostly deals with U.S. international trade, not domestic trade.

"Jones" is Senator Wesley Livsey Jones, a Republican from the State of Washington who then served as Commerce Committee chairman. Jones is rightly associated with the 1920 Merchant Marine Act. He was involved from the beginning to the end, culminating in congressional passage on Friday, June 4, 1920—the next to the last day of the congressional session.

The 1920 Act, as a whole, was a landmark U.S. maritime policy law—and not because of the section dealing with domestic commerce. Specifically, it rejected U.S. government ownership of commercial vessels in favor of private ownership and established a U.S. vessel support program in international trade that informed subsequent efforts to promote the U.S. merchant marine.

The "Jones Act" is consequently more than one law when we include all the laws reserving U.S. domestic maritime commerce to U.S.-flag vessels. And it is an Act that encompasses more than domestic maritime trade. Finally, the confusion is compounded by the fact that another section in the 1920 Merchant Marine Act having to do with merchant mariner injury recovery is also commonly referred to as the "Jones Act."

Some explanation of this background is necessary to frame this book, which focuses on the 1920 Act, the original "Jones Act" as a whole. It examines how the United States developed merchant marine policies starting in 1776, culminating in the 1920 Act. It is the premise of this book that to understand the 1920 Merchant Marine Act—and subsequent U.S. maritime policies adopted and policy choices available—it is necessary to trace the journey of the 1920 Act from the beginning of U.S. national merchant marine policy making.

This is partly because the policy makers who created the 1920 Merchant Marine Act were steeped in U.S. maritime policy history. One of the 1920 congressional hearing exhibits, for example, was a survey of English navigation acts going back to the fourteenth century.[1]

This is also because the economic conditions faced by U.S. maritime policy makers in 1920 were fundamentally the same as those the U.S. has faced since the Civil War to this day. Throughout that time, U.S. vessel operating costs and capital costs have generally been higher than comparable costs elsewhere in the world. Since ocean-going vessels can go anywhere and compete everywhere, U.S.-flag vessels have historically been at a cost disadvantage wherever ocean-going trade was open to vessels of every nation. That cost disadvantage must be met somehow if there is to be a U.S.-flag merchant marine in the international trade today as it existed in 1865 and 1920.

Therefore, to understand the Jones Act, the journey matters. It explains the policy choices available, made, and foregone, as well as the successes and failures of the policies adopted. Those choices are just as relevant today as in 1920. The events, policy choices, and people who played their part over time are the key to understanding both the 1920 Act and U.S. merchant marine policy before and after.

---

[1] U.S. Congress, Senate, Commerce Committee, Hearings before the Senate Commerce Committee on the Establishment of an American Merchant Marine, 66th Congress, 2nd Session (1920), 2080-83.

Dramatis Personae

Alexander, Joshua W. (1852–1936). Member of Congress (D-MO), 1907–19; chairman, House Merchant Marine and Fisheries Committee, 1911–19; secretary of commerce, 1919–21.

Baker, Bernard N. (1854–1918). Prominent Baltimore vessel owner; sold vessels to the United States in the Spanish-American War; nominated among the first commissioners to the U.S. Shipping Board in 1917 but did not serve.

Baker, Newton D. (1871–1937). Mayor of Cleveland, 1912–15; secretary of war, 1916-21.

Benson, William S. (1855–1932). U.S. Navy officer; first U.S. Navy Chief of Naval Operations, 1915–1919; chairman, U.S. Shipping Board, March 1920–June 1921; commissioner, U.S. Shipping Board, 1921–28.

Blaine, James G. (1830–93). Member of Congress (R-ME), 1863–76; speaker of the House, 1869–75; senator (R-ME), 1876–81; lost 1884 presidential election to Grover Cleveland; secretary of state, March 1881–December 1881, 1889–92.

Campbell, Ira A. (1878–1963). Admiralty lawyer; counsel, U.S. Shipping Board, 1918–19; special assistant to U.S. attorney general for Admiralty, 1919–20; chief architect of the Ship Mortgage Act included in the Merchant Marine Act, 1920.

Chamberlain, Eugene Tyler (1856–1929). Commissioner, Bureau of Navigation, 1893-1921. Highly influential expert on shipping matters across multiple presidential administrations.

Clark, William L. (unknown). Seattle lawyer and lobbyist for Pacific Steamship Company; testified in 1920 Merchant Marine Act hearings and wrote coastwise changes to existing law.

Clarke, James P. (1854–1916). Governor of Arkansas, 1895–97; senator (D-AR), 1903-1916; Chairman, Senate Commerce Committee, 1913–16.

Codman, John (1814–1900). Prolific maritime writer and one of the chief private advocates for "free ships."

Colby, Bainbridge (1869–1950). Commissioner, U.S. Shipping Board, 1917–19; secretary of state, 1920–21.

Collins, Edward K. (1802–78). Ship owner (New York and Liverpool United States Mail Steamship Company known as the "Collins Line"), one of the first U.S. subsidized shipping lines.

Cramp, Charles Henry (1828–1913). President of one of the largest U.S. shipyards located in Philadelphia (William Cramp & Sons Shipbuilding Co.); active in U.S. merchant marine policy matters.

Dean, Robert Augustus (1881–1924). Attorney, assistant chief counsel, and then chief counsel, U.S. Shipping Board, 1918-21.

Deane, Silas (1737–89). Merchant, First Continental Congress agent to France, played a role in the exclusion of the colonies from the English Navigation Act system.

Denman, William (1872–1959). West coast admiralty attorney; chairman, U.S. Shipping Board, January 1917–July 1917; judge, U.S. Court of Appeals for the Ninth Circuit, 1935–59.

Dewey, George (1837–1917). U.S. Navy officer; commander of the Navy Asiatic Squadron at the 1898 Battle of Manila Bay; president, General Board of the Navy Department.

Dingley, Nelson Jr. (1832–99). Governor of Maine, 1874–76; member of Congress (R-ME), 1881–99.

Donald, John A. (1858–1922). Ship owner; commissioner, U.S. Shipping Board, 1917-21.

Elkins, Stephen B. (1841–1911). Member of Congress (R-NM); secretary of war, 1891-1893; senator (R-WV), 1895–1911.

Eustis, Frederic A. (1877–1958). Amateur yachtsman who assisted with the early U.S. Shipping Board plan to build wooden vessels.

Farquhar, John M. (1832–1918). Civil War Medal of Honor winner; member of Congress (R-NY), 1885–91; chairman, House Merchant Marine & Fisheries Committee, 1889–91.

Fithian, George W. (1854–1921). Member of Congress (D-IL), 1889–95; chairman, House Merchant Marine and Fisheries Committee, 1893–95.

Fletcher, Duncan U. (1859–1936). Senator (D-FL), 1909–36; chairman, Senate Commerce Committee, 1916–19.

Franklin, Philip Albright Small (A. S.) (1871–1939). Head of the White Star Line office in New York when the *Titanic* sank; president and chairman, International Mercantile Marine Company, 1916–36; chairman, Shipping Control Committee, 1918–19.

Frye, William P. (1830–1911). Member of Congress (R-ME), 1871–81; senator (R-ME), 1881–1911; chairman, Senate Commerce Committee, 1887–93, 1895–1911.

Furuseth, Andrew (1854–1938). Leading American maritime labor leader; secretary, Sailor's Union of the Pacific, 1887–1935; president, International Seamen's Union, 1908–1935.

Gallatin, Abraham Alfonse Albert (1761–1849). Member of Congress, 1795–1801 (DR-PA); secretary of the treasury, 1801–14; lead U.S. negotiator for the 1815 commercial treaty with Britain that set the U.S. on the road of free maritime trade.

Gallinger, Jacob H. (1837–1918). Member of Congress (R-NH), 1885–89; Senator (R-NH), 1891–1918; chairman, Senate Republic Conference, 1913–17.

Goethals, George Washington (1858–1928). U.S. Army officer; chief engineer, Panama Canal, 1907–14; first governor of Panama Canal Zone, 1914–17; general manager, Emergency Fleet Corporation, April 1917–July 1917; acting quartermaster general of the Army, 1917–19.

Greene, William S. (1841–1924). Member of Congress (R-MA), 1898–1924; chairman, House Merchant Marine Committee, 1907–11, 1919–24.

Griscom, Clement A. (1841–1912). Ship owner; co-led the creation of the International Mercantile Marine Company with J. P. Morgan.

Hale, Eugene (1836–1918). Member of Congress (R-ME), 1869–79; senator (R-ME), 1881–1911; chairman, Senate Committee on Naval Affairs, 1897-1909.

Hanna, Marcus (Mark) A. (1837–1904). Cleveland businessman; chairman, Republican National Committee, 1896–1904; senator (R-OH), 1897–1904.

Humphrey, William E. (1862–1934). Member of Congress (R-WA), 1903–17; member, Federal Trade Commission, 1925–33.

Hurley, Edward Nash (1864–1933). Highly successful businessman and inventor; chairman, U.S. Shipping Board, July 1917–July 1919.

Jones, Wesley Livsey (1863–1932). Father of the "Jones Act"; member of Congress (R-WA), 1899–1909; senator (R-WA), 1909–32; chairman, Commerce Committee, 1919–30; chairman, Appropriations Committee, 1930–32.

Kirlin, J. Parker (1861–1927). Admiralty lawyer; general counsel, Shipping Control Committee; counsel to White Star Line in *Titanic* litigation.

La Follette, Robert M. (1855–1925). Member of Congress (I-WI), 1885–91; governor of Wisconsin, 1901–06; senator (I-WI), 1906–25.

Lasker, Albert D. (1880–1952). Advertising pioneer; chairman, U.S. Shipping Board, 1921–23.

Lodge, Henry Cabot (1850–1924). Senator (R-MA), 1893–1924; active on maritime policy relating to the Philippines, President Wilson's ship purchase legislation, and the 1920 Merchant Marine Act.

Long, John D. (1838–1915). Member of Congress (R-MA), 1883–1889; governor of Massachusetts, 1880-1883; secretary of the Navy, 1897–1902.

Lynch, John (1825–1892). Member of Congress (R-ME), 1865–73; led the first congressional committee investigation of the state of the U.S. merchant marine in 1870.

Maguire, James G. (1853–1920). Lawyer; member of Congress (D-CA), 1893–99; early promotor of seamen's rights.

Marvin, Winthrop Lippit (1863–1926). Journalist; secretary, 1905 Gallinger Merchant Marine Commission; author, including of *The American Merchant Marine; Its History and Romance from 1620 to 1902*.

McAdoo, William Gibbs Jr. (1863–1941). Secretary of the treasury, 1913–18. Formulated the idea for the U.S. government's purchase of vessels and promoted the legislation that became the Shipping Act 1916.

Morgan, J. Pierpoint (1837–1913). Business mogul; co-led the creation of the International Mercantile Marine Company.

Morse, Charles W. (1856–1933). Business mogul convicted of fraud; established the Virginia Shipbuilding Company in Alexandria, Virginia.

Nelson, Knute (1843–1923). Member of Congress (R-MN), 1883–89; governor of Minnesota, 1893–1895; senator (R-MN), 1895–1923.

Payne, John Barton (1855–1935). Lawyer; chairman, U.S. Shipping Board, August 1919–March 1920; secretary of the interior, March 1920–March 1921; chairman, American Red Cross, 1920–35.

Payne, Sereno E. (1843–1914). Member of Congress (R-NY), 1883–87, 1889–1914; first House majority leader, 1899–1911; chairman, House Ways and Means Committee, 1899–1911.

Piez, Charles A. (1866–1933). Mechanical engineer and manufacturer; vice president, Emergency Fleet Corporation; general manager, U.S. Shipping Board, 1917–19.

Redfield, William C. (1858–1932). Member of Congress (D-NY), 1911–13; first Secretary of Commerce, 1913–19.

Roach, John (1815–87). Founder of one of the largest U.S. shipyards in Chester, PA (John Roach & Sons); active in U.S. merchant marine policy matters.

Root, Elihu (1845–1937). U.S. attorney for the Southern District of NY, 1883–1885; secretary of war, 1899–1904; secretary of state, 1905–09; Senator (R-NY), 1909–15; winner, Nobel Peace Prize, 1912.

Rosseter, John H. (1871–1936). Vice president and general manager, Pacific Mail Steamship Company; director of operations, U.S. Shipping Board, 1917-19.

Schwab, Charles M. (1862–1939). Business mogul; president, United States Steel Corporation; president and chairman, Bethlehem Steel Corporation; director general, Emergency Fleet Corporation, April 1918-November 1918.

Stevens, Raymond B. (1874–1942). Member of Congress (D-NH), 1913–15; vice chairman, U.S. Shipping Board, 1917–20.

Underwood, Oscar W. (1862–1929). Member of Congress (D-AL), 1897–1915; House majority leader, 1911–15; senator (D-AL), 1915–27; Senate minority leader, April 1920–December 1923.

Vest, George G. (1830–1904). Confederate member of Congress (D-MO), 1862–1865; Confederate senator (D-MO), January 1865–May 1865; senator (D-MO), 1879–1903.

Walsh, Joseph (1875–1946). Member of Congress (R-MA), 1915–22; chairman, House Select Committee on United States Shipping Board Operations, 1919–21 (known as the "Walsh Committee").

Wickersham, James (1857–1939). Delegate to the U.S. House of Representatives (R-AK), 1909–17, January 1919–March 1919, March 1921–March 1921, 1931–33.

Wilson, William B. (1862–1934). International secretary-treasurer, United Mine Workers of America, 1900–08; member of Congress, (D-PA), 1907–13; first secretary of labor, 1913–21.

*Senator Wesley Livsey Jones, circa 1921,
Library of Congress*

Chapter 1—Introduction

The journey to the Jones Act began in England in the late fourteenth century, with one of the first forms of economic regulation of maritime trade. In 1381, England, for the first time, reserved its foreign trade to vessels giving their allegiance to the king. By the time of Queen Elizabeth I in 1563, a law was enacted also reserving English domestic maritime trade to English vessel owners.

The English Navigation Acts of 1651 and 1660, which were the most prominent and famous of such acts, reserved English foreign, domestic, and colonial trade to English vessels. That remained the case until the mid-nineteenth century. In the seventeenth century, England also set forth what it meant to be an English vessel in terms of where it was built, who owned it, who commanded it, and where the crew came from.

America's Founding Fathers knew that they would likely need an American navigation system to replace the English Acts once independence was achieved. The 1776 "Plan of Treaties" written by John Adams was the plan for that system. The plan sought free markets for American vessels and U.S. goods around the world rather than managed trade. The premise of the American plan was that the newly freed colonies could compete with anyone on a level playing field. How to get that level playing field dominated early American merchant marine national policy-making for decades.

When the colonies formally achieved independence, there was a short period of time when Britain considered letting them retain at least some of their Navigation Act privileges to maintain existing trading relationships beneficial to Britain. However, ultimately, Britain chose the opposite, and the colonies were excluded from certain trades controlled by Britain, especially trade with Britain's Caribbean colonies (referred to as the "West Indies").

JOURNEY TO THE JONES ACT

During the Confederation period, that of America's first national government, efforts failed to get the states to unify around a law that would permit trade retaliation against countries that discriminated against American vessels and goods. Those efforts were doomed by the lack of trade authority in the Confederation constitution.

Indeed, the imperative to make possible effective international trade policy spurred adoption of the U.S. Constitution. The goal was accomplished by giving the new federal government the commerce power and rejecting an approach that would have required two-thirds vote of the House and the Senate to adopt any "navigation act" dealing with ocean commerce. The North-South sectional compromise that made that possible was based on permitting the slave trade to continue until 1808. But for that compromise, it would have been difficult for the United States to ever have adopted any meaningful merchant marine policy, including the "Jones Act."

The first U.S. Congress in 1789 immediately set to work to adopt discriminating import duties and tonnage taxes on vessels, both to force open markets and to fund the new government. Representative James Madison led the effort. By the early acts adopted, the United States established the principles of promoting American vessels in the foreign trade and of reserving its domestic maritime trade to American vessels. In the domestic (called "coastwise" or "coasting") trade, the United States made the tonnage taxes payable by foreign vessels more than eight times as high as the tax on American-owned vessels.

The War of 1812 was fought primarily to defend American international commercial trade rights. The United States succeeded in the 1815 peace that followed in obtaining reciprocal free direct trade with Britain but not free trade with the West Indies. Lack of open access to these colonies animated subsequent U.S. maritime policy.

The United States enacted a series of retaliatory laws aimed at Britain and other countries that discriminated against American vessels from 1817 to 1828. These rested on the foundation of the 1815 commercial treaty with Britain, which expressly permitted unilateral U.S. action. The purpose was to end mutual discrimination. The laws were not intended to reserve a market for U.S. vessels.

Landmark legislation was the Act of March 1, 1817, signed by President James Madison just before he ended his second term in office. That Act provided, for the first time on a permanent basis, an outright reservation of U.S. coasting trade to vessels wholly owned by U.S. citizens. Other parts of the 1817 law were patterned on the 1651/1660 English Navigation Acts. The major difference was that the U.S. law expressly invited reciprocal treatment by foreign countries by promising the relaxation of U.S. restrictions in return.

The 1817 Act did not restrict U.S. domestic trade to U.S.-registered vessels but rather to vessels owned by U.S. citizens, even if they were registered in another country. U.S.-owned, foreign-flag vessels could still participate in U.S. domestic trade upon the payment of a stiff tonnage tax. It was not until 1898 that the 1817 Act was amended to restrict U.S. domestic trade to U.S.-registered vessels, excluding U.S. citizen-owned foreign-registered vessels.

The discriminating tonnage taxes the United States adopted opened foreign markets to American vessels. These laws were also associated with the rise of the U.S. fleet of wooden sailing vessels, which peaked in the 1850s. After the Civil War, many persons argued that these discriminating trade practices caused the expansion of the U.S. merchant marine.

In fact, the U.S.-flag merchant marine maintained a leading position in many worldwide trades from about 1830 to 1860. U.S.-flag wooden sailing vessels, for example, dominated the North Atlantic trade into the 1830s. However, the first crossing of the North Atlantic by British wooden steamships in April 1838 signaled the end of that dominance.

By the 1840s, the British had established regular, government-subsidized service from Liverpool to North America with wooden side-wheel steamships. The subsidized British company came to be known as the Cunard Steamship Company. The U.S. government matched the British subsidy with the Collins Line in 1850, but by 1858, that company was bankrupt. Another subsidized U.S. company—Pacific Mail Steamship Company—was later (in the 1870s) embroiled in a congressional bribery scandal. The experience with these two companies contributed to decades of opposition to direct government vessel subsidies.

International troubles for the U.S. merchant marine became evident by the 1850s as the fleet started to lose ground. A worldwide leader in the construction and operation of wooden sailing vessels, the U.S. fleet was slow to adapt to iron steamships. Britain did so partly out of necessity since Britain had exhausted much of its useful timber, and partly out of opportunity because of ample domestic coal and iron resources available to it in favorable locations.

By the end of the Civil War, Britain was well on its way to dominating world shipping as it shifted to iron steamships. The United States, which had been its equal, was left behind.

The Civil War accelerated this divergence. The trade disruption caused directly and indirectly by Confederate commerce-raiding vessels decimated the U.S.-flag fleet at that critical juncture of technological transformation. After the war, the U.S. economy moved away from its historical focus on maritime industries, turning inward with resources flowing to open the continent. Still, the merchant marine in the U.S. domestic trade continued to expand after the Civil War.

The lack of an effective industry or government response to the decline of the U.S.-flag fleet in international trade prompted a long period of national hand-wringing. Extensive congressional hearings were held in 1870, 1882, 1890, and 1905. Every Congress actively considered merchant marine legislation. Private industry lobbied vigorously for assistance. Books, pamphlets, and articles about the diminished U.S.-flag fleet trading internationally were written in a continuous stream, particularly in the late nineteenth century and early twentieth century.

These efforts occurred when the U.S. merchant marine was an important U.S. industry. Merchant marine issues were national political issues. Both major political parties adopted planks of general support for the U.S. merchant marine, and presidents routinely spoke about shipping.

During that fifty-nine-year period, from 1865 to 1914, the national push and pull between free trade versus protected trade also occurred in the shipping industry. The political parties divided on trade protection for the merchant marine along the same lines that they divided on general industry tariffs.

Republicans were generally in support of high tariffs to protect domestic industry. They were correspondingly in favor of subsidizing the merchant marine either through mail subsidies, which was a quasi-cargo preference, or direct subsidies called "bounties" or "subventions" to countervail the effect of the tariffs and high U.S. labor and material costs caused by those tariffs.

In contrast, Democrats were generally against high tariffs and maritime subsidies in any form and argued in favor of permitting U.S. vessel owners to be able to purchase their vessels anywhere in the world as a tonic that would solve all merchant marine problems. At the time, all U.S.-registered vessels, including vessels in international trade, had to be built in the United States. This Democratic initiative became known as the "free ship" policy.

The parties divided less uniformly on whether to reinstate discriminating duties in favor of U.S.-flag vessels. The culmination of the reinstatement effort prior to the 1920 Act was the inclusion of a discriminating duty in the Underwood Tariff Act of 1913. This was later nullified by the U.S. Supreme Court as being in contravention of America's free trade commercial treaties. Senator Jones, who advocated for discriminating duties throughout his time in the U.S. Congress starting in 1899, unsuccessfully tried to revive the idea in the 1920 Act.

It was not until the adoption of the Ocean Mail Act of 1891 that the U.S. re-entered the realm of general cargo vessel subsidies. That program, however, had been significantly watered-down from what was proposed and was never able to make a substantial impact.

The need to do something about the merchant marine in international trade became even more prominent as the United States took control of non-contiguous territories and fought overseas wars. Congress treated trade with Alaska, Hawaii, and Puerto Rico as U.S. domestic trade when those territories were acquired. Cuba was expressly left out, and coverage of the Philippines was very much a live issue before and during consideration of the 1920 Merchant Marine Act.

The inclusion of Alaska into the U.S. domestic trade reservation led to issues of interpretation and the exploitation of loopholes because of the ability of cargo shippers to use Canadian ports, railroads, and vessels to evade the reservation. Congress tried to close these loopholes by amending the 1817 Act several times. For example, section 27 of the 1920 Act—one of the provisions usually cited as *the* "Jones Act"—addressed a loophole created by a 1913 U.S. attorney general opinion.

The Spanish-American War highlighted the danger of relying heavily on foreign vessels. The United States managed to acquire a fleet of vessels to support operations in the Caribbean and in Asia during the war, but at substantial expense. The country had been fortunate that the main theater of operations was nearby and that the war was brief and did not involve other European antagonists. Had the war had more participants or taken longer to conclude, the United States could have failed to achieve its war aims, as its warships would have been denied access to neutral vessels and ports.

The inclusion of the Philippines as a U.S. territory due to that war led to the adoption of the first defense-related government cargo reservation law—the Cargo Preference Act of 1904–

-first proposed by then-Representative Wesley Jones. This was the first expansion of the government-impelled cargo policy outside the realm of ocean mail and remains a law today.

During the late nineteenth and early twentieth century, U.S. seamen organized into unions and drew national attention to the antiquated laws applicable to mariners. Those laws, for example, provided for imprisonment for failing to report for duty. Safety concerns arising from a series of maritime disasters, including the sinking of the *Titanic* in 1912, boosted seamen's reform efforts that culminated in the Seamen's Act of 1915. That Act included measures intended to equalize worldwide wages and working conditions with American standards as an alternative to subsidizing the U.S. merchant marine trading internationally.

The early twentieth century saw the extension of the industry trust from land to the ocean with the formation of J. P. Morgan's International Mercantile Marine Company (IMM). The express intention was to consolidate and eliminate competition in the North Atlantic trade. The White Star Line, owner of the *Titanic*, was part of that combination, which ultimately failed.

By the early twentieth century, virtually all ocean routes served by common carriers, referred to as "lines," were subject to agreements among those carriers in groups called "conferences." The IMM combination and the prevalence of conferences alarmed cargo shippers, who feared price fixing and discrimination. Both the British government and the U.S. Congress reacted with extensive investigations of carrier practices. The U.S. investigation resulted in U.S. government oversight over conferences included in the Shipping Act, 1916 and expanded in the 1920 Act.

The 1899-1902 Boer War spotlighted another maritime danger to the United States. Specifically, it demonstrated how dependent the U.S. economy was on foreign (especially British) vessels. The war soaked up shipping capacity and drove up shipping rates for U.S. goods in certain trade lanes, even though the United States was not involved in the war.

JOURNEY TO THE JONES ACT

The worldwide voyage of President Teddy Roosevelt's "Great White Fleet" of U.S. warships in 1907-09 again emphasized the lack of U.S.-flag commercial vessels to support worldwide U.S. military operations. The fleet's voyage was only made possible through the chartering of foreign vessels to deliver U.S.-mined coal to various foreign ports. Had the fleet been engaged in an operation against a hostile nation, support vessels might not have been available due to alliance and neutrality obligations. The lesson was nevertheless not acted upon.

The construction of the Panama Canal focused attention on another potential cargo reservation, namely for the cargoes purchased for constructing the canal. In fact, "buy American" was enacted for the canal construction, but "ship American" was not.

For a short time, it appeared as though U.S.-flag vessels engaged in the domestic trade would also be exempt from Panama Canal tolls. However, that exemption was repealed just before the canal was opened in 1914. Senator Jones kept the toll exemption issue alive and was a staunch proponent of reinstating it for U.S. vessels engaged in the West Coast to East Coast trade.

The outbreak of World War I repeated the Boer War effect on worldwide merchant shipping on a grander scale. U.S. international trade suffered, leading to demands for action.

A limited free ships policy had already been included in the Panama Canal Act of 1912 to bring in relatively new foreign-built vessels in the U.S. flag but without U.S. coastwise trading privileges. That policy failed, and no vessels were reflagged because of relatively high U.S.-flag vessel operating costs. In the context of World War I, the policy was made less restrictive and tried again in the Ship Registry Act of 1914, with substantial success. This occurred mainly because American-owned foreign-registered vessels then needed the relative safety of the U.S. flag as a neutral nation.

The Panama Canal Act had been the first relaxation of the U.S.-build requirement actively sought by the free ship movement since the Civil War. But neither that Act, nor the Ship Registry Act, nor the provision of war risk insurance by the U.S. government in 1914 were enough to provide for a U.S.-flag fleet of vessels sufficient for the country's commercial needs. The Wilson administration proposed in early 1915 the unprecedented step of broad U.S. government ownership of commercial vessels through a government-owned corporation to serve U.S. international commerce.

The administration's proposal was heavily opposed by Republicans in Congress—including Senator Jones—and a breakaway group of Democratic senators. Opponents cried "socialism" and worried about neutrality violations, and so the proposal languished despite Democratic control of both chambers of Congress. As it gradually became more evident that the United States might be drawn into the war anyway, opposition softened.

The Wilson vessel acquisition bill was eventually supported by a change in public sentiment in favor of war preparedness. The administration also compromised many provisions to assuage opposition, particularly agreeing that U.S. Government ownership would sunset five years after the end of the war (a provision that did not survive the war's aftermath).

The 1916 Shipping Act, finally adopted, was one of the major U.S. war mobilization acts enacted prior to U.S. entry into the war. In terms of politics, the 1916 Act, which was adamantly opposed by Republicans, was the product of Democrats. The 1920 Act, which had to adapt the 1916 Act to post-war circumstances, was the product of many of the same Republicans, like Senator Jones, who had opposed U.S. government shipping intervention in the first place.

The 1916 Shipping Act set up the United States Shipping Board, which in turn formed the Emergency Fleet Corporation to purchase, own, operate, and build vessels. For the first few months of its existence, the board was consumed by personality conflicts and policy disputes, including whether to supplement steel vessel construction with wooden vessels. Although the shipping board had barely gotten off the ground by the time the United States declared war on Germany on April 6, 1917, it nevertheless served as the mechanism by which the U.S. government acquired and built one of the largest fleets of commercial vessels in the world.

Sometimes lost in the focus on the enormous U.S. new vessel-building effort was the fact that most of the U.S. tonnage that served in the war either already existed when the U.S. entered the conflict or was already under construction when the U.S. government requisitioned it. While the United States was neutral, both U.S. and foreign owners had already filled U.S. shipyards with orders. Most of the existing fleet came from vessels enrolled in the mail subsidy program or engaged in U.S. domestic trade, vessels reflagged under the Ship Registry Act, and vessels requisitioned from belligerents (German) or neutrals (Dutch).

The massive U.S. building effort, the largest industrial mobilization effort to that time, mainly came too late because the conflict ended before the operation could kick into high gear. That fleet was built in anticipation of a long war, an increased U.S. Army presence in Europe in 1919, and a continued vigorous German submarine campaign.

Even in the middle of 1918, the U.S. Army was planning on putting as many as 4.3 million men in Europe versus the 2.1 million force initially planned. Had that occurred, the Shipping Board's building effort may not have been enough. As it was, there were not enough vessels during the winter of 1918-1919 to simultaneously bring home all the foreign armies (Canadian, Australian, etc.), address the famine in Europe, and renew commercial trade.

When World War I ended, the United States was still building vessels and would continue to do so for some time because of the impracticality of telling shipyards and their subcontractors employing thousands around the country to halt operations abruptly. By 1920, the building program had contributed to a substantial worldwide oversupply of vessels, even though many of the U.S.-built emergency vessels were laid up or scrapped.

The enormous effort to build vessels hurriedly led to graft and waste, which was revealed in congressional investigations. The most egregious findings related to the wooden vessels the Fleet Corporation had ordered and the enormous green field shipyard built on Hog Island near Philadelphia (where Philadelphia's airport now stands).

The primary impetus for the 1920 Act was the question of what to do with all these U.S. government-owned vessels. There was a strong but not universal national feeling that the government should get out of the commercial vessel business as soon as possible. But there was a difference of opinion as to whether to dump the vessels into the commercial market or to engage in judicious sales over time with continued government ownership and operation of commercial vessels.

The latter approach won out, and the Shipping Board would be reconstituted in the 1920 Act to manage the fleet until it could be gradually sold. Private U.S. companies were hired to manage vessels, which the government could not sell except at a severe discount from the construction cost on trade routes not served by privately owned U.S.-flag vessels.

The huge government-owned fleet also appeared to present an opportunity to finally achieve the dream of reestablishing a substantial worldwide U.S.-flag shipping presence. Toward that end, and to pressure Paris peace negotiators to agree to Wilson's peace aims, the Wilson administration attempted to hold back the sale of U.S.-flag vessels to other countries that were clamoring for shipping capacity after the end of the war.

The administration also made it known that the U.S. government was willing to lose money to rationalize world shipping, including worldwide adoption of 1915 Seamen's Act mariner rights. The effort was doomed by the need to address famine in Europe and to forestall U.S. domestic discontent by permitting U.S. shipyards to take foreign orders to take the place of government orders.

The program of judicious sales with the hope of establishing a worldwide merchant marine presence ran into a decline in international trade in the war's aftermath and an oversupply of vessels. The pre-war high U.S. cost disadvantage re-emerged, and the lack of a commercial merchant marine infrastructure eventually made the whole 1920 Act program a substantial drain on the U.S. Treasury, a problem that had to be addressed in subsequent merchant marine legislation.

Congress also adopted U.S.-flag foreign trading fleet support measures in the 1920 Act. In particular, the Act required preferential rail rates within the United States for U.S.-flag vessels, re-imposition of discriminating duties favoring U.S.-flag vessels, and finally, after years of effort, a reservation of trade to the Philippines to American vessels. Each of these provisions was highly controversial at the time, and none of them was, in fact, implemented. Whether these measures would have succeeded in sustaining a commercially viable privately owned fleet in the international trade is unknown because they were never tried.

In addition, the 1920 Act became a vehicle for many other changes. This included amendments to ocean carrier antitrust oversight provisions enacted as part of the 1916 Shipping Act, re-invigoration of modest mail subsidies for U.S.-ocean carriers, refinement of the merchant mariner rights enacted as part of the 1915 Seaman's Act, a long-sought Ship Mortgage Act to facilitate the financing of American vessels, and provisions to help the U.S. merchant marine with war taxes and vessel depreciation.

Of course, the 1920 Act amended the pre-existing domestic maritime reservation for which it is famous. That section refined and restated the application of the reservation primarily in reaction to the way that the prior 1898 law had been interpreted in 1913 and did not change long-standing U.S. maritime policy that reserved U.S. domestic trade to U.S. vessels.

Finally, the 1920 Act expressly established by law the national maritime policy of the United States that had been implicit to that time. That policy was that the United States should have a commercial merchant marine, that such a merchant marine should be large enough to support the United States in a national emergency and to carry a substantial portion of U.S. international trade, and that the merchant marine should consist of privately-owned and -operated, not government-owned or -operated, vessels. These principles have endured and are, as much as anything, the legacy of the "Jones Act."

King Charles II of England, School of Peter Lely, Bolton Museum and Art Gallery, Lancashire, UK

Chapter 2 — English Origins

Back to Discriminating Duties

On May 20, 1920, during the consideration of the 1920 Merchant Marine Act, there was a colloquy between Senator Henry Cabot Lodge (R-MA) and Senator Jones on the Senate floor.[1] The subject was import duties (a tax on imports) that discriminated in favor of cargoes carried by the U.S. merchant marine. The discussion concerned whether the United States should reintroduce discriminating import duties to promote the U.S. merchant marine, as it had successfully done from 1789 to the mid-nineteenth century but had long abandoned.

Lodge had just turned seventy on May 12 and was, at the time, Senate majority leader. His long academic and political career had focused on maritime policy issues repeatedly. Lodge's acquaintance with the world of ships had started early. His father was a merchant with an office on the Boston docks, and Lodge spent early summers wandering the docks and making friends with mariners.[2]

Lodge thereafter had frequent interaction with commercial maritime policy. He had written a biography in 1883 of Alexander Hamilton, an early thought leader on import duties and whether they should be used for revenue generation or as tools of maritime policy.[3] He chaired the Senate Philippines Committee from 1899 to 1911 (also known as the "Lodge Committee"), which attempted to apply the U.S. maritime laws to those islands. As one of the ten members of Congress who formed the 1905 Merchant Marine Commission, he was also a strong advocate for subsidizing the U.S. merchant marine. And he was an ardent and active opponent of Woodrow Wilson's "Ship Purchase Bill," which became the 1916 Shipping Act.[4]

During the colloquy with Jones, Lodge inquired about a section in the pending legislation that stated that it was the "judgment of Congress" that treaty provisions restricting the right of the United States to discriminate against foreign vessels "should be terminated." The president was also "authorized *and directed*" to give the requisite treaty notices.[5] There were in fact over thirty such commercial agreements. This was one of the most controversial bill sections at the time, and possibly the least understood and mentioned since then.

Lodge pointed out that the imposition of discriminating duties favoring U.S. vessels had been the policy of the country from its beginning until the U.S.-Great Britain Commercial Convention of 1815, which followed the 1814 Treaty of Ghent ending the War of 1812.[6] In fact, those discriminations had prompted the thirty or so bilateral commercial treaties that would be upended by the provision under consideration.

In that 1815 convention, both the U.S. and Britain had accorded vessels of the other "national treatment" in the direct trade between the two countries. Each country would treat vessels of the other as if they were their own (known as "reciprocal national treatment").

Lodge pointed out that the 1815 Convention "had destroyed the tonnage discrimination which up to that time had been settled policy of the United States." In this he was not entirely accurate since such "destruction" occurred mainly via subsequent U.S. laws enacted between 1817 and 1828 and the resulting commercial treaties.[7]

The proposed section, he said, appeared to "return to the old policy of the country at the beginning of the last century." He asked for information but not, as he pointed, in a "hostile spirit" to the provision. He further noted that the section "opens the door for a return to that policy, which has been advocated by both political parties."

Jones, as the floor leader for the legislation, responded that the section was meant to start a process—"it is unshackling us"—to respond to changing economic conditions after the world war. He further reported that many countries had renounced or were considering renouncing their commercial treaty obligations.

Jones also argued that American discriminating duties had worked to support the U.S. merchant marine and that he believed that the abandonment of those duties starting in 1815 "was ultimately the cause of the decrease in our merchant marine." After the end of the discussion, the section passed the Senate by voice vote.

CHARTA MARITIMA[8]

The Senate floor discussion in May 1920 alluded to when the United States was born into a world dominated by economic nationalism, or mercantilism, where discriminating duties were common. U.S. trade policy at that time had to account for these attributes or accept the trade policies of other nations as a fait accompli. As put in a 1785 Congressional report authored by James Monroe—if the individual American states could not combine to counteract the discriminations of foreign countries, "their system will prevail."[9]

The most important navigation regulation system for the United States, both to counteract and to emulate, was that of England. Although England appears to have had earlier laws, most historians point to a law enacted in 1381 in the fifth year of the reign of King Richard II as England's first direct navigation—meaning shipping trade—law.[10] King Richard, the son of Edward known as the Black Prince, was then about fifteen years of age and was to die in prison in 1400 at the age of thirty-two.

This law was known to American policy makers. John Adams wrote to Thomas Jefferson in 1785, urging each state to adopt the same 1381 shipping restrictions.[11] The law was also quoted by Senator Jones on the Senate floor in September 1913 in connection with Congressional consideration of the re-adoption of discriminating duties favoring American vessels.[12] On that day, Jones also referenced England's subsequent navigation acts as models for U.S. legislation.

The 1381 shipping reservation was the embodiment of mercantilism.[13] The law declared that it was a "great Mischief which the Realm suffereth, and long hath done" for gold, silver, and other valuables to be "carried out of the Realm," which would lead to the "Destruction of the same Realm, which God prohibit." Such exportation was therefore restricted with certain exceptions, such as by licensed merchants and from specified ports, and with the "special Leave and License had of the King."

The law also contained a shipping provision "to increase the Navy of England, which is now greatly diminished." Specifically, the law stated—"that none of the King's liege People do from henceforth ship any Merchandize in going out or coming within the Realm of England, but only in Ships of King's Liegance" and any shipment "in any other Ships or Vessels upon the Sea, than of the said Liegance, shall forfeit to the King all his Merchandises shipped in other Vessels."

In the first year of the reign of Queen Elizabeth I in 1558, the prior navigation restrictions were all repealed.[14] The reason given in the law was that other countries had followed suit and had retaliated with their own navigation restrictions such that there had "growen greate displeasure between the forreyne Prynces and the Kinges of this Realme."

In the fifth year of Elizabeth's reign in 1563 appeared the first clear restriction on domestic maritime trade. The law was called "An Acte towching certayne Politique Constitutions made for the maintenance of the Navye."[15] It required that only wholly English-owned vessels could transport "fish, victuals, wares or things" between English "ports or creeks" upon penalty of the forfeiture of the goods carried or the value thereof. Current U.S. law—which restricts U.S. domestic maritime trade of "merchandise" between "points in the United States" and is often referred to as the "Jones Act"—is similar to this 1563 law.[16]

The purpose of such navigation laws was summarized by Thomas Mun, a director of the English East India Company, in a book published in 1664.[17] He argued that imports could be limited if we "soberly refrain from excessive consumption of forraign wares in our diet and rayment."—in other words, foreign luxury goods. With respect to vessels, Mun argued that the "value of our exportations likewise may be much advanced when we perform it our selves in our own Ships, for then we get only not the price of our wares as they are worth here, but also the Merchants gains, the charges of ensurance, and fraight to carry them beyond the seas."

English navigation acts also restricted colonial commerce largely to England—especially the English Navigation Acts of 1651 and 1660. These Acts later served as models for American navigation and domestic commerce laws, particularly the U.S. navigation Act of March 1, 1817, discussed in detail in a later chapter.

The 1651 and 1660 Acts were regarded by many then and since as the epitome of mercantilism applied to shipping and trade. The 1660 Act was referred to later in the seventeenth century by English economists as the "Sea Magna Charta" or the "Charta Maritima" because of its prominence, and it governed English trade well into the nineteenth century.[18] By 1847, when the Navigation Acts had lost their luster, Osman Ricardo, a member of Parliament and the son of the economist David Ricardo, said, "The real object of the Navigation Act, call it by what name they pleased—the *Charta Maritima*, or any other magnificent title—was to protect British shipowners, in other words, to raise freights unnaturally."[19]

The 1651 Act was enacted by Oliver Cromwell's Rump Parliament which was the Parliament that authorized the process leading to the execution of King Charles I. The primary instigation for the Act was the growing dominance of international trade by the Dutch, which had started with the termination of the Spanish embargo of Holland in 1647.[20] Though Holland is not specifically mentioned in the 1651 Act, the "terms of the law were obviously designed to cripple the carrying and entrepôt trade of the Dutch."[21] The "entrepôt trade" was the transshipment trade where Holland served as the focal point for goods arriving from foreign destinations to be re-shipped elsewhere.

The 1651 Act itself, which contained elements from prior navigation acts, divided the world into trade with Europe versus trade elsewhere.[22] With respect to trade with Europe, foreign vessels could be used for imports only if they were from the place where the foreign good or commodity originated or was usually shipped from. That each country should use only its own vessels for its own trade was a principle with a long history.[23] This provision effectively prevented the Dutch entrepôt trade with England.

With respect to "Asia, Africa, or America, or of any part thereof"—that is to include the North American colonies—all "Goods or Commodities whatsoever, of the Growth, Production or Manufacture" had to be transported to England on vessels the "Owners thereof; and whereof the Master and Mariners are also for the most part of them, of the People of this Commonwealth."

The 1651 Act increased tension between the England and Holland and was a contributing cause of the First Anglo-Dutch War of 1652-1654.[24] The war ended in April 1654 with the signing of the Treaty of Westminster with no clear victor, and the commercial rivalry between the nations continued both in Europe and abroad, leading to further conflict.

The connection between the 1651 Act and the subsequent Anglo-Dutch war was recalled in 1920 to criticize the potential revival of a Navigation Act type discriminatory duty which by then the United States had abandoned. Eugene Tyler Chamberlain, the long running commissioner of the U.S. Bureau of Navigation, wrote in 1920 that the new proposed duty was "mediæval rather than merely 'antiquated' originating in the fourteenth century. Its best-known application resulted in three years of naval warfare of 1651-1654 between England and Holland."[25]

The period between the reigns of Charles I and Charles II, known as the "Interrregnum," effectively ended with Oliver Cromwell's death on September 3, 1658. Following the return to England of Charles II in 1660, the Convention Parliament, which restored the king, again considered the question of navigation.

In September 1660, the Convention Parliament enacted "An Act for the Encourageing and increasing of Shipping and Navigation," which was later confirmed by the Cavalier Parliament (the Royalist Parliament) in July 1661.[26] That act was one of the few laws passed during the Interregnum to be retained with the return of the monarchy.[27]

The 1660 Act required any goods or commodities shipped to England from "Africa, Asia or America" to be transported in English-owned (including colonial-owned) vessels commanded by an English master where three-fourths of the mariners would be English. The 1660 Act further enumerated which products of the colonies could only be exported to England, including including sugar, tobacco, cotton, wool, indigo, and "dyeing wood." This "enumerated list" was altered and amended substantially over time.

The vessel restriction was also applied, like the Elizabethan law of 1563, to domestic shipping. Goods or commodities shipped from Europe (when the 1660 Act was amended in the 1662 Act of Frauds) to England could only be brought in vessels from the place of origin of such goods or commodities or in English-built or English-owned vessels, with the English-connected vessels having to have an English master and three-fourths crew of English mariners.[28] Further changes were made over time to this system.[29]

The Navigation Acts were not without cost to the English economy but were stoutly defended in the seventeenth century and later in the interest of maintaining a greater portion of the shipping to serve national defense. For example, Samuel Fortrey in 1673 argued that "whatever it costs the dearer to the purchaser here, is no prejudice to the publick, when our own nation receives the profit of it; especially it being by the increase of that, which consists the greatest honour and safety of the kingdom."[30] Director of the East India Company and noted economist Josiah Child argued that without the Acts, England would have fewer ships and seamen and it "would expose us to the receiving of all kind of Injuries and Affronts from our Neighbours."[31]

JOURNEY TO THE JONES ACT

Adam Smith, in his famous book *An Inquiry into the Nature and Causes of the Wealth of Nations*, published on March 9, 1776, came to a similar conclusion.[32] When he made the case for free international trade, he excepted two situations where it would "be advantageous to lay some burden upon foreign for the encouragement of domestic industry"—(1) "when some particular sort of industry is necessary for the defence of the country," and (2) "when some tax is imposed at home upon the produce" of domestic industry and an "equal tax" should be imposed on foreign goods.

With respect to the former, he pointed to the British "act of navigation," which "very properly endeavors to give the sailors and shipping of Great Britain the monopoly of the trade of their own country" even though the "act of navigation is not favourable to foreign commerce." He concluded that "as defence, however, is of much more importance than opulence, the act of navigation is, perhaps, the wisest of all commercial regulations of England."

This navigation act system also resulted in considerable commercial maritime integration between the American colonies and England.[33] The colonies developed as a center of ship construction building on natural advantages such as ready access to timber, pitch, and other vessel-building materials, an abundance of sheltered harbors, and shipbuilding expertise from England and elsewhere. English vessel owners routinely ordered ships to be constructed in the American colonies, and colonial-owned ships carried a significant portion of the trade not only between the American colonies and England but also among the North American colonies and between those colonies and English colonies in the Caribbean. In fact, the growth of the British empire, particularly in comparison to continental European rivals dealing with timber shortages and lacking a vessel-building colony, can be attributed in part to this integration.[34]

---

[1] 59 Cong. Rec. 7350-53 (May 20, 1920).
[2] Henry Cabot Lodge, Early Memories (New York: Charles Scribner's Sons, 1913), 22–25.

3 Henry Cabot Lodge, Alexander Hamilton, ed. John T. Morse, Jr. (Boston: Houghton, Mifflin, 1883); Henry Cabot Lodge, ed., The Works of Alexander Hamilton (Federal Ed., (New York: G. P. Putnam's Sons, 1904).

4 U.S. Congress, Senate, Report of the Merchant Marine Commission, 58th Cong., 3rd sess., 1905, S. Rep. 58-2755; The American Merchant Marine: Speech of Hon. H. C. Lodge of Massachusetts, in the Senate of the United States, January 30, 1906 (Washington, DC: Government Printing Office, 1906).

5 41 Stat. 988, 1007 (June 5, 1920).

6 8 Stat. 228 (July 3,1815), Treaty Series 110.

7 3 Stat. 351 (March 1, 1817); 4 Stat. 308 (May 24, 1828).

8 A comprehensive list of English navigation laws is contained in Lawrence A. Harper, The English Navigation Laws: A Seventeenth-Century Experiment in Social Engineering (New York: Octagon Books, 1973), "Table of Statutes Cited."

9 "Reports of Committees for Increasing the Powers of Congress by Recommendations to the States," in The Writings of James Monroe, ed. Stanislaus Murray Hamilton (repr., New York: G. P. Putnam's Sons, 1898-1903), 80–83.

10 Harper, English Navigation Laws, 19n1 (1381 is referred to as the "conventional point of departure"); Henry C. Hunter, How England Got Its Merchant Marine 1066-1776 (New York: National Council of American Shipbuilders, 1935), 17.

11 "Letter from John Adams to Thomas Jefferson (August 7, 1785)," in The Works of John Adams, ed. Charles Francis Adams (Boston: Little, Brown, 1853), vol. 8, 313.

12 50 CONG. REC. 4494–98 (September 8, 1913).

13 5 Ric. II, c. 2, 3.

14 1 Eliz., c. 13.

15 5 Eliz., c. 5.

16 46 U.S.C. § 55102(b) & (c).

17 A Selection of Early English Tracts on Commerce, from the Originals of Mun, Roberts, North, and Others (London: Printed for the Political Economy Club, 1856), 127-29.

18 Josiah Child, A New Discourse of Trade (London: John Everingham, 1693), preface; Francis Brewster, Essays on Trade and Navigation in Five Parts (London: Tho. Cockerill, 1695) (first part), 92.

19 Hansard HC Deb. vol. 89, col. 1012 (February 9, 1847).

20 That dominance started even earlier. Lawrence Stone, "Elizabethan Overseas Trade, 2 The Economic History Review (1949): 30–58.

21 Harper, English Navigation Laws, 49.

22 Harper, English Navigation Laws, 49; Acts and Ordinances of the Interregnum, 1642–1660, eds. C. H. Firth, and R. S. Rait (London: His Majesty's Stationery Office, 1911), vol. 2, 559–62.

23 Harper, English Navigation Laws, 39.

24 For example, J. E. Farnell, "The Navigation Act of 1651, the First Dutch War, and the London Merchant Community," Economic History Review 16 (1964): 439–54.

[25] U.S. Commissioner of Navigation, Annual Report of the Commissioner of Navigation to Secretary of Commerce for Year Ended June 30, 1920 (Washington, DC: Government Printing Office 1920), 31—32.

[26] Acts and Ordinances of the Interregnum, 559.

[27] Edward Channing, "The Navigation Laws," Proceedings of the American Antiquarian Society 6 (October 1889): 160–79, 163–64.

[28] 14 Car. II, c. 11.

[29] Harper, English Navigation Laws, 59–62. Vessel-build restrictions accumulated over time in Great Britain and the absolute restriction of Great Britain's domestic trade to British-built vessels was not enacted until 1825. Hamilton A. Hill, The Navigation Laws of Great Britain and the United States (Boston: Albert J. Wright, 1878), 6.

[30] Samuel Fortrey, "Englands Interest and Improvement" (1673), in A Select Collection of Early English Tracts on Commerce from the Originals of Mun, Roberts, North, and Others (London: Political Economy Club, 1856), 242–43.

[31] Josiah Child, A New Discourse of Trade (London: T. Sowle, 1698), 4th ed., 112, 115.

[32] Adam Smith, An Inquiry into the Nature and Causes of the Wealth of Nations, ed. Edwin Cannan (London: Methuen, 1904), vol. 1, 427—29.

[33] John G. B. Hutchins, The American Maritime Industries and Public Policy, 1789–1914 (Cambridge: Harvard University Press, 1941), chap. 5.

[34] Hutchins, American Maritime Industries, 154–6.

Silas Deane, attributed to William Johnson, circa 1766, Webb Deane Stevens Museum

Chapter 3—Setting the American Maritime Policy Stage

It is uncertain what role the English Navigation Acts played in the American Revolution. The Declaration of Independence included as a "cause" for seeking independence the "cutting off our Trade with all parts of the world," which is exactly what the Navigation Acts were designed to do. The inclusion of this phrase lends credence to the view that the colonies chafed under the Navigation Acts.[1]

Another view is that the Navigation Acts did little overall economic harm to the American colonies and bound the colonies to the mother-country in ways that were mutually beneficial.[2] It was only when England started a heavy-handed policy to raise revenues in 1764 that the seeds of revolution were sown.

That policy accelerated with the arrival of newly appointed commissioners of customs in Boston in 1767, who were charged with enforcing British customs laws.[3] The case of the sloop *Liberty*, owned by John Hancock and seized by British authorities in 1768, is a good example of this new level of enforcement.

The Sloop Liberty[4]

The Navigation Acts required that all goods shipped to the colonies had to travel via England, where they were landed and inspected, and applicable duties were paid before the goods were shipped to the colonies.[5] Thus, England became by law the entrepôt of the colonial trade. Certain items were exempted from this requirement, such as "Servants or Horses" from Scotland or Ireland and "Medera's Wines."

Madeira wine, which was fortified with alcohol so as not to spoil during the long sea voyage, became very popular in the colonies.[6] George Washington, among others, was fond of Madeira and regularly ordered it for his estate and then during his service in the Continental Army. The wine came to play a role in the deteriorating relationship between the British Crown and the colonies as England incurred a substantial debt in fighting the Seven Year's War against the French (the "French and Indian War") and sought revenue from the colonies to help repay it. The first revenue act was the famous Sugar Act of 1764.[7] Although the Act reduced the tax on molasses, it also contained tax increases, including a new stiff tax on Madeira wine.[8]

The colonials reacted by evading the tax through even more smuggling or by bribing customs officials than they had done before. A typical ruse was to declare only part of the actual cargo upon arrival and to bribe the customs official to ignore the undeclared portion. Britain reacted with the Commissioners of Customs Act of 1767, which created a board of five commissioners to be headquartered in Boston to oversee enforcement for all the American colonies.[9]

When the commissioners first arrived in Boston in November 1767, Sir Francis Bernard, governor of the Province of Massachusetts Bay, requested that the corps of cadets, the governor's ceremonial bodyguard commanded by John Hancock, act as the guard of honor for the commissioners.[10] Hancock refused. Later, he also refused to attend a ceremonial dinner for the new arrivals.

An unruly group of Bostonians actually met the commissioners at the dock wearing messages that said "Liberty, Property, and no Commissioners."[11] The commissioners, expecting they may need military assistance to enforce the customs laws, requested that warships be sent from Halifax, and the substantial man-of-war *H.M.S. Romney* and two armed sloops were sent.[12] All were in Boston harbor when the authorities seized the *Liberty* on June 10, 1768.

The 90-ton *Liberty* owned by Hancock arrived in Boston from Madeira on May 9, 1768. Twenty-five casks of Madeira were declared, and the duties paid.[13] That was a cargo size much smaller than the vessel's capacity. In later litigation, it was alleged that the vessel had, in fact, had a cargo of 100 "pipes" of Madeira, which was a standard shipping measurement each holding about 110 gallons.[14] The two customs officials who boarded the vessel did not report, however, anything untoward—at the time.

A new cargo of two hundred barrels of whale oil and twenty barrels of tar were later loaded onto the vessel. On June 10, customs officials showed up at the dock unannounced and had the vessel seized by the *Romney* crew, who towed her out into the harbor. One of the British officers who participated in the operation recorded in his journal that the "Towns people... pelted us very severely with Stones."[15]

The seizure pretext was the failure to post a bond *before* such cargoes were loaded onto the vessel.[16] The long-standing practice had been the posting of a bond *after* the vessel was fully loaded but before the vessel departed. In other words, the seizure arose from the new cargo, not the cargo of Madeira. The commissioners were technically correct in the application of the law—but acted contrary to everyone's reasonable expectation, as evidenced by the fact that this was the first such enforcement.[17]

A riot started to protest the seizure.[18] Adding to the mob's anger was the fact that the *Romney* was forcibly taking men from inbound vessels at the time to serve as British Navy sailors. Writing to a colonial agent in England on June 16, Lt. Gov. Thomas Hutchinson said that "it is unfortunate that in the midst of these diff. the *Romney* has been pressing Seamen."[19]

In the same letter, Hutchison described the scene as the *Liberty* was taken from the pier: a "Mob presently gathered and insulted the Custom H Offic and carried them in triumph as trespassers up the Wharffe tore their cloaths and bruised and otherways hurt them until one after another they escaped."[20] The mob also hauled the collector of customs' private boat out of the water and burned it.

The commissioners fled for their lives to the *Romney* and later to Castle Williams in Boston harbor and did not return to

Boston until November when there were three British Army regiments in Boston.[21] The presence of British Army troops in the city would lead to other problems regarding quartering and, later, the Boston Massacre in 1770.

After the *Liberty* was condemned and sold in September, a related case was brought against Hancock in Admiralty Court, where the case would be tried without a jury. The charge was smuggling Madeira. One of the customs officials who had boarded the *Liberty* in May and had not reported anything amiss immediately after that visit changed his story. In early June, he claimed that he had been manhandled, offered a bribe, and locked in a cabin so as not to see what other cargo was being unloaded.[22]

The claimed penalty amount was substantial based on the punitive damages provision in the Sugar Act—more than enough to make the governor and customs officials rich since they would receive a portion of any paid fines and possibly financially ruin Hancock.[23]

John Adams ably defended Hancock, arguing that the treatment of Hancock had put him "below the Rank of an Englishman."[24] Due to that defense, or perhaps because the evidence against Hancock was flimsy (including the changed, arguably perjured, story), or maybe because it had become clear in Britain that the colonial officials were engaged in a shake-down of Hancock, the charges were dropped in March 1769.[25]

The *Liberty* was to play another role in colonial dissatisfaction. She had been seized, condemned, and purchased by British customs officials and converted into a customs enforcement vessel, the *H.M.S. Liberty*. Her commander, William Reid, became notorious for his zealousness.[26]

On July 17, 1769, the *Liberty* escorted to Newport, Rhode Island, two detained vessels—a brig commanded by Joseph Packwood and a sloop, the *Sally*, commanded by Edward Finker.

JOURNEY TO THE JONES ACT

It turned out that Captain Packwood had filed all his necessary paperwork and so the seizure was unwarranted. While his paperwork was being checked, Packwood went back to his vessel anchored in the harbor to retrieve his sword and clothing. The officer then in command of the *Liberty* "refused to let him bring away, and 'tis said, offer'd him Violence; which reduced Capt. Packwood to the necessity of drawing his Sword, to force his Way into his Boat, whereupon the Officer call'd to the Liberty's People to fire on Capt. Packwood as he was going ashore."[27]

According to subsequent public notices, then "a great Number of People, riotously and tumultuously assembled together, in the Evening of the 19th of July last, and having, by Force and Arms, attacked and secured the said Captain Reid and his Men, and taken Possession of both Vessels; they set Fire to, and sunk the Liberty."[28] The two small boats of the *Liberty* were also burned after being taken to the site of what is now Equality Park in Newport, and the *Sally* escaped during the tumult. Captain Reid was unharmed.[29]

In 1949, a plaque was placed where the boats were burned. It reads, "On this old common the boats of H.M.S. Liberty were burned July 19, 1769 by the citizens of Newport who had previously fired upon and destroyed the sloop. This was the first overt act of violence against Great Britain in America."[30]

In the war of independence that followed, the colonies had to deal with the possibility of no longer being within the British Navigation Act system if they achieved independence. Revolutionary leaders had to anticipate a period of commercial disengagement and subsequent re-engagement as an independent nation into the international economic system. Such re-engagement would occur on a country-by-country basis with France as the test case.

THE PLAN OF TREATIES

On June 7, 1776, Richard Henry Lee offered a three-part resolution in the Continental Congress: to declare the independence of the colonies from Britain, "to take the most effectual measures for forming foreign Alliances," and to prepare a plan of confederation.[31] This was the famous "Lee Resolution," also known as "The Resolution for Independence."

On June 11, 1776, Congress appointed a committee "to prepare a plan of Treaties to be proposed to foreign Powers" consisting of John Dickinson, Benjamin Harrison, Robert Morris, and Benjamin Franklin.[32] John Adams was chosen by the committee to prepare a treaty draft to be proposed first to France and then to be used as a model for later treaties.

Much is lost to time regarding the deliberations of the committee because it perforce conducted its proceedings in secret.[33] What is apparent is that John Adams envisioned focusing on commerce rather than the political and seeking trade reciprocity rather than free trade.

It was thought by many American leaders that France would be eager to avenge its humiliation after the Seven Years' War, in which it lost most of its North American colonies. One enticement that the United States could offer to France was open and direct commerce between the two countries, which was prohibited by the British Navigation Acts.

As Adams stated in his diary for June-August 1776, "I contended for the same Principles, which I had before avowed and defended in Congress, viz. That We should avoid all Alliance, which might embarrass Us in after times and involve Us in future European Wars. That a Treaty of commerce, which would opperate as a Repeal of the British Acts of Navigation as far as respected Us and Admit France into an equal participation of the benefits of our commerce... would be an ample Compensation to France for Acknowledging our Independence."[34]

In preparing his draft, Adams liberally copied from other treaties. Yet he probably drafted one of the most important clauses in the model treaty on his own: reciprocal national treatment.[35] Those first two articles of the model treaty provided for "perfect" reciprocity, meaning that U.S. citizens would be treated as French citizens in France and French citizens treated as U.S. citizens in the United States without conditions.

Although the draft was modified, the reciprocal national treatment paragraphs remained essentially untouched in the final model treaty draft. The September 24, 1776 instructions to the American negotiators in France (Silas Deane, Arthur Lee, and Benjamin Franklin), however, gave them leeway to accept most favored nation status in lieu of reciprocal national treatment.[36] Under a reciprocal most favored nation principle, each country would agree to treat the nationals of the other country no worse than the "most favored" nationals of other countries.

The actual commercial treaty signed by France and the colonies in 1778 contained a "conditional" most favored nation provision falling short of full reciprocity.[37] The condition was to dilute the commitment such that if another country obtained a concession from France in exchange for some commercial concession, that would not automatically be extended to the United States unless the United States made some equivalent concession to France.[38]

Adams's other concept that the United States should not agree to a treaty of political alliance with France was overridden. The two countries signed a Treaty of Alliance on February 6, 1778.[39]

The most favored nation formulation would also leave future treaty partners free to discriminate against American vessels as they would vessels from other countries so long as the treatment was no worse for the Americans. The struggle to escape such discrimination later shifted to the new American national government under the Articles of Confederation drafted pursuant to the Lee Resolution.

Although reciprocal national treatment was not adopted, the model treaty written by John Adams has been called "perhaps the most important document written by him as a member of the Continental Congress."[40] The principle of reciprocity, as set forth in that treaty, interpreted at the time to mean freedom of navigation for American vessels, became an enduring national objective. However, before Adams's vision unfolded, it was not clear at the end of the Revolutionary War how Britain would treat the newly independent colonies in international trade. Silas Deane, an American businessman and diplomat, played a critical role in how that turned out.

SILAS DEANE AND LORD SHEFFIELD

Silas Deane, an American from Connecticut sent to France as America's first foreign commercial and political agent, is usually overshadowed by Ben Franklin in the historical memory. But Deane was important to early French aid and played a key part in the decision to exclude the newly independent United States from the British Navigation Acts in 1783. Deane also had an unsavory reputation at the time and has been referred to both as a patriot/hero and as a traitor/embezzler.[41]

Deane's Role in the Revolutionary War. Deane was born in Ledyard, Connecticut in 1737.[42] His father and grandfather were blacksmiths. He studied Latin and went to Yale, graduating in 1758 and going on to marry wealthy widows twice. He taught school by day and studied law by night. Edward Bancroft, one of his students, was later the secretary of the American delegation in Paris. Deane passed the bar in 1761 and established a practice in Wethersfield, Connecticut, south of Hartford, where he was also a prominent merchant, counting Benedict Arnold among his friends.

The house he built in 1769 in Wethersfield, not too far from the Silas Deane Highway and the Silas Deane Middle School, still exists and is part of the Webb-Deane-Stevens Museum. There are obviously people in Connecticut who believe that Deane was a patriot.

His second marriage brought him political connections. His wife was the granddaughter of a former governor of the colony of Connecticut, and Deane was appointed a state assemblyman in 1768. He became involved in revolutionary politics including being appointed as a representative from Connecticut to the First Continental Congress in 1774.

JOURNEY TO THE JONES ACT

In 1775, he played a role in financing the expedition to take Fort Ticonderoga from the British—one of America's first military victories.[43] He did so by diverting state money without authorization, which was approved after the fact.[44] Thereafter, he was sometimes referred to as "Ticonderoga."[45] Benedict Arnold was one of the leaders of the expedition to take the fort.

In the Continental Congress, he served on several committees, including the Committee of Secrecy, created on September 18, 1775, to procure arms and ammunition.[46] He was not, however, re-elected as a representative to Congress in the fall of 1775. John Trumbull (the famous Revolutionary War painter) explained in a November 14, 1775, letter to John Adams that Deane was "a man, whose freedom of Speech and pointedness of Sarcasm has made him as many enemies, as have been raised against him by envy—and both together form a large Party."[47]

Out of Congress, Deane entered into an agreement with the Continental Congress to purchase items in Europe to help secure allies among Native American tribes.[48] In February 1776, he was party to an agreement with the Committee of Secrecy to exchange goods for arms and ammunition in the amount of two hundred thousand Continental dollars.[49] In the latter venture, his partners were all members of Congress, including Robert Morris.[50] As compensation, he would receive a 5 percent commission on business transactions—a point noted in congressional proceedings decades later.[51]

Separately, the Committee for Secret Correspondence, formed to conduct the colonies' foreign affairs, appointed Deane commercial and political agent in France.[52] Deane's mission was to contact the French government and determine whether there was a possibility of a commercial agreement or military alliance and to secure equipment for twenty-five thousand men.[53] Thus, Deane, America's first political and diplomatic agent, went to France with mixed objectives.[54]

In France, Deane was later credited by the U.S. Congress with substantial success in arranging for the shipment of military supplies.[55] Arthur Lee, who was a congressional agent in London and who had started the negotiations with the French government, felt that he deserved the credit.[56] A portion of those supplies landed in Portsmouth, New Hampshire in 1777 in time to equip the army that later won the Battle of Saratoga in October 1777.[57]

To keep up his connections in the French court, Deane was prevailed upon to offer officer's commissions in the Continental Army to well-connected persons. Some—like Johann von Robais, Baron de Kalb, and his protégé, Gilbert du Motier, Marquis de Lafayette—worked out well for the colonies.[58] In honor of this history, "Dekalb" was used as a vessel name for a U.S. troop transport in World War I.

Others did not work out as well. The parade of officers arriving in America claiming contracts signed by Deane caused great friction in Congress and was a key factor in Deane's subsequent ouster. Washington wrote to Deane on August 13, 1777, that the "difficulty of providing those Gentlemen in a matter suitable to the former ranks of some, and the expectations of many, has not a little embarrassed Congress and myself."[59]

Following the Declaration of Independence, Congress sent Arthur Lee and Ben Franklin to join Deane and, in September 1776, made all three commissioners to the court of France.[60] All three signed America's first foreign treaty—a treaty of alliance with France—on February 6, 1778.[61]

While Franklin and Deane got along, Lee did not get along with either of the other two, but especially not with Deane. The rivalry became intense and soon Arthur Lee began alleging in reports to Congress that Deane was commingling private and public transactions and was embezzling public money.[62]

The Committee on Foreign Affairs (formerly "for Secret Correspondence") sent Deane an order in late 1777 to return to Congress. The order implied that the purpose was to "be well informed of the state of affairs in Europe."[63] Deane arranged to return on a French warship in 1778 before he could arrange for full settlement of his business transactions in France.[64]

In the meantime, Lee's reports had created substantial suspicions. Deane stayed in Benedict Arnold's lodgings when he arrived in Philadelphia in July 1778 (Arnold was then the military governor of Philadelphia).[65] Congress gave him the cold shoulder. It neither charged him with any specific offense nor permitted him to leave, and he was subsequently brushed off with a never-ending series of audits.[66]

After months of congressional run around, Deane showed his frustration by publishing an exposé in the *Philadelphia Packet* in December 1778 of his treatment by Congress.[67] In doing so, he ignited a political firestorm. Thomas Paine, then secretary (meaning the clerk) of the Foreign Affairs Committee and still writing under the pseudonym "Common Sense," answered Deane's charges in January 1779 in the same publication.[68]

To imply that Deane had embezzled funds, Paine quoted from Arthur Lee's confidential reports to Congress stating that the early French aid was a donation which was not actually the case since it was a loan.[69] Worse, Paine appeared to give official sanction to the fact of French aid. The assistance was widely known but had been structured through intermediaries to give the French government plausible deniability.[70]

Conrad Alexandre Gérard de Rayneval, the first French minister to the United States who had negotiated and signed the Treaty of Alliance, wrote two angry letters to Congress demanding an official retraction.[71] Congress acquiesced and denied in public that there had been any secret aid prior to the treaty of alliance or that there was a donation.[72] John Adams recorded in his diary for February 8, 1779, that he was so disgusted by Deane going public that he likened Deane to a "wild boar, that ought to be hunted down for the benefit of mankind."[73]

The "Deane Affair" languished further until Deane was finally discharged by Congress in August 1779 "in order that he may settle his accounts without delay."[74] He returned to France in July 1780. In Paris, then in Ghent, and finally in London, Deane pursued commercial ideas, but none panned out and he became destitute and forced to rely on the charity of friends.

From May to June 1781, he wrote a series of confidential letters suggesting that the colonies would lose the war and they should reconcile with Britain. Those letters wound up in British hands under circumstances that remain mysterious to this day. They may have been on a vessel intercepted by the British or they may have been diverted by Edward Bancroft and given to the British government.[75] Bancroft was a British double agent, but this was not confirmed until late in the nineteenth century.[76] In any event, the letters were published in New York in the *Rivington Royal Gazette* starting on October 20, 1781—one day after Cornwallis surrendered at Yorktown.[77]

The timing could not have been worse for Deane for multiple reasons, as he wrote to Robert Morris on October 10, 1783:

> The series of misfortunes which from my leaving France in 1778 to return to Philadelphia, wanted but that of the publication of my letters to overwhelm me. My fortune in America well-nigh ruined by depreciation, the funds which I had left in France wasted or misapplied by those in whose hands I had placed them... and publicly stigmatized both in America and in France as a defaulter and a traitor, I did not think it prudent to attempt to withstand the general torrent, and therefore retired into an exile as obscure and low as the circumstances to which I was reduced.[78]

His exile may have been "low," but it was not "obscure."

Deane and Sheffield. In November 1782 a preliminary peace treaty was signed in Paris between the colonies and Britain and presented to Parliament on January 27, 1783.[79] William Petty, the Second Earl of Shelburne, was then serving as prime minister. Shelburne advocated for a conciliatory policy toward the American colonies in order to pry the colonies away from

France and to maintain a market for British manufactures. He therefore favored a continuation of trade on a similar basis as before the war. The Americans proposed reciprocal national treatment, to include the English Caribbean colonies.[80] A May 1783 royal proclamation maintained the pre-revolutionary commercial status quo.[81]

At about that time, Deane moved to London and met John Baker Holroyd, the First Earl of Sheffield, a strong believer in the Navigation Acts. Later, Deane admitted that he provided Sheffield with data on British-American trade.[82] That data was used by Sheffield to produce a pamphlet first published in May 1783 entitled *Observations on the Commerce of the American States*.[83] Many argued at the time that Deane had actually written the pamphlet.[84] In fact, there is evidence that the data was copied and re-arranged, which looked bad for Deane.[85] Richard Henry Lee wrote to Samuel Adams on November 18, 1784, that "Silas Deane & [Benedict] Arnold are in frequent conversations with British Ministers" and "it is said" that Deane "composed part of the book adopted by Lord Sheffield."[86]

In the pamphlet, Sheffield argued that the long-standing trade between the American colonies and the British colonies in the "West Indies" (meaning the Caribbean) could be replaced with trade from Canada, Ireland, and Britain. He concluded that the newly independent colonies should be treated as a foreign country outside the Navigation Acts.[87] The pamphlet was very influential and popular and went through six editions by July 1784.[88]

In March 1783 the Shelbourne administration introduced the "American Intercourse Bill," which would have retained much of the colonies' previous status. Sheffield spoke out against it, arguing that the Navigation Acts "gave us the trade of the world" and if Britain altered those acts, it would have "sacrificed the marine of England."[89] The Sheffield pamphlet and another one by George Chalmers provided the economic arguments in support of opposition to the Intercourse Bill.[90] The tide turned against free trade with the former colonies and the bill was abandoned.

An Order in Council published on July 5, 1783, decided the issue by effectively excluding American vessels from the West Indies trade.[91] Subsequent Orders in Council and enactments would extend the exclusion until 1830.[92]

But for the Sheffield pamphlet, the trade outcome could easily have been different.[93] Edward Gibbon, the famous English historian, said of his friend Lord Sheffield, "The Navigation Act, the palladium of Britain was defended, and perhaps saved, by his pen; and he proves, by the weight of fact and argument, that the mother-country may survive and flourish after the loss of America."[94]

When the Order in Council became known in Paris where Benjamin Franklin, John Adams, and John Jay were negotiating a peace treaty, the "effect upon the American Commissioners of this drastic change in policy was decisive."[95] The result was that most of the commercial articles in the draft treaty were immediately dropped and left for future negotiation.[96]

American policy makers were aware of the impact of *Observations*. For example, James Madison wrote Edmund Randolph on August 30, 1783, that a "Pamphlet has lately come over from G. Britain which appears to be well adapted to retard if not prevent a commercial Treaty, & which is said to be much attended to."[97]

In his letters, Deane argued that the "newspapers" had made up the closeness of his association with Sheffield and that he never agreed to the pamphlet's conclusions.[98] As Deane said in a May 3, 1784 letter to John Jay, "It is true that I am in the habits of intimacy and of friendship with Lord Sheffield, but we never meet without a dispute on the subject of his pamphlet."[99] His protestations notwithstanding, some have speculated that Deane was paid for his work, and it is hard to believe that there were no payments involved given his destitute financial circumstances.[100]

The mysteries of Deane's life followed him to his end. He finally decided to return to America in 1789 and was on a vessel in September when he became gravely ill. The vessel returned to England due to weather, Deane was put ashore, and died soon thereafter. At the time, it was popularly believed that he overdosed on opium.[101] Some have since theorized that he was poisoned by his former student Edward Bancroft to prevent Deane from "outing" him.[102] Bancroft was a doctor, chemist, and specialized in poisons so the speculations are not without basis. More current interpretations, however, point to death from natural causes.[103]

The saga continued after Deane's passing. In 1838, Philura Deane Alden, Deane's granddaughter, petitioned Congress for redress.[104] As a result, a final accounting was ordered on August 10, 1842, vindicating Deane's claims of rectitude in the conduct of the country's business in France in 1776—78.[105]

---

[1] Larry Sawers, "The Navigation Acts Revisited," Economic History Review 45, no. 2 (May 1992): 262—84.

[2] For example, Oliver M. Dickerson, The Navigation Acts and the American Revolution (Philadelphia: University of Pennsylvania Press, 1951; repr., New York: Octagon Books, 1974).

[3] Dickerson, Navigation Acts and the American Revolution, 208.

[4] George G. Wolkins, "The Seizure of John Hancock's Sloop 'Liberty,'" Massachusetts Historical Society, Proceedings: October, 1921–June, 1922, 55 (1923): 239–84; Oliver M. Dickerson, "John Hancock: Notorious Smuggler or Near Victim of British Revenue Racketeers," Mississippi Valley Historical Review 32, no. 4 (March 1946): 517–40; Dickerson, Navigation Acts and the American Revolution, 231-250; John Philip Reid, In a Rebellious Spirit: The Argument of Facts, the Liberty Riot, and the Coming of the American Revolution (University Park, PA: The Pennsylvania State University Press, 1979); and Massachusetts Historical Society, Adams Papers: Digital Edition, https://www.masshist.org/publications/adams-papers.

[5] 15 Car. II, c. 7.

[6] David Hancock, Oceans of Wine: Madeira and the Emergence of American Trade and Taste (New Haven, CT: Yale University Press, 2009).

[7] 4 Geo. III, c. 15.

[8] Wolkins, "Seizure of John Hancock's Sloop 'Liberty,'" 240.

[9] 7 Geo. III, c. 41.

[10] Dickerson, "John Hancock," 527–28.

[11] Dora Mae Clark, "The American Board of Customs, 1767—1783," American Historical Review 45, no. 4 (July 1940): 777–806, 785.
[12] The commissioners requested navy support on February 12, 1768. "Letter from Commissioner of Customs to Comm. Hood (February 12, 1768)," Wolkins, "Seizure of John Hancock's Sloop 'Liberty,'" 278.
[13] Dickerson, "John Hancock," 517—18.
[14] Hancock, Oceans of Wine, 20. The later "Information" against John Hancock charged that the Liberty unlawfully put ashore without paying the duty on one hundred "pipes" of wine. "Sewall v. Hancock, Admiralty—Revenue Jurisdiction," Massachusetts Historical Society, Legal Papers of John Adams, vol. 2, Adams Papers Digital Edition, https://www.masshist.org/publications/adams-papers/index.php/volume/ADMS-05-02.
[15] James C. Brandow, ed., "Memoirs of a British Naval Officer at Boston, 1768—1769: Extracts from the Autobiography of William Senhouse," Proceedings of the Massachusetts Historical Society 3rd series 105 (1993): 74–93, 80.
[16] Dickerson, "John Hancock," 518–20 ("The riot was undesired by the Boston leaders and unfortunate; but it was such a plain case of public plunder.").
[17] Dickerson, "John Hancock," 519—20; Dickerson, Navigation Acts and the American Revolution, 219—21.
[18] Dickerson, "John Hancock", 520–21.
[19] Wolkins, "Seizure of John Hancock's Sloop 'Liberty,'" 283.
[20] "Letter from Gov. Bernard to Earl W. Hill (June 11, 1768)," Colonial Society of Massachusetts, Vol. LXXXVI: The Papers of Francis Bernard, vol. 4: 1768, no. 623, https://www.colonialsociety.org/node/2861.
[21] Clark, "American Board of Customs, 1767–1783," 787.
[22] Wolkins, "Seizure of John Hancock's Sloop 'Liberty,'" 251–52.
[23] David S. Lovejoy, "Rights Imply Equality: The Case against Admiralty Jurisdiction in America, 1764-1776, William and Mary Quarterly 16, no. 4 (October 1959): 459–84, 479.
[24] Josiah Quincy, Jr., Reports of Cases Argued and Adjudged in the Superior Court of Judicature of the Province of Massachusetts Bay, between 1761 and 1772 (Boston: Little, Brown, 1865), app. I, 460.
[25] Dickerson, "John Hancock," 538–40.
[26] Constance D. Sherman, "An Account of the Scuttling of His Majesty's Armed Sloop Liberty," American Neptune 20, no. 4 (October 1960): 243–49.
[27] "Newport, July 22," Connecticut Journal, July 28, 1769, 4; "Newport, July 22," Connecticut Currant, July 31, 1769, 3.
[28] "Advertisement by the Commissioners of His Majesty's Customs," Newport Mercury, (Rhode Island), August 21, 1769, 1; "A Proclamation by the Honorable Joseph Wanton, Esquire, Governor, Captain-General, and Commander in Chief, of and over the English Colony of Rhode Island, and Providence Plantations, in New England, in America." Newport Mercury, Rhode Island), July 24, 1769, 3.

[29] Sherman, "An Account of the Scuttling," 248.
[30] Brian M. Stinson, Newport Firsts: A Hundred Claims to Fame (Charleston, SC: History Press, 2018), chap. 13.
[31] Journals of the Continental Congress 1774–1789, vol. 5, 425–26.
[32] Journals of the Continental Congress 1774–1789, vol. 5, 431.
[33] Gregg L. Lint, "John Adams on the Drafting of the Treaty Plan of 1776," Diplomatic History 2, no. 3 (Summer 1978): 313-–20.
[34] John Adams autobiography, part 1, "John Adams," through 1776, sheet 24, page 4 [electronic edition], Adams Family Papers: An Electronic Archive, Massachusetts Historical Society, https://www.masshist.org/digitaladams/archive/doc?id=A1_24&bc=%2Fdigitaladams%2Farchive%2Fbrowse%2Fautobio1.php.
[35] "Editorial Note," Adams Papers: Digital Edition, Massachusetts Historical Society, Papers of John Adams, volume 4, www.masshist.org/publications/adams-papers/index.php/view/PJA04d170; Lint, "John Adams on the Drafting of the Treaty Plan of 1776," 315.
[36] William B. Willcox et al., eds., The Papers of Benjamin Franklin (New Haven, CT: Yale University Press, 1982), vol. 22, 624–30.
[37] Treaty of Amity and Commerce between the United States of America and His Most Christian Majesty, 8 Stat. 12 (February 6, 1778).
[38] Vernon G. Setser, The Commercial Reciprocity Policy of the United States 1774–1829 (New York: Da Capo Press, 1969), 19.
[39] Treaty of Alliance between the United States of America and His Most Christian Majesty, 8 Stat. 6 (February 6, 1778).
[40] Lint, "John Adams on the Drafting of the Treaty Plan," 319.
[41] For example, Charles J. Stillé, "Silas Deane, Diplomatist of the Revolution," Pennsylvania Magazine of History and Biography 18, no. 3 (1894): 273–92; George Larkin Clark, Silas Deane, a Connecticut Leader in the American Revolution (New York: G. P. Putnam's Sons, 1913); Coy Hilton James, Silas Deane: Patriot or Traitor (East Lansing: Michigan State University Press, 1975); Milton C. Van Vlack, Silas Deane: Revolutionary War Diplomat and Politician (Jefferson, NC: McFarland, 2013); Kalman Goldstein, "Silas Deane: Preparation for Rascality," Historian, 43, no. 1 (November 1980): 75–97.
[42] Van Vlack, Silas Deane, 11-36; James, Silas Deane, 1–10.
[43] Clark, Silas Deane, 28–29.
[44] For example, "Letter from Col. S. Parsons to J. Trumbull (June 2, 1775)," Collections of the Connecticut Historical Society (Hartford, CT, 1860), vol. 1, 181–84 ("Mr. Deane and myself first undertook and projected taking that fort &c, and with the assistance of three other persons procured money, men &c, and sent out this expedition without any consultation with Assembly or others.") That volume also contains the promises to repay the amounts from Deane and others and the

accounting which approved the proper disbursement of those funds. Collections of the Connecticut Historical Society, vol. 1, 184–88.

[45] For example, "Letter from S. Deane to E. Deane (June 18, 1775)," New York Historical Society, The Deane Papers 1774–1777 (1886), vol. 1, 60–62.

[46] Journals of the Continental Congress 1774–—1789, vol. 2, 253–55.

[47] "Letter from J. Trumball to J. Adams (November 14, 1775)," Adams Papers: Digital Edition, Massachusetts Historical Society, Adams Papers: Digital Edition, Papers of John Adams, vol. 3, https://www.masshist.org/publications/adams-papers/index.php/volume/PJA03/pageid/PJA03p298.

[48] Deane Papers 1774-1790, vol. 23, 245; Journals of the Continental Congress 1774–1789, vol. 4, 96.

[49] Papers of Benjamin Franklin, vol. 22, 354–56.

[50] Papers of Benjamin Franklin, vol. 22, 354–-56.

[51] The private bill finally authorizing payment to Deane's heirs signed by President John Tyler in 1842 limited the application of the 5 percent commission to $200,000 of purchases. 6 Stat. 857 (August 11, 1842).

[52] The Papers of Benjamin Franklin, vol. 22, 369 (Committee of Secret Correspondence Certificate for Silas Deane).

[53] The Papers of Benjamin Franklin, vol. 22, 369–74 (Committee of Secret Correspondence Instructions to Silas Deane).

[54] U.S. Congress, Senate, Re Petition of Horatio Alden and Philura Alden, 27th Cong., 2nd sess., 1842, S. Rep. 27-88, 2.

[55] Re Petition of Horatio Alden and Philura Alden, S. Rep. 27-88, 2.

[56] Van Vlack, Silas Deane, 4-5.

[57] The British were aware of the arrival of the two vessels—the Amphitrite and the Mercury—and their importance: "great Succours, greater I believe than ever were furnished by a Nation pretending to be at Peace, has raised the Spirits of the Rebels and of their numerous Well-wishers here." "Letter from Lord Stormount to Lord Weymouth (July 2, 1777)," in Naval Documents of the American Revolution, ed. William James Morgan (Washington, DC: Naval Historical Center, 1986), vol. 9, 452–53. A useful timeline appears in Elizabeth S. Kite, "The Continental Congress and France – Secret Aid and the Alliance 1776–1778," Records of the American Catholic Historical Society of Philadelphia 39, no. 2 (June 1928): 155–74.

[58] "Silas Deane to the Committee of Secret Correspondence (November 28, 1776)," in The Diplomatic Correspondence of the American Revolution, ed. Jared Sparks (Boston: N. Hale and Gray & Bowen, 1829), vol. 1, 67, 73; "Silas Deane to the Committee of Secret Correspondence (May 25, 1777)," in Diplomatic Correspondence of the American Revolution vol. 1, 291, 295; Journals of the Continental Congress 1774–1789, vol. 8, 721–23.

[59] "Letter from G. Washington to S. Deane (August 13, 1777)," Founders Online, National Archives, https://founders.archives.gov/documents/Washington/03-10-02-0593.

[60] Journals of the Continental Congress 1774–1789, vol. 5, 827.

[61] Treaty of Alliance between the United States of America and His Most Christian Majesty, 8 Stat. 6 (February 6, 1778). The Treaty of Amity and Commerce with France was signed on the same day. 8 Stat. 12. Simeon Deane, Silas's brother, delivered the two agreements to Congress on May 2, 1778. Journals of the Continental Congress 1774–1789, vol. 11, 417.

[62] Much has been written about the origins of the feud between Lee and Deane cited in Goldstein, "Silas Deane: Preparation for Rascality," 76n2.

[63] Journals of the Continental Congress 1774–1789, vol. 8, 605; Diplomatic Correspondence of the American Revolution, vol. 1, 117–18.

[64] James, Silas Deane, 57–60.

[65] Van Vlack, Silas Deane, 165.

[66] An 1842 report of the U.S. Senate Committee on Revolutionary Claims concluded that from 1778 to 1785, Deane "unceasingly, perserveringly, and pertinaciously, endeavored to procure a settlement with the Government, and claimed a large balance was due him. He tried every means, devised every plan, and made every offer to affect a settlement, which seemed to be the first wish of his heart." Re Petition of Horatio Alden and Philura Alden, S. Rep. 27-88.

[67] Silas Deane, "To the Free and Virtuous Citizens of America," Philadelphia Packet, December 5, 1778, 3.

[68] "Common Sense to the Public, on Mr. Deane's Affair," Pennsylvania Packet, January 2 and 5, 1779, 3 & 2.

[69] Journals of the Continental Congress 1774—1789, 13: prefatory note, 8 ("The year opened with the injudicious blurting out of state secrets by Thomas Paine...".).

[70] Journals of the Continental Congress 1774-1789, vol. 13, 30–38.

[71] Diplomatic Correspondence of the Revolution, vol. 3, 11–12, 16–17.

[72] "Resolution of January 12, 1779," Pennsylvania Packet, January 16, 1779, 3; Journals of the Continental Congress 1774–1789, vol. 13, 54–55.

[73] Charles Francis Adams, The Works of John Adams (Boston: Charles C. Little and James Brown, 1851), vol. 3, 187.

[74] Journals of the Continental Congress 1774–1789, vol. 14, 929–30.

[75] For the speculation that the letters were intercepted rather than captured: Van Vlack, Silas Deane, 176–77.

[76] Thomas J. Schaeper, Edward Bancroft: Scientist, Author, Spy (New Haven, CT: Yale University Press, 2011).

[77] Alexander Davidson Jr., "James Rivington and Silas Deane," The Papers of the Bibliographical Society of America 52, no. 3 (3rd Quarter 1958): 173–78.

[78] Deane Papers 1774-1790, vol. 23, 201.

[79] William Cobbett, The Parliamentary History of England from the Earliest Period to the Year 1803 (London: T. C. Hansard, 1814), vol. 23, 354.

[80] Setser, Commercial Reciprocity Policy of the United States 1774–1829, 40–51.
[81] London Gazette, no. 12440 (from May 13 to May 17, 1783), 1.
[82] "Letter from Deane to Ben Franklin (October 19, 1783)," Deane Papers 1774–1790, vol. 23, 212, 214 (in the same letter Deane disavows working with Arnold saying that Arnold sought him out in London and Deane did not want to have anything to do with him).
[83] John Lord Sheffield, Observations on the Commerce of the American States, new and enlarged ed. (Dublin: Luke White, 1784).
[84] Walter E. Minchinton, "Silas Deane and Lord Sheffield's 'Observations on American Commerce,'" Revista da Universidade de Coimbra 28 (1980): 83–98, 98; J. P. Brissot De Warville, New Travels in the United States of America: Performed in 1788 (Dublin: W. Corbet, 1792), v-vi (translator's preface).
[85] Minchinton, "Silas Deane and Lord Sheffield's 'Observations on American Commerce,'" 85.
[86] James Curtis Ballagh, ed., The Letters of Richard Henry Lee (New York: Macmillan, 1914), vol. 2, 294–95.
[87] John J. McCusker, "The Rise of the Shipping Industry in Colonial America," in America's Maritime Legacy: A History of the U.S. Merchant Marine and Shipbuilding Industry since Colonial Times, ed. Robert A. Kilmarx (Boulder, CO: Westview Press, 1979): 1–19, 13–15.
[88] John L. Bullion, "George III on Empire, 1783," William and Mary Quarterly 51, no. 2 (April 1994): 305—10, 310n9.
[89] Cobbett, Parliamentary History of England, vol. 23, 762–64.
[90] George Chalmers, Opinions on Interesting Subjects of Public Law and Commercial Policy Arising from American Independence (London: J. Debrett, 1784).
[91] London Gazette, no. 12455 (from July 5 to July 8, 1783), 1; 23 Geo. III, c. 39 (law enabling the Order in Council).
[92] Herbert C. Bell, "British Commercial Policy in the West Indies, 1783–93," English Historical Review, 31, no.123 (July 1916): 429–41.
[93] Vincent T. Harlow, Founding of the Second British Empire, 1763–1793 (London: Longmans, 1964), vol. 1, 221-222.
[94] Edward Gibbon, The Memoirs of the Life of Edward Gibbon, ed., George Birkbeck Hill (New York: G.P. Putnam's Sons, 1900), 226.
[95] "Letter from Nathaniel Falconer to Benjamin Franklin (July 8, 1783)," in Papers of Benjamin Franklin, May 16 through September 15, 1783, ed. Ellen R. Cohn (New Haven, CT: Yale University Press, 2011), vol. 40, 288--89; Harlow, Founding of the Second British Empire, vol. 1, 477.
[96] For example, "The American Peace Commissioners to Robert R. Livingston (July 27, 1783)," in Papers of Benjamin Franklin, vol. 40, 388–389.
[97] "Letter from J. Madison to E. Randolph (August 30, 1783)," available at Founders Online, National Archives, https://founders.archives.gov/documents/Madison/01-07-02-0166.

[98] "Letter from S. Deane to R. Morris (October 10, 1783)," Deane Papers 1774—1790, vol. 23, 200, 205 (regarding reports that he met frequently with British officials and was "intimate with General Arnold" and "to have furnished Lord Sheffield with materials for a pamphlet on American commerce, &c." -- "I can only assure you, and I have no interest to deceive you, that there is not the least foundation in truth for any of these reports.").

[99] The Deane Papers 1774-1790, vol. 23, 299. John Adams placed Deane in league with Sheffield: "Letter from J. Adams to R. Livingston (Aug. 2, 1783)," Deane Papers 1774—1790, vol. 23, 184 ("My advices from England are that Lord Sheffield with his friends Deane, Arnold, Skeane, and P. Wentworth, are making a party unfriendly to us.").

[100] Minchinton, "Silas Deane and Lord Sheffield's 'Observations,'" 86.

[101] Dennis Kent Anderson and Godfrey Tryggve Anderson, "The Death of Silas Deane: Another Opinion," New England Quarterly 57, no. 1(March 1984): 98–105, 98–99.

[102] Julian P. Boyd, "Silas Deane: Death by a Kindly Teacher of Treason?" William and Mary Quarterly 16, no. 2 (April 1959): 165–87; 16, no. 3 (July 1959): 319–42; and 16, no. 4 (October 1959): 515–50.

[103] William Stinchcombe, "A Note on Silas Deane's Death," William and Mary Quarterly 32, no. 4 (October 1975): 619–24; Anderson and Anderson, "Death of Silas Deane."

[104] Referenced in Re Petition of Horatio Alden and Philura Alden, S. Rep. 27-88.

[105] 6 Stat. 857 (August 11, 1842).

President James Madison, 1816, artist John Vanderlyn, White House Historical Association

Chapter 4—Early American Navigation Policy

The former American colonies had to find a way to convince or force other countries not to discriminate against American vessels. James Madison led the long effort to adopt a national commercial policy to counteract such discrimination.[1] As a member of Congress in 1789, Madison directed the congressional effort to discriminate against Britain and in favor of France. In 1812, as president, he went to war with Britain over neutral shipping rights which eventually opened direct trade with Britain. And he finally achieved his overall goal when he signed the Act of March 1, 1817, the American "Charta Maritima," which included the first outright reservation of U.S. domestic commerce to U.S.-citizen-owned vessels.[2]

Articles of Confederation Policy Failure

America's first federal government was formed under the Articles of Confederation, which came into force on March 1, 1781. The first article established that the "style of this confederacy shall be, 'The United States of America.'"[3] The national government resided in "the United States in Congress assembled," with each state having one vote.

Congress was expressly denied the authority to adopt any "treaty of commerce," and the Confederation had no direct taxation authority. Thus, the Confederation government was hobbled from the beginning in adopting anything to prefer or protect American vessels.

Unsurprisingly, other countries took advantage of the Confederation's weakness. When the American Revolutionary War ended officially on September 3, 1783, England, Spain, and France all took steps to exclude American vessels from their colonies in the West Indies and elsewhere.[4]

Madison knew that the solution was to adopt policies preferring American vessels. In a letter to Edmund Randolph in May 1783 even before the infamous Order in Council was issued, Madison wrote that the United States should look to the "example of old and intelligent nations," particularly Britain, concerning which, he rhetorically asked, "does she not still make a preference of her own Vessels and her own mariners the basis of her maritime power?"[5]

Several proposals were made to amend the Articles of Confederation to impose national import duties in place of state tariffs. A recommendation approved by congressional delegates in April 1783 later served as model for the first duties adopted by the U.S. Congress in 1789.[6] The 1783 proposal recommended to the states a series of import duties for specific goods (such as tobacco) and a 5 percent proportionate duty (referred to as "*ad valorem*") on non-enumerated goods for a period of twenty-five years. The sole purpose of the proposal was to discharge national debts.

Unanimous state approval was required to adopt the amendment. By the time the last state agreed—New York in 1786—it did so with conditions that would have required re-approval by all other states.[7] Therefore, despite widespread approval in principle of the idea to amend the articles to permit the imposition of import duties, the necessity to obtain unanimous approval doomed the effort.[8]

The Continental Congress also sought to address directly the British Orders in Council. It formed a committee that reported in September 1783 that the new orders "are highly injurious to the welfare and commerce of these United States."[9] The committee determined that "it is of importance to counteract these systems so injurious to the United States"—but nothing was done.[10]

A 1785 congressional trade committee led by James Monroe similarly reported that discrimination had to be fought with discrimination.[11] Monroe warned that if the United States did not counter foreign policies, the "prospects of national consequence must decline, their merchants become only the agents and retailers of those of foreign powers, their extensive forests be hewn down and laid waste to add to their strength and national resources, and the American flag be rarely seen upon the face of the seas."[12]

That same year, John Jay, serving as secretary of foreign affairs, wrote to John Adams and wondered "whether the United States should withdraw their attention from the ocean and leave foreigners to fetch and carry for them, or whether it is more their interest to look forward to naval strength and maritime importance, and take and persevere in the measures proper to attain it."[13]

Adams, then minister to Britain, believed that the answer to Jay's charge was to retaliate rather than have "foreigners fetch and carry" for the United States. Thus, Adams wrote frequently to Jay and others that the country had to adopt navigation acts to gain a foothold in international trade.[14] One October 1785 letter to Jay is typical: "The Commerce of America will have no Relief at present, Nor, in my Opinion, ever, until the United States Shall have generally passed Navigation Acts. If this Measure is not adopted, We shall be derided, the more We suffer, the more will our Calamities be laugh'd at."[15]

The inability of the Confederation government to protect U.S. foreign commerce and to obtain revenues through duties in a coordinated way was one of the principal motivators for a new federal constitution.

CONSTITUTIONAL CONVENTION—SLAVERY AND NAVIGATION

The Confederation government's weaknesses finally became overwhelming, and a convention was called starting in Philadelphia on May 14, 1787. Every state sent a delegation except Rhode Island.

The Confederation period brought into sharp relief the different sectional views on navigation laws.[16] Southern states were concerned that the northern states would adopt a navigation act that reserved imports and exports to American vessels thereby likely to raise freight rates.[17] Northern states believed they needed a navigation act to get fair access to international trade.

In an August 1785 letter to Madison, Richard Henry Lee wrote that it was clear to him that giving Congress "a power to legislate over the trade of the Union would be dangerous in the extreme to the five Southern or staple States, whose want of ships and seamen would expose their freightage and their produce to a most pernicious and destructive monopoly."[18] Lee also expressed the view that giving Congress the ability to enact a U.S. navigation act would be worse "than even the crabbed, selfish system of Great Britain."[19]

The basic politics were described by Alexander Hamilton: "There are navigating and non-navigating states."[20] The northern states wanted "no restraints on their navigation, and they should have full power, by a majority in Congress, to make commercial regulations in favor of their own, and in restraint of the navigation of foreigners." The southern states—"apprehensive that the restraints of a navigation law would discourage foreigners, and, by obliging them to employ shipping of the Northern States, would probably enhance their freight"—sought "that two-thirds in Congress should be the requisite to pass an act in regulation of commerce."

In the summer of 1787, a committee was formed—the "Committee of Detail"—to set down the agreements made at the convention to that point. On August 6 that committee issued a report that would have granted to Congress the general power "to regulate commerce with foreign nations and among the several States."[21] The report also recommended inclusion of two controversial provisions—that "no Tax or Duty shall be laid, by the Legislature, on Articles exported from any State" and "no Navigation Act shall be passed without Assent of two-thirds of the Members present in each House."[22]

Oliver Ellsworth (CT) argued in favor of the export tax ban because an export tax "will discourage industry" and would likely not fall uniformly which "would engender incurable jealousies."[23] Elbridge Gerry (MA) (later Madison's vice president for a time and for whom the term "gerrymander" is named) argued similarly that the export power would permit the national government "to oppress the States, as much as Ireland is oppressed by Great Britain."[24]

James Wilson (PA) and others countered that taking away the power over exports would impede the government's ability to regulate trade.[25] The motion to remove the limitation failed and an alternative to grant power over exports but only upon a two-thirds vote of each House offered by Madison was also defeated.[26] Ultimately, the U.S. Constitution would include general commerce power given to the federal government and the restriction on the export taxes.

The Committee of Detail also recommended inclusion of a provision authorizing states to continue to import slaves. Gouverneur Morris (PA), who had called slavery a "nefarious institution" and a "curse of heaven on the states where it prevailed," proposed that the slave importation issue be linked" to the navigation issue and considered by a new committee.[27] He believed that "these things may form a bargain among the Northern & Southern States."[28]

On August 22, 1787, the convention referred the matters to a "Committee of Eleven." That committee's August 24 report recommended a compromise: that slave importation be permitted but end in 1800 in exchange for congressional authority to impose a duty on the importation of slaves and elimination of the two-thirds navigation act approval requirement.[29]

George Mason (VA) confirmed the compromise at the Virginia state ratification convention on June 21, 1788. According to Mason, there were eight votes in favor of retaining the two-thirds navigation act voting requirement "till a compromise took place between the northern and southern states; the northern states agreeing to the temporary importation of slaves; and the southern states conceding, in return, that navigation and commercial laws should be on the footing on which they now stand."[30]

On August 29, the convention debated a motion made by Charles Cotesworth Pinckney (SC) to reinstate the two-thirds navigation act vote requirement. George Clymer (PA) and Roger Sherman (CT) argued against the motion because they did not want to see a repeat of the "embarrassing" inaction of the Confederation government.[31] Gouverneur Morris argued that a navigation act would increase the number of American vessels and thereby make the shipment of southern staples cheaper.[32]

John Rutledge (SC) "reminded the House of the necessity of securing the West India trade to this country. That was the great object, and a navigation Act was necessary for obtaining it."[33] Edmund Randolph (VA) argued that the draft constitution was already "so odious" that a "rejection of the motion [to reinstate the two-thirds super majority for navigation acts] would compleat the deformity of the system."

At the end of the debate, the motion to reinstate the two-thirds vote requirement failed on a procedural motion by a vote of four to seven with South Carolina voting with the northern states, and the report of the Committee of Eleven was adopted.[34] South Carolina also had commercial interests favoring the navigation act authority as confirmed by a later Charleston, South Carolina shipbuilders' communication to the new U.S. Congress in favor of a navigation act.[35]

The tragedy and travesty were that the compromise necessary to obtain navigation act authority resulted in a slave trade that lasted until January 1, 1808.[36] Many years later, in 1901, Senator George G. Vest (D-MO), a former Confederate congressman, nevertheless captured the moment when he said that the navigation laws "came from an infamous coalition between the shipping interests of New England and the African slave trade."[37]

JOURNEY TO THE JONES ACT

David A. Wells, a prominent proponent in the late nineteenth century of freeing U.S. maritime commerce from the navigation laws the United States adopted under this constitutional authority, wrote in 1883:

> Such, then, is a brief history of the inception and growth of our present navigation laws. Conceived in sin and brought forth in iniquity, they seemed to have entailed a curse... general for the whole country, but more especially on that section whose fathers sold their honor to accomplish the result, and who thereby merited execration for having entailed, for eighteen long years, the horrors of the African slave-trade. And when one journeys through New England, and sees how thick are the graves of her sons, slain in a war which slavery originated, the question might suggest itself: Would these graves exist, had the ancestors of those who fill them not consented to strengthen and perpetuate domestic slavery as a consideration for the privilege of doing another wrong; namely, that of restricting their fellow-citizens from freely exchanging the products of their labor?[38]

Despite these criticisms, the convention did in fact make possible subsequent U.S. merchant marine policy which supported the great U.S. merchant marine of the pre-Civil War era. John Rutledge, during South Carolina's ratifying convention, summed up the benefit. Rutledge warned that United States could never "expect to become a great nation until we were powerful on the waters." He added, "If we are a great maritime people, what have we to fear? Nothing."[39]

THE SECOND AND THIRD ACTS OF THE REPUBLIC

When the first U.S. Congress convened in the spring of 1789, there was no president (the votes of the electors had not even been officially tallied), no executive departments of government, no sources of revenue, and no one to collect the revenue if there were sources. The U.S. Constitution was more of an outline than a book on government. The first U.S. Congress had to start building out that outline.

One given was that government needed revenue to function and to repay the debts of prior American governments. The new federal government had agreed to assume those debts under article VI of the U.S. Constitution.[40]

Another given was that such revenue would have to come predominantly from import and tonnage duties because no other form of taxation was politically acceptable. What was not a given was how to set the duty rates in general and specifically whether to discriminate against other countries or in favor of U.S. vessels.

The first U.S. Congress met for the first time on March 4, 1789, at the Federal Hall in New York at 26 Wall Street, although it was not until April 1 that the House of Representatives achieved a quorum. The U.S. Senate achieved a quorum on April 6 and immediately proceeded to count the votes of the electors in the choice of president and vice president. George Washington was elected with sixty-nine electoral votes. At a time when the second-place candidate became vice president, John Adams was elected to that position with thirty-four. John Jay came in third with nine votes.

On April 9, following enactment of a law for the administration of oaths required by article VI of the U.S. Constitution, the House turned to considering a resolution offered by Madison on "duties on imports." With reference to the Confederation era, which he referred to as a "state of imbecility," Madison recommended the quick and temporary adoption of the 1783 Confederation duty program.[41]

The object, according to Madison, was to generate revenue and for the "general regulation of commerce; which, in my opinion, ought to be as free as the policy of nations will admit."[42] He also recommended "the addition of a clause or two on the subject of tonnage," or in other words, a tax on vessels in addition to the tax on their cargoes.[43] Madison's simple plan eventually became more complex with the negotiation of a long list of enumerated duty categories swallowing the general 5 percent ad valorem duty.

In the tonnage clauses, Madison proposed a three-way differentiation. He proposed one rate for U.S.-built vessels "belonging wholly" to U.S. citizens, a second rate for vessels "belonging wholly to the subjects of Powers with whom the United States have formed treaties," and a third rate for all other vessels. Thus U.S.-owned/U.S.-built vessels would pay the lowest rate and treaty vessels would be preferred over non-treaty vessels. In other words, French vessels would be preferred over British vessels since there was a commercial treaty with France and none with Britain.

Many American merchants resented the exclusion of U.S. vessels from the trade with the British Caribbean colonies brought about by the 1783 Order in Council and, as Madison wrote in 1785, "animosities" against Britain "of our citizens remains strong" while there remained a favorable sentiment toward France.[44]

In contrast, Alexander Hamilton, who was to become the first secretary of the treasury, was focused on putting the U.S. government on a sound fiscal footing.[45] He and much of the Senate believed that any discrimination against Britain would be counter-productive to such revenues. They expected Britain to retaliate rather than acquiesce if France were treated better than Britain, which would likely lead to a trade war between the United States and Britain, reduced trade volume, and reduced import duty and tonnage tax revenue.

Prior to the ratification of the Constitution, Hamilton had argued *both* the revenue and fair-trade points of view. In Federalist Paper no. 11, he argued that American independence "has already excited uneasy sensations in several of the maritime powers of Europe" which would use whatever means "of depriving us, as far as possible, of an ACTIVE COMMERCE in our own bottoms."[46] Hamilton cautioned that the "maritime nations...

would in all probability combine to embarrass our navigation in such a manner as would in effect destroy it, and confine us to a PASSIVE COMMERCE." America's response, he argued, should be to adopt "prohibitory regulations."

In Federalist Paper no. 12 he argued that a "nation cannot long exist without revenues" and that if such revenues were not "withdrawn from commerce" then the burden "must fall with oppressive weight upon land" (in terms of property taxes).[47] He also pointed out that Britain relied mainly on import duties and excise taxes and that in "America, it is evident that we must long depend for the means of revenue chiefly on such duties."

For their part, Madison, Jefferson, and Washington held to the view that the United States benefited most from free trade and free trade could not be achieved in a mercantilist world without tough unilateral measures.[48] As Madison said in the House floor debate, "I am a friend to free commerce, and, at the same time, a friend of such regulations as are calculated to promote our own interest, and this on national principles."[49]

On the discrimination in favor of treaty countries, Representative John Laurance of New York carried the arguments against. Laurance (sometimes spelled Lawrence) has been called "The Immigrant Founding Father America Never Knew."[50] Laurance was the second judge advocate general of the Continental Army, a member of Congress, a senator, a federal judge, and an expert in admiralty in his private law practice.

Laurance argued that the tonnage duty would inevitably fall on U.S. commodity exports which would suffer because there were not enough American vessels.[51] He questioned whether public sentiment was truly in favor of discriminating against Britain.[52]

Laurence also pointed out that American vessels had something to lose if there was British retaliation. American vessels were already on "equal footing" with British vessels in the direct trade between the two countries by British policy. Britain could reverse that policy at any time putting American vessels at a disadvantage.[53] Laurance concluded his arguments by noting that "it is good policy to let commerce take its own course, and not to attempt discrimination, which may eventually prove more injurious to us than we at present conceive."[54]

Madison countered that public sentiment favored discrimination against non-treaty countries, as evidenced by exactly such discriminations in the duties imposed by states like Virginia in the Confederation era.[55] He also asked the rhetorical question, "Is it not also of some importance, that we should enable nations in treaty with us to draw some advantage from our alliance?"[56]

Madison could have also pointed to petitions received from shipbuilders in Maryland, Pennsylvania, and South Carolina in early 1789 that begged the new government to adopt a navigation law.[57] The petition from "Baltimore Town" pointed out (quoting Josiah Child) that the colonial fleet was larger than the English fleet when the English 1660 Navigation Act was enacted and that the newly formed United States was therefore in a better position to provide for the carriage of its own products than England was at that time.

Madison moreover made a national defense argument, "I consider that an acquisition of maritime strength is essential to this country; if ever we are so unfortunate as to be engaged in war, what but this can defend our towns and cities upon the sea-coast?" he declared, "Or what but this can enable us to repel an invading enemy?"[58]

Madison also emphasized that, "if it is expedient for America to have vessels employed in commerce at all, it will be proper that she have enough to answer all the purposes intended; to form a school for seamen, to lay the foundation of a navy, and to be able to support itself against the interference of foreigners." With respect to the disparity in tariff rates favoring American vessels, Madison recognized that "owners of American shipping will put a considerable part of the difference in their pockets," although this "sacrifice is but small" and was "a tax we must pay for the national security."[59]

While considering the import duty proposal, two changes were made to promote U.S. shipping aside from the discriminating tonnage tax. First, at the suggestion of Representative Thomas Fitzsimons (PA), a provision was added to favor U.S.-built vessels in the importation of tea from China and India. Second, William Smith (MD) moved to add a "drawback" (reduction) of 10 percent on all duties paid on goods imported on American vessels.[60] These were the first two provisions under U.S. law to prefer U.S. vessels and fittingly signed into law by President Washington as the second act of the Republic on July 4, 1789.

On May 7, the House proceeded with a separate tonnage resolution which ultimately (with some revisions) became the third act.[61] As it was agreed to in the House, the tonnage law maintained the gradation Madison offered by providing tonnage tax amounts of 6 cents, 30 cents, and 50 cents per ton, respectively. It also would have accorded the 6 cents both to U.S. and foreign-built vessels wholly owned by U.S. citizens.[62] In addition, the resolution would have restricted the U.S. coastwise trade "in the transportation of the produce or manufactures of the United States" outright to U.S.-built, U.S. citizen-owned vessels. On May 29, the bill was sent to the U.S. Senate for concurrence.[63]

The Senate struck the coastwise trade provision, permitting such trade subject to the payment of the 50 cent per ton duty, and the House agreed on June 27.[64] The Senate also proposed striking the discrimination in favor of treaty country vessels, sparking a sharp discussion. Madison favored abandoning the legislation altogether rather than agreeing with the Senate. In contrast, Laurance argued that the House should cave to the Senate because revenue to be had from the bill was too important to risk in the face of stiff Senate opposition.

Senator William Maclay (PA) noted in his contemporaneous journal that the Senate could not be swayed. He referred to speaking against the "villainous amendments" to be "in vain" and attributing the Senate's position to "influence of this [New York]."[65] Maclay also referred to Laurance as "a mere tool for

British agents and factors."[66] On July 1, Madison lost as the House voted thirty-one to nineteen to accept the Senate's last amendments.[67]

Maclay further explained the compromise that had to be struck in a description of the balance between protected and free maritime trade that could be applied at any point in U.S. history:

> There were two extremes in commercial relations equally to be avoided. The principle of the Navigation Act might be carried so far as to exclude all foreigners from our ports. The consequences would be a monopoly in favor of the mercantile interest. The other was an unlimited license in favor of foreigners, the consequence of which would be a monopoly in favor of the cheapest carriers, and in time a total dependence on them.[68]

The United States chose the middle course in 1789. Two of the first three laws enacted by the U.S. Congress preferred American vessels, but not absolutely.[69]

Yet, Congress was not finished with laws preferring American vessels via duties or tariffs. It has been estimated that between 1789 and 1828, Congress also passed about fifty tariff laws directly or indirectly preferring American vessels.[70]

The U.S. merchant marine also received support at the highest levels of the U.S. government. In his second Annual Message to Congress (in other words, the State of the Union address) delivered in December 1790, Washington urged Congress to consider "such encouragements to our own navigation as will render our commerce and agriculture less dependent on foreign Bottoms, which may fail us in the very moments most interesting."[71]

As secretary of state, Jefferson delivered to Congress influential maritime policy reports in 1791 and 1793. The 1791 report was on U.S. fisheries an important source of both mariners and work for U.S. shipyards.[72] Jefferson argued that the "loss of seamen, unnoticed, would be followed by other losses in a long train." He suggested that it "is easier, as well as better, to stop this train at its entrance, than when it shall have ruined or banished whole classes of useful and industrious citizens."

In his December 1793 report, Jefferson expanded on the importance of a U.S. merchant marine.[73] Notably, this report was cited with approval by the 1905 Merchant Marine Commission.[74]

The 1793 report contains a statement that was to be repeated in substance by later statesmen and could be said to have predicted America's situation in 1914 exactly, "When those nations who may be our principal carriers, shall be at war with each other, if we have not within ourselves the means of transportation, our produce must be exported in belligerent vessels, at the increased expense of war-freight and insurance, and the articles which will not bear that, must perish on our hands." At the outset of World War I, the principal carrier of U.S. goods was Britain, a belligerent, and the United States, lacking "the means of transportation," suffered "the increased expense of war-freight and insurance" and much of its exports "perished" at the docks.

Although the role of the U.S. discriminations in supporting the U.S merchant marine is unclear, it is undeniable that the U.S. merchant marine expanded substantially after 1789. The U.S. fleet, which comprised about 200,000 tons at the end of 1789, grew to almost 1.4 million tons at the end of 1815 about the time the United States signed its treaty of commercial reciprocity with Britain.[75] From 1820 to 1830, American vessels carried roughly 90 percent of U.S. foreign trade.[76]

---

[1] "James Madison played a crucial role in the 1780s–arguably the crucial role–in the definition of American commercial policy at both the congressional and state levels." John E. Crowley, The Privileges of Independence: Neomercantilism and the American Revolution (Baltimore: Johns Hopkins University Press, 1993), 95 (emphasis in original).

JOURNEY TO THE JONES ACT

[2] William W. Bates, American Navigation: The Political History of Its Rise and Ruin and the Proper Means for Its Encouragement (Boston: Houghton, Mifflin, 1902), dedication.
[3] Articles of Confederation of 1781.
[4] Setser, Commercial Reciprocity Policy of the United States, 53n2.
[5] "Letter from J. Madison to E. Randolph (May 20, 1783)," available at Founders Online, National Archives, https://founders.archives.gov/documents/Madison/01-07-02-0037.
[6] Journals of the Continental Congress 1774–1789, vol. 24, 257–61.
[7] Douglas A. Irwin, "Revenue or Reciprocity? Founding Feuds over Early U.S. Trade Policy," National Bureau of Economic Research, NBER Working Paper Series, Working Paper 15144, July 2009, 6.
[8] E. James Ferguson, The Power of the Purse: A History of American Public Finance 1776–1790 (Williamsburg, VA: University of North Carolina Press, 1961), 336.
[9] Journals of the Continental Congress 1774–1789, vol. 25, 628.
[10] Journals of the Continental Congress 1774–1789, vol. 25, 629.
[11] "Reports of Committees for Increasing the Powers of Congress by Recommendations to the States," found in The Writings of James Monroe, ed. Stanislaus Murray Hamilton (New York: G. P. Putnam's Sons, 1898), vol. 1, 80–83.
[12] Hamilton, The Writings of James Monroe, vol. I, 82–85.
[13] "Report on the Algerine Declaration of War (October 20, 1785)," available at Founders Online, National Archives, https://founders.archives.gov/documents/Jay/01-04-02-0094.
[14] Setser, Commercial Reciprocity Policy of the United States, 97–98.
[15] "Letter from J. Adams to J. Jay (October 12, 1785)," available at Founders Online, National Archives, https://founders.archives.gov/documents/Adams/06-17-02-0275.
[16] Charles Warren, Making of the Constitution (Boston: Little, Brown, 1928), 580 ("It is impossible to understand properly the fight over the adoption of the Constitution in the Convention... unless this fear of the South at Northern domination of its commerce is thoroughly realized.").
[17] For example, "Letter from G. Washington to J. McHenry (August 22, 1785)," available at Founders Online, National Archives, https://founders.archives.gov/documents/Washington/04-03-02-0184.
[18] "Letter to J. Madison from R. Lee (August 11, 1785)," available at Founders Online, National Archives, https://founders.archives.gov/documents/Madison/01-08-02-0180.
[19] "Letter from R. Lee to unidentified recipient (October 10, 1785)," in The Letters of Richard Henry Lee 1779–1794 (New York: MacMillan, 1914), vol. 2, 387–90.
[20] "New York Ratifying Convention Remarks (Francis Child's Version) (June 20, 1788)," available at Founders Online, National Archives, https://founders.archives.gov/documents/Hamilton/01-05-02-0012-0005.

[21] Warren, Making of the Constitution, 570.
[22] Crowley, Privileges of Independence, 96–98.
[23] Farrand, Max, ed., The Records of the Federal Convention of 1787, Library of Congress, Digital Collections, A Century of Lawmaking for a New Nation: U.S. Congressional Documents and Debates 1774 to 1875, vol. 2, 359–60.
[24] Farrand, Records of the Federal Convention of 1787, vol. 2, 362.
[25] Farrand, Records of the Federal Convention of 1787, vol. 2, 362.
[26] Farrand, Records of the Federal Convention of 1787, vol. 2, 363.
[27] Elliot, Jonathan, ed., Debates in the Several State Conventions, on the adoption of the Federal Constitution, as Recommended by the General Convention at Philadelphia in 1787, Library of Congress, Digital Collections, A Century of Lawmaking for a New Nation: U.S. Congressional Documents and Debates 1774 to 1875, vol. 5, 392-93.
[28] Farrand, Records of the Federal Convention of 1787, vol. 2, 374.
[29] Farrand, Records of the Federal Convention of 1787, vol. 2, 396.
[30] Farrand, Records of the Federal Convention of 1787, vol. 3, 334.
[31] Farrand, Records of the Federal Convention of 1787, vol. 2, 450.
[32] Farrand, Records of the Federal Convention of 1787, vol. 2, 450.
[33] Farrand, Records of the Federal Convention of 1787, vol. 2, 450.
[34] Farrand, Records of the Federal Convention of 1787, vol. 2, 453.
[35] American State Papers: Commerce and Navigation, vol. 1, 5.
[36] 2 Stat. 426 (March 2, 1807).
[37] 34 Cong. Rec. 1334 (January 23, 1901).
[38] David A. Wells, Our Merchant Marine: How It Rose, Increased, Became Great, Declined and Decayed (New York: G. P. Putnam's Sons, 1883), 73–74. This passage was quoted by Eugene T. Chamberlain, the long serving commissioner of the Bureau of Navigation, in the Congressional hearings on the Shipping Act, 1916. U.S. Congress, House, Committee on Merchant Marine and Fisheries, Hearings before the House Merchant Marine and Fisheries Committee on Creating a Shipping Board, A Naval Auxiliary and a Merchant Marine, 64th Cong., 1st sess., 1916, 179.
[39] Elliot, Debates on the Adoption of the Federal Constitution, vol. 4, 299.
[40] Constitution of the United States, Art. VI, cl. 1.
[41] Annals of Congress, vol. 1, 106–08.
[42] Abridgment of the Debates of Congress from 1789 to 1856 (New York: D. Appleton, 1860), vol. 1, 22.
[43] Annals of Congress, vol. 1, 106–08.
[44] "Letter from J. Madison to T. Jefferson (August 20, 1785)," available at Founders Online, National Archives, https://founders.archives.gov/documents/Madison/01-08-02-0182.
[45] Irwin, "Revenue or Reciprocity?" 25.
[46] Alexander Hamilton, "The Utility of the Union in Respect to Commercial Relations and a Navy," Federalist Papers, no. 11.

47 Alexander Hamilton, "The Utility of the Union in Respect to Revenue," Federalist Papers, no. 12.
48 For example, Jefferson wrote in 1785 that Americans wish to engage in trade "by throwing open all the doors of commerce and knocking off it's shackles" but "this cannot be done for others, unless they will do it to us" so a system was needed to "shackle them in our ports as they do us in theirs." "Letter from T. Jefferson to G. Van Hogendorp (October 13, 1785)," available at Founders Online, National Archives, https://founders.archives.gov/documents/Jefferson/01-08-02-0497.
49 Annals of Congress, vol. 1, 192.
50 Keith Marshall Jones III, John Laurance: The Immigrant Founding Father America Never Knew (Philadelphia: American Philosophical Society, 2019).
51 Annals of Congress, vol. 1, 184–85.
52 Annals of Congress, vol. 1, 191–92.
53 Bates, American Navigation, 53.
54 Annals of Congress, vol. 1, 192.
55 Bates, American Navigation, 47–48.
56 Annals of Congress, vol. 1, 190.
57 American State Papers: Finance, vol. 5, 9; American State Papers: Commerce and Navigation, vol. 7, 5-6.
58 Annals of Congress, vol. 1, 246–47.
59 Annals of Congress, vol. 1, 246–47.
60 Bates, American Navigation, 62; Annals of Congress, vol. 1, 343.
61 Bates, American Navigation, 62.
62 Annals of Congress, vol. 1, 290.
63 Annals of Congress, vol. 1, 416.
64 Annals of Congress, vol. 1, 632.
65 Edgar S. Maclay, Journal of William Maclay, United States Senator from Pennsylvania 1789–1791, Library of Congress, Digital Collections, A Century of Lawmaking for a New Nation: U.S. Congressional Documents and Debates 1774 to 1875, 78.
66 Maclay, Journal of William Maclay, 47.
67 Annals of Congress, vol. 1, 643.
68 Maclay, Journal of William Maclay, 77.
69 1 Stat. 24 (July 4, 1789); 1 Stat. 27 (July 20, 1789).
70 Walter T. Dunmore, Ship Subsidies: An Economic Study of the Policy of Subsidizing Merchant Marines (Boston: Houghton Mifflin 1907), 14.
71 George Washington, Second Annual Address to Congress, December 8, 1790, UC Santa Barbara, The American Presidency Project, accessed September 20, 2023, https://www.presidency.ucsb.edu/documents/second-annual-address-congress-0.
72 American State Papers: Commerce and Navigation, vol. 1, 8–22.
73 "Final State of the Report on Commerce (December 16, 1793)," available at Founders Online, National Archives, https://founders.archives.gov/documents/Jefferson/01-27-02-0503-0004.

[74] Report of the Merchant Marine Commission, S. Rep. 58-2755, 24–25.
[75] Annual Report of the Commissioner of Navigation to the Secretary of the Treasury (1884), 118.
[76] Annual Report of the Commissioner of Navigation to the Secretary of the Treasury (1884), 21.

Abraham Alfonse Albert Gallatin, artist Daniel Huntington, Harvard Art Museum

Chapter 5—Era of Free Trade Reciprocity

The war between Britain and France under Napoleon Bonaparte from 1803 to 1814 brought the United States and Britain back into conflict in the War of 1812. Britain enforced a blockade of France, which led both to the forcible impressment of sailors from American vessels needed to man the British Navy and aggressive interpretations of the limits of the neutral trade conducted by the United States with France. Napoleon's abdication on April 11, 1814, relieved much of the maritime pressure as Britain ended the blockade of France. By early 1814 the United States was already negotiating with Britain.

1815 U.S.—Great Britain Commercial Convention

Leading the U.S. delegation in Europe was Swiss-born Abraham Alfonse Albert Gallatin.[1] Gallatin was a former member of Congress and President Jefferson's secretary of the treasury.[2] As soon as Britain signed the Treaty of Ghent in December 1814 ending the war between the two countries, Gallatin drew up a commercial treaty proposal.[3] Gallatin's negotiations to end the war and re-establish commercial relations with Britain ushered in an era of free trade reciprocity for the United States.[4]

The American proposal was divided into two sets of articles. One was purely commercial and the other concentrated on "belligerent and neutral collisions."[5] Specifically, Gallatin tried to end British impressment in exchange for excluding British seamen from U.S. vessels, to clarify neutral rights, and to open up the "West Indies" and "East Indies" (primarily India) trades.[6] In other words, Gallatin sought to address both some of the causes of the War of 1812 as well as the long-standing trade issues.

At the time, there was no commercial treaty between the United States and Britain. The "Jay Treaty," a Federalist Party product, had expired in 1807.[7] That treaty had been aggressively criticized by Gallatin and Madison and other members of the Democratic-Republican Party. It had permitted Britain to retaliate for American discriminating duties in the direct trade between the countries, although it had permitted limited free trade by American vessels in the West Indies.

Negotiations would not be easy. Britain did not seriously consider the set of American proposed articles on neutral relations.[8] It was also "freely avowed on the British side that, with respect to the American trade with the West Indies, they could do nothing."[9]

The British negotiators expected an equivalent American concession on "East Indies" trade (they suggested fur trade concessions in the "north west" North American territories).[10] Since the United States had no colonial inducements to offer, the British thought themselves generous to open up the trade temporarily to American vessels.[11] On direct trade, the British were willing to provide for mutual national treatment. Gallatin thus failed on most of his objectives.[12]

At numerous points, William Clay and John Quincy Adams, Gallatin's fellow negotiators, wanted to walk away from the negotiations because they thought the treaty would be worthless to the United States. But Gallatin persisted.[13] Gallatin and Clay, in a May 18, 1815, letter to James Monroe, admitted that the British moved forward with the negotiations only when the U.S. negotiators announced they were leaving London.[14]

The best Gallatin could achieve on the crucial West Indies trade was to get an agreement to reserve rights, which made subsequent congressional retaliatory action possible.[15] Getting Britain to agree to potential U.S. retaliation was a considerable achievement. The British had wanted the same rights in U.S. ports for British vessels coming from the West Indies as British vessels coming from Britain—without providing reciprocal rights for American vessels in West Indies ports.[16] As Gallatin pointed out in a January 4, 1816, letter to Clay, "the words adopted fully imply the right of laying an additional duty on British vessels from British West Indies."[17]

Gallatin saw the benefit of regularizing direct trade. In a September 1815 letter to Madison, he said, "the convention, such as it is, must, so far as relates to them, be considered as an evidence of friendly disposition. The campaign of 1814 had made us respected and gave us peace."[18] By the "campaign of 1814," Gallatin was likely referring to the repulse of the British force in Baltimore and Andrew Jackson's victory in New Orleans.

Madison's response was incisive.[19] He replied that it was not to be expected "that the British government, on the pinnacle of its elevation would look with solicitude on her relations to the United States." Nevertheless, he said, "the convention is a proof... that she does not wish the sort of conflict which her countervailing duties would be likely to produce" and the "equalization stipulation on the subject is valuable to both parties." Expecting that the West Indies trade would be included "was promised neither by experience nor by the circumstances of the moment."

Madison predicted that "the want of reciprocity in that trade whilst Great Britain permits her own vessels to come to our ports, will be more and more felt, particularly by the Eastern States, and will sooner or later produce invitations to the other States to concur in counteracting regulations." He concluded, "I retain my opinion that effectual ones might be adopted without incurring any very sensible inconvenience to our commerce, much less any risk to the peace between the two countries." Such "effectual counteracting regulations" would not be long in coming although they took many years to achieve their full intended effect.

March 1, 1817, Navigation Act

The U.S. Shipping Board reported in 1922 that in "1815 came the great change from discrimination to reciprocity."[20] That was evident not only in the 1815 Commercial Convention but also in March 3, 1815, legislation. This law, which preceded the convention, repealed U.S. discriminating duties for any direct trade if the foreign country ceased discriminating against U.S. vessels.[21] The law thus invited the world to trade freely with the United States on a reciprocal basis.

The 1815 law was the carrot, but a stick was needed to make it effective. Getting the stick commenced with an attempt by President Madison to diffuse future tension with Britain over the impressment of mariners. An 1813 law had taken a step in that direction by requiring that U.S vessels have U.S. citizen crews. But there was a loophole for the hiring of citizens of countries that did not exclude U.S. citizens.[22] Madison, in a special February 1815 message to Congress, recommended that the law be made even more restrictive in favor of U.S. citizens. He also wanted to ensure that U.S. commerce did not overly rely on foreign mariners who might be "recalled by their Governments under circumstances the most inconvenient to the United States."[23]

In his December 1815, Message to Congress, Madison repeated his mariner recommendation. Madison hoped that the 1815 Commercial Convention would be improved over time and that "Congress will decide on the expediency of promoting such a sequel by giving effect to the measure of confining the American navigation to American seamen."[24] A motion made to advance Madison's request, however, failed.[25]

Congress instead focused on the failure of the Commercial Convention to open the West Indies trade. When the Senate ratified the convention on December 19, 1815, it adopted a resolution advising Madison to negotiate further with Britain.[26] This advice reflected negative public sentiment toward the West Indies exclusion.[27]

In 1816 Congress proceeded with consideration of navigation legislation to address the inadequacies of the 1815 Commercial Convention. Three proposals were considered: One was to adopt the formulation contained in the English 1660 Navigation Act to prohibit the indirect import trade to the U.S. in foreign vessels. An American twist was added—the prohibition would be repealed if American vessels were granted indirect trade access.[28] The second proposal would have provided for a duty on goods and a tonnage tax on vessels for goods imported from any port from which American vessels were excluded.[29] The third would have turned this duty into a prohibition of any foreign vessel from coming to the United States from any port from which American vessels were excluded.[30]

All three would eventually become law. The first idea became the Act of March 1, 1817, the second a law signed on March 3, 1817, and the third—after the second discriminating duty law failed to open the British West Indies ports—became law on April 18, 1818.[31]

Madison raised the general navigation issue arising from the 1815 Commercial Convention in his December 1816 message to Congress.[32] He attributed the "depressed state of our navigation" to "its exclusion from the colonial ports of the nation most extensively connected with us in commerce, and from the indirect operation of that exclusion." In other words, British vessels were enjoying the West Indies-related trades to the exclusion of U.S. vessels.

However, Madison did not recommend a particular course of action. Newspapers at the time speculated that the reason he did not do so was to avoid alienating "agriculturists and manufacturers" if he favored "the navigating class or shipowners." Those American exporters, it was noted, made a profit "whether they chartered a Danish, English, or American vessel."[33]

On December 23 the U.S. House started to make its wishes known when a simple two-section prohibition on indirect trade was reported by Representative John Forsyth (GA), chairman of the Foreign Relations Committee, modeled after the first two sections of the English 1660 Navigation Act.[34] According to this prohibition, "goods, wares, or merchandise" could only be imported in American vessels or in vessels carrying those items from their own country. The American version also had a reciprocity proviso.

An alternative non-intercourse bill was considered in the House on January 21, 1817, by Representative Samuel Smith (MD).[35] The bill's title expressed its purpose, "To prohibit all commercial intercourse with ports or places into, or with which, the vessels of the United States are not ordinarily permitted to enter and trade."[36] If the Forsyth bill was a scalpel, the Smith bill was a sledgehammer.

A petition (then called a "memorial") submitted to Congress by a group of prominent New York merchants dated January 17, 1817, recommended legislation based on the principles of both the indirect prohibition and non-intercourse bills.[37] The merchants argued that "if foreigners want our bread, our cotton, our tobacco, our lumber, our naval stores, we only ask to be allowed a fair and reasonable share in the carriage of the same to them" with the wish that eventually "all restrictions be removed" by all countries.

Henry Wheaton, a noted New York lawyer who among other things was the plaintiff in the U.S. Supreme Court's first copyright case in 1834, was appointed to represent the group in Washington.[38] Wheaton wrote to Representative Forsyth arguing Gallatin's point that "the right to enact a navigation law is untouched by the late commercial convention with Great Britain."[39] Other memorials were also submitted from other states to the same effect.[40]

The press reported that the non-intercourse bill was "understood to be agreeable to the wishes of the ship owners... who have indeed petitioned its passage."[41] Others argued "that it will injure the agriculturist in proportion as it benefits the ship owner, and that its beneficial influence on our Commerce is questionable."

On January 29, 1817, the more moderate indirect trade prohibition was considered by the House.[42] Representative William Lowndes (SC) moved to delete the reciprocity proviso to steer the legislation in the direction of the non-intercourse bill. That motion was voted down. Then the House tabled the bill.[43]

Representative Lowndes moved to add five sections to the indirect trade prohibition bill, including adding a direct reservation of the U.S. coastwise trade to American-owned vessels. Lowndes's amendment was close to what would become law.[44] There is no explanation in the *Annals of Congress* as to why the domestic reservation was included although the provision was like English Navigation Acts provisions going back to the Elizabethan law of 1563.

Modern historians have speculated that the inclusion of the coastwise reservation was due to the broadness of the reciprocity invitation in the Act of March 3, 1815.[45] That law permitted the president to repeal "duties on the tonnage of ships and vessels," which could be read to include the discriminating duties first enacted in 1789 favoring U.S.-flag vessels in the domestic trade. The purpose of the Lowndes provision would then be to take away that possibility so that the coastwise trade would be reserved to U.S.-owned vessels regardless of whether other countries opened their coastwise trade to U.S-owned vessels.

The legislation was revised on February 1, 1817, largely as it was subsequently enacted.[46] This included the Lowndes proposed coastwise trading provision. The law also exempted American vessels with U.S. citizen officers and two-thirds citizen crew from a new 50 cents per ton duty for American vessels trading coastwise. Notably, the congressional debate focused on the foreign intercourse and reciprocity provisions, not on the coastwise trade restriction.[47]

As finalized, the law excluded from the carriage of "goods, wares, or merchandise" between U.S. ports any "vessel belonging wholly or in part to a subject of any foreign power."[48] In 1843, the U.S. attorney general had the occasion to interpret this exclusion. He concluded that foreign-registered vessels owned wholly by U.S. citizens could transport items between two U.S. ports subject only to a higher duty than the duty paid by U.S.-owned vessels.[49] It was not until 1898 that Congress amended the 1817 Act to restrict U.S. domestic trade to "vessels of the United States," i.e., U.S-flag vessels, as it is today.[50]

Madison signed the measure into law as the Navigation Act of March 1, 1817, three days before the end of his second term and about two weeks before his sixty-sixth birthday. A modern Madison biographer believes that "in a sense this bill... was Madison's going-away present from Congress," fulfilling Madison's early ambitions for the country's navigation to be free from foreign discrimination.[51]

In his letters, Madison focused on foreign trade and Britain. In a February 1817 letter to Jefferson, Madison said that the bill copied "the great principle of the British Acts" and "will be felt deeply in G.B. [Great Britain] in its example, if not in its operation."[52] In a March 31, 1817, letter to Gallatin, Madison noted that Congress had shied away from the non-intercourse bill and referred to the legislation as enacted as including "the Navigation Act which applies to G.B. & her imitators, the rule of her General Navigation Act of Chs. II [Charles II]."[53]

Despite Madison's comparison of the Act of March 1, 1817, to the English 1660 Navigation Act, the two had a major difference. The 1817 Act was predominantly a means to end, which was to open the British West Indies to American vessels and to remove or to prevent similar discriminations imposed by other countries. In contrast, the English Navigation Acts were the policy end (reserving a market for British vessels and tying the colonial empire together), regardless of what other countries did.

For this reason, the U.S. attorney general in 1842 referred to the law as the "Reciprocity Act of 1817."[54] The offer of reciprocity to any country that did not discriminate against American vessels was the key element.[55]

The 1817 Act was also only the beginning of a discrimination policy to achieve open markets. These efforts culminated in laws offering reciprocity on all trades for any country enacted on May 24, 1828 (and, more specifically, for Britain on May 29, 1830) upon a finding by the president that U.S.-flag vessels were not being discriminated against.⁵⁶ Britain responded positively. President Andrew Jackson signed the non-discrimination proclamation on October 5, 1830.⁵⁷

From then on, to this day, vessels of the two countries engaged in direct and indirect trade have moved freely without discrimination. In 1913 Senator Jones, who believed that the United States should not have stopped discriminating, referred to the 1828 law offering full reciprocity to the world as "the Act that has destroyed our shipping power."⁵⁸

Once the goal of reciprocity was achieved, what remained of the 1817 Act's substance was the coastwise trade reservation. This occurred even though its adoption in 1817 took place without fanfare or recorded discussion, probably because it was unremarkable. Reservation of domestic trade was long a provision of the English Navigation Acts. And the discriminating duties enacted in 1789 had effectively reserved U.S. domestic trade before 1817. An enhanced reservation was not a big policy step.

The coastwise trade reservation endured and has been U.S. law ever since. Section 27 of the 1920 Merchant Marine Act amended and restated the 1817 Act, which had already been amended several times in the intervening years. As foreign free trade reciprocity was achieved, the U.S.-flag fleet in the foreign trade prospered. That prosperity faded in the mid-nineteenth century and the defining moment in the downturn was the Civil War. Before that, the United States dabbled with subsidizing U.S.-flag vessels in international trade.

---

[1] Henry Adams, The Life of Albert Gallatin (Philadelphia: J. B. Lippincott, 1879), 549.
[2] Henry Cabot Lodge, Albert Gallatin (New York: Charles Scribner's Sons, 1879); Adams, Life of Albert Gallatin; John Austen Stevens, Albert Gallatin (Boston: Houghton, Mifflin, 1899); Raymond Walters Jr., Albert Gallatin: Jeffersonian Financier and Diplomat (New York: The Macmillan Company, 1957); and Nicholas Dungan, Gallatin: America's Swiss Founding Father (New York: New York University Press, 2010).
[3] Walters, Albert Gallatin, 289.

4 Henry Hall, American Navigation with Some Account of the Causes of Its Recent Decay, and of the Means by Which Its Prosperity May Be Restored, Restored (New York: D. Appleton, 1880), 46.
5 Charles Francis Adams, ed., Memoirs of John Quincy Adams, Comprising Portions of His Diary From 1795 to 1848 (Philadelphia: J. B. Lippincott, 1874), vol. 3, 208.
6 American State Papers: Foreign Relations, vol. 4, 9; Walters, Albert Gallatin, 291.
7 Treaty of Amity, Commerce and Navigation, between His Britannick Majesty and The United States of America, by Their President with the Advice and Consent of Their Senate, 8 Stat. 116, Treaty Series 105.
8 Adams, Memoirs of John Quincy Adams, Comprising Portions of His Diary from 1795 to 1848, vol. III, 210-211; American State Papers: Foreign Relations, vol. 4, 11.
9 Adams, Memoirs of John Quincy Adams, Comprising Portions of His Diary From 1795 to 1848, vol. III, 211; American State Papers: Foreign Relations, vol. 4, 10.
10 American State Papers: Foreign Relations, vol. 4, 13.
11 Adams, Memoirs of John Quincy Adams, vol. 3, 211, 225. Clay and Gallatin asserted in a May 18, 1815, letter to Monroe that the trade should be opened because it benefited both parties since U.S. vessels carried Indian exports paid for in hard currency. American State Papers: Foreign Relations, vol. 4, 9.
12 Adams, Life of Albert Gallatin, 551.
13 Adams, Memoirs of John Quincy Adams, 219, 222, 230.
14 American State Papers: Foreign Relations, vol. 4, 8.
15 F. Lee Benns, American Struggle for the British West India Carrying–Trade, 1815–1830 (Bloomington: Indiana University Studies), vol. 10, study no. 56 (March 1923), 32.
16 Benns, American Struggle for the British West India Carrying-Trade, 32; The Writings of Albert Gallatin, ed. Henry Adams (Philadelphia: J. B. Lippincott, 1879), vol. 1, 680, 681 and 682.
17 Adams, Writings of Albert Gallatin, vol. 1, 682.
18 Adams, Writings of Albert Gallatin, vol. 1, 650–51.
19 Adams, Writings of Albert Gallatin, vol. 1, 652–53.
20 U.S. Shipping Board, Report on the History of Shipping Discriminations and on Various Forms of Government Aid to Shipping (Washington, DC: Government Printing Office, 1922), 7.
21 3 Stat. 224 (March 3, 1815).
22 2 Stat. 809, 810—11 (March 3, 1813).
23 "Message from J. Madison to Congress (February 25, 1815)," available at Founders Online, National Archives, https://founders.archives.gov/documents/Madison/03-09-02-0030.
24 "Annual Message from J. Madison to Congress (December 5, 1815)," available at Founders Online, National Archives, https://founders.archives.gov/documents/Madison/03-10-02-0061.
25 Annals of Congress, vol. 29, 27–30 (motion by Rep. Nathan Sanford of New York).

26 U.S. Congress, Senate, Journal of the Executive Proceedings of the Senate of the United States 3, 7, December 19, 1815, https://memory.loc.gov/cgi-bin/ampage?collId=llej&fileName=003/llej003.db&recNum=14&itemLink=D?hlaw:1:./temp/~ammem_wLCU::%230030015&linkText=1.
27 Benns, American Struggle for the British West India Carrying Trade, 43 (collects newspaper articles).
28 U.S. Congress, House, Bills and Resolutions, "Concerning the Navigation of the United States," HR 32, 14th Cong., 2nd sess., December 23, 1816, https://memory.loc.gov/cgi-bin/ampage?collId=llhb&fileName=046/llhb046.db&recNum=599. This bill was reported to the House of Representatives by Rep. John Forsyth of Georgia on December 21, 1816. Annals of Congress, vol. 30, 356–57.
29 U.S. Congress, House, Bills and Resolutions, "Supplementary to the act, regulating duties on Imports and Tonnage, passed twenty-seventh April, one thousand eight hundred and six," HR 33, 14th Cong., 2nd sess. December 23, 1816, https://memory.loc.gov/cgi-bin/ampage?collId=llhb&fileName=046/llhb046.db&recNum=601.
30 Annals of Congress, vol. 30, 695–696 (Senate) & 247, 308–09 (House; became H.R. 66).
31 3 Stat. 369 (March 3, 1817); 3 Stat. 432 (April 18, 1818).
32 "Annual Message from J. Madison to Congress (December 3, 1816)," available at Founders Online, National Archives, https://founders.archives.gov/documents/Madison/03-11-02-0557.
33 Littleton W. Tazewell, A Review of the Negociations between the United States of America and Great Britain, Respecting the Commerce of the Two Countries, and More Especially Concerning the Trade of the Former with the West Indies (London: John Murray, 1929), 36.
34 Annals of Congress, vol. 30, 356–57.
35 Annals of Congress, vol. 30, 696–97.
36 U.S. Congress, House, Bills and Resolutions, "To prohibit all commercial intercourse with ports or places into, or with which, the vessels of the United States are not ordinarily permitted to enter and trade," HR 66, 14th Cong., 2nd sess., January 21, 1817, https://memory.loc.gov/cgi-bin/ampage?collId=llhb&fileName=046/llhb046.db&recNum=684.
37 "Memorial on Navigation," Niles' Weekly Register (Baltimore) 11, no. 23 (February 1, 1817): 374–75.
38 Wheaton v. Peters, 33 U.S. 591 (1834).
39 "On the Policy of a Navigation Act, &c.," Colombian, February 26, 1817, 2.
40 For example, Annals of Congress, vol. 30, 105.
41 "Friday, January 31," National Intelligencer, February 1, 1817, 1.
42 Annals of Congress, vol. 30, 770.
43 Annals of Congress, vol. 30, 770–842.

[44] U.S. Congress, House, Journal of the House of Representatives of the United States 10, 309, January 29, 1817, https://memory.loc.gov/cgi-bin/ampage?colIId=llhj&fileName=010/llhj010.db&recNum=1191&itemLink=D?hlaw:6:./temp/~ammem_fKIz::%230101192&linkText=1. Text of amendments at U.S. Congress, House, Bills and Resolutions, "Amendments proposed by Mr. Lowndes to the Bill, entitled 'A Bill concerning the Navigation of the United States,' No. 32," H.R. __ [unnumbered], 14th Cong., 2d sess., January 29, 1817, https://memory.loc.gov/cgi-bin/ampage?colIId=llhb&fileName=046/llhb046.db&recNum=732.

[45] Bates, American Navigation, 206 (to put the domestic trading reservation "safely out of hand of our diplomats"); Gerald R. Jantscher, Bread upon the Waters: Federal Aids to the Maritime Industries (Washington, DC: Brookings Institution, 1975), 46 n 3.

[46] Annals of Congress, vol. 30, 841–42 (an amendment by Rep. Forsythe to require 100 percent U.S. citizen crews on fishing vessels receiving U.S. government bounties failed 71-72 with the Speaker of the House casting the deciding vote).

[47] Annals of Congress, vol. 30, 770–842.

[48] 3 Stat. 361 (March 3, 1817).

[49] U.S. Attorney General, "Employment of Foreign Vessels in the Coasting Trade," Op. Att'y Gen. 4, no. 188 (July 20, 1843).

[50] 30 Stat. 248 (February 17, 1898).

[51] Robert Allen Rutland, James Madison: The Founding Father (Columbia: University of Missouri Press, 1987), 238.

[52] "Letter from J. Madison to T. Jefferson (February 15, 1817)," available at Founders Online, National Archives, https://founders.archives.gov/documents/Jefferson/03-11-02-0071.

[53] "Letter from J. Madison to A. Gallatin (March 31, 1817)," available at Founders Online, National Archives, https://founders.archives.gov/documents/Madison/04-01-02-0021.

[54] U.S. Attorney General, "Reciprocity Act of 1817," Op. Att'y Gen. 4, no. 69 (June 30, 1842).

[55] Lloyd W. Maxwell, Discriminating Duties and the American Merchant Marine (New York: H. W. Wilson, 1926), chap. 2.

[56] 4 Stat. 308 (May 24, 1828); 4 Stat. 419 (May 29, 1830).

[57] U.S. Congress, House, Tariff Acts Passed by the Congress of the United States from 1789 to 1909, 61st Cong., 2nd sess., 1909, H. Doc. 61-671, 94.

[58] 50 Cong. Rec. 4495 (September 8, 1913).

Collins Line steamship Baltic, lithograph by N. Currier, circa 1852, Library of Congress

Chapter 6—First Government Subsidies

The first U.S. government direct monetary support for the U.S. merchant marine started with a refund of duties payable to the government by fishing vessels. That was included in the first U.S. duty act in 1789.[1] In 1792, Congress replaced the refund with an "allowance" payable to the vessel's owner. This payment was divided between the owner and the crew as prescribed by law.[2] These allowances would continue until 1866.[3]

The 1905 Merchant Marine Commission would later cite this long-standing subsidy as "an exact and authoritative precedent" for general vessel subsidies based on "the example of the fathers of the Republic."[4] The commission claimed that the motives were the same: "to create a sea militia, a force of naval volunteers, brave and hardy men, inured to the ocean, who should be prepared to defend the flag in war." The 1905 commission also claimed that fishermen had provided the bulk of Navy crews in the War of 1812, the Mexican American War of 1848, and the Civil War.

Consideration of more general subsidies was prompted by the formation of subsidized transatlantic British shipping lines. The introduction of wooden steamships led to the creation of regular service on direct lines, such as between Liverpool and New York. Britain issued its first transatlantic steamship mail contract in 1839 to Samuel Cunard and Robert Napier.[5] The subsidy was successful in supporting a regular service that was, for about ten years, a monopoly until the advent of the American "Collins Line" in 1850. The Cunard/Napier company went on to become a household name when in 1879 the firm was officially reorganized as the Cunard Steamship Company.

Charlie Papavizas

The Unlucky Collins Line[6]

U.S. general maritime subsidies started in 1845 as mail carriage contracts awarded to steamship lines. Mail subsidy contracts were to be the primary U.S. government direct financial support of the U.S. merchant marine until the Merchant Marine Act, 1936. One of the most famous of the early ocean mail subsidies was an 1847 contract with the "New York and Liverpool United States Mail Steamship Company," known as the "Collins Line."

The namesake of that shipping line was Edward Knight Collins who was born in 1802 in Truro, Cape Cod, Massachusetts.[7] By the age of fifteen, he was a clerk in a store in New York City and was making trips to the West Indies as "supercargo" (representative of the vessel's owner on the vessel). These adventures included "experiencing several hair-breath escapes from pirates and two disastrous shipwrecks on the coasts of Cuba and Florida."[8]

After several successful sailing vessel ventures, Collins constructed in the 1830s the biggest wooden sailing vessels of the time, including the *Shakespeare* delivered in 1834. Collins named three similar new vessels after other actors and playwrights and the service between Liverpool and New York became known as the "Dramatic Line."[9]

Although the Dramatic Line was successful, the appearance of the first steamships to cross the Atlantic in April 1838 (the *SS Sirius* and the *SS Great Western*) changed the game. Although the Dramatic Line vessels kept to a schedule, they could not easily compete with steamships. Collins recognized the problem immediately and vowed to build bigger and better steamships to compete with Cunard.[10]

Believing that he needed U.S. government subsidies to compete with the British subsidies, Collins submitted an unsolicited proposal to the government for that purpose.[11] Collins's three-paragraph proposal provided that, in exchange for a ten-year contract paying $385,000 per annum, he would build five steamships of at least 2,000 tons and 1,000 horsepower "sufficiently strong for war purposes." He pledged to deliver four of them within eighteen months and carry U.S. mail between New York and Liverpool on a regular schedule.

These terms turned out to be over-promises, which were later used against Collins. At the time, the House Naval Affairs Committee noted that Collins was offering bigger and more efficient vessels than those employed by Cunard. Collins also required less subsidy than either Cunard or the other American proposal that had been submitted.[12]

Congress had earlier granted the postmaster general the first authority to enter into international contracts for the carriage of mail on March 3, 1845.[13] The first mail transportation contract was awarded to the Ocean Steam Navigation Company for service between New York and "Bremen Haven, Germany" via Southampton, England.

The 1847 "Collins Act" granted to the secretary of the Navy authority to "cause to be built and equipped four first-class seagoing steamships via the acceptance of the "proposals of E. K. Collins and his associates."[14] One of those "associates" was the merchant banker James Brown, of the famous firm Brown Brothers & Co., who in fact invested more in the enterprise than Collins.[15] Thus, Collins received a sole-source, ten-year government contract by legislation. Brown's role vis-à-vis Cunard was lost to history until the mid-1970s.[16]

Collins took three years to finance his new venture and build four wooden side-wheel steamships, the *SS Arctic*, *SS Atlantic*, *SS Baltic*, and *SS Pacific*. Collins outdid himself with vessels of between 2,700 and 2,850 tons and about 280 feet in length. They were larger than his government contract requirement and faster and better appointed than any Cunard vessel at the time. Service commenced on April 27, 1850.

To beat the Cunard vessels and meet the requirements of his government contract, the Collins vessels often burned exorbitant quantities of coal and required frequent repairs. Collins had obtained from Congress advances on the contract in 1848 to help finance the construction of the vessels. He also obtained a contract extension in 1849 because of construction delays.

The vessels came in way over budget.[17] In a letter to Congress, Collins blamed the difference on his effort to build "the four largest and swiftest steamers in the world."[18] The service provided by the vessels was in fact acceptable to the postmaster general, who said "the ships of this line have preserved their early reputation for unrivalled speed and sea-worthiness."[19] On average, the Collins vessels were about a day faster than the Cunard vessels.[20]

The problem was that the Collins Line was operating at a substantial financial loss.[21] This was sympathetically reported to Congress by the Senate Post Office Committee in 1852, which noted that "on the score of elegance and convenience the American ships are at least ten years in advance of the British."[22]

Collins approached Congress in early 1852 for a substantial increase in the subsidy. Opposition came from many quarters, including from Southern members of congress. They argued that the U.S. government was not getting anything in return for its money.[23] Collins's inability to make a profit was also held against him.

To sway Congress, Collins arranged to sail the *Baltic* to Washington, DC for a public relations trip. Due to her draft, the vessel could only reach as far as Alexandria, Virginia. There, she was opened to invited guests and members of the public.[24] Senator Solon Borland (D-AR) objected strenuously to Collins publicity efforts, saying that Collins was acting on "a proposition which is an insult in itself—that the nearest way to the hearts and understanding of Senators is down their throats."[25] As a sign that there was already substantial disharmony in Congress when it came to Collins, the motion to adjourn to permit members to visit the vessel barely passed by a vote of 21 to 19.[26] In the end, however, the president, members of Congress, foreign ministers, cabinet officials, and Army and Navy officers visited the vessel.[27]

JOURNEY TO THE JONES ACT

Possibly because of the visit, Congress voted the increase sought by Collins, and President Millard Fillmore signed it into law at the end of August 1852.[28] The leading advocate for the Collins Line was Charles Seward (W-NY), who argued that to let the Collins Line fail would be to "surrender the whole nation's cause without a blow."[29]

Collins had also sold the increase as being necessary to match Cunard. Many analyses then and later focused on the Cunard-Collins rivalry as the reason the Collins Line struggled.[30] Subsequent scholarship, however, has focused on the connection of major investors in the two lines. James Brown on the American side was matched by his brother William Brown, senior partner in a British banking firm, who was a major investor in Cunard. The two had entered a secret pooling and rate-setting agreement between the lines.[31] When this was discovered long after the fact, it was remarked that "while legal in form"—at the time—the agreement "was indeed, *had* to be—a matter of collusion."[32]

The agreement was only rendered inoperative by circumstance. On September 27, 1854, the *SS Arctic* on its westward voyage collided with the French vessel *Vesta* off the coast of Newfoundland in fog. The *Vesta* was an iron-hulled, screw-propelled vessel ferrying fishing employees.[33] Her bow was almost destroyed, and she looked at first to be the more heavily damaged vessel.[34]

The *Vesta*'s wound was in fact survivable because she had transverse bulkheads, but the damage to the *Arctic* was fatal since she did not. When that became obvious, the *Arctic*'s captain James F. Luce decided to steam directly to the nearest land. When the flooding extinguished the vessel's boilers, panic overwhelmed the lifeboats (one had been sent to assist the *Vestas* and there were not enough to begin with). None of the women and children on board survived, including Collins's wife and two of his children. Eight members of the Brown banking family were also on board and all perished. A monument still stands for them in the Green-Wood Cemetery in Brooklyn, New York.[35] Of about four hundred aboard, approximately eighty-eight survived—mostly members of the crew and especially engineers.

As the *New York Times* later reported, "there was unquestionably a lamentable lack of discipline and good conduct on board the *Arctic* at the time of the wreck."[36] As his crew commandeered the lifeboats, Luce and his eleven-year-old son stayed with the vessel to the end. Luce went down with the vessel but was sucked to the surface. There, a broken-off paddle-box narrowly missed him but struck and killed his son. Luce floated on top of the paddle box until he was picked up by a passing vessel two days later. He was greeted as a hero when he finally arrived in New York.[37]

The *Arctic's* sinking was a front-page story in the *New York Times* and in other newspapers around the country receiving *Titanic*-level national attention.[38] In the first reports, Luce was presumed lost.[39] As reports of the sinking and the conduct of the crew began to circulate, outrage followed.[40]

A federal grand jury in New York was convened to consider whether criminal charges should be brought against the crew.[41] The grand jury instead recommended significant policy changes. These included requiring that vessels have lifeboats sufficient for all on board, and that the engineers' department be under the direct command of the captain (the engineers were among the first to abandon ship). The recommendations were not adopted until after later shipping disasters.

Despite the agreement between the Browns, and an increase in subsidy secured by Collins in 1852, the Collins Line continued to lose money.[42] An effort to continue the extra subsidy and grant the Collins Line two additional years of subsidies to replace the *Arctic* passed Congress in 1855 but was vetoed by President Franklin Pierce.[43] By 1856, Collins's congressional welcome was wearing out, and Congress reversed the 1852 increase.[44] President Pierce's message stated that continuation of the subsidy would "establish a monopoly, in violation of the soundest principles of public policy, and of doubtful compatibility with the Constitution."[45]

JOURNEY TO THE JONES ACT

The Collins Line suffered a second catastrophe in 1856 when the *Pacific* was lost without a trace.[46] She left Liverpool in January 1856 and disappeared, despite several searches.[47] Incredibly, a note in a bottle was found in 1861 in the Scottish Hebrides islands apparently written by a passenger, which said:

> On board the Pacific, from L'pool to N. York. Ship going down. (Great) confusion on board. Icebergs around us on every side. I know I cannot escape. I write the cause of our loss, that friends may not live in suspense. The finder of this will please get it published. Wm. Graham.[48]

William Graham was a British sea captain sailing on the *Pacific* as a passenger.

The Collins Line had constructed the *SS Persia* in 1852 and the *SS Adriatic* in 1856. The *Adriatic* was the last wooden sidewheeler built for transatlantic service and was thought to be too inefficient from the time she was delivered.[49] Regardless, after being sold to another line, she set the speed record for completing a passage eastward in 1859 of nine days and seven hours.[50]

By January 1858 the Collins Line had ceased sailing. A last-gasp effort was undertaken to get Congress to reinstate the Collins Line contract, which had lapsed. By then the balance had tipped to opposition led by many Democratic U.S. senators who happened to later serve in the Confederate government. The Collins Line subsidy became a sectional football.[51] Senator Jefferson Davis (D-MS) said that "I see no reason why, if we can get our mails carried in British vessels across the Atlantic, we should establish a line of American vessels" and "the vanity of the attempt has been illustrated by the results."[52] Senator Robert A. Toombs (D-GA), later a Confederate general, argued that "if letters cannot be carried without a subsidy... I think we had better let England do it."[53]

All the mail contracts were terminated in legislation enacted in 1858, in favor of appropriating funds for the carriage of mail. There was only a marginal preference for U.S.-flag vessels.[54] In the Collins Line insolvency proceedings, the creditors fought off contract default claims asserted by the U.S. Navy and the vessels were sold at auction.[55] Collins left shipping and went to Ohio to pursue mining and other business interests.[56] He died in 1878 at the age of seventy-five without fanfare, leaving behind a small estate, and is buried without a marker.[57]

The Collins Line episode was a preview of how difficult it would be to meet international subsidized competition with mail or other subsidies. In the meantime, subsidies led to another problem in the case of the Pacific Mail Steamship Company.

The Pacific Mail Steamship Company

On June 15, 1846, the United States and Britain signed a treaty settling the long-standing Oregon territory boundary dispute between the two countries.[58] Congress separately authorized the secretary of the Navy in the March 1847 Collins Act "to contract... for the transportation of the mail from Panama to such port as he may select in the Territory of Oregon, once a month each way, so as to connect with the mail from Havana to Chagres across the isthmus."[59] Chagres was then the chief Atlantic port in Panama.

The Postal Service awarded the subsidy contract to the Pacific Mail Steamship Company in 1848.[60] Pacific Mail wound up being one of the most famous U.S. shipping lines and continued until 1916 when it was taken over by Grace Line management.[61] The first manager of the company was William H. Aspinwall, related on his mother's side to John Howland, a signer of the Mayflower Compact.[62]

Pacific Mail's Pacific service was matched to a service from New York via Charleston, Savannah, and from Havana to the Atlantic coast of Panama. Then the mail (as well as passengers and other cargo) would proceed across the Panamian isthmus, at first by mule and boat, and later by the Panama Canal Railway which opened in 1855.[63] Aspinwall was also prominent in the construction of the railway and a new town named "Aspinwall" (now Colon) at the Atlantic terminus, replacing Chagres in the trans-isthmian trade.

Pacific Mail started its West Coast service with three purpose-built wooden side-wheel steamships: the *SS California*, *SS Oregon*, and *SS Panama*. Because of the California gold rush, this service was so successful that it survived the termination of the mail contracts in 1858. From 1848 until the completion of the transcontinental railroad in 1869, Pacific Mail formed the main connection between the two U.S. coasts.[64]

The Pacific Mail's service was again subsidized by the U.S. government for the carriage of mail in 1865 to Asian destinations.[65] As with the Collins Line, Pacific Mail later requested a subsidy increase.

The proposed 1872 postal appropriation legislation would have doubled the stipend between San Francisco and Japan and China in exchange for increased service. It also would have provided a stipend for service to the Hawaiian Islands (referred to as the "Sandwich Islands") and to Brazil.[66] The stipends were tied directly to national defense, and the vessels had to meet certain criteria to make them militarily useful.

Congressmen complained that, although the subsidy to Asia would be competitively bid, there very likely would be only one bidder, Pacific Mail.[67] It was also pointed out that the current stipend was already excessive for the service performed and that more frequent service would increase the controversial immigration from China.[68] The opposition was summed up by Senator Oliver H. P. T. Morton (R-IN): "I am not willing to vote an enormous subsidy of $1,000,000 a year to a single steamship line unless there is some evidence—and up to this time there has been none—that this line cannot be put on semimonthly without this subsidy."[69]

Senator John Sherman (R-OH) of antitrust fame countered that Pacific Mail was the only carrier that had been willing to step up to the plate to provide the necessary service, that the original subsidy had been enacted by a unanimous Senate, and the "general results of the contract have been favorable to the Government of the United States."[70]

The increased and expanded subsidies became law in the postal appropriations act signed by President Ulysses S Grant on June 1, 1872.[71] The act named the Pacific Mail Steamship Company, but there were provisos. If that company was awarded the subsidy contract, it would have to maintain its service from New York to San Francisco via the Panamanian isthmus.

The increase was to be short-lived. In February 1873, LeGrand Lockwood (the son) alleged that the subsidy increase had been obtained by bribery.[72] LeGrand Lockwood (the father), a New York businessman, was a director of the Pacific Mail Steamship Company when he died in 1872.[73] He presumably had passed on evidence of bribery to his son.

The U.S. House of Representatives adopted a resolution calling for an investigation. The Ways and Means Committee alleged "that a large sum of money was used to secure the passage through Congress of an increased annual appropriation to the Pacific Mail Steamship Company."[74] Several House of Representatives and Senate committees undertook investigations in 1874-75 of the "China Mail Service" with the object of unearthing whether corrupt payments had been made.[75]

The Ways and Means Committee issued an inconclusive report in February 1875.[76] The committee attributed the failure to get to the bottom of the matter to key witnesses who avoided process and otherwise did not provide full evidence. The committee concluded that substantial funds were unaccounted for but that it was not clear where the money went or that bribery had occurred. Congress ended the matter by repealing the authority to contract with Pacific Mail in March 1875 and thus ended U.S. mail subsidy efforts until 1891.[77]

The Pacific Mail company kept up its trans-Pacific service and Panama/U.S. West Coast services, although the Panama service suffered following the opening of the transcontinental railroad in 1869. Southern Pacific Railroad took control of Pacific Mail in 1893, tying ocean movements with U.S. rail movements. This business plan was upended when the Panama Canal Act of 1912 restricted steamship companies owned by railroads from using the Panama Canal.[78]

Enactment of the Seamen's Act of 1915 was another blow since Pacific Mail had relied on Chinese seamen to compete with subsidized Japanese lines: that Act made such arrangements difficult. Pacific Mail's four largest steam vessels were sold to International Mercantile Marine Company (IMM) in August 1915 for the North Atlantic route. The rest of the fleet and the name was sold to Grace Line later that year.

---

[1] 1 Stat. 24, 27 (July 4, 1789).
[2] 1 Stat. 229, 230 (February 16, 1792).
[3] 14 Stat. 328 (July 28, 1866); Edwin M. Bacon, Manual of Ship Subsidies: An Historical Summary of the Systems of all Nations (Chicago: A. C. McClurg, 1911), 69. The laws pertaining to bounties paid to fishing vessels are listed in the Annual Report of the Commissioner of Navigation to the Secretary of Commerce and Labor (1909), appendix O.
[4] Report of the Merchant Marine Commission, S. Rep. 58-2755, 20–21.
[5] Francis E. Hyde, Cunard and the North Atlantic 1840-1973—A History of Shipping and Financial Management (London: MacMillan, 1975).
[6] Ralph Whitney, "The Unlucky Collins Line," American Heritage 8, no. 2 (February 1957): 48–53, 100–02.
[7] "Obituary – Edward K. Collins," New York Tribune, January 23, 1878, 5.
[8] George W. Sheldon, "Old Shipping Merchants of New York," Harper's New Monthly Magazine 84, no. 501 (February 1892): 457—71, 468.
[9] Whitney, "Unlucky Collins Line," 51.
[10] Sheldon, "Old Shipping Merchants of New York," 471.
[11] Edward W. Sloan, "Collins versus Cunard: The Realities of a North Atlantic Steamship Rivalry, 1850-1858," International Journal of Maritime History 4, no. 1 (June 1992): 83—100, 99.
[12] U.S. Congress, House, Ocean Steamers, 29th Cong., 1st sess., 1846, H. Rep. 29-685, 5—6.
[13] 5 Stat. 732 (March 3, 1845) (section 14 – to contract with "any steamboat plying upon the Western or other waters of the United States" provided price no greater "than the average rate paid for such service" under any prior contract).

[14] Marguerite M. McKee, "The Ship Subsidy Question in United States Politics," Smith College Studies in History 8, no. 1 (October 1922): 5—60, 22; 9 Stat. 187 (March 3, 1847) (the same law directed that a contract be entered into with A. G. Sloo, of Cincinnati, for a service between New York and New Orleans).
[15] Sloan, "Collins versus Cunard," 86.
[16] Sloan, "Collins versus Cunard," 87.
[17] U.S. Congress, Senate, June 15, 1852 Report, 32nd Cong, 1st sess., 1852, S. Rep. 32-267, 7.
[18] U.S. Congress, Senate, Memorial of E.K. Collins and His Associates, 32nd Cong., 1st sess., 1852, S. Misc. 32-17, 2.
[19] U.S. Congress, Senate, Message from the President of the United States to the Two Houses of Congress: Report of the Postmaster General, 32nd Cong., 2nd sess., 1852, S. Ex. Doc 32-1, 643.
[20] Sheldon, "Old Shipping Merchants of New York," 471.
[21] June 15, 1852 Report, S. Rep. 32-267, 7–8.
[22] June 15, 1852 Report, S. Rep. 32-267, 9.
[23] Edward W. Sloan, "The Baltic Goes to Washington: Lobbying for a Congressional Steamship Subsidy, 1852," Northern Mariner 5, no. 1 (January 1995): 19–32, 20–21.
[24] Sloan, "The Baltic Goes to Washington," 20–21.
[25] Cong. Globe, 32nd Cong., 1st sess. (March 1, 1852), 658.
[26] Cong. Globe, 32nd Cong., 1st sess., 659.
[27] For example, Alexandria Gazette, March 2, 1852, 1; "Latest Intelligence – The Grand Entertainment on Board the Baltic to the President, Cabinet, Members of Congress, &c., &c.," New York Times, March 3, 1852, 2.
[28] 10 Stat. 15, 21 (July 21, 1852).
[29] Whig Party; Cong. Globe, 32nd Cong., 1st sess. (April 27, 1852), 1199–202.
[30] For example, Hutchins, American Maritime Industries, 356–57.
[31] Sloan, "Collins versus Cunard," 87.
[32] Sloan, "Collins versus Cunard," 99 (emphasis in original).
[33] For example, "Horrible Catastrophe—The Steamer Arctic in Collision with an Iron Propeller," Baltimore Sun, October 12, 1854, 1.
[34] "The Arctic – Rescue of Capt. Luce and Nine Others by the Bark Cambria," New York Times, October 16, 1854, 1.
[35] "Brown Family, Steamer Arctic Sinking (1854)," Green-Wood, https://www.green-wood.com/2010/brown-family-steamer-arctic-sinking-1854/.
[36] "Opinion: The Wreck of the Arctic," New York Times, December 4, 1854, 4; "Opinion: The Arctic and her Owners," New York Times, December 1, 1854, 4.
[37] "The Arctic – Proposed Testimonial to Capt. Luce," New York Times, October 19, 1854, 1; "Capt. James C. Luce Dead," New York Times, July 11, 1879, 8.

[38] For example, "Loss of the Arctic," New York Times, October 12, 1854, 1; "The Arctic," New York Times, October 13, 1854, 1; "The Arctic," New York Times, October 14, 1854, 1.
[39] For example, "Loss of the Arctic," New York Times, October 12, 1854, 1.
[40] "The Wreck of the Arctic: Mr. Dorian's Reply to the Letter of Mr. John Collins, Jr.," New York Times, December 1, 1854, 1.
[41] "Law Intelligence – Presentment of the Grand Jury," New York Times, January 22, 1855, 6.
[42] 10 Stat. 15, 21 (July 21, 1852).
[43] "From Washington—The Collins Triumph—Matters in Congress," New York Times, (March 2, 1855), 4.
[44] 11 Stat. 101 (August 18, 1856).
[45] Cong. Globe, 33rd Cong., 2nd sess. (March 3, 1855), 1156.
[46] "The Missing Pacific," New York Times, February 11, 1856, 4; "The Pacific," New York Times, February 12, 1856, 4.
[47] "One Week Later from Europe – Unsuccessful Search for the Pacific," New York Times, April 24, 1856, 1.
[48] "A Message from the Sea," Express (London), July 24, 1861, 2; "Reminiscence of the Lost Steamship Pacific," New York Times, August 7, 1861, 5.
[49] "The Steamships of the Collins Line," Scientific American 13, no. 33 (April 24, 1858): 261.
[50] "The Collins' Liner 'Adriatic,'" Marine Engineer (London) 14 (April 1, 1892): 9–10.
[51] For example, Winthrop Lippitt Marvin, The American Merchant Marine: Its History and Romance from 1620 to 1902 (New York: Charles Scribner's Sons, 1910), 276–79; John H. Morrison, History of American Steam Navigation (New York: W. F. Sametz, 1903), 414–15.
[52] Cong. Globe, 35th Cong. 1st sess. (June 9, 1858), 2832.
[53] Cong. Globe, 35th Cong. 1st sess. (June 10, 1858), 2833.
[54] 11 Stat. 364 (June 14, 1858).
[55] "AW Intelligence," New York Times, April 2, 1858; "Sea and Ship News," New York Times, April 12, 1858, 5.
[56] "Obituary – Edward K. Collins," New York Tribune, January 23, 1878, 5.
[57] Whitney, "The Unlucky Collins Line," 102.
[58] 18 Stat. 320 (June 15, 1846), TS 120.
[59] 9 Stat. 187 (March 3, 1847).
[60] John Haskell Kemble, "The Genesis of the Pacific Mail Steamship Company," California Historical Society Quarterly 13, no. 4 (September 1934): 240–54; A. H. Cathcart, "Pacific Mail—Under the American Flag around the World," Pacific Marine Review 17 (July 1920): 53–58.
[61] René De La Pedraja, A Historical Dictionary of the U.S. Merchant Marine and Shipping Industry: Since the Introduction of Steam (Westport, CT: Greenwood Press, 1994), 469–73.

[62] "Obituary—William H. Aspinwall," New York Times, (January 19, 1875), 8.
[63] D Alessandro Arseni, "The Panamá Route 1848-1851," Postal Gazette no. 2 (November 2006): 10–11.
[64] John Haskell Kemble, "The Panama Route to the Pacific Coast, 1848-1869," Pacific Historical Review 7, no. 1 (March 1938): 1–13.
[65] 13 Stat. 430 (February 17, 1865).
[66] 17 Stat. 199 (June 1, 1872).
[67] Cong. Globe, 42nd Cong., 2nd sess. (May 7, 1872), 3146–47.
[68] Cong. Globe, 42nd Cong., 2nd sess. (May 3, 1872), 3027.
[69] Cong. Globe, 42nd Cong., 2nd sess. 3025.
[70] Cong. Globe, 42nd Cong., 2nd sess. 3030–33.
[71] 17 Stat. 199 (June 1, 1872).
[72] For example, "Lobby Legislation–The Investigation Concerning the New York Stock Exchange," New York Herald, February 18, 1873, 5.
[73] "Obituary—LeGrand Lockwood," New York Times, February 25, 1872, 3.
[74] Cong. Globe, 42nd Cong., 3rd sess. (February 20, 1873), 45.
[75] Paul Maxwell Zeis, American Shipping Policy (Princeton: Princeton University Press, 1938), 238 (lists the various Congressional reports issued).
[76] U.S. Congress, House, China Mail-Service, 43rd Cong., 2nd sess., 1875, H. Rep. 43-268. Zeis argues that "it was proved" that money was paid out by the company for bribes. Zeis, American Shipping Policy, 24.
[77] 18 Stat. 340, 342 (March 3, 1875).
[78] 37 Stat. 560, 566-67 (August 24, 1912).

Rear Admiral Raphel Semmes, Confederate Navy, circa 1863, Library of Congress

Chapter 7 – American Civil War

The U.S. merchant marine had a golden age from the opening of trade with Britain in 1830 to the Civil War. In 1861 the U.S.-flag fleet engaged in foreign trade reached an apex unmatched until the twentieth century.[1] The same year, the U.S.-flag fleet engaged in the U.S. coastwise trade was slightly larger. As a point of comparison (and noting that the United States and Britain measured vessel tonnage differently at the time), the total U.S. registered fleet of about 5.2 million tons was comparable to the overall British fleet of 5.9 million tons, the largest in the world.[2]

There were many contributing factors.[3] It was an age before iron steamships became economical, and the United States was a world leader in large wooden vessel construction. The cotton trade increased six-fold from 1830 to 1860. The passenger trade to the U.S. increased exponentially: about 25,000 passengers arrived in 1830 and 315,000 in 1850. The whaling industry peaked in 1858 in terms of vessels engaged. And the Crimean War (1853-56) temporarily increased international shipping rates.

The California gold rush, starting in 1848, also provided a substantial boost to American shipping.[4] The U.S. Treasury Department interpreted the 1817 Act to apply to both direct sailing voyages from the East Coast to California around the tip of South America and to indirect voyages via the Panamanian isthmus.[5] An 1854 law confirmed the interpretation by providing that goods shipped from the East Coast to the West Coast did not leave U.S. customs territory.[6]

U.S. advantages began to dissipate in the 1850s. But the Civil War provided the catalysts that accelerated the decline—particularly a decline in the cotton trade and the actions of rebel commerce raiders.[7]

JOURNEY TO THE JONES ACT

At the outset of the war, the Confederacy immediately sought to obtain vessels to be used as commerce raiders. By destroying Union vessels and their cargoes and driving up insurance rates, the raiders hoped to put economic pressure on the Union. The thirteen colonies in the Revolutionary War and the United States in the War of 1812 had successfully engaged in extensive commerce raiding.[8] The Confederate States of America wanted to repeat that success. The most famous commerce raider was the *C.S.S. Alabama.*

C.S.S. ALABAMA

The *Alabama* story was a subject of fascination during the Civil War on both sides of the Atlantic.[9] Although she was deadly to U.S. commerce, she is generally considered to have fought with boldness and élan. In accord with the rules of warfare of the time, the *Alabama* vouchsafed the crews and passengers of vessels she burned and sank.[10]

The *Alabama* story starts with James Dunwoody Bulloch, a former U.S. Navy officer and the half-brother of Theodore Roosevelt's mother, Martha Bulloch. Bulloch served as a Confederate agent in Europe in the rebels' attempts to acquire vessels. Many years later, Roosevelt maintained a fondness for his uncle, who encouraged him to write his 1882 book *The Naval War of 1812*.[11] In the preface, Roosevelt expressed his "sincerest thanks to Captain James D. Bulloch, formerly of the United States Navy." Roosevelt did not mention Bulloch's service to the rebellion.

Bulloch was most famous for his role in the construction of the *C.S.S. Alabama.* She was ordered in 1861 as the future *Enrica* (hull number 290) from Laird Brothers of Birkenhead on the River Mersey opposite Liverpool. U.S. consular officials immediately took note of her, as her lack of cargo capacity indicated her intended function as a warship.

Bulloch also sought to build two iron steamships fitted with rams. These were to be built at the same shipyard and were known as the "Laird Rams" (hull numbers 294 and 295). William Aspinwall, of the Pacific Mail Steamship Company, was sent to Britain by Secretary of the Navy Gideon Welles to interfere in Confederate vessel acquisition efforts, including the Laird Rams project.[12] The U.S. minister to Britain, Charles Francis Adams, son of John Quincy Adams and grandson of John Adams, also informed the British government that delivery of the Rams to the Confederate States of America would mean war between the United States and Britain.[13] Both of those vessels were ultimately purchased by the Royal Navy.

With respect to the future *Alabama*, Adams demanded that the British government satisfy its obligation as a neutral country and prevent an instrument of war from getting into rebel hands. The British argued that their only obligation arose under domestic law, the Foreign Enlistment Act of 1819, which had been invoked on May 13, 1861, by Queen Victoria's Proclamation of Neutrality.[14] The Enlistment Act required proof of aggressive intent. By the time an order was received to detain the vessel in August 1862, the *Alabama* had left for "sea trials"—never to return.

The British government's handling of the affair was later challenged by the U.S. government. The British claimed the proof from the Americans came too late to stop the vessel. The international Alabama Claims Tribunal found in 1872 that, based at least on the neutrality standard applied to the American claims (not the Foreign Enlistment Act standard), the British government had failed in its obligations.

As stated by the tribunal, this failure occurred "notwithstanding the warnings and official representations made by the diplomatic agents of the United States during the construction of the said number '290.'" Richard Cobden, a leading Member of Parliament, said in a May 1864 speech that it was "a cruel satire" "to say that our laws have been found sufficient to enforce our neutrality."[15]

JOURNEY TO THE JONES ACT

The vessel sailed to the Azores where she was outfitted with weapons and provisions before setting out to capture and destroy U.S.-flag vessels. Her crew consisted mainly of British nationals. She became the Confederacy's most successful commerce raider, burning or sinking sixty-five American vessels all over the world in less than two years.

In the summer of 1864, she returned to Europe and went to Cherbourg in France for repairs and refit. By then, the captain of the *Alabama* and former U.S. Navy officer Raphael Semmes had already begun to run out of vessels to attack because so much of the U.S.-flag fleet had been reflagged in other countries.

The *U.S.S. Kearsarge*, which had been tracking the *Alabama* and was a comparable vessel in terms of size and armament, also sailed toward Cherbourg and waited for the *Alabama* to exit the protection of neutral French waters.[16] A battle ensued on June 19, 1864, watched by thousands of onlookers on shore and in boats. An early shot fired by the *Alabama* lodged in the *Kearsarge's* rudder but did not explode (the rudder and cannon ball are housed at the Washington Navy Yard Navy Museum).

Had the cannon ball exploded, the *Alabama* probably would have been able to destroy the *Kearsarge* or at least been able to escape. The more accurate fire from the *Kearsarge* eventually told the tale. The *Alabama* started to sink, and Semmes ordered the colors struck. Most of the crew were rescued from the water. Semmes was picked up by a British yacht that had come to watch the battle. He was taken to England where he received a hero's welcome.

The United States requested that Britain turn Semmes over; the British refused. When the *Alabama* was sunk, the *New York Times* reported that "the English feel in their hearts as if the conflict was their own. It was fought with an English-built vessel, with English guns and English powder, and an English crew."[17]

The *Alabama* and Semmes were famous at the time and since.[18] In the report of the centennial celebration of Semmes's birth in September 1909 in Baltimore, it was reported that his completely unrepentant account—*Memories of Services Afloat*—had impressed Kaiser Wilhelm II of Germany.[19] Supposedly the German emperor said in 1894 that he revered Semmes and viewed him as "the greatest Admiral of the nineteenth century."[20] Works continue to be written about the Confederate commerce raiders, and the wreck of the *Alabama* found in 1984 has been the subject of archaeological exploration.[21]

Perhaps the greatest impact of the Confederate commerce raiders was that U.S. maritime policy attention at a critical time became backward-looking rather than forward looking. The focus shifted to the effects of the war and how to get compensation from Britain and away from the underlying deterioration of the market position of the U.S.-flag wooden sailing fleet and what, if anything, to do about it.

The American Claims—Treaty of Washington

Semmes may have been a hero in the South and in England, but he was a pirate pure and simple to the Union. The last straw to many Northerners was when Semmes returned to England on a British yacht. Then the British government refused to hand him over to the U.S. government.

The bad blood had started with Queen Victoria's May 1861 Neutrality Proclamation implicitly recognizing the rebel states as a belligerent country. Even though arguably justifiable, and maybe even brought on by the Union announcement of a "blockade," it was viewed by many in the North as an act of betrayal. Then there were the commerce raiders and blockade runners built in England. Finally, there was Britain's role in helping vessels evade the Union blockade, with British authorities often looking the other way when vessels transshipped cargoes in British Caribbean colonies.

Frederick Milnes Edge, a British citizen living in the United States, in an open 1864 letter to Lord Earl Russell (the British foreign secretary), stated that "the most serious cause of hostile feeling against Great Britain remains to be told, namely, the fitting out, arming, and building of Confederate ships of war in English ports, and the fearful effect upon American commerce produced by the marauders."[22] Americans, he said, viewed the Confederate commerce raiders as nothing more than "English pirates." After the war, the U.S. Congress referred to the Confederate commerce raiders as "English piratical vessels sailing under the confederate flag."[23] Edge went on to state that "were it not for English participation in the chimerical projects of southern slaveholders, the rebellion would, long ere this, have been crushed, and the trade and commerce of the United States not be suffering from the terrible devastations from privateers which, without England's intermediary, would never have had existence."[24]

Senator Charles Sumner (R-MA), then chairman of the Senate Foreign Relations Committee, went so far as to argue in a widely read and impassioned speech that the British had caused both direct and indirect damages and demanded they pay for both. He alleged that, by ignoring the international law of neutrality, Britain had prolonged the war by two years.[25]

President Andrew Johnson summed up the American view in his message to Congress in December 1865. Specifically, he complained that British efforts had "the effect, to a great extent, to drive the American flag from the sea, and to transfer much of our shipping and our commerce to the very power whose subjects had created the necessity for such a change."[26]

Even before the Civil War ended, the U.S. government sought compensation from Britain for what it considered neutrality violations. After many unsuccessful attempts at compromise, the United States and Britain agreed in the 1871 Treaty of Washington to have all commerce raider claims—referred to as the "'Alabama Claims'"—resolved by a "Tribunal of Arbitration" in Geneva.[27] The treaty also addressed boundary and fishing disputes between the two countries, including granting "free navigation" to the citizens of both Canada and the United States on the Yukon River. This subject later complicated U.S. attempts to close loopholes in its coasting law, discussed in an upcoming chapter.[28]

The tribunal consisted of one representative from the United States and Britain and three neutral arbitrators. President Ulysses S Grant appointed Charles Francis Adams to represent the United States.

The treaty established certain "rules" regarding the duties of a neutral country to be used by the tribunal in rendering its judgment.[29] Among those duties was "to use due diligence to prevent the fitting out, arming, or equipping within its jurisdiction, of any vessel which it has reasonable ground to believe is intended to cruise or to carry on war against a Power with which it is at peace...."[30]

The tribunal issued an award largely in favor of the United States in September 1872, with the arbitrators voting separately on the claims relating to each commerce-raiding vessel. Church bells were rung, and cannons were fired in Geneva when the award was announced. The vote on the *Alabama* was unanimous—that Britain had violated its duties as a neutral as framed by the Treaty of Washington. The tribunal by a vote of four to one awarded $15.5 million in gold to the United States.[31]

It was a substantial amount for 1872, but it was much less than the direct damages suffered by U.S. vessel owners (about 237 vessels, or 5 percent of the total, were lost).[32] The tribunal's decision nevertheless served as the model for the 1907 Hague Convention and the 1909 London Declaration on neutral duties and rights. These conventions became important at the outset of World War I when the U.S. was a neutral country.[33]

THE GREAT FLAG EXODUS

The direct harm addressed by the tribunal was dwarfed by the indirect harm to the U.S. merchant marine caused by the commerce raiders. The raiders caused havoc by driving up war risk insurance rates, making shipping economically prohibitive.[34]

JOURNEY TO THE JONES ACT

Vessel owners were left with no choice but to either tie up their vessels for the duration of the war, sell them to foreign interests, or attempt to retain control under a foreign flag.[35] The Civil War set a precedent for later use of foreign registries to preserve vessel neutrality.[36]

The Confederate commerce raiders had much more of a negative effect on the U.S. merchant marine than the 5 percent total loss indicates. At the time, it was estimated that the approximately 110,000 tons of shipping lost to the raiders were dwarfed by the 800,000 or so tons reflagged (about 700 vessels).[37] More modern estimates point to over 1,000 vessels reflagged and about 237 destroyed.[38]

As stated by Adams in an 1865 letter to Lord Russell, Britain's policy had resulted in "the destruction of the whole mercantile navigation belonging to the people of the United States." Furthermore, Britain was "fast acquiring the entire maritime commerce of the United States by reason of the acts of a portion of her Majesty's subjects engaged in carrying on war against them on the ocean during a time of peace between the two countries."[39]

The effect on the international presence of the U.S.-flag fleet was profound. In 1855, U.S.-flag vessels carried over 80 percent of the direct trade with Britain. In 1865 that percentage was 28 percent and thereafter the slide continued until it was only about 7 percent in 1895.[40]

After the end of the Civil War, the U.S. Congress turned its attention to what to do about the vessels that had left the U.S. registry to be flagged in Britain or elsewhere and whether a stimulus was needed to revive the merchant marine. The House of Representatives in February 1865 requested advice from the Treasury Department on both subjects.

In a January 1866 letter, the Treasury Department reminded Congress that "existing laws exclude from the privileges of the American flag... vessels of domestic build which, after having been once documented under those laws, are transferred to foreign ownership."[41] Treasury advised neither to relax the reflagging law nor to provide "any additional encouragement of shipbuilding." The House also received in January 1866 a "remonstrance of shipowners at Bangor, Maine, against issuing American registers to vessels who changed registers during the rebellion."[42]

Representative John Lynch (R-ME) offered a resolution in January 1866, which was unanimously approved. It stated that "all vessels once American, whose national character has been changed, or which have been placed under a foreign flag or a foreign register... should never again be allowed an American register."[43] The reason was that such owners had abandoned "the flag of their country during a period of war."

Representative Lynch followed up with legislation which became law in February 1866.[44] It closed the loophole that had existed for vessels registered abroad but whose beneficial owners remained American.[45] Such registrations likely involved a fraud on the foreign registry where ownership was limited to the nationals of the registering country. This bar against vessels returning to the U.S. flag was not relaxed until 1897. At that time, U.S.-built vessels could be reflagged in the U.S. if purchased by Americans and provided the vessel had not been "enlarged or undergone change" abroad in the meantime.[46]

Thus the U.S. Congress made the war-induced flag exodus permanent and probably cut off its nose to spite its face. Some later argued that the United States was better off anyway because most of the lost vessels were wooden sailing vessels whose commercial utility was waning.[47] No one knows for sure what damage the reflag prohibition did to the U.S. merchant marine in terms of lost financial capital and expertise. But subsequent events were to prove that the U.S.-flag fleet would have a very difficult recovery from the Civil War.[48]

---

[1] Annual Report of the Commissioner of Navigation to the Secretary of the Treasury (1901), 562.
[2] Annual Report of the Commissioner of Navigation to the Secretary of the Treasury (1901), 471.

[3] Hutchins, American Maritime Industries, 264—72; U.S. Congress, House, Foreign Commerce and Decadence of American Shipping: Letter from the Secretary of the Treasury, 41st Cong., 2d sess., 1870, H. Exec. Doc. 41-111, 6.

[4] Hutchins, American Maritime Industries, 266; Marvin, American Merchant Marine, 391; Hall, American Navigation, 51. A law was also enacted in 1848 permitting U.S.-flag vessels enrolled and licensed for the coastwise trades to stop and trade at one or more foreign ports, which had not previously been permitted. 9 Stat. 232 (May 27, 1848).

[5] Robert Mayo, ed., "Treasury Department Circular no. 21 (Oct. 7, 1848)," in A Synopsis of the Commercial and Revenue System of the United States as Developed by Instructions and Decisions of the Treasury Department for the Administration of the Revenue Laws (1847), vol. 1, 9 (As a result of peace treaty "California became a part of the American Union."); "Decision of Treasury Department regarding Trade between Pacific and Atlantic Ports of the U.S. Via Aspinwall and Panama—A Coasting Trade Prohibited to Foreign Vessels," in Synopsis of Sundry Decisions Rendered by the Treasury Department under the Tariff and Other Acts, during the Year Ending December 31, 1868 (Washington, DC: Government Printing Office, 1869), 16 ("Such trade is regarded as, to all intents and purposes, a trade between ports and districts of the United States, and is therefore actually and truly coastwise, and falls completely within the reasons which have prompted the legislation upon the coasting trade. Nor can the fact that the voyage is accomplished by a combination of two or more vessels with each other, instead of by one alone, affect the character of the voyage under the statute, both the commencement and termination of the journey (of the merchandise) being in American ports."); U.S. Treasury Department, Report on the Internal Commerce of the United States (Washington, DC: Government Printing Office, 1885), 41 ("Under our navigation laws only American vessels can engage in trade between Atlantic and Pacific ports of the United States, it being regarded as a branch of the coastwise or domestic trade of the country.").

[6] 10 Stat. 270, 272 (March 28, 1854).

[7] Hutchins, American Maritime Industries, 321.

[8] Bruce A. Elleman and S.C.M. Paine, eds., Commerce Raiding: Historical Case Studies, 1755-2009 (Newport, RI: Naval War College Press, 2013), chaps. 2 and 4.

[9] James Tertius deKay, The Rebel Raiders: The Astonishing History of the Confederacy's Secret Navy (New York: Ballantine Books, 2002) and United Nations, "Alabama Claims of the United States of America against Great Britain (May 8, 1871)," in Reports of International Arbitral Awards, 2012, vol. 29, part 9.

[10] For example, "The Pirate Alabama—How Capt. Semmes Treats His Prisoners and Watches His Crew—A Description of the Vessel," New York Times, (February 26, 1863), 2. Many in the Union nevertheless considered the Confederate commerce raiders as "pirates" and not "belligerents." For example, "Are They Pirates?", New York Times, (June 23, 1861), 4.

[11] Theodore Roosevelt, The Naval War of 1812 (New York: G. P. Putnam's Sons, 1882), preface.

[12] "Obituary – William H. Aspinwall," New York Times, January 19, 1875, 8.
[13] Douglas H. Maynard, "The Forbes-Aspinwall Mission," Mississippi Valley Historical Review 45, no. 1 (June 1958): 67–89.
[14] 59 Geo. III, c. 69; London Gazette, no. 22510 (May 14, 1861), 2046.
[15] HC Deb. (May 13, 1864), vol. 175, col. 497.
[16] One of the earliest accounts of the engagement is in Frederick Milnes Edge, An Englishman's View of the Battle between the Alabama and Kearsarge (New York: Anson D. F. Randolph, 1864). Other accounts include John McIntosh Kell, Recollections of a Naval Life, Including the Cruises of the Sumter & Alabama (Washington, DC: Neale, 1900), 244–51; and deKay, Rebel Raiders, ch. 21.
[17] "English Feeling at the Sinking of the Alabama," New York Times, July 8, 1864, 4.
[18] For example, "The Rebel Pirates – The Alabama, Georgia and Tuscaloosa at the Cape of Good Hope–Enthusiastic Reception Extended to the Confederates," New York Times, October 8, 1863, 1.
[19] Raphael Semmes, Memories of Service Afloat during the War between the States (Baltimore: Kelly, Piet, 1869).
[20] R. A. Brock, ed., "Centennial of Birth of Admiral Raphael Semmes, Born in Charles County, MD., September 27, 1809," Southern Historical Society Papers 38 (January-December 1910): 22–27, 24.
[21] "CSS Alabama Wreck Site (1864): A Confederate Shipwreck in France," Naval History and Heritage Command, Sites and Projects, Shipwreck Sites, https://www.history.navy.mil/research/underwater-archaeology/sites-and-projects/shipwrecksites/css-alabama.html.
[22] Frederick Milnes Edge, The Destruction of the American Carrying Trade: A Letter to Earl Russell (London: William Ridgway, 1863), 11.
[23] U.S. Congress, House, Causes of the Reduction of American Tonnage, 41st Cong., 2nd sess., 1870, H. Rep. 41-28, 9.
[24] Edge, Destruction of the American Carrying Trade, 26.
[25] Cong. Globe, 41st Cong., spec. sess. (April 13, 1869), appendix 21–26; deKay, Rebel Raiders, chap. 24.
[26] Andrew Johnson, First Annual Message, December 4, 1865, available at UC Santa Barbara, The American Presidency Project, https://www.presidency.ucsb.edu/documents/first-annual-message-10.
[27] 17 Stat. 863, Treaty Series 133 (1871).
[28] Annual Report of the Commissioner of Navigation to the Secretary of the Treasury (1898), 65.
[29] These rules became part of U.S. law in the Act of June 15, 1917, 40 Stat. 217 (1917).
[30] 17 Stat. 863, Treaty Series 133, Art. IV (1871).
[31] United Nations, "Alabama Claims of the United States of America against Great Britain (May 8, 1871)," 133–34.

[32] Spencer C. Tucker, "CSS Alabama and Confederate Commerce Raiders during the U.S. Civil War," in Commerce Raiding: Historical Case Studies, 1755—2009, chap. 5, 86.

[33] 36 Stat. 2310, Treaty Series 540 (1907).

[34] George W. Dalzell, The Flight from the Flag: The Continuing Effect of the Civil War upon the American Carrying Trade (Chapel Hill: University of North Carolina Press, 1940), 238–42.

[35] The process of finding a "nominal" British owner to re-register the vessel under British flag was noticed. "American Ships under the British Flag," North American and United States Gazette, March 5, 1861, 2; "Piracy and Marine Insurance," New York Times, April 28, 1861, 8.

[36] Rodney Carlisle, "Flagging-Out in the American Civil War," Northern Mariner/le marin du nord 22, no. 1 (January 2012): 53–65, 55.

[37] U.S. Congress, House, Mercantile Marine: Letter from the Secretary of the Treasury, 39th Cong., 1st sess., 1866, H. Ex. Doc. 39-25.

[38] Carlisle, "Flagging-Out in the American Civil War," 60. Carlisle also points out that many vessels owned by Confederates also "flagged out" and those vessels are not usually included in the tallies. Rodney Carlisle, Rough Waters: Sovereignty and the American Merchant Flag (Annapolis, MD: U.S. Naval Institute Press, 2017), 958—88.

[39] "Letter from C. Adams to E. Russell (April 7, 1865)," Papers Relating to Foreign Affairs, Accompanying the Annual Message of the President to the First Session Thirty-Ninth Congress, U.S. Department of State, Office of the Historian, Historical Documents, Document 173, https://history.state.gov/historicaldocuments/frus1865p1/d173.

[40] Report of the Merchant Marine Commission, S. Rep. 58-2755, 1769.

[41] U.S. Congress, House, Mercantile Marine, 39th Cong., 1st sess., 1866, H. Exec. Doc. 39-25. The restriction to U.S.-built vessels was contained in the Act of December 31, 1792—the restriction when a vessel is transferred to foreign ownership was contained in the Act of June 27, 1797. 1 Stat. 287 (December 31, 1792); 1 Stat. 523 (June 27, 1797).

[42] U.S. House Journal, 39th Cong., 1st sess., January 10, 1866, 127. There is evidence for this view elsewhere as well, for example "Another Word to Ship-Owners," New York Times, September 8, 1865, 4 (Owners who reflagged "are entitled to little sympathy or consideration, and those of our merchants who nobly stood by the flag and caused it to float proudly over their ships when Anglo-rebel pirates scoured the seas, and steadily refused to barter away their honor as well as their ships to foreign colors, should protect against this outrage upon our integrity as true Americans.").

[43] U.S. House Journal, 39th Cong., 1st sess., January 18, 1866, 163.

[44] 14 Stat. 3 (February 10, 1866).

[45] Carlisle, "Flagging-Out in the American Civil War," 55–57.

[46] 29 Stat. 687, 689 (March 3, 1897).
[47] John Roach, The American Carrying Trade (New York: H. B. Grose, 1880), 28–29.
[48] William H. Lincoln of the New England Ship-Owners Association argued in 1887, for example, that U.S. vessel owners were poised to re-enter the foreign trade if they had been permitted to do so with foreign-built vessels. Proceedings of the Convention of the Department of the North Atlantic Coast of the American Shipping and Industrial League Held at Boston, Mass., October 21st and 22nd, 1887 (Washington, DC: Judd & Detweiler Printers, 1887), 37.

Representative John Lynch, circa 1860, Library of Congress

Chapter 8—Lynch Committee

Much was written starting in the 1860s about why the U.S.-flag commercial fleet did not recover from the Civil War. In 1922 the U.S. Shipping Board gave five reasons.[1]

First, the board noted that the "advantage we had in cheap wood and skillful building was overcome in the late thirties [1830's] by England's advantage with iron." The board claimed the effects were masked because the California gold rush put a premium on large wooden sailing ships.

Second, the Civil War had not only deprived the United States of reflagged vessels—it had also driven American cargo shippers to British carriers. And these were not to be easily recovered as customers. This occurred during and after the Civil War, a time when the Northern states had a booming economy.[2]

Third, "labor and capital have been attracted to other more lucrative fields of employment... Railways, manufacturing, and industry generally commanded high rates of return without apparent risks, which were considered incidental, necessarily, to shipping."

Fourth, the U.S. import tariffs adopted during the Civil War made building vessels more expensive in the United States and "stimulating American manufactures had induced capital to enter that field. The unprotected shipping industry naturally suffered for lack of capital."

Fifth, Lloyd's Register in London changed its classification ratings. Iron vessels were given priority over wooden vessels resulting in high insurance rates for predominantly wooden U.S.-built vessels. Lloyd's Register was the first national organization to rate vessels for insurance purposes. This was referred to as "classification." These policies were often cited as part of a deliberate effort by Britain to disadvantage the U.S. merchant marine.[3]

These reasons can be easily supplemented from a cottage industry of books and pamphlets claiming to know why the U.S. merchant marine in the foreign trade declined and how to revive it.[4] It was in this context that the U.S. Congress entered the field by forming a Select Committee in 1870 to study the problem.

LYNCH COMMITTEE REPORT

Representative John Lynch was chosen to chair the select committee. It produced a landmark February 1870 report entitled "Causes of the Reduction of American Tonnage."[5] The Lynch Committee report was to be the first of several congressional reports on the state of the U.S. merchant marine over the ensuing decades.[6]

The Lynch Committee acknowledged that the Civil War had occurred during a revolution in naval architecture but disagreed with the idea that America could not compete in building and operating iron steamships. The committee argued that the attention of the country had been "diverted from the pursuits of peace to the preservation of our national existence." Britain, "under the guise of neutrality, was making war upon our commerce for the benefit of its own."[7] The committee urged the United States not to "become the mere commercial dependency of the nation for whose advantage we have been thus spoiled and reduced."

The committee argued that the statistics provided a "striking refutation of the assumption that the revival of our shipping will follow the increase of our exports."[8] The committee also noted that both Britain and France provided ample subsidies to their national shipping lines and the lines of those countries were free of taxation. U.S. shipping companies bore the weight of war-time and state taxation: "in a contest so unequal there can be but one result, and that is the total loss of our foreign carrying trade and the destruction of our merchant marine."[9]

The committee set forth many of the policy options that were to inform the long running debate about reviving the U.S. merchant marine. The committee rejected a proposal to let vessels that had registered in another country in the Civil War return to the U.S. flag because such vessel owners had "identified their interest with those of our enemy."[10]

The committee also considered a modification of American navigation laws to permit foreign-built vessels to be registered in the United States either free of duty "or on the payment of a moderate duty." This was rejected. The committee believed that the U.S. shipbuilding industry would be destroyed if foreign-built vessels were freely permitted under U.S. registry.

Moreover, the committee was concerned that permitting foreign-built vessels under the U.S. registry "would deprive us of the mechanical skill requisite to build our navy in time of war." It would mean the United States would require "a large naval force entirely useless as a peace establishment, but necessary to preserve and defend the national honor and interests in case they were menaced."[11] The committee nevertheless acknowledged that an "American shipowner must... be able to purchase as cheap as the foreigner, or he must obtain better ships; otherwise, he is deprived of that equality of ability to compete."

The committee also addressed subsidies for steamships and urged several financial aids to be adopted. One was a refund or drawback of import duties paid on raw materials such as imported iron used in vessel construction. The U.S. government had imposed import duties on most materials used in vessel construction in 1861 to raise war revenues.[12] The subsequent Revenue Act of 1864 also imposed a two percent tax on all vessel hulls once finished.[13]

The committee also recommended the adoption of direct subsidies to be paid to vessels running to the British North American provinces and to steamers to worldwide ports. The committee considered relieving U.S.-flag vessels of tonnage duties but implicitly acknowledged that treaty obligations prevented that unless foreign vessels were also so relieved.

Finally, the committee suggested but did not propose that the U.S. Government build vessels useful in times of peace and war and give "free use of such ships in time of peace to merchants who would take care of them until required for national defense."[14] This was an early preview of the Shipping Act, 1916.

The committee defended its overall proposal on the basis that a similar policy program was working for Britain, and that it would provide for the maritime industry no more than what was provided "with lavish liberality" to U.S. railroads and interior water communications. Moreover, the committee believed that the "prosperity of the country in time of peace, as well as its security in time of war, is largely dependent upon an efficient merchant marine."[15]

JOHN CODMAN ("CAPTAIN RINGBOLT")

Lynch's principal adversary in the effort to subsidize the U.S. merchant marine was Capt. John Codman, a private lobbyist. On May 26, 1870, Lynch had the following to say on the House floor about Codman who apparently was in the gallery at the time:

> Pamphlets have been laid upon our tables signed by Captain John Codman, who represents the interests of the iron shipbuilders of the Clyde. This gentleman came here immediately after the opening of Congress, and has since squat at the ear of every man who would give him audience and listen to his statements in favor of British shipbuilders as against the shipbuilders of his own country, whom he has ridiculed, misrepresented, and abused.[16]

By Clyde, Lynch was referring to the River Clyde in Scotland, which flows through Glasgow, where many of the leading British shipyards were then located. Lynch urged the House not to be taken in by Codman's misrepresentations.

Later that evening, there was a physical fight between Representative James S. Negley (R-PA) and Codman at the Arlington Hotel.[17] That hotel was one of Washington's leading hotels after the Civil War and stood at Vermont Avenue and I Street near the Treasury Building and the White House. The Department of Veterans Affairs building now stands in that location.[18]

The press reported that "Negley charged that Mr. Codman opposed the bill in the interest of Clyde shipbuilders and… was a paid agent of these gentlemen." Codman said that this was either a joke or a lie, to which "Negley at once struck Codman a sharp blow in the face," whereupon Codman retaliated by striking Negley "with a cane he carried." It was reported that the two were broken up by bystanders "before they could inflict further damage on each other." This incident was one of many from 1870 to 1900 involving Codman and the U.S. merchant marine.

Codman was born in 1814 in Dorchester, Massachusetts in the Boston area.[19] His father, a Harvard graduate, was a Congregational minister who preached at the Second Church of Dorchester, still in existence in the town's "Codman Square District." His great-great-grandfather was Robert Codman, who settled in Salem, Massachusetts, in 1630.

In 1823, Codman entered Phillips Academy at Andover. One of his schoolmates was Oliver Wendell Holmes Sr., the famous poet and physician. Codman later went to Amherst College for two years before dropping out to go to sea.

Codman sailed around the world on clipper ships. In 1837 he happened to be in England as the second mate of the vessel *Globe* and watched eighteen-year-old Queen Victoria's coronation. He recounted his experience at the time of the Queen's Diamond Jubilee in an 1897 *New York Times* article.[20] Codman and his mates bribed some guards to sit on the wall of Devonshire House on Piccadilly; he recalled, "Little could the Yankee sailors who sat upon that wall foresee what that gaudy pageant that passed before them might presage."

He also served at a young age as the captain of the brig (a two masted cargo sailing ship) the *Argyle*. By the 1840s he had made a fortune in shipping as a merchant. In 1847 he got married and published his first book under a pseudonym "Captain Ringbolt." It was a tome about his sea experiences called *Sailor's Life and Sailor's Yarns*.[21] Herman Melville reviewed the book in the first volume of the *Literary World* published in 1847.[22] A "ringbolt" is a bolt made with a ring for passing a rope through.

In 1854 Codman took command of the U.S.-flag wooden steamship *William Penn*, a vessel chartered by France for the Crimean War. Codman kept notes and wrote a book in 1896 about the experience, entitled *An American Transport in the Crimean War*.[23] He later claimed that his experience in the Black Sea, where numerous iron steamships served together with wooden sailing vessels, convinced him to advocate for free ships.[24]

During the Civil War, Codman commanded for a time the armed steamer *U.S.S. Quaker City*, a civilian steam vessel chartered to the U.S. Navy. After the war, she returned to commercial service and was the scene of a travel log written by Mark Twain, compiled in the book *The Innocents Abroad*.[25]

In 1864 Codman was hired to deliver the American armed cruiser *Cotopaxi* to Brazil. Later in 1867 he wrote about his experiences in the book *Ten Months in Brazil*.[26]

When he returned to the United States after the Civil War, Codman established himself as a newspaper columnist, writing on a variety of topics under the names "J.C.," "John Codman" and "Captain Ringbolt." Among the topics he returned to over and over was international trade and U.S. navigation laws. He consistently advocated until his death in 1900 for free trade and "free ships" and was referred to as "the old apostle of free ships."[27]

Codman, for example, wrote in a November 1869 letter to Lynch's committee (provocatively from the town of "Dumbarton on the Clyde" where the British shipyards were located) arguing for free ships and against subsidies. In that letter, published in the *New York Times*, he argued that "our ridiculously absurd navigation laws prevent us from purchasing such ships" and "our action *quo ad hoc* is neither more or less than national suicide!"[28]

Later in the 1870s he traveled west to Idaho and became a ranch owner. He wrote about his experiences in the book *Winter Sketches from the Saddle* and became committed to what he called "equestrianopathy," the belief that riding horses was healthful.[29]

In the winter of 1886, at the age of seventy-five, he rode a horse, named "Grover Cleveland," from New York to Boston, and the adventure was covered in the *New York Times*.[30] Writing right up until his death, he passed away in Boston on April 6, 1900.[31]

Lynch Committee Proposed Legislation

The legislation on which Lynch tangled with Codman was introduced in February 1870. The bill would have reduced and refunded duties on shipbuilding inputs, like iron and steel. It also would have imposed a system of bounties to be paid per ton for certain U.S.-flag vessels.[32] A later April 1870 version added a special bounty for trade via Panama between U.S. coasts but limited the bounties to ten years.[33]

Lynch argued that "the state of the merchant marine was positively disgraceful" and, although "the loss of our commerce was our misfortune; our failure to regain it, if we do fail, will be our fault."[34] The American people, Lynch said, should "resolve that the principle of economy shall never be carried to such an extent as to leave us entirely at the mercy of any foreign nation."[35]

Representative Erastus Wells (D-MO) pointed to a "gratuitous lobby" of foreigners arguing against the legislation noting that "our desks and the hotels are flooded with pamphlets deprecating all aid to American shipping interests, and secret agencies are at work to control the action of Congress."[36] Wells argued that if the Lynch bill was defeated, "the work of the Alabama and Stonewall [another Confederate commerce raider] will be complete."

Lynch also argued that a free ships policy was unfair because it would put foreign-built vessels, which did not pay U.S. duties during their construction, in the same position as U.S.-built vessels that were burdened with such duties.[37] Lynch made the case that vessels in the foreign trade were "exports" since they competed directly with foreign-built vessels for the same cargoes. The obvious solution, he argued, was to equalize the burdens by having the U.S. government refund duties paid on shipbuilding inputs like iron.

The opposition was stiff. Representative Fernando Wood (D-NY), the former mayor of New York and an opponent of both the Civil War and the Thirteenth Amendment to the U.S. Constitution (abolishing slavery), argued on May 17 that commerce was more important than who carried the goods.[38] He also argued that if the United States wanted more vessels under its flag, all it had to do was permit American owners to buy foreign-built vessels.

Much later, in 1896, Codman recounted in the *New York Times* that the Wood's free-ship idea died even before it was formally proposed because of U.S. shipbuilder lobbying. He claimed that the morning after Wood made his proposal, a group of shipbuilders came from Philadelphia, "breakfasted at the Arlington [Hotel], then marched over to Mr. Wood's house, and the obnoxious clause was eliminated."[39]

Representative Benjamin F. Butler (R-MA) proposed, as a substitute, to re-introduce discriminating duties favoring U.S.-flag vessels.[40] Representative Eugene Hale (R-ME), a freshman congressman who was to resurface later as a policy maker for the merchant marine and U.S. Navy, argued that such duties had worked for Britain and for the United States in its early days and that such duties could work again.[41] Representative

John Coburn (R-IN) responded that such discriminating duties would invite retaliation by other countries and was "a dangerous experiment; more expensive, more extravagant than the original bill."[42]

Others echoed the free ships refrain. Representative Coburn said, "If it were proposed to encourage commerce and navigation a man of common sense would say, 'Let our citizens buy ships where they can buy them the cheapest.'"[43] Despite Lynch's efforts, his bill failed to advance.[44]

Still, Lynch and his allies did not give up attacking free ships as an alternative to subsidies. Representative John Farnsworth (R-IL) pointed out that it was inconsistent to oppose refunds on duties imposed on shipbuilding inputs but then support the importation of foreign-built vessels without any duty.[45]

Lynch posed the question to the House regarding letting foreign-built vessels into the U.S. registry:

> Will an American Congress after England has for the advantage of her own commerce destroyed the merchant marine of our country, now, while the claim for this spoliation remains unsettled, and while the remembrance of the wrong still rankles in the breast of every true American, break down those navigation laws which have stood from the foundation of the Government, and under the operation of which we attained the highest rank as a maritime Power, that the English shipbuilder may build our shipping?[46]

Lynch was also forceful in calling out foreign lobbyists, including Codman. He pointed out that "three-fourths of all the ship owners that came before the committee were opposed to the proposition which has been urged here on their behalf."[47] He sarcastically noted that whenever the bill touched "English interests those gentlemen who are here under false colors, these disguised agents of the Clyde shipbuilders, go around and supply facts and figures and plausibly deceptive arguments, ostensibly in the interests of American shipowners, but really in the interests of shipbuilders and shipowners of England."

More than once in the proceedings Lynch had to engage in floor bickering and procedural fights to move the legislation forward. He also, on several occasions became frustrated and lashed out at who he thought was behind the interruptions and tactics: namely foreign interests. At one point, the *New York Times* reported there were "calls to order, and much confusion."[48] It was at this point that Representative Negley came to blows with Codman at the Arlington Hotel.[49]

In late May 1870 toward the end of the debate, Lynch lambasted Representative Robert C. Schenck (R-OH), who was raising an objection about continuing the debate. Lynch said that the opposition "does not rise here" and "I understand where it originates and the purpose of it" implying that foreign vessel owners were influencing the debate.[50] Schenck took offense, and Lynch withdrew his remarks. The *New York Times* reported that Lynch had "impugned the motives of those attempting to close debate."[51]

Lynch attempted to salvage matters on May 31 by proposing a substitute with only the duty provisions. That bill nevertheless failed by a greater margin than earlier proposals.[52] The Butler substitute to reimpose discriminating duties also failed.[53] The worsening vote totals indicated that Lynch had overstayed his welcome.

The fight, however, was not completely over. The portent of war between France and Prussia in the summer of 1870 caused the Grant administration to address vessel registration. The administration suggested to Congress that foreign-built vessels be permitted to reflag in the U.S. to avoid being treated as belligerent vessels.[54] Neither legislative chamber was able to act in time prior to July 16, 1870, when France declared war on Prussia. Many years later, Codman and the shipbuilder Charles H. Cramp argued in the press about whether Grant was convinced to back down or whether the legislation had simply run out of time.[55] The *Congressional Record* indicates the latter, and the emergency passed because the Franco-Prussian War was so short (lasting roughly six months).

---

[1] U.S. Shipping Board, Report on the History of Shipping Discriminations and on Various Forms of Government Aid to Shipping, 13—14.

[2] Dalzell, Flight from the Flag, 247–48.

[3] For example, Charles S. Hill, History of American Shipping: Its Prestige, Decline, and Prospect (New York: American News, 1883), 181—83; William W. Bates, Shipping Restoration—The Causes of Decline Examined; Justice of the Demand for Proper Legislation (Denver: Smith-Brooks, 1907), 44.

[4] For example, Bates, American Navigation; John Codman, Free Ships (New York: G. P. Putnam's Sons, 1881); Dunmore, Ship Subsidies; Hall, American Navigation with Some Account of the Causes of its Recent Decay, and of the Means by Which Its Prosperity May Be Restored; Hill, History of American Shipping; Hamilton A. Hill, American Shipping: Its Decline and the Remedies (Boston: J. H. Eastburn's Press, 1869); Roach, American Carrying Trade; David A. Wells, Our Merchant Marine: How It Rose, Increased, Became Great, Declined, and Decayed (New York: G. P. Putnam's Sons, 1882). The U.S. Naval Institute published numerous articles on the merchant marine in the nineteenth century listed in Library of Congress: A List of Books on Merchant Marine Subsidies, 2nd ed. (Washington, DC: Government Printing Office, 1903), such as French E. Chadwick, "Our Merchant Marine: The Causes of Its Decline, and the Means to Be Taken for Its Revival," U.S. Naval Institute Proceedings 8, no. 4 (January 1882): 75–120.

[5] Causes of the Reduction of American Tonnage H. Rep. 41-28.

[6] For example, "American Commerce—The Causes of Its Decline— The Congressional Committee in Session," New York Times, October 15, 1869, 8.

[7] Causes of the Reduction of American Tonnage, H. Rep. 41-28, 10.

[8] Causes of the Reduction of American Tonnage, H. Rep. 41-28, 5.

[9] Causes of the Reduction of American Tonnage, H. Rep. 41-28, 10.

[10] Causes of the Reduction of American Tonnage, H. Rep. 41-28, 11.

[11] Causes of the Reduction of American Tonnage, H. Rep. 41-28, 14.

[12] 12 Stat. 178 (March 2, 1861).

[13] 13 Stat. 223, 267 (June 30, 1864).

[14] Causes of the Reduction of American Tonnage, H. Rep. 41-28, 17.

[15] Causes of the Reduction of American Tonnage, H. Rep. 41-28, 16.

[16] "Washington," New York Times, May 27, 1870, 5; "Washington," New York Herald, May 27, 1870, 10.

[17] "Washington," New York Times, May 27, 1870, 5; "Washington," New York Herald, May 27, 1870, 10; "From Washington," New York World, May 27, 1870, 2.

[18] Thomas J. Carrier, Washington, D.C., a Historical Walking Tour (Charleston, SC: Arcadia, 1999), 77.
[19] Biographical information regarding John Codman, except where otherwise referenced, comes from John Codman, Winter Sketches from the Saddle (Long Riders' Guild Press ed., 2001), forward by Brandon R. Schrand (originally published by G. P. Putnam's Sons, 1888), http://www.lrgaf.org/articles/codman-schrand.htm, and American Council of Learned Societies, Dictionary of American Biography, ed. Allen Johnson and Dumas Malone (New York: Charles Scribner's Sons, 1930), 259.
[20] Capt. John Codman Dead," New York Times, April 7, 1900, 1; "A Victorian Retrospect–John Codman's Recollection of Scenes in Piccadilly on Coronation Day Sixty Years Ago," New York Times, June 21, 1897, 4.
[21] Captain Ringbolt, Sailor's Life and Sailor's Yarns (New York: S. Francis, 1847).
[22] Herman Melville, "Book Review of Sailor's Life and Sailor's Yarns," Literary World 1, no. 5 (March 6, 1847): 105–06.
[23] John Codman, An American Transport in the Crimean War (New York: Bonnell, Silver, 1896).
[24] "'Free Ships' at the Reform Club – Captain John Codman Makes an Eloquent Plea for a National Necessity," New York Herald, March 18, 1894, 13.
[25] Mark Twain, The Innocents Abroad or the New Pilgrims' Progress (Hartford, CT: American Publishing, 1869).
[26] John Codman, Ten Months in Brazil (Boston: Lee and Shepard, 1867); "Ten Months in Brazil," Boston Semi-Weekly Advertiser, July 31, 1867, 4 ("Captain John Codman's 'Ten Months in Brazil' is a pleasant and readable little book.").
[27] For example, "Our Shipping," Boston Herald, November 27, 1887, 17; "Free Ships the Thing—John Codman Exposes Fallacious Reasoning of Opponents of the Fithian Bill," New York Herald, (July 4, 1894, 12; "Plea for Free Ships—Capt. Codman Addresses the Free Trade League," Boston Herald, March 6, 1898, 22; "Codman Answers Cramp's Arguments," New York Herald, March 25, 1894, 5; "Ship Builder and Owner—Responsibility for Loss of the American Carrying Trade," New York Times, April 20, 1896, 10.
[28] "Free Ships for Free Commerce," New York Times, December 22, 1869, 4.
[29] John Codman, Winter Sketches from the Saddle (New York: G. P. Putnam's Sons, 1888).
[30] "Capt. Codman's Ride," New York Times, December 3, 1886, 4.
[31] "Capt. John Codman Dead," New York Times, April 7, 1900, 1.
[32] H.R. 1261, 41st Cong., 2nd sess. (February 17, 1870).
[33] H.R. 1889, 41st Cong., 2nd sess. (April 28, 1870).
[34] Cong. Globe, 41st Cong., 2nd sess. (May 11, 1870), 3369–74.
[35] U.S. Congress, House, Message from the President of the United States and Accompanying Documents, 41st Cong., 3rd sess., 1870, H. Exec. Doc. 41-1, part 1, 16.

[36] Cong. Globe, 41st Cong., 2nd Sess. (May 11, 1870), 3372.
[37] Cong. Globe, 41st Cong., n2d Sess. (May 12, 1870), 3412.
[38] Cong. Globe, 41st Cong., 2nd Sess. (May 17, 1870), 3522–29.
[39] "Ship Builder and Owner—Responsibility for Loss of American Carrying Trade," New York Times, April 20, 1896, 10.
[40] H.R. 1889, 41st Cong., 2nd sess. (May 16, 1870) (Butler Substitute).
[41] Cong. Globe, 41st Cong., 2nd sess. (May 19, 1870), 3619–20.
[42] Cong. Globe, 41st Cong., 2nd sess. (May 24, 1870), 3764.
[43] Cong. Globe, 41st Cong., 2nd sess. 3763.
[44] Cong. Globe, 41st Cong., 2nd sess. 3768.
[45] Cong. Globe, 41st Cong., 2nd sess. (May 26, 1870), 3856—57.
[46] Cong. Globe, 41st Cong., 2nd sess., 3861.
[47] Cong. Globe, 41st Cong., 2nd sess., 3861.
[48] "Forty-First Congress," New York Times, May 27, 1870, 5.
[49] "Washington – The Northern Pacific Railroad," New York Times, May 27, 1870, 5.
[50] Cong. Globe, 41st Cong., 2nd sess. (May 31, 1870), 3955.
[51] "House of Representatives—The Revival of Commerce," New York Times, June 1, 1870, 5.
[52] Cong. Globe, 41st Cong., 2nd sess. (May 31, 1870), 3958.
[53] Cong. Globe, 41st Cong., 2nd sess., 3956.
[54] Cong. Globe, 41st Cong., 2nd sess. (July 14, 1870), 5561; U.S. Congress, Senate, Message of the President of the United States, 41st Cong., 2nd sess., 1870, S. Exec. Doc. 41-115.
[55] Codman offered one version of what transpired in "Some Fallacies of Ship Builders—Captain Codman Points Out Those in an Article Written by Charles Cramp–-Grant's Call for Free Ships," New York Herald, April 12, 1894, 12.

Senator Willaim P. Frye, circa 1880, Mathew Benjamin Brady, photographer, Library of Congress

Chapter 9 — Subsidies vs. Free Ships

The Collins Line failure and the Pacific Mail scandal inhibited further serious subsidy discussion, and nothing substantive was accomplished on mail subsidies until 1885. In the meantime, other measures that might promote the U.S. merchant marine were considered.

A good example was an 1878 proposal made by John Roach, a prominent shipbuilder from Philadelphia. Roach's proposal was to have the U.S. government pay a postal subsidy for a shipping line he started between the United States and Brazil.[1] There were favorable factors, including a promise by Brazil to provide matching funds. Nevertheless, and despite an energetic lobbying campaign, Democrats in control of the House of Representatives refused to approve the proposal and the service had to be suspended.

To recall, the Democratic Party supported free ships together with general opposition to import tariffs and subsidies. The Republican Party backed retaining the nation's long-standing U.S.-build policy and supporting the U.S. merchant marine with subsidies.

Subsidies or free ships thus tended to advance depending on which party was in power. When Grover Cleveland was president from 1885 to 1889 and then again from 1893 to 1897, free ships made headway, but the policy was not enacted into law. When Benjamin Harrison was president from 1889 to 1893 and William McKinley, Theodore Roosevelt, and Howard Taft from 1897 to 1911, subsidies and bounties were ascendant, including enactment of the Ocean Mail Act of 1891. A limited free ships policy was enacted as part of the Panama Canal Act of 1912 and expanded in the 1914 Ship Registry Act under President Wilson, but substantial subsidies had to wait until 1936.

JOURNEY TO THE JONES ACT

Three Republican political leaders from Maine took up Lynch's cause as the leading subsidy proponents and free ships opponents: James G. Blaine, William P. Frye, and Nelson Dingley, Jr., all born within two years of each other (1830-32). At least one of them was in Congress at any given time from 1863 to 1911. Although they were leaders of many failed legislative attempts, they nevertheless succeeded in beating back free ships and in enacting modest reform legislation in 1884, mail subsidies in the Postal Appropriations Act of 1885, and the 1891 Ocean Mail Act.

Their motivation may be gleaned from the state of U.S. shipbuilding and vessel ownership at the time. Maine, which had wood but not ready supplies of iron, dominated the construction of large wooden sailing vessels. Ninety-one large wooden vessels (about one-third in Bath) were built in Maine during the year ended June 30, 1890. Their average size was about 544 tons.[2] Only four steam vessels were built in Maine in the same period. Meanwhile, Pennsylvania, Michigan, and Ohio dominated the building of iron steam vessels.

The Maine concentration also applied to vessel ownership. During an era when owners would choose a local port as the port of registry for ease of access to physical documents, Maine was the second largest place of registry for sailing vessels in the United States, second only to New York in terms of tonnage.[3] Conversely, Maine was not a significant place of registry of steam vessels.

Senator George G. Vest (D-MO), a leading vessel subsidy opponent, invoked Shakespeare to draw out the Maine connection. He said about Senator Frye in 1890 that, "he represents a shipbuilding people. Take away the shipbuilding from Maine and 'Othello's occupation's gone.'"[4]

THE THREE MAINERS

Blaine had an illustrious career as a politician from 1863 to 1892, but he also had the unwanted distinction of being the only Republican nominated for president from 1860 to 1912 (among nine candidates altogether) who was not elected to that office at least once. Harrison also lost once, but after serving as president. Blaine narrowly lost to Cleveland in 1884.[5]

Blaine served as a U.S. representative from Maine from 1863 to 1876 and was speaker of the House from 1869 to 1875 when the Lynch Committee was active.[6] He served in the Senate from 1876 to 1881, becoming secretary of state in March 1881.

His first short stint at State ended when President James Garfield was shot on the morning of July 2, 1881, in Washington, DC at the depot of the Baltimore and Potomac Railroad (approximately where the East Gallery of the National Gallery of Art now stands). Blaine was "arm in arm" with the president when Garfield was shot.[7] Blaine was not a favorite of Vice President Chester Arthur (whom he later defeated in 1884 for the Republican Presidential nomination) and so he resigned as secretary of state effective December 1881.

From then until he ran for president in 1884 and after that loss, Blaine also spent time writing. He did not return to government until 1889, serving as President Harrison's secretary of state. He served until 1892, resigning a few days before the Republican national convention. Despite being in poor health, he had the second most votes at that convention. Blaine's health continued to deteriorate, and he died on January 27, 1893.

Blaine paved the way for Frye and Dingley as a strong U.S. merchant marine supporter. He led the effort in support of the Roach postal subsidy, arguing that the subsidy requested was a small amount in comparison to what was being spent on the U.S. Navy's "South Americas squadron to protect a commerce that does not exist... and have our officers go ashore and display our flag from the harbors and have some good balls and receptions."[8]

In his 1884 political history, *Twenty Years of Congress*, Blaine stated that if the U.S. government had supported the U.S. merchant marine the way it had supported the railroads, the U.S. fleet would have recovered from the Civil War.[9] He argued that free ships would have "meant simply that American capitalists might secure the registry of the United States for vessels built in English shipyards."

Frye served as one of Blaine's campaign managers in 1876 when Blaine sought the nomination to run for president. Blaine supported Hayes in the general election and asked Hayes to nominate Frye as the U.S. attorney general which Hayes did not do.[10] Frye again served as one of Blaine's national campaign managers in 1880 and succeeded Blaine as chair of the Maine Republican state committee in 1881.

Frye was a state legislator, the mayor of Lewiston, Maine, and served in the U.S. House of Representatives from 1871 to 1881. When Blaine became secretary of state for a second time in 1889, Frye succeeded Blaine in the U.S. Senate. He served there until August 9, 1911, when he died in office.

In his Senate career, Frye worked tirelessly to enact subsidies to support the fleet, to tighten U.S. coastwise laws, and to defeat free ships. A contemporary description of vessel subsidy efforts said that Frye "has had the subject at heart for many years" and that he was "prompted by patriotic zeal."[11] Eugene Tyler Chamberlain, the long-serving commissioner of the Bureau of Navigation, called him American shipping's "staunchest friend."[12]

Chamberlain also wrote after Frye died that his career was "unequaled in congressional history in the dignity, duration, and extent of its disinterested efforts to promote American commerce and navigation."[13] The press referred to Frye as the "father of postal subsidy" after enactment of the 1891 Ocean Mail Act, also called the "Frye-Farquhar bounty bill."[14]

Still, Frye was not without his critics. For example, Frye had his moment in David Graham Phillips' sensationalist 1906 *The Treason of the Senate* series in *Cosmopolitan* magazine. Journalist Bill Moyers has described the nine-part series as having "exploded in the consciousness and conversation of the country;" furthermore, "the series fueled the growing drive by reformers to confront the power of large corporations and financial interests on Wall Street."[15] Although Phillips's treatment of Frye was muted in comparison to how harshly he characterized other politicians, he nevertheless wrote that Frye's "chief public occupation since 1901 has been urging a ship-subsidy grab… promised an influential group of 'campaign contributors.'" [16]

The *Outlook* magazine attempted to meld competing views on Frye after he died in an article entitled "A Statesman of the Old School:"[17]

> Frye may fairly be described as belonging to the better of two divisions in which conservative leaders of a generation ago may be classed; he was not a petty politician, and yet he was a politician in the main, rising sometimes to statesmanlike qualities, and never becoming a mere tool of great interests.

In a historical oddity, a vessel named in Frye's honor built in Maine in 1901 was the first U.S.-flag vessel sunk by the German Navy in World War I.[18] The German commerce raider was the *SS Prinz Eitel Friedrich*. Later, a "Liberty" ship built in Maine named for Frye was sunk by a German U-boat in World War II.[19]

Only a few months after sinking of the *Frye* and short of fuel and provisions, the *Friedrich* went into a U.S. port and was interned under U.S. neutrality laws.[20] She was seized by the U.S. government when the United States entered the war, was refurbished, and served as a U.S. troopship as the *DeKalb*, named after Johann von Robais, Baron de Kalb who had served in the Continental Army in the Revolutionary War.

De Kalb (mentioned in an earlier chapter as one of the officers recommended by Silas Deane) had been born in Germany and served in the French Army before service in America. When the vessel was seized and renamed in 1917, President Woodrow Wilson wrote that its naming after a German who had served in the French and American armies had "a poetic property about it!"[21]

Dingley succeeded Frye in the House when the Maine legislature appointed Frye to the Senate. His district included the shipbuilding center of Bath. Dingley had met Blaine in 1854 when Blaine was the editor and part owner of the *Kennebunk Journal*. At the time, Dingley was the owner of the *Lewiston Journal*.[22] Dingley was also a law clerk in the firm of Fessenden & Frye in Lewiston, Maine, in 1855.[23] Dingley served in the Maine state legislature and, for a short time, as the governor of Maine. He was a U.S. congressman from 1881 to January 13, 1899, when he died in office at the age of sixty-six.[24]

Like Frye, Dingley was a strong advocate for the U.S. merchant marine and a determined free ships opponent. He was responsible for the creation of the Bureau of Navigation in the Treasury Department in 1884 intended to bring together U.S. maritime policymaking in one place.[25]

Codman was a regular Frye and Dingley opponent. For example, Codman and Dingley wrote competing prescriptions for the U.S. merchant marine in April 1884 in the *North American Review*, entitled "The Decline of American Shipping."[26]

Dingley was also known for his orthodox Republican views on high tariffs. He was the prime architect as chairman of the Ways and Means Committee of a return to high tariffs in what is known as the "Dingley Tariff Act of 1897."[27] The Dingley tariffs were the highest protective tariffs in U.S. history and lasted until the enactment of the Revenue Act of 1913.[28]

On the subject of the merchant marine, Dingley pronounced himself an advocate of the U.S. merchant marine in an April 20, 1882, House floor speech. Dingley was responding to an April 15 speech by Representative Benton McMillin (D-TN), an avid U.S. tariff opponent.[29] McMillin argued that the U.S.-flag fleet had flourished with commercial trade reciprocity in the 1840s and 1850s and that the industry had been "given the most ample protection that the loudest clamorer for special privileges could wish." He also pointed out that requiring vessels to be U.S. built for the U.S. registry was a "suicidal policy." With "commercial freedom," he argued, "the shackles will fall from our commerce as did Peter's chains at the angel's touch."

Dingley forcefully pushed back, by enumerating a list of burdens borne by the U.S.-flag fleet—burdens not borne by British vessels.[30] He sarcastically punctuated items in his list with phrases like, "Is this another of the 'protective props' to which the gentlemen from Tennessee referred?" Dingley concluded that "we have not only avoided the protection and encouragement of American shipping under the influence of free-trade teachings but we have also neglected to modify our navigation laws so as to remove burdens on the running of vessels which England has removed from her shipping."

1882 Dingley Committee

Dingley was appointed in August 1882 to a congressional joint select committee on American shipping, consisting of three Senators and six Representatives.[31] Although Dingley was not the chairman, this came to be known as the "Dingley Committee," and for good reason. The committee report was issued under his name and the focus was on the burdens Dingley identified in his April 1882 floor speech.[32]

The chief free ships proponents on the select committee were Representative Samuel S. Cox (D-NY) and Senator Vest. Cox unsuccessfully ran for speaker of the House in 1883 when the House switched to a Democratic majority and was known for his witty speeches.[33] He was a free trader generally and argued in the minority report that the committee's recommended burdens bill did not go far enough.

Vest, known for his oratory skill and who had previously served as a member of the Confederate congress, would prove to be a recurring thorn in the side of subsidy proponents while serving in the Senate from 1880 to 1903.[34] Vest was famous as a lawyer for recovering damages in an 1870 case on behalf of the owner of a hunting dog, "Old Drum," which had been killed by a sheep farmer.[35] The phrase "a man's best friend is his dog" is attributed to his closing speech to the jury. In an episode of the 1960s television series *Death Valley Days* entitled "Tribute to the Dog," President Ronald Reagan played the role of Vest.[36] Vest has also been credited with popularizing the phrase "History is written by the victors and framed according to the prejudices and bias existing on their side."[37] He used this phrase in an 1891 speech to a convention of former Confederates.

The Dingley Committee analysis of the causes of merchant marine decline was a reprise of the Lynch Committee report.[38] It recommended that Congress address a series of operating cost "burdens." The committee sought to aid shipbuilding by providing for refunds from the U.S. government of import duties applied to certain shipbuilding components such as iron plates. The committee also recommended that the U.S. Navy build vessels in private shipyards and not just in Navy-owned shipyards. Finally, it tried to improve the treatment of seamen, as discussed in an upcoming chapter.

1884 DINGLEY ACT

Legislation to implement the Dingley report advanced at the end of the Forty-Seventh Congress in early 1883. However, Congress did not finish the job and had to be addressed again, in 1884, at the beginning of the Forty-Eighth Congress.[39] Dingley and Cox drew the battle lines on free ships. Responding to Dingley's argument that U.S. laws needed to be modernized, Cox argued:

> Go on, gentlemen! Modify your shipping laws, remove burdens, extend privileges, copy the British code! We will aid you in the experiment as far as you go and would bid you go further, to fare better.
>
> Do more! Out of your Treasury, or out of the tonnage fund, mostly collected from foreign shipping, make a sort of allowance for the use of certain American materials in building ships; and yet like

the young man in Scripture, one thing ye will lack. You may copy the English statutes, as liberalized in 1849 in allowing Englishmen to buy ships where they pleased, and in 1854, when they opened their coasting trade to all the world.[40]

Here, Cox was referring to the fact that Britain had repealed its foreign trading navigation acts in 1849 and then its domestic trading navigation act in 1854.[41] Vest made the same argument, noting that Dingley's aim to lift certain cost burdens on U.S.-flag vessels was "insectivorous compared to the deadly blight which had stricken down the merchant marine of the United States" and that free ships was needed to avoid "the relic of barbarism adopted in the days of Oliver Cromwell" (meaning the English 1650 Navigation Act).[42]

On the other side, Dingley argued that the change in law permitting British owners to purchase vessels anywhere for British registry had not given Britain any advantage. Rather, that was due "solely to the accidental revolution in the ocean carrying trade which saved her from being distanced more and more by our wooden clipper ships."[43] Britain had laid the groundwork for the switch to iron, steam-propelled vessels, according to Dingley. For its part, the United States had failed to do so because the Civil War tied its hands.

Dingley also argued strenuously against the dangers of relying on foreign-built vessels, referring to Britain's Civil War involvement: "What would have become of our ports... if at the breaking out of the war we had been obliged to resort to the nation which tried to crush us?"[44] In that eventuality, the United States "would suffer more than the belligerents themselves." Where vessels are built "is more than a question of business... It is a question of whether the nation shall be able to defend itself; it is a question of national security and national independence."[45]

A version of the Dingley legislation was re-introduced in early 1884 by Representative Henry Warner Slocum (D-NY).[46]

He cooperated with Dingley and Frye to get the legislation enacted in the Democratic majority House. (Slocum had been one of the youngest generals in the U.S. Army in the Civil War, played important roles at Gettysburg and General Sherman's "March to the Sea" campaign, and was, among other things, a prime mover behind the building of the Brooklyn Bridge.[47] Statutes of him stand at Gettysburg, Pennsylvania and at Grand Army Plaza in Brooklyn.)

As with the earlier bill, the legislation advanced by Slocum focused on consensus measures to bring U.S. law in line with British law.[48] Despite Slocum's protestations that a free ship amendment would doom the bill in the Senate, Cox persisted and offered an amendment to permit foreign-built iron or steel steamships of not less than 3,000 tons to be freely U.S. registered.[49] Such vessels would not have U.S. domestic trading privileges.

Dingley pointed out that U.S. operating costs were higher than British operating costs. Without domestic trading privileges, U.S. owners would prefer to own British-built/British-flag vessels rather than British-built/U.S.-flag vessels–even with a free ship law.[50] This was to prove prophetic: when a free ship law was made part of the Panama Canal Act of 1912 but excluded U.S. domestic trading privileges, no vessels reflagged into the U.S. registry. Despite Dingley's arguments, the Cox free ships amendment passed the House on April 26, 1884.[51]

Free ships, however, failed in the Senate although a favorable mail subsidy for U.S.-flag vessels was included in the final legislation. During Senate consideration, Frye, like Lynch before him, called out the influence of Codman—"Who is Capt. John Codman?" he asked. "He is the drum-major of the whole 'free-ship' band, and the magic of his wand sets the tune which will be played."[52]

Frye also quoted from an article regarding foreign steamship owners who employed Codman and used funds "freely to influence the New York press, and whenever necessary, to influence official action in Washington."[53] Senator Zebulon B. Vance (D-

NC) rose to Codman's defense: "I am authorized by him to denounce as false any statement to the effect that he is suborned or in the pay of foreign shipowners."[54] Moreover, "he is entitled to quite as much respect as Mr. John Roach, who seeks to plunder the American people in the name of patriotism by high protective laws."

Ultimately, the Senate also added a Frye amendment to eliminate the postmaster general's authority to impose arbitrary rates on U.S.-flag vessels. This would become important after Congress enacted the law to authorize substantial mail subsidies.[55]

A conference committee to resolve the House and Senate legislation differences—including Dingley, Frye, Slocum, and Vest but not Cox—found middle ground by removing both the free ships provision *and* the mail subsidy provision. It kept the repeal of arbitrary postal rates.[56] The legislation also retained relief of certain cost burdens and required that all officers on U.S.-flag vessels – not just the captain or the vessel master – be U.S. citizens. Moreover, the law limited advances and allotments paid to mariners (discussed in a subsequent chapter). President Chester A. Arthur signed the bill into law on June 26, 1884.[57]

1891 Ocean Mail Act

The next merchant marine policy battleground was the Post Office Appropriation Act of 1885 signed into law on March 3, 1885 by President Arthur.[58] That Act aimed to increase the mail carriage rates paid to American carriers. President Grover Cleveland (an opponent of subsidies) was sworn in the next day, March 4, 1885, and William F. Vilas, Cleveland's postmaster general refused to agree to the higher rates. The postmaster general reported that the current rates were already adequate and that Congress should "plainly convey the purpose and impose the duty" if the purpose of the higher rates were to subsidize the U.S. merchant marine.[59]

Subsidy supporters had to wait for the inauguration of President Benjamin Harrison in early 1889 to make good on that suggestion. Not only were both the House and the Senate under Republican control that year for the first time since 1875 but the 1888 Republican national platform was firmly against free ships and in favor of "rehabilitation of our American merchant marine."[60]

The pro-merchant marine interests also organized themselves in the 1860s into a national "American Shipping and Industrial League."[61] That league was the first private group organized to promote the U.S. merchant marine.[62] An early leader was Capt. Ambrose Snow, also president of the Marine Society of New York (chartered by King George III in 1770). Snow was the national league's first vice president and one of its Washington lobbyists.[63]

Snow appears to have been successful at getting access. For example, he was the coxswain on a barge with rowers from the Marine Society who ferried Harrison ashore from his vessel in the East River in New York in April 1889.[64] Harrison was in New York for a centennial naval parade and the very same society had rowed George Washington to Manhattan in 1789.[65] The *New York Herald* referred to the twelve rowers as "lusty but venerable, white bearded oarsmen" and Snow as the "white mustached but tough looking old gentleman."

The Shipping and Industrial League coalesced around the "French system" of merchant marine support.[66] Known as the "Tonnage Bill," it would provide a government payment of a certain amount for miles travelled in the foreign trade, regardless of the type of vessel.[67] It did not have presidential support, however. President Harrison, in his December 1889 annual message to Congress, instead recommended ocean mail service be made "liberally remunerative" to "encourage the establishment and in some fair degree equalize the chances of American steamship lines in the competitions which they must meet."[68]

Frye reported a bill for each idea.[69] Describing the direct payment bill as the "Shipping League tonnage bill," he pointed out that it had the support of numerous boards of trade, chambers of commerce, and other organizations.[70] The express purpose of the bill was to meet the subsidizing by England, France, and Germany of their national vessels. All subsidized vessels would be required to have U.S. citizen officers and an increasing number of American seamen over time.

Unlike the tonnage bill, the mail subsidy bill would pay higher rates for vessels of greater capability divided into classes. Each of the first three classes would have to be built in accordance with Navy plans and specifications so the vessels would be convertible to "auxiliary cruisers." The highest rate would be paid to iron steam vessels of at least 8,000 tons, capable of a continuous speed of 20 knots.

The criteria were not devised at random and were repeated in 1892 legislation that provided a special, narrowly drawn permission for two foreign-built vessels to register in the U.S.[71] The main condition was that the vessel owner had to contract to build in the U.S. two vessels at least as capable as the reflagged vessels.

The only vessels that met the criteria were the *SS City of New York* and the *SS City of Paris*, two twin-screw transatlantic passenger liners built in Scotland and owned by the Philadelphia-based International Navigation Company (INC). The company had taken over the British Inman Line when that line became insolvent. The British government then withdrew the line's subsidy because of the American ownership—as further discussed in a subsequent chapter.[72]

Clement A. Griscom, the president of INC, had informed Congress that he would reflag the vessels to the United States and build two vessels in that country if he also obtained the U.S. mail service contract between the United States and Britain. Congress obliged. Those vessels were in fact reflagged and the two vessels, *SS St. Louis* and *SS St. Paul*, were built at the Cramp & Sons shipyard in Philadelphia. All four vessels served in the U.S. Navy in the Spanish-American War.

Vest led the opposition to both bills. Relying on the writings of Codman, he argued that the U.S. merchant marine had done best in the first half of the nineteenth century without subsidies.[73] Expecting exports to increase because there was more U.S.-flag service was a "monstrous fallacy," according to Vest who further claimed that "commerce will not follow the flag. The flag will follow commerce. The flag will follow self-interest; and until you make the interest of the people of foreign countries to export to us and to buy our exports, they will never follow any other flag but the flag that puts money into their own pockets." Both bills nevertheless passed the Republican Senate in July 1890.[74]

The process proved trickier in the House. In early 1890 Representative John M. Farquhar (R-NY), chairman of the Merchant Marine Committee, introduced a tonnage bill and held hearings in 1890.[75] Dingley also served on the Committee. Among the witnesses were Captains Snow and Codman as well as William W. Bates, who was the first commissioner of navigation. Bates had been a Great Lakes shipping man and was a strong advocate for discriminating duties.[76] Vessel owners, such as William P. Clyde, and shipyard representatives, such as Charles H. Cramp, also testified. Some subsidy opponents thought at the time that Bates was beholden to the Shipping League, to the point that Representative Hilary A. Herbert (D-AL) called him "a creature of the league." [77]

In the summer of 1890, Farquhar's committee recommended the tonnage bill but there was no further House consideration of that bill.[78] Representative George W. Fithian (D-IL), who was to serve as chairman of the Merchant Marine Committee from 1893-95, wrote a scathing minority report.[79] Three other Democrats, including Representative Joseph "Fighting Joe" Wheeler (AL), also opposed the bill. Wheeler was a U.S. Army officer before the Civil War, a general in the Confederate army, and a general in the U.S. Army during the Spanish-American War.

By early 1891 the Farquhar Committee again approved the Senate's tonnage bill with reduced subsidy amounts.[80] Fithian was once more one of the leaders of the opposition. He argued that the French tonnage system was a failure and that the subsidies would not reduce freight rates.[81] Rather, "reason will dictate, that after the subsidy is granted the subsidized shipowner would take his subsidy and charge current rates." Fithian was also not shy about resorting to hyperbole arguing that "of all its foes, socialism is the most dangerous to our system of government, and the proposition to pay subsidies or bounties to ships or any other industry is but a step in that direction."

Most of the opposition came from representatives of agricultural districts who were unhappy with tax dollars subsidizing ocean service. They argued these would not benefit American farmers. Representative Joseph H. Outhwaite (D-OH), for example, offered an amendment requiring vessel owners who received bounties to rebate 50 percent in the form of reduced freight charges to exporters of American products.[82]

On February 27, 1891, the House consideration of the bounty bill went through multiple gyrations in a matter of hours. The deliberation was described in the press as "one of the most determined and closely contested struggles ever seen in Congress."[83]

After the House soundly rejected a Fithian free ships amendment, Representative Joseph G. Cannon (R-IL) (then on the Rules Committee) maneuvered the Senate tonnage bill out of consideration and substituted a diluted version of the mail subsidy bill in its place.[84] The key procedural vote was 143 in favor, 142 against and 44 not voting.[85] The chair had to make multiple procedural rulings to permit the original bill to be instantaneously recommitted to the Merchant Marine Committee and to permit Chairman Farquhar to simultaneously report the mail subsidy substitute for a vote.

Subsidy advocates settled for what they could get.[86] Farquhar concluded that while "this bill does not come up to all of my expectations as a friend of the merchant marine in the foreign trade, yet as a loyal citizen and one who desires to see the flag of his country on every sea I accept its condition."[87] In a speech in Philadelphia in 1900, Frye said that the "bill had been emasculated" and that he "was a good deal discouraged by that attempt."[88]

Representative William M. Springer (D-IL), one of the chief opponents, was happy at the defeat of that "stupendous scheme" of tonnage bounties and on the members of Congress resisting "the most persistent lobby that has ever visited Washington."[89] One magazine editorialized that "having by navigation laws and rapacious tariffs driven our mercantile fleet from the ocean as effectually as fifty *Alabamas* could have done it, the Republicans in Congress vehemently demanded subsidies for ships" and that only by following Britain's free trade example could the fleet be revived.[90]

The chaotic House result stood despite Frye's effort to force a conference committee.[91] President Harrison signed the legislation on March 3, 1891.[92]

As enacted, the postmaster general was authorized to enter into contracts with U.S. citizens of not less than five years and not more than ten years in duration for the carriage of international mail.[93] Such contracts were to be bid and awarded to the lowest responsible bidder. All vessels had to be U.S.-flag steamships owned and officered by U.S. citizens with the crew being initially comprised of one-fourth U.S. citizens.

The principal beneficiary of the mail subsidies was INC's "American Line." Other lines that benefited were Pacific Mail Steamship Co., Oceanic Co., the New York & Cuba Mail Co., and the Red "D" Line.[94] Although the Ocean Mail Act was criticized as being inadequate to revive the U.S. merchant marine in the foreign trade, twenty vessels were built in the United States under the Act from 1895 to 1907.[95] Those vessels provided valuable service in both the Spanish-American War and World War I.

1893-1895 FREE SHIP LEGISLATION

The magic moment for free ships should have been the Fifty-Third U.S. Congress, which met from 1893 to 1895, when both the House and the Senate were under Democratic control, Cleveland was the president, and Fithian, a strong free ships advocate, was the chairman of the Merchant Marine Committee. Moreover, Cleveland had appointed Eugene Tyler Chamberlain the new commissioner of navigation in December 1893. He was also a forceful advocate for free ships and against discriminating duties—the exact opposite of Bates, his predecessor.

Fithian introduced free ships legislation in both the Fifty-Second and Fifty-Third Congresses (the Democrats had taken control of the House in the Fifty-Second Congress, 1891-93).[96] The legislation would have permitted any vessel built outside the United States to be registered under U.S. flag, regardless of whether it was used or new construction and completely free from duty. In the Fifty-Third Congress (1893-95), the legislation would not have permitted the vessel to engage in the U.S. domestic trade.

The Fithian Committee asserted that subsidies had been a failure whenever and wherever tried.[97] Instead, the United States should follow the example of Britain, which adopted its own free ships law for international trade in 1849. According to the committee, this did not result in a loss of British shipbuilding opportunities, but rather permitted British owners to purchase U.S.-built wooden sailing vessels. The committee did not appear to consider that permitting British owners to purchase outmoded vessels occurred at a moment of technological transformation. There was no apparent similar opportunity awaiting U.S shipyards in 1893 when British yards were ascendant.

Chamberlain, in his first *Annual Report*, argued that the U.S. merchant marine could only be promoted through a free ship policy combined with subsidies to match those of foreign countries.[98] The requirement that vessels be built in the United States for the U.S.-flag had "accomplished nothing for shipbuilding," he said, and "stunted the development of American navigation."

Chamberlain also argued in multiple annual reports and in the press that Congress should duplicate writ large the 1892 reflag law which had resulted in the building of the *St. Louis* and *St. Paul*.[99] The *New York Times* editorialized that the law should be expanded in a column entitled "Why Stop There."[100]

Free ships advocates received outspoken support from Cleveland and the "progressive" press, even in the unlikeliest of places.[101] In November 1894, Mrs. Frances Cleveland christened the vessel *SS St. Louis* in Philadelphia.[102] Despite the occasion being to honor a U.S.-built vessel, and before about twenty thousand people, President Cleveland stubbornly advocated for foreign-built free ships in his remarks. *The Philadelphia Inquirer* noted that "he advocated free ships, unmindful of the practical lessons of the day" and in what was probably quite an understatement—"considerable surprise was expressed when the President advocated free ships" at the launching of one of the largest U.S.-built liners.[103]

In his December 1894, annual message to Congress, President Cleveland stuck with the anti-navigation law argument: "The ancient provision of our law denying American registry to ships built abroad and owned by Americans appears in the light of present conditions not only to be a failure for good at every point, but to be nearer a relic of barbarism than anything that exists under the permission of a statute of the United States."[104]

Despite this support, and the favorable political conditions, neither the Fithian free ships legislation nor the expansion of the 1892 reflag permission advanced beyond committee in either legislative chamber. Free ships continued to be advocated but did not advance during the subsequent extended period of Republican control until the Panama Canal Act of 1912.

---

[1] Leonard Alexander Swann, Jr., John Roach, Maritime Entrepreneur (Annapolis, MD: U.S. Naval Institute, 1965), chap. 5.
[2] Annual Report of the Commissioner of Navigation to the Secretary of the Treasury (1890), 335.
[3] Annual Report of the Commissioner of Navigation to the Secretary of the Treasury (1890), 307.
[4] 21 CONG. REC. 6919 (July 2, 1890).

[5] Blaine was the subject of an episode of "The Contenders—They Lost the Election but Changed Political History," produced by C-Span, which first aired on September 16, 2011. C-Span, The Contenders Series, "James Blaine, Presidential Contender," https://www.c-span.org/video/?301269-1/james-blaine-presidential-contender.

[6] "Biographies of the secretaries of states: James Gillespie Blaine (1830—1893), U.S. Department of State, Office of the Historian, https://history.state.gov/departmenthistory/people/blaine-james-gillespie.

[7] "A Great Nation in Grief – President Garfield Shot by Assassin," New York Times, July 3, 1881, 1.

[8] 8 CONG. REC. 1589 (February 19, 1879).

[9] James G. Blaine, Twenty Years of Congress from Lincoln to Garfield (Norwich, CT: Henry Bill, 1886), vol. 2, 614.

[10] Ronald F. Banks, "The Senatorial Career of William P. Frye," MA diss., University of Maine (1958), 5.

[11] "The Progress of the World—Congress at Work," American Monthly Review of Reviews 22, no. 1 (January 1901): 15—18, 15.

[12] U.S. Congress, Senate, William Pierce Frye—Memorial Addresses Delivered in the Senate and the House of Representatives of the United States, 62nd Cong., 3rd sess., 1913, S. Doc. 62-1145, 109—10.

[13] Annual Report of the Commissioner of Navigation to the Secretary of Commerce and Labor (1911), 11.

[14] "Effect of the Subsidy Bill," New York Tribune, March 5, 1891, 2; Zeis, American Shipping Policy, 32.

[15] David Graham Phillips, The Treason of the Senate, December 16, 2014, https://billmoyers.com/2014/12/16/treason-senate-aldrich-head.

[16] David Graham Phillips, The Treason of the Senate (New York: Monthly Review Press, 1953), 94.

[17] "A Statesman of the Old School," Outlook 98 (August 19, 1911): 857.

[18] "Von Bernstorff Defends Sinking of American Ship by German Raider Eitel," Evening World (New York), (March 13, 1915), 2; Carlton Savage, ed., Policy of the United States toward Maritime Commerce in War (Washington, DC: Government Printing Office, 1936), vol. 2, 38—40 (discussing negotiations between the U.S. and German governments to settle claims arising from the sinking).

[19] Rodney Carlisle, Sovereignty at Sea: U.S. Merchant Ships and American Entry into World War I (Gainesville: University of Press of Florida, 2009), 36—37.

[20] "DeKalb (Id. No. 3010): 1917-1919," Naval History and Heritage Command, www.history.navy.mil/research/histories/ship-histories/danfs/d/dekalb.html.

[21] "Letter from W. Wilson to E. House (May 7, 1917)," in The Papers of Woodrow Wilson Digital Edition, ed. Arthur Link (Charlottesville, VA: University of Virginia Press, Rotunda, 2017), vol. 42, 235.

[22] Edward Nelson Dingley, The Life and Times of Nelson Dingley, Jr. (Kalamazoo, MI: Ihling Bros. & Everard, 1902), 48.

[23] William Pierce Frye: Memorial Addresses Delivered in the Senate and the House of Representatives of the United States, S. Doc. 62-1145, 85.

[24] "Tributes to the Late Representative Dingley," Boston Herald, January 15, 1899, 4.

[25] 23 Stat. 118 (July 5, 1884). The Dingley Committee Report had recommended the creation of such a position. U.S. Congress, House, American Shipping, 47th Cong., 2nd sess., 1882, H. Rep. 47-1827, 13. The history of the Bureau of Navigation is set forth in Lloyd M. Short, The Bureau of Navigation, Its History, Activities and Organization (Baltimore: Johns Hopkins Press, 1923).

[26] Nelson Dingley Jr. and John Codman, "The Decline in American Shipping," North American Review 137, no. 329 (April 1884): 313–35.

[27] 30 Stat. 151 (July 24, 1897); 28 Stat. 570 (August 27, 1894).

[28] 38 Stat. 114 (October 3, 1913).

[29] 13 Cong. Rec. 2917-2918 (April 15, 1882).

[30] 13 Cong. Rec. 3109-3110 (April 20, 1882).

[31] American Shipping, H. Rep. 47-1827, 1 (contains the resolution). There was also a similar report in the prior Congress. U.S. Congress, House, Causes of the Decadence of Our Merchant Marine; Means for Its Restoration and the Extension of Our Foreign Commerce, 46th Cong., 3d sess., 1881, H. Rep. 46-342.

[32] American Shipping, H. Rep. 47-1827.

[33] For example, "The Democratic Candidates for Speaker—Who and What They Are," Cleveland Leader, October 1, 1883, 5 ("His sarcastic tongue has made him many enemies, and he is the prince of repartee in Congress.").

[34] "Ex-Senator Vest Dies at Sweet Springs, MO," New York Times, Aug. 10, 1904, 7.

[35] Robert C. Byrd, The Senate 1789-1989, Classic Speeches 1830-1993, ed. Wendy Wolff (Washington, DC: Government Printing Office, 1994), vol. 3, 437–41.

[36] "Death Valley Days Series: Tribute to the Dog," IMDb, https://www.imdb.com/title/tt0556919/.

[37] "Vest on Secession," Abilene Weekly Reflector, (August 27, 1891), 1.

[38] American Shipping, H. Rep. 47-1827, 15-24.

[39] H.R. 7061 is available at 14 Cong. Rec. 925–26 (January 6, 1883).

[40] 14 Cong. Rec. 931.

[41] 17 & 18 Vict. c. 5 (March 23, 1854).

[42] 15 Cong. Rec. 977 (February 8, 1884).

[43] 14 Cong. Rec. 935 (January 6, 1883).

[44] 14 Cong. Rec. 941.

[45] 14 Cong. Rec. 941.

[46] 15 Cong. Rec. 319 (January 9, 1884).

[47] "Gen. Henry W. Slocum Dead," New York Times, April 15, 1894, 16; "Brilliant Solder's Record," New York Times, April 15, 1894, 16.

[48] 15 Cong. Rec. 3427-3428 (April 26, 1884); U.S. Congress, House, American Ship-Building and Ship-Owning Interests, 48th Cong., 1st sess., 1884, H. Rep. 48-5.
[49] 15 Cong. Rec. 3447 (April 26, 1884).
[50] 15 Cong. Rec. 3448.
[51] 15 Cong. Rec. 3451.
[52] 15 Cong. Rec. 3647 (May 1, 1884).
[53] 15 Cong. Rec. 3647; quoted in "Capt. Codman on Free Ships," Republican Journal (Belfast, ME), May 8, 1884, 12.
[54] 15 Cong. Rec. 3859 (May 6, 1884).
[55] 15 Cong. Rec. 975–77 (February 8, 1884).
[56] 15 Cong. Rec. 5452 (June 21, 1884).
[57] 23 Stat. 53 (June 26, 1884).
[58] 23 Stat. 385 (March 3, 1885).
[59] U.S. Congress, House, Ocean Mail Service, 51st Cong., 1st sess., 1890, H. R. Rep. 51-2889, 9-10, 51—53.
[60] Republican Party Platform of 1888, June 19, 1888, UC Santa Barbara, the American Presidency Project, Republican Party Platforms, https://www.presidency.ucsb.edu/documents/republican-party-platform-1888.
[61] "The National Shipping League," New York Tribune, June 14, 1886, 3; "Our Merchant Marine—Efforts of the National Shipping League to Revive It," Daily Critic (Washington, DC), June 23, 1886, 1; "A New Shipping League," New Haven Register, September 1, 1886, 1.
[62] Pedraja, Historical Dictionary of the U.S. Merchant Marine, 47.
[63] "Money for American Ships—A Subsidy Bill Proposed by the Shipping League," New York Times, (January 19, 1888), 3.
[64] "Will Row President Harrison," Daily Inter Ocean (Chicago), April 7, 1889, 2.
[65] "Old Boys at The Oar—The Veteran American Shipmasters Who Will Row President Harrison Ashore at the Centennial Naval Pageant," New York Herald, April 7, 1889, 14.
[66] "Money for American Ships—A Subsidy Bill Proposed by the Shipping League," New York Times, January 19, 1888, 3.
[67] Proceedings of the Convention of the Department of the North Atlantic Coast of the American Shipping and Industrial League Held at Boston, Mass., October 21st and 22nd, 1887 (Washington, DC: Judd & Detweiler Printers, 1887), 15-16 (explained by Captain Snow).
[68] Benjamin Harrison, First Annual Message, December 3, 1889, UC Santa Barbara, the American Presidency Project, https://www.presidency.ucsb.edu/documents/first-annual-message-14.
[69] 21 Cong. Rec. 4175–76 (May 3, 1890) (S. 3738 & S. 3739).
[70] 21 Cong. Rec. 4175–76 and (July 2, 1890), 6908–09.
[71] 27 Stat. 27 (May 10, 1892).

[72] U.S. Congress, Senate, Revival of the Merchant Marine, 56th Cong., 1st sess., 1900, S. Doc. 56-149, 100–09; "Ready to Sail Under Our Flag," New York Times, August 14, 1892, 2.
[73] 21 CONG REC. 7175 (July 12, 1890)
[74] 21 CONG REC. 7188, 7189.
[75] U.S. Congress, House, Committee on Merchant Marine and Fisheries, Hearings before the House Merchant Marine Committee on H.R. Bill no. 4663, Known as the 'Tonnage Bill,'" 51st Cong., 1st sess., 1890.
[76] "Capt. William W. Bates," Cleveland Plain Dealer, November 18, 1889, 2; for example, Bates's testimony before the Farquhar Committee, Hearings before the House Merchant Marine Committee on H.R. Bill no. 4663, Known as the 'Tonnage Bill," 220–262; and Bates, American Navigation.
[77] 22 CONG. REC. 3473 (February 27, 1891).
[78] U.S. Congress, House, American Merchant Marine in the Foreign Trade, 51st Cong., 1st sess., 1890, H. Rep. 51-1210. The mail subsidy bill was reported separately by the Committee on the Post-Office and Post-Roads. Ocean Mail Service, H. Rep. 51-2889.
[79] American Merchant Marine in the Foreign Trade, H. Rep. 51-1210, 39.
[80] U.S. Congress, House, American Merchant in the Foreign Trade, 51st Cong., 2nd sess., 1890, H. Rep. 51-3273.
[81] 22 CONG. REC. 1044–54 (January 8, 1891).
[82] 22 CONG. REC. 3476–78 (February 27, 1891).
[83] "For American Shipping—The Senate Postal Subsidy Bill Passed by the House," New York Tribune, February 28, 1891, 1; "Shipping Bill Passed," Philadelphia Inquirer, February 28, 1891, 1 ("After a memorable session lasting until midnight...").
[84] 22 Cong. Rec. 3501–02 (February 27, 1891).
[85] 22 CONG. REC. 3506–07.
[86] "Thankful for a Little," New York Tribune, March 7, 1891, 5.
[87] 22 CONG. REC. 3510.
[88] "Expansion of Territory, Expansion of Trade—An Address by Hon. William P. Frye, U.S. Senator from Maine, Before the Union League of Philadelphia, March. 17, 1900," https://babel.hathitrust.org/cgi/pt?id=loc.ark%3A%2F13960%2Ft80k2g87c&seq=10, 23.
[89] 22 CONG. REC. 3511 (February 27, 1891).
[90] "Editorial Department: Cleveland's Letter," Belford's Magazine 6, no. 34 (March 1891): 705–10, 708.
[91] "Postal Subsidies Given," New York Times, March 3, 189), 2.
[92] 22 CONG. REC. 3511 (February 27, 1891).
[93] 26 Stat. 830 (March 3, 1891).
[94] Jesse E. Saugstad, Shipping and Shipbuilding Subsidies: A Study of State Aid to the Shipping and Shipbuilding Industries in Various Countries of the World, U.S. Department of Commerce, Trade Promotion Series no. 129 (1932), 60—64; Annual

Report of the Commissioner of Navigation to the Secretary of the Treasury (1897), 190–92.

[95] Zeis, American Shipping Policy, 33; American Registries for Certain Seagoing Vessels, H. Rep. 62-405, 7.

[96] H.R. 5441, 52nd Cong., 1st sess. (1892), 23 CONG. REC. 892 (February 5, 1892); H.R. 285 and H.R. 2655, 53rd Cong., 1st sess. (1893), 25 CONG. REC. 1275 (September 6, 1893) & 25 CONG. REC. 1427 (September 12, 1893).

[97] U.S. Congress, House, American Registry of Ships Built in Foreign Countries, 52nd Cong, 1st sess., 1892, H. Rep. 52-966; U.S. Congress, House, Free Admission to American Registry of Ships Build in Foreign Countries, 53rd Cong., 1st sess., 1893, H. Rep. 53-148.

[98] Annual Report of the Commissioner of Navigation to the Secretary of the Treasury (1894), 18.

[99] For example, Annual Report of the Commissioner of Navigation to the Secretary of the Treasury (1897), 15–17; Eugene Tyler Chamberlain, "A Present Chance for American Shipping," North American Review 158, no. 448 (March 1894): 277–82.

[100] "Why Stop There," New York Times, (May 16, 1892), 4.

[101] Several "progressive" press opinions favoring free ships were collected in Chips Scattered by the Hammers of the New York Progressive Press Bearing upon the Navigation Laws and Other Obstructions to Commerce and Industry (Boston: Rockwell and Churchill, 1894).

[102] The christening of the St. Louis and the St. Paul is described in William Henry Flayhart III, The American Line (1871-1902) (New York: W.W. Norton, 2000), chap. 9.

[103] "The St. Louis Is Now Afloat," Philadelphia Inquirer, November 13, 1894, 1.

[104] Grover Cleveland, Second Annual Message (second term), December 3, 1894, UC Santa Barbara, the American Presidency Project, https://www.presidency.ucsb.edu/documents/second-annual-message-second-term.

Senator Oscar W. Underwood, circa 1910, Library of Congress

Chapter 10 – Discriminating Duties Return

Percolating alongside subsidies and free ships as potential solutions were efforts to re-introduce discriminating import duties. Discriminating duties, unlike subsidies and free ships which were highly partisan issues, crossed political party lines.

The 1896 Republican national party platform stated, "We favor the early American policy of discriminating duties for the upbuilding of our merchant marine."[1] McKinley's August 26, 1896, nomination acceptance letter endorsed this policy and said that it "should be again promptly adopted by Congress and vigorously supported until our prestige and supremacy on the seas is fully attained."[2]

For Democrats, the 1896 Maine state convention endorsed the policy and the 1905 Merchant Marine Commission Minority Report, authored by three Democrats, proposed free ships *and* discriminating duties.[3] A leading proponent of discriminating duties was Representative Oscar W. Underwood (D-AL), majority leader and chairman of the Ways and Means Committee from 1911 to 1915 (and then senator from 1915 to 1927). Underwood was Senate minority leader when Congress enacted the 1920 Merchant Marine Act.

Discrimination proponents argued simplistically that the United States had developed a substantial commercial fleet under the protection of discriminating duties and that the fleet declined when the protections were removed. Therefore, they asserted, the protections caused the expansion of the fleet, and the removal of protections hampered the fleet. Senator Jones often expressed this argument: that the United States had made a mistake in opening its shipping trade to the world on a reciprocal non-discrimination basis.

JOURNEY TO THE JONES ACT

Opponents of discriminating duties frequently pointed out that such association of circumstances did not necessarily mean cause and effect. They believed that the U.S.-flag fleet had declined for reasons unrelated to the imposition or absence of government trade restrictions. One of the most prominent persons making this counterargument was Eugene Tyler Chamberlain, the highly influential commissioner of the Bureau of Navigation who served in that role from 1893 to 1921.

EUGENE TYLER CHAMBERLAIN

Chamberlain was at the center of every U.S. maritime policy debate during his twenty-seven-year tenure as the commissioner, which put him in touch with the movers and shakers of the day. He even impressed his fellow Harvard University alumni. The Fiftieth Anniversary Report of the Harvard Class of 1878 noted, "He has probably come into contact, during his official life in Washington, with more of the great and near-great of the past fifty years than anyone else in the Class."[4]

Chamberlain was born in Albany, New York on September 28, 1856.[5] One of his family relations was Joshua Lawrence Chamberlain, the Union hero of Gettysburg, and also the governor of Maine and president of Bowdoin College. In 1908, Chamberlain and his more famous cousin served together on the Committee on History of the Chamberlain Association of America.[6]

Chamberlain attended the Albany Academy (founded in 1813) and then Harvard College. An accomplished student at Harvard, he was an editor of the *Harvard Advocate*, Harvard's literary magazine, a Phi Beta Kappa member, and a commencement speaker (his topic was "Progress in Philosophy").[7]

He started meeting the "great and near-great" at Harvard, among them Theodore Roosevelt, Class of 1880. Chamberlain, tongue-in-cheek, related in 1928 that he had agreed when the O.K. Society, a Harvard literature club, rejected Roosevelt for membership because Roosevelt "spent his time on rocks, birds and butterflies" and not "the serious affairs that the O.K. was accustomed to discuss." However, Chamberlain admitted that Roosevelt was a "fine fellow."

Following graduation from Harvard, Chamberlain eventually joined the staff of the Albany *Evening Journal* as associate editor. In his new position, he renewed his acquaintance with Roosevelt, a Republican New York state assembly member from 1882 to 1884, and came to know the state's governor, Grover Cleveland.

The connection to Cleveland became so strong that the Cleveland campaign asked Chamberlain to write a candidate biography for the 1884 presidential race.[8] Chamberlain also campaigned for Cleveland.[9] Many years later, Senator Robert M. La Follette (D-WI), a Chamberlain critic, said that "Mr. Chamberlain wrote an effusive biography of President Cleveland, and as a reward he was named to be Commissioner of Navigation."[10]

Chamberlain continued his press career at the *Albany Argus* in 1887, succeeding Daniel S. Lamont, who became Cleveland's assistant and later secretary of war in the second Cleveland administration.[11] Upon his appointment to the *Argus*, the *New York Times* reported that Chamberlain "is a bright, terse, and entertaining writer, well informed on all subjects, foreign and domestic" and "a great admirer of Grover Cleveland."[12]

In 1889 Chamberlain appeared on the maritime stage when he was appointed the secretary of the American delegation to the International Maritime Conference held in Washington, DC.[13] Both William T. Sampson, then a U.S. Navy captain and later commander of the North Atlantic Squadron in the Spanish-American War, and Clement Griscom, then-president of the INC, were members of the U.S. delegation.[14] The conference recommended revised rules of the road for vessels to help prevent collisions at sea, as adopted by the United States in 1896.[15]

In 1892 there was a fight for the presidential nomination between Senator David Bennett Hill (D-NY) and former president Grover Cleveland as to who should be the party's nominee for president. Hill's supporters called for state "snap conventions" without notice to Cleveland supporters. But Cleveland won the national Democratic Party nomination anyway.[16] The *Argus* and Chamberlain opposed the snap convention tactic.

In 1893 the *Argus* was sold to anti-Cleveland owners and Chamberlain resigned. When the *Argus* was sold, the *New York Times* referred to Chamberlain as "one of the brightest editorial writers in this section of the State, and the ablest tariff writer in the State outside of New-York City."[17]

Perhaps because of his work with the International Maritime Conference, Cleveland appointed Chamberlain commissioner of navigation in December 1893. When Chamberlain's appointment was announced, he was referred to in the press as an "anti-snapper" and part of the "Cleveland machine in the State of New York."[18] Some questioned whether he was qualified for the position, arguing "that he would not be able to distinguish a dingy from a whaler."[19] One called him a "young fresh water politician" "full of enthusiasm for the 'free ship' humbug as if he hailed from the banks of the Catfish Creek or the Tombigbee."[20]

Chamberlain nevertheless proved over time to be a capable commissioner. A 1912 magazine article found him to be "a clean, clear-headed, energetic, big-hearted man—a typical American gentleman; quick and concise in speech and action, immediately convincing one that he means what he says and says what he means, and demanding instinctive confidence. No better man could be found for the position which he occupies."[21]

Chamberlain also proved politically adept. He was appointed by a Democratic president (Cleveland) and was retained by three Republican presidents (McKinley, Roosevelt, and Taft), as well as Presidents Woodrow Wilson and Warren G. Harding. Of course, Chamberlain knew Roosevelt personally. Chamberlain's ability to work for both political parties proved useful at a time when most government positions were at the whim of the president.

Generally, Chamberlain sought the middle policy ground. He tried to straddle the political divide by arguing strenuously for free ships. But he also said that "free registry and subsidies are not alternative or conflicting propositions, but independent methods of dealing with two different subjects."[22] Meaning, free registry dealt with construction costs and subsidies dealt with operating costs.

In 1897 he joined a group, led by Frye, which came up with proposed subsidy legislation.[23] In his 1899 *Annual Report*, Chamberlain announced that the free ships policy was politically hopeless and economically fruitless because of the unfavorable U.S.-foreign operating cost differential.[24] In later years, Chamberlain returned to considering free ships a legitimate option. But he was not at all sanguine about its chances for success once free ships was enacted in a limited form in the Panama Canal Act of 1912.[25]

Democrats viewed these practical position adjustments unfavorably. For example, Vest said in 1901 that Chamberlain had undergone an "extraordinary conversion" and that he, "metaphorically speaking, stepped out on the back porch one sunny morning and looking up at the kitchen chimney saw that the smoke was drifting toward the Republican camp, and the commissioner drifted with the smoke."[26] Vest also lamented that Chamberlain had fallen "under the seductive influence of my friend from Maine [Frye]."[27]

Similarly, during the great seamen's reform effort of the period, Chamberlain advocated for mariner emancipation but against the full panoply of economic rights sought by labor leader Andrew Furuseth and Senator La Follette.[28] Chamberlain argued that while Congress should address the excesses, the U.S.-flag fleet should not be made even more non-economic than it already was via expanded seaman's rights.[29]

La Follette disagreed and declared on the Senate floor in 1913, "Did it ever occur to any of you gentlemen on the other side that the present Commissioner of Navigation has managed to weather several administrations?"[30] La Follette ignored the nuance in Chamberlain's position, arguing that "he was for free ships under Cleveland. When a new administration that favored ship subsidies came in he faced about and in his reports was a vehement advocate for subsidies." La Follette concluded that "he has always been for the shipowners. He is always for the administration. He is always for this job. [Laughter.]."

But there was one subject where Chamberlain could not be accused of deviating: he consistently opposed discriminating duties. His first *Annual Report* explained that the "belief entertained in some quarters that the early history of the United States shows that discriminating taxes are a successful means of upbuilding an American merchant marine finds no warrant in the facts or discussions of the period."[31] Rather, the duties were invoked merely as a "matter of reprisal for discrimination made against American vessels in foreign ports, and the policy was given up as soon as it had been effective in putting an end to those discriminations."

On the issue of the U.S. domestic trade, Chamberlain advocated for the American (versus the British) view of international law. This stipulated that U.S. coastwise trade laws encompassed territories under U.S. political sovereignty, reserving trade to U.S.-flag vessels regardless of how far they were from the continental United States. Consequently, Chamberlain was in favor of extending the U.S.-flag reservation to Alaska, Hawaii, and Puerto Rico and helped draft the relevant statutes.[32] The British view was that trade with non-contiguous territories was colonial, not domestic, trade.[33]

He wrote constantly on maritime policy subjects and on promotion of the U.S. merchant marine.[34] In 1897, for example, he wrote, "We have created the navy to protect. It now apparently remains to create the merchant fleet to be protected."[35] He also was known for his compilations of navigation laws.[36]

As often occurs in government, Chamberlain's position as chief expert of merchant marine matters provided him with substantial policy influence. For example, Representative John A.

Martin (D-CO) said in 1912 that Chamberlain "is a very responsible and high authority… in my judgment the highest and most responsible and best qualified in the service of the Government, far above the Secretary of War or the Secretary of Commerce and Labor."[37]

His marine safety accomplishments were numerous.[38] He had significant roles, for example, in the revision of rules to prevent collisions at sea and in the formulation of the International Convention of 1914 on Safety of Life at Sea convened in London because of the *Titanic* disaster. Chamberlain was also proud of the fact that he was a leader in building and supporting a fleet of vessels with which the United States went to war in 1917.[39]

Chamberlain was asked to resign as commissioner in August 1921, which he did, within a month of turning sixty-five. Rather than fully retire, he took a job in the U.S. Department of Commerce and Labor as a clerk/analyst, which he described as being "less active." During this "less active" period, he authored books on, among other things, the Italian ship-subsidy system, liner predominance in transoceanic shipping, and the Geneva conference on ocean shipping.[40]

He responded to an April 1916 appeal in *Life* magazine seeking help for war orphans in France and later called it his "main purpose of my present life."[41] He helped more than thirty French families, including almost one hundred children. In 1928, he called his correspondence with these families and children "my most precious possession." Those papers now reside with the U.S. Library of Congress.[42] In July 1921 President Alexandre Millerand of France awarded Chamberlain the Legion of Honor for his service. Chamberlain quipped that he could not wear such an award "under the American Constitution" but that he counted "when my time comes, upon presenting it to St. Peter as a passport to Paradise." Chamberlain died in October 1929 at the age of seventy-three.[43]

JOURNEY TO THE JONES ACT

1894 Tariff

As commissioner, Chamberlain had his hands full. Proponents of discriminating duties pursued their passage from 1894 to 1920. The main battleground was the periodic tariff bills passed by Congress, which affected virtually every aspect of the economy.[44] The Tariff Act of 1894, for example, itemized tariffs on 690 items ranging from acids to zinc.[45]

The tariff acts of the late nineteenth century and early twentieth century built on the foundation of early versions of U.S. discriminating duty statutory language favoring American vessels. In 1790 the United States had adopted a 10 percent *surcharge* to the duty on imports otherwise payable, unless the items were transported in U.S.-flag vessels.[46] This replaced the 10 percent *discount* in the first 1789 duty act if U.S.-flag vessels were utilized.[47] The 1817 Act also prohibited the indirect trade by foreign vessels where U.S.-flag vessels were prohibited from carrying that trade.[48] An 1824 tariff act was the first to directly exempt foreign vessels from the 10 percent discriminating duty when so "entitled by treaty, or by any act of Congress."[49] A similar formulation was included in periodic tariff acts thereafter.[50]

In the age of reciprocity, countries gradually eliminated their discriminations against U.S.-flag vessels and obtained an exemption from these U.S. requirements in return. Both the Tariff Act of 1883 (known as the "Mongrel Tariff Act" because of its patchwork nature) and the Tariff Act of 1890 (known as the "McKinley Tariff") contained these same 10 percent discriminating surcharges and the indirect trade prohibition forgiven with reciprocity. However, the Acts made them effectively inoperable because they did not apply to vessels from countries that did not discriminate against U.S.-flag vessels under the 1824 tariff act version.[51]

The 1894 Tariff Act was the first act where there was an attempt to reverse treaty reciprocity. Frye noted that the 10 percent duty in prior acts "is to-day of no earthly account because we have given away every advantage, we ought to derive from it by reciprocal legislation and by treaties."[52] He proposed an amendment that would make the 10 percent duty stick by abrogating or amending treaties where necessary to revert to the pre-reciprocity policy of the U.S. government. Frye was turned back, and nothing came of the effort in 1894.[53]

1897 Dingley Tariff

Senator Stephen B. Elkins (R-WV) made a second attempt to reintroduce meaningful discriminating dues in the lead up to the Dingley Tariff Act of 1897.[54] The son-in-law of a U.S. senator, Elkins was secretary of war from 1891 to 1893 (the town of Elkins in West Virginia is named after him). Elkins's proposal would have reversed the treaty/Act of Congress exemption by abrogating all treaties "in contravention" of the 10 percent duty and repealing all contrary acts of Congress.

Elkins argued that because of the "policy of protection to our manufactures and to shipping in the coastwise trade, the United States is now the leading nation in manufacturing, and our coastwise trade is the largest in tonnage and the most prosperous on the world."[55] The application of the same policy to the foreign maritime trade, he continued, would create the same results.

When a conference committee (Dingley was the lead House negotiator) adopted the Elkins' amendment, its text changed under what were later called mysterious circumstances. Elkins's aims were in fact out in the open. He stated, for example, that "the Canadian Pacific Railroad is the natural enemy of the transportation interests of the United States."[56]

Rather than abrogate treaties and repeal laws, the new language would add a 10 percent duty on "goods, wares, or merchandise... which being the production or manufacture of any foreign country not contiguous to the United States" that enters the United States "from such contiguous country."[57] The provision also deleted reciprocity when it occurred via "Act of Congress." In other words, the text disadvantaged any U.S. imports coming via Canada or Mexico if those goods did not originate in Canada or Mexico.

JOURNEY TO THE JONES ACT

House and Senate members asked questions about the provision adopted by the conference committee. In the House, Dingley asserted that the provision had been carried over from prior tariff acts and that it did not apply to any country that had a commercial agreement with the United States.[58] Notably, Dingley did not draw attention to the contiguous country change. Senator William B. Allison (R-IA), the lead Senate negotiator, stated that current law was unchanged except to prevent evasion.[59]

After enactment in July 1897, the provision immediately became notorious and controversial. It was interpreted by John K. Richards, the U.S. solicitor general, to apply to goods coming over Canadian railroads through Canadian ports from other countries destined for the United States, regardless of treaty obligations.[60] Opposition to the provision arose immediately, accompanied by questions as to how the provision had been enacted without greater scrutiny.

It was argued in the press that there was "evidence that it was not fully explained in either house" and that it had exceeded the conference committee's authority.[61] There were also "charges that Mr. Dingley was either negligent or lacking in candor." Elkins, as the author, "knew what he wanted" implying that a substantial law change was intended all along.[62] The *New York Times* editorialized by calling the provision the "Elkins Discriminating Duty" and "Legislation by 'Slip' and 'Trick.'"[63]

Elkins eventually admitted that he had a hand in amending the statute, but he defended the provision and asserted it was warranted.[64] He stated later that "there will be no halt until adequate protection is secured for our American shipping and against the privileges of the Canadian railroads."[65]

Elkins met in person several times with President McKinley and Joseph McKenna, the U.S. attorney general, arguing in favor of an interpretation to give the provision effect.[66] He told McKinley and McKenna that he knew the statute was "open to two constructions" but, as "the apostle of protection," McKinley should "not allow his protection of American interests to stop at the water's edge."

Unconvinced, McKenna reversed the solicitor general's interpretation.[67] McKenna alluded to the possibility that the "purpose of the amendment was to relieve the American transcontinental railroads in competition with the Canadian Pacific Railroad," but that such a purpose was not explained in Congress. Further, it did not fit with the shipping purpose of the discriminating duty statute, which the United States had had since 1824. The better interpretation, McKenna indicated, was that Congress intended the provision to prevent evasion of the 10 percent discriminating duty applicable to ocean vessels as Senator Allison said on the Senate floor.

One newspaper greeted the McKenna opinion with the headline, "The Schemers Have Suffered a Defeat."[68] Another newspaper lamented that a "Good Law" was "Rendered Inoperative."[69] In any event, the changes contained in the Dingley Tariff regarding shipping fell in line with prior interpretations. It appeared to impose a discriminating duty, only to have it taken away by treaty or act of Congress.

1913 Underwood Tariff

No substantive action was taken again on vessel related discriminating duties until the Revenue Act of 1913, known as the "Underwood Tariff," signed into law by President Woodrow Wilson in October 1913.[70] The Underwood Tariff lowered tariffs overall and instituted a federal income tax. This was authorized by the Sixteenth Amendment to the U.S. Constitution, adopted in February 1913. The legislation reflected Wilson's goals of reducing tariffs to make them less burdensome on the U.S. consumer and replacing the lost revenue with an income tax.

Oscar Underwood had run for president in 1912 and was among several candidates who had lost the nomination to Wilson. He was an opponent of the Ku Klux Klan, women's suffrage, and the Prohibition. For his Klan opposition, he was the subject of the first episode of the television show *Profiles in*

JOURNEY TO THE JONES ACT

Courage which aired on November 8, 1964.[71] The series was inspired by John F. Kennedy's Pulitzer Prize-winning book *Profiles in Courage* published in 1956.[72]

The episode focused on the 1924 Democratic Convention where Underwood was again a candidate for president along with former treasury secretary William G. McAdoo. At the convention, Underwood forced a vote to condemn the Klan by name. McAdoo opposed the resolution, which was narrowly defeated. Neither Underwood nor McAdoo was nominated.

As early as 1910, Underwood was advocating for a return to vessel discriminating duties.[73] Underwood did not agree to fight other countries' subsidies with U.S. subsidies because, in his view, the "Constitution of the United States contemplated the raising of taxes for specific governmental purposes... but clearly did not contemplate... the right to subsidize special interests out of the Federal Treasury."

In anticipation of a tariff overhaul, Underwood conducted extensive hearings starting in January 1913.[74] Those hearings took a detour to address a domestic maritime trade issue. Representative William E. Humphrey (R-WA) requested that the proposed tariff legislation impose foreign import duties on goods shipped from the U.S. East Coast to Vancouver and then overland to the United States. He viewed such practices as an evasion of U.S. coastwise laws.[75]

Humphrey had also complained in 1912 about the carriage of passengers from Seattle to Alaska via Vancouver.[76] Here, he was reacting to a January 4, 1913 opinion by U.S. Attorney General George W. Wickersham that the coastwise laws did not apply to mixed water and land shipments between the Seattle and Alaska via Canada.[77]

In Underwood's view, the U.S. coastwise trade reservation was "one of the most iniquitous laws we have on the statute books." He was also concerned that the change sought by Humphrey would have unintended effects on other transshipments through Canada.

James Wickersham, the delegate from Alaska, added his opposition because much of the Alaskan freight came through Canada. In his diary, Wickersham said that Underwood "smilingly said that he did not think it was necessary for me to take any time presenting my objections... whereupon I, too, smiled and left the remnant of the bill with the Com—dead."[78] The committee did not act on the Humphrey proposal as Wickersham surmised.

In the tariff legislation developed in the House, Underwood followed through with a 5 percent discount when U.S. vessels were utilized.[79] In the press, the provision was called a "ship subsidy in disguise."[80] The Underwood proposal, as amended, was subject to a proviso "that nothing in this subsection shall be construed as to abrogate or in any manner impair or affect the provisions of any" U.S. treaty obligation.[81]

Senator Wesley Jones played an active part in the discriminating duty provision debate. On September 8, 1913, Jones offered an amendment to replace the 5 percent discount with a 10 percent surcharge discriminating duty. The amendment contained the addition that the "President is directed to cause to be abrogated without unnecessary delay... all treaties which contravene this provision."[82] In other words, Jones proposed in 1913 what Frye had proposed in 1894 and Elkins had proposed in 1896.

In support of his amendment, Jones quoted from Underwood's 1910 speech on discriminating duties. Jones also referred admiringly to the English Navigation Act of 1651 ("Cromwell's drastic but successful policy"). He referred to the 1828 Act, which was the culmination of U.S. open trade reciprocity policy, as "the Act that has destroyed our shipping power." He made the same prediction that Jefferson made in 1793, Dingley made in 1883, and Frye made in 1900 about what would happen to the United States because of its dependence on British shipping if Britain went to war:

> Suppose England should engage in a war with a great power. Thousands of her ships would be

taken for transports and other thousands might be destroyed. Our foreign commerce would be destroyed, and the products we now send abroad would be left on our hands, glutting our markets and bringing upon us industrial ruin and widespread commercial disaster.[83]

Jones also responded to those who said that other countries would retaliate—this, he said, "is the cry of weakness, of cowardice" and "other nations can not [sic] complain any more than we can complain at their system of subsidies."[84]

The Senate did not adopt Jones's amendment. The 5 percent discount provision, although it became law, was not enforced by the Wilson administration. The U.S. Supreme Court then put the final nail in the 5 percent duty coffin in the "Five Percent Discount cases."[85] In these 1917 cases, the court said that the law "relies upon future negotiations to make the change effective and suspends action while the present treaties remain in force." Jones took heed with the language he proposed in 1919 on discriminating duties, which wound up in the 1920 Merchant Marine Act.

---

[1] Republican Party Platform of 1896, June 18, 1896, UC Santa Barbara, The American Presidency Project, Republican Party Platforms, https://www.presidency.ucsb.edu/documents/republican-party-platform-1896.

[2] 30 CONG. REC. 587 (April 5, 1897) (referenced in the remarks of Senator Stephen B. Elkins).

[3] Bates, American Navigation, 417; Report of the Merchant Marine Commission, S. Rep. 58-2755, liii.

[4] Harvard College Class of 1878 Fiftieth Anniversary Report 1878-1928 (Cambridge, MA: Riverside Press, 1928), 38 (the source for information regarding Chamberlain not otherwise specifically cited).

[5] Harvard College Class of 1878 Fiftieth Anniversary Report 1878—1928, 38–47.

[6] The Chamberlain Association of America, Report of Annual Meetings Held in Boston, Massachusetts, in 1908, 1909 and 1910 (Portland, ME: Smith & Sale, Printers, 1911), 152.

[7] "Editors," Harvard Advocate 24, Index (1877-1878): i; "Items," 24 The Harvard Advocate 24, no. 9 (September 26, 1877): 106–07, 107; "Items," Harvard Advocate 25, no. 8 (February 15, 1878): 95.

[8] Thomas W. Handford, Early Life and Public Services of Hon. Grover Cleveland, the Fearless and Independent Governor of the Empire State (Chicago: Belford, Clarke, 1884). The biography to this day does not bear Chamberlain's name a fact the New York Times attributed in 1891 to "personal reasons." "Albany's New Editor–Eugene Tyler Chamberlain in Charge of the 'Argus,'" New York Times, August 10, 1891, 1.

[9] Harvard College, Class of 1878, Secretary's Report no. III (Cambridge, MA: Riverside Press, 1892), 35–36.

[10] 50 Cong. Rec. 5779 (October 23, 1913).

[11] "Daniel S. Lamont," Harper's Weekly 30, no. 1515 (January 2, 1886), 58.

[12] "Albany's New Editor," New York Times, August 10, 189), 1.

[13] "A Great American Legal Navigator," Pacific Marine Review 18 (December 1921): 717.

[14] Protocols of Proceedings of the International Marine Conference held in Washington, D.C., October 16 to December 31, 1889 (Washington, DC: Government Printing Office, 1890), vol. 1, 4.

[15] 26 Stat. 320 (August 19, 1890); Grover Cleveland, Proclamation 39: Enforcement of an Act to Prevent Collisions at Sea, December 31, 1896, UC Santa Barbara, The American Presidency Project, www.presidency.ucsb.edu/documents/proclamation-391-enforcement-act-prevent-collisions-sea.

[16] For example, "Albany Democrats Moving—A Thousand Names in One Day to the Snap-Convention Protests," New York Times, April 28, 1892, 3.

[17] "Sale of the Albany Argus," New York Times, March 30, 1893, 1.

[18] "A New Commissioner—Mr. E. T. Chamberlain to be Head of the Navigation Bureau," Evening Star, (Washington, DC), November 27, 1893, 1; "An Anti-Snapper Rewarded—Appointment of E. T. Chamberlain of Albany, Commissioner of Navigation," New York Tribune, November 28, 1893, 2.

[19] "An Anti-Snapper Rewarded."

[20] "Helping the Enemy," Boston Journal, July 7, 1894, 6.

[21] "Men We Are Watching: Eugene Tyler Chamberlain," Independent, A Weekly Magazine 72, no. 3324 (August 15, 1912): 364–65.

[22] Annual Report of the Commissioner of Navigation to the Secretary of the Treasury (1894), 18.

[23] 34 Cong. Rec. 31 (December 4, 1900).

[24] Annual Report of the Commissioner of Navigation to the Secretary of the Treasury (1899), 34–35.

[25] In 1911, for example, in an article which appeared in Scientific American, Chamberlain repeated his view that subsidies and free ships were two compatible policies. Eugene Tyler Chamberlain, "The American Merchant Marine," Scientific American 55, no. 3 (July 15, 1911): 44–45.

[26] 34 Cong. Rec. 1332 (January 23, 1901).

[27] 34 Cong. Rec. 1341.

[28] For example, Chamberlain applauded the reforms on advances and allotment notes included in the 1884 Dingley Act and argued in favor of reduced imprisonment for failing to report or desertion, but not for eliminating all penalties. Annual Report of the Commissioner of Navigation to the Secretary of the Treasury (1895), 31–45.

[29] "The methods and practices of competing rival nations must be held constantly in mind if our experiments are not to end in the growth of our rivals at the expense of our own shipping." Annual Report of the Commissioner of Navigation to the Secretary of the Treasury (1897), 30.

[30] 50 CONG. REC. 5779 (October 23, 1913).

[31] Annual Report of the Commissioner of Navigation to the Secretary of the Treasury (1894), 22.

[32] Harvard College Class of 1878 Fiftieth Anniversary Report 1878–1928, 42.

[33] Eugene Tyler Chamberlain, The Geneva Conference and Ocean Shipping, U.S. Department of Commerce, Trade Information Bulletin no. 202 (March 3, 1924), 8–9.

[34] For example, "Significant Statistics as to Navigation Compiled by Eugene Chamberlain," New York Times, (July 5, 1894), 4; Chamberlain, "A Present Chance for American Shipping," 277.

[35] "An American Merchant Marine," Catholic Telegraph 66, no. 42 (October 21, 1897): 3.

[36] "Men We Are Watching—Eugene Tyler Chamberlain," 365 ("He is known the world over thru his compilation of navigation laws and thru frequent articles on maritime subjects.").

[37] U.S. Congress, House, Committee on Interstate and Foreign Commerce, Hearings before the House Interstate and Foreign Commerce Committee on the Panama Canal, 62nd Cong., 2nd sess., 1912, 876.

[38] "Men We Are Watching – Eugene Tyler Chamberlain," 364–70.

[39] Harvard College Class of 1878 Fiftieth Anniversary Report 1878–1928, 44.

[40] Chamberlain, The Geneva Conference and Ocean Shipping; Eugene Tyler Chamberlain, Liner Predominance in Transoceanic Shipping, U.S. Department of Commerce, Trade Bulletin no. 448 (1926); and Eugene Tyler Chamberlain, Italian Ship-Subsidy System, U.S. Department of Commerce, Trade Information Bulletin no. 529 (1928).

[41] Harvard College Class of 1878 Fiftieth Anniversary Report 1878–1928, 46–47.

[42] The "Eugene Tyler Chamberlain Collection Relating to French Orphans of World War I" is available in the U.S. Library of Congress Manuscript Division.

[43] "Maritime Expert Dies in Baltimore—Eugene Tyler Chamberlain Served Under Cleveland as Navigation Commissioner," Evening Star (Washington, DC), October 29, 1929, 11.

[44] When extensive revisions to the tariff laws were considered in early 1913 by the House Ways and Means Committee chaired by Representative Oscar W. Underwood, the result was a hearing record in seven volumes containing about sixty-five

hundred pages of testimony and statements. U.S. Congress, House, Tariff Schedules: Hearings before the Committee on Ways and Means, 62nd Cong., 3rd sess., 1913, H. Doc. 62-1447.

[45] 28 Stat. 509 (August 27, 1894).
[46] 1 Stat. 180, 181 (August 10, 1790).
[47] 1 Stat. 24, 27 (July 4, 1789).
[48] 3 Stat. 351 (March 1, 1817).
[49] 4 Stat. 25, 29 (May 22, 1824).
[50] U.S. Attorney General, "Dingley Tariff Act: Discriminating Duty," Op. Att'y Gen. 21, no. 597, 602 (September 20, 1897).
[51] 22 Stat. 488, 491 (March 3, 1883); 26 Stat. 567, 616–17 (October 1, 1890).
[52] 26 CONG. REC. 6570 (June 20, 1894).
[53] 26 CONG. REC. 6574.
[54] 28 CONG. REC. 2473 (March 5, 1896); 30 Stat. 151, 209 (July 24, 1897).
[55] 30 CONG. REC. 580–600 (April 5, 1897).
[56] "Attacks the Canadian Pacific – Stephen B. Ellis Poses as Protector of American Railways." New York Times, April 5, 1896, 12.
[57] 30 CONG. REC. 2800 (July 21, 1897).
[58] 30 CONG. REC. 2711 (July 19, 1897).
[59] 30 CONG. REC. 2800 (July 21, 1897).
[60] U.S. Attorney General, "Discriminating Duty: Dingley Tariff Act," Op. Att'y Gen. 21, no. 591 (August 11, 1897).
[61] "The Discriminating Duty—How It Was Inserted in the Dingley Bill by the Conferees," New York Tribune, August 30, 1897, 2.
[62] "The Discriminating Duty—How the Provision Formerly in Force Was Amended in Conference," New York Times (August 16, 1897),
[63] "Legislation by 'Slip' and 'Trick,'" New York Times, September 2, 1897, 6; "The Elkins Discriminating Duty," New York Times, September 22, 1897, 6.
[64] , "Senator Elkins Did It—Confesses to Having Framed Section 22 of Tariff Law, Milwaukee Journal, September 21, 1897, 2; "The History of 'Section 22,'" Plain Dealer (Cleveland), September 29, 1897, 4.
[65] "To Fight for Discriminating Duties," New York Tribune, September 23, 1897, 1.
[66] "The History of 'Section 22,'" Plain Dealer (Cleveland), September 29, 1897, 4.
[67] "Dingley Tariff Act: Discriminating Duty," Op. Att'y Gen. 21, no. 597.
[68] "The Schemers Have Suffered a Defeat—Attorney General McKenna Hands Down a Decision Against the Steve Elkins Interpretation of Section 22," Minneapolis Journal, September 21, 1897, 1.
[69] "A Good Law Rendered Inoperative," Indiana State Journal, (September 29, 1897), 4.
[70] 38 Stat. 114 (October 3, 1913).
[71] "Profiles in Courage: Oscar W. Underwood," IMDb, https://www.imdb.com/title/tt0679743/?ref_=ttep_ep1.

[72] John F. Kennedy, Profiles in Courage (New York: Harper Brothers, 1956).
[73] 45 CONG. REC. 2475–78 (February 26, 1910).
[74] U.S. Congress, House, Committee on Ways and Means, Hearings before the Committee on Ways and Means: Tariff Schedules, 62nd Cong., 3rd sess., 1913, H. Doc. 62-1447, vol. 6, 6154–61.
[75] Committee on Ways and Means, Hearings before the Committee on Ways and Means: Tariff Schedules, H. Doc. 62-1447, vol. 6, 6154–61.
[76] U.S. Congress, House, Amending Laws Relating to Navigation, 62nd Cong., 2rd sess., 1912, H. Rep. 62-653.
[77] U.S. Attorney General, "Transportation of Merchandise from Seattle to Fairbanks," Op. Att'y Gen. 30, no. 3 (January 4, 1913).
[78] Alaska State Library. Historical Collections. Alaska Digital Archives. Diary of James Wickersham, February 1, 1913, https://vilda.alaska.edu/digital/collection/cdmg21/id/6113/rec/26.
[79] 50 CONG. REC. 743—45 (April 28, 1913) and 4499 (September 8, 1913); "Urges Duty in Favor of American Ships," New York Times, December 26, 1911, 11; 38 Stat. 114, 196–97 (October 3, 1913).
[80] For example, "Ship Subsidy in Disguise," Oregonian, May 22, 1913, 10.
[81] U.S. Congress, House, Tariff Act of 1913, 63rd Cong., 1st sess., 1913, H. Rep. 63-86, 20.
[82] 50 CONG. REC. 4494 (September 8, 1913).
[83] 50 CONG. REC. 4494–98.
[84] 50 CONG. REC. 4498.
[85] U.S. v. M.H. Pulaski Company, 243 U.S. 97 (1917). The 5 percent discount law was repealed in 1922. 42 Stat. 858 (September 21, 1922).

U.S.S. Nanshan, circa 1920, U.S. Naval History and Heritage Command

Chapter 11—The Spanish-American War

The Spanish-American War, in which the United States defeated Spain and acquired overseas possessions in the Caribbean and Asia, was short in duration (about 120 days), was fought mainly in America's backyard (the Caribbean) and involved only one other country (Spain). This combination of conditions was not likely to be repeated nor give rise to overarching merchant marine "lessons." The war nevertheless illuminated issues with the U.S. ability to muster sufficient auxiliary, supply, and transport vessels to prosecute an overseas war.

Subsidy advocates would argue that the war proved that the United States needed a more vibrant merchant marine. Why? The next war might make commercial vessels not so easily accessible, the vessels procured and chartered were barely enough even for a short war, and limited mail subsidies were not sufficient for supporting an adequate merchant marine.

Subsidy opponents argued that the war proved that the United States could acquire what it needed from the worldwide commercial market and that mail subsidies had failed to provide the needed vessels (usually those making this point would omit the fact that the Ocean Mail Act of 1891 provided only a small portion of the assistance originally proposed).[1] Advocates pursued both these arguments in subsequent merchant marine policy discussions.

The U.S. merchant marine felt another effect of the Spanish-American War. As a result of the war, the United States expanded to Puerto Rico and the Philippines (as well as Guam). This made national imperatives of the incorporation of Hawaii and the construction of a Panama Canal as discussed in later chapters. By that expansion, the United States had to consider whether to apply U.S. coastwise laws and provide shipping services to those territories and to how to deal with vessels registered in those territories prior to United States takeover.

A Mongrel Fleet[2]

As a result of U.S. support for Cuban independence, Spain declared war on the United States on April 23, 1898. By early 1898 the U.S. Navy's war planning was already advanced.[3] The Navy entered the war with a plan approved by a war planning board convened by Secretary of the Navy John D. Long on June 30, 1897.[4]

Although the plans differed as to certain strategies—such as whether to attack ports in Spain after seizing a base in the Canary Islands—the later plans consistently identified the need to acquire merchant vessels for various Navy needs. The planning board advocated the purchase or charter of a "large number" of "merchant steamers of fast speed, and mounting a few guns each."[5] An earlier plan recommended that the blockade force "be increased by a large number of small fast armed steamers from the steam yacht and coastwise shipping."[6]

The planning board was also "in favor of calling the fleet largely by means of colliers moving to the stations of the ships, rather than by too exclusive reliance upon coaling stations." A "collier" was a vessel designed to carry coal in bulk and could be used to offload it onto a vessel at sea.

In anticipation of war and in accord with Navy planning, Assistant Secretary of the Navy Teddy Roosevelt appointed a "Board of Auxiliary Cruisers" in March 1898 to assess the market for suitable vessels to acquire or charter.[7] During the war, that board and the Army purchased about one hundred merchant vessels. They were converted into auxiliary cruisers, supply ships, troopships, colliers, and gunboats. The Navy spent about $20 million to acquire the vessels and make them suitable for naval service.[8]

JOURNEY TO THE JONES ACT

Another five large passenger steamships were chartered: the *City of Peking* from Pacific Mail Steamship Company, and the *St. Paul, St. Louis, New York,* and *Paris* from the International Navigation Company. The large, fast, INC vessels were armed, U.S. Navy officers took over, and the civilian crews remained without being enlisted.[9] During the war, the vessels served with distinction as auxiliary cruisers and later as troopships.[10]

The U.S. government purchased seven British-flag vessels owned by the Atlantic Transport Line headed by Bernard N. Baker of Baltimore.[11] Baker described in 1905 testimony how he arranged the transfer of the vessels from British flag to U.S. flag at President McKinley's personal behest.[12] According to Baker, the transfer had to occur from the British company owner (he owned most of the stock) to him personally and then to the U.S. government—in order to evade British neutrality laws, which would have been violated, he believed by direct transfer.

The Navy also organized an "Auxiliary Naval Force" for coastal defense which eventually comprised of about forty-one vessels.[13] The Naval War College had referred to these vessels as the "mosquito flotilla."[14] That force, which received a separate $3 million appropriation in May 1898, consisted of tugs, yachts, and coastal monitors (most were up to date versions of the original *Monitor*).[15] Designated to patrol significant U.S. ports and tend to mine fields laid in harbor entrances, these vessels were largely manned by the state naval militia.

As war preparations proceeded, the Navy received many tenders from U.S. companies to transport coal, but all but one backed out when war commenced.[16] As a result, the Navy had to purchase cargo steamships, mostly foreign (seventeen out of nineteen), for the purpose of converting them into colliers.[17] The Navy reported that "there were but few vessels in this country suitable for the transportation of coal" and the owners "generally demanded exorbitant prices."[18] Even boosters of the Navy's effort argued that many of the vessels purchased abroad were "to be grotesquely unfit for the purposes for which they were secured."[19]

The Army had to acquire its own vessels and stood second in line to the Navy's priorities. From April 1898 to September 1898, the Army purchased fifteen vessels for Atlantic/Gulf operations and two for Pacific operations, and chartered forty-four and seventeen vessels, respectively, in those two theaters of operation.[20] Most of the chartered vessels were "time chartered," meaning that they were provided fully crewed.[21]

The War Department also pressured Congress to grant special permissions to certain foreign-built vessels to register in the United States. At the time, Senator Frye stated that "I dislike exceedingly to admit to American registry foreign-built ships but the War Department is levying blackmail, and I recognize the necessity of sending men to Manila."[22] The *Zealandia*, for example, owned by the Claus Spreckels's Oceanic Steamship Company and registered in Hawaii, received such special permission.[23]

The official history of the process of assembling a naval auxiliary was that the Navy was able "to get vessels at very reasonable prices" once competition kicked in.[24] Contemporary Navy reports, however, complained about the prices paid for foreign colliers, although the most expensive collier was the U.S.-flag *Merrimac*, whose story is set out in a later chapter.[25]

Secretary John Long argued after the war that "several hundred vessels were offered to the department, some at extortionate prices" and that "some American owners displayed more greed than patriotism."[26] Years later, Treasury Secretary McAdoo asserted that the United States had been "utterly unprepared" for the Spanish-American War in terms of naval auxiliaries. He argued that the nation had "paid fabulous prices" and "there is no officer of the navy who knows about these purchases who won't admit that most of these vessels were junk."[27] In early 1915 evidence was presented in Congress that the U.S. government took enormous losses on the vessels it purchased and then sold after the war.[28]

Despite these criticisms, most of the vessels purchased for the Spanish-American War were still in the Navy or transferred to the War Department by the outset of World War I.[29] The *Nanshan*, for example, acquired by Commodore George Dewey for the Philippines campaign in 1898, served in World War I and was not decommissioned until 1922.[30]

One of the issues that arose regarding the U.S. government-purchased vessels after the war was whether they could be registered as U.S.-flag vessels with coastwise trading privileges.[31] The Army and Navy preferred that result to increase the value of the vessels upon sale.[32] But this option was not permitted by law according to Chamberlain and the U.S. attorney general.[33]

Several things are also notable about vessel manning in this context. At the time, U.S.-registered vessels engaged in the foreign trade—except those subject to ocean mail contracts such as the four INC vessels—did not have to have American crews except the master and any officer standing watch.[34] Purchased vessels retained civilian crews if they remained non-commissioned vessels. Only if the vessels were commissioned as Navy vessels did they take on Navy crews, which meant that many of the sailors in the auxiliary fleet were both civilians and not U.S. citizens.[35] Some foreign crewmembers may have left their vessels to avoid potential foreign enlistment liability imposed by other countries.[36]

Even U.S. Navy warships recruited from foreign merchant mariners.[37] There was no U.S. Navy reserve at the time, although there were state naval militia and retirees. The state militia first emerged in Massachusetts in 1888 and varied substantially in their ability to man vessels.[38] According to the Navy, "of the total force of 24,123 enlisted men employed in the Navy during the war, 4,216 were mustered in from naval militia organizations."[39]

With respect to non-citizens, the Navy Bureau of Navigation reported that 74 percent and 77 percent of its enlisted personnel were U.S. citizens for the fiscal years ended 1897 and 1898, respectively. However, about half of the non-citizens had indicated an intention to become U.S. citizens.[40]

The presence of foreigners in the U.S. Navy occasioned mockery from Spanish officials. For example, the commanding Spanish general in the Philippines proclaimed on April 23, 1898, that the islands would soon face "a squadron manned by foreigners, possessing neither instruction nor discipline."[41] Dewey had the proclamation read to his crews while in route to the Philippines and it was greeted with derision and laughter.

U.S. Navy officers had nevertheless expressed concerns about the reliability and loyalty of foreign crew members. An 1890 Naval Institute *Proceedings* article complained about how the Navy repelled Americans because of a lack of advancement opportunities. As a result, "all languages are heard on our decks" and we have an "international navy."[42]

Foreign citizens were especially numerous in Dewey's Asiatic Squadron. The employment of Chinese on Navy vessels stationed in Asia was common for years although discouraged by the Navy Department.[43] Dewey later attempted to gain U.S. admission for about fifty Chinese nationals who had served on his warships. At the time, the Chinese Exclusion Act of 1882 prevented Chinese from immigrating.[44] Hoping for an exception for his men, Dewey wrote Secretary Long in May 1898 saying that "it seems unreasonable that men who have battled for our country should be excluded from it."[45] His lobbying, however, was rebuffed by Congress.

NANSHAN AND ZAFIRO

A good illustration of the haphazard, but nevertheless successful, U.S. approach to merchant vessels is the case of the steamships *Nanshan* and *Zafiro*.

On February 25, 1898, Roosevelt, in Secretary Long's absence, sent his famous telegram to Dewey. Roosevelt ordered the fleet to "keep full of coal" and "in the event declaration of war Spain, your duty will be to see that the Spanish squadron does not leave the Asiatic coast."[46] The next day, Secretary Long reiterated to Dewey to "keep full of coal—the best that can be had."[47]

JOURNEY TO THE JONES ACT

Dewey responded on February 27 about the "great scarcity of coal within the limits of the station. It is suggested that coal and ammunition should be sent from San Francisco without delay." Dewey reiterated the lack of available coal on March 11. Long immediately authorized Dewey to contract for delivery of five thousand tons of coal and to "order coal from England if necessary."

On April 4 Long asked Dewey to find out if he could purchase a steamship, and a Dewey message simultaneously informed Long that he had chartered the British steamship *Nanshan* containing three thousand tons of coal. As a point of reference, Dewey's flagship, the *U.S.S. Olympia*, had an internal capacity of about eleven hundred tons of coal.[48] On April 6 Long ordered Dewey to purchase the *Nanshan*, which he did, and another vessel for supplies, which was the *Zafiro*, another British steamship. With these two vessels, Dewey had coal and supplies for about five months of operations.[49]

On April 24 Long ordered Dewey to the Philippines, and the Asiatic Squadron destroyed the Spanish fleet on May 1 with the loss of only one American sailor. Both the *Nanshan* and the *Zafiro* accompanied the squadron to Manila.

Dewey adopted unorthodox methods for the two vessels to preserve their utility given neutrality laws. He had no choice because the nearest secure source of supplies was San Francisco, seven thousand miles from Hong Kong. What Dewey was worried about was that neutral countries, such as Britain (meaning Hong Kong), would deny access to warships of both Spain and the United States for the duration of the war.[50] In fact, the British governor of Hong Kong asked Dewey's warships to leave on April 25 because of Britain's neutrality obligations.[51]

What Dewey counted on was the fact that the obligations of a neutral country were malleable. A neutral port might bar merchant vessels carrying war material (i.e., "contraband"), such as ammunition, but not bar the same vessels access for the purpose of acquiring coal or food for a fleet of warships. Dewey thus purchased and documented the *Nanshan* and *Zafiro* "to enable them to resort to neutral ports."[52]

The purchaser on the bills of sale was George Dewey as an individual.[53] The U.S. Navy did not commission either vessel, even though Dewey indicated in an April 9 cable to Long that he would "arm, equip, and man" the *Zafiro*.[54] The *Nanshan* was in fact not commissioned until 1914; the *Zafiro* was never a Navy-commissioned vessel.

In his autobiography, Dewey wrote that "we registered them as American merchant steamers" and by claiming that they were in route to Guam, "we had a free hand in sending them to English, Japanese or Chinese ports to get any supplies we might need."[55] The law of neutrality permitted belligerent vessels to refuel and take on supplies in a neutral port for the purpose of returning home.

As we know from Chamberlain's and the attorney general's guidance, the *Nanshan* and *Zafiro* were not in fact entitled to be registered as "vessels of the United States" because they were foreign-built. However, it was necessary that the vessels fly the flag of a country to be able to enter ports to re-supply Dewey's squadron.

The "work-around" was that the American consul accompanying the Asiatic Squadron likely delivered certificates to each of the vessels, permitted by U.S. consular regulations certifying that the vessel owner was a U.S. citizen.[56] Chamberlain explained the technicality—"any foreign-built vessel, purchased entirely and in good faith by an American citizen, is entitled to the flag and protection of the United States" even if it is not entitled to U.S. registry as a "vessel of the United States."[57]

Dewey also entered into contracts with the Chinese sailors and some of the British officers on board the vessels, agreeing to pay them double their wages to stay on.[58] That pay was to be paid in silver "Mexican dollars," then a common form of international exchange.[59] There is one account indicating that the crew "gave notice of their intention to become United States citizens."[60] In Dewey's words, the crew "shipped merchant service."[61] It is not clear how the British officers did not run afoul of British foreign enlistment laws, since they served on vessels that were arguably U.S. Navy auxiliaries.[62]

Dewey placed a single Navy officer and a handful of enlisted men on each vessel, all armed, plus a single small one pounder cannon for self-defense against boats.[63] Dewey claimed that the Navy officers "exercised control over the movements of the ship and gave all orders concerning her," but the crew answered to the British officers.[64]

In the Philippines, the Chinese crew of the *Zafiro* went ashore on May 4, 1898, and allegedly looted homes and stores. In an international arbitration between Britain (on behalf of the property owners) and the United States, the arbitrators determined that the vessels "were registered as American vessels" and concluded that "from all evidence… the *Zafiro* was a supply ship, acting in Manila Bay as part of Admiral Dewey's force, and under his command through the naval officer on board for that purpose and the merchant officers in charge of the crew." The United States was therefore responsible for the actions of the vessel (and potentially for the crew even when ashore). The panel awarded about 6,000 Mexican dollars to the claimants.

The two vessels were also involved in a 1903 Supreme Court opinion in a group of cases referred to as "The Manila Prize Cases."[65] Those cases concerned whether the U.S. Navy owed the crews in Dewey's squadron a portion of the proceeds from the sale of wrecked Spanish vessels and other captured property. The court agreed with the claimants that a portion of the proceeds were indeed "prize" and therefore the Navy should have distributed such proceeds to the Navy crews. But as to the *Nanshan* and the *Zafiro*, the Court determined that the vessels were not "part of the fighting force of the Navy in the battle" and "participated neither actually nor constructively in the captures" and so their crews did not merit a portion of the prize proceeds.

In other words, the uncertain character of the *Nanshan* and the *Zafiro* meant that they were simultaneously part of the Navy for liability purposes and not part of the Navy for purposes of sharing in prize money.

---

[1] For example, Zeis American Shipping Policy, 34–36.

[2] Jeffrey Michael Dorwart, "A Mongrel Fleet: America Buys a Navy to Fight Spain, 1898," Warship International 17, no. 2 (1980): 128–55.

[3] John A. S. Grenville, "American Naval Preparations for War with Spain, 1896-1898," Journal of American Studies 2, no. 1 (April 1968): 33–47.

[4] Mark L. Hayes, "War Plans and Preparations and their Impact on U.S. Naval Operations in the Spanish-American War (March 23, 1998)," Naval Historical Center, Spanish-American War, www.history.navy.mil/research/library/online-reading-room/title-list-alphabetically/s/spanish-american-war-war-plans-and-impact-on-u-s-navy.html.

[5] "Plan of Operations against Spain (June 30, 1897)," Naval History and Heritage Command, Documentary Histories, Spanish-American War www.history.navy.mil/research/publications/documentary-histories/united-states-navy-s/pre-war-planning/plan-of-operations-a-1.html.

[6] "Plan of Operations against Spain (December 17, 1896)," Naval History and Heritage Command, Documentary Histories, Spanish-American War, www.history.navy.mil/research/publications/documentary-histories/united-states-navy-s/pre-war-planning/plan-of-operations-a-3.html.

[7] U.S. Navy Department, Annual Reports of the Navy Department for the Year 1898 (Washington, DC: Government Printing Office, 1898), 5, 21; "Auxiliary Cruisers—A Special Bureau of the Navy Department to Begin Work in This City To-day," New York Times, March 14, 1898, 1 ("The naval officials say there will be no difficulty experienced in obtaining all the vessels that are desired, as there are hundreds available." Forty vessels were immediately identified for inspection "if their owners desire to part with them.").

[8] The amount spent on vessels has been widely reported to have been $18 million. For example, David F. Trask, The War with Spain in 1898 (New York: Macmillan, 1981), 82. But that number appears to include funds spent acquiring warships such as the Amazonas and otherwise does not square with the amounts reported by the Navy to Congress in 1898. Annual Reports of the Navy Department for the Year 1898, 687–89; Spencer C. Tucker, ed., The Encyclopedia of the Spanish-American and Philippine-American Wars (Santa Barbara, CA: ABC-CLIO, 2009), 432.

[9] Daniel Roberts, "A Navy of Foreigners, Mercenaries, and Amateurs: Naval Enlistment in the Spanish-American War," International Journal of Naval History 13, no.

1 (April 2016), https://www.ijnhonline.org/a-navy-of-foreigners-mercenaries-and-amateurs-naval-enlistment-in-the-spanish-american-war.

[10] William H. Flayhart III, "Four Fighting Ladies," America Spreads Her Sails—U.S. Seapower in the 19th Century, Clayton R. Barrow, Jr., ed. (Annapolis, MD: U.S. Naval Institute Press, 1973); Marvin, American Merchant Marine, 426–28.

[11] Report of the Merchant Marine Commission, S. Rep. 58-2755, 467. Atlantic Transport Company acquired the Wilson and Furness-Leyland Line, Limited to replace the vessel capacity sold to the U.S. Government. "Steamship Line Transfer," New York Times, June 30, 1898, 12.

[12] Report of the Merchant Marine Commission, S. Rep. 58-2755, 467; Bernard N. Baker, "How We Can Have American Ships for the Panama Canal," North American Review 191, no. 650 (January 1910): 29–38, 29–30.

[13] Annual Reports of the Navy Department for the Year 1898, 106, 114–15.

[14] Annual Reports of the Navy Department for the Year 1898, 106.

[15] 31 CONG. REC. 5159 (May 24, 1898); 31 CONG. REC. 5170 (May 25, 1898).

[16] Annual Reports of the Department of the Navy, 1898, 270; W. A. M. Goode, With Sampson through the War (New York: Doubleday, 1899), 8; John D. Long, The New American Navy (New York: Outlook, 1903), vol. 1, 155–56.

[17] Annual Reports of the Navy Department for the Year 1898, 584.

[18] Annual Reports of the Navy Department for the Year 1898, 270.

[19] Marvin, The American Merchant Marine, 430.

[20] Report of the Commission Appointed by the President to Investigate the Conduct of the War Department in the War with Spain (Washington, DC: Government Printing Office, 1899), 29–30, 32.

[21] William Joe Webb, "The Spanish-American War and United States Army Shipping," American Neptune XL, no. 3 (July 1980): 167–91, 173; Annual Report of the Quartermaster-General of the Army to the Secretary of War for the Fiscal Year Ended June 30, 1898 (Washington, DC: Government Printing Office, 1898), 13.

[22] 31 CONG. REC. 5108 (May 23, 1898); 31 CONG. REC. 5162 (May 24, 1898); "Registry for a British Ship," New York Times, May 24, 1898, 2.

[23] 30 Stat. 421 (May 27, 1898). A list of all vessels documented by Act of Congress in fiscal year 1898 is contained in Annual Report of the Commissioner of Navigation to the Secretary of the Treasury (1898), 246.

[24] Annual Reports of the Navy Department for the Year 1898, 94.

[25] Dorwart, "A Mongrel Fleet: America Buys a Navy to Fight Spain, 1898," 136–38.

[26] Long, New American Navy, 152-153.

[27] U.S. Congress, Senate, A Naval Auxiliary Merchant Marine: Speech of Hon. W. G. McAdoo, Secretary of the Treasury, before the Chamber of Commerce of Indianapolis, Ind., October 13, 1915, 64th Cong., 1st sess., 1915, S. Doc. 64-5, 3–4.

[28] 52 CONG. REC. 2005–06 (January 21, 1915).

[29] 52 CONG. REC. 2005–06.

30 "Nanshan," Naval History and Heritage Command, https://www.history.navy.mil/research/histories/ship-histories/danfs/n/nanshan.html#:~:text=Nanshan%20was%20launched%20in%201896,British%20Marine%20Service%20in%20comma.

31 Another issue which arose was whether U.S.-flag vessels registered in neutral countries could return to the U.S.-flag after the war. The Treasury Department declined to address the issue because U.S. law would require continuous U.S. citizen ownership which would be contrary to neutrality requirements. Treasury Decisions under Tariff, Internal Revenue, Immigration, Navigation Laws, Etc., vol. 1, January 1, to June 30, 1898 (Washington, DC: Government Printing Office, 1898), 833–34.

32 Annual Report of the Commissioner of Navigation to the Secretary of the Treasury (1899), 86 ("The price for which they can be sold will be considerably greater if by legislation the vessels can engage in the coasting trade of the United States.").

33 Lyman J. Gage, ed., "Treasury Department Circular no. 157 (August 12, 1898)," Circular Instructions of the Treasury Department Relative to the Tariff, Navigation, and Other Laws for the Year Ending December 31, 1898 (Washington, DC: Government Printing Office, 1898); U.S. Attorney General, "American Registry," Op. Att'y Gen. 22, no. 566 (August 11, 1899); The Merritt, 84 U.S. 582 (1873).

34 29 Stat. 188 (May 28, 1896).

35 "The Auxiliary Fleet–Purchase of Four Steamers of the Morgan Line Concluded by the Government," New York Times, April 6, 1898, 2.

36 U.S. Congress, House, Employment of Vessels of the United States for Public Purposes, 58th Cong., 2nd sess., 1904, H. Rep. No. 58-1893, 3; Alfred G. Smith of the New York and Cuba Mail Steamship Co. (known as the "Ward Line") testified in 1905 that many foreign crewmembers left their vessels because of foreign enlistment acts. Report of the Merchant Marine Commission, S. Rep. 58-2755, 129.

37 Frederick S. Harrod, Manning the New Navy: The Development of a Modern Enlisted Force, 1899-1940 (Westport, CT: Greenwood Press, 1978), 34–36.

38 Charles Oscar Paullin, Paullin's History of Naval Administration 1775-1911 (Annapolis, MD: U.S. Naval Institute Press, 2012), 425–26.

39 Annual Reports of the Navy Department for the Year 1898, 143.

40 Annual Reports of the Navy Department for the Year 1898, 320–21; Annual Reports of the Navy Department for the Year 1897, 222.

41 Long, New American Navy, 183–85.

42 W. F. Fulham, "The System of Naval Training and Discipline Required to Promote Efficiency and Attract Americans," U.S. Naval Institute Proceedings 16, no. 55 (October 1890): 473—95, 479.

43 Roberts, "A Navy of Foreigners."

44 22 Stat. 58 (May 4, 1882).

45 "Chinese on Dewey's Ships–The Admiral Says They Fought Bravely and Should Be Nationalized," New York Times, July 16, 1898, 7; "Dewey's Chinese Seamen–They

Fought Like Heroes, but Cannot Enter American Ports," New York Times, February 23, 1899, 5.

[46] Annual Reports of the Navy Department for the Year 1898, appendix 65–68.

[47] "Battle of Manila Bay," Naval History and Heritage Command, Publications, Documentary Histories, www.history.navy.mil/research/publications/documentary-histories/advanced-search.html?isListOfDocuments=true&edition=united-states-navy-s&topic=united-states-navy-s/the-battle-of-manila.

[48] John Brady, "Olympia, Icon of the Navy," Sea History 170 (Spring 2020): 20–25.

[49] Annual Reports of the Navy Department for the Year 1898, 666.

[50] For example, George Dewey, Autobiography of George Dewey Admiral of the Navy (New York: Charles Scribner's Sons, 1913), 190–91, 240–41.

[51] George Dewey, The War with Spain: Operations of the United States Navy on the Asiatic Station: Reports of Rear-Admiral George Dewey on the Battle of Manila Bay, May 1, 1898, and on the Investment and Fall of Manila, May 1 to August 13, 1898 (Washington, DC: Government Printing Office, 1900), 7, 67.

[52] "'Zafiro' Case," American Journal of International Law 20, no. 2 (April 1926): 385–90, 386.

[53] American and British Claims Arbitration, 'Zafiro' Case, Claims of D. Earnshaw, A. Young and G. Gilchrist: Answer of the United States (Washington, DC: Government Printing Office, 1924), 23–26.

[54] Annual Reports of the Navy Department for the Year 1898, appendix 66.

[55] Dewey, Autobiography of George Dewey Admiral of the Navy, 191–92. Dewey's Autobiography is cited by the Zafiro International Arbitration Tribunal. "'Zafiro' Case," American Journal of International Law, 386.

[56] Regulations Prescribed for the Use of The Consular Service of the United States (Washington, DC: Government Printing Office, 1896), 133–34, para. 343; Robert Rienow, The Test of the Nationality of a Merchant Vessel (New York: Columbia University Press, 1937, 161–64.

[57] "Treasury Department Circular no. 157 (Aug. 12, 1898)," Circular Instructions of the Treasury Department Relative to the Tariff, Navigation, and Other Laws for the Year Ending December 31, 1898.

[58] American and British Claims Arbitration, 'Zafiro' Case, Claims of D. Earnshaw, A. Young and G. Gilchrist: Answer of the United States, 29; "Notices," Army and Navy Journal 35, no. 39 (May 28, 1898): 778.

[59] A. Piatt Andrew, "The End of the Mexican Dollar," Quarterly Journal of Economics 18, no. 3 (May 1904): 321–56.

[60] Adelbert M. Dewey, The Life and Letters of Admiral Dewey (Akron, OH: Werner, 1899), 230–31.

[61] American and British Claims Arbitration, 'Zafiro' Case, Claims of D. Earnshaw, A. Young and G. Gilchrist: Answer of the United States, 30.

[62] The Great Britain Proclamation of Neutrality dated April 26, 1898, prohibited any "British subject" from accepting or agreeing "to accept any commission or engagement in the military or naval service of any foreign state at war with any foreign state at peace with Her Majesty." Proclamations and Decrees During the War with Spain (Washington, DC: Government Printing Office, 1899), 31–37.
[63] American and British Claims Arbitration, 'Zafiro' Case, Claims of D. Earnshaw, A. Young and G. Gilchrist: Answer of the United States, 30.
[64] American and British Claims Arbitration, 'Zafiro' Case, Claims of D. Earnshaw, A. Young and G. Gilchrist: Answer of the United States, 30.
[65] U.S. v. Dewey, 188 U.S. 254 (1903).

Senator George G. Vest, Library of Congress

Chapter 12—The Great Subsidy Stalemate

After the Spanish-American War there was a renewed effort to subsidize the U.S. merchant marine, with the most intense activity occurring between 1898 and 1911. A congressional critic of vessel subsidies described the subsidy advocates during this period as "the most active, persistent, influential, and unblushing lobby... hounding the life out of both branches of Congress."[1] A leading maritime policy historian called this period of activity the "Great Subsidy Offensive," but it could just as easily be called the "Great Subsidy Stalemate."[2]

Both U.S. owners and shipyards supported operating subsidies in the international trade. The reasons for this are not obvious, since a natural reaction of U.S. owners engaged in the international trade could logically have been to support free ships so as to be able to acquire vessels at an international price. Shipyards in turn might have focused their attention on construction subsidies while opposing free ships.

Vessel owners as a group likely opposed free ships because the group was dominated by owners in the domestic trade not engaged in international competition. They had no incentive to acquire foreign-built vessels.[3] Shipyards likely supported subsidies because they believed that a prosperous U.S.-flag merchant marine in the international trade was necessary to support their order book.[4]

That the commonality of interest existed is nevertheless evident. When Senator Frye brought together a diverse group in 1897 to promote the U.S. merchant marine (including vessel owners), they all agreed to support subsidies and to oppose free ships.[5] In testimony before the 1905 Gallinger Commission, all the major U.S. vessel owners were asked directly whether they would reflag foreign-built vessels. They all answered that they would not or would do so only with subsidies.[6] U.S. shipyards concentrated on the Delaware River agreed."

THE DELAWARE RIVER—THE AMERICAN CLYDE

During the second half of the nineteenth century, the locus of iron steel shipbuilding on the U.S. ocean coastline (as distinct from the Great Lakes) was the Delaware River from Wilmington, Delaware to Philadelphia.[7] Pennsylvania was a national leader in the mining of coal and iron, and furnaces and iron working facilities were established in the Philadelphia area. Many evolved into the business of building vessels and vessel engines, as had occurred on the Clyde River in Scotland.

Although the United States lagged far behind Britain in the mass production of iron steamships, a substantial U.S. iron/steel steamship building industry developed on the Delaware River.[8] Two shipyards were particularly significant: William Cramp & Sons Shipbuilding Company (Port Richmond in Philadelphia) and John Roach & Sons (Chester, south of Philadelphia). The presence of those yards and other facilities led some to call the Delaware River "the American Clyde."[9] The principals of both yards were outspoken proponents of subsidies and equally outspoken opponents of free ships.

Cramp & Sons. The Cramp (changed from "Krampf" or "Krampp") family were among the first settlers from Germany in the Philadelphia area in the early 1700s.[10] William Cramp, born near Philadelphia in 1806, started his first vessel construction facility in 1830 building wooden vessels.

The yard benefited from the demand for large wooden sailing vessels, it constructed six of them for the California trade from 1849 to1853. The yard also was an early adopter of screw propulsion (versus paddle wheels) and constructed the first screw-propelled tug in the United States in 1846 (the *Sampson*). Charles H. Cramp, one of William's sons born in 1828, took the operation to the next level with the adoption of industrial processes and the construction of iron steamships.

The Cramp shipyard built one of the most noteworthy vessels of the Civil War. In anticipation of the construction of Confederate ironclad warships, the U.S. Navy ordered the famous *U.S.S. Monitor*, which was constructed in early 1862 in a U.S. Navy shipyard. Spreading its bets, the Navy also ordered two more conventional steam screw-propelled wooden vessels with iron armor, one of which was the *U.S.S. New Ironsides* delivered by the Cramp shipyard in late 1862. The construction of that vessel was important to the transition of the Cramp shipyard into the construction of all iron vessels.

Charles (known as "Charley") Cramp was also an active advocate for U.S. shipbuilding and the U.S. merchant marine.[11] For example, he testified before the Lynch Committee on December 2, 1869.[12] In his testimony, he attributed attacks on the U.S.-build policy to the British desire to "overrun" the U.S. market.[13] Had free ships succeeded, he argued, "there would not now be a first-class shipyard in existence on our soil and we would have been, like Chili and Japan, forced to dicker on the banks of the Clyde for the construction of our new navy, if we had one at all."

Codman was a frequent Cramp opponent. When Cramp defended the U.S-build requirement as having come from the country's Founding Fathers, such as Madison, Codman was quoted as saying that U.S. navigation laws had "nothing to do with the motives that actuated our Revolutionary fathers... any more than we have to do with the motives of Noah in building his ark."[14]

Charles's son Edwin S. Cramp, who was vice president of the company until 1907, subsequently took on the advocacy mantle.[15] Testifying before the 1905 Merchant Marine Commission, Edwin made familiar arguments for mail subsidies and discriminating duties and against free ships.[16] He also argued against what he called "'whitewashed' tramps." These were vessels wrecked and salvaged in the United States that had attained U.S. registry privileges by virtue of having a certain amount spent in a U.S. shipyard (discussed in a later chapter).

JOURNEY TO THE JONES ACT

Over time, the Cramp & Sons operations grew enormously, from less than one hundred employees in 1830 to about eight thousand in 1902. During World Wars I and II, their ranks reached a high of ten thousand or more. Cramp & Sons eventually built over five hundred vessels, many of which were notable. Significant ocean liners included four Pennsylvania-class vessels delivered in 1873-74 for the American Steamship Company (the "American Line" owned at the time by the Pennsylvania Railroad Company), the *St. Louis* and *St. Paul* delivered in 1894-1895 for the International Navigation Company, the *Kroonland* and *Finland* delivered to International Mercantile Marine Company (International Navigation Company's successor) in 1902, the *Great Northern* and *Northern Pacific* delivered to the Great Northern Steamship Co., and the *Malolo* (renamed later the *Matsonia* and then later *Queen Frederica*) for Matson Line delivered in 1927 and not scrapped until 1977 after passing through several owners.[17]

Cramp & Sons was also a major warship builder. It built the first U.S. warships designated as "battleships": the *U.S.S. Indiana* (BB-1), the *U.S.S. Massachusetts* (BB-2), and the *U.S.S. Iowa* (BB-4), delivered from 1895 to 1897. All these vessels were instrumental in the Spanish-American War. Cramp also built America's first "dreadnought" battleship, the *U.S.S. South Carolina* (BB-26), as well as warships for foreign navies such as the cruiser *Kasagi* for Japan in 1898. During World War I, the yard delivered forty-six torpedo destroyers (many served in World War II) and delivered one cargo vessel and four tankers for the U.S. Shipping Board from 1919 to 1921. In World War II, the yard mainly built Navy cruisers, submarines, and tugs.

The transition from larger naval vessels to smaller naval vessels reflected increased competition in naval shipbuilding from the Newport News Shipbuilding and Drydock Company and New York Shipbuilding Corporation. The Washington Naval Treaty of 1922 restricted naval combatant construction to 10,000-ton cruisers, which increased the price pressure on smaller naval construction, and the dearth of commercial building opportunities in the 1920's led to the closure of the Cramp shipyard in 1927.[18] At that time, the company already was no longer controlled by the Cramp family, which had sold their interest in July 1915. From 1919 until its closure, the company operated under the control of W. Averell Harriman's American Ship and Commerce Corporation.

Roach & Sons. John Roach (originally "Roache") was born in Ireland in 1815, was left an orphan, and emigrated to the United States at the age of sixteen.[19] After initially working at a New Jersey iron works, he later co-founded a foundry in New York City, which he expanded over time and merged with the Morgan Iron Works, a manufacturer of marine steam engines. Also, about that time, he bought in 1871 a shipyard in Chester, Pennsylvania, which he renamed the Delaware River Iron Shipbuilding and Engine Works.

From 1871 to 1885, Roach & Sons, as the firm came to be known, was the largest and most productive iron U.S. shipbuilder. It constructed over 125 iron vessels for both commercial and government customers. By the time of John's death in 1887, Roach & Sons had built 90 percent of the American steamships in the U.S. international trade, and he was referred to as "the Father of American Iron Shipbuilding."[20]

There were, however, bumps in the road. Pacific Mail Steamship Company ordered seven vessels from Roach & Sons in 1872 to meet the requirements of the 1872 mail subsidy authorized by Congress.[21] When the bribery and fraud crisis engulfed Pacific Mail, Pacific Mail defaulted on its progress payments.[22] The shipyard was almost bankrupted.

Roach & Sons delivered the first two vessels, the *City of Peking* and *City of Tokyo,* in 1874.[23] They were the largest vessels built in the United States at the time (and there was only one British vessel larger), about 420 feet in length capable of carrying about 2,000 passengers and making the voyage between Yokohama, Japan, and San Francisco in seventeen days. The *City of Peking* had an illustrious history, making 116 round trips between those ports from 1875 to 1903 and serving as a U.S. troop ship in the Spanish-American War.

JOURNEY TO THE JONES ACT

The launch of the Pacific Mail vessels was accompanied by an April 1874 dinner to honor Roach at Delmonico's restaurant in New York. The dinner was attended by New York mayor William F. Havemeyer, New York state judge John R. Brady (who in 1881 administered the oath of office to Chester A. Arthur when President Garfield died), Major Gen. Winfield Scott Hancock (of Gettysburg fame), and Representative Samuel S. Cox (Roach was his constituent, but Cox would later advocate for free ships).[24]

According to one report, the best wine vintages Delmonico's had to offer "flowed with the profuseness of vin ordinaire at a political barbecue."[25] Roach said that he hoped that "we are not here to-night because one man has built a ship, or even because that ship is a good one, but because we hope she is the forerunner of whole fleets of ships."[26]

Roach backed up his hope by being a persistent advocate for the U.S.-flag vessels. According to his *New York Times* obituary in 1887, Roach "devoted the best years and energies of his life to building up an American merchant marine. He was possessed by this idea, and never wearied in advocating the restoration of the ocean carrying trade."[27]

He was also the listed author of several books, appeared as a witness in Congress, gave speeches, and appeared frequently in the press.[28] For example, the *New York Times* interviewed him in 1879 on the subject of "Why We Have No Ships—Mr. John Roach's Opinion."[29] Roach's answer was that the main difference between England's success and America's failure was a lack of U.S. government support.

In his advocacy, he was an adamant opponent of free ships and frequently had uncivil interactions with Codman.[30] At a Dingley Committee hearing in November 1882 where both Codman and Roach had testified earlier, Roach asked for a further chance to speak. At that point, the press reported that Roach "showed his anger by a very red face and very emphatic gesticulations as he pointed at Capt. Codman," accusing him of providing questions to Representative Cox. Roach claimed he had no right to do that since Codman had "no occupation connected with shipbuilding" and had hidden employers presumably meaning British shipyards.[31] Codman responded that he represented "fifty millions of people who want free ships." On November 24, Roach seeking the last word, wrote to the *New York Herald* that the fifty million Codman mentioned was likely a reference to the population of Britain rather than the United States.[32]

Roach's ambition led to his downfall. The failure to obtain a U.S. government subsidy for his Brazilian line resulted in substantial losses.[33] Compounding matters, his well-known support for Republicans also put him on the political firing line.[34]

Roach & Sons entered into a contract in July 1883 to build the first four steel warships ever ordered by the U.S. Navy, known as the "ABCD" ships as their names were the *U.S.S. Atlanta*, *U.S.S. Boston*, *U.S.S. Chicago*, and *U.S.S. Dolphin*. By this point, Roach & Sons had been involved in many government contract controversies going back to 1867, in which favoritism and kickbacks had been alleged. Charles Cramp, who had been substantially underbid by Roach on the ABCD vessels, alleged bid collusion. Further contributing to an air of impropriety, the secretary of the Navy was William E. Chandler, Roach's friend and lawyer since 1868.[35] The stage was therefore set for critics and enemies to pounce if there was trouble with this new contract.

The first vessel to be delivered—the *U.S.S. Dolphin*—passed her sea trials during the Republican Arthur administration but was rejected by the Navy in the Democratic Cleveland administration in 1885. The U.S. attorney general opined that the performance defects amounted to an invalidation of the contract.[36] The potential loss of payments for the four vessels plus the loss of shipyard investments already made for them strained the yard's finances.

Already physically sick from what turned out to be cancer, Roach put his company into receivership, saving the shipyard since his overall assets exceeded his liabilities.[37] Ultimately, the yard completed the *Dolphin* and U.S. Navy shipyards completed the other three vessels. Despite the controversy, the *Dolphin*, delivered in 1884, served in the U.S. Navy until 1921.

After Roach died in 1887 and the debts of the company were paid, the Chester shipyard and Morgan Iron Works were taken over by John Baker Roach, Roach's eldest son.[38] The firm built another eighty-one vessels from 1887 to 1907.

The *New York Times* opinion on his passing characterized Roach as a successful but tragic figure and noted that he was "an ardent and aggressive protectionist."[39] The yard, like that of Cramp and Sons, was later sold to W. Averell Harriman; it delivered an additional forty vessels for the U.S. Shipping Board in World War I.

Roach's family sought vindication for the *Dolphin* incident and the funds spent on the other three vessels. It was not until 1898 that the U.S. Congress obliged.[40] Congress enacted two laws in 1898 to pay the Roach heirs for what the yard spent on the three vessels other than the *Dolphin* and for completing the latter.[41]

Hanna-Payne-Frye Bounty Bills

The 1896 McKinley election made possible an intensified effort to enact vessel operating support, called "bounties."[42] The renewed effort lasted until the Democrats took control of House in 1911.

The principal leaders at the beginning of the lobbying campaign were Senator Frye, Senator Marcus A. Hanna (known as "Mark") (R-OH) and Representative Sereno E. Payne (R-NY). (Hanna was a wealthy businessman from Cleveland, was Republican National Committee chairman, and had managed McKinley's presidential campaign. Payne was the chairman of the Merchant Marine Committee from 1895 to 1899 and was a staunch protectionist.)

Frye created an *ad hoc* merchant marine committee in 1897 comprising prominent shipping-related persons including several Republican members of Congress like Senators Hanna and Elkins, shipbuilders like Charles H. Cramp, leading vessel owners like Clement A. Griscom, Theodore C. Search (the president of the National Manufacturers' Association), and Aaron Vanderbilt, secretary of the American Shipping and Industrial League and a distant relative of Cornelius Vanderbilt, and one U.S. government official, Eugene Chamberlain.[43] Chamberlain provided the supporting data. Griscom was the chairman. The committee hired George F. Edmunds, a former Vermont Republican Senator, as counsel.[44]

The consensus of the Frye *ad hoc* committee was that the only potentially viable merchant marine promotion path was "bounties" set at rates intended to equalize the cost differential between U.S.-flag vessel and foreign vessels.[45] The first legislative salvo was fired by Hanna and Payne who introduced bills in December 1898 about the same time as the peace treaty was signed with Spain ending the Spanish-American War.[46]

The bills provided for a ten-year program of bounties, to be paid to U.S.-flag vessels for foreign voyages with the highest bounties paid for fast ocean passenger steamships, analogous to foreign bounty systems.[47] Bounty contract applicants had to be U.S. citizens. Over time, many changes were made in subsequent bill iterations, including a cap on expenditures in what otherwise worked like an entitlement (bounties paid for miles sailed regardless of the number).

Chamberlain, who had strongly advocated for free ships while Cleveland was president, called that cause politically hopeless in his 1899 *Annual Report*. He recommended adopting bounties as the only workable approach to promoting the U.S. merchant marine in the international trade.[48]

When Chamberlain became a leading bounty advocate, Codman (like Vest quoted above) targeted him with criticism.[49] In an 1899 letter to the *New York Times* Codman proclaimed that bounties were "schemes of robbery" and that "when Mr. McKinley was elected Mr. Chamberlain succeeded in some mysterious manner in retaining his position, and as will be observed... is now the pliant tool of the men whose intrigues he so diligently endeavored to thwart."[50] In a February 13, 1900, letter to the *Times*, Codman also sarcastically referred to the draft legislation produced by the *ad hoc* committee as the "McKinley-Payne-Hanna-Frye-Cramp-Griscom-Edmunds bill."[51]

Codman did not credit that the Hanna-Payne legislation contained a modified free ship aspect. The legislation would have permitted foreign-built vessels to be registered under U.S.-flag, provided that a similar vessel was built in a U.S. shipyard within five years.[52] The one-for-one idea was patterned on the Act of May 10, 1892 which resulted in the construction of the *St. Louis* and the *St. Paul* at Cramp Shipyard.[53]

The House Merchant Marine and Senate Commerce Committees (chaired by Payne and Frye, respectively) recommended passage of the *ad hoc* committee's bill in January 1899, and the Treasury Department submitted supporting information to the Senate.[54] But the legislation was not actively considered by the Fifty-Fifth Congress, which ended March 4, 1899.

Frye introduced similar bills in 1900 and 1902 with the support of Presidents McKinley and Roosevelt.[55] In his inaugural speech on March 4, 1987, McKinley urged "prompt attention to the restoration of our American merchant marine."[56] In his last speech before being shot in Buffalo on September 5, 1901, McKinley said "we must have more ships. They must be under the American flag, built and manned and owned by Americans."[57] In his first Annual Message to Congress in December 1901, Roosevelt wrote "immediate remedial action" was needed and that it was "unwise for the United States to continue to rely upon ships of competing nations for the distribution of our goods."[58]

The party divide on providing subsidies could not have been starker. The 1900 Democratic national platform opposed such "barefaced frauds upon the taxpayers as the shipping subsidy bill with the false pretense of prospering American shipbuilding," which "would put unearned millions into the pockets of favorite contributors to the Republican campaign fund."[59] In contrast, without mentioning bounties, the 1900 Republican national platform stated that dependence on foreign vessels presented "a serious danger to our trade, for its sudden withdrawal in the event of European war would seriously cripple our expanding foreign commerce," which provided "a compelling reason for legislation which will enable us to recover our former place among the trade-carrying fleets of the world."[60]

Meanwhile, Frye argued that a U.S. merchant marine was necessary to promote U.S. international commerce.[61] In response, the *New York Times* editorial page pointed out that the United States already was a leading exporter despite the lack of a national fleet, "for there is something a little absurd in the notion of a people of such tremendous powers of expansion being checked in its growth by the lack of subsidized carriers—a Samson of trade bound with green withes by foreign steamship companies."[62]

Frye also accurately predicted what in fact happened in 1914:

> Our short and decisive war with Spain compelled us to hunt the seas over for transports and colliers; to purchase or charter forty ships from foreign nations. Suppose the war had lasted a year, or had been with a more powerful nation, and neutrality had been enforced, as it should be, we would have been in most serious straits. As it was, our producers paid heavy penalties in increased freight rates. Great Britain in her war with the Boers had transports enough, but even then rates were seriously advanced in the East. Suppose there should be a European war or a conflict between Great Britain and Germany, what would become of our enormous export trade? Who would be our carriers? Who would pay the war insurance premiums on our cargoes, even if carriers could be found? We

should suffer almost as seriously as either of the combatants. Our farmers, manufacturers, and wage-earners would pay almost as much as a cost of the war as they.[63]

In response, Vest argued that the "Senator from Maine draws a ghastly picture of a naval war between Germany and England" but that such a situation could be easily remedied by opening the U.S. registry to foreign-built vessels at that time.[64]

Although Vest made a valid point, Frye had the better of the argument. In 1914, U.S. international trade did suffer exactly as Frye predicted. The United States permitted foreign-built vessels to come under the U.S-flag as Vest predicted, but such reflagging proved inadequate and did not account for the effects of German submarine warfare, neutrality and other laws (many countries enacted laws preventing their vessels from reflagging), and the enormous increase in the flow of trade needed to support the war effort.

Vest also argued that the application of funds from the general treasury to support a particular industry was unconstitutional because it was neither covered by the commerce clause of the U.S. Constitution nor subject to an enumerated constitutional power.[65] Senator George Turner (D-WA) joined Vest in arguing that the "legislation is not Democratic or Republican; it is Socialistic" and "the purest and baldest kind of paternalism and socialism."[66] Turner also referred to the legislation as a "lawless and piratical raid by shipowners and shipbuilders on the Treasury."[67]

Where Vest and others were effective was in echoing the Democratic national platform by putting a spotlight on the bounty beneficiaries.[68] Vest argued that providing bounties "to wealthy corporations that do not need it is naked robbery under the forms of law."[69] He also claimed that the major recipients of the intended law, like INC, were well off companies.

Senator Hanna had introduced the legislation with a long speech that had ended with "applause in the galleries."[70] Vest noted how Hanna had "closed his strong and forcible speech in a burst of patriotic ardor" that reminded him of an actor in Kentucky "who always brought down the house at the close of the last act by wrapping himself in the American flag, while the orchestra, consisting of one violin and a bass drum, played Yankee Doodle, rushing to the footlights, firing off a horse pistol, and screaming like the American eagle. [Laughter]."[71]

Both Vest and Turner also made frequent mention of the fact that the legislation was the product of a hand-picked committee with a commercial interest in the legislation. Vest noted that it only "ostensibly" came from the Commerce Committee but really came from "a committee of promotion."[72]

Senator Alexander S. Clay (D-GA) (father of U.S. Army General Lucius D. Clay who played a leading role in the Berlin Airlift in 1948-1949) joined Turner in arguing that the bounties would not help farmers because the vessels which would receive the most subsidy were fast steamships, which mainly carried passengers and specialty cargoes.[73]

The last gasp of the Hanna-Payne-Frye subsidy legislation was a bill which passed the Senate on March 17, 1902 (no Democrats voted in favor and two Republicans voted against).[74] Two important amendments were adopted at the last minute affecting the creation of IMM, an international shipping trust formed by Clement Griscom and J. P. Morgan.

One amendment was to foreclose the grant of subsidies to any foreign-built vessel, which appeared to make sure that any British-flag vessels IMM acquired could not obtain U.S. subsidies. This amendment appears to have persuaded Morgan to make peace with the British government in 1902 about keeping acquired vessels under British flag.[75] The second amendment, which was helpful to IMM, made it clear that any subsidy participant could also own a foreign steamship line.

Chamberlain was to claim that some good came of the effort anyway, since at least eight vessels were ordered in U.S. shipyards (in anticipation of enactment which all proved useful during World War I). Those vessels included the *Kroonland* and *Finland,* delivered to IMM's Red Star Line in 1902 by Cramp & Sons.[76] Both vessels were used as troopships in World War I. The *Finland* also transported and housed the U.S. Olympic team for the 1912 Summer Olympics in Stockholm.

After the legislation died in 1902, there was a lull in subsidy activity and the protagonists changed. Vest ended his service in the Senate in March 1903 and died on August 9, 1904. Hanna died in office on February 15, 1904. Payne was no longer chairman of the Merchant Marine Committee starting in 1900. It was President Teddy Roosevelt who revived the effort with a new subsidy proponent, Senator Jacob Gallinger of New Hampshire.

THE MERCHANT MARINE (GALLINGER) COMMISSION

Roosevelt set out to break the log jam in his 1903 Annual Message to Congress. He noted that a majority of Americans wanted to promote U.S. shipping but "hitherto the differences of opinion as to the proper method of reaching this end have been so wide that it has proved impossible to secure the adoption of any particular scheme."[77] Roosevelt recommended that a commission be formed of both executive branch officials and Members of Congress.

Congress established "The Merchant Marine Commission" in 1904, although it limited it to ten members of Congress.[78] In its report recommending the creation of the commission, the Merchant Marine Committee quoted at length an article by Winthrop L. Marvin, editor of the *Boston Journal.*

Specifically, Marvin had pointed out that shipbuilding for the foreign trade was in "'a condition of absolutely arrested development."[79] Marvin had previously written the widely read book *The American Merchant Marine: Its History and Romance from 1620 to 1902,* dedicated to Theodore Roosevelt and sympathetic to subsidies.[80] Marvin had also testified before Congress against the admission of foreign-built vessels to the U.S. registry.[81]

Senator Gallinger chaired the commission, and he was joined by four senators (including Senator Lodge) and five representatives with the majority in each group being Republicans. Gallinger had already indicated support for prior subsidy legislation.[82]

Marvin, who came from a Portsmouth, New Hampshire shipping and fishing family, was appointed commission secretary.[83] Marvin later (from 1919 to 1926) served as the vice president and general manager of the American Steamship Association and from 1922 the owner of the *Marine Journal*.[84]

The political makeup of the commission was noteworthy. A 1905 editorial in the *Boston Herald* said that "if this was not a 'packed jury,' so far as 'free ships' was concerned, it would be difficult to form one which was more so."[85] Marvin was singled out by the *Boston Herald* referring to him as a "subsidy pleader."[86] Marvin indignantly responded that everyone joined the commission with an open mind and the eighteen hundred pages of testimony of vessel-owning interests who presumably would benefit from free ships and yet opposed it was evidence of the lack of prejudice.[87]

Commission Report. The commission itself was sensitive to the charge that its results were preordained. Its January 1905 Report took pains to state that the commission was "open minded as to the best policy of relief for our vanishing ships and seamen."[88]

The commission concluded that the "real dominant factor" in more costly U.S. vessels was not the cost of steel but "the high wages of the skilled American workmen who fashion the plates and beams into the finished ship."[89] Similarly, the commission believed that U.S.-flag crew wages were higher than foreign wages because U.S.-flag vessels were hired in U.S. ports where the standard of living was high. The commission report analogized U.S.-flag vessels to a "floating factory" and "the "difference in wages and in style of living is not greater between an American and a foreign ship than between an American and foreign factory."[90]

The commission complained that "American shipping in the foreign trade has been for forty to fifty years the only American industry exposed directly to foreign competition that has not been protected by the Government."[91] This, while other American industries had prospered behind a high tariff wall. The commission also noted that other nations were supporting their foreign trading fleets.[92]

The majority report did not dwell on discriminating duties.[93] The minority report by three of the four Democrats on the Commission, on the other hand, strongly advocated a return to that policy.[94] The minority was not impressed by threats of foreign retaliation.[95] Nor was it troubled by the long "free list" of items not subject to import duties where percentage based discriminating duties would have no effect.[96]

The minority report prompted the majority to write a separate response on discriminating duties.[97] The majority determined that retaliation would fall on U.S. exports. Also, the markets, such as in South America which the commission wanted to serve with expanded U.S. merchant marine service, were the ones with the longest "free lists."

The commission instead made a series of recommendations, including expanding and increasing mail subsidies and introducing a new annual "subvention" (an amount per gross ton of vessel pursuant to an annual contract renewable for up to ten years) for vessels engaged full time in the foreign trade. Subsidized vessels would have to meet several requirements, including agreeing to carry a proportion of "naval volunteers" as part of the crew, to make the vessel available for requisition by the U.S. government for "national defense or for any public purpose," and to agree to make all repairs in the United States.[98]

In its report, the commission claimed that there was "an exact and authoritative precedent" for "subventions" in the bounties paid to U.S. deep sea fishermen and deep sea fishing vessels from 1792 to 1866 (as mentioned in a previous chapter).[99] According to the report, many of the Navy's sailors in the

War of 1812 and the Mexican War were deep sea fishermen and, the commission's view, "subventions" stood upon a "policy, founded under Washington, through the counsel of Jefferson, stood under Madison and Jackson as well as the younger Adams."[100]

The minority opposed "subventions."[101] They asserted that the "chief difference from former direct subsidy bills is that it is not as honest as these bills were." The minority argued that the U.S. Congress should not be fooled by "the substitution of the more euphonious title 'subvention' for 'subsidy.'"

The commission called in the U.S. Navy to support its position on subventions. The commission heard from two of the most famous Navy theoreticians of the day and of all time: Rear Admiral (ret.) Stephen B. Luce and Captain (ret.) Alfred Thayer Mahan.[102] Luce was the founder and first president of the Naval War College. Mahan was the second president of the college and by 1904 was already a famous author who had influenced policymakers around the world with his writings, particularly his book *The Influence of Sea Power upon History, 1660-1783*, originally published in 1890.[103]

Luce testified that the merchant marine was the source of seamen for the Navy and that "the greater part" of the expanded officer pool in the Civil War came from the merchant marine.[104] He also quoted from Marvin's book to the effect that the Spanish-American War had "'proved that the merchant marine of the United States in 1898 was not sufficient to provide the indispensable naval reserve for even a brief conflict with a third-rate (fourth-rate) power."[105] Mahan testified that "it seems reasonable to suppose that the larger the number of Americans who are engaging in seafaring pursuits the greater will be the reserve for the Navy, and that in order to have a large number of Americans so engaged you must also have a very large American shipping...."[106]

Both Luce and Mahan were careful, however, not to endorse any method for merchant marine promotion.[107] In *The Influence of Sea Power*, Mahan doubted that the United States could have a navy without a merchant marine.[108] At the hearing, however, Mahan said he was "not at all in a position to speak" on how to support a U.S.-flag fleet, which he referred to as the "economical and industrial features of a merchant marine."[109]

Congressional Action on the Commission Report. Legislation proposed by the commission passed the U.S. Senate on February 14, 1906.[110] All the votes in the affirmative were by Republicans. Five Republicans, all from farming states, voted with the Democrats, seeking to defeat the bill. Democrats voting in a bloc against the Gallinger legislation, combined with Republican defections, was to be the pattern in subsequent votes.

The commission sought to improve the record with supplemental information, including a report from Admiral Dewey, then-president of the Navy General Board.[111] Dewey was supportive but guarded, as were Luce and Mahan. He focused on the need to support fast vessels to serve as scouts and "squadron colliers" (coaling vessels of sufficient speed to keep up with the battle fleet). This supported the commission's position to prefer fast vessels in the subsidy amounts. Dewey's report did not express any concern, however, regarding the ability to acquire slow vessels in time of war.

Another report from the Army War College was more supportive of the commission's position.[112] That report indicated that the current "force for which our military establishment is maintained can not [sic] be exerted over sea" and "this condition can not [sic] improve until the American steam seagoing merchant marine has increased in tonnage to approximately two and one-half times its present volume."[113]

The War College also noted that the expedition to Cuba in the Spanish-American War had only met success because of good weather and "a severe storm encountered would have scattered the fleet, probably with great loss of life, and would have defeated the object of the expedition."

Additional support came from Secretary of State Elihu Root, who said that the American shipowner was not pitting his "intelligence, skill, industry, and thrift" in a contest with foreign shipowners, but rather in "a contest against his competitors and his competitors' governments and his own Government also." In his view, "plainly, these disadvantages created by governmental action can be neutralized only by governmental action."[114] The only practical government action available were subsidies since, according to Root, discriminating duties and free ships would be self-defeating.

President Teddy Roosevelt echoed Secretary Root in a January 1907 message to Congress.[115] Roosevelt pointed out, as had the commission, that U.S. maritime wages and conditions had to be improved, not reduced, to attract U.S. citizens back to seafaring. The president argued that if subsidies were not enacted, the United States would be ceding American commerce to rivals.

The commission legislation divided the House Merchant Marine Committee, chaired by Charles H. Grosvenor (R-OH), which reported in January 1907 a substantially paired down bill.[116] Even that diluted bill was strenuously opposed in a minority report signed by five Democrats. It was led by Representative Thomas Spight (D-MS), who indicated that the Congress should consider adopting free ships and, if necessary, reintroducing discriminating duties.[117] Spight began the Civil War a Confederate private and rose to the rank of captain.

The legislation failed the first vote in the House on March 1, 1907.[118] With Speaker of the House Joseph G. Cannon (R-IL) personally gaveling the proceedings, the House then proceeded to table a motion to reconsider and to vote on the House substitute for the Senate bill by a vote of 162 to 150.[119] This favorable vote came too late for the Senate to act in the Fifty-Ninth Congress, which ended on March 3, and the legislation died.

Gallinger again garnered the support of President Roosevelt in the latter's 1908 Annual Message and renewed and sharpened the presentation in favor of legislation in early 1908.[120] The legislation passed the Senate but failed in the House at the end of the Sixtieth Congress on March 2, 1909, by a vote of 172 in favor with 175 against.[121] President Taft renewed the call for legislation in his 1909 Annual Message, and Gallinger again modified the bill seeking support but it nevertheless failed to advance.[122] Subsidy legislation would not again come so close to enactment until after World War I.

The 1909 phase of congressional consideration of the subsidy legislation was marred by bribery accusations. Among the handful of Republicans voting against the legislation was Representative Halvor Steenerson (R-MN). Steenerson spoke against the bill on the floor of the House and put in the *Congressional Record* a February 28 *Journal of Commerce* editorial entitled "Enemies of the Merchant Marine." The article asserted that the "clamor for subsidies are animated by selfish motives."[123] Steenerson had also stated in a letter that the Merchant Marine League, formed in 1904 in Cleveland to promote the U.S. merchant marine, was promoting subsidies only "to get big contracts."[124]

The league, which prided itself on having a membership not consisting of either vessel owners or shipyards, responded with an article in its publication entitled "Congressman Steenerson of Minnesota—Does He Represent the Foreign Shipping Interests or His Own District?"[125] The article referred to Steenerson as being "uninformed or malicious" and alleged, via a thirdhand report, that bribery by foreign interests was mainly behind opposition to subsidies.

Steenerson was outraged and demanded a congressional investigation to disprove the bribery allegations.[126] A special committee was formed that interviewed numerous witnesses and produced a lengthy report in 1911.[127] Acrimonious accusations flew during the inquiry, but the results were inconclusive.[128]

Probably the most sensational testimony was provided by two brothers, John W. Dodsworth (managing editor) and A. W. Dodsworth (business manager) of the *Journal of Commerce*. They testified that they had been offered substantial sums of money to write editorials favoring subsidies.[129] The allegations were carried by newspapers around the country as if they were fact, but neither brother could attach any names to the supposed offerors.[130]

During the last consideration of subsidy legislation in 1911, Senator Wesley Jones said he was reluctantly supporting the legislation even though he never believed it would succeed.[131] He argued that the better method of promotion was to re-introduce discriminating duties. Inviting a tariff war by abrogating non-discrimination treaties was more likely to succeed than a "mail-contract war."[132]

The continuing division in the body politic created by subsidies was vividly on display in the Senate at the very end of the subsidy consideration. On February 2, 1911, the Gallinger legislation passed in a tie vote—39 to 39 with 13 not voting—broken by Vice President John S. Sherman.[133] Fifty-nine of the ninety-one senators at the time were Republicans. Twelve of them voted against the bill, and no Democrats voted for it.

No action was taken in the last month of the Sixty-First Congress. The Sixty-Second Congress, which entered office on April 4, 1911, effectively ended subsidy consideration since the Democrats took control of the House. Senator Frye, the great champion of the U.S. merchant marine who had served in the U.S. Senate for just over thirty years, died in office on April 27, 1911.

Mail subsidies again became a topic in the 1920 Merchant Marine Act, but it was not until the enactment of the Merchant Marine Act, 1936 that the original aim of the Gallinger Commission, generally subsidizing U.S.-flag vessels engaged in the foreign trade, was achieved.

When the 1936 Act was proposed to the U.S. Congress by President Franklin D. Roosevelt in March 1935, Roosevelt confronted head-on the "subsidy" boogeyman that had vexed the Hanna-Payne-Frye and Gallinger efforts by saying that we should "end this subterfuge" of indirect support for the merchant marine and provide such support "honestly" by calling a "subsidy by its right name."[134] And so, the 1936 Act adopted both construction and operating subsidies, which persisted into the early 1980s.

Before and during the subsidy consideration, there was one merchant marine policy area where there was consensus—to preserve and extend the U.S. coastwise trade reservation, which had existed since 1789.

---

[1] Employment of Vessels of the United States for Public Purposes, H. Rep. 58-1893, part 2, 1.
[2] Zeis, American Shipping Policy, 29–30.
[3] This theory of how U.S. vessel owners came to align their interests with U.S. shipyards is espoused by several historians. For example, Zeis, American Shipping Policy, 29—30; and Vivian Vale, The American Peril: Challenge to Britain on the North Atlantic 1901–1904 (Manchester, UK: Manchester University Press, 1984), 42–47.
[4] For example, Charles H. Cramp, "The Merchant Marine and the Subsidy Bill," Independent 53, no. 2720 (January 17, 1901): 130–32.
[5] 34 CONG. REC. 31 (December 4, 1900).
[6] Report of the Merchant Marine Commission, S. Rep. 58-2755, 70–73.
[7] For example, in 1900, about 250,000 tons of vessels were built on the U.S. coasts and about 130,000 tons on the Great Lakes. Report of the Merchant Marine Commission, S. Rep. 58-2755, 433.
[8] Hutchins, American Maritime Industries, 448–70.
[9] "The American Clyde," Harper's New Monthly Magazine 56, no. 335 (April 1878): 641–52; David B. Tyler, The American Clyde: A History of Iron and Steel Shipbuilding on the Delaware from 1840 to World War I (New York: University of Delaware Press: 1958); Thomas R. Heinrich, Ships for the Seven Seas: Philadelphia Shipbuilding in the Age of Industrial Capitalism (Baltimore: Johns Hopkins University Press, 1997).
[10] Except where noted, the source of the description of the William Cramp & Sons Shipbuilding Company is Gail E. Farr and Brett F. Boswick, Shipbuilding at Cramp & Sons (Philadelphia: Philadelphia Maritime Museum, 1991) and "Story of the Cramp Shipyard," Nautical Gazette 97, no. 8 (November 22, 1919): 197–99.
[11] "American Shipbuilders," Plain Dealer, (Cleveland) (December 19, 1886), 13; for example, Charles H. Cramp, "The Steamship Merger and American Shipbuilding," North American Review 175, no. 548 (July 1902): 5–16.
[12] Causes of the Reduction of American Tonnage, H.R. Rep. 41-28, 156–57.
[13] Charles H. Cramp, "Our Navigation Laws," North American Review 158, no. 459 (April 1894): 433–45, 436.
[14] "Some Fallacies of Ship Builders—Captain Codman Points Out Those in an Article Written by Charles Cramp," New York Herald, April 12, 1894, 12.

[15] "Edwin S. Cramp Resigns – None of the Family Now in Shipbuilding Company," New York Times, February 15, 1907, 1.

[16] Report of the Merchant Marine Commission, S. Rep. 58-2755, 422–35.

[17] Tim Colton, "Shipbuilding History: Construction Records of U.S. and Canadian Shipbuilders and Boatbuilders," https://shipbuildinghistory.com/shipyards/large/cramp.htm.

[18] "Cramp's Will Quit Building Ships – Naval and Merchant Marine Depression Forces Yard at Philadelphia to Shut Down," New York Times, (April 27, 1927), 20.

[19] Except where noted, the sources of the description of the John Roach & Sons are Howard Grose, John Roach. Born December 25, 1813. Died January 10, 1887 (New York: Atlantic Publishing and Engraving, 1887); Leonard Alexander Swann, Jr., John Roach, Maritime Entrepreneur (Annapolis, MD: U.S. Naval Institute Press, 1965); and Tyler, American Clyde.

[20] Grose, John Roach. Born December 25, 1813. Died January 10, 1887.

[21] Swann, John Roach, Maritime Entrepreneur, 80.

[22] Swann, John Roach, Maritime Entrepreneur, 81–83. "Pacific Mail—A Crisis in Its Affairs," New York Times, August 20, 1873, 8.

[23] "Another Great Steam-Ship—Launch of the City of Tokio at Chester, Penn.," New York Times, May 14, 1874, 8.

[24] "The Pacific Mail's Plea—Testimony Heard by the Congressional Committee," New York Times, November 22, 1882, 7.

[25] "Dinner to John Roach—The Great Ship-Builder Presented with a Service of Plate," New York World, May 1, 1874, 5.

[26] "The John Roach Dinner—Last Night's Gathering at Delmonico's," New York Times, May 1, 1874, 5.

[27] "John Roach's Life Ended—Death of America's Most Noted Shipbuilder," New York Times, January 11, 1887, 3.

[28] For example, Roach, American Carrying Trade; John Roach, The Successful Maritime Policy: An Investigation into the Causes of the Decline of Our Shipping Interest (New York: American Protectionist Publishing, 1880); John Roach, England's Maritime Policy: The Cause of the Decline of American Shipping (1881); John Roach, Shall American Build Ships? (New York: H. B. Grose, 1881); Report of The Tariff Commission (Washington, DC: Government Printing Office, 1882), 1905–1935 (testimony of John Roach); "John Roach on the Stand," New York Times, September 13, 1883, 3; "Mr. Roach Carries the Day–Resolutions Embodying His Views Adopted by the Board of Trade," New York Times, January 22, 1884; "American and English Ships—Mr. John Roach Challenges Mr. Park's Statements Before the Post Office Committee," New York Times, April 20, 1888, 2.

[29] "America's Few Vessels—The Carrying Trade and Foreign Ships—Why We Have No Ships—Mr. John Roach's Opinion," New York Times, January 5, 1879, 5.

[30] For example, "Reviving the Mercantile Marine," New York Times, January 15, 1884, 8 (Roach and Codman made presentations to the Board of Trade and Transportation).
[31] "The Pacific Mail's Plea – Testimony Heard by the Congressional Committee," New York Times, November 22, 1882, 7.
[32] "John Roach and Captain Codman," New York Herald, November 25, 1882, 9.
[33] Swann, John Roach, Maritime Entrepreneur, 122–23.
[34] Henry Hall, ed., America's Successful Men of Affairs—An Encyclopedia of Contemporaneous Biography (New York: New York Tribune, 1895), 544.
[35] For example, "Some Serious Charges," Harrisburg Patriot (Pennsylvania), July 28, 1883, 2; "Roach's Bids—Secretary Chandler Accused of Having Tricked a Competing Contractor," San Francisco Bulletin, July 18, 1883, 3.
[36] U.S. Attorney General, "Dispatch Boat Dolphin," Op. Att'y Gen. 18, no. 207 (June 30, 1885).
[37] "John Roach Dying—Attacked by a Cancer Like That of Gen. Grant," New York Times, January 4, 1887, 1.
[38] "Death of John Roach—The Great American Shipbuilder at Rest," Philadelphia Inquirer, January 11, 1887, 1.
[39] "Mr. John Roach," New York Times, January 11, 1887, 4.
[40] "Claim Bills Approved—Favorable Reports for John Roach's Heirs and the Erie Railroad," New York Times, December 15, 1897, 3.
[41] 30 Stat. 1409 (April 9, 1898); 30 Stat. 1450 (June 3, 1898).
[42] Grosvenor M. Jones, Government Aid to Merchant Shipping: Study of Subsidies, Subventions, and Other Forms of State Aid in Principal Countries of the World, U.S. Department of Commerce, Special Agent Series no. 119, 1916, 8; Saugstad, Shipping and Shipbuilding Subsidies: A Study of State Aid to the Shipping and Shipbuilding Industries in Various Countries of the World, U.S., 10–11.
[43] 34 Cong. Rec. 31 (December 4, 1900).
[44] "For the Merchant Marine—Representatives of American Shipping Interests Meet in Washington to Consider Legislation," New York Times, April 8, 1897, 3.
[45] 34 Cong. Rec. 31 (December 4, 1900).
[46] S. 5024; H.R. 11312, 55th Cong., 2nd sess. (1899). S. 5590 was reported as a substitute for S. 5024 by the Senate Commerce Committee.
[47] Annual Report of the Commissioner of Navigation to the Secretary of the Treasury (1899), 35–75 and appendix A.
[48] Annual Report of the Commissioner of Navigation to the Secretary of the Treasury (1899), 34–35. This did not mean that Chamberlain completely gave up on the free ships policy. In 1911, for example, in an article that appeared in Scientific American he repeated his view the subsidies and free ships were two compatible policies. Eugene Tyler Chamberlain, "The American Merchant Marine," Scientific American 1-5, no. 3 (July 15, 1911): 44–45.

[49] For example, "Subsidies for Steamships—The Hanna-Payne Bill Is Not Extravagant in Payments to Encourage American Shipping Interests," New York Times, August 21, 189), 7 ("Chamberlain, who has prepared much of the information for members of Congress that has enabled them to support the Hanna-Payne Shipping Bill..."); "The Subsidy Bill's Fate– President's Sanction Has Not Insured Its Passage," New York Times, February 13, 1900, 5 (Chamberlain "who has supplied a great deal of information to the promoters of the Subsidy bills... "); "Pushing the Subsidy Bill," New York Times, February 20, 1900, 8 (House Republican conf. held and Griscom, Clyde, and Chamberlain were present).

[50] "The Subsidy and Bounty Bill," New York Times, August 27, 1899, 18.

[51] "Commerce and the Flag," New York Times, February 13, 1900, 6.

[52] Annual Report of the Commissioner of Navigation to the Secretary of the Treasury (1899), 42—43 and appendix A.

[53] Annual Report of the Commissioner of Navigation to the Secretary of the Treasury (1899), 42 and appendix A. Chamberlain had recommended to Congress that the Paris/New York precedent be made a general law applicable to any person willing to reflag a vessel and construct one in the United States. Annual Report of the Commissioner of Navigation to the Secretary of the Treasury (1897), 17.

[54] U.S. Congress, House, Promotion of Commerce and Increase of Foreign Trade, Etc., 55th Cong., 3rd sess., 1899, H. Rep. 55-1866; U.S. Congress, Senate, Promotion of Commerce and Increase of Foreign Trade, Etc., 55th Cong., 3rd sess., 1899, S. Rep. 55-1551; U.S. Congress, Senate, Promotion of Commerce and Increase of Foreign Trade, Etc., 55th Cong., 3d sess., 1899, S. Doc. 55-60; "Our Merchant Marine—Shipping Interests Heard before a House Committee," New York Times, January 11, 1899, 5; U.S. Congress, Senate, Navigation Laws of Foreign Nations, 55th Cong., 3rd sess., 1899, S. Doc. 55-91.

[55] U.S. Congress, Senate, National Merchant Marine, 56th Cong., 1st sess., 1900, S. Rep. 56-473.

[56] William McKinley, Inaugural Address, March 4, 1897, UC Santa Barbara, the American Presidency Project, https://www.presidency.ucsb.edu/documents/inaugural-address-43.

[57] William McKinley, President McKinley's Last Public Utterance to the People in Buffalo, New York, September 5, 1901, UC Santa Barbara, the American Presidency Project, https://www.presidency.ucsb.edu/documents/president-mckinleys-last-public-utterance-the-people-buffalo-new-york.

[58] Theodore Roosevelt, First Annual Message, December 3, 1901, UC Santa Barbara, the American Presidency Project, https://www.presidency.ucsb.edu/documents/first-annual-message-16.

[59] Republican Party Platform of 1900, June 19, 1900, UC Santa Barbara, The American Presidency Project, Republican Party Platforms, https://www.presidency.ucsb.edu/documents/republican-party-platform-1900.

[60] 1900 Democratic Party Platform, July 5, 1900, UC Santa Barbara, The American Presidency Project, Democratic Party Platforms, https://www.presidency.ucsb.edu/documents/1900-democratic-party-platform.
[61] 34 Cong. Rec. 30 (December 4, 1900).
[62] "An American Statesman," New York Times, April 28, 1899, 6.
[63] 34 Cong. Rec. 30 (December 4, 1900).
[64] 34 Cong. Rec. 1333 (January 23, 1901).
[65] 34 Cong. Rec. 1336.
[66] 34 Cong. Rec. 1608 (January 29, 1901); 34 Cong. Rec. 1832 (February 2, 1901).
[67] 34 Cong. Rec. 1608 (January 29, 1901).
[68] 34 Cong. Rec. 1607–19 (January 29, 1901).
[69] 34 Cong. Rec. 1336 (January 23, 1901).
[70] 34 Cong. Rec. 266–75 (December 13, 1900).
[71] 34 Cong. Rec. 1336 (January 23, 1901).
[72] 34 Cong. Rec. 1331–32.
[73] 34 Cong. Rec. 225–30 (December 11, 1900).
[74] 35 Cong. Rec. 2906–07 (March 17, 1902).
[75] Thomas R. Navin and Marian V. Sears, "A Study in Merger: Formation of the International Mercantile Company," Business History Review 28, no. 4 (December 1954): 291–328, 316–17.
[76] Annual Report of the Commissioner of Navigation to the Secretary of the Treasury (1901), 18.
[77] Theodore Roosevelt, Third Annual Message, December 7, 1903, UC Santa Barbara, The American Presidency Project, https://www.presidency.ucsb.edu/documents/third-annual-message-16.
[78] 33 Stat. 561 (April 28, 1904).
[79] U.S. Congress, House, Development of American Merchant Marine, 58th Cong., 2d sess., 1904, H. Rep. 58-418, 3.
[80] Marvin, American Merchant Marine. Favorable quotes were provided for book advertisements by John D. Long, the former secretary of the Navy, Charles H. Cramp and Chamberlain. "Advertisement," Boston Journal, January 17, 1903, 7; Roosevelt thanked Marvin for the dedication. "Letter from T. Roosevelt to W. Marvin (October 22, 1902)," www.theodorerooseveltcenter.org/Research/Digital-Library/Record/ImageViewer?libID=o183353.
[81] For example, Winthrop L. Marvin, "The American Ship in 1902," Scribner's Magazine 32, no. 5 (November 1902), 577–83, 583. Marvin appeared at the House Merchant Marine hearing in February 1904 to oppose the reflagging of six foreign built vessels "for the shipping interests of Boston." "Oppose Registry of Foreign Ships," Boston Herald, February 7, 1904, 7.
[82] For example, Promotion of Commerce and Increase of Foreign Trade, Etc., S. Doc. 55-60.

[83] "Editor on the Board—Winthrop L. Marvin of the Journal Nominated as Civil Service Commissioner by Gov. Crane," Boston Herald, January 24, 1901, 3.
[84] The American Steamship Association was initially called the "National American Merchant Marine Association" and Marvin was its first secretary. "Vote to Organize Private Marine," Boston Herald, January 24, 1919, 8; "American Steamship Owners' Association," Nautical Gazette 98, no. 26 (June 26, 1920): 960–61; "W. L. Marvin Dies of Stroke at 62," New York Times, February 4, 1926, 23.
[85] "Subsidies and Free Ships," Boston Herald, August 16, 1905, 6.
[86] "The American Merchant Marine," Boston Herald, July 29, 1905, 6.
[87] "Experts Oppose Free Ship Plan—Winthrop L. Marvin, Secretary of the Merchant Marine Commission, Says Expedient Was Rejected as Valueless by Them," Boston Herald, August 16, 1905, 6.
[88] Report of the Merchant Marine Commission, S. Rep. 58-2755, 3.
[89] Report of the Merchant Marine Commission, S. Rep. 58-2755, 10.
[90] Report of the Merchant Marine Commission, S. Rep. 58-2755, 11–12.
[91] Report of the Merchant Marine Commission, S. Rep. 58-2755, 11.
[92] Report of the Merchant Marine Commission. S. Rep. 58-2755, 15.
[93] Report of the Merchant Marine Commission, S. Rep. 58-2755, 38—39. Testimony received by the commission from Chamberlain described the history of the U.S. reciprocity policy and how discriminating duties were solely meant to open markets to U.S.-flag vessels and not to continue once those markets had been opened. Report of the Merchant Marine Commission., S. Rep. 58-2755, 1758—86.
[94] Report of the Merchant Marine Commission, S. Rep. 58-2755, part 2.
[95] Report of the Merchant Marine Commission, S. Rep. 58-2755, 53–54.
[96] Report of the Merchant Marine Commission, S. Rep. 58-2755, 54.
[97] U.S. Congress, Senate, Paper Relating to Discriminating Duties, 58th Cong., 3d sess., 1905, S. Doc. 58-169.
[98] Report of the Merchant Marine Commission, S. Rep. 58-2755, 46–51.
[99] Report of the Merchant Marine Commission, S. Rep. 58-2755, 20—21. The fishing bounty laws are set forth in Appendix E to the Commission Report, 73.
[100] Report of the Merchant Marine Commission., S. Rep. 58-2755, 21.
[101] Report of the Merchant Marine Commission, S. Rep. 58-2755, 60–61.
[102] "Veteran Admiral Not to See Fleet—P.F. Harrington, Oldest of All Annapolis Graduates, Will Go to Academy Instead," New York Times, May 27, 1934, 72.
[103] Alfred Thayer Mahan, The Influence of Sea Power upon History, 1660—1783 (Boston: Little, Brown, 1890).
[104] Report of the Merchant Marine Commission, S. Rep. 58-2755, 1738.
[105] Report of the Merchant Marine Commission, S. Rep. 58-2755, 1739.
[106] Report of the Merchant Marine Commission, S. Rep. 58-2755, 1746.
[107] Although often cited in support of a U.S. merchant marine, Mahan seems to have been ambivalent about the need for such an establishment. In his writings,

Mahan pointed out that a merchant marine tended to generate the need for a naval force to protect it and that the presence of a merchant marine tended to support and boost prospects for a robust naval force. However, neither tendency was an absolute: "It seems reasonable to say that, where merchant shipping exists, it tends logically to develop the protection which is called naval; but it has become perfectly evident, by concrete examples, that a navy may be necessary where there is no shipping." Allen Wescott, ed., Mahan on Naval Warfare: Selections from the Writings of Rear Admiral Alfred T. Mahan (Mineola, NY: Dover Publications, 1999, unabridged reprint of 1941 edition published by Little, Brown, Boston), 355. Indeed, Mahan wrote that "the United States, with no aggressive purpose, but merely to sustain avowed policies, for which her people are ready to fight, although unwilling to prepare, needs a navy both numerous and efficient, even if no merchant vessel ever again flies the United States flag." Wescott, Mahan on Naval Warfare, 358. At the same time, he wrote that a merchant marine was useful: "A broad basis of mercantile maritime interests and shipping will doubtless conduce to naval efficiency, by supplying a reserve of material and personnel." Wescott, Mahan on Naval Warfare, 355.

[108] Mahan, Influence of Sea Power upon History, 99.

[109] Report of the Merchant Marine Commission, S. Rep. 58-2755, 1745.

[110] 40 CONG. REC. 2551 (February 14, 1906) (The five Democrats were Elmer J. Burkett [NE], Jonathan P. Dolliver [IA], Robert M. La Follette Sr. [WI], John C. Spooner [WI] and William Warner [MO]).

[111] U.S. Congress, House, Development of the American Merchant Marine and American Commerce, 59th Cong., 1st sess., 1905, H. Doc. 59-56; U.S. Congress, House, Development of the American Merchant Marine and American Commerce, 59th Cong., 1st sess., 1906, H. Doc. 59-564; Development of the American Merchant Marine and American Commerce, H. Doc. 59-564, 3–13.

[112] Development of the American Merchant Marine and American Commerce, H. Doc. 59-564, 14–20.

[113] "Army Faces Collapse in War, Says Staff—Helpless to Strike Quick Blow without a Merchant Marine, New York Times, January 15, 1906, 4.

[114] "Root's Plea to Nation for Ship Subsidies," New York Times, November 21, 1906, 6.

[115] U.S. Congress, House, American Merchant Marine, 59th Cong., 2nd sess., 1907, H. Doc. 59-553; "President for Subsidy Bill," New York Times, May 18, 1906, 1.

[116] "Sharp Committee Tilt on Ship Subsidy Bill," New York Times, December 14, 1906) 7; U.S. Congress, House, Development of the American Merchant Marine and American Commerce, 59th Cong., 2nd sess., 1907, H. Rep. 59-6442.

[117] Development of the American Merchant Marine and American Commerce, H. Rep. 59-6442, part 2.

[118] 41 CONG. REC. 4372-4376 (March 1, 1907).

[119] Representative Wesley Jones voted on each occasion in favor of the legislation.

[120] Theodore Roosevelt, Eighth Annual Message, December 8, 1908, UC Santa Barbara, The American Presidency Project, https://www.presidency.ucsb.edu/documents/eighth-annual-message-4; U.S. Congress, Senate, Development of the American Ocean Mail Service and American Commerce, 60th Cong., 1st sess., 1908, S. Doc. 60-225; U.S. Congress, Senate, Trade Follows the Flag, 60th Cong., 1st sess., 1908, S. Doc. 60-375.

[121] 42 Cong. Rec. 3647 (March 20, 1908); 43 CONG. REC. 3694 (March 21, 1909).

[122] William Howard Taft, First Annual Message, December 7, 1909, UC Santa Barbara, The American Presidency Project, https://www.presidency.ucsb.edu/documents/first-annual-message-17; "Taft Favors Ship Subsidy," Times-Picayune, October 1, 1909, 15; "The Ship Subsidy Grab Defeated," Times-Picayune, March 3, 1909, 6; "Ship Subsidy in Congressional Disfavor," Seattle Daily Times, October 4, 1909, 1.

[123] 43 CONG. REC. 3681–83 (March 2, 1909).

[124] "Congressman Steenerson of Minnesota, Does He Represent the Foreign Shipping Interests or His Own District?" American Flag 8 (December 1, 1909), 3–15.

[125] "Congressman Steenerson of Minnesota, Does He Represent the Foreign Shipping Interests or His Own District?" 4–15.

[126] 45 CONG. REC. 2555 (March 1, 1910).

[127] U.S. Congress, House, Report and Hearings of the Select Committee Appointed to Investigate Certain Charges Under House Resolution 543, 61st Cong., 3rd sess., 1911, H. Rep. 61-2297.

[128] "Steamship Lobby Hard to Corner," New York Times, November 29, 1910, 3; "Ship Subsidy Lobby Inquiry," New York Times, December 1, 1910, 4.

[129] Report and Hearings of the Select Committee Appointed to Investigate Certain Charges Under House Resolution 543, H. Rep. 61-2297, 1374–88.

[130] For example, "Ship Subsidy Probe Develops a Scandal–Money Offered to Buy Influence of a Newspaper," Times-Picayune, January 26, 1911, 3; "Tells of Subsidy Bribes," Baltimore Sun, January 26, 1911, 2; "Charges Bribery for Ship Subsidy," Plain Dealer (Cleveland), January 26, 1911, 5.

[131] 46 CONG. REC. 1822 (February 2, 1911).

[132] There was reason to believe that U.S. subsidies would be met by new or increased foreign subsidies. For example, "Our Subsidy Scheme Frightens Britishers," New York Times, February 16, 1905, 2.

[133] 46 CONG. REC. 1825 (February 2, 1911).

[134] U.S. Congress, House, Views and Two Reports on Subject of Adequate Merchant Marine, 74th Cong., 1st sess., 1935, H. Doc. 74-118, 2.

Falls of Clyde, circa 1900, National Maritime Historical Society

CHAPTER 13—COASTWISE TRADE

While the foreign trading fleet suffered after the Civil War, the domestic or coastwise trading fleet prospered. From 1865 to 1914, the aggregate tonnage of vessels predominantly in the foreign trade declined from about 1.6 million tons to about 1.1 million tons.[1] The aggregate tonnage of vessels predominantly in the domestic trade increased from about 3.5 million tons to 6.7 million tons.[2]

The fleet grew in tandem with an expansive American view of what should be reserved for U.S.-flag vessels in terms of both activity and geography. In terms of activity, the 1817 Act cargo reservation was expanded expressly to cover carriage of passengers as well as dredging.[3] In terms of geography, the domestic reservation started as a "coastal" or "coasting" concept, which encompassed voyages along a single coastline—like a portion of the East Coast—and grew to encompass trade between the East and West Coasts when the goods were transshipped by land across the Panamanian isthmus. Subsequently, the concept was expanded across oceans, as the United States added Alaska, Hawaii, and Puerto Rico to its dominion.

PASSENGERS AND DREDGING

The 1817 Act restricted U.S.-flag vessels to the importation of "goods, wares, or merchandise" from one U.S. port to another U.S. port. The absence of any mention of passengers or other activities was eventually felt.

Specifically, it became apparent by the 1880s that there was an exploitable loophole in the law since there was no penalty to be paid by foreign vessels transporting passengers in the coastwise trade. A penalty of two dollars per passenger was enacted in 1886.[4] Dingley, the floor leader for the legislation, pointed out that a problem arose because of "Canadian vessels on the lakes" and "it has been suggested by the Treasury Department that the penalty... will be sufficient to break up this practice."[5]

Although the law was simple, it nevertheless acquired the grand name "Passenger Vessel Services Act" or "PVSA."[6]

It turned out that the penalty was insufficient, particularly "on long and expensive voyages from the Pacific coast of the United States to Alaska"; consequently, Treasury requested an increase to $200 per passenger in 1898.[7] Congress increased the penalty and tightened the reservation to make it applicable to the transportation of passengers "either directly or by way of a foreign port."[8]

The impetus to cover dredging, as with passengers, started with foreign vessels entering the U.S. market. The foreign dredge *Holm* was contracted to assist in grade raising in Galveston in the years following the devastating 1900 hurricane. She was owned by an American corporation and arrived to start work in June 1904.[9] Several more German-built, American-owned dredges were also ordered for the Galveston work.[10] Newspapers started to warn of a potential "invasion of dredges from Europe."[11]

Chamberlain noted that "the use of the dredge is contrary to the spirit of the law which restricts the coasting trade to vessels of the United States." But he also opined that dredging did not violate the 1817 Act unless there was "transportation" involved.[12] The Justice Department concurred.[13]

The House Merchant Marine Committee recommended enactment of legislation to prohibit foreign dredging but to grandfather the existing foreign dredges, so long as they continued their existing contracts.[14] Congress agreed to name five grandfathered dredges in the law, including one that had been ordered but not yet delivered.[15] The law did not define "dredging," leaving the definition to be fleshed out by administrative interpretation over time.[16]

The Galveston dredging episode was associated with tragedy. One of the dredgers ordered from Europe, the *Texas,* sank off the coast of Ireland on December 24, 1904, with the immediate loss of thirty-one crew members.[17] Thirteen men made it to a single lifeboat, with twelve surviving for fourteen days until rescued. The rescue occurred just as the survivors were in the process of choosing lots as to who to eat.

Another dredge—the *Galveston*—was also ordered from a German shipyard by an American company.[18] The American contractor doing the work in Galveston rejected the *Galveston* as being defective, leaving her in legal limbo.[19] According to newspapers reports, the vessel captain claimed the crew – consisting of "one American, one Porto Rican, seven Norwegians, three Swedes, three Germans, three Englishmen, one Irishman, one Dane and two Spaniards" – then mutinied when the vessel sailed from Havana to New Orleans (the crew claimed they were only defending themselves.)[20] There was also a Chilean and two Italians, but they were among the five missing crew members who had jumped ship and presumably drowned to escape the captain.

One headline read, "Fights and Free Use of Arms, with Five Men Missing from Ill-Fated Vessel." The *Galveston* was arrested in federal court in New Orleans by the crew and a contractor seeking unpaid wages and payments.[21] The case was eventually settled, and the *Galveston* was sold to the Canadian government.[22] It was said that the vessel "holds the record for getting into trouble."[23]

Philippines and Hawaii

The Spanish-American War brought the United States into possession of the former Spanish colonies in Cuba, Guam, Philippines, and Puerto Rico and indirectly into possession of Hawaii. The nation relinquished control over Cuba over time, leaving trade between the United States and Cuba to bilateral trade negotiations.[24] Puerto Rico, of course, was not relinquished.[25] Vessels owned by Puerto Rican nationals prior to the date of annexation became eligible for the U.S. registry as of the date of annexation, as had occurred with the Louisiana Purchase and the acquisition of Alaska.[26] How the Philippines and Hawaii were to be treated, however, presented their own unique problems.

Philippines. Spain ceded the Philippine Islands to the United States under the Treaty of Paris signed on December 10, 1898, ending the war.[27] The United States also agreed "to admit Spanish ships and merchandise to the ports of the Philippine Islands on the same terms as ships and merchandise of the United States" for ten years.

The interpretation in the Philippines was that the country was still foreign territory for customs purposes. In August 1898, shortly after the fall of Manila, the U.S. commanding general issued an order reopening the customs house in Manila and mandating that pre-existing Spanish tariffs and duties continue to apply.[28] President William McKinley also restricted trade between the United States and Puerto Rico to U.S.-flag vessels, but not with the Philippines.[29]

The U.S. peace negotiators in Paris appeared to agree with that approach. They issued a treaty interpretation that the agreement "to place Spanish vessels and merchandise on the same footing as American *is not intended to be exclusive.*"[30] As Chamberlain indicated, "It is the understanding of the Bureau that the navigation laws generally are not, under the treaty of Paris, to be applied to trade between the United States and the Philippines" because of this interpretation.[31]

The U.S. Supreme Court complicated matters with several Puerto Rico decisions, particularly *Huus v. New York & Porto Rico Steamship Company,* rendered in 1901.[32] The court determined that trade with Puerto Rico became domestic trade "since the treaty of annexation." This, together with annexation legislation that followed, had placed Puerto Rico "substantially upon the coast of the United States." Together with a series of other Supreme Court decisions, known as the "Insular Cases," the court grappled with the meaning of territories like the Philippines.[33]

These events put Chamberlain betwixt and between. Having stated that the navigation laws would not apply (i.e., the Philippines was foreign), Chamberlain nevertheless issued a Treasury

Department circular stating that no tonnage tax would be collected from vessels coming from the Philippines because no such tax was collected from vessels coming from a U.S. port.[34]

Whether the Philippines was part of the United States for purposes of the coastwise trade came up in the consideration of the 1902 Philippine Organic Act. The 1902 Act was later superseded in 1916 by the Philippine Autonomy Act, also confusingly known as the "Jones Act" after Representative William A. Jones (D-VA).[35] The 1902 Act was shepherded through the Senate by Senator Henry Cabot Lodge, chairman of the Committee on the Philippines, known as the "Lodge Committee."

Democrats took the opportunity to embarrass Republicans with the incongruity of having added the Philippines to the United States but not having extended U.S. navigation laws to that territory. Senator Augustus O. Bacon (D-GA), who had been a captain in the Confederate army and was an opponent of overseas U.S. expansion, needled Lodge. He argued that anything the War Department and the Treasury Department had done not to reserve the trade between the Philippines and the United States or among Philippine islands to U.S. vessels had been illegal because the Philippines had been ceded to the United States.[36]

Lodge admitted that permitting foreign vessels into the Philippines' "domestic trade" "is of necessity unlawful," but pressing the point would simply paralyze trade because of the lack of qualified U.S.-flag vessels.[37] He said that the War Department "trusted that Congress" would back up their decisions. Bacon argued that "no emergency can authorize an officer of a department of this Government to violate the statute law." Senator John H. Mitchell (R-OR) retorted, "Would the Senator from Georgia... arraign the Secretary of the Treasury... for permitting certain foreign vessels to clear to our outlying possessions?"[38]

Another criticism came from Senator Stephen Mallory II (D-FL), the son of the former Confederate secretary of the Navy, who argued that U.S. coastwise laws already applied as confirmed by the *Huus* case and noted the incongruity of considering giving bounties to U.S. vessel owners and then denying them the benefits of the coastwise trade.[39] As he said, "our statutes do not recognize any other than the two distinct divisions of maritime or water-borne commerce than the foreign and the coastwise trade," and so the Philippines had to be in one or the other.

The 1902 Act as proposed would have affirmed those administrative acts. It would have treated the Philippines as foreign territory by expressly putting off the application of the coastwise laws to the Philippines indefinitely. Lodge argued that postponing the application of the coastwise laws was necessary because of the lack of U.S.-flag vessels for the trade. But that trade restriction would be imposed as soon as that situation was remedied.[40] Lodge accepted a two-year definite commencement of the coastwise restriction, and that is how the law was enacted.[41]

The Philippine Commission, which had been appointed to govern the Philippines, and the War Department then agitated to extend the date. Secretary of War William H. Taft wrote to Representative Charles Grosvenor in April 1904 about the "disaster which would follow the application of the coastwise laws to the interisland trade in the Philippine Islands."[42] The commission argued that "nothing could be more disastrous to these islands" than having the coastwise laws go into effect in 1904.[43] Further, "it would be selfish exploitation of these islands of an indefensible character to exclude vessels now in the trade and... would furnish just ground for reproach against a government professing good will and doing evil."[44] Congress in 1904 extended the date to 1906, and in 1906 postponed it again to April 11, 1909, when the Treaty of Paris concession to Spanish vessels (and arguably all vessels) would expire.[45]

The Philippine Commission argued in 1908 that "nothing further appears necessary to establish the wisdom" of a permanent extension of the application of the coastwise laws than the fact that notwithstanding the various acts, only 13 of the 366 steam ships cleared by customs in trade between the Philippines and the United States in the fiscal year ended June 30,

1908, were American.⁴⁶ And so in 1908, a permanent extension of the non-application of the coastwise laws was enacted.⁴⁷

Hawaii. The Kingdom of Hawaii, long an independent sovereign nation, signed a commercial treaty with the United States in 1875, leading to a boom in American-controlled sugar plantations. Many Hawaiians had been fearful that the treaty would increase U.S. influence over the islands and lead to calls for U.S. annexation. Those fears were well-founded and eventually borne-out by the January 17, 1893, overthrow of the government of Queen Lili'uokalani by a group including U.S. citizens. Their goal was U.S. annexation. The controversial overthrow was aided by the American minister to Hawaii, who requested that U.S. Marines from the cruiser *U.S.S. Boston* (one of the original "ABCD" vessels with Dewey at Manila Bay) land for the ostensible purpose of protecting American property.

Annexation divided American opinion at the time. Chamberlain, for example, wrote in December 1893 in an article entitled "The Invasion of Hawaii" that "the theory of insular colonial expansion by conquest... will find scant favor among the people of the United States."⁴⁸ One hundred years later, in 1993, the U.S. Congress adopted a resolution signed by President Bill Clinton apologizing "for the overthrow of the Kingdom of Hawaii."⁴⁹

One annexation issue was the Hawaiian vessel registry. Hawaii had been registering vessels since the early nineteenth century under the "Sandwich Island Registry."⁵⁰ The U.S. Government alleged as early as 1848 that the Hawaiian register was too lax in its oversight of registry eligibility.⁵¹

The mechanism usually employed was to have Hawaiian citizens present themselves as the vessel's owner. This was accomplished by having the non-Hawaiian owner transfer title to a Hawaiian citizen. That citizen would simultaneously mortgage or charter the vessel back to the non-Hawaiian together with a power of attorney in favor of the non-Hawaiian true owner.⁵²

JOURNEY TO THE JONES ACT

The U.S. government communicated on February 17, 1893, to the Hawaiian provisional government its opposition to "a movement... to place a number of foreign vessels under Hawaiian registry, with a view to eventually obtain the benefits of United States registry."[53] This was occurring because U.S. annexation was anticipated as inevitable. Those behind the "movement" noticed that the U.S. had granted U.S. registry to vessels built outside the United States and owned by citizens of Louisiana in 1804 and Alaska in 1868 when those territories were acquired.[54]

Among those intent on taking advantage of the situation was Claus Spreckels, a leading U.S. industrialist, who also owned a substantial Hawaii sugar farm and a shipping line, the Oceanic Steamship Company, that served Hawaii.[55] Spreckels boasted in March 1893 that he would save millions in U.S. vessel-building costs by registering non-U.S. built vessels in Hawaii and then have those vessels be grandfathered into the U.S. flag upon annexation of Hawaii.[56]

The entry into the U.S. flag of vessels via the Hawaii back door alarmed U.S. shipping interests. In June 1897 Senator William Frye informed the Hawaiian foreign minister that annexation was being impeded by provisional vessel registration, and he wrote to President McKinley to the same effect.[57] The Hawaiian government cabled its consuls to stop the provisional registry practice in July 1897, but registrations continued.[58]

The Hawaiian government reacted by refusing permanent registry of such vessels.[59] A test case arose before the Hawaiian Supreme Court involving the foreign-built steamship *China* registered by George W. Macfarlane. He had served as colonel of the military staff of Hawaiian king Kalākaua and was his final chamberlain.[60] The typical arrangement of transferring title and mortgaging the vessel back to the real owner was used.

The Hawaii collector-general of customs refused to register the vessel, and Macfarlane sued to force the registration.[61] It was disclosed in the initial court proceedings that the refusal was because Hawaii had assured the United States that no more foreign vessels would be registered. The Circuit Court judge wrote that Hawaiian law did not prohibit trust arrangements in favor of a non-citizen, unlike U.S. registration law. The lack of such prohibition meant that the only factor for consideration was legal title—which Macfarlane patently had.

On September 27, 1897, the Hawaii Supreme Court agreed that Hawaiian law only required that the vessel be "wholly owned by a subject... of this Kingdom." Macfarlane was such a "subject" and the bill of sale meant he "wholly owned" the vessel. The *China* decision opened the door to several other vessels that were registered under similar circumstances.[62]

Hawaii finally made its registry law more stringent in May 1898 by copying a portion of U.S. registration law.[63] All applicants had to swear "that there is no citizen or subject of any foreign Prince or State directly or indirectly by way of trust, confidence or otherwise interested in such vessel," which would seem to have closed the door on the schemes.[64] The *Hawaiian Star* newspaper opined that registry law change was "an annexation measure pure and simple," intended to remove annexation opposition.[65]

A U.S. congressional resolution followed in July 1898 known as the "Newlands Resolution" after Representative Francis G. Newlands (D-NV) annexing Hawaii.[66] Hawaiian state sovereignty was transferred to the United States on August 12, 1898. Dewey's victory at Manila Bay in May 1898 highlighted the importance of Hawaii as a base and likely spurred annexation, which had languished since 1893.[67] The Newlands Resolution also formed a commission to recommend appropriate legislation and made Hawaii's international relations subservient to U.S. foreign policies. But it reserved to the interim Hawaiian government "municipal legislation" not inconsistent with U.S. law. This was the final vessel loophole.

The congressional commission recommended that "commerce between the United States and Hawaii... should be so protected by our navigation laws and vessel registry... as to give to our country and to our newly acquired people all the advantages which should properly come to either."[68] The commission also recommended that "all vessels carrying Hawaiian registers immediately prior to the transfer of sovereignty of the Hawaiian Islands to the United States shall be entitled to be registered as American vessels."[69] The commission's report was conveyed to Congress on December 6, 1898.[70]

About two weeks later, on December 21, Capt. William Matson—the founder of Matson Navigation Company—took over the British-flag iron hull four-masted sailing vessel the *Falls of Clyde* and obtained a provisional register from the Hawaiian consul in San Francisco.[71] Reports conflicted as to whether the beneficial owner was Matson or the John D. Spreckels Bros. Company. Matson had a close connection to the Spreckels having served as the captain of the family yacht.[72]

The legal owner of the *Falls of Clyde* was Arthur Morgan Brown, then the marshal of the Republic of Hawaii. Again, the Hawaiian government resisted registration and again was overruled by the Hawaii Supreme Court on June 5, 1899.[73] The court decided that vessel registration was a "municipal law" and not a matter of foreign relations.

The U.S. government had had enough. The Treasury Department and the U.S. attorney general took the position that the Newlands Resolution removed Hawaii government authority to register vessels.[74] President McKinley issued an executive order on September 18, 1899, ordering the cessation of any further Hawaiian vessel registration.[75]

The question then turned to what to do about vessels like the *Falls of Clyde*, which had been registered by Hawaii in June 1899 after the formal annexation of Hawaii had occurred on August 12, 1898, but before the McKinley order.[76] The question was resolved in the Organic Act which provided for a Hawaii territorial government and became law on April 30, 1900. That Act included the commission-recommended provision that vessels registered prior to August 12 owned by either U.S. citizens or Hawaiian citizens would become U.S.-flag vessels.[77] In addition, five vessels were specifically enumerated in the Organic Act as being eligible for U.S. registry including the *Falls of Clyde*.[78]

Members of Congress viewed the enumeration of these vessels with suspicion. Senator Richard F. Pettigrew (R-SD), for example, called one of the vessel purchases a sham. Although usually loath to permit exceptions to the U.S.-build requirement, Frye defended the enumeration.[79] He argued that there were only a few affected vessels, they were "engaged in the sugar trade and peculiarly fitted for it," and "there was no really good reason given why it should not be extended to them."[80]

The five named vessels were included in the law plus those registered before August 1898.[81] Other vessels also obtained special permissions by law.[82] It was later reported that sixty-three vessels obtained U.S. registry via the Organic Act, although many were small vessels.[83]

In retrospect, Chamberlain reported that the withdrawal of British and Japanese passenger vessels from the Hawaii trade as a result of the imposition of U.S. coastwise law had affected Hawaii negatively but that U.S.-flag interests were "rapidly beginning to remove any embarrassment on this ground by providing transportation facilities which will be superior to those hitherto possessed by the island."[84] He also stated that the "application of the coasting laws to Hawaii has already been a powerful stimulus to American shipbuilding."[85]

The *Falls of Clyde* was operated by Matson until 1907, making about sixty voyages to and from Hawaii and then was sold. Much later, after several vessel iterations, she was placed in museum status in Hawaii. There were, at one time, plans to take her to Glasgow (where she was built) for a full restoration.[86]

COASTWISE WHACK-A-MOLE

Wrecked Vessels—the Merrimac. The U.S. Congress routinely enacted special legislation in the early nineteenth century to permit U.S. registration of named foreign vessels wrecked in the United States and substantially repaired in U.S. shipyards.[87] In 1852 Congress decided to regularize the practice with a law permitting the Treasury Department to grant U.S.-flag privileges to foreign-built vessels wrecked in the United States. They had to be owned by U.S. citizens and at least three-fourths of the final value had to be expended on "repairs" in a U.S. shipyard.[88]

The law ran into trouble because the Justice Department interpreted what constituted "repairs" broadly. Justice permitted, for example, dockage fees to be counted as "repairs" meaning that a vessel might satisfy the value test by just being tied up to a pier long enough.[89] In 1898 Senator Elkins attempted to restrict reflagged vessels to the foreign trade and make them ineligible for the coastwise trade.[90] The Senate Commerce Committee reported at the time that existing law "furnishes an opportunity for fraudulent statements and estimates as to the cost of repairs."[91] In 1906 Representative Charles Grosvenor said that "some of the most rascally performances that have come to our knowledge... have been the fraudulent introduction of these ships that have pretended to be wrecked and very often had not been wrecked at all."[92]

The most famous of these "wrecked" vessels was the collier *Merrimac*, which played an outsized role in the Spanish-American War. She was built as the *Solveig* in Britain in the town of Wallsend in November 1894. In early 1897, she was damaged in a pier fire while in Newport News, Virginia.[93] Subsequently, she was purchased by a U.S. company and an application was made to register her under the U.S. flag.[94]

The Navy purchased her in April 1898 to be used as a collier for the highest price paid for a U.S.-flag collier during the war ($342,000;[95] for comparison, the *Nanshan*, which served Dewey, cost about $155,000).[96] Representative John W. Gaines (D-TN) threatened an investigation since it was alleged that the Navy Board of Auxiliary Cruisers had first turned down purchasing the vessel at $100,000.[97] The criticism continued after the war. For example, some noted that "nothing has been bought by the government during this war in which there has not been a steal."[98]

The *Merrimac* was found to be in poor condition when she joined the fleet blockading Cuba. Commodore Winfield Scott Schley cabled Secretary John Long on May 27, 1898, reporting that the vessel had to be towed to Key West, delaying the movements of U.S. naval vessels.[99] Temporary repairs were made in Key West to enable her to at least able to sail on her own.[100]

When a squadron of Spanish warships evaded the U.S. blockade and managed to make it into Santiago harbor in Cuba, a plan was hatched to sink a vessel in the narrow channel and block the exit of those vessels. The *Merrimac* was considered the most expendable candidate. "Naval Constructor" Lt. Richmond Pearson Hobson was chosen to make the vessel ready for the daring mission.[101]

Hobson, from Alabama, had graduated first in his class from the U.S. Naval Academy. However, he was not always popular because he did not drink or smoke.[102] Later in life, he was Democratic member of Congress from Alabama from 1907 to 1915 and a leading speaker for the Anti-Saloon League, as was Senator Wesley Jones. Hobson apparently prevailed on Rear Admiral William Thomas Sampson to lead the mission and six volunteers joined him for what was commonly thought to be a suicide run. A seventh stowed away.

The vessel sailed under cover of darkness on June 2, 1898, and made it into the channel but was then fired upon by the Spanish.[103] A fortuitous shot disabled the *Merrimac's* steering gear and only some of the explosive charges worked. But the vessel sank, only not in a place to block the harbor exit. None of the *Merrimac's* crew were severely injured. They swam to a raft and were captured next morning by a launch with the commander of the Spanish fleet, Adm. Pascual Cervera y Topete, on board.[104] The press derisively referred to the *Merrimac* as "an expensive cork."[105]

JOURNEY TO THE JONES ACT

Even before Hobson and his seven comrades had been exchanged for Spanish prisoners, they had become instant U.S. celebrities and the story of their mission appeared in hundreds of newspapers.[106] Hobson kissed so many women at publicity events as he crossed the country by train for his next posting in the Philippines (for example, reportedly five hundred in Denver) that it became somewhat of a national embarrassment.[107]

All eight of the *Merrimac* crew were later awarded Medals of Honor. In his message to Congress on December 5, 1898, President McKinley said that the episode "thrilled not alone the hearts of our countrymen but the world by its exceptional heroism."[108] The Navy said in its 1898 *Annual Report* that "probably one hundred persons can claim that the sinking of the *Merrimac* was due to their having suggested it to the Department."[109]

The fact that the *Merrimac* entered the U.S. flag via the wrecked-vessel exception was not neglected. In his 1905 Merchant Marine Commission testimony, the shipbuilder Edwin Cramp adamantly opposed the wrecked-vessel exception. He referred to the process of approving vessels for reflagging as a "commercial crime" and wrecked vessels "whitewashed tramps" and "floating coffins."[110] He called the *Merrimac* "the most celebrated" of these vessels which "saved her reputation by being sunk at Santiago."

Chamberlain complained in 1905 that the U.S. attorney general had so interpreted the law that the "literal words" were "far from conveying the precise meaning of the operation of the act."[111] He also wrote that twenty-two of the fifty-six U.S.-flag vessels built abroad as of June 1905 had come in under the wrecked-vessel exception (the rest mainly via individual acts of Congress and the Hawaii annexation).

Frye introduced legislation in 1906 to repeal the wrecked-vessel exception and resume the practice of granting such reflag permissions only by act of Congress. Representative David A. De Armond (D-MO) objected, arguing that the legislation "is in the interest of a comparatively few shipbuilders... and in perpetuation of a policy [the U.S. build requirement] which has well-nigh driven the American merchant marine from the seas."[112] Representative Charles Grosvenor argued that the administrative process had proven unworkable and the legislation was requested by the secretary of commerce.[113] Republicans were then in control of both chambers of the Fifty-Ninth Congress. The repeal legislation became law after a party line vote in the House.[114]

Beginning in 1913, the tables turned in the Sixty-Third Congress when Democrats were in control of both chambers. Senator Duncan U. Fletcher (D-FL), a staunch defender of the Confederate cause and Senator Jones's immediate predecessor as chairman of the Senate Commerce Committee from 1916 to 1919, introduced legislation to reinstate the wrecked-vessel exception. It included changes to help prevent fraud. The accompanying Senate report claimed that it was "manifestly absurd" for a vessel salvaged and repaired in the United States at substantial expense to only be able to obtain U.S. registry via an Act of Congress.[115] Despite Republican and Commerce Department opposition, the legislation nevertheless was enacted in 1915 and is still the law today.[116]

Port-to-Port Evasions. The 1817 Act contained a simple definition, proven naïve by subsequent events, of what constituted restricted domestic trade. As Chamberlain indicated in 1898, voyages of "mixed description" were not "contemplated when our laws were framed."[117] The Act governed the transportation of merchandise from "one port of the United States to another port of the United States." Both transshipment and mixed land and water evasions developed to avoid using U.S.-flag vessels mainly in connection with Alaskan trade.

The first change to the 1817 Act, enacted in 1866, was specifically designed to prevent foreign transshipment of cargoes between two U.S. ports, but only when the merchandise was shipped from a port "on the northern, northeastern, or northwestern frontiers" of the United States.[118] In other words, Canadian transshipments were targeted. The compilers of the U.S. statutes added to that provision the Treaty of Washington guarantee of "free navigation" on the Yukon and other rivers.[119]

JOURNEY TO THE JONES ACT

In 1892 the law was tested by a shipper of 250 kegs of U.S. manufactured nails shipped from New York to Antwerp in a Belgian vessel. Then the nails were shipped on another foreign vessel to the U.S. west coast.[120] U.S. Customs sought to forfeit the kegs when they arrived at their destination as being shipped in violation of the 1817 Act. A federal district court determined that the shipment was a "palpable evasion" of the law, but not prohibited because the 1817 Act only prohibited direct shipment from one U.S. port to a second one.

Congress moved to close the "250 kegs of nails" foreign transshipment loophole.[121] The phrase "via any foreign port" was added to the 1817 law in 1893 at the instigation of Representative Dingley and Senator Frye.[122]

A further loophole developed with respect to voyages where a U.S.-flag vessel only undertook part of the overall transportation. Frye and Sereno Payne, then chairman of the Merchant Marine Committee, explained in early 1898 that there were plans to ship cargo from Seattle to Vancouver in a U.S.-flag vessel, land it, and then load it on a foreign vessel for shipment to Alaska.[123] They sought to add the words "or for any part of the voyage" to close the loophole by requiring that a U.S.-flag vessel or vessels undertake the entirety of the voyage.

In a colloquy with Representative William H. Moody (R-MA), Payne said that the provision did not affect transportation by rail and "refers entirely to goods brought in vessels and transferred to other vessels."[124] The law, enacted February 17, 1898, also limited the U.S. coastwise trade for the first time to "vessels of the United States."[125]

The next momentous evasion occurred in 1912 and concerned mixed land and water transportation. The question arose whether it was lawful to ship cargo by a U.S.-flag vessel from Seattle to Skagway, Alaska, then by rail to Whitehorse, Canada, and finally by river on Canadian vessels to Fairbanks, Alaska.

In a January 1913 opinion, U.S. Attorney General George W. Wickersham found the transportation lawful because the

1898 amendment concerned only water transportation and did not proscribe mixed land and water transportation.[126] He was persuaded in part by the floor statements regarding the purpose of the 1898 law and the Payne-Moody colloquy that the law did not affect rail transportation.

This was the opinion that Representative William Humphrey tried to interest Representative Oscar Underwood in addressing, without success, in connection with the Underwood Tariff Act of 1913.[127] The Wickersham opinion, combined with expanded Canadian rail service in western Canada, were the main reasons for amending U.S. coastwise law in the 1920 Merchant Marine Act.

---

[1] Annual Report of the Commissioner of Navigation to the Secretary of the Commerce (1914), 172.
[2] Both "registered" and "enrolled and licensed" vessels had to meet the same criteria to be considered "vessels of the United States." A registered vessel could engage in international trade but had to surrender its certificate of registry to be enrolled and licensed to engage in the domestic trade. Similarly, an enrolled and licensed vessel had to trade in its enrollment and license for a certificate of registry to trade foreign. Tax rates, fees, and documentation varied depending on whether a vessel was sailing within the same "collection district" or going to another "collection district" or to another "great district." Laws of the United States Relating to Navigation and the Merchant Marine (Washington, DC: Government Printing Office, 1895); Robert O. McDonald, "Documentation and Transfer of Vessels; Transfer of United States Vessels to Aliens," Tulane Law Review 47, no. 3 (April 1973): 511–34, 511–15.
[3] 24 Stat. 79, 81 (June 19, 1886).
[4] 24 Stat. 79, 81 (June 19, 1886).
[5] 17 Cong. Rec. 1108 (February 3, 1886).
[6] 24 Stat. 79, 81 (June 19, 1886); U.S. Customs and Border Protection, for example, in its current administration of the U.S. coastwise laws refers to that penalty section as the "Passenger Vessel Services Act" or "PVSA." U.S. Customs and Border Protection, an Informed Compliance Publication, What Ever Member of the Trade Community Should Know About: The Passenger Vessel Services Act (An Informed Compliance Publication: April 2010).
[7] 31 Cong. Rec. 1729–30 (February 15, 1898).
[8] 30 Stat. 248 (February 17, 1898).

JOURNEY TO THE JONES ACT

[9] "Raising Galveston's Grade—Dredge Holm Commences Operation on the Canal," Dallas Morning News, July 2, 1904, 4; "Galveston–A Story of Rehabilitation," Dallas Morning News, June 18, 1905, 4-5.

[10] "Dredge for Galveston–Last of Grade Raising Fleet Sail from Holland," San Antonio Express, December 20, 1904, 3.

[11] "How the Holm Got In," Sun and New York Press, December 22, 1904, 9.

[12] Annual Report of the Commissioner of Navigation to the Secretary of the Treasury (1904), 25—26.

[13] U.S. Congress, Senate, Foreign-Built Dredges, 59th Cong., 1st sess., 1906, S. Rep. 59-2384.

[14] U.S. Congress, House, Foreign-Built Dredges, 59th Cong., 1st sess., 1906, H. Rep. 59-1341. The same legislation as amended was reported favorably by the Merchant Marine Committee at the end of the 58th Congress. U.S. Congress, House, Foreign-Built Dredges, 58th Cong., 3rd sess., 1905, H. Rep. 58-4591.

[15] 34 Stat. 204 (May 28, 1906). Opponents of the grandfather provision requested that it only apply after a federal judge had adjudicated whether existing coastwise laws prohibited the dredging activities undertaken by the foreign dredges. Foreign-Built Dredges, S. Rep. 59-2384.

[16] For example, U.S. Customs and Border Protection, Customs Service Decision 79-331 (December 28, 1978).

[17] "Galveston Dredge Foundered at Sea," San Antonio Express, January 12, 1905, 6; "Awful Suffering of Dredge's Crew," Baltimore American, March 2, 1905, 8; "Story of Suffering– Captain of Wrecked Dredge Boat Texas Reaches New York," Dallas Morning News, March 2, 1905, 6.

[18] "United States District Court – Hearing on the Galveston Case," Times Picayune, December 8, 1905, 5; "In the Courts—The Dredge Galveston Pronounced American, but Not Registered," Times Picayune, December 22, 1905, 4.

[19] "To Return Dredge—Contractors to Send Galveston back to Germany," Dallas Morning News, June 27, 1905, 2; "Dredge Released on Bond–Galveston, after Perils of All Sorts, Goes Free Again," Dallas Morning News, November 29, 1905, 9.

[20] "Mutiny and Desperate Encounters on Galveston—Fights and Free Use of Arms, with Five Men Missing from Ill-Fated Vessel," Times-Picayune, September 22, 1905, 8; "Forced Three Men into the Sea—Rest of Crew of Dredge Galveston Were Then Almost Starved by Brutal Captain," Pensacola Journal, September 23, 1905, 9.

[21] "United States District Court—Hearing on the Galveston Case," Times Picayune, December 8, 1905, 5.

[22] "The Galveston Dredge Case Settled," Times Picayune, January 21, 1906, 4.

[23] "Dredge Galveston Sold," Times Picayune, April 30, 1906, 5.

[24] Report of the Merchant Marine Commission, S. Rep. 58-2755, 1786–87 (Chamberlain testimony).

[25] 31 Stat. 77 (April 12, 1900) (known as the "Foraker Act").

[26] By an 1899 executive order, vessels owned by inhabitants of Puerto Rico and the Philippines were entitled, after meeting certain conditions, to receive a U.S. government-issued "certificate of protection entitling the vessel to which it is issued to the protection and flag of the United States" like the consular certificates likely issued to Nanshan and the Zafiro. Annual Report of the Commissioner of Navigation to the Secretary of the Treasury (1899), 205–10. Laws in 1804 and 1868 performed the same function for Louisiana and Alaska. 2 Stat. 259 (February 25, 1804), § 1; 15 Stat. 240 (July 27, 1868), § 3.

[27] 30 Stat. 1754, 1755 (December 10, 1898).

[28] Annual Reports of the War Department for the Fiscal Year Ended June 30, 1899, Report of the Major-General Commanding the Army (Washington, DC: Government Printing Office, 1899), 313–14.

[29] Annual Report of the Commissioner of Navigation to the Secretary of the Treasury (1899), 84. There was confusion in Congress whether a similar order had been issued for to the Philippines. 35 CONG. REC. 1058 (January 28, 1902).

[30] U.S. Congress, Senate, A Treaty of Peace between the United States and Spain, 55th Cong., 3d sess., 1899, S. Doc. 55-62, part 1, 218 (emphasis added).

[31] Annual Report of the Commissioner of Navigation to the Secretary of the Treasury (1899), 84.

[32] Huus v. New York & Porto Rico Steamship Company, 182 U.S. 392 (1901). There were also similar cases such as De Lima v. Bidwell, 182 U.S. 1 (1901) and Dooley v. U.S., 182 U.S. 222 (1901).

[33] For example, Fourteen Diamond Rings v. U.S., 183 U.S. 176 (1901) (also known by the name of the claimant, Emil J. Pepke, a U.S. soldier who had purchased diamond rings in the Philippines while there on duty and had brought them back to the United States without entering them with U.S. Customs or paying duty).

[34] "Treasury Department Circular no. 103 (December 3, 1901)," Treasury Decisions Under Tariff and Navigation Laws, Etc. (Washington, DC: Government Printing Office, 1902), vol. 4 (January–December,1901), 917.

[35] 39 Stat. 545 (August 16, 1916).

[36] 35 CONG. REC. 825, 829–31 (January 21, 1902)

[37] 35 CONG. REC. 825.

[38] 35 CONG. REC. 830.

[39] 35 CONG. REC. 1909–10 (February 19, 1902).

[40] 35 CONG. REC. 1389 (February 6, 1902).

[41] 35 CONG. REC. 2112 (February 24, 1902); 32 Stat. 54 (Mar. 8, 1902).

[42] U.S. Congress, House, Philippines and Coastwise Shipping Laws, 58th Cong., 2nd sess., 1904, H. Doc. 58-660. Congressional hearings were held on whether there was adequate U.S. shipping capacity to require the use of U.S.-flag vessels in 1904. U.S. Congress, Senate, Shipping between United States and Philippines, 58th Cong., 2nd sess., 1904, S. Doc. 58-124; U.S. Congress, House, Committee on Merchant

Marine and Fisheries, Shipping between Ports of United States and Ports in Philippine Islands, Etc., 58th Cong., 2nd sess., 1904, H. Rep. 58-1904; U.S. Congress, Senate, Philippine Shipping Bill, 58th Cong., 2nd sess. 1904, S. Doc. 58-182.

[43] Bureau of Insular Affairs, War Department, Fourth Annual Report of the Philippine Commission, 1903 (Washington, DC: Government Printing Office, 1904), part I, 71.

[44] Fourth Annual Report of the Philippine Commission, 1903, part 1, 72.

[45] 33 Stat. 181 (April 15, 1904); 34 Stat. 154 (April 30, 1906).

[46] War Department, Annual Reports, Report of the Philippine Commission to the Secretary of War, 1908 (Washington, DC: Government Printing Office, 1909), part 1, 4.

[47] 35 Stat. 70 (April 29, 1908).

[48] Eugene Tyler Chamberlain, "The Hawaiian Situation: The Invasion of Hawaii," North American Review 157, no. 445 (December 1893): 731–35.

[49] 107 Stat. 1510 (November 23, 1993).

[50] Agnes C. Conrad, "Hawaiian Registered Vessels," Hawaiian Journal of History 3 (1969): 31–41.

[51] Conrad, "Hawaiian Registered Vessels," 32—33 (1848 correspondence from the U.S. Commissioner Anthony Ten Eyck to the Hawaiian government). U.S. law penalized foreign-built vessels owned by U.S. citizens in the U.S.-foreign trade vs. the foreign-to-foreign trade. John Bassett Moore, A Digest of International Law (Washington, DC: Government Printing Office, 1906), vol. 2, § 323, 1007–43.

[52] The 1846 Hawaiian registry law only required that vessels be "owned wholly, or in part, by some subject native or naturalized of His Majesty." Statute Laws of His Majesty Kamehameha III, King of the Hawaiian Islands (Honolulu: Charles E. Hitchcock, Printer, 1846), vol. 1, 84.

[53] U.S. Congress, House, Hawaiian Correspondence: Message from the President of the United States, 53d Cong., 2nd sess., 1893, H. Ex. Doc. 53-48.

[54] 2 Stat. 259 (February 25, 1804), § 1; 15 Stat. 240 (July 27, 1868), § 3.

[55] Jacob Adler, "The Oceanic Steamship Company: A Link in Claus Spreckels' Hawaiian Sugar Empire," Pacific Historical Review 29, no. 3 (August 1960): 257–69.

[56] "Claus Spreckels' Plans—He Will Enter Vessels Under the Hawaiian Flag, to Be Americanized Later," New York Herald, March 12, 1897, 19; "How Annexation Will Aid Spreckels," New York Daily Tribune, March 12, 1893, 9; "Tariff Helps Spreckels," New York Times, August 29, 1897, 5 (speculating that the 10 percent discriminating duty discount in the 1897 Dingley Tariff would help Spreckels).

[57] William Adam Russ, Jr., The Hawaiian Republic (1894–1898) (Selingsgrove, PA: Susquehanna University Press, 1961), 244; 33 CONG. REC. 2325 (February 27, 1900).

[58] Conrad, "Hawaiian Registered Vessels," 35; "Foreign-Built Vessels in Hawaii," New York Times, July 18, 1897, 9.

[59] Conrad, "Hawaiian Registered Vessels," 35.

[60] "In the Matter of the Application of George W. Macfarlane for a Writ of Mandamus," Reports of Decisions Rendered by the Supreme Court of the Hawaiian Islands, March 25, 1897 to April 20, 1899 (Honolulu: Hawaiian Gazette, 1899), vol. 11, 166–78; "Under the Hawaiian Flag," New York Times, July 21, 1897, 5; "A Hawaiian Ship," Pacific Commercial Advertiser, September 28, 1897, 2; "Hawaiian Registry for the China," New York Times, October 9, 1897, 3.

[61] "Hawaii's Status Unchanged," New York Times, August 22, 1897, 10.

[62] Conrad, "Hawaiian Registered Vessels," 36.

[63] "Hawaiian Registry," Pacific Commercial Advertiser, March 8, 1898, 2.

[64] "Act 32," Pacific Commercial Advertiser, May 21, 1898, 5.

[65] "The Registry Act," Hawaiian Star, May 14, 1898, 5; "Registering Vessels," Hawaiian Star, April 21, 1898, 5.

[66] 30 Stat. 750 (July 7, 1898).

[67] Thomas J. Osborne, "The Main Reason for Hawaiian Annexation in July, 1898," Oregon Historical Quarterly 71, no. 2 (June 1970): 161—78.

[68] U.S. Congress, Senate, Hawaiian Commission, 55th Cong., 3d sess., 1898, S. Doc. 55-16, 11.

[69] Hawaiian Commission, S. Doc. 55-16, 42.

[70] In the meantime, more vessels had been issued provisional registry by Hawaiian consuls. "For Hawaiian Registry–Two More Vessels Coming under Obsolete Hawaiian Flag," Daily Bulletin (Honolulu), (December 1, 1898), 2; "Mazama Now Kilohana," Hawaiian Star, (December 1, 1898), 6.

[71] "Two English Vessels Now Owned Here," San Francisco Call, December 21, 1898, 8 ("now owned by William Matson and others"); "Purchased English Vessels," Daily Bulletin (Honolulu), December 30, 1898, 2 ("now owned by William Matson and others"); "Hawaiian 4-Masted Ship," Hawaiian Star, January 20, 1899, 2 ("purchased some time ago, on behalf of John D. Spreckels Bros. Company").

[72] Fred A. Stindt, Matson's Century of Ships (Modesto, CA: Fred A. Stindt, 1982), 14.

[73] "In the Matter of the Application of L.D. Spencer et. al for a Writ of Mandamus," Reports of Decisions Rendered by the Supreme Court of the Hawaiian Islands, May 1, 1899 to June 20, 1900 (Honolulu: Hawaiian Gazette Company, 1899), vol. 12, 66–75.

[74] U.S. Attorney General, "Vessels: Registers: Hawaii," Op. Att'y Gen. 22, no. 578 (September 30, 1899).

[75] William McKinley, "Discontinuing Issuance of Registers to Vessels by Authorities of Hawaii," Executive Order no. 122 (September 18, 1899).

[76] "Status of Hawaii's Flag," New York Times, February 3, 1899, 5; "Hawaii and the British Claims," San Francisco Chronicle, November 6, 1899, 3.

[77] 31 Stat. 141, 161, § 98 (April. 30, 1900).

[78] U.S. Congress, House, Government for the Territory of Hawaii, 56th Cong., 1st sess., 1900, H. Rep. 56-305, 25.

[79] 33 Cong. Rec. 2325–26 (February 27, 1900), 4465 (April 20, 1900) and 4650 (April 25, 1900).
[80] 33 Cong. Rec. 2324.
[81] 31 Stat. 141, 161 (April 30, 1900).
[82] 30 Stat. 432 (June 7, 1898). War Department, Annual Reports of the War Department for the Fiscal Year Ended June 30, 1898, Report of the Major-General Commanding the Army (Washington, DC: Government Printing Office, 1898) (including the Catania, Unionist, and Zealandia, at 30 Stat. 420 (May 21, 1898), 30 Stat. 475 (June 18, 1898), and 30 Stat. 421 (May 27, 1898), respectively). A list of all vessels documented by Act of Congress in fiscal year 1898 is contained in Annual Report of the Commissioner of Navigation to the Secretary of the Treasury (1898), 246.
[83] Conrad, "Hawaiian Registered Vessels," 39.
[84] Annual Report of the Commissioner of Navigation to the Secretary of the Treasury (1900), 54. The registry process for former Hawaiian-flag vessels was set out in "Treasury Department Circular no. 62 (May 3, 1900)," Treasury Decisions under Tariff and Navigation Laws, Etc., January–December,1900 (Washington, DC: Government Printing Office, 1901), vol. 3, 403.
[85] Annual Report of the Commissioner of Navigation to the Secretary of the Treasury (1901), 30.
[86] Sandra Dick, "Piece of Maritime History Prepares to Return Home to the Clyde," Herald (Scotland), (December 13, 2020); Annalisa Burgos, "Hawaii's Iconic Falls of Clyde Ship at Honolulu Harbor to Soon Lose Historic Designation," Hawaii News Now, (June 28, 2023), https://www.hawaiinewsnow.com/2023/06/29/hawaii-delist-falls-clyde-ship-register-historic-places/.
[87] For example, 6 Stat. 313 (May 21, 1824). A list of the special acts naming individual vessels appears in an 1877 Opinion of the U.S. attorney general. U.S. Attorney General, "Wrecked Vessel – Issue of Register," Op. Att'y Gen. 15, no. 402 (December 5, 1877).
[88] 10 Stat. 149 (December 23, 1852).
[89] For example, U.S. Attorney General, "Repairs Upon a Wrecked Foreign-Built Vessel," Op. Att'y Gen. 5, no. 674 (February 14, 1853); U.S. Attorney General, "Wrecked Vessel: Issue of Register," Op. Att'y Gen. 15, no. 402 (December 5, 1877).
[90] U.S. Congress, Senate, Preservation of American Coastwise Shipping Trade, 55th Cong., 2nd sess., 1898, S. Rep. 55-1129.
[91] Preservation of American Coastwise Shipping Trade, S. Rep. 55-1129, 2.
[92] 40 Cong. Rec. 2611 (February 15, 1906).
[93] "Big Fire at Newport News," New York Times, April 28, 1897, 14.
[94] "The Lone Star Lines—Will Have Trouble over Their New Ship, the Solvieg," Times-Picayune, November 18, 1897, 2; "Protest Merrimac's Registry," Sun and New York Press, November 18, 1897, 10.
[95] U.S. Navy Department, Annual Reports of the Department of the Navy for 1898, 270.

96 "Purchase of the Merrimac," New York Times, June 8, 1898, 4.

97 "Purchase of Merrimac May Be Investigated by Congress," Boston Journal, June 7, 1898, 2; 31 CONG. REC. 5614 (June 7, 1898). Roosevelt explained the discrepancy in a letter to Secretary Long in 1900 as a change in circumstances—when the Merrimac was first offered, it was thought it was not needed, but when the Spanish fleet sailed for the Caribbean, the need for more colliers suddenly became acute. "Letter from Theodore Roosevelt to John D. Long (March 5, 1900)," Papers of John Davis Long 1897–1904, ed. Gardner Weld Allen, the Massachusetts Historical Society (Norwood, MA: Plimpton Press, 1939), 316–17.

98 "The Secretary of War," The Political Nursery II, no. 4 (September 1898), 1.

99 "Cable from Commodore Winfield S. Schley, Commander, Flying Squadron, to Secretary of the Navy John D. Long (May 27, 1898)," Naval History and Heritage Command, Documentary Histories, Spanish-American War, www.history.navy.mil/research/publications/documentary-histories/united-states-navys/the-flying-squadron/commodore-winfield-s-5.html.

100 "Journal of Rear Admiral William T. Sampson, Commander, North Atlantic Fleet (May 29, 1898)," Naval History and Heritage Command, Documentary Histories, Spanish-American War, www.history.navy.mil/content/history/nhhc/research/publications/documentary-histories/united-states-navy-s/the-flying-squadron/journal-of-rear-admi-1.html.

101 For example, "Lieut. Hobson's Deed," New York Times, June 6, 1898, 1.

102 Barton C. Shaw "The Hobson Craze," U.S. Naval Institute Proceedings 102, no. 876 (February 1976): 54–60.

103 For example, Goode, With Sampson through the War, 149–53.

104 "Cable from W. T. Sampson to Sec. Long (Jun. 3, 1898)," U.S. Navy Department, Annual Reports of the Navy Department for the Year 1898, 437.

105 "Merrimac an Expensive Cork," Daily Illinois State Register, June 6, 1898, 1.

106 Shaw, "The Hobson Craze," 57–58.

107 For example, "Hobson's Kissing Excites to Anger and Official Vexation," Buffalo News, December 21, 1891, 1; "Admiral Hobson, War Hero, 66 Dies," New York Times, March 17, 1937, 25.

108 William McKinley, Second Annual Message, December 5, 1898, UC Santa Barbara, The American Presidency Project, https://www.presidency.ucsb.edu/documents/second-annual-message-15.

109 U.S. Navy Department, Annual Reports of the Navy Department for the Year 1898, 319.

110 Report of the Merchant Marine Commission, S. Rep. 58-2755, 428–29.

111 Annual Report of the Commissioner of Navigation to the Secretary of Commerce and Labor (1905), 20–21 & 211–13.

112 40 CONG. REC. 2612 (February 15, 1906).

113 40 CONG. REC. 2611. U.S. Congress, House, Committee on Merchant Marine and Fisheries, Registry of Repaired Foreign Wrecks, 59th Cong., 1st sess., 1906, H. Rep.

59-926; U.S. Congress, Senate, Committee on Commerce, Registry of Repaired Foreign Wrecks, 59th Cong., 1st sess., 1906, S. Rep. 59-114.

[114] 34 Stat. 17 (February 22, 1906).

[115] U.S. Congress, Senate, Register and Enrollment of Vessels Built in Foreign Countries under Certain Circumstances, 63rd Cong., 2nd sess., 1914, S. Rep. 63-816, 4. The legislation was also considered earlier. U.S. Congress, House, Register and Enrollment of Foreign Vessels, 62nd Cong., 2nd sess., 1912, H. Rep. 62-1043.

[116] 52 Cong. Rec. 3961 (February 17, 1915); 38 Stat. 812 (February 24, 1915); 46 U.S.C. § 12107.

[117] Annual Report of the Commissioner of Navigation to the Secretary of the Treasury (1898), 65.

[118] 14 Stat. 178, 182 (July 18, 1866).

[119] Annual Report of the Commissioner of Navigation to the Secretary of the Treasury (1898), 65; U.S. Congress, House, Committee on Merchant Marine and Fisheries, 55th Cong., 2nd sess., 1898, H. Rep. 55-441.

[120] U.S. v. 250 Kegs of Nails, 52 F. 231 (S.D. Ca. 1892). There was a similar 1904 unreported decision regarding passengers decided by the U.S. District Court for the Western District of Washington captioned U.S. v. The Foreign Steamer Princess Beatrice concerning a voyage from Seattle to Victoria in one vessel and then from Victoria to Skagway in another vessel—found not to violate the Passenger Vessel Services Act. U.S. Attorney General, Coastwise Carrying Trade: Foreign Vessel Taking Tourists around the World and Landing at Different Port, Op. Att'y Gen. 28, no. 204 (February 26, 1910). Rep. Humphrey offered legislation to remedy the situation which did not advance. Amending Laws Relating to Navigation, H. Rep. 62-653.

[121] U.S. Congress, House, Transportation of Merchandise between Ports of the United States, 52nd Cong., 2nd sess., 1893, H. Rep. 52-2288.

[122] 27 Stat. 455 (February 15, 1893).

[123] 31 Cong. Rec. 1609–10 (February 10, 1898).

[124] 31 Cong. Rec. 1729–31 (February 15, 1898).

[125] 30 Stat. 248 (February 17, 1898); 30 Stat. 248 (February 17, 1898).

[126] U.S. Attorney General, "Transportation of Merchandise from Seattle to Fairbanks," Op. Att'y Gen. 30, no. 3 (January 4, 1913).

[127] Discussed in the "Underwood Tariff Act of 1913" section.

"The Great White Fleet," probably leaving Virginia, 1907, Naval History and Heritage Command

Chapter 14 — Cargo Preferences, Tolls, and Free Ships

The Spanish-American War highlighted the lack of U.S.-flag commercial vessels to support U.S. armed forces overseas. The Boer War from 1899 to 1902 highlighted the lack of U.S.-flag commercial vessels to support U.S. international trade when Britain was at war because of Britain's dominance of the world trading fleet of vessels. Both effects recurred in World War I.

Britain had to transport troops, animals, equipment, and supplies thousands of miles for the war against the Boer republics in South Africa. U.S. trade was disrupted due to the withdrawal of a substantial portion of the British fleet of steamships serving North Atlantic commerce.[1] According to the *Financial Times* of London, "the natural effect of their withdrawal has been to cripple the opportunities afforded for sending freight to and from America, and to raise freights."[2]

The 1905 Gallinger Commission determined that Britain withdrew from commercial service about 250 steamships, aggregating about one million tons.[3] The entire fleet of U.S-flag iron and steel steamships engaged in the foreign trade in 1900 was 124 vessels aggregating about 270,000 tons.[4]

The negative effect on the U.S. economy was substantial. A 1919 U.S. Chamber of Commerce report determined that British commandeering of vessels caused U.S. cargo rates to increase by an average of 30 percent.[5] Representative William Humphrey wrote dramatically that "during the little Boer War, England withdrew a sufficient number of ships to increase freight rates from some of our ports 150 per cent."[6] The Gallinger Commission staff summarized by saying that "the practical result, of course, was that our shrewd transatlantic kinsmen thereby forced the farmers and ranchmen of the western States and the planters of the South to contribute to the cost of subduing the Boer republics of South Africa."[7]

The United States had already fought its overseas war, against Spain. As a result, the nation had armed forces located in overseas territories from the Caribbean to the Philippines and they had to be rotated and supplied. A natural question arose. Was the movement of those personnel and cargoes to be reserved to U.S.-flag vessels following the British example or should the U.S. government be flag blind like American commercial shippers?

1904 Cargo Preference Act

When the U.S. government became a substantial shipper of cargo for the first time after the Spanish-American War, no provision was made to prefer U.S.-flag vessels. Statutes of the period required both the Army and Navy to ship goods based on the lowest bidder without exception.[8]

Compounding the situation, the War Department utilized vessels it acquired in the war to provide service to the territories in competition with both U.S. and foreign private lines. The Gallinger Commission found "that the Government itself was directly and powerfully contributing to the decline of American merchant shipping... by operating rival lines of foreign-built craft."[9]

Representative Wesley Jones was one of the first to propose that privately owned U.S.-flag vessels should be preferred for the carriage of War Department cargoes. Jones introduced a bill in May 1902 to authorize the Secretary of War to favor U.S.-flag service to the Philippines when vessels owned by the government were unavailable.[10] The legislation, as approved in committee and as supported by the War Department, would have included a 10 percent cap over foreign rates.[11]

Opposing the proposal, Representative James L. Slayden (D-TX) declared it was "nothing but another form of the ship-subsidy bill" and "it is a plain, frank proposition to take money out of the Treasury of the United States and vote it into the treasure box of private shipowners."[12] Jones responded that the simple proposition seems to me to be "'Do we prefer our own Government to transport its own supplies under foreign flag and in foreign ships, thereby employing foreign labor and capital, rather than in our own ships, under our own flag, and employing our own capital and labor, even if it costs a few cents more?'" You may vote for the foreign ship; I will vote for the American ship, and I have no fears of the verdict of the American people on such a proposition. [Applause][13] Despite Jones's efforts, the legislation was tabled.

Frye renewed the debate when he introduced legislation in early 1904 that would have required the use of privately owned U.S.-flag vessels to transport Army or Navy supplies. This could only be waived "in the interests of national defense."[14] Secretary of War Elihu Root wrote that his department was in favor of the preference concept. However, the department favored the Jones formulation of a fixed differential cap rather than the Frye proposal, although it was willing to raise the cap from 10 percent to 25 or 30 percent.[15] Frye objected and Root wrote in a follow-up letter that the department would agree to a differential of 50 or even 100 percent, but there should be some numerical limit.[16]

The House and Senate reports in favor of the legislation pointed out that Britain, Germany, and France all used their own vessels to transport military supplies.[17] Senator Eugene Hale (R-ME) stated "it is a reproach for us that what every other great nation does—transport its military supplies in its own ships—we should not do in our own case."[18]

Opposition was fierce. Senator Edward W. Carmack (D-TN) called the Frye amendment "a sort of legislative jimmy by which a lot of burglarious shipowners are trying to break into the Treasury of the United States."[19] The Navy chimed in that it should not "be the one to pay all the subsidy for building up the American merchant marine."[20]

The most persistent criticism was the open-ended nature of the U.S.-flag preference, regardless of cost. One of the most consequential limitations offered by Senator Porter J. McCumber (R-ND) was agreed to without objection.[21] That amendment provided that U.S.-flag charges to the Army and Navy could not be greater than those charged to private customers.[22]

The House Merchant Marine Committee added another limitation, namely that U.S. rates could not be "excessive and unreasonable," which also found its way into the law.[23] Every effort to quantify what was "excessive and unreasonable"—in terms of a percentage cap—was rejected, including a 100 percent differential.[24] The bill was signed into law by President Roosevelt on April 28, 1904, and remains today a measure of support for privately owned U.S.-flag vessels.[25]

Voyage of the Great White Fleet

The 1904 Cargo Preference Act became significant in the context of the 1907-09 voyage of the "Great White Fleet."

The spark for the voyage was tension with Japan which arose from a California nativist movement seeking to exclude and segregate Japanese immigrants.[26] Those tensions led President Roosevelt to request options from the Navy for defending U.S. territorial possessions, such as Hawaii. The Navy General Board, chaired by Admiral Dewey, recommended in June 1907 that most of the Atlantic fleet of battleships, the main force of the Navy, be assembled and sent to the Pacific.[27]

The administration went to great pains to avoid the public message that the voyage was to counter Japan.[28] No purpose for the voyage of sixteen battleships to the West Coast was provided when it was first publicly discussed by the Roosevelt administration in August 1907.[29] Moreover, there was no indication of the route the fleet would take to return to the East Coast.

The Japanese government was equally careful not to indicate any alarm. For example, Japanese Adm. Baron Gomel Yamamoto, who had been Navy minister during the war with

Russia and later twice premier of Japan, assured reporters in New York upon his arrival in July 1907 that Japan did not view the movement of the fleet as a threat.[30] Upon announcement of the battleships going to the Philippines, the Japanese government in fact invited the fleet to visit Japan.[31]

The plan was nevertheless decried publicly for unnecessarily risking war.[32] Roosevelt was also heavily criticized for exposing the fleet far from ready sources of repair and supply, for the unnecessary expense, and for making obvious the fleet's dependence on foreign supply vessels.[33]

In Roosevelt's defense, Alfred Mahan wrote that the U.S. Navy had to be prepared to defend both the East and West Coasts and that such ability was not a threat to Japan—any more than having an Atlantic fleet was a threat to European nations.[34] Since the U.S. battle fleet was not sufficiently large to have two fleets and defend both coasts simultaneously, the only practical alternative was to train the fleet to be able to switch coasts (a voyage that prior to the opening of the Panama Canal, took about three months) and to show the world that the United States had that capability. This very same reason was given by Roosevelt in his December 1907 Annual Congressional Message.[35]

None of this provided a rationale, however, for the fleet continuing west to circumnavigate the world after its voyage to the West Coast. No one knows for sure how those factors were weighed by Roosevelt.[36] Roosevelt indicated in his 1913 autobiography that it was his decision alone to undertake the world tour and that he had several reasons for ordering it. He sought to promote peace and show other navies that the U.S. Navy could do it in the face of domestic and foreign skepticism; but at the same time, he wrote, his "prime purpose" was to stimulate interest in the U.S. Navy.[37]

It was common at the time for warships to visit other countries and to engage in naval "parades" or "pageants."[38] Roosevelt decided to use the fleet in the grandest parade of all. The voyage started on the East Coast and proceeded to the West Coast, then to Hawaii and the Philippines and then finally back to the East Coast through the Suez Canal and the Mediterranean to arrive home prior to the end of his term on March 4, 1909.[39]

Roosevelt responded to the lack of U.S. supply vessels to support the voyage by announcing that U.S.-flag colliers would be preferred, up to a 50 percent premium, but that he was, in any event, confident that foreign colliers could be contracted to transport U.S. coal to various ports to be used as coaling stations.[40] At the time, the only two places in the world that mined high-energy, low-smoke coal were Appalachia and Wales. So, most of the coal burned by the fleet would have to come from the U.S. East Coast and be positioned around the world.

The Navy's Bureau of Equipment, which had the job of making sure the fleet was provided with coal, was not as sanguine as the president.[41] The bureau indicated in November 1908 that supplying the fleet on the around the world voyage was a "serious problem," that the "few colliers possessed by the navy were utterly inadequate," and that the total number of U.S.-flag vessels available for purchase or charter was also insufficient. Its report concluded that "had foreign complications arisen, or had a combination been effected between foreign shipowners, our fleet might have had to remain lying helpless in some foreign port." One newspaper headlined the report as "Lack of Colliers Cripples Big Fleet."[42]

Three legal issues also arose in the use of foreign colliers, all resolved by the U.S. attorney general in favor of such use.[43] The first was whether the existing 1898 U.S. coastwise law prohibited the hiring of foreign vessels to transport coal between the U.S. coasts. The attorney general determined that the law did not apply to U.S. government cargo.[44] Second, the question arose under the 1904 Cargo Preference Act whether the U.S. government could utilize foreign vessels if U.S.-flag vessels were not available. Here, the attorney general also gave the Navy latitude.[45] Finally, the attorney general opined that the government ownership of the cargo exempted it from the tonnage tax.[46]

JOURNEY TO THE JONES ACT

The necessity to use foreign colliers was a frequent topic of public discussion. For example, at the December 1907 annual meeting of the Merchant Marine League, Assistant Secretary of the Navy Truman H. Newberry reminded the audience that Admiral Dewey had testified in 1905 that there was an immediate need for Navy fleet colliers. Newberry added that the collier "deficiency in this regard cannot long continue without inviting calamity."[47]

Foreign navies took note of the U.S. fleet's Achilles' heel. Count Ernst von Reventlow, a German naval analyst, wrote that 90 percent of the colliers used for the worldwide voyage would be British, and Britain "could use this fact to advantage in case of future complications between the United States and Japan."[48] At the time, Britain and Japan were allies. Winthrop Marvin wrote a letter to the *New-York Daily Tribune* agreeing with Reventlow. In it, he noted that the German had "winged a keen shaft at us" and that what Reventlow was saying was "mortifyingly true and undeniable."[49]

The focus on foreign collier dependence appeared well justified when the fleet was in Australia in July and August 1908 and foreign colliers did not show up.[50] The Navy had to scramble to purchase local, inferior, Australian coal to keep to the schedule. Rear Admiral Charles S. Sperry, then in command of the fleet, wrote that "not the least significant lesson of the cruise was that colliers chartered under foreign flags failed to deliver 27,000 tons of coal as ordered in New Zealand and Australia and if we cannot have a suitable commercial marine of our own, then the government should own sufficient colliers."[51]

U.S. senators focused on the problem as well. During one of the debates on the Gallinger Commission legislation in early 1908, Senator Francis Newlands offered an amendment to form a "Foreign Commerce Commission" to build up to twenty-seven vessels to be owned by the U.S. government to serve as colliers and other auxiliary vessels in times of national need. They were to be chartered to private interests in times of peace for the purpose of promoting foreign trade and commerce.[52] This was probably the first ever proposal for U.S. government ownership of commercial vessels, something the 1870 Lynch Committee had considered but not proposed.[53]

Senator Eugene Hale, then chairman of the Naval Affairs Committee, agreed but urged Newlands to offer his amendment in the Navy appropriation legislation instead.[54] Hale argued that the progress of the fleet was a "melancholy spectacle" and that the fleet was "absolutely dependent upon its motion, upon its existence as a moving fleet, on the indulgence of foreign powers."[55] Hale also quoted Samuel Taylor Coleridge's poem *The Rime of the Ancient Mariner* to describe the fleet without foreign colliers: "As idle as a painted ship—Upon a painted ocean."

Despite the issues with colliers, the voyage was generally thought of as a success. Winthrop Marvin, for example, called it "the greatest naval cruise of modern times" arguing that it would improve battleship efficiency substantially (the fleet conducted training exercises throughout the voyage), was little more expensive than similar training closer to home and would promote better international relations.[56]

The fleet set off from Hampton Roads on December 16, 1907, in a grand review, attended by Roosevelt, and sailed south toward the Caribbean.[57] The fleet, painted white during peacetime, was eventually called the "great white fleet" in the press and the phrase caught on.[58] In its fourteen-month journey, the fleet was manned by about fourteen thousand sailors, travelled forty-two thousand miles, and made twenty port calls. Wherever the fleet went, it was heroically received earning it the moniker "Greatest Show on Earth."[59] The fleet arrived back at Hampton Roads on February 22, 1909, reviewed by President Roosevelt.[60]

Scientific American captured the pride of the nation upon the return of the fleet: "In view of the bitter criticism with which it was assailed... the return of this same fleet to Hampton Roads after a 42,000-mile cruise around the world, with every ship in first-class shape and the *morale* of officers and men greatly improved, is a tribute to the far-signed sagacity which projected the voyage."[61] It was also noted that "one of the most gratifying results of the cruise has been the enthusiastic and unmistakably friendly reception which was accorded at every port where the ships let go anchor" and "our vessels have lived fully up to their designation as *seagoing* battleships." The only negative was "our great shortage of colliers."

Contemporaneously, the U.S. Navy planning for possible war with Japan determined that one hundred foreign colliers would be needed.[62] The movement of troops to capture and hold island bases and to defend the Philippines would have required "another armada of foreign ships."[63]

For all the agonizing about the lack of colliers and other Navy auxiliary vessels, the deficiency was not fully remedied prior to the U.S. entry into World War I. In terms of Navy auxiliaries, there were thirty auxiliary vessels in the U.S. Navy in 1907 and only twenty-five in 1916.[64] The only Navy colliers available upon the outbreak of World War I were five authorized in the 1909 naval program and two already under construction at that time. These were larger than typical commercial vessels and better equipped to transfer coal.[65]

In terms of revitalizing the U.S. merchant marine, the subsidy efforts had failed by 1911. Those efforts were replaced in part by the 1904 Cargo Preference Act. Attempts were also made in connection with the opening of the Panama Canal to prefer U.S.-flag vessels for canal cargoes and canal tolls and, finally, to adopt a free ships policy.

Panama Canal Act

The voyage of the Great White Fleet accentuated the need for a canal across the isthmus of Panama to permit the U.S. to shift its Navy from ocean to ocean as needed. The United States had taken over construction of the canal in 1904, and it was opened to vessels in August 1914. Several merchant marine policy issues arose with respect to the canal.[66]

Panama Canal Cargo Preference. Following the U.S. takeover of the Panama Canal operation, the Isthmian Canal Commission was formed in February 1904 to oversee the project. One issue faced by the commission was whether to prefer the purchase of U.S. materials if they were more expensive than foreign-sourced materials.

The commission initially said that it would purchase items needed wherever they were cheapest.[67] The commission recognized that this policy "is certain to produce, every time that a large contract is awarded to a foreign manufacturer or dealer, an outcry on the part of the American unsuccessful competitors."

The canal commission muddled along until the spring of 1906, when it tendered for the construction of two dredges. A Scottish shipyard submitted the lowest offer. A Maryland firm offered a price difference of only 10 percent.[68] Probably hoping to pass the political buck, Secretary of War Taft wrote to President Roosevelt in May 1906 about the situation, which Roosevelt passed on to Congress.[69]

Congress responded with a June 25, 1906, joint resolution signed by the president, providing that "purchases of material and equipment" for the Canal had to be sourced from the United States "unless the President shall, in any case, deem the bids or tenders therefor to be extortionate or unreasonable."[70] The resolution did not address ocean transportation services.

This omission became important in early 1908 when the canal commission issued an invitation for one of its largest contracts. It stipulated a transport of about one million tons of cement from the United States to the canal over a three-year period.[71] Senator Frye introduced a joint resolution similar to the "material and equipment" resolution requiring use of privately owned U.S.-flag vessels, provided their rates were not "extortionate or unreasonable."[72]

JOURNEY TO THE JONES ACT

The favorable Senate Commerce Committee report said that "it is more than a question of 'cheapness.'"[73] No serious opposition surfaced in the Senate. The debate largely focused on ensuring that cargoes would move even if no U.S.-flag vessel was available, and the Senate passed the resolution by consent on March 13, 1908.[74]

The House was a different matter. Although the Commerce Committee recommended the legislation, a substantial minority of the committee asserted that the law "would interfere to a serious degree" with the construction of the Canal.[75] The minority pointed to a letter from General George Washington Goethals, then chairman of the commission and later, among other things, the first governor of the Panama Canal Zone. (When Goethals died in 1928, the *New York Times* referred to him as the "Builder of the Panama Canal.)"[76]

Goethals wrote to the president that "while I have a very friendly feeling for American shipping," "the burden of encouraging" American shipping "should not be thrown upon the Isthmian Canal Commission."[77] The minority view prevailed, no action was taken on the legislation in the House, and Frye's canal cargo preference provision died.

The Great Tolls Controversy. One of the most contentious policy issues arising from the construction of the Panama Canal was whether to exempt U.S.-flag vessels engaged in the coastwise trade from tolls.

The issue was joined in December 1910 with one of Frye's last official acts. Specifically, Frye introduced legislation to have the Treasury pay Panama Canal tolls for U.S.-flag vessels.[78] Chamberlain supported the proposal and argued that this formulation was consistent with the principle of not charging U.S. vessels tolls on any U.S. interior canal or river improved for navigation.[79]

Of relevance to the setting of tolls was a treaty between the United States and Britain known as the Hay-Pauncefote Treaty of 1901 regarding the construction of an Isthmian canal.[80] That treaty contained a clause drawn from prior international experience "that there shall be no discrimination against any such nation, or its citizens or subjects, in respect of the conditions or charges of traffic, or otherwise." Chamberlain argued that Frye's proposal did not violate this non-discrimination clause because the same tolls would be assessed against all vessels using the canal.[81]

Chamberlain also warned, bordering on the frantic, that the United States would surely eventually open the coastwise trade to foreigners if the country abandoned the long-standing principle that the U.S. coastwise trade was free of tolls."[82] Representative John A. Martin (D-CO), one of the chief opponents of exempting the coastwise trade from tolls, questioned Chamberlain aggressively in the House Commerce Committee hearings. He was particularly dogged about Chamberlain's contention that the coastwise trade would inevitably be ruined if tolls were charged.[83] Martin interrupted his colleagues so often that Chamberlain said that "this is getting to resemble... the wireless interference with which we are dealing in another committee [Laughter.]."[84]

Meanwhile, the congressional debate had moved to an outright exemption from tolls for vessels in the coastwise trade considered by the House Commerce Committee and rejected in March 1912. However, the committee majority claimed that such an exemption would not have violated U.S. treaty obligations.[85]

There was also a nationalist view reflected in a May 1912 address by Samuel L. Barker, financial editor of the *North American*, who argued that "sentiment and false generosity should be thrust aside by the American Nation in this matter."[86] Citing to Frye's legislation and Chamberlain's support, Barker argued that having built the canal, and having to maintain it, Americans "have a just right to claim and take for themselves its larger benefits."

A leading proponent of the coastwise toll exemption was Representative Frank E. Doremus (D-MI). In advancing the tolls exemption, Doremus cited to the 1911 *Annual Reports* of the secretaries of war and commerce.[87] The secretary of war wrote that "an examination of the treaty and the surrounding circumstances to my mind leaves no doubt as to the right of the United States, both legally and morally, to pay the tolls on its vessels."[88] The issue left unaddressed was how the tolls would be set if U.S.-flag vessels were exempted and whether that would place the whole toll burden on foreign carriers.

Numerous resolutions from around the country were put in the record in support of no tolls on U.S. vessels.[89] Senator Henry Cabot Lodge placed in the record an article written by Winthrop Marvin, "The American Flag in the Panama," which predicted that subsidized British lines would benefit the most from the canal if tolls were imposed on U.S. vessels. Eventually, the author argued, U.S.-flag coastwise service would decline to the point that the trade would have to be opened to foreign vessels.[90] The worrisome prospect was that British vessels would transport goods, such as timber, from Vancouver to the East Coast cheaper than U.S.-flag vessels would transport timber from Seattle. This became a preoccupation of Senator Wesley Jones in later years.[91]

Doremus, like Chamberlain, argued that imposing tolls for domestic U.S. commerce "is at war with the fundamental policy of this Government for 125 years—a policy which, coupled with a national system of internal improvements, has made the domestic commerce of the United States the marvel of the civilized world."[92] Doremus also argued that exempting U.S.-flag vessels from tolls was a continuation of the policy set down in 1789 reserving U.S. coastwise trade to U.S. vessels.[93]

Representative Joshua W. Alexander (D-MO), chairman of the House Merchant Committee, also made the emotional exemption case, "I say we should discriminate in favor of American shipping, both in the coastwise trade and in the foreign trade. That is my view [Applause.]"[94] And, he said, "I would give to our merchant marine every possible benefit in the competition of this, the world's greatest engineering triumph."[95] Alexander was often referred to as "Judge Alexander" because of his prior service as a Missouri state judge.[96]

The Doremus exemption amendment passed the House on May 18, 1912.[97] The British government protested on July 8, 1912, arguing that relieving U.S.-flag vessels of tolls by whatever method would violate the Hay-Pauncefote Treaty because it would increase the burden on foreign vessels to pay for canal expenses.[98] Congress nevertheless included the coastwise trade tolls exemption in the Panama Canal Act of 1912.[99] In his message upon enactment in August 1912, President Taft wrote that "I feel confident that the exemption of the coastwise vessels... is not a violation of the Hay-Pauncefote treaty" even if lawyers may differ.

Shortly before the Canal Act was signed into law by President William Howard Taft on August 24, 1912, Woodrow Wilson, by that point a candidate for president, endorsed the coastwise trade exemption.[100] The 1912 Democratic national party platform also favored the exemption.[101]

By early 1913 leading Democrats who had voted for the toll exemption had a change of heart.[102] The New York Chamber of Commerce came out against the exemption.[103] The *New York Times* editorialized that the tolls exemption "is merely a subsidy to an interest already enjoying a monopoly" (referring to the domestic trade reservation to U.S.-flag vessels).[104] Wilson apparently had already made up his mind to seek repeal of the exemption.[105]

By October 1913 President Wilson was openly supporting repeal, stating that he believed it violated the Hay-Pauncefote Treaty.[106] On March 5, 1914, in an address to Congress, Wilson requested the repeal, saying "we are too big, too powerful, too self-respecting a Nation to interpret with too strained or refined a reading the words of our own promises just because we have power enough to give us leave to read them as we please."[107]

JOURNEY TO THE JONES ACT

The repeal was enacted on June 17, 1914, and the canal opened on August 15 without the coastwise trade toll exemption.[108] Senator Jones voted to retain the exemption.[109] Years later, in 1921, Senator Jones, Senator William E. Borah and others attempted without success to again exempt U.S.-flag vessels from canal tolls.[110]

Free Ships. Neither Codman, Dingley, Frye, nor Vest lived to see it, but free ships finally had a breakthrough in the Panama Canal Act of 1912. It began with an increase in free ships promotion when Democrats took back the House in November 1910. The effort accelerated when Woodrow Wilson was elected two years later.

The revived free ships initiative started with an amendment offered by Senator William J. Stone (D-MO) to the Gallinger subsidy legislation on February 2, 1911. This would have permitted foreign-built vessels to be U.S. registered for the foreign trade and trade to the Philippines.[111] The amendment narrowly failed. Minutes later, the subsidy legislation passed the Senate in the tie vote broken by the vice president. Senator Jones voted for the free ship amendment and then also for the bill—the only Republican to do so.

The next day a free ship amendment passed the House. Under the amendment, only steel steamships of 2,500 tons or more owned entirely by U.S. citizens could enter the U.S. flag. And then they would be without eligibility for mail subsidies or the coastwise trade.[112] The legislation was not acted upon further by that Congress.

Representative Joshua Alexander succeeded Representative William Greene as the chairman of the Merchant Marine Committee in April 1911 and introduced free ship legislation starting in May 1911.[113] The legislation would have permitted U.S. registry for foreign-built vessels no more than five years of age.[114] Such vessels would be eligible to trade with the Philippine Islands, Guam, and Tutuila (American Samoa), but not in the U.S. coastwise trade. They would not receive the benefit of any canal toll exemption. The legislation as initially proposed would have required all U.S. corporations owning any U.S. reflagged vessel to be 100 percent owned by U.S. citizens. U.S. corporations regardless of the shareholder ownership qualified to register U.S.-flag vessels since at least 1858.[115]

To soften the blow to U.S. shipyards, the proposed legislation also would have paired "free ships" with "free materials." U.S. shipyards would not pay duties on materials used in the construction of vessels such as imported steel.[116] As the House Merchant Marine Committee reported the bill, it also added the right of reflagged vessels to participate in the 1891 Ocean Mail Act subsidies and to receive any toll benefits accorded U.S.-flag vessels in the *foreign* trade. The majority wrote that some incentive had to be given to U.S. owners to reflag, given high U.S. operating costs.

The minority led by Representatives Greene and Humphrey lashed out at the mail subsidy eligibility and pointed to the likelihood that the law would not work because of high U.S. operating costs.[117] On the mail subsidy, the minority wrote that "no nation to-day pays mail subsidy to any foreign-built vessel" and the Democratic party, which "with blind prejudice vociferously denounces anything in the form of a subsidy for American ships" now favors "it for foreign cheap ships built by foreign cheap labor." The Republican minority also expected that reflagged vessels, which were likely to lose money, "would bring tremendous pressure upon Congress to permit these foreign-built ships to engage in the coast-to-coast trade of the United States."

On August 8, 1912, Senator John S. Williams (D-MS) offered a scaled down amendment simply to permit foreign-built vessels into the registry.[118] Williams was anti-tariff, pro-segregation, and pro-Wilson. In 1906, he offered an amendment to the Navy appropriations bill to change the name of the next U.S. battleship to "Skeered o' Nothin." He suggested the U.S. battleship meet the British battleship *Dreadnought* in a "duel à l'outrance" near Long Island (presumably a reference to President Roosevelt's house at Sagamore Hill) with Roosevelt and his cabinet "entertained on the quarter-deck as guests of the ship and the nation."[119]

Senator Gallinger led the opposition to the Williams amendment.[120] He argued that the amendment was not germane to the Panama Canal legislation and that it could do harm but would not likely do any good. He pointed out that his 1905 commission had approached U.S. investment banks to ask whether they would invest in American ships if they could be bought anywhere in the world but without U.S. coastwise trading privileges. They uniformly said they would not.

However, the die was cast in favor of doing something to revive the U.S. merchant marine in the foreign trade. Some Republican stalwarts like Senators Elihu Root (R-NY) and Jones said they would vote in favor of the amendment even though they did not believe it would do much good.[121] The Williams amendment passed comfortably.[122]

Gallinger re-grouped and offered a second-degree amendment to exclude reflagged vessels from U.S. mail subsidies. Williams agreed once it was made clear that vessels built to U.S. Navy specifications would still be eligible for the subsidies and the Gallinger amendment was added by consent. This was not likely to occur with foreign construction.[123]

What emerged from a conference committee was close to Alexander's proposal. Reflagged vessels would have to be less than five years of age, wholly owned by U.S. citizens (even if via a corporation) and entitled to ocean mail subsidies—but only if they met U.S. Navy specifications. "Free materials" was also included. The conference version became law in the Panama Canal Act of 1912.[124]

---

[1] Annual Report of the Commissioner of Navigation to the Secretary of the Treasury (1901), 29.
[2] "Transatlantic Shipping and the War," Financial Times, (London), April 23, 1900, 2.

[3] U.S. Congress, House, Committee on Merchant Marine and Fisheries, Hearings before the House Merchant Marine Committee on the Development of the American Merchant Marine and American Commerce, 59th Cong., 1st sess., 1906, 487.
[4] Annual Report of the Commissioner of Navigation to the Secretary of the Treasury (1900), 11.
[5] Hearings before the Senate Commerce Committee on the Establishment of an American Merchant Marine, 538.
[6] William E. Humphrey, "The Pending Shipping Legislation," North American Review 182, no. 592 (March 1906): 446–55, 450.
[7] Hearings before the House Merchant Marine and Fisheries Committee on the Development of the American Merchant Marine, 489.
[8] U.S. Congress, Senate, Employment of United States Vessels for Public Purposes, 58th Cong., 2nd sess., 1904, S. Rep. 58-182.
[9] Report of the Merchant Marine Commission, S. Rep. 58-2755, 39.
[10] H.R. 14441, 57th Cong., 1st sess., 35 CONG. REC. 5532 (May 15, 1902).
[11] U.S. Congress, House, Transportation of Government Supplies to the Philippines, 57th Cong., 1st sess., 1902, H. Rep. 57-2348.
[12] 35 CONG. REC. 6889 (June 16, 1902).
[13] 35 CONG. REC. 6891.
[14] 38 CONG. REC. 2408 (February 26, 1904).
[15] U.S. Congress, Senate, Transportation of Government Supplies from the United States to the Philippine Islands, Etc., 58th Cong., 2nd sess., 1904, S. Doc. 58-94.
[16] 38 CONG. REC. 2469 (February 27, 1904).
[17] Employment of Vessels of the United States for Public Purposes, S. Rep. 58-182; Employment of Vessels of the United States for Public Purposes, H. Rep. 58-1893.
[18] 38 CONG. REC. 2409 (February 26, 1904).
[19] 38 CONG. REC. 2597 (March 1, 1904).
[20] 38 CONG. REC. 2417 (February 26, 1904).
[21] 38 CONG. REC. 2414.
[22] The "McCumber Amendment" was interpreted in Sea-Land Service, Inc. v. Danzig, 211 F. 3d 1371 (Fed. Cir. 2000).
[23] Employment of Vessels of the United States for Public Purposes, H. Rep. 58-1893.
[24] 38 CONG. REC. 2596 (March 1, 1904).
[25] 33 Stat. 518 (April 28, 1904); 10 U.S.C. § 2631(a).
[26] Kenneth Wimmel, Theodore Roosevelt and the Great White Fleet (Dulles, VA: Brasseys, 1998), 214–18.
[27] James R. Reckner, Teddy Roosevelt's Great White Fleet (Annapolis, MD: U.S. Naval Institute Press, 1988), 9.
[28] For example, "The Fleet Will Go," New York Times, September 27, 1907, 1.
[29] "Roosevelt Plans Fleet's Sailing," New York Times, August 24, 1907.

30 "Japanese Admiral Here Talking Peace–Nations' Friendship Not to Be Broken by Passing Storm, Says Yamamoto," New York Times, July 11, 1907, 2.
31 "Fleet Going to Japan at Mikado's Wish," New York Times, March 21, 1908, 1.
32 For example, "Walker Hires Hall, Scolds Roosevelt–Says Sending the Fleet to the Pacific is Invitation to Japan to Fight," New York Times, September 8, 1907, 5.
33 Annual Reports of the Navy Department for the Fiscal Year 1908 (Washington, DC: Government Printing Office, 1908), 5–6; "Pacific Trip Costs $1,229,280 in Coal," New York Times, October 13, 1907, 4; Park Benjamin, "Warships as Playthings," Independent 64, no. 3096 (April 2, 1908): 737–40; Charles A. Sidman, "Feeding the Battle-Ship Squadron on Its Cruise," Harper's Weekly 51, no. 2655 (November 9, 1907): 1666; "Navy Lacks Colliers," New York Times, August 27, 1907, 4.
34 Alfred T. Mahan, "The True Significance of the Pacific Cruise," Scientific American 97, no. 23 (December 7, 1907): 407, 412–13.
35 Theodore Roosevelt, Seventh Annual Message, December 3, 1907, UC Santa Barbara, the American Presidency Project, https://www.presidency.ucsb.edu/documents/seventh-annual-message-4.
36 Speculations abound, such as in Lori Bogle, "Why T.R. Sent the Great White Fleet," Daybook 12, no. 2, Hampton Roads Naval Museum (October 2007): 7–9.
37 When the fleet arrived in Mexico before heading to California, foreign observers expressed surprise that the fleet arrived intact without any stragglers. For example, "Berlin, March 17," New York Times, March 18, 1908, 3; Theodore Roosevelt: An Autobiography (New York: Macmillan, 1913), 592, 594–95.
38 Robert A. Hart, The Great White Fleet: Its Voyage around the World 1907-1909 (Boston: Little, Brown, 1965), 15–23.
39 "Battleship Fleet to Circle World," New York Times, September 5, 1907, 1.
40 "The Fleet Will Go," New York Times, September 27, 1907, 1.
41 Annual Reports of the Navy Department for the Fiscal Year 1908, 297.
42 "Lack of Colliers Cripples Big Fleet," Washington Times, November 28, 1908, 13.
43 "Can Use Foreign Colliers? –Belief That Department of Justice Upholds Navy Department," New York Times, October 4, 1907, 5.
44 U.S. Attorney General, "Coal for Navy: Transportation in Foreign Vessels," 26 Op. Att'y Gen. 415 (October 3, 1907). Rep. C. E. Littlefield (R-MA) wrote in opposition to the interpretation that U.S. government cargo was exempt from the U.S. coastwise laws. "Disagrees with Bonaparte–Littlefield Says Collier Decision Is Based on Misconception of Statute," New York Times, October 29, 1907, 10.
45 "Coal for Navy: Transportation in Foreign Vessels," Op. Att'y Gen. 26, no. 415.
46 U.S. Attorney General, "Coal for Navy: Transportation in Foreign Vessel: Tonnage Tax," Op. Att'y Gen. 26, no. 426 (October 9, 1907).
47 "Plead for Strong Merchant Marine–Naval Deficiency Cannot Long Continue without Inviting Calamity, Says Newberry," New York Times, December 22, 1907, 6.
48 "Berlin, Dec. 17," New York Times, December 18, 1907, 2.
49 "Weak Point in National Armor," New-York Daily Tribune, December 21, 1907, 7.

[50] U.S. Congress, Senate, Operations of Pay Department of the Atlantic Fleet on Cruise around the World, 61st Cong., 2nd sess., 1910, S. Doc. 61-646, 23–24.

[51] Daniel Joseph Costello, "Planning for War: A History of the General Board of the Navy, 1900–1914," Ph.D. diss., Fletcher School of Law and Diplomacy (1968), 570, https://archive.org/details/planningforwarah00cost.

[52] 42 CONG. REC. 3633–36 (March 20, 1908). Newlands offered an amendment again in opposition to Gallinger Commission legislation in 1911 to build thirty vessels for the Navy to be used in commercial service which failed 37 to 39 with 15 not voting. Senator Wesley Jones voted with the Democrats in favor of the amendment. 46 CONG. REC. 1819–21 (February 2. 1911).

[53] Zeiss, American Shipping Policy, 51; Causes of the Reduction of American Tonnage, H. Rep. 41-28, 17, 19–21.

[54] 42 CONG. REC. 3636 (March 20, 1908). Funds were later appropriated for the purchase of U.S.-flag colliers. "Rejects Bids for Colliers–Navy Department Refuses to Purchase High-Priced Vessels," New York Times, July 30, 1908, 12.

[55] 42 CONG. REC. 3636 (March 20, 1908); "Navy Need of Colliers—Senator Hale Says Fleet is at Disadvantage without Them," New York Times, March 21, 1908, 1. Only nine U.S.-flag Navy colliers participated in the operation. Information Relative to the Voyage of the United States Atlantic Fleet Around the World, December 16, 1907 to February 22, 1909 (Washington, DC: Government Printing Office, 1910), 15.

[56] Winthrop L. Marvin, "The Greatest Naval Cruise of Modern Times," American Review of Reviews 37I, no. 4 (April 1908): 456–63.

[57] "Plans Completed for Naval Review—Maritime Pageant Will Surpass Anything of the Kind Seen in American Waters," New York Times, November 10, 1907, 4.

[58] For example, "When the Big Fleet Comes to San Francisco," San Francisco Call, July 28, 1907, 5; "New Rank for Fighting Bob," Pacific Commercial Advertisor, November 9, 1907, 10; "Fleetitis Raged in Australia," Sun, October 4, 1908, 4. The fleet of United Fruit Company vessels painted white was also called the "Great White Fleet." Pedraja, A Historical Dictionary of the U.S. Merchant Marine, 614–15.

[59] Hart, Great White Fleet, chap. 1.

[60] "Navy-Mad Throngs at Hampton Roads," New York Times, February 21, 1909, 1.

[61] "Lessons and Results of the Battleship Cruise," Scientific American 100, no. 8 (February 20, 1909): 140 (each emphasis in original).

[62] Edward S. Miller, War Plan Orange–The U.S. Strategy to Defeat Japan, 1897-1945 (Annapolis, MD: U.S. Naval Institute Press, 1991), 126. The relationship of U.S. war planning to coal logistics is also discussed in Michael Vlahos, "The Naval War College and the Origins of War-Planning against Japan," Naval War College Review 33, no. 4 (July–August 1980): 23–41.

[63] Miller, War Plan Orange, 127.

[64] "US Ship Force Levels," Naval History and Heritage Command, www.history.navy.mil/research/histories/ship-histories/us-ship-force-levels.html#1904.

[65] Miller, War Plan Orange, 130.
[66] Another issue was whether to permit railroad-owned ocean lines to utilize the canal. Congress determined that they should not be so permitted. 37 Stat. 560, § 11 (August 24, 1912). As later determined by a court, "Congress specifically designed the Canal Act to protect independent water carriers from unfair competition by rail-owned water carriers." Water Transport Ass'n v. I.C.C., 715 F. 581, 583 (D.C. Cir. 1983).
[67] Letter of the Secretary of War transmitting The First Annual Report of the Isthmian Canal Commission, December 1, 1904 (Washington, DC: Government Printing Office, 1905), 12.
[68] U.S. Congress, House, Purchase of Material and Equipment for Use in Construction of the Panama Canal, 59th Cong., 1st sess., 1906, H. Rep. 59-4878, 1–2.
[69] Purchase of Material and Equipment for Use in Construction of the Panama Canal, H. Rep. 59-4878.
[70] 40 Cong. Rec. 7278 (May 23, 1906) & 9250 (June 26, 1906).
[71] Employment of United States Vessels for Public Purposes, S. Rep. 60-182.
[72] 42 Cong. Rec. 1105 (January 27, 1908).
[73] Employment of United States Vessels for Public Purposes, S. Rep. 60-182.
[74] 42 Cong. Rec. 3035–3045 (March 9, 1908), 3200–06 (March 12, 1908) and 3264–73 (March 13, 1908).
[75] U.S. Congress, House, Transportation by Sea of Material and Equipment for Use in Construction of Panama Canal, 60th Cong., 1st sess., 1908, H. Rep. 60-1534, 12–15.
[76] "Gen. Goethals Dies after Long Illness—Builder of Panama Canal and Once Ruler of the Isthmus Succumbs Here at 70," New York Times, January 22, 1928, 1.
[77] Transportation by Sea of Material and Equipment for Use in Construction of Panama Canal, H. Rep. 60-1534, 14–15.
[78] 46 Cong. Rec. 54 (December 7, 1910).
[79] Annual Report of the Commissioner of Navigation to the Secretary of Commerce and Labor (1911), 11.
[80] 32 Stat. 1903, Treaty Series 401 (February 31, 1902).
[81] Annual Report of the Commissioner of Navigation to the Secretary of Commerce and Labor (1911), 22.
[82] Annual Report of the Commissioner of Navigation to the Secretary of Commerce and Labor (1911), 22.
[83] U.S. Congress, House, The Panama Canal: Hearings before the Committee on Interstate and Foreign Commerce, 62nd Cong., 2nd sess., 1912, H. Doc. 62-680, 1912, 805–922.
[84] The Panama Canal: Hearings before the Committee on Interstate and Foreign Commerce, H. Doc. 62-680, 880.
[85] U.S. Congress, House, Operation of Panama Canal, 62nd Cong., 2nd sess., 1912, H. Rep. 62-423.

[86] U.S. Congress, Senate, The Panama Canal and Restoration of American Merchant Marine, 62nd Cong., 2nd sess., 1912, S. Doc. 62-881, 4, 10–11.
[87] 48 Cong. Rec. 6692 (May 17, 1912).
[88] War Department Annual Reports, 1911 (Washington, DC: Government Printing Office, 1912), 58.
[89] For example, 48 Cong. Rec. 6597–6601 (May 16, 1912), 6654 (May 17, 1912) and 6761–6762 (May 18, 1912).
[90] 48 Cong. Rec. 9353 (July 20, 1912).
[91] For example, 51 Cong. Rec. 13720–26 (August 14, 1914).
[92] 51 Cong. Rec. 6602 (May 16, 1912).
[93] 51 Cong. Rec. 6602–03.
[94] 51 Cong. Rec. 6690 (May 17, 1912).
[95] 51 Cong. Rec. 6694.
[96] "J. W. Alexander, Wilson Aide, Dies," New York Times, February 28, 1936, 21.
[97] 51 Cong. Rec. 7019–20.
[98] Theodore Roosevelt, Seventh Annual Message, December 3, 1912, UC Santa Barbara, the American Presidency Project, https://www.presidency.ucsb.edu/documents/seventh-annual-message-4.
[99] 37 Stat. 560, 562 (August 24, 1912).
[100] William S. Coker, "The Panama Canal Tolls Controversy: A Different Perspective," Journal of American History 55, no. 3 (December 1968): 555–64, 556.
[101] 1912 Democratic Party Platform, June 25, 1912, UC Santa Barbara, The American Presidency Project, Democratic Party Platforms, https://www.presidency.ucsb.edu/documents/1912-democratic-party-platform.
[102] "Democrats Shift on Tolls," New York Times, January 25, 1913, 8.
[103] "Commerce Chamber Hits Free Tolls Law," New York Times, February 14, 1913, 8.
[104] "Democrats and the Toll Bill," New York Times, February 20, 1913, 10; "The Panama Tolls Subsidy," New York Times, May 21, 1913, 10.
[105] David F. Houston, Eight Years with Wilson's Cabinet, 1913-1920: With a Personal Estimate of the President (Garden City, NY: Doubleday, Page, 1926), vol. 1, 59–60.
[106] Coker, "The Panama Canal Tolls Controversy: A Different Perspective," 559; "Grey Answers Knox on Tolls Dispute," New York Times, March 1, 1913, 7.
[107] 51 Cong. Rec. 4313 (March 5, 1914).
[108] 38 Stat. 385, 386 (June 17, 1914).
[109] 51 Cong. Rec. 10247–48 (June 11, 1914).
[110] For example, "Panama Canal Tolls Question Reopened," Evening Journal (Delaware), (May 5, 1921), 5.
[111] 46 Cong. Rec. 1825 (February 2, 1911).

[112] 46 CONG. REC. 1921 (February 3, 1911). The amendment and its rationale are described in U.S. Congress, House, Merchant Marine and Fisheries Committee, American Merchant Marine in Foreign Trade and the National Defense, 61st Cong., 2nd sess., 1910, H. Rep. 61-502, 14-15. Representative Alexander signed the minority report led by Representative Spight that objected to the subsidies, called for discriminating duties in favor of U.S.-flag vessels, and said that the free ship provision in the Republican proposal was just "'bait' to catch Democratic 'suckers'" because it was so constrained that it was bound to fail. American Merchant Marine in Foreign Trade and the National Defense, H. Rep. 61-502, parts 2 and 3.

[113] H.R. 8765, 62nd Cong., 2nd sess. (1911). Earlier versions and a later version (H.R. 16692) are described in U.S. Congress, House, American Registries for Certain Seagoing Vessels, 62d Cong., 2d sess., 1912, H. Rep. 62-405.

[114] American Registries for Certain Seagoing Vessels, H. Rep. 62-405.

[115] 11 Stat. 313 (June 11, 1858) (repealed 4 Stat. 129, § 5 (March 3, 1825) which required the president or secretary of any company registering a vessel to swear that "no part of such steamboat or vessel has been, or is then, owned by any foreigner or foreigners."). The authority of a U.S. corporation owned by non-citizens to register a "vessel of the United States" was confirmed in administrative decisions. For example, U.S. Attorney General, Registry and Enrollment of Vessels, Op. Att'y Gen. 29, no. 188 (July11, 1911).

[116] S. 1672, 62nd Cong., 2nd sess. (1911).

[117] American Registries for Certain Seagoing Vessels, H. Rep. 62-405, part 2.

[118] 48 CONG. REC. 10437 (August 8, 1912).

[119] 40 CONG. REC. 6959 (May 16, 1906).

[120] 48 CONG. REC. 10438–44 (August 8, 1912).

[121] 48 CONG. REC. 10441.

[122] 48 CONG. REC. 10443–44.

[123] 48 CONG. REC. 10444.

[124] 37 Stat. 560 (August 24, 1912).

AMERICAN LINE.

THE AMERICAN STEAMSHIP COMPANY

OF PHILADELPHIA.

Weekly Mail Steamship Service between

PHILADELPHIA AND LIVERPOOL,

CALLING AT QUEENSTOWN.

Sailing every Thursday from Philadelphia and every Wednesday from Liverpool.

| PENNSYLVANIA, | INDIANA, | ABBOTSFORD, |
| OHIO, | ILLINOIS, | *KENILWORTH. |

PRICES OF PASSAGE IN CURRENCY.

First Cabin, $75 to $100, according to accommodations.
Intermediate and Steerage tickets to and from all points at lowest current rates.
Steamers marked with a star do not carry intermediate.
Passenger accommodations for all classes unsurpassed. Ample attendance is provided. Every steamer carries a surgeon and stewardess.
These steamers are supplied with Life-Rafts, in addition to the usual Life-Boats and Life-Preservers.
Through tickets and through bills of lading issued between all prominent points.
For passage, rates of freight and other information, apply to

PETER WRIGHT & SONS, General Agents,

No. 307 Walnut St., Philadelphia.

RICHARDSON, SPENCE & CO., Liverpool.   N. & J. CUMMINS & BROS., Queenstown.

American Line Advertisement, 1874,
Pennsylvania Illustrated Advertiser

Chapter 15—Combinations and Conferences

The advent of steamships made it possible for vessels to keep to an announced schedule and to offer common carriage, regardless of whether they were full of cargo or not.[1] Vessels still "tramped" (meaning they went wherever the cargo was) to where they could obtain cargoes that were not on a schedule, but travelers and certain cargoes migrated to regular, scheduled service.

Vessels sailing on a regular schedule regardless of cargo strongly incentivized vessel owners to fill their vessels at almost any rate necessary. This tended to lead to rate wars.[2] When overall business was down, such as when a trade lane had too many vessels, competition could be fierce for cargoes which led to freight rate races to the bottom.

There was also keen competition to offer the best service to capture premium passenger and cargo traffic in the North Atlantic. Every generation of steamship was faster, larger, and better appointed than the previous generation. There was an advantage in offering more frequent service, leading to the need for more and more capital. Moreover, no line could afford to sit still with their existing vessels or risk extinction. There were no barriers to entry, vessels could sail to whatever trade lane was the most lucrative, and anyone with sufficient capital could order vessels for international trade. As a result, there was a strong tendency to overcapacity. This contributed to, and exacerbated, the rate wars.

Carriers reacted where possible with rate "truces," reflected in agreements among competitors to fix minimum rates. These were known as "conferences."[3] In a similar vein, and long after the first conference was formed, an American company financed and promoted by J. Pierpoint Morgan attempted to dominate the important North Atlantic trade by trying to gather all the significant ocean carriers in one combination.

THE AMERICAN PERIL[4]

Although the origins of the International Mercantile Marine Company, or IMM, are hazy, the idea of a dominant combination of carriers in the North Atlantic taking advantage of the growing U.S. export trade likely came from Clement A. Griscom.[5] J. P. Morgan also played an essential role in financing and organizing the company.[6] The *Boston Herald* in 1912 credited both men: "Napoleon of Shipping Dead—Clement A. Griscom Engineered J. P. Morgan's Ocean Combination."[7]

Born in 1841 to a prominent Philadelphia family, Griscom graduated from the Friends' Academy in 1857 at the age of sixteen and went to work as a clerk in the prominent Quaker ship brokerage and steamship agency firm of Peter Wright & Sons.[8] He was a partner by the time he was twenty-two. In 1871, the Peter Wright firm was appointed the agent for the American Steamship Company. That company was controlled by the Pennsylvania Railroad Company, which operated U.S.-flag vessels in what was known then as the "Keystone Line" between Liverpool and Philadelphia.

In the same year, Peter Wright & Sons and the railroad formed International Navigation Company (INC)—with Griscom as vice president and James A. Wright, Peter Wright's oldest son, as president. According to Griscom family lore, the port of Antwerp was chosen as a locus of the new line by triangulating pins and lines on a wall map from northern European manufacturing centers.[9] At the time, Antwerp was underutilized because it lagged with port improvements. Griscom was chosen to go to Antwerp and make a deal.

In Belgium, Griscom negotiated a joint venture between INC and the newly formed Belgian company Société Anonyme de Navigation Belgo-Américaine. The joint venture ordered its first three vessels to be constructed in Britain and to focus its service on Antwerp under the Belgian flag and with Belgian crews.

That service was known as the "Red Star Line" after its stack symbol: a white stripe with a red five-pointed star.

By the time the Red Star Line had ceased operations in 1935, it had transported more than 2.5 million persons to North America and was one of the major lines transporting Jewish refugees from Europe.[10] Since 2013 there has been a museum in Antwerp commemorating the company's emigration history.[11]

In 1873 Griscom also became the manager of the American Steamship Company, later acquired by INC in 1884. Peter Wright & Sons had been the American agents of the Inman Steamship Company since 1874.[12] Inman was a prominent British company subsidized by British ocean mail subsidies and was a rival of Cunard Line and the White Star Line. As mentioned in a previous chapter, INC bought Inman out of bankruptcy,[13] and in 1888, Griscom became President of INC. Inman was then merged into American Steamship Company (the "American Line") in 1893.

The purchase of Inman created a problem when the British government withdrew mail subsidies because the company came under American control.[14] This was a harbinger of what was to come with INC's acquisitions of other British lines.

Inman had already ordered two vessels to upgrade its fleet, which had to be accounted for in the merger. Griscom, who studied marine architecture and was the first president of the Society of Naval Architects and Marine Engineers (SNAME), helped design the two vessels with innovative features. This included twin-screw propellers, transverse bulkheads, and watertight compartments.[15] The vessels were more reliable than single screw vessels and the danger of sinking was greatly lessened since localized damage would not flood the entire hull. The vessels—the *City of New York* and the *City of Paris*—were delivered in 1888. For a while, they were the most luxurious vessels operating on the North Atlantic.

Reacting to the loss of British subsidies, Griscom then conducted a political campaign to permit the U.S. registry of these two vessels (despite being foreign-built) in exchange for the company's commitment to construct two comparable vessels in the United States—a bargain discussed previously in connection with construction of the *St. Louis* and *St. Paul* at Cramp Shipyard.

The next stage of expansion for INC came through a connection with J. P. Morgan. Griscom's prominence brought him into regular contact with politicians and other business leaders, including Morgan.[16] For example, he met Senator Hanna and Morgan on holiday at the thermal baths in Aix-les-Bains in France in 1898.[17] In 1900 during the Republican national convention, Hanna stayed in Griscom's home in Haverford, a Main Line town outside of Philadelphia.

On maritime policy, Griscom was a delegate to the International Maritime Conference in 1889, where he worked with Chamberlain. He was chairman of Frye's 1897 *ad hoc* committee to promote the merchant marine. And he was an active supporter of operating subsidies.[18] Griscom also testified before congressional committees to promote the U.S. merchant marine.[19]

Griscom's vision was to create a combination of American-owned carriers that could serve the entire North American coast with substantial U.S.-flag participation, supported by U.S. government subsidies.[20] When Griscom met Morgan in 1899 in connection with the refinancing of INC, he shared his vision, and the two went to work to make it a reality.

INC, with Morgan's backing, made the first moves in December 1900 by getting Bernard Baker to agree to merge Atlantic Transport Company into INC. Morgan helped finance the acquisition and the construction for Baker of new U.S.-built vessels in anticipation of U.S subsidies under the Hanna-Payne-Frye legislation.[21] Baker had been in publicized negotiations to merge with the British Leyland Line, and this reportedly prompted Griscom/Morgan's move.

Baker then assisted Morgan with the acquisition of Leyland in 1901.[22] Unlike Griscom's purchase of the Inman Line, the Leyland Line was fully solvent, and Morgan's reputation of going big gave notice to the British of more to come.[23] In his various negotiations, Morgan added that his aim was to amalgamate U.S. railroad interests with shipping companies to provide the whole extent of the transportation of cargoes.[24]

In early 1902 Morgan negotiated a cooperation agreement with the two largest German lines, Hamburg-American Line and North German Lloyd Line. He also secured an agreement with Harlan & Wolff located in Belfast to build INC's vessels at that shipyard.[25] Those two German lines had refused to be amalgamated.

Morgan followed these moves up in April 1902 by announcing the acquisition of the White Star Line, the most profitable British line (and later the smaller Dominion Line). White Star's largest shareholder was the estate of Thomas H. Ismay, and a sale to some third party had been likely to settle the estate.

Morgan undertook these efforts even though the shipping market had turned bearish. In March 1902, the U.S. Senate adopted an amendment to the Hanna-Payne-Frye subsidy legislation prohibiting foreign-built vessels from receiving subsidies.[26] Morgan went to Washington and had lunch with Hanna to discuss the legislation's prospects immediately after adoption of that amendment.[27] After the meeting, Morgan made retaining British subsidies under British flag a priority.

The overall result was "the largest and most completely equipped steamship company in the world," with 136 ocean steamships of over 1 million tons.[28] Hamburg-American, the next largest, had vessels of aggregating about 600,000 tons. Despite the impressive size of the company, the common view was that Morgan overpaid for both Leyland and White Star which later hobbled IMM.[29] In addition, IMM only owned roughly one-third of the North Atlantic trade capacity, which was not enough to give it sufficient market power to control rates.[30]

Furthermore, the combination of so many lines under American ownership alarmed Britain.[31] The new conglomerate was variously referred to in British newspapers as "The Trust Octopus," "The Ocean Octopus," and "A National Peril."[32] Sensing "Peril," the *London Daily News* editorialized that "it is the ownership and control of the steamers rather than the flag they fly that is the real menace." Several White Star vessels were enrolled in the British Navy's "merchant cruiser" list, and, according to Winthrop Marvin, "it was almost as if the Yankees had surreptitiously acquired a section of his Majesty's navy."[33]

There was speculation that the combination would eventually encompass Cunard and large Belgian and Dutch lines.[34] Griscom's involvement also led some to believe that the vessels would be reflagged, along the lines of the 1892 reflag legislation, and that the true threat was U.S. subsidies.[35] Griscom was later quoted in the House of Commons to that effect.[36] INC leaders frequently denied that this was their intention.[37] Still, the threat was perceived as being so dire that some urged Britain to consider reestablishing its navigation laws abandoned mid-nineteenth century.[38]

In the United States, Morgan was called the "real ruler of the world's marine."[39] Yet to retain British subsidies and not suffer the Inman Line experience, Morgan negotiated a confidential twenty-year agreement with the British government, promising to keep British vessels under British flag with British management and British crews.[40]

The *New York Times* criticized the agreement, arguing that the vessels owned by American interests could thus be used against the nation or against a country toward which the United States was neutral. This, in fact, occurred in World War I.[41] Chamberlain agreed that American and British interests could diverge, putting the vessels in an awkward position.[42] The agreement, which was not fully revealed at the time, was used as evidence by Senator Wesley Jones in 1921 of British dominance of worldwide shipping when he placed it in the *Congressional Record*.[43]

The agreement was also criticized by the British for permitting the vessels to remain under British flag, despite U.S ownership.[44] The British government granted special subsidies to Cunard in a companion agreement to keep Cunard under British ownership, which increased the economic pressure on INC.[45]

In October 1902, the combination was made official with the reorganization of INC as the International Mercantile Marine Company or IMM. Griscom was the first president. The board of directors would be dominated by Americans. But, reflecting the sensitivities about who was in control, there would be a "British Committee" to manage the British lines.[46] J. Bruce Ismay, the son of Thomas Ismay, was made a director on the British committee.

In late 1907 the British government provided grants to Cunard to build the liners *Lusitania* and *Mauretania*. IMM responded in 1908 with the order to build the vessels *Olympic*, *Titanic*, and *Britannic*. Meanwhile, IMM's management had changed earlier, when Bruce Ismay replaced Griscom as president of IMM in 1904.

Philip A. S. Franklin, placed in charge of Atlantic Transport when IMM was formed, also became one of IMM's vice presidents. Franklin was to play significant roles in the mobilization of the U.S. merchant marine in World War I and in the formulation of the 1920 Merchant Marine Act.

However, Franklin first became famous for another reason. He oversaw the White Star Line office in New York in April 1912 when the news of the *Titanic* disaster was received. His first public statement on the morning of April 15 was to claim that the vessel was un-sinkable and everyone was safe.[47] Franklin later had to admit that the *Titanic* had gone down and that he had held back bad news.[48] The misstep did not hurt Franklin's career.

Bruce Ismay, on the other hand, was on the *Titanic* and was one of the few male passengers who survived.[49] He was played by Jonathan Hyde in the 1997 movie *Titanic*.[50] He was severely criticized in the press as a coward although he was cleared of any wrongdoing in subsequent investigations.[51] He tortured himself for surviving when so many had been lost. He became a recluse dying at the age of seventy-four in 1937.

Bad news seemed to follow IMM thereafter. The two leading German shipping lines ended their arrangement with IMM in May 1912.[52] Griscom died in June 1912; Morgan died in March 1913.[53] An antitrust suit brought by the U.S. government in 1911 was ongoing. The government alleged that the rate coordination agreements among the lines violated U.S. antitrust laws. That case did not conclude until 1916 when the U.S. Supreme Court determined it was mooted by the world war.[54] The *New York Times* headlined the suit in 1912 as "The Ship Trust That Has Drawn Uncle Sam's Fire." The article focused on an unflattering German exposé of how IMM came together.[55]

IMM was never able to find efficiencies in its size sufficient to overcome the capital outlays to acquire the lines necessary to form the combination. Rate wars continued until World War I. Ultimately, the steamship trust came to be called "J. P. Morgan's Greatest Failure."[56]

IMM entered receivership in 1915 and, although there was a substantial revival in World War I under Franklin's management, the British lines were sold following the war. In 1943, IMM merged with United States Lines Co., its then principal subsidiary. IMM/United States Lines occupied No. 1 Broadway in New York until 1979.[57]

Winthrop Marvin, a defender of IMM, argued that "the chief service which Mr. Morgan's merger has thus far rendered to his country is in demonstrating that American capital is now ready to seek the sea—that our wealth is no longer absorbed in purely domestic development."[58] Marvin, however, overstated the case. IMM's chief contribution to maritime policy was focusing government attention on both sides of the Atlantic on anti-competitive behavior.[59]

JOURNEY TO THE JONES ACT

ROYAL COMMISSION ON SHIPPING RINGS

Perhaps the first shipping "conference" was the 1850 agreement among the Brown Brothers, which apportioned the trade between Cunard and the Collins Line.[60] The first widely recognized rate-setting conference among ocean carriers operating between British ports and Calcutta was the 1875 "Calcutta Conference."[61]

Under the Calcutta conference agreement, carriers agreed not to offer preferential rates or concessions, which large volume shippers demanded. Deferred rebates were introduced in 1877 to address shipper demands. A deferred rebate is defined as the portion of the freight paid by the shipper to the carrier, returned by the carrier to the shipper in the future (deferred)—if the shipper remained loyal to the conference.[62] These rebates incentivized large shippers without freezing out small shippers.[63] A U.S. congressional report later concluded that, "between 1875 and 1906, the deferred rebate system came into almost universal use."[64]

British and colonial chambers of commerce complained to the British government about the rebate system, particularly in the South African trade.[65] A Royal Commission on Shipping Rings was charged in November 1906 to examine the system of deferred rebates "and to report whether such operation have caused, or are likely to cause injury to British or Colonial trade."[66] Arthur Cohen, who had been junior counsel to the British member of the Alabama Claims Tribunal, was appointed the chairman of the Royal Commission.[67]

The Royal Commission produced an extensive report backed by a multi-volume record. For the first time, it delineated common practices in ocean shipping conferences.[68] Like a splintered Supreme Court decision, the majority commission report was signed by eleven members. But two had reservations, and there was a minority report signed by five members, with one member having reservations. The extensive testimony was often candid about how conferences benefited the conference members.[69]

The commission focused on deferred rebates and determined that such rebates were created to "tie" shippers to carriers. This was because shippers who did not remain loyal would not only lose rebates for the current period, but also for a prior period. The commission observed that conferences were weak in certain trade lines, like the North Atlantic. It attributed that weakness to the importance of passengers in that trade who obviously were unaffected by a deferred rebate incentive.

The commission determined that a conference "formed and safeguarded by such a tie as the deferred rebate, necessarily created a certain kind of monopoly." But there are limitations on the power of the monopoly, such as the presence of shipping capacity outside the conference by tramp carriers. And the lack of conference cohesion on ancillary activities, such as cargo storage and handling facilities, restrained the monopoly power of the conferences.[70]

The advantages of the conference system, as indicated by shippers to the Commission, were that it tended to provide regular and fixed service, serving a range of ports on a stable basis. Conferences also tended to provide equality of service among similarly situated shippers. Shippers found this valuable.[71] The commission found that "a large proportion (we are disposed to believe a large majority) of the regular shippers regarding Shipping Conferences making use of the system of deferred rebates as the necessary means by which the advantages supplied under an organised service can be attained."[72] It concluded that "where regular and organised service is required, the Conference system, fortified by some tie upon the shipper, is as a general rule necessary."

The commission also identified disadvantages of the conference system along the lines of the usual market disadvantages of monopolies. Although the evidence was inconclusive, it was alleged that conferences charged arbitrarily high rates.[73]

Given the advantages, the commission rejected outlawing deferred rebates and direct government intervention.[74] Instead, it recommended that the British government encourage associations of shippers to countervail conference influence, that the British Board of Trade monitor conferences (including requiring confidential filing of conference agreements with the Board), and that conferences be required to publish tariffs.[75] The commission was particularly hopeful that "counter-combinations" of shippers would rein in conference abuses, since "shipowners conducting the operations of Conference Lines are public-spirited men fully alive to the desirability of encouraging trade."[76]

The commission minority determined that conferences were inefficient, that shippers paid higher than necessary rates in the conference system, and that there was no evidence that conferences have "appreciably increased regularity of sailing or greatly improved the quality of steamers."[77] But, the minority nevertheless hesitated to recommend strong action echoing the majority's view of the "high character" of conference lines. Instead, the minority recommended a difference in degree by seeking to strengthen British government oversight over conferences and by giving greater power to shipper associations than was provided by the commission majority.

The most striking thing about the minority report is that even those who thought that the conference disadvantages outweighed the advantages were not prepared to recommend strenuous measures. It was left to the U.S. Congress to take meaningful action.

ALEXANDER COMMITTEE REPORT

Ocean shipping-related combinations and conferences were also criticized in the United States. As early as 1904 and 1905, the U.S. Interstate Commerce Commission (ICC) was investigating U.S. inland railroad agreements for the transportation of grain. The ICC sought to prevent railroads from disadvantaging any U.S. port.[78]

In 1907 Peter Wright & Sons brought a complaint before the ICC. It alleged that the Hamburg-American Line, North German Lloyd, and other lines operated in a pool that controlled U.S.

inland and ocean transportation.[79] The action was unsuccessful, however, as the ICC agreed with the defendants that it did not have jurisdiction, even though a portion of the shipping occurred in the United States

Representative William Humphrey, who had protested about how the Panama Canal would benefit Vancouver over Seattle, also complained that foreign conferences were manipulating and disadvantaging U.S. businesses. In February 1911, citing the dismissal of the Peter Wright ICC complaint, Humphrey introduced legislation that would have given the Justice Department the authority to deny access to U.S. ports of foreign lines that violated U.S. antitrust laws.[80]

The House Merchant Marine Committee report about the Humphrey proposal stated that "these combinations of foreign ships practice the same thing in the same way for the doing of which domestic trusts have been enjoined, dissolved, and their agents fined and sent to prison."[81] The legislation received favorable press and was supported by the Justice Department.[82] However, it was not acted on before the end of the Sixty-First Congress on March 3, 1911.[83]

Humphrey tried again in early 1912 with the introduction of a similar bill, a step approved by the Merchant Marine Committee.[84] This time Humphrey had the active support of Chairman Alexander.[85] Alexander explained that the bill was written with the Justice Department to make it possible to enforce the Sherman Anti-Trust Act against foreign vessels in the U.S. foreign trade.[86] The legislation passed the House without objection but was not actively considered by the Senate.[87]

In March 1912, the U.S. House had already authorized the Merchant Marine Committee to investigate shipping conferences.[88] The extensive investigation concluded with a landmark report issued in March 1914. This report, widely called the "Alexander Committee Report," was authored by Solomon S. Huebner on assignment to the committee.[89] Huebner was later known as a pioneer in insurance education as a professor at the Wharton School of the University of Pennsylvania. He assisted on marine insurance matters in connection with the 1920 Merchant Marine Act.[90]

The committee created a voluminous record, following on the work of the Royal Commission, and found that "it is the almost universal practice for steamship lines engaged in the American foreign trade to operate... under the terms of written agreements, conference arrangements or gentlemen's understandings." There were about eighty such agreements covering American trade.[91]

Like the Royal Commission, the Alexander Committee recognized that regular and sustained service was an advantage of the conference system. This should be retained, in its view, but there were also abuses such as discrimination among shippers and price gouging. The committee pointed out that "all monopolies are liable to abuse."[92]

At the same time, the committee was not optimistic about engendering open competition merely by prohibiting conferences, writing that "there is no happy medium between war and peace when several lines engage in the same trade."[93] Moreover, any attempt to dissolve all cooperative arrangements could harm U.S. trade.[94] The *New York Times* summarized the view with the headline "Find Shipping Pools Too Useful to End."[95] The path forward was "overwhelmingly in favor of some form of government regulation of steamship carriers engaged in this country's foreign trade" to address the abuses.[96]

The committee made separate, although similar, recommendations for U.S. foreign and domestic trade. In both instances, the committee recommended expanding the authority of the ICC to encompass review of all cooperative agreements involving U.S. trade, which would have to be filed with the ICC. For agreements in the foreign trade, the ICC which would be given the power to reject those "discriminating or unfair in character, or detrimental to the commercial interests." The ICC would also be given investigatory power. Freight rate rebating, discrimination between shippers or ports, and "fighting ships" would be prohibited. A "fighting ship" was a vessel employed by a conference to undercut the rates of a non-conference member to force them off a trade route.[97]

As to the domestic trade, the committee noted that the Panama Canal Act had required "divorcing of common carriers by water from the railroads under certain conditions."[98] The committee recommended preventing railroads from preferring or disadvantaging water carriers via rate disparity, terminal access or otherwise.[99]

The *New York Times* editorialized its support for the middle ground approach, writing that it was "welcome as proof that reason is returning to its throne in American economic legislation."[100] Ultimately, the committee's work reflected the confidence of the era that government could tamp down on market abuses while retaining the advantages of a competitive market.[101]

Alexander introduced legislation in June 1914 to implement the committee's recommendations.[102] Alexander argued that the purpose of the bill "was to preserve to shippers, through effective government control, the advantages obtainable only by permitting the several carriers in any given trade to cooperate through some form of rate and traffic arrangement, and that the same time prevent the abuses which the committee found to exist."[103] No action was taken on the legislation before the outbreak of World War I, at which point the attention of American policy makers immediately turned to the trade disruptions caused by that war in the summer of 1914.

---

[1] Royal Commission on Shipping Rings, Report of the Royal Commission on Shipping Rings with Minutes of Evidence and Appendices (London: Darling & Son, 1909), vol. 1, 10; J. Russell Smith, "Ocean Freight Rates and Their Control through Combination," Political Science Quarterly 21, no. 2 (June 1906): 237–63.

[2] For example, E. Robert Seaver & Edward Schmeltzer, "The Role of Conferences and the Dual-Rate System in Ocean Foreign Trade," Law and Contemporary Problems 24 (Fall 1959): 605–21, 606–08.

[3] Report of the Royal Commission on Shipping Rings with Minutes of Evidence and Appendices, vol. 4, 416.

⁴ Vale, The American Peril, 223–24.
⁵ Navin, "Study in Merger," 291–92.
⁶ Navin, "Study in Merger," 293–94 (Morgan's role "can best be described as a collateral position to a Philadelphian named Clement Acton Griscom.").
⁷ "Napoleon of Shipping Dead—Clement A. Griscom Engineered J. P. Morgan's Ocean Combination," Boston Herald, November 11, 1912, 5.
⁸ Dumas Malone, ed., Dictionary of American Biography (New York: Charles Scribner's Sons, 1932), 6-7; Dexter Marshall, "Clement Acton Griscom," Cosmopolitan 35, no. 1 (May 1903): 57–59; and Lawrence Perry, "The Head of the International Shipping Corporation," World's Work 5, no. 2 (December 1902): 2857–60.
⁹ Lloyd Carpenter Griscom, Diplomatically Speaking (New York: Literary Guild of America, 1940), 10–11.
¹⁰ Eugene Van Mieghem, One Foot in America: The Jewish Emigrants of the Red Star Line (Antwerp, Belgium: BAI Publishers, 2009).
¹¹ Grace Bello, "Museum in Antwerp Recalls the Ships That Brought Einstein and Irving Berlin to America," Tablet Magazine (November 26, 2013), https://www.tabletmag.com/sections/community/articles/red-star-line-museum-antwerp.
¹² Edward Needles Wright, "The Story of Peter Wright & Sons Philadelphia Quaker Shipping Firm 1818–1911," Quaker History 56, no. 2 (Autumn 1967): 67–89 (the author was the great-grandson of Peter Wright).
¹³ "Buying the Inman Line," New York Times, October 20, 1886, 10.
¹⁴ U.S. Congress, Senate, Commerce Committee, Hearings before the Senate Commerce Committee on the Bill "To Promote the Commerce and Increase the Foreign Trade of the United States, and to Provide Auxiliary Cruises, Transports, and Seamen for Government Use When Necessary" (Washington, DC: Government Printing Office, 1899), 26–27 (Testimony of Clement A. Griscom); Winthrop Marvin, "The Great Ship 'Combine,'" American Monthly Review of Reviews 26, no. 6 (December 1902): 679–88.
¹⁵ "Griscom, Founder of Ship Trust, Dead," New York Times, November 11, 1912, 11; Perry, "The Head of the International Shipping Corporation," 2857–60.
¹⁶ For example, "Hanna in Philadelphia," New York Times, (December 12, 1896), 1; "Senator Hanna Coming Here—Will Be Guest of Clement A Griscom on Latter's Yacht, and Then Go to Oyster Bay," New York Times, September 13, 1902, 1.
¹⁷ Griscom, Diplomatically Speaking, 127–28.
¹⁸ For example, "Hanna Will Push Ship Subsidy Bill," Philadelphia Inquirer, December 2, 1900, 7 (meeting at the Arlington Hotel in Washington, DC).
¹⁹ For example, Revival of the Merchant Marine, S. Doc. 56-149, 99–107.
²⁰ Navin, "Study in Merger," 302; Marshall, "Clement Acton Griscom," 57–59.
²¹ Navin, "Study in Merger," 300–01.
²² "J.P. Morgan & Co., Buy the Leyland Line," New York Times, April 30, 1901, 2.
²³ For example, "Mr. Carnegie and the Deal," Sheffield Daily Telegraph, May 1, 1901, 4; "Big Shipping Deal—American Railway Interests and the Leyland Line," Lloyd's List, April 30, 1901, 10.

24 Bernard Huldermann, Albert Ballin (London: Cassell, 1922), chap. 5.
25 These agreements appear in the Appendix to the Annual Report of the Commissioner of Navigation (1902).
26 35 CONG. REC. 2906 (March 17, 1902).
27 Navin, "Study in Merger," 316.
28 Annual Report of the Commissioner of Navigation (1902), 67.
29 For example, M. J. Fields, "The International Mercantile Marine Company—An Ill-Conceived Trust," Journal of Business of the University of Chicago 5, nos. 3 and 4 (July and October 1932): 268–82 and 362–79.
30 For example, J. Russell Smith, "Ocean Freight Rates and Their Control through Combination," Political Science Quarterly 21, no. 2 (June 1906): 237–63, 250, 258–59.
31 For example, "Morgan Alarms British," Oregonian, April 22, 1902, 5; "Comment on Morgan's Big Steamship Trust—The Combination Causing Considerable Perturbation in Great Britain," Times-Picayune, April 22, 1902, 9.
32 "The Trust Octopus," Weekly Dispatch (London), April 27, 1902, 1; "The Ocean Octopus," Dundee Evening Post, April 25, 1902, 5; "A National Peril," London Daily News, April 25, 1902, 6.
33 Marvin, "The Great Ship Combine."
34 For example, "The Shipping Trust," London Daily News, April 24, 1902, 12.
35 For example, W. Wetherrell, "American Millionaires and British Shipping," Fortnightly Review 77 (January to June 1902): 511–23; "The North Atlantic Shipping Trade," Times (London), April 28, 1902, 7.
36 124 Parl. Deb. H.C. (4th ser.) (July 2, 1903), column 1132.
37 "The North Atlantic Shipping Trust–A Statement of the Right Hon. W. J. Pirrie, Chairman of the Firm of Harland and Wolff," Times (London), (May 13, 1902), 8; Marvin, "The Great Ship Combine," 683.
38 Calchas [pseud.], "The Ocean Trust and National Policy." Fortnightly Review 426 (June 1, 1902): 942–56.
39 "Ocean Lines to Be Combined," Cleveland Leader, April 20, 1902, 1.
40 "The Agreement between the British Government and the Cunard and Morgan Combine Mercantile Fleets," Scientific American 84, no. 11 (September 12, 1903): 2. The U.S. government may not have known fully about these agreements until 1919. "Letter from E. Hurley to W. Wilson (January 20, 1919)," Papers of Woodrow Wilson, vol. 54, 171.
41 "The Ship Trust and the British Government," New York Times, April 3, 1903, 8; "The Cunard Company and the Shipping Combine," New York Times, July 21, 1903, 8.
42 Annual Report of the Commissioner of Navigation (1902), 68–69.
43 60 CONG. REC. 1856–60 (January 22, 1921).
44 "Britain and the Ship Trust," New York Times, April 23, 1903, 1.

[45] "Cunard Agreement Approved," New York Times, August 13, 1903, 5; Eugene Tyler Chamberlain, "The New Cunard Steamship Agreement," North American Review 177, no. 5631 (October 1903): 533–43.

[46] "Combination of Six Steamship Companies—International Corporation to Have a Capital of $120,000,000," New York Times, October 2, 1902, 1.

[47] For example, "Women Sob as News Bulletins Appear," New York Times, April 16, 1912, 5; "She Cannot Sink, Says Official of White Star Line," Evening World, April 15, 1912, 2.

[48] "Franklin Held Back Bad News–It Was Too Discouraging to Be Told, White Star Official Admits," New York Times, April 17, 1912, 2.

[49] For example, Stephen Cox, The Titanic Story, Hard Choices, Dangerous Decisions (Chicago: Open Court, 1999), chap. 2.

[50] Available at "Titanic," AFI Catalog (December 19, 1997), https://catalog.afi.com/Catalog/moviedetails/55202.

[51] Andrew Wilson, Shadow of the Titanic: The Extraordinary Stories of Those Who Survived (New York: Atria Books, 2011), chap. 6.

[52] "German Lines' Pool with Morgan Ended," New York Times, May 10, 1912, 1.

[53] "Griscom, Founder of Ship Trust, Dead," New York Times, November 11, 1912, 11.

[54] U.S. v. Hamburg-Amerikanishe Packetfahrt-Actien Gesellschaft, 239 U.S. 466 (1916).

[55] New York Times, June 23, 1912, 51.

[56] "J. P. Morgan's Greatest Failure–The Steamship Trust," Current Literature 53, no. 2 (August 1912): 172–174.

[57] "International Mercantile Marine Company Building," Landmarks Preservation Commission (September 19, 1995), http://s-media.nyc.gov/agencies/lpc/lp/1926.pdf.

[58] Winthrop L. Marvin, "The American Ship in 1902," Scribner's Magazine 32, no. 5 (November 1902), 577–83, 583.

[59] Vale, American Peril, 223.

[60] William Sjostrom, "Competition and Cooperation in Liner Shipping," Centre for Policy Studies, University College Cork, National University of Ireland, Working Paper no. 2009-02 (December 2009), 4.

[61] U.S. Congress, House, Special Subcommittee on Steamship Conferences, Hearings before the Special Subcommittee on Steamship Conferences of the House Merchant Marine and Fisheries Committee on the Steamship Conferences, 86th Cong., 1st sess., 1959, 254.

[62] 46 U.S.C. § 40102(10).

[63] Daniel Marx Jr., International Shipping Cartels: A Study of Industrial Self-Regulation by Shipping Conferences (Princeton, NJ: Princeton University Press, 1953), 47.

[64] Hearings before the Special Subcommittee on Steamship Conferences of the House Merchant Marine and Fisheries Committee on the Steamship Conferences Steamship Conference Study, 255.

[65] "Letter from D. Lloyd George to Arthur Cohen (Oct. 30, 1906)," in Lucy Cohen, Arthur Cohen, A Memoir by His Daughter for His Descendants (London: Bickers & Son, 1919), 181–82.

[66] Report of the Royal Commission on Shipping Rings, with Minutes of Evidence and Appendices, i.

[67] Tom Bingham, "The Alabama Claims Arbitration," International and Comparative Law Quarterly 54, no. 1 (January 2005); 1–25, 19.

[68] Kenneth J. Kryvoruka, "American Ocean Shipping and the Antitrust Laws Revisited," Journal of Maritime Law and Commerce 11, no. 1 (October 1979): 67–108, 73.

[69] John S. McGee, "Ocean Freight Rate Conferences and the American Merchant Marine," University of Chicago Law Review 27, no. 2 (Winter 1960): 191–314, 212.

[70] Report of the Royal Commission on Shipping Rings, vol. 1, 77.

[71] Report of the Royal Commission on Shipping Rings, vol. 1, 77–78.

[72] Report of the Royal Commission on Shipping Rings, vol. 1, 78.

[73] Report of the Royal Commission on Shipping Rings, vol. 1, 78.

[74] Report of the Royal Commission on Shipping Rings, vol. 1, 81–84.

[75] Report of the Royal Commission on Shipping Rings, vol. 1, 85–90.

[76] Report of the Royal Commission on Shipping Rings, vol. 1, 85.

[77] Report of the Royal Commission on Shipping Rings, vol. 1, 114.

[78] "In the Matter of Differential Freight Rates to and from North Atlantic Ports," I.C.C. Reports 11, no. 13 (April 27, 1905).

[79] "Cosmopolitan Shipping Company v. Hamburg-American Packet Company et. al.," I.C.C. Reports 13, no. 266 (March 9, 1908).

[80] 46 CONG. REC. 1520 (January 26, 1911).

[81] U.S. Congress, House, American Trade and Foreign Shipping Monopolies, 61st Cong., 3d sess., 1911, H. Rep. 61-2058.

[82] For example, "Foreign Steamship Trusts Arraigned," Boston Journal, January 28, 1911, 9; "Humphrey Aims to Curb Foreign Ship Trust," Albuquerque Journal, January 28, 1911, 1.

[83] Humphrey also introduced resolutions in the last session of the Sixty-First Congress and the first session of the Sixty-Second Congress for a joint House-Senate investigation of shipping line conferences. H. J. Res. 277, 61st Cong., 3rd sess. (1911); H. J. Res. 72, 62nd Cong., 2nd sess. (1911). The House Rules Committee also conducted a hearing in December 1911 on H. J. Res. 72. Hearings before the House Rules Committee on House Joint Resolution No. 72 Providing for an Investigation of the So-Called Shipping Trust (December 18, 1911) (Washington, DC: Government Printing Office, 1912).

[84] U.S. Congress, House, American Trade and Foreign Shipping Monopolies, 62nd Cong., 2nd sess., 1912, H. Rep. 62-632; "For Barring Ships of Foreign Trusts—House Committee Urges Bill Closing Our Ports to Those Run in Restraint of Trade," New York Times, May 2, 1912, 7.

[85] 48 Cong. Rec. 6849–51 (May 20, 1912).
[86] 48 Cong. Rec. 7563 (June 3, 1912).
[87] 48 Cong. Rec. 7563.
[88] H. Res. 425, 62nd Cong., 2nd sess. (1912); 48 Cong. Rec. 2836 (March 5, 1912).
[89] Proceedings of the Committee on the Merchant Marine and Fisheries in the Investigation of Shipping Combinations under House Resolution 587 (Washington, DC: Government Printing Office, 1913).
[90] "Dr. Solomon S. Huebner Dead; Pioneer in Insurance Education," New York Times, July 18, 1964, 19; Hearings before the Senate Commerce Committee on Establishment of an American Merchant Marine, 1334–68.
[91] Proceedings of the Committee on the Merchant Marine and Fisheries in the Investigation of Shipping Combinations under House Resolution 587, vol. 4, 415.
[92] Proceedings of the Committee on the Merchant Marine and Fisheries in the Investigation of Shipping Combinations under House Resolution 587, vol. 4, 304.
[93] Proceedings of the Committee on the Merchant Marine and Fisheries in the Investigation of Shipping Combinations under House Resolution 587, vol. 4, 416.
[94] Proceedings of the Committee on the Merchant Marine and Fisheries in the Investigation of Shipping Combinations under House Resolution 587, vol. 4, 416.
[95] "Find Shipping Pools Too Useful to End—Any Attempt to Dissolve Them Would Cripple Trade, Is House Committee's Conclusion," New York Times, March 2, 1914, 6.
[96] Proceedings of the Committee on the Merchant Marine and Fisheries in the Investigation of Shipping Combinations under House Resolution 587, vol. 4, 307–308.
[97] "Fighting ship" was defined in the Shipping Act, 1916 as "a vessel used in particular trade by a carrier or group of carriers for the purpose of excluding, preventing, or reducing competition by driving another carrier out of said trade." 39 Stat. 728, 733 (September 7, 1916).
[98] Proceedings of the Committee on the Merchant Marine and Fisheries in the Investigation of Shipping Combinations under House Resolution 587, vol. 4, 422.
[99] Proceedings of the Committee on the Merchant Marine and Fisheries in the Investigation of Shipping Combinations under House Resolution 587, vol. 4, 423–24.
[100] "Shipping Trusts," New York Times, March 3, 1914, 8.
[101] McGee, "Ocean Freight Rate Conferences and the American Merchant Marine," 195.
[102] 51 Cong. Rec. 10705 (June 18, 1914).
[103] "Federal Control for Water Lines," New York Times, June 15, 1914, 9.

Andrew Furuseth, circa 1918, Library of Congress

Chapter 16—Seamen's Rights

One of the enduring parts of the 1920 Merchant Marine Act is section 33 relating to the recovery by seamen for workplace injuries often referred to as *the* "Jones Act." That section, however, was not the only change made to U.S. law regarding seamen's rights in 1920. Many laws, including the 1884 Dingley Act, were amended. Those changes were the result of an almost continuous evolution in the treatment of seamen under U.S. law from 1790 to 1920.

Special Status of Seamen

Seamen have had a special status around the world since at least the Middle Ages, as reflected in maritime codes like the thirteenth century "Laws of Oleron."[1] This status stems from the unique maritime workplace. Seamen work in a hostile environment under adverse work conditions where the ability to find better employment is circumscribed

This special status has been governed for centuries by a contract called "ship's articles" or "shipping articles," with a duration of a single or round-trip voyage. This contract is executed between the seaman and the vessel, represented by the vessel master.[2] The current U.S. Code still refers to "shipping articles agreements."[3]

Pursuant to the articles, a seaman agrees to obey the vessel's master.[4] The safety of the vessel, its crew, its passengers, and its cargo depends on a system of obedience to a single captain who must have absolute authority. The U.S. Supreme Court in 1942 described the connection—the vessel's master "must command and the crew must obey. Authority cannot be divided. These are actualities which the law has always recognized."[5] Little wonder that the recurring signing of articles for consecutive employments has been likened to "a series of short-term enlistments in the military."[6]

The United States early on followed the British example, which provided seamen some protections against economic and physical coercion but leaned in the direction of discipline and bondage to the vessel.[7] In 1790, the U.S. Congress enacted its first mariner law. It required that seamen be hired only in writing for foreign voyages and large vessels on domestic voyages, that a seaman could demand payment of one-third of his wages at every port where cargo was either loaded or unloaded, that vessels could be declared "too leaky, or... otherwise, unfit," and that a medicine chest and minimum food requirements (water, salted beef, and bread) be provided.[8]

In practice, these protections often did not amount to much. The vessel unfitness provision, for example, was rarely invoked because both the crew majority *and* the chief mate (working for the vessel owner) had to agree that the vessel was unsafe.[9]

These seamen protections were balanced by provisions that penalized deserting seamen and anyone who harbored them. Once a seaman or "Jack" signed his articles, he was required to report to the vessel.[10] The law provided harsh consequences to the seaman who failed to report or deserted. The penalties included permitting the capture and imprisonment of seamen by government authorities, forfeiture of remaining wages, and the loss of possessions on the vessel.

These penalties first enacted in 1790 for seamen were largely copied in the Fugitive Slave Act enacted in 1793.[11] The maritime labor reform movement would refer to the 1790 mariner law as the "fugitive sailor law."[12]

An 1829 law provided for the arrest and delivery back to their vessels of foreign seamen who deserted in the United States.[13] U.S. citizens were exempt from delivery to foreign vessels in the United States, but the U.S. government included reciprocal rights in its consular treaties. This meant that U.S. consuls abroad could use local enforcement authorities to capture and return deserting U.S. seamen to U.S. vessels.[14]

Eventually laws were enacted that governed virtually every aspect of a seaman's economic life. The U.S. Code still provides the requirement contained in the 1915 Seamen's Act that vessels must have "a space of at least 120 cubic feet and at least 16 square feet, measured on the floor or deck of that place, for each seaman or apprentice lodged in the vessel."[15] How much space and how well it was ventilated in the forecastle (pronounced FOLK-s'l) (where crew quarters on sailing vessels were located) was a major reform issue in the late nineteenth and early twentieth centuries. The phrase "before the mast" stems from the fact that the forecastle on sailing vessels is forward of the vessel's mast or masts.

Although U.S. federal courts referred to seamen as "wards" who needed judicial protection, they were nevertheless reluctant to hold vessel masters accountable for harsh punishments.[16] In the 1806 case of *Thorne v. White*, the judge determined that a sailor, assaulted by his master, should not suffer forfeiture of his wages because of disobedience, but, at the same time, noted that it was "the duty of seamen to bear even the ill-temper of the master, and to get out of his way, when instances of passion occur."[17] In the 1831 case of *Butler v. McClellan*, the judge awarded damages to a seaman but noted that courts would not interfere in corporal punishment unless "unusual or unlawful instruments have been used, or the punishment has been manifestly excessive and disproportionate to the fault."[18]

The classic 1840 work written by Richard Henry Dana, *Two Years before the Mast,* focused the American public on the harshness of sea discipline, which included flogging.[19] In one famous instance recounted by Dana, a sailor asked why he was being flogged. "'Have I ever refused any duty, sir? Have you ever known me to hang back, or be insolent, or not to know my work?'". The captain replied that 'it is not that that I flog you for; I flog you... for asking questions.' And when the man 'writhed under the pain' and called out 'Oh, Jesus Christ! O, Jesus Christ!,' the captain replied *'he can't help you. Call on Captain T------. He's the man! He can help you! Jesus Christ can't help you now!'*"[20] It was not until 1898 that all forms of corporal punishment were outlawed on U.S.-flag vessels.[21] Flogging was outlawed in 1850, although no penalty for violating the law was then provided.[22]

At the time Dana served on board a U.S.-flag sailing vessel in the late 1830s, the entire crew had to be U.S. citizens by law. This requirement, imposed in 1813, was a reaction (as was noted in a prior chapter) to the British Navy impressment of sailors leading up to the War of 1812.[23] Prior to 1813 only the vessel captain (also referred to as the "master") had to be a U.S. citizen.[24]

This crew requirement lasted until 1864 when, despite the exodus of U.S.-flag vessels due to rebel commerce raiding, the needs of the U.S. Navy to sustain the blockade of the South resulted in a mariner shortage.[25] Congress responded by partially repealing the 1813 requirement and fully repealing the 1817 Act extra import duty applicable to vessels with less than two-thirds U.S. citizen crews.[26]

It was not until the 1915 Seaman's Act, which required that at least 75 percent of the crew understand the language of their officers, that the tide started to shift back to having U.S. citizen crews.[27] In 1936 a 75 percent crew citizenship requirement was enacted for all U.S.-flag vessels. Later the same year, in the Merchant Marine Act, 1936 this requirement was made 100 percent for subsidized vessels.[28]

The removal of the crew requirement, combined with a generally strong American economy, harsh U.S. mariner laws, and low prospects for advancement, turned many Americans away from the sea.[29] Most U.S.-flag crews after the Civil War until the 1920 Merchant Marine Act had a substantial number of foreigners.[30] Foreign seamen largely displaced black American seaman, who formed a substantial portion of the crews aboard U.S.-flag vessels prior to the Civil War.[31]

As Americans turned from the sea, on-board discipline by U.S. officers became harsher than before and was administered by "bucko" mates (officers). The vessels where harshness prevailed were called "hell-ships."[32] The harsh discipline made it even more difficult to recruit Americans resulting in low-quality sailors, which led to more harsh discipline.

The 1946 movie version of *Two Years before the Mast* illustrated both the harsh discipline and one manner of crewing vessels.[33] Brian Donlevy played Richard Henry Dana, the Harvard student who chose to go to sea, kept a journal, and turned it into a book. One slice of drama introduced in the movie was that Alan Ladd, the movie lead, was supposedly a spoiled son of a vessel owner who had been "shanghaied" aboard the vessel owned by his father.[34]

"Shanghaiing," the kidnapping of men to serve as sailors, was not a term that came into wide use until the 1850s, but it was one of the many land-side problems that plagued seamen.[35] The world ashore in the nineteenth and early twentieth centuries was filled with persons who manipulated and took advantage of seamen. In his fourth book, based in part on his experiences as a sailor and originally published in 1849, Herman Melville wrote:

> Besides, of all sea-ports in the world, Liverpool, perhaps, most abounds in all the variety of land-sharks, land-rats, and other vermin, which make the hapless mariner their prey. In the shape of landlords, bar-keepers, clothiers, crimps, and boarding-house loungers, the land-sharks devour him, limb by limb; while the land-rats and mice constantly nibble at his purse.[36]

The situation was no better in New York, San Francisco, or Portland, Oregon. The 1915 Seaman's Act was meant to remedy these problems, as well as other issues relating to discipline and working conditions at sea.

LAND-SHARKS, LAND-RATS, AND OTHER VERMIN

Shipping for a defined period meant that seamen were released someplace in the world, usually with money in their pocket (since much of their wages were paid when the voyage finished). There, they had to find a place to stay until they could find a vessel for their next articles. Of course, they came ashore with pent-up energy after being in a dangerous, smelly, unhealthy environment for weeks or months at a time. Vessel captains arriving at their final port had to find a new crew for the next voyage. When vessels arrived in places like San Francisco, seaman were tempted to leave the profession and look for gold or find land-side employment. This made it difficult for vessels to crew up for that next voyage.

These conditions led to the spontaneous creation of an industry intent on relieving seamen of their money and of serving as intermediaries between vessel masters and seamen to entice or force seamen, one way or another, back onto a vessel for the next voyage.[37] As an 1887 California state report indicated, a sailor "from the day he arrives in port, until the day of his departure, he is never out of the hands of sharpers, who coax, wheedle, debauch, and pander to his worst vices, until his last dollar is gone."[38]

One of the key contributors to the land-side conditions was the advance payment of wages and unrestricted wage allotments.[39] The purpose of the system was wholesome enough, which was to require vessel owners to pay seamen an advance on wages to buy clothes and supplies and permit seamen to allot money for their families ashore. But, to prevent pre-voyage desertion, advances were usually held by the owner in credit payable by an agent.

Boarding houses took in seamen and charged them for room, board, liquor, clothing, and other services in exorbitant amounts. These expenses usually equaled the seaman's pay off amount (if earned) plus the full amount of the advance. The result was that the seaman sailed on his next voyage in debt to the vessel (the amount of the advance).[40]

Vessel masters also had an incentive to encourage seamen to "jump ship" before being paid off because they would pocket the pay-off amount.[41] Boarding house keepers had an incentive to get seaman off their vessels and into their "care" as soon as possible, to encourage turn over. The process of enticing men to jump ship before being paid off might begin before a vessel even docked, or in the middle of an unloading period. Boarding house "runners" were employed with vessel master encouragement to row out to vessels with liquor and promises, to encourage seamen to come to a particular boarding house.[42]

Boarding house keepers were sometimes also "shipping masters" who were paid a fee for "finding" seamen to man vessels, in addition to providing overpriced housing, clothing, etc. This fee was known as "blood money" and these shipping masters were referred to as "crimps."[43]

The system effectively made a seaman "a commercial slave rather than a free man" since the only way to obtain another job was to work through a crimp.[44] The evils of the system were long recognized. An 1834 Boston newspaper reported:

> The detestable boarding-house landlords' system of advance wages which prevails, and has not a single redeeming feature, is a disgrace to civil society from the first to the last. It is a tissue of villainy and frauds, in violation of the laws of God and man, which, if unmasked and fully brought to light, would stir up a general burst of indignation. Its history is briefly told. It meets the sailor miles away from the wharf with a bottle of poison, securing his promise to board with him, who thus gets a mortgage on him, and generally gets the seaman to agree that when he is paid off the kind-hearted and benevolent landlord shall be his banker, he being assured that otherwise he is in danger of falling in with land privateers. But in a few days the landlord offers his man for sale to the party that will pay the most *"advance."* It is a traffic in the flesh of human beings[45]

As bad as this system was, there was an even more sinister side, also depicted in *Two Years before the Mast*. Seamen were not just cajoled and tricked into the boarding house and onto vessels—they were also provided to vessels through forcible kidnapping. Particularly where sailors were hard to come by, experienced seamen, or just any man unlucky enough to have gone into the wrong bar at the wrong time might be drugged, intoxicated or physically knocked out and then shipped onto a vessel.[46] The term "shanghaied" is associated with this practice, although it is also used generally to describe the procurement of seamen via crimping.[47] Once someone unlucky enough to be "shanghaied" violently regained consciousness, they were usually on a vessel which had already set sail. They had no choice but to work as sailors for the balance of the voyage.

Over time "shanghaiing" by crimps has been romanticized. For example, a 1967 episode of the television show *Death Valley Days* was entitled "Shanghai Kelly's Birthday Party," starring Robert Taylor as James "Shanghai" Kelly. Kelly was a notorious crimp in San Francisco in the 1870s.

The story goes that Kelly was engaged to provide crews for three vessels. To do so, he announced a birthday cruise in San Francisco Bay with free liquor. On board, ninety men were supposedly drugged with opium and then distributed to the three vessels. Subsequent research casts doubt on the authenticity of the story, but it nevertheless continues to be told.[48] The band *Gaelic Storm*, for example, which appeared in the movie *Titanic* released in 1998, has written a song called "Shanghai Kelly" with this last verse:

> Well a lot of us, we hit the floor
> Ninety men or maybe more
> They rolled us up in blankets
> And they dragged us to the door
> They sold us to the Reefer just before she passed the Golden Gate
> Before we all got sober, we were married to our fate
> And miles away from all I knew
> Stranded with this rotten crew
> With naught but work for us to do until we reached Peru
> With blistered hands we'd haul the line

> Man the sails, swab the deck
> And dream of Shanghai Kelly with a rope around his neck![49]

It was not until 1906 that "shanghaiing" was made illegal.[50]

The boarding house-crimp system persisted because it was not entirely one-sided. One of the reasons that it survived for so long, despite long-standing union and public criticism, was that it worked to provide employment to mariners and crews to vessels. Another reason it survived was the boarding house owners formed associations and were adept at exerting municipal political influence to avoid significant change.[51]

Eventually, however, the shift to steamship lines reduced the demand for middlemen, as the lines established their own shore-side employment offices.[52] Moreover, economic conditions, particularly on the West Coast in the coastwise fleet, permitted mariners to organize into unions and to advocate for change. The undeniable leader of that U.S. movement was Andrew Furuseth.

Andrew Furuseth

Andrew (also, "Anders" and "Andy") Furuseth was so important to the U.S. seafaring labor movement from 1887 until his death in 1938 that it is hard to imagine the enactment of the many reforms during that period without him. By these reforms, he is said to "have destroyed the power of the crimps and freed all seamen who come under American law."[53] Unsurprisingly, then, he was known as the seamen's "Emancipator" and the "Viking Sailor."[54] In 1916, the *New Republic* observed that you might disagree with him, but "it is not possible to withhold admiration from Andrew Furuseth," as he has fought for "the rights of man at sea, as very few modern men will fight for anything."[55]

Furuseth was born in Norway in 1854 in a large and poor farming family.[56] His father's last name was Nilsen, but Andy took the name Furuseth from the name of a local village. At the age of eight, he was "fostered away" to another family where he received some schooling. He went to sea in 1873 at the age of nineteen and served for about seven years on sailing vessels with a variety of nationalities, later becoming a commercial fisherman on the Columbia River.[57]

Until 1889, when he became a full-time union leader, he alternated between fishing and serving on U.S. coastal vessels. It was a time when Scandinavians so dominated the sailing trade on the West Coast sailing fleet that it was known as the "Scandinavian navy."[58]

Furuseth also experienced the power of the crimping system in San Francisco when he started sailing in the coastal fleet.[59] From 1880 to 1884, he had no trouble finding work, provided he stayed at a boarding house run by a crimp. Not surprisingly, he remained unemployed when he went to a rooming house.

While Furuseth was away fishing, the Coast Seamen's Union was formed in March 1885 in San Francisco.[60] Furuseth joined the Union when he returned. When the secretary of the Union died in January 1887, Furuseth, who was on the union finance committee, was elected secretary, the titular head of the Union. Furuseth bounced back and forth between union duties and fishing over the next few years, until June 1892, when he took a leadership position for good until 1935.[61]

Furuseth was instrumental in adopting a publicity strategy to shame the public into supporting the union's aims.[62] The union started a newspaper, the *Coast Seamen's Journal* (later the *Seamen's Journal*), in 1887. It included a column called "The Red Record" which detailed examples of cruelty and abuses at sea.[63] It was modeled on the *Red Record* authored by Ida B. Wells, which chronicled lynchings in the South.[64] In 1895, these columns were published as a pamphlet, sent to major newspapers all over the country, and used to lobby the U.S. Congress.[65]

Furuseth also had sought a state investigation of shore-side conditions. In the summer of 1887, the California commissioner of the Bureau of Labor Statistics confirmed all the nefarious aspects of the boarding house/crimp system.[66]

Meanwhile, the disparate elements of organized maritime labor began to come together.[67] In 1888 Furuseth set forth his idea at a convention of the American Federation of Labor of a single national seamen's organization. Furuseth was to be a lifelong friend and supporter of Samuel Gompers, founder and longtime leader of the AFL, and an active participant in AFL affairs. The two men shared the philosophy that distinct craft unions should work within the political system to improve working conditions contradicting more radical approaches.

In 1891 the Coast Seamen's Union joined the Steamship Sailor's Union to form the Sailor's Union of the Pacific, or SUP.[68] By 1895 the Atlantic and Great Lakes seaman unions had affiliated with the SUP. In 1892 they comprised three districts in the International Seamen's Union of America. In 1908 Furuseth was elected president of that umbrella union and he remained so until his death.

A key factor powering the SUP was how the Shipping Commissioners Act of 1872 was interpreted by the courts.[69] That Act provided for federally appointed "shipping commissioners" in U.S. ports to combat abusive practices. The Act required that shipping articles be signed and pay offs occur in front of a commissioner.

Congress exempted domestic voyages from this process in 1874.[70] In so doing, the 1874 Act also was interpreted to repeal desertion penalties.[71] This made a variety of anti-vessel owner tactics possible, such as signing articles and then jumping ship. This type of behavior resulted in a loss of partial wages and articles left on the vessel, but not imprisonment. Vessel owners reacted by convincing Congress in 1890 to again amend the 1872 Act so that the penalties applied for all articles signed before a commissioner.[72]

Having not taken a very active political role before the 1890 law, the SUP drafted an "Appeal to Congress" in 1892.[73] The appeal listed a number of grievances, including "involuntary servitude" and "insecurity of wages contracted for, caused first by the system of advances or allotments." The SUP also decided to endorse former judge James G. Maguire, a Democrat, for Congress representing San Francisco.[74] Maguire served in Congress until 1899 and was a strong supporter of the SUP agenda.

From 1892 to 1893, the SUP struggled with vessel owners over wages and "blood flowed freely on the waterfront... as the crimps fought the Union for control of shipping."[75] The 1893 economic depression ended the battle in the vessel owner's favor, and the union agreed to reduced wages.[76]

The capstone of the union's troubles was a bombing which occurred on September 24, 1893, in front of a crimp's boarding house in San Francisco leaving four dead and four wounded.[77] The press blamed the union. A *San Francisco Chronicle* story included the headlines "Fiends at Work" and "Murderous Attack by Union Sailors."[78] Furuseth, after disclaiming any Union responsibility for the attack, preached that "peace, even the Christian peace of turning the other cheek, must be our policy in the future." Furuseth urged the union members to "remember that tomorrow is also a day," which became a union motto.[79]

In late 1893, Maguire requested that someone be sent to Washington to explain the union's legislative agenda. It fell to Furuseth to do so.[80] From 1894 to the end of his life, Furuseth spent much of his time in Washington, DC, where he became well acquainted with members of the press and Congress—such as Senator Robert M. La Follette Sr. (P-WI), whom he met in 1909.[81]

Furuseth was a charismatic figure. He was well read, particularly regarding the maritime laws of the world and the history of the law of seamen. He was argumentative.[82] And he spoke with conviction and personal experience regarding seafaring conditions. In a 1915 article entitled "Andrew Furuseth and his Fifteen-Year Siege of Congress," he was described as having "bulldog pertinacity."[83] Although he had no wealth and no political power, "he had a Cause and burning devotion to it." That cause was to free the sailor, so that sailor could pursue the best economic opportunities without restraint just as if his job was on land.[84]

In 1915 La Follette would look back on his first meeting with Furuseth and say that, when he met Furuseth, he found him to be a "tall, bony, slightly stooped man, with a face bespeaking superior intelligence and lofty character."[85] La Follette thought he was a "master of his subject" and "logical, rugged, terse, quaint, and fervid with conviction."

Furuseth's devotion and honesty were reflected in his austere life.[86] He never married and only took as a salary the amount he would have been paid as a seaman.[87] He lived in seaman's quarters whenever he could find them, wore simple clothes, and allegedly became "class-unconscious."[88] He said on many occasions that "a union official to be efficient should have nothing of his own and want nothing for himself."[89] When he was threatened with imprisonment for contempt by a San Francisco judge, he said (something like this, as there are various versions):

> You cannot make me any more lonely than I have always been. You cannot give me food worse than I have always had. My sleeping quarters will be no more cramped than they have been at any time.[90]

When La Follette asked Furuseth if he had provided for his retirement, Furuseth responded, "When my work is finished, I hope to be finished. I have no provision against old age; and I shall borrow no fears from time."[91]

Furuseth did not belong to any organized religion and referred to some ministers and priests by the slang term "sky pilots."[92] In a 1927 Labor Day address to University of California students, he said that "work is worship—to labor is to pray, because that is to exercise the highest, the divine faculties implanted in us as the sons of God."[93]

He had a high-pitched voice and never entirely lost his accent. When he railed against the use of court injunctions in labor disputes, he called them "inyunctions." Not everyone found this charming. A 1908 opinion piece in the *Oregonian* said that Furuseth "is an excellent example of parasitical growth on the labor body" and he "has never taken the trouble to learn the language of our people" with his "glib talk about 'yobs and inyunctions."[94]

Although he was a prolific writer, Furuseth was publicity-shy and averse to having his picture taken, as pointed out by Carl Sandburg.[95] Furuseth did not want to outshine the seafarers' freedom movement, and only when the 1915 Seamen's Act became law did he finally consent to have his picture taken. This was proudly displayed on the cover of the April 1915 issue of *La Follette's Magazine* under the headline "The Face of Andrew Furuseth."[96]

Sandburg wrote about Furuseth:

In every American Federation of Labor convention, his lean, crouched figure rises. His eyes glow. His face is screwed with intensity. His shrill voice tells of the seamen's fight for better things. They all watch for the time when Furuseth is going to get the floor.[97]

Following his great triumph in enacting the 1915 Seamen's Act, Furuseth had to spend years defending the law, seeking to make sure it was enforced and trying to prevent the courts from watering it down.[98] Attention was diverted by World War I, which ramped up wages and increased the size of the seagoing unions tremendously.[99]

A shipping depression following the war drove wages down and put substantial pressure on all seagoing unions.[100] Meanwhile, the Industrial Workers of the World (IWW, known as "Wobblies") were making inroads with the SUP membership. They advocated more radical and aggressive approaches and joint action with other trades, including longshoremen.

Furuseth, for his part, remained wedded to craft unionism. He opposed industrial unions comprised of the sailors, firemen, cooks, and stewards, as well as land-side labor. He also opposed radical approaches, such as seeking to upend capitalism.[101] A disastrous strike in 1921 all but ended union influence over bargaining for a decade. The ISU's membership decreased in a single year from 115,000 members in 1920 to 50,000 members in 1921 and declined further in the 1920's.[102]

By the time the SUP recovered in the 1930s, it was no longer Furuseth's union.[103] He was viewed by many as fighting the battles of the sailing age and ignoring the battles of the steamship age. He spent less and less time in San Francisco while trying to enforce the 1915 Seamen's Act. Local union leaders took advantage of his absence to turn the union away from him.[104]

Radicals had formed the Marine Workers' Industrial Union in 1932 and attacked Furuseth, calling him "Andy Barnacle" and "Weeping Willow Andy Feroshus."[105] Furuseth was convinced that communists had taken over the SUP.[106] The division between the SUP and International Seamen's Union became so extreme that in 1936 Furuseth engineered the expulsion of the SUP from the International Seamen's Union. He likened the effort "to throwing his only child out of the house."[107]

In those years, Furuseth's health was already failing him, and he died on January 22, 1938, in Washington, DC at the age of eighty-three.[108] He was the first labor leader to lie in state at the U.S. Department of Labor building. He had seventy-one honorary pall bearers, including the secretary of labor, numerous members of Congress, Supreme Court justices, and labor leaders.[109] His *New York Times* obituary stated that he won "through a long life filled with hard labor and noble endeavor... the title 'the Abraham Lincoln of the Sea.'"[110]

1915 SEAMEN'S ACT

The union's 1892 "Appeal to Congress" was ignored until Representative James Maguire was elected to Congress. He introduced in 1894 a series of bills addressing the union's grievances.[111] The shipping masters and the crimps had brought shipping to a standstill, by refusing to provide seamen as required under the 1884 Dingley Act's prohibitions of advances and allotments.[112] Congress re-introduced limited allotment payments in 1890 and Chamberlain later said that "it is a matter of profound regret that the law concerning allotments and advances of wages as passed in 1884 [the Dingley Act] was not allowed a fair trial."[113]

Vessel owners criticized the Maguire reform bills, beginning with complaints that they had not had an adequate opportunity to digest the provisions.[114] Representative Henry H. Bingham (R-PA) led that effort. (Bingham was known as "General Bingham" for his exemplary service in the Union Army during the Civil War (he was a Medal of Honor recipient), including at the Battle of Gettysburg).

Bingham reportedly was prompted by the Cramps of Philadelphia to oppose the Maguire bills.[115] He prevented consideration of legislation at the end of the second session of the Fifty-Third Congress in July 1894.[116] Vernon C. Brown, on behalf of the New York Maritime Association, argued that the bills were "radical in many respects, and show clearly that some other mind than 'Poor Jack's' framed their sections."[117] Both sides made their cases before Congress in hearings.[118]

In the end, most of the reforms were dropped, but the Maguire Act of 1895 undid some of the harm done by Congress in 1890, especially with desertion penalties.[119] The bill was a compromise among Dingley, Frye, and Furuseth.[120] Ultimately, however, the Maguire Act's intent to reverse the 1890 Act did not survive the 1897 *Arago* Supreme Court case.

That case started when four seamen from the barkentine *Arago* (a four-masted vessel) jumped ship in Astoria, Oregon in 1895. The vessel was on a voyage from San Francisco to Chile.[121] The men who jumped ship and claimed cruel treatment were arrested and imprisoned in San Francisco. The case was pursued all the way to the Supreme Court where Representative Maguire argued on behalf of the seamen.[122]

JOURNEY TO THE JONES ACT

In an infamous interpretation of the Thirteenth Amendment to the U.S. Constitution prohibiting "slavery" and "involuntary servitude," the court determined that the amendment could not have been intended to apply to "voluntary" shipping articles.[123] Basing its decision on a review of maritime laws going back to ancient times, the court ruled that imprisonment for failing to report for duty or for jumping ship was still permitted by the U.S. Constitution.

In his dissent, Justice John Marshall Harlan argued that the holding of a person against their will "for the purpose of compelling him to render personal service to another in a private business, places the person so held in custody in a condition of involuntary servitude, forbidden by the Constitution of the United States." Criticism of the decision was swift and harsh, with some likening it to a "second Dred Scott Decision" after that infamous slave recovery case.[124]

Furuseth and the unions harnessed the outrage at the *Arago* decision and, together with Maguire, pursued further legislation.[125] Their efforts resulted in the White Act of 1898, named for Senator Stephen M. White (D-CA). Maguire led the House effort.[126] The White Act again started out as a package of reforms but was paired down by pro-vessel owner legislators like Senator Frye.[127]

The legislation nevertheless ended up declaring all forms of corporal punishment unjustified. It eliminated jailing for jumping ship in the United States on both domestic and foreign voyages, and authorized prison terms for masters and mates who assaulted seamen (vessel owners were not made liable, which was changed in the 1915 Seamen's Act). Although a distinct step forward, the 1898 White Act left much in the way of reform unfinished and was soon undermined by state laws permitting imprisonment for desertion.[128]

The SUP, like much of the labor community, also sought to restrict immigration and, specifically, to exclude Asian seamen from U.S.-flag vessels.[129] Chinese seamen dominated the crews of U.S-flag vessels engaged in the Pacific trades, like those of the Pacific Mail Steamship Company.[130] Legal efforts to exclude Asians were shot down by the U.S. attorney general and the courts, by rejecting the argument that alien exclusion laws applied to the crews of U.S.-flag vessels. It was determined that U.S.-flag vessels were not literally U.S. "territory" for purposes of those exclusion laws.[131]

In this effort, Furuseth was an openly racist opponent of Chinese seamen.[132] In an article provided to Congress in 1913, he wrote that "the drift from the sea on the part of the Caucasian is general and growing. There must be a change; it must be fundamental, and it must be soon, or the sea must become the domain of the Oriental."[133]

Furuseth also opposed efforts by vessel owners to seek subsidies because he did not believe that subsidies would result in increased U.S. citizen manning.[134] For Furuseth, the key to sea power was more U.S. citizen seamen, not more U.S.-flag vessels with non-citizen crews.[135] He argued that reserving the coastwise trade had done nothing to bring in U.S. citizens to man U.S.-flag vessels. Therefore, he argued, there was no reason to expect that subsidies in the foreign trade would either.

Furuseth rejected the notion that U.S.-flag vessels were not competitive because of labor rates.[136] He noted that U.S.-flag vessels were already manned predominantly by non-U.S. citizens. The rates paid at the time were those which the market set in the port where a seaman shipped out, not based on vessel registry or crew nationality.[137]

For their part, foreign owners fought against the possibility of having to hire at U.S. wages by paying off their crews outside the United States. The U.S. government cooperated in maintaining this system through the consular treaties. These were sometimes referred to as "slave-catching treaties" where foreign governments agreed to capture and return deserting seamen to vessels.[138]

Furuseth's solution to the U.S.-flag merchant marine's lack of competitiveness was to seek worldwide emancipation, which he believed would create an international market for seamen. Meeting resistance abroad to direct emancipation, Furuseth sought to be included in reform legislation provisions to apply U.S. manning, hour, safety, and other standards to foreign vessels trading in the United States. He also proposed requiring that at least 75 percent of the crews on U.S.-flag vessels understand the language of the officers and that foreign sailors be permitted to collect half their wages upon jumping ship in the United States.[139] The half-wage requirement would help make it economically possible for seamen to abandon their vessels and seek more remunerative employment at U.S. rates.

Representative Edward J. Livernash, (D-CA) introduced the new comprehensive package of reforms in 1904.[140] Livernash explained to the House that the legislation was needed to get Americans to sail again. To do that, the following conditions had to be addressed: "The forecastle is, as a rule, unfit for habitation, crimping suffered to exist, payment of wages not safeguarded, no standard of skill provided, under-manning permitted, Asiatics employed, involuntary servitude protected."[141]

The package was expanded and re-introduced in 1906, 1908 and 1909 by Representative Thomas Spight, who had served in the Confederate army. No action was taken on his legislative proposals.[142] The proposed legislation began to pick up steam in 1907 when Representative William B. Wilson (D-PA) was elected to Congress, and when Furuseth later met Senator La Follette and enlisted his support. Representative Wilson had been secretary of the United Mine Workers and had worked with Furuseth at the American Federation of Labor.

Various congressional hearings were held from 1910 to 1914.[143] Vessel owners and Atlantic Coast International Seamen's Union representatives objected especially to the requirement that at least 75 percent of each crew department understand the language of the officers, since many Atlantic Coast members spoke Spanish as their native language.[144] The half-pay at every port provision was also attacked because it allegedly "legalizes desertion and would put vessel owners at the mercy of seamen and the "seamen's union."[145]

Spight and La Follette first added a provision in 1910 to the proposed legislation to abrogate the "slave-catching" consular treaties.[146] This was the key to implementation of Furuseth's program to raise foreign wages to the U.S. level in the U.S. foreign trade.[147]

This consular treaty provision proved to be one of the most controversial parts of the legislation and a similar provision was almost the undoing of the 1915 Seaman's Act. This was due to the perceived interference in the internal affairs of foreign vessels and its effect on long-established commercial agreements even though applying U.S. economic law to foreign vessels in U.S. ports was not unprecedented. The 1884 Dingley Act section prohibiting allotments also applied to foreign vessels in U.S. ports. Any foreign vessel which violated the prohibition could be denied port clearance.[148]

Favorable conditions accelerated in 1912 when both national political parties' platforms endorsed action in favor of seamen.[149] On August 3, 1912, the U.S. House passed the Wilson seamen's bill by voice vote.[150] According to the Merchant Marine Committee report, the bill would "give freedom to the sailor," "promote safety at sea," and "equalize the operating expenses of foreign and domestic vessels engaged in over-sea [sic] trade and tend to build up our merchant marine."[151]

Representative Humphrey, together with Representative Greene writing in the minority, strongly objected to the bill because they believed it did nothing for the U.S. merchant marine. They argued that it mainly helped foreign seaman since the bill only applied to the foreign trade where there was little U.S.-flag presence.[152]

The legislation was referred to a Senate subcommittee of the Commerce Committee chaired by Senator Theodore E. Burton (R-OH). He held hearings in December featuring vessel owners opposing the legislation.[153] A Commerce Committee substitute was developed which abolished imprisonment in foreign ports but watered-down many of the safety provisions.[154] The legislation was so watered-down that Furuseth at first advocated for killing the bill rather than accepting it.[155]

The legislation came together on Sunday March 2, 1913. Senator Burton explained that "bitter antagonism has arisen between the advocates and the opponents of this bill" and that the committee alternative was an attempt to compromise those divergent views.[156] La Follette offered a series of amendments to try to bring the substitute closer to the House bill without success.[157] A conference committee hastily convened, and the House accepted the Senate's final version.[158]

On March 4, 1913, on his last day in office, President Taft "pocket vetoed" the bill (by not signing it within ten days of a congressional adjournment). He wrote that the bill "conflicts in its operation with the treaty obligations of the United States."[159] President Woodrow Wilson, who was inaugurated later the same day, was to be troubled for the exact same reason, two years later, when he was presented with a seamen's reform bill. Notably, Taft's pocket veto was issued even though the *Titanic* disaster of April 15, 1912, had drawn attention to the lack of safety aboard passenger vessels, including the inadequate number of experienced seamen to man lifeboats.[160] Furuseth was untroubled and said that it was the union's good fortune that Taft pocket vetoed the legislation because it later resulted in much better legislation.[161]

In the new Congress, which commenced in March 1913, Democrats controlled both chambers of Congress. Committee Chairman Alexander re-introduced the union's version of the seamen's legislation.[162] Senator Knute Nelson re-introduced the watered-down version Taft had pocket vetoed.[163] William Wilson, now secretary of labor, and William C. Redfield, secretary of commerce, recommended Senator Nelson's legislation.[164]

A La Follette version passed the U.S. Senate on October 21, 1913. With Furuseth in the Senate gallery, La Follette said that "this bill is the evolution of a struggle of nineteen years, not only to emancipate thousands of men from slavery, but also it is the work of able, patriotic men who would see the American merchant marine restored to a place of importance in the commerce of the world by legitimate, honest, and economic methods, rather than by some dishonest subsidy scheme."[165]

It was at this time that La Follette also called out Chamberlain as a tool of shipowners and the administration.[166] After the debate, Furuseth was overcome with emotion and said, "This finishes the work Lincoln began."[167] Further action on the legislation was not, however, to occur until after the results of the International Conference on Safety of Life at Sea, held in London starting in November 1913.

Wilson appointed Furuseth to the U.S. delegation along with Chamberlain.[168] Alexander was the chairman of the U.S. commission to the Conference. Furuseth feared that the conference would only marginally improve safety and he called Chamberlain "a chameleon commissioner" serving owner's interests.[169]

Some of Furuseth's fears were realized, as the conference only required lifeboats sufficient for 75 percent of the passengers to be manned by "boat handlers." The La Follette bill required 100 percent lifeboat capacity and two able-bodied seamen for each boat. Furuseth resigned from the American delegation in disgust in late December 1913.[170]

Meanwhile, vessel owners demanded additional hearings, which were held by the House Merchant Marine Committee from December 1913 to March 1914.[171] Nothing came of the hearings, which Furuseth described as a "perfect carnival of criticism."[172]

President Wilson presented the London Convention to the Senate on March 20, 1914.[173] Furuseth was concerned that ratification of the convention would sate the public's desire for improved safety. He promoted an amendment to the ratification instrument, making it clear that the United States reserved the right to impose higher standards. The Senate ratified the convention on December 16, 1914, with that amendment.[174]

JOURNEY TO THE JONES ACT

In the meantime, Chairman Alexander had reported a version of the seamen's legislation on June 19, 1914, which was substantially watered-down to the convention standards.[175] Alexander adamantly opposed the provisions that required foreign vessels to pay their seamen half their wages upon demand in a U.S. port and prohibited such vessels from honoring allotments made by foreign seamen.[176] That bill passed the House by voice vote on August 27, 1914.[177]

Finally, the Senate disagreed, and a conference committee was appointed. It did not issue its report until February 24, 1915.[178] Furuseth despaired that the bill would again be killed and blamed Wilson and Chamberlain.[179] The goal of getting foreign vessels to register in the United States (permitted by the 1914 Ship Registry Act discussed in a subsequent chapter) without the ambiguity of pending legislation spurred action.[180]

Final congressional approval was anti-climactic. The House approved the conference report on February 25, and the Senate passed the bill on February 27 by voice vote.[181] An attempt to force reconsideration in the Senate was defeated.[182] Senator Wesley Jones voted in favor of reconsideration, even though he claimed he would have voted for the conference report anyway "with very much misgiving" if there had been a recorded vote.[183]

As finally compromised, the legislation abolished imprisonment for desertion, allowed seamen to receive half-pay in every loading or unloading port, forbade the "master's option" to force seamen to sign their rights away, improved habitation requirements, prohibited all advance payments and allotments, and required sufficient lifeboats for the full passenger complement (with a Great Lakes exception) with at least one able seaman for each lifeboat. Most of these provisions were also made applicable to foreign vessels while in U.S. ports and required the government to give notice to abrogate "articles in treaties and conventions," in conflict with the law's provisions.[184] Finally, the legislation required that 75 percent of the crew had to understand the language of the officers.

Lobbying of the Wilson administration intensified immediately.[185] Furuseth had already met twice with Secretary of State William Jennings Bryan in January.[186] On February 27, La Follette telephoned the White House seeking to meet the president.[187]

On March 1 Robert Lansing, counselor to the State Department and later secretary of state, cited the potential war-time commerce disruption and argued against signing the legislation.[188] He also argued that it would be impossible to abrogate only a portion of the affected treaties and that full abrogation would have negative, unintended consequences. Bryan conveyed the advice on the same day to the president suggesting Wilson veto the legislation.[189] Also on March 1, Furuseth wrote the president seeking his support saying that "it is very difficult for us seamen, Mr. President, to understand how any nation can justly make any complaint because the United States chooses to make the seaman a free man."[190]

On March 2 Secretary Bryan amplified Lansing's advice to the president. Although he was "very much impressed by the arguments in favor of the bill on its general merits," he recommended Wilson send the legislation back to Congress and indicated he would sign it if the treaty abrogation provision was removed.[191]

On the same day, Wilson replied to Furuseth, saying that what "is troubling me just at this moment is that it demands of the Government what seems a truly impossible thing, namely, the denunciation of some twenty-two commercial treaties." He also claimed that he had been advised that the denunciation of a particular clause of a treaty is not feasible."[192] On March 2, a group of seven senators led by Senator John W. Kern (D-IN) met with the president and urged him to sign the bill.

The flurry of activity culminated in a March 2 evening meeting among Wilson, La Follette, and Furuseth. The only record of what happened in the meeting is from a La Follette biography, where it is claimed that "Andy went down on his knees to the President" and "begged him to make him a freeman who had a right to walk the streets and live his life as other citizens did, which right he did not have as a seaman."[193] Furuseth's principal biographer believes that this recollection is an embellishment because it was so out of character.[194]

La Follette stayed behind for about twenty minutes alone with the President after Wilson met with Furuseth.[195] Joseph P. Tumulty, Wilson's personal secretary, apparently told La Follette two days later about something the president had said to him: "'Tumulty, I have just experienced a great half-hour, the tensest since I came to the White House. That man La Follette pushed me over tonight on the Seamen's bill.'"

Wilson signed the law on March 4 on the last day of the Sixty-Third Congress. On March 5 Wilson wrote Newton D. Baker, who had represented the Great Lakes Carriers' Association and was Wilson's secretary of war, saying that he "finally determined to sign it because it seemed the only chance to get something like justice done to a class of workmen who have been too much neglected by our laws."[196] On March 6 Furuseth wrote to Wilson that "in signing the Seamen's Bill you gave back to seamen, so far as the United States can do it, the ownership of their own bodies, and thus wiped out the last bondage existing under the American flag."[197]

However, the fight for Furuseth and the SUP was far from over.[198] Vessel owners worked in the Administration, Congress, and the courts to overturn or dilute the Act's requirements.[199] Pacific Mail Steamship sold five vessels blaming the Act.[200] This led La Follette to blame vessel owners for working against the law instead of seeking to comply.[201]

Furuseth's immediate opponent was the U.S. Department of Commerce, which watered-down the Act in its "Circulars."[202] Circular no. 265 issued September 18, 1915, for example, interpreted the crew language requirement to mean that the crew merely had to be able to execute officers' orders, even if given in pidgin English. Seamen also only had to understand the orders from officers in their own department.[203] In other words, seamen in the engineering department did not need to understand officers in the deck department. This undermined one of the main safety purposes of the law.[204]

The U.S. attorney general also limited the application of U.S. safety standards to foreign vessels, even though one of the main purposes of the Seamen's Act was to equalize standards.[205] Furuseth wrote that the law "failed to meet its purpose... because of the action of the Commissioner of Navigation, Mr. Eugene Tyler Chamberlain."[206]

With the Commerce Department generally siding with the vessel owners, Furuseth pursued litigation to enforce the Seamen's Act, with some success.[207] For example, the Supreme Court determined that the Act was not an unconstitutional interference in the right to contract[208] and upheld the watch system advocated by Furuseth.[209] But, there were also many losses such as with liability issues.

For example, in the 1918 case of *Chelentis v. Luckenbach S. S. Co.*, the Supreme Court examined section 20 of the Seamen's Act, which sought to make vessel owners fully liable for acts of the vessel officers.[210] In *Chelentis*, a seaman was injured and later lost his leg when ordered on deck during a storm. There was no allegation that the vessel was unseaworthy, which is how the vessel owner might be liable, only that the officer who gave the order was negligent.

Under a 1903 Supreme Court case (*The Osceola*), officers were considered "fellow servants" of the crew and the vessel owner was not liable if an officer's order led to injury of a seaman except to the extent of "maintenance and cure."[211] Under that concept, a vessel owner was only liable to pay the seamen's wages under the articles, daily living expenses until the seamen recovered from his injury ("maintenance"), and his medical expenses ("cure"). The only exception where more could be recovered—such as lost future income—was when it was proved that the vessel was unseaworthy.

The Seamen's Act provided that "in any suit to recover damage for any injury sustained on board vessel... seamen having command shall not be held to be fellow-servants with those under their authority."[212] Somehow, the Supreme Court in *Chelentis* determined that this provision did not wipe away vessel owners' pre-existing fellow servant liability shield. The *Chelentis* case spurred enactment of section 33 in the 1920 Merchant Marine Act, which is one of the two sections popularly referred to today as the "Jones Act."

One of the most controversial sections—the abrogation of consular treaties providing for the arrest of deserting seamen—was very similar to a provision in the 1920 Merchant Marine Act intended to permit the re-imposition of discriminating duties. The State Department implemented the Seamen's Act provision by providing notice to affected countries. Those countries generally agreed to modify the treaties.[213] The same did not occur in 1920 to permit the re-imposition of discriminating duties.

The Seamen's Act advanced Furuseth's theories and had a modest positive effect on the employment of U.S. citizens and the equalization of wages.[214] But a combination of a long shipping recession in the 1920s after World War I's temporary boost in employment ended and the dilution of provisions by the courts and the executive branch reduced the Act's effectiveness. In summary, the Act was "never given a real opportunity to demonstrate its effectiveness because of the opposition of foreign shipowners in American courts and because of interpretations and constructions by the Department of Commerce unfavorable to the seamen's understanding of the law."[215]

---

[1] Also referred to as the "Rules of Oleron," *Benedict on Admiralty*, 7th ed. revised, vol. 1 (New York: Matthew Bender, 1988) § 6; *The Troop*, 118 F. 769 (D. Wa. 1902).
[2] Dingley Act expressly permitted round trip voyage articles or articles for a definite time. 23 Stat. 53, 58 (June 26, 1884).
[3] 46 U.S.C. §§ 10302 and 10502.
[4] U.S. law defines the "master" as "the individual having command of a vessel." 46 U.S.C. § 10101.
[5] Southern S.S. Co. v. National Labor Relations Board, 62 S. Ct. 886, 890–91 (1942).
[6] Alex Roland, W. Jeffrey Bolster, and Alexander Keyssar, *The Way of the Ship: America's Maritime History Reenvisioned, 1600–2000* (Hoboken, NJ: John Wiley & Sons, 2008), 226. Indeed, the U.S. government argued in the infamous Supreme

Court case of *Robertson v. Baldwin*, 165 U.S. 275 (1897), that seamen were indistinguishable from enlisted service members. Brief for the United States at 10 cited in James Gray Pope, "The Thirteenth Amendment at the Intersection of Class and Gender: *Robertson v. Baldwin's* Exclusion of Infants, Lunatics, Women, and Seamen," Seattle University Law Review 39 (Spring 2016): 901–26.

[7] Craig J. Forsyth, William B. Bankston, and Carol Thompson, "The Merchant Marine Desertion Penalty: A Study in Legal Evolution," International Review of Modern Sociology 19, no. 1 (Spring 1989): 53–67, 59–60.

[8] 1 Stat. 131 (July 20, 1790).

[9] 1 Stat. 131 (July 20, 1790), § 3; U.S. Congress, House, Hearings before the Committee on Merchant Marine and Fisheries on Sundry Bills Relating to the American Merchant Marine, Known as the 'Maguire' Bills, 53rd Cong., 2nd sess., 1894, H. Misc. Doc. 53-206, 4–5 (testimony of Andrew Furuseth).

[10] Ronald Hope, Poor Jack: The Perilous History of Merchant Seamen (London: Chatham Publishing, 2001).

[11] 1 Stat. 302 (February 12, 1793).

[12] For example, "Toilers and Their Doings—Sailors Celebrate Their Anniversary," San Francisco Chronicle, March 15, 1897, 10.

[13] 4 Stat. 359 (March 2, 1829).

[14] The 1880 consular convention with Belgium had typical wording: "The respective Consul-General, Consuls, Vice-Consuls and Consular Agents may cause to be arrested the officers, sailors, and all other persons making part of the crews, in any matter whatever, of ship of war or merchant vessels of their nation, who may be guilty, or accused, of having deserted said ships and vessels, for the purpose of sending them on board or back to their country." U.S. Congress, Senate, Treaties, Conventions, International Acts, Protocols and Agreements between the United States of American and Other Powers, 61st Cong., 2nd sess., 1910, S. Doc. 61-357, 94, 98.

[15] 46 U.S.C. § 11101(a).

[16] Martin J. Norris, "The Seaman as Ward of the Admiralty," Michigan Law Review 52, no. 4 (February 1954): 479–504, 504n1.

[17] 1 Pet. Adm. 168 (D. Pa. 1806).

[18] 1 Ware 220, 4 F. Cas. 905 (D. Ma. 1831).

[19] Richard Henry Dana, Two Years before the Mast (New York: Harper & Brothers, 1840).

[20] Dana, Two Years Before the Mast, 126–27 (emphasis in original).

[21] 30 STAT. 755 (DECEMBER 21, 1898).

[22] 9 Stat. 513, 515 (September 28, 1850); E. Kay Gibson, "Flogging Wasn't the Worst of It: Protecting America's Seamen in the Waning Days of Sail," Sea History 121 (Winter 2007–08): 10–13; E. Kay Gibson, Brutality on Trial (Gainesville: University of Florida Press, 2006).

[23] 2 Stat. 809 (March 3, 1813).

[24] 1 Stat. 55 (September 1, 1789); 1 Stat. 287 (December 31, 1792).
[25] Annual Report of the Commissioner of Navigation to the Secretary of Commerce (1915), 41 (U.S. citizen restriction "removed [except as to officers] as a war measure.").
[26] 13 Stat. 201 (June 28, 1864) (repealed all prior manning laws provided "That officers of vessels of the United States shall in all cases be citizens of the United States."); revised in 29 Stat. 188 (May 28, 1896).
[27] 38 Stat. 1164, 1169 (March 4, 1915).
[28] 49 Stat. 1930, § 5 (June 25, 1936) (the requirement was then amended to require 75 percent of the seamen and 100 percent of the officers to be U.S. citizens "unless the Secretary of Commerce shall, upon investigation, ascertain that qualified citizen seamen are not available, when, under such conditions, he may reduce the above percentages."); 49 Stat. 1985, § 302 (June 29, 1936).
[29] Andrew Furuseth blamed U.S. laws most of all. "Says Americans Have Quit Going to Sea on Account of Laws," Duluth News-Tribune, February 25, 1910, 4.
[30] Annual Report of the Commissioner of Navigation to the Secretary of the Treasury (1897), 24—25 (about 70 percent foreign in 1897); Annual Report of the Commissioner of Navigation to the Secretary of Commerce (1915), 41 (about two-thirds foreign in 1915); Annual Report of the Commissioner of Navigation to the Secretary of Commerce (1920), 48 (majority foreign in 1919).
[31] W. Jeffrey Bolster, "'To Feel like a Man': Black Seamen in the Northern States, 1800–1860," Journal of American History 76, no. 4 (March 1990): 1173–99.
[32] Paul S. Taylor, The Sailors' Union of the Pacific (New York: Ronald Press, 1923), 21–23.
[33] "The Screen in Review–'Two Years before the Mast,'" New York Times, September 25, 1946, 39.
[34] "The Screen in Review – 'Two Years Before the Mast,'" New York Times, September 25, 1946 (described by the New York Times critic as "a typical Hollywood packet sailing under papers that have been conveniently forged").
[35] Richard H. Dillon, Shanghaiing Days (New York: Coward-McCann, 1961).
[36] Herman Melville, Redburn: His First Voyage (Boston: L. C. Page, 1924), 137.
[37] Willis J. Abbot, American Merchant Ships and Sailors (New York: Dodd, Mead, 1902), 370 ("The seaman landing with money in his pocket in any large town is like a hapless fish in some of our much angled streams.").
[38] California Bureau of Labor Statistics, Investigation into Condition of Men Working on the Waterfront and on Board Pacific Coast Vessels, San Francisco, June 29—July 10, 1887 (Sacramento: 1887), 4.
[39] Georgia Smith, "Shanghaiing Historical Essay," Found SF, The San Francisco Digital History Archive, https://www.foundsf.org/index.php?title=Shanghaiing (advances were "the taproot of the shanghaiing system").
[40] Annual Report of the Commissioner of Navigation to the Secretary of the Treasury (1885), 163–64.

[41] California Bureau of Labor Statistics, Investigation into Condition of Men, 5.
[42] This process is described in California Bureau of Labor Statistics, Investigation into Condition of Men, 4–6; Annual Report of the Commissioner of Navigation to the Secretary of the Treasury (1899), appendix N.
[43] Bill Pickelhaupt, Shanghaied in San Francisco (Mystic Seaport–The Museum of America and the Sea, CT: 1996, repr. 2007), 169.
[44] Pickelhaupt, Shanghaied in San Francisco, 169.
[45] U.S. Congress, House, Advance Wages of Seamen in Merchant Service, 47th Cong., 1st sess., 1882, H. Rep. 47-1757, 1–2 (quoting the Boston Daily Advertiser).
[46] Shanghaiing in Portland, Oregon was the subject of a series of articles in the Oregonian newspaper in 1933 starting with "Shanghai Days in the City of Roses," Sunday Oregonian, October 1, 1933, 49.
[47] Pickelhaupt, Shanghaied in San Francisco, 171.
[48] Pickelhaupt, Shanghaied in San Francisco, 16–17.
[49] Gaelic Storm, "Shanghai Kelley," Go Climb a Tree (2017).
[50] 34 Stat. 551 (June 28, 1906). "Shanghaiing" was defined in the law as to "procure or induce or attempt to procure or induce another by force, threats, or representations which the person making them knows or believes to be untrue, or while the person so induced or procured is intoxicated or under the influence of any drug, to go on board of any such vessel" in order to have that person "perform service or labor of any kind on board of any vessel of any kind engaged in trade and commerce among the several States or with foreign nations."
[51] Annual Report of the Commissioner of Navigation to the Secretary of the Treasury (1895), 28 ("In our large seaports the boarding-house keepers are strongly organized...".); Paul S. Taylor, The Sailors' Union of the Pacific (New York: Ronald Press, 1923), 49.
[52] René De La Pedraja, A Historical Dictionary of the U.S. Merchant Marine and Shipping Industry since the Introduction of Steam (Westport, CT: Greenwood Press, 1994), 157–58.
[53] Taylor, Sailors' Union of the Pacific, 3–4.
[54] Samuel Gompers, "Seamen Freed–Their Emancipator," American Federationist 22, no. 4 (April 1915): 272–74; Hyman Weintraub, Andrew Furuseth–Emancipator of the Seamen (Berkeley, CA: University of California Press, 1959); "In memory of the Emancipator of Seamen—Andrew Furuseth, 150th Anniversary," West Coast Sailors (March 12, 2004, special edition); "The Viking Sailor Who Won 21-year Fight for Freedom of Seamen," Milwaukee Journal, January 29, 1938, 4.
[55] "Andrew Furuseth," The New Republic 9, no. 106 (November 11, 1916): 40–42, 40.
[56] Bernt A. Sosveen, "Andrew Furuseth," in Silas B. Axtell, A Symposium on Andrew Furuseth (New Bedford, MA: Darwin Press, 1948), 51-60; Knut Gjerset, Norwegian Sailors in American Waters – A Study in the History of Maritime Activity on the

Eastern Seaboard (Northfield, MN: Norwegian-American Historical Association, 1933), 172; Weintraub, Andrew Furuseth, 1—4.

[57] Robert M. La Follette, "Andrew Furuseth and His Great Work," La Follette's Magazine 7, no. 4 (April 1915), 2.

[58] Stephen Schwartz, Brotherhood of the Sea: A History of the Sailor's Union of the Pacific 1885-1985 (London: Routledge, 1986, repr. 2019), 42.

[59] Weintraub, Andrew Furuseth, 7.

[60] "In memory of the Emancipator of Seamen," West Coast Sailors, 1—2.

[61] Weintraub, Andrew Furuseth, 11–27.

[62] "In memory of the Emancipator of Seamen," West Coast Sailors, 4.

[63] Felix Reisenberg, Jr., Red Record: Historical Essay," Found SF, the San Francisco Digital History Archive, https://www.foundsf.org/index.php?title=Red_Record. The stories of brutality were widely disseminated to the press. For example, "Brutality aboard Ship," New York Tribune, January 31, 1896, 1.

[64] Christopher M. Sterba, "Transcultural San Francisco: Andrew Furuseth, Olaf Tveitmoe, and the Forgotten Scandinavian American Experience," Pacific Historical Review 85, no. 1 (February 2016): 72–109, 86.

[65] The Red Record: A Brief Resume of Some of the Cruelties Perpetrated upon American Seamen at the Present Time (San Francisco: Coast Seamen's Print, 1897).

[66] California Bureau of Labor Statistics, Investigation into Condition of Men Working on the Waterfront.

[67] Arthur E. Albrecht, "International Seamen's Union of America—A Study of Its History and Problems," Bulletin of the United States Bureau of Labor Statistics 342 (Washington, DC: Government Printing Office, 1923), 3–15.

[68] Albrecht, "International Seamen's Union of America."

[69] 17 Stat. 273 (July 7, 1872).

[70] 18 Stat. 64 (June 9, 1874).

[71] Schwartz, Brotherhood of the Sea, 43.

[72] 26 Stat. 320 (August 19, 1890); U.S. Congress, House, Laws Relating to Shipping Commissioners, 53rd Cong., 2nd sess., 1894, H. Rep. 53-911.

[73] Peter B. Gill, "The Sailor's Union of the Pacific from 1885-1929," University of Washington, University of Washington Libraries, Pacific Northwest Historical Monographs (1942), 205, https://digitalcollections.lib.washington.edu/digital/collection/pnwhm/id/1030/rec/4.

[74] Weintraub, Andrew Furuseth, 32.

[75] "In memory of the Emancipator of Seamen," West Coast Sailors, 2.

[76] John L. Mathews, "The Coming Ashore of Andrew Furuseth," Everybody's Magazine 25, no. 1 (July 1911): 60-71, 64 ("Two hundred men in jail, thirteen shot dead by masters or police for refusing to go aboard or stay aboard ship and work—that was the situation when the Union gave up and the men went to work at half pay.").

[77] Gill, "Sailor's Union of the Pacific," 127–29.
[78] "Fiends at Work," San Francisco Chronicle, September 24, 1893, 20.
[79] For example, Paul Hall, "'Tomorrow Is Also a Day,'" Seafarers Log 8, no. 11 (March 15, 1946): 3.
[80] Weintraub, Andrew Furuseth, 32–33.
[81] "Andrew Furuseth and His Great Work," La Follette's Magazine 7, no. 4 (April 1915): 2. Furuseth may have come to La Follette's attention in 1907—1908 when he sided with the graft prosecution of labor leader Abe Ruef in San Francisco. Leon Fink, Sweatshops at Sea (Chapel Hill: University of North Carolina Press, 2011), 95.
[82] Arthur Ruhl, "The Sailor's Side," Collier's, The National Weekly 47, no. 18 (July 22, 1911): 18-20, 18 ("He reminds one of some character of Ibsen's—with whose plays, by the way, he is thoroughly familiar."); Weintraub, Andrew Furuseth, 192.
[83] "Andrew Furuseth and His Fifteen-Year Siege of Congress," Current Opinion 59, no. 1 (July 1915), 18–19.
[84] Mathews, "The Coming Ashore of Andrew Furuseth," 60 ("For the seamen of the world the most important event of the nineteenth century was the Coming Ashore of Andrew Furuseth").
[85] "Andrew Furuseth and His Great Work," La Follette's Magazine 7, no. 4 (April 1915): 2.
[86] Weintraub, Andrew Furuseth, 192 ("No one, not even Furuseth's worst enemies, ever accused him of personal dishonesty"); "Letter from Mae E. Waggaman: Former Private Secretary to Andrew Furuseth (Feb. 25, 1947)," in Silas B. Axtell, A Symposium on Andrew Furuseth 35—37; "Friends to Hail 'Andy' Furuseth, Labor Chief Who 'Freed' Seamen," New York Times, March 12, 1954, 43 ("Unionist Died Penniless in '38 after a Lifetime of Helping Mariners Gain Security").
[87] Weintraub, Andrew Furuseth, 91–92.
[88] Mathews, "Coming Ashore of Andrew Furuseth," 67, 71 ("A seaman's pay, a seaman's ration, a seaman's dwelling-space satisfy him.").
[89] Axtell, Symposium on Andrew Furuseth, 10.
[90] "'The Sailors' Lincoln,'" New York Times, (January 24, 1938), 22. For a discussion of the origins of this "credo" see Archie Green, "Furuseth's Credo," West Coast Sailors (March 12, 2002), 8—11. A different version of this "credo" appears on the bust of Furuseth in front of the Sailors' Union of the Pacific Headquarters in San Francisco.
[91] La Follette, "Andrew Furuseth and His Great Work," 2.
[92] Weintraub, Andrew Furuseth, 88.
[93] "Furuseth's Labor Day Talk," Seamen's Journal 41, no. 10 (October 1, 1927): 11–13.
[94] "The Sailor's Mistletoe," Oregonian, (October 17, 1908), 8.
[95] Weintraub, Andrew Furuseth, 256 (select list of Furuseth publications); "Seeks No Publicity," San Francisco Call, (August 3, 1913), 47; Carl Sandburg, "The Face of Andy Furuseth," La Follette's Magazine 7, no. 4 (April 1915): 1.

[96] "The Face of Andrew Furuseth," La Follette's Magazine.
[97] "The Face of Andrew Furuseth," La Follette's Magazine.
[98] Weintraub, Andrew Furuseth, chaps, 8 and 9; Gill, "The Sailor's Union of the Pacific," 446–59.
[99] Elmo Paul Hohman, History of American Merchant Seamen (Hamden, CT: Shoe String Press, 1956), 48–49.
[100] John H. Kemble and Lane C. Kendall, "The Years between the Wars: 1919–1939,"149–55, in Kilmarx, America's Maritime Legacy.
[101] Andrew Furuseth, "Second Message to Seamen—His Relationship to the Harbor Workers and the Shipowners" (Chicago: International Seamen's Union of America, 1919), 24–25 (disparaging the "'One Big Union'" idea); Weintraub, Andrew Furuseth, 195.
[102] Albrecht, "International Seamen's Union of America," 27.
[103] Welntraub, Andrew Furuseth, 194.
[104] Weintraub, Andrew Furuseth, 194–200.
[105] Weintraub, Andrew Furuseth, 195–96.
[106] Weintraub, Andrew Furuseth, 197.
[107] "In memory of the Emancipator of the Seamen," 12.
[108] "Furuseth Death Brings Tribute—Champion of Sailors to the End," San Francisco Chronicle, January 23, 1938, 85.
[109] "In memory of the Emancipator of the Seamen," West Coast Sailors, 12.
[110] "Andrew Furuseth Labor Leader, Dies," New York Times, January 23, 1938, 9.
[111] Weintraub, Andrew Furuseth, 32 (listed in note 15).
[112] 24 Stat. 79 (June 19, 1886).
[113] Annual Report of the Commissioner of Navigation to the Secretary of the Treasury (1895), 31 (Chamberlain also referred to the 1884 Dingley Act "as one of the most liberal and humane of our statutes for the protection of seamen.").
[114] Gill, "Sailor's Union of the Pacific," 210.
[115] Axtell, Symposium on Andrew Furuseth, 117.
[116] 26 CONG. REC. 7944–45 (July 27, 1894).
[117] "Not for the Sailors Good–Vernon C. Brown Shows the Evils of the Maguire Bills," New York Times, June 10, 1894, 9. Furuseth's response appeared in a subsequent article. "Favors the Shipping Bills–An Answer to Objections Made by Vernon C. Brown, New York Times, June 16, 1894, 9.
[118] U.S. Congress, House, Committee on Merchant Marine and Fisheries, Hearings before the Committee on Merchant Marine and Fisheries on Sundry Bills Relating to the American Merchant Marine, Known as the 'Maguire' Bills, 53rd Cong., 2nd sess., 1894, H. Misc. Doc. 53-206.
[119] 28 Stat. 667 (February 18, 1895).
[120] Gill, "The Sailor's Union of the Pacific from 1885-1929," 211.

[121] Finn J. D. John, "'Arago Four' Decision Literally Declared Sailors as Slaves," Redmond Spokesman, November 11, 2020, https://www.redmondspokesman.com/arago-four-decision-literally-declared-sailors-as-slaves/article_00566a06-1e15-11eb-bdcc-1f4e73be8b5d.html.

[122] "Famous Arago Case on Appeal," San Francisco Call, May 2, 1897, 2; Gill, "The Sailor's Union of the Pacific," 225.

[123] Robertson v. Baldwin, 165 U.S. 275 (1897).

[124] "The Sailor and the Law—Is Jack Bond or Free?" San Francisco Chronicle, January 31, 1897, 26.

[125] For example, "Wrongs of the Sailors," New York Times, March 26, 1897, 1. In the meantime, the Act of March 3, 1897, simplified proof of cruel treatment removing the requirement of proving that the treatment was inspired by malice, hatred, or revenge. 29 Stat. 687, 691 (March 3, 1897).

[126] 30 Stat. 755 (December 21, 1898).

[127] "Senator Frye Gets a Roast–A Mass-Meeting That Spoke Out Loud for 'Poor Jack,'" San Francisco Call Bulletin, February 3, 1897, 8.

[128] Schwartz, Brotherhood of the Sea, 151.

[129] For example, U.S. Congress, Senate, Employment of Chinese on Vessels Flying the American Flag, Etc., 57th Cong., 1st sess., 1902, S. Doc. 57-281, 2 (contains the recommendation of the SUP, American Federation of Labor and many other labor organizations to make it unlawful to employ Chinese on U.S.-flag vessels "for the sake of the nation as well as for the sake of Caucasian seamen.").

[130] Annual Report of the Commissioner of Navigation to the Secretary of the Treasury (1898), 20 ("The crews of our own steamships plying to China and Japan are almost wholly Chinese and Japanese, shipped before American consuls at foreign ports where the vessels enter and clear.").

[131] Summarized in Scharrenberg v. Dollar S.S. Co., 245 U.S. 122 (1917).

[132] For example, "Wants No Chinese Sailors," Oregonian, February 5, 1902, 1.

[133] U.S. Congress, Senate, The Decay of Seamanship, 63rd Cong., 1st sess., 1913, S. Doc. 63-216.

[134] Weintraub, Andrew Furuseth, 117, 172.

[135] Weintraub, Andrew Furuseth, 173.

[136] Weintraub, Andrew Furuseth, 117–18.

[137] For example, Andrew Furuseth, "Subsidies in Relation to Sea-Power," American Federationist 7, no. 4 (April 1900): 92–96.

[138] Gill, "The Sailor's Union of the Pacific," 395.

[139] Weintraub, Andrew Furuseth, 115, 171, 174.

[140] H.R. 13771, 58th Cong. 2nd sess. (1904).

[141] 38 Cong. Rec. 2093–01, 2094 (February 19, 1904).

[142] H.R. 17724, 59th Cong., 1st sess. (1906); H.R. 14655, 60th Cong., 1st sess. (1908); and H.R. 11193, 61st Cong., 1st sess. (1909).

[143] For example, U.S. Congress, House, Committee on Merchant Marine and Fisheries, Hearings before the House Merchant Marine Committee on House Bill 11372, 62nd Cong., 2nd sess., 1911; U.S. Congress, House, Committee on Merchant Marine and Fisheries, Hearings before the House Merchant Marine and Fisheries Committee on S. 136, 63rd Cong., 2nd sess., part 1, 1913.
[144] Weintraub, Andrew Furuseth, 117.
[145] 49 Cong. Rec. 4575 (March 2, 1913) (statement of the Chamber of Commerce of the State of New York).
[146] U.S. Congress, House, Committee on Merchant Marine and Fisheries, Hearings before the House Merchant Marine Committee on American Seamen, 61st Cong., 2d sess., 1910, 8.
[147] Weintraub, Andrew Furuseth, 115.
[148] 23 Stat. 53, 55—56 (June 26, 1884).
[149] 1912 Democratic Party Platform, June 25, 1912, UC Santa Barbara, the American Presidency Project, Democratic Party Platforms, https://www.presidency.ucsb.edu/documents/1912-democratic-party-platform; Republican Party Platform of 1912, June 8, 1912, UC Santa Barbara, the American Presidency Project, Republican Party Platforms, https://www.presidency.ucsb.edu/documents/republican-party-platform-1912.
[150] 48 Cong. Rec. 10172 (August 3, 1912).
[151] U.S. Congress, House, Free and Efficient Seamen, 62nd Cong., 2nd sess., 1912, H. Rep. 62-645.
[152] Free and Efficient Seamen, H. Rep. 62-645, part 2; "Merchant Marine Policy Attacked– Congress Destroyed It, Yet Favors Bill Benefiting Foreign Sailors, Says Humphrey," New York Times, May 23, 1912, 15.
[153] U.S. Congress, Senate, Commerce Committee, Hearings before the Senate Subcommittee of the Commerce Committee on H.R. 23673 on Involuntary Servitude Imposed Upon Seamen, 62nd Cong., 3rd sess., 14 parts, 1912-1913.
[154] 49 Cong. Rec. 4563-4565 (March 2, 1913); U.S. Congress, Senate, Desertion of Seamen from United States Vessels, 62nd Cong., 2nd sess., 1912, S. Rep. 62-482 (letter of Department of Commerce and Labor in support of S. 5757).
[155] "Report and Debate on Bill," Coast Seamen's Journal 26, no. 2217 (March 19, 1913): 1.
[156] 49 Cong. Rec. 4565 (March 2, 1913).
[157] 49 Cong. Rec. 4581—88.
[158] l49 Cong. Rec. 4806.
[159] U.S. Congress, House, Report on Pocket Veto: Message from the President of the United States, 70th Cong., 2nd sess., 1928, H. Doc. 70-493, 41; "Congress Lingers till Last Minute," New York Times, March 5, 1913, 5.
[160] Weintraub, Andrew Furuseth, 120.
[161] Weintraub, Andrew Furuseth, 121.

[162] 50 Cong. Rec. 1085 (May 3, 1913) (H.R. 4616).
[163] 50 Cong. Rec. 54 (April 7, 1913) (S. 136).
[164] Desertion of Seamen from United States Vessels, S. Rep. 62-482.
[165] 50 Cong. Rec. 5777 (October 23, 1913).
[166] 50 Cong. Rec. 5779.
[167] Weintraub, Andrew Furuseth, 124.
[168] "Letter from A. Furuseth to W. Wilson (October 29, 1913)," Papers of Woodrow Wilson, vol. 28, 469.
[169] "Chamberlain and Uhler Exposed! –U.S. Government Officials in Role of Twin Servants to the Shipping Interests," Coast Seamen's Journal 27, no. 2274 (April 22, 1914): 1.
[170] U.S. Congress, Senate, Foreign Relations Committee, Hearings before the Senate Foreign Relations Committee on an International Convention Relating to Safety of Life at Sea, Signed at London, 63rd Cong., 2d sess., 1914, 40.
[171] Hearings before the House Merchant Marine and Fisheries Comm. on S. 136, part 2.
[172] Weintraub, Andrew Furuseth, 126.
[173] U.S. Congress, Senate, International Conference on Safety of Life at Sea, 63rd Cong., 2nd sess., 1914, S. Doc. 63-463.
[174] "Amends Sea Safety Plan," New York Times, December 17, 1914, 12.
[175] U.S. Congress, House, Welfare of American Seamen and Safety of Life at Sea, 63rd Cong., 2nd sess., 1914, H. Rep. 63-852.
[176] Weintraub, Andrew Furuseth, 128.
[177] 51 Cong. Rec. 14362 (August 27, 1914).
[178] U.S. Congress, House, Seaman's Bill, 63rd Cong., 3rd sess., 1915, H. Rep. 63-1439.
[179] For example, "Chamberlain and Uhler Exposed!—U.S. Government Officials in Role of Twin Servants to the Shipping Interests," Coast Seamen's Journal 27, no. 2274 (April 22, 1914): 1; "General Uhler Shown Up!" Coast Seamen's Journal 27, 2281 (June 10, 1914): 1.
[180] "Modified Seamen's Bill Passes the House," Survey 32, no. 23 (September 5, 1914): 555–56, 555.
[181] 52 Cong. Rec. 4654 (February 25, 1915).
[182] 52 Cong. Rec. 4817.
[183] 52 Cong. Rec. 4818.
[184] 38 Stat. 1164 (March 4, 1915).
[185] "Letter from F. Simmons to J. Tumulty (December 31, 1914)," Papers of Woodrow Wilson, vol. 32, 554 ("I am strongly of the opinion that the passage of this bill will be full of embarrassment, not only to our relations with foreign governments but also to the programme of the Administration looking to the rehabilitation of the merchant marine.").
[186] Weintraub, Andrew Furuseth, 131.

[187] "Note from the White House Staff (February 27, 1915)," Papers of Woodrow Wilson, vol. 32, 294.
[188] "Letter from R. Lansing to W. Bryan (March 1, 1915)," Papers of Woodrow Wilson, vol. 32, 302.
[189] "Letter from W. Bryan to W. Wilson (March 1, 1915)," Papers of Woodrow Wilson, vol. 32, 302.
[190] "Letter from A. Furuseth to W. Wilson (March 1, 1915)," Papers of Woodrow Wilson, vol. 32, 304.
[191] "Letter from W. Bryan to W. Wilson (March 2, 1915)," Papers of Woodrow Wilson, vol. 32, 309.
[192] "Letter from W. Wilson to A. Furuseth (March 2, 1915)," Papers of Woodrow Wilson, vol. 32, 309.
[193] Belle Case La Follette and Fola La Follette, Robert M. Follette, June 14, 1855–June 18, 1925 (New York: Macmillan, 1953), 535.
[194] Weintraub, Andrew Furuseth, 132n77.
[195] La Follette, Robert M. Follette, 535–36.
[196] "Letter from W. Wilson to N. Baker (March 5, 1915)," Papers of Woodrow Wilson, vol. 32, 324.
[197] "Letter from A. Furuseth to W. Wilson (March 6, 1915)," Papers of Woodrow Wilson, vol. 32, 333.
[198] Andrew Furuseth, "The Dawn of Another Day," American Federationist 22, no. 9 (September 1915): 717–21.
[199] "Seamen's Law Condemned—The Nation's Business Publishes Views of Shipping Interests," New York Times, July 20, 1915, 20.
[200] "Pacific Mail Sells 5 Liners to Ship Trust—La Follette's Seamen's Act Drives Ships from Oriental Service," New York Tribune, August 14, 1915, 1.
[201] "La Follette Defends Bill – Senator Accuses the Shipowners of Being in a Conspiracy," New York Times, July 22, 1915, 18.
[202] Weintraub, Andrew Furuseth, 134–37.
[203] "No. 265 (Bureau of Navigation) –Language Test under the Seamen's Act (Sep. 18, 1915)," Circulars of the Department of Commerce in Effect July 1, 1917 (Washington, DC: Government Printing Office, 1917), 153—54. This circular was later changed to align more closely with the original intent of the law. Albrecht, "International Seamen's Union of America—A Study of Its History and Problems," 40–41.
[204] "The Seamen's Boomerang Law," New York Times, August 16, 1915, 8.
[205] Op. Att'y Gen. 30, no. 441 (August 25, 1915); "Studies Seamen's Law—Safety Rules for Foreign Ships Pondered by President," New York Times, August 10, 1915, 7.
[206] Furuseth, "The Dawn of Another Day," 721.
[207] Weintraub, Andrew Furuseth, 164–65.
[208] Strathearn S. S. Co. v. Dillon, 252 U.S. 348 (1920).
[209] O'Hara v. Luckenbach Steamship Co., 269 U.S. 364 (1926).
[210] 247 U.S. 372 (1918).

[211] 198 U.S. 158 (1903).
[212] 38 Stat. 1164, 1185 (March 4, 1915).
[213] Jesse S. Reeves, "The Jones Act and the Denunciation of Treaties," American Journal of International Law 15, no.1 (January 1921): 33–38, 37.
[214] Paul S. Taylor, "Eight Years of the Seamen's Act," American Labor Legislative Review 15, no. 1 (March 1925): 52–63.
[215] Albrecht, "International Seamen's Union of America," 52.

Senator Wesley Livsey Jones, Harris & Ewing, photographer, Library of Congress

Chapter 17 – Wesley Livsey Jones

Jones had a long career in the U.S. House of Representatives and the U.S. Senate and was an effective legislator, an astute politician, one of the hardest working senators of his era, and always viewed as honest and forthright. His many legislative successes include the Federal Water Power Act of 1920, the Merchant Marine Act, 1920, the Jones-Miller Anti-Narcotic Act of 1922, the Flood Control Act of 1928 (relating to the Mississippi and Sacramento Rivers), and the Merchant Marine Act, 1928. He was among the first to propose a U.S. government cargo preference law, which became the Cargo Preference Act of 1904.

But what he was best known for during most of his legislative career was serving as a national leader of the "dry" movement in support of Prohibition. Uncharacteristically, he lost his political perspective and began to steadily lose support in the late 1920s and early 1930s as the country turned its back on that social policy. In fact, the most famous "Jones Act" was the 1929 "Increased Penalties Act," which turned, for the first time, Prohibition violations into felonies.[1] This last act defined him most of all and contributed to the one and only election he lost, in 1932, shortly before his death.

Yakima Jones[2]

Jones was born on October 9, 1863, in southern Illinois in an area known as "Little Egypt" shortly after his father died serving in the Union army.[3] By the age of ten, he was hired out to do farm work and went to school only in the winter. At age sixteen, he began teaching school to earn his way through Southern Illinois "College," a Cumberland Presbyterian institution located in Enfield, Illinois.[4]

JOURNEY TO THE JONES ACT

Enfield was a small town where no liquor was sold; there were, however, four churches.[5] William E. Borah, the future senator from Idaho, a staunch isolationist, and leading opponent of President Woodrow Wilson's League of Nations, was a fellow classmate. One of Borah's biographers wrote that Jones "was considered something of a prodigy at the College."[6] Jones's son later said that Jones thought Borah was too flamboyant.[7]

After receiving his degree, Jones moved to Chicago and studied law by day and taught school by night. He was admitted to the bar in 1886 at the age of twenty-two. Around this time, he married Minda Nelson from Enfield with whom he had two children. While in Illinois, he campaigned for Blaine in 1884 and Harrison in 1888.[8] After trying to establish a law practice in Decatur, he moved in 1889 to North Yakima, Washington at the age of twenty-six. His reasons for doing so were never made public.[9] In Yakima, he worked in a real estate firm for a while and then as a partner in a small law firm.

As he had in Illinois, Jones started volunteering for the Republican Party and eventually caught the eye of Washington state leadership.[10] Possibly because Republican leadership thought that they were going to lose in 1898 (Democrat William Jennings Bryan had won the state with about 57 percent of the vote in 1896), they picked Jones to run for one of the state's at-large U.S. House seats.[11]

The state press described him as "'Yakima' Jones," "a plain solid looking sort of man… of medium height, broad shouldered and strong, he looks what he is, a man of intelligence."[12] He gave his acceptance speech "in a strong, clear voice, slightly metallic, perhaps, but that has a pleasant ring to it when he emphasizes his words." Moreover, "there was nothing light or frivolous about his words, he eschewed flippancy, talked in an earnest and impassioned way, dealt in cold facts, and kept his audience listening attentively. He was loudly cheered."

One of Jones's opponents for the congressional seat was J. Hamilton Lewis. Known as "Col. Lewis," he had served in the Spanish-American War as a colonel in the Washington National

Guard. He was also known for fancy dress and flowery speeches.[13] After Lewis lost to Jones in the 1898 election, he later moved to Illinois. There, he was elected a U.S. senator from 1913 to 1919 and again from 1930 to 1939 when he died. Lewis was with Congressman Alexander, Chamberlain, and Furuseth in London in 1914 at the International Convention on Safety of Life at Sea as the U.S. Senate representative.

Jones gained fame in an October 22, 1898 debate with Lewis in Walla Walla.[14] The *Seattle Daily Times*, which supported Lewis, reported that Lewis "burnt the skin off him, making him [Jones] the laughing stock of the packed Republican audience" including calling out Jones for not serving during the Spanish-American War.[15] The Seattle *Post-Daily Intelligencer* saw things differently: "'Yakima' Jones Vanquishes Col. Lewis" and "Orator Loses His Temper at His Good-Humored Opponent."[16] That debate stayed with Jones. Pro-Jones news articles in 1932 referenced the debate when "Young 'Wes' Defeated 'Dude' Lewis."[17] Jones was fortunate that 1898, the year of the victory over Spain, favored Republicans, and Jones and his fellow Republican, Francis W. Cushman, were both elected over Lewis and William C. Jones. [18]

After the election, Jones was greeted enthusiastically by a packed opera house in Yakima on November 12.[19] In what was almost certainly an overstatement, the event was reported as being an "immense gathering," which "went fairly wild over his masterly and statesmanlike patriotic address." Likely closer to the truth was the report that Jones's speech was "broadly patriotic and strictly non-partisan."

In 1898 and later campaigns, Jones's personal qualities, his reputation as being honest, hardworking, cautious, practical, and without pretense or noticeable ambition, served him well. As one historian wrote, "Jones was a tall, sincere, devout former lawyer from Yakima. He did not drink, gamble, smoke, or swear. He was dedicated to middle-class American values and to the Republican party, both of which he in many ways personified."[20]

JOURNEY TO THE JONES ACT

The *Oregonian* wrote in 1920 that Jones "has gone far with moderate ability" but it was "ability re-enforced by sound character, honest convictions, genuine desire to serve."[21] James Michener in the novel *Alaska*, even though a work of fiction, wrote that Jones was a "hardworking, amiable Republican... whose devotion to duty had elevated him to the chairmanship of the important Senate Commerce Committee."[22]

His hardworking style was legendary: "The dominant legend of his life is one of toil" and "it is probable that he puts in more time in the Senate Chamber than does any other member of the upper house."[23] In the lead up the 1920 Merchant Marine Act, he oversaw thirty-seven hearings in fifty-one days, including six Saturdays taking testimony from over one hundred witnesses.[24] These qualities were played up in his campaigns and he was called the "Blacksmith Senator."[25] Jones's steady, middle-of-the-road approach earned him both praise ("he has steady grown, both in popularity and influence" and "he has the facility of sticking to his own way without giving offense") and criticism (an "average western Congressman").[26]

How he spent his spare time also spoke to his character. It was reported that he only went to the theater or to hear music once a week with his wife and avoided serious or tragic shows.[27] After Jones died, his son wrote, "'My father's only recreations... were golf and tramping in the mountains.'"[28] He played at the golf courses at the Old Soldiers' Home close to Catholic University and East Potomac Park, both in Washington, DC. His golfing partner for about fifteen years was Representative William B. Oliver (D-AL), an eleven-term congressman. Oliver shared at the Jones Congressional memorial that, "when we were in Washington, unless heavy snow or rainstorm forebade, we met at daybreak at golf links within the District, returning always to our homes in time for 8 o'clock breakfast... There were no caddies, no wagers of any kind on the game, but simply a meeting of friends in the early morning hours for wholesome exercise."[29]

A 1919 story was used to illustrate Jones's common man attributes. Jones was driving to Washington, DC with his wife, son, and daughter-in-law when his car broke down in Delaware. They knocked on a farmhouse door and the only available place to stay was in a barn. This episode was turned into a campaign staple because the farmer was a tenant of a "Dupont" and the story was told as "Jones stayed at Dupont's barn," although it turned out that the "Dupont" was not Senator Henry A. Dupont.[30]

In terms of his political philosophy, Jones liked to refer to himself as a "conservative progressive," by which he meant that he did not favor what were considered radical approaches but was sympathetic to both the political and social reforms animating the progressive movement.[31] For example, on race relations, he wrote to President Woodrow Wilson and other government officials, protesting Wilson's segregation of black government employees: "It is hard to believe that any discrimination is being made by officials of the National Government in regard to any of the citizens of this country."[32] In 1914 he offered an amendment to an agricultural extension appropriations bill to restrict funding to segregated institutions and provide for equal funding of predominantly black institutions.[33] These efforts earned him the support of Booker T. Washington and the NAACP.[34]

Jones also supported women's suffrage, asking rhetorically in 1913 when the Senate considered a constitutional amendment granting women the right to vote: "What peculiar sexual difference is there that entitles man to vote and prevents woman? Can anyone point out any such peculiarity? No one has ever done so."[35] Jones was not, however, in the least bit in favor of immigration. When confronted as to whether he had the same solicitude toward Japanese immigrants as he did to blacks, Jones said that the difference was that blacks were U.S. citizens and Japanese were not and "I hope they never will be."[36]

On labor rights, he tried to thread a narrow path between business interests and labor reform.[37] For example, we have seen that he was wary of the Seamen's Act.[38] In 1916 Jones advanced complaints of shipowners about their inability to crew their vessels, allegedly caused by that legislation. Although, he claimed he was not in opposition to the law.[39] At the time, the Seamen's Act was regularly attacked in the Seattle newspapers.[40] Jones's son claimed that Jones was nevertheless fond of Furuseth and that improving on the Seamen's Act was one of Jones' prime motivations in getting the 1920 Merchant Marine Act passed with Seaman's Act modifications.[41]

Jones's overall strategy worked: he was re-elected and served five terms in the U.S. House of Representatives in total, although he pined for the Senate.[42] An opportunity arose in 1907 when Washington State adopted a non-binding Senate preferential primary law for the first time as a prelude to direct elections, rather than election by the state legislature.[43]

Jones, then forty-five years old, campaigned hard in the primary and defeated the incumbent senator, who had not had to campaign publicly before. Jones was then easily elected by the Republican-dominated legislature in early 1909.[44] Jones ran as the reform candidate and his reputation for honesty, modesty, and forbearance served him well.

On most issues, Jones was cautious and politically nimble. Senator Clarence C. Dill (D-WA) said in eulogy, "'Senator Jones never knocks any flies. He bunts and always plays low ball. That is why he is always safe.'"[45] Jones's political adeptness failed him in two major instances. Each time, he started from a principled position but held on too long after the position became a political loser: U.S. neutrality prior to World War I and, as already mentioned, Prohibition.

Jones was a leader of the movement to avoid provocations that would embroil the United States in World War I. He was adamantly opposed to Americans traveling into war zones or on belligerent vessels.[46] After the sinking of the *Lusitania*, he was widely quoted as saying that he would "rather resign my seat in the United States Senate than by my vote place the right of a citizen to go abroad above the right of my country to enjoy peace."[47]

In 1916, he said that an American who "persists in travelling for pleasure or profit in the danger zone and in a belligerent ship shows that he is utterly lacking in patriotism" and such a person "is entitled to no consideration whatever."[48] In this he clashed with former president Theodore Roosevelt, who wrote to the contrary—any leader who argued that "we need not take action" for the deaths of American on lawful travel "occupies a position precisely and exactly as base and as cowardly... as if his wife's face were slapped on the public streets and the only action he took was to tell her to stay in the house."[49]

The neutrality issue came to a head with Wilson's early 1917 proposal to arm merchant vessels. This practice was known as "armed neutrality." Jones was one of the senators who urged that the armed neutrality legislation be approached with caution since it effectively would put the United States at war with Germany.[50] He eventually signed on to ending a La Follette-led filibuster of the Wilson proposal—but with reservations.[51]

There was enormous acrimony directed toward the filibustering senators referred to by Wilson as "a little group of willful men."[52] Although Jones was not one of those singled out, he was tarnished in his home state as being unpatriotic and pro-German.[53] The *Seattle Times* called Jones out on his attempt to argue sides of the debate claiming that Jones's reservations would have turned privately armed U.S.-flag vessels into pirates, making the situation worse than if the vessels were unarmed.[54] The *Seattle Star* argued that Jones had "failed pathetically on the one big thing in his generation."[55]

Perhaps to make up for his earlier opposition, Jones became an avid supporter of the war effort once war was declared.[56] He continued, however, to moralize, and it later defined his career. For example, Jones offered an amendment to the Army conscription legislation known as the "Selective Service Act of 1917." It prevented the establishment of "houses of ill fame, brothels, or bawdy houses within 10 miles of any military camp," which became part of the law.[57] Jones also was a leader in amending the law to authorize the president to prevent the sale of liquor near Army camps claiming that many of the states had already gone "dry" (by July 1917, twenty-six states were

JOURNEY TO THE JONES ACT

indeed dry).[58] Prohibition was to be critical to the rest of Jones's Senate career.

THE FIVE-AND-TEN SENATOR[59]

One of Jones's first legislative moves on Prohibition was a 1912 amendment he offered to District of Columbia legislation. He proposed giving family members the right to sue any inn that sold liquor to anyone whose family had informed the establishment not to sell liquor to their relative.[60] That first step started him on a path where he eventually become "the leading defender of the faith." His "portrait hung conspicuously in the office of the Anti-Saloon League [which led the Prohibition political campaign] for as long as the organization existed under that name."[61]

In the 1914 election, Jones tried to find middle ground when there was a Washington state prohibition ballot initiative. He knew it divided the state and generated strong feelings (the ballot succeeded with 52.58 percent of the vote).[62] Jones was reelected in 1914 only because the opposition vote was split among four candidates, with Jones receiving only about 38 percent of the total vote.[63] In supporting Prohibition efforts, Jones was therefore doing, at least at first, no more than the people of the State of Washington appeared to want.[64]

In 1918 he advanced an amendment to the annual agricultural appropriations legislation to impose prohibition as a nationwide war measure.[65] Congress had given the president authority to impose prohibition in 1917 at his discretion. Jones's amendment made it mandatory.[66] Jones argued that a large portion of the U.S. population "feel that prohibition now would be one of the most effective means of doing what everybody says we seek to do—win the war."[67] The reasoning was the grains used to produce liquor were needed to feed people both in the United States and abroad.

After passage of the Eighteenth Amendment and the "National Prohibition Act of 1919," known as the "Volstead Act," Jones insisted on enforcement.[68] In 1921, he argued "there is no such thing as personal liberty in a Republic" and the "law must be enforced or orderly government will fall."[69]

The *New York Times* remembered this phrase in 1929.[70] The *Times* editorialized that Jones was a "felon-maker" and that "for him the Constitution is the Eighteenth Amendment."[71] The *Times* sarcastically requested that "Senator Jones ought to create some more felonies."

The *Times* was referring to the "Increased Penalties Act" of 1929 which made felonies of certain Volstead Act offenses, colloquially referred to as the "Five-and-Ten law" after the possible five years in jail or maximum $10,000 fine.[72] The law was also called the "Jones-Stalker Act" or just the "Jones Act" or "Jones Law."[73]

Even before enactment of that law, Jones had become thoroughly mixed up in Prohibition enforcement in the State of Washington.[74] Jones arranged for the appointment of the chief Treasury enforcement agents in the state and was in regular contact with them.[75] Those agents, who had served Jones in various political capacities prior to their appointments, became controversial because of violence and alleged corruption. When Jones defended them despite criticism, the bad publicity that followed Prohibition enforcement in Washington began to eat away at his political support.

Jones's Five-and-Ten Law sponsorship came to define him much to Jones's surprise.[76] He argued that it would only affect commercial bootleggers and not individual consumption and that Americans should be "good sports" about complying with the law.[77] He defended the law as being necessary to stop the commercialization of liquor traffic and believed it would be effective.[78]

Over time he came to resent the law being associated with him and him alone and sought to spread the blame.[79] For example, he pointed out that it passed the Senate in a 65 to 18 vote and that it was he who offered an amendment to alleviate any potential harshness.[80]

His defense and protestations were to no avail. Jones became the "author of the 'five-and-ten' law," the "Daddy of the Jones Law," and the "five-and-ten Senator."[81] Even sympathetic treatments of his role pointed out that he had persistently offered prohibition amendments to war emergency measures.[82] Moreover, Jones burnished his stern reputation, arguing that tourists who smuggled liquor should be prosecuted and lawyers who defended "wet" clients should be disbarred.[83]

By the spring of the 1932 election year, it was obvious that Jones's Prohibition leadership was going to hurt him politically. He started to argue that if the people of Washington State wanted it, then he would favor letting the people vote on "reversion." [84] When he did so, the *New York Times* reported that, "here in Washington nobody could be led to believe that Senator Jones could have a sincere change of heart. His dryness is the sort which might well be described as desiccated."[85]

At the time, Jones was also closely identified with the unpopular President Herbert Hoover, whom he admired and supported.[86] The level of criticism Hoover faced during the ongoing economic depression upset Jones to the point that he defended the president in a prominent February 1932 radio address.[87]

In his last two years in the Senate, from 1930 to 1932, Jones was Appropriations Committee chairman. He told friends that this time was the "height of my ambition as far as positions are concerned."[88] Jones had already served as Republican whip from 1924 to 1929. He was proud of his efforts to cut federal expenditures and his adherence to orthodox Republican fiscal conservatism.[89] The message of a federal government doing less rather than more to help the country was not popular during the ongoing economic depression.

Jones was too ill to campaign in 1932 and was handicapped by his Prohibition positions and Hoover alignment. He only received about 33 percent of the vote, which was slightly less than the vote received by Hoover in Washington State.[90] Jones had had abdominal operations in 1928 and 1929 and had never fully recovered.[91] He died on November 19, 1932, less than two weeks after his first and only election defeat.

Jones was remembered at the time as a national leader on irrigation, waterpower, Alaska, and the merchant marine.[92] On maritime matters he was often remembered more for the 1928 Merchant Marine Act than the 1920 Merchant Marine Act.[93] But even more so, the focus was on Prohibition and his role with the "Five-and-Ten Law." The *New York Times* summary of Jones's career was that he was the "long leading dry."[94]

Critics of Jones's character at the time of his death were scarce. Most typical were plaudits for the traits he had exhibited throughout his public career, ranging from when he started as "Yakima Jones" to when he became the "Five-and-Ten Senator." Representative William Humphrey, his House colleague, eulogized Jones as follows:

> He performed every duty—he evaded no responsibility. He practiced no deception. Honesty was one of the outstanding qualities of his rugged character. He was intellectually honest. He was honest with himself and with others. There was about him no cant or hypocrisy. What he preached he practiced. That which his conscience dictated was done. In public and in private life, I have never known a cleaner man.[95]

---

[1] For example, "The Jones Law," New York Times, March 18, 1929, 24.

[2] For example, "Meeting for Jones," Yakima Herald, (January 29, 1908), 1 ("'Yakima Jones for senator' is to be the slogan of the Jones Club which will be organized in this city at once.").

[3] "Jones, Wesley Livsey, 1863-1932," Biographical Directory of the United States Congress, https://bioguide.congress.gov/search/bio/J000257; William Stuart Forth, "Wesley L. Jones: A Political Biography," (PhD diss., University of Washington,1962); Keith Murray, "Research Suggestions: The Wesley L. Jones Papers," Pacific Northwest Quarterly 36, no. 1 (January 1945): 65–68; Memorial Services Held in the House of Representatives of the United States, Together with Remarks Presented in Eulogy of Wesley L. Jones (Washington, DC: Government Printing Office, 1933); "Wesley L. Jones," United States Law Review 66 (1932): 686; "Jones, 'Blacksmith Senator,' Enjoys Work Family Once Slept in Barn on Auto Trip," Seattle Daily Times, October 30, 1932, 26; Ray T. Tucker, "Jones of Washington—A Portrait of the Author of the 'Five and Ten' Law," Outlook and Independent 152, no. 7 (June 12, 1929): 247—49, 273; Joe Mitchell Chapple, "Affairs at Washington," National Magazine 31, no. 5 (February 1910): 457—86, 477—82; An Illustrated History of Klickitat, Yakima and Kittitas Counties (Interstate Publishing Company, 1904), 538; John A. Campbell, ed., A Biographical History with Portraits of the Prominent Men of the Great West (Chicago: Western Biographical and Engraving, 1902), 685.

[4] Tucker, "Jones of Washington," 248–49.

[5] Waldo W. Braden, "Some Illinois Influences on the Life of William E. Borah," Journal of the Illinois State Historical Society 40, no. 2 (June 1947): 168–75, 172–73.

[6] Claudius O. Johnson, Borah of Idaho (New York: Longmans, Green, 1936), 11.

[7] Forth, Wesley L. Jones, 435 n1.
[8] 60 CONG. REC. 926 (January 4, 1921).
[9] Forth, Wesley L. Jones, 7—8 (Forth interviewed Jones's son who did not know the reason for the Yakima move.).
[10] Tucker, "Jones of Washington," 249.
[11] Tucker, "Jones of Washington," 249.
[12] "Republicans of Washington Turn Solid Front to the Foe," Seattle Post-Intelligencer, (September 22, 1898), 1, 2; "Convention Report in Detail," Seattle Post-Intelligencer, (September 22, 1898), 2.
[13] Memorial Services Held in the House of Representatives and Senate of the United States, Together with Remarks Presented in Eulogy of James Hamilton Lewis (Washington, DC: Government Printing Office, 1939), 5.
[14] Forth, Wesley L. Jones, 51–52.
[15] "Opinion," Seattle Daily Times, October 24, 1898, 5.
[16] J. Howard Watson, "'Yakima' Jones Vanquishes Col Lewis," Seattle Post-Intelligencer, October 23, 1898, 1.
[17] "Jones, 'Blacksmith Senator," Enjoys Work—Family Once Slept in Barn on Auto Trip," Seattle Daily Times, October 30, 1931, 26.
[18] Forth, Wesley L. Jones, 51.
[19] "Republican Victory Is Royally Celebrated," Seattle Post-Intelligencer, November 13, 1898, 1.
[20] Norman H. Clark, The Dry Years: Prohibition and Social Change in Washington (Seattle: University of Washington Press, 1988), rev. ed., 179–80.
[21] "Senator Jones," Oregonian, September 17, 1920, 8.
[22] James A. Michener, Alaska: A Novel (New York: Random House, 1987), 816; Tucker, "Jones of Washington, 248.
[23] "Senator Jones Defends the Jones Law," New York Times Magazine, May 5, 1929, 3.
[24] Hearings before the Senate Commerce Committee on the Establishment of an American Merchant Marine.
[25] "Jones 'Blacksmith Senator,' Enjoys Work," Seattle Daily Times, October 30, 1932, 26.
[26] Ira E. Bennett, "Western Affairs at Washington," The Pacific Monthly 18, no. 6 (December 1907): 666—79, 674; "Mr Jones Takes All Credit–Allows Ankeny None," Seattle Daily Times, July 1, 1908, 6. The Seattle Daily Times frequently attacked Jones during that election cycle. For example, "Jones is Deficient in Dignity," Seattle Daily Times, July 17, 1908, 20. By 1932, the paper was extolling Jones's virtues. "Jones, 'Blacksmith Senator,' Enjoys Work.
[27] Tucker, "Jones of Washington," 248.
[28] "Party Loyalty Kept Senator on Go to the Last," Seattle Sunday Times, November 20, 1932, 7.

[29] Memorial Services Held in the House of Representatives of the United States, Together with Remarks Presented in Eulogy of Wesley L. Jones, 46.

[30] "Jones, 'Blacksmith Senator,' Enjoys Work;" "Senator Wasn't in Col. Dupont's Barn," Evening Journal (Delaware), June 30, 1919, 2.

[31] Forth, Wesley L. Jones: A Political Biography, 253.

[32] "Letter from W. Jones to W. Wilson (September 29, 1913)," Papers of Woodrow Wilson, vol. 28, 344; "Letter from W. Jones to W. McAdoo (September 29, 1913)," Papers of Wesley Livsey Jones, University of Washington University Libraries, Pacific Northwest Historical Documents Collection, box 220, folder 11; "Uplifters Advise Negroes," New York Times, May 4, 1914, 4.

[33] 51 CONG. REC. 2929 (February 5, 1914).

[34] For example, "Letter from B. Washington to W. Jones (February 18, 1914)," Papers of Wesley Livsey Jones, box 220, folder 9; "Letter of B. Riley to W. Jones (February 6, 1914)," Papers of Wesley Livsey Jones, box 220, folder 2.

[35] 50 CONG. REC. 5120 (September 18, 1913); "Demands Suffrage Debate–Senator Jones Wants Action on Amendment to Enfranchise Women," New York Times, September 19, 1913, 8.

[36] 51 CONG. REC. 2934 (February 5, 1914).

[37] Forth, Wesley L. Jones, 350–54.

[38] 52 CONG. REC. 4818 (February 25, 1915).

[39] 53 CONG. REC. 7291 (May 3, 1916).

[40] For example, "Scuttling American Ships," Seattle Daily Times, May 7, 1915, 6.

[41] Forth, Wesley L. Jones, 503n44.

[42] Forth, Wesley L. Jones, 761.

[43] Forth, Wesley L. Jones, 99.

[44] "Elections in Other States," New York Times, January 20, 1909, 3.

[45] Memorial Services Held in the House of Representatives of the United States, Together with Remarks Presented in Eulogy of Wesley L. Jones, 39.

[46] For example, "Stay in U.S., Says Jones," Washington Times, March 9, 1917, 4.

[47] For example, "Lister Occupies Olympia Pulpit," Seattle Daily Times, May 17, 1915, 18; "Washington Senator Is Peace Advocate," Denver Post, May 17, 1915, 2.

[48] 53 CONG. REC. 505 (January 15, 1916).

[49] Theodore Roosevelt, Fear God and Take Your Part (New York: George H. Doran, 1916), 35.

[50] 54 CONG. REC. 4898–4900 (March 3, 1917).

[51] Forth, Wesley L. Jones, 376—79.

[52] "Sharp Words by Wilson—Indicts Little Group for Halting Legislation in Perilous Time," New York Times, March 5, 1917, 1 (text of president's statement reprinted). The episode led to the adoption of the Senate's first cloture rule. 55 CONG. REC. 45 (March 8, 1917).

[53] For example, "Jones' Resignation as Senator Is Demanded," Washington Standard, March 16, 1917, 7; "Have You Requested That Jones Resign?" Tacoma Times, March 19, 1917, 3.

[54] For example, "Jones Convicts Himself," Seattle Daily Times, March 27, 1917, 6. Jones defended himself saying that all he asked for was deliberation on such an important issue. "Jones Stands for U.S. Rights, He Says," Seattle Daily Times, March 27, 1917, 7.

[55] "Inglis to Jones?" Seattle Star, September 7, 1920, 2.

[56] 55 CONG. REC. 1295–96 (April 27, 1917).

[57] 55 CONG. REC. 907 (April 21, 1917).

[58] 55 CONG. REC. 5587 (July 31, 1917).

[59] Don Charles, "The Five-and-Ten Senator," Brooklyn Daily Eagle, August 4, 1929, 70.

[60] U.S. Congress, Senate, Liquor Traffic in the District of Columbia, 62nd Cong., 2nd sess., 1912, S. Rep. 62-651.

[61] Clark, Dry Years, 179.

[62] "Washington Initiative 3, Alcohol Prohibition Measure (1914)," Encyclopedia of American Politics, Ballotpedia, https://ballotpedia.org/Washington_Initiative_3,_Alcohol_Prohibition_Measure_(1914).

[63] Available at ourcampaigns.com.

[64] "Washington Tires of State Dry Law," New York Times, May 1, 1932, 5 ("Years before the Eighteenth Amendment was adopted, the Washington law was regarded by the Anti-Saloon League as the ideal statutory enactment.").

[65] For example, 56 CONG. REC. 4121–29 (March 27, 1918).

[66] 40 Stat. 1045, 1046 (November 21, 1918).

[67] 56 CONG. REC. 9635–38 (August 29, 1918) (also putting in the record evidence that liquor consumption reduced efficiency of production).

[68] 41 Stat. 305 (October 28, 1919).

[69] 61 CONG. REC. 7705 (November 15, 1921).

[70] "Map First Defense in Jones Law Case," New York Times, March 21, 1929, 5.

[71] "Jones, The Felon-Maker," New York Times, April 11, 1929, 28.

[72] 45 Stat. 1446 (March 2, 1929).

[73] "Prohibition—The Five & Ten," Time Magazine, March 25, 1929; "Coolidge Signs Bill for Stiff Dry Penalties—Two Are Arrested at Capital under New Law," New York Times, March 3, 1929, 3; "Dry Penalties Bill Passed by Senate–Jones Measure for Five Years in Jail or $10,000 Fine Gets 65 to 18 Vote," New York Times, February 20, 1929, 1.

[74] Clark, Dry Years, 150–60, 183–85.

[75] "Letter from W. Jones to H. Gilham (January 23, 1924)," Papers of Wesley Livsey Jones, box 4, folder 7; Forth, Wesley L. Jones, 640––66.

[76] Tucker, "Jones of Washington," 247.

[77] "Senator Jones Defends the Jones Law," New York Times Magazine, May 5, 1929, 3; Nell Ray Clarke, "$10,000 Fine or 5 Years in Jail–United States Senator Wesley Jones Explains the Law Bearing His Name," Times-Picayune, May 19, 1929, 76; Nell

Ray Clarke, "Author of Jones Law Predicts Show-Down on Enforcement," Sunday Star (Washington, DC), May 19, 1929, 89.

[78] For example, "Jones Predicts Plan Will Solve Liquor Problem," Springfield Daily Republican, March 12, 1929, 19.

[79] "Prohibition: The Five & Ten," Time Magazine.

[80] "Jones, 'Blacksmith Senator,' Enjoys Work," Seattle Daily Times, October 30, 1932, 26.

[81] "In Senator Jones's State," New York Times, May 27, 1930, 24; "'Dampest Dozen' List Names Leading Drys," New York Times, October 23, 1930, 11; "The Daddy of the Jones Law," Spokane Chronicle, May 10, 1929; "Senator Jones Dies; Long Leading Dry," New York Times, November 20, 1932, 28.

[82] Tucker, "Jones of Washington," 247 ("not a fanatic on the subject of individual drinking; in fact, it is doubtful if there is a more broad-minded dry in or out of Congress.").

[83] "Jones for Applying His Law to Tourists," New York Times, April 29, 1929 ("'Travelers smuggling liquor into the United States are clearly offenders against the recently enacted law."), 1; "Jones Denounces Wet Lawyers Here–Senator, in Newark, Says They Will Violate Oath in Aiding Dry Law Offenders," New York Times, April 11, 1929, 4.

[84] "Senator Jones of '5 and 10' Declares for Resubmission," New York Times, August 21, 1932, 19.

[85] "Washington Tires of State Dry Law," New York Times, May 1, 1932, 5.

[86] Forth, Wesley L. Jones, 802–05.

[87] 75 CONG. REC. 4210–12 (February 18, 1932).

[88] "Letter from W. Jones to S. Chowder (January 8, 1930)," Papers of Wesley Livsey Jones, box 22, folder 13.

[89] "Saving by Congress More Than Billion," New York Times, July 17, 1932, 14.

[90] Forth, Wesley L. Jones, 815–19; ourcampaigns.com.

[91] "Senator Wesley Jones under Knife," New York Times, May 22, 1928, 27; "Senator Wesley Jones Operated On," New York Times, July 11, 1929, 23.

[92] "Northwest Mourns for Senator Jones," Oregonian, November 20, 1932, 1; "Condolences of U.S. Pay Tribute to Senator Jones," Seattle Sunday Times, November 20, 1932, 7.

[93] For example, "Praised by Both Sides in Congress," New York Times, November 20, 1932, 28 (R. J. Baker of the American Steamship Association said upon his death–"While his name has been associated with other forms of legislation, it will always be as the author of the Jones-White shipping act that he will be remembered.").

[94] "Senator Jones Dies; Long Leading Dry," New York Times, November 20, 1932, 28; "Jones, Five and Ten Liquor Enforcement Act Sponsor, is Dead," Dallas Morning News, November 20, 1932, 1; "Wesley L. Jones, Author of Rigid Liquor Law, Dies," Times-Picayune, November 20, 1932, 13.

[95] Memorial Services Held in the House of Representatives of the United States, Together with Remarks Presented in Eulogy of Wesley L. Jones, 35.

Secretary of the Treasury William Gibbs McAdoo, circa 1913, Harris & Ewing photographer, Library of Congress

Chapter 18 – 1916 Shipping Act

The onset of World War I in August 1914 paralyzed the world shipping markets. The freight market froze because currency became unavailable, German cruisers caused havoc, war risk insurance became unavailable, and many shippers held their orders to determine whether the war would be short (a common expectation) or long.[1] It was estimated that half the available ocean tonnage had been taken off the market virtually overnight.[2]

U.S. exports, particularly in staples such as wheat and cotton, stopped moving at a time when there were bumper harvests.[3] Railroads no longer moved commodities to ports because there was no place to put them.[4] The Treasury Department reported to Congress that "at a time when we have the most to sell and customers abroad are eager to buy, the fact that our ocean carrying facilities are in the hands of others subject to war risks and controlled by interests not our own stares us in the face."[5]

The lack of currency was associated with a run on the banks and a suspension of stock exchange operations. This shortage was addressed by Treasury through the issuance of emergency currency.[6] Treasury determined that "the demoralization of foreign exchanges and credits and the disorganization of ocean transportation produced a situation of exceeding gravity."

It became apparent by the fall of 1914 that war might be long and the demand for staples increased substantially. Governments ameliorated the currency and war risk insurance issues. But freight rates increased because of the loss of German/Austrian vessels to the market (they had been interned in neutral ports).[7] Also, commercial shipping now faced the threat posed by German submarines.[8] Treasury reported to the U.S. Senate in December 1914 that rates for the carriage of wheat, flour, and cotton between New York and Liverpool increased from three to five times as much as pre-war rates.[9]

JOURNEY TO THE JONES ACT

The Wilson administration leapt into action to respond to the crisis. The most controversial proposal was to have the U.S. government own and operate vessels in what was known as the "Ship Purchase Bill," which was eventually merged into the Shipping Act, 1916. The originator of this idea and its principal promoter was William Gibbs McAdoo, Jr.[10]

WILLIAM GIBBS MCADOO, JR.

McAdoo, like Wesley Jones, grew up poor, after the Civil War, in rural America.[11] Born in October 1863 in Marietta, he lived in Milledgeville, Georgia, until he was thirteen years old.[12]

McAdoo was the fourth of seven children. His father was from Tennessee and served as a lieutenant with the Tennessee volunteers in the Mexican American War. That was after he taught school, attended East Tennessee University (later the University of Tennessee), and studied to be a lawyer. McAdoo's father also served in the Confederate Army as a captain.

Although McAdoo's father was educated and accomplished (twice elected attorney general for Knoxville, for example), the family was poor and lacked the means to move to Knoxville after the Civil War until the senior McAdoo accepted a professorship at the University of Tennessee in 1877.

In Knoxville, McAdoo attended the University of Tennessee for two years. At the age of eighteen, he left the university to serve as the deputy clerk for the federal court in Chattanooga. In November 1885 he married his first wife, Sarah Hazelhurst Fleming, with whom he would have six children who lived past infancy. The same year, he was admitted to the bar in Tennessee and practiced in Chattanooga.

Early on, McAdoo established railroad and political connections. He saw an opportunity when Knoxville decided to electrify its streetcar system and used his savings to acquire the Knoxville Street Railroad Company. There ensued a battle with a competing company, which included a street fight when

McAdoo attempted to complete a street line.[13] The legal battle ended in 1892 with the insolvency of his company.

McAdoo managed to get released from this debt and decided to move to New York. There, he established a law practice and became acquainted with people who had started a tunnel under the Hudson River to connect New Jersey and New York by rail.[14] Seizing the moment, he organized the Hudson and Manhattan Railroad Company, of which he was president. "H&M," as it was known, completed two mid-town tunnels in 1908, overcoming substantial engineering hurdles and opposition from commercial interests, like the railroads operating Hudson River ferries.

The original terminus in Manhattan at Nineteenth Street under Sixth Avenue opened on February 26, 1908 (that station has been closed since August 1, 1954).[15] H&M was extended all the way to Thirty-Third Street and Sixth Avenue, the Union Square area, in November 1910. In July 1909 two downtown tunnels were opened connecting Jersey City with lower Manhattan. H&M also constructed at the lower Manhattan station twin twenty-two story buildings, the largest office buildings in the world at the time.[16]

When H&M became insolvent in 1962 and was purchased by the New York Port Authority, the Manhattan buildings were demolished and became part of the World Trade Center site, completed in 1973. At that time, the name of the train service was also changed to the "Port Authority Trans-Hudson" or "PATH," as it is known to this day. "H&M" signs still exist in the New York area.

H&M was a huge success and McAdoo received enormous favorable publicity as a hands-on, can-do administrator who treated both the railroad's customers and his employees fairly.[17] His motto was "the public be pleased," to contrast with other railroads that had acted as if their motto was "the public be damned."[18] His approach was backed by his belief that corporations had a social responsibility. In a 1910 lecture delivered to the Harvard University Business School, he argued that "every corporation has a soul" and that soul "is the soul of its dominant individual—usually the president."[19]

McAdoo was, according to one of his leading biographers, "one of the ablest Americans of his time" and "the very epitome of ideological and political flexibility."[20] Walter Lippman, the famous journalist, wrote that McAdoo "does not hesitate or brood or procrastinate or reflect at length. Instinctively he prefers the bold and the decisive to the prudent and tepid course, for he is a statesman grafted upon a promoter."[21]

Newton Baker, who was secretary of war from 1916 to 1921 and served in the Wilson cabinet with McAdoo, wrote in 1923 that McAdoo "has an unconscious love of power" and he is "restless and unhappy, unless he is doing something that either makes a flash or a loud noise."[22] A jingle made the rounds in 1920 about McAdoo along these lines:

> The Who, pre-eminently Who
> Is William Gibbs, the McAdoo...
> He's always up and McAdooing;
> From to Sun to Star and Star to Sun
> His work is never McAdone.[23]

McAdoo wrote in his memoirs that he met Woodrow Wilson by accident in February 1909.[24] He went to Princeton to visit his son, and happened to meet Wilson, then-president of Princeton University, at the train station. McAdoo became an important supporter not only in Wilson's 1910 New Jersey governor's race but in early efforts to get Wilson nominated to run for president in 1912.

When Wilson did poorly in the presidential primaries, McAdoo stayed optimistic and urged him to persist.[25] After Wilson was nominated, he arranged to have McAdoo appointed vice chairman of the National Democratic Committee. Underwood, who was one of the candidates who had lost to Wilson at the convention, wrote to McAdoo just after the election that "there is no one man among us all that is entitled to more credit than you are for the proper handling of the political situation."[26]

Although McAdoo had joined Wilson's campaign stating that he was not doing it to obtain a future position, he changed his mind and accepted the offer to be the secretary of the Treasury.[27] He did so even though he was worried that he could not afford to live on a secretary's salary with a large family in Washington.

McAdoo proved an enlightened choice, serving from March 1913 to December 1918. He played a substantial role in the enactment of the Federal Reserve Act in 1913, probably the most important financial legislation between the Civil War and President Franklin Roosevelt's New Deal legislation. He was key in stabilizing the U.S. banking system and economy with currency infusions when World War I started.[28] Moreover, he spearheaded the "Liberty Loans" program to help finance U.S. participation in the war.[29] McAdoo was also central to the U.S. maritime response to the war, including enactment of the 1914 Ship Registry Act and the 1916 Shipping Act, discussed in the next sections.

Like Jones, McAdoo was both personally and politically dry.[30] And, like Jones, McAdoo stood on the political ground that once the country had adopted a dry policy with the enactment of the Eighteenth Amendment and the Volstead Act, it should be enforced or repealed.[31] Prohibition promised to be a divisive issue in the 1924 Democratic convention when McAdoo was a presidential candidate.[32]

On race matters, he supported Wilson's segregation of the federal government. McAdoo rationalized the policy by advancing the "separate but equal" argument.[33] When he was later director general of railroads, he ordered that there be no pay discrimination between black and white employees.[34] At the same time, the Ku Klux Klan supported McAdoo for president in 1924, after first opposing him.[35] Although McAdoo apparently did not solicit the support, he also did not repudiate it and opposed the Underwood anti-Ku Klux Klan plank at the convention.[36]

JOURNEY TO THE JONES ACT

McAdoo's first wife died in February 1912 after a prolonged fight with rheumatoid arthritis.[37] McAdoo became friendly with Wilson's youngest daughter, Eleanor, and they were married in the White House in May 1914.[38] McAdoo was fifty-one and Eleanor was twenty-five. McAdoo offered to resign from his position to avoid charges of nepotism, but Wilson asked McAdoo to stay on.[39] The blurring of official and family roles was to be remarked in the press and among the other cabinet members during the rest of McAdoo's tenure.[40]

McAdoo's overwhelming focus on this public life appears to have taken a toll on his family. His six children from the first marriage and the two he had with Eleanor had numerous marriages, divorces, substance abuse episodes, failed businesses, and arrests.[41] His marriage to Eleanor ended in divorce.[42]

After he resigned as Treasury secretary in December 1918, McAdoo co-founded a law firm in New York—McAdoo, Cotton & Franklin. McAdoo had told Wilson that he was resigning to replenish his financial resources.[43] To the press, McAdoo cited poor health after six years of work in Washington.[44]

McAdoo in fact had an expensive lifestyle. By 1919 he had four homes, a ranch in Arizona, an airplane with a pilot, several automobiles, and a chauffeur. He was also a member of several private clubs.[45] McAdoo had few passions other than work, but he loved fast cars and more than once survived life-threatening accidents.[46]

When he founded the law firm in New York, McAdoo had not practiced law in twenty years and there were mumblings about him trading on his administration access rather than his talent as an attorney. One of his first clients was the Virginia Shipbuilding Corporation, which was under investigation by the U.S. Shipping Board for fraud centering on Charles W. Morse (discussed in a later chapter). Another client was Edward L. Doheny, the recipient of sweetheart oil leases in the Harding administration summarized as the "Teapot Dome Scandal."[47] McAdoo was hired by Doheny to help with Mexican government expropriation of oil interests and there was no connection to the domestic scandal, but political damage was done.[48] McAdoo later resigned from the New York firm in 1922 to move to California.[49]

The *Nation* wrote in February 1924 that "some men leave office to practice law. Mr. McAdoo left to practice son-in-law."[50] And—"it is impossible to believe that he could actually separate William G. McAdoo, the lawyer, from William G. McAdoo, the son-in-law, or William G. McAdoo, ex-cabinet member."

McAdoo ran for president in both 1920 and 1924. In each case he had the most delegates at the beginning of the nominating convention but was not nominated.[51] It took 103 ballots at the heavily contested 1924 Convention at Madison Square Garden for him to lose the nomination.[52] He was elected U.S. senator from California in 1932 in the same year Jones lost and served a single term. McAdoo helped deliver the California delegation to Franklin Roosevelt at the 1932 nominating convention, and thereafter supported FDR for re-election in 1936 and 1940.[53]

After losing the California Democratic party nomination in 1938, McAdoo was appointed by the U.S. Maritime Commission (a successor to the U.S. Shipping Board) to be the chairman of the Board of American President Lines.[54] That company became insolvent as the Dollar Steamship Company or "Dollar Lines," and the commission had assumed control over it in August 1938.[55] The commission then renamed the company, which had been naming its passenger vessels after American presidents, as "American President Lines." McAdoo turned the company around heading into World War II serving until 1940.

After his divorce from Eleanor Wilson was final, McAdoo married Doris Isabel Cross, a twenty-six-year-old nurse who had served in the McAdoo household in Santa Barbara.[56] On February 1, 1941, while visiting Washington, DC to attend FDR's January 20 inauguration, he died of a heart attack, at the age of seventy-seven. The *New York Times* wrote that he had had "a truly great career," that he was the "strong man of the

JOURNEY TO THE JONES ACT

Wilson cabinet," and that "Congress gave him extraordinary powers, yet he used them wisely."[57]

Before McAdoo drifted briefly into the public's consciousness in 2017 when another presidential son-in-law worked in the White House, his role was recognized by Hollywood.[58] Namely, McAdoo achieved fame in the 1944 feature film *Wilson*, produced by Darryl F. Zanuck. It won five Academy awards (although not for best picture, best director, or best actor).[59] McAdoo was played by Vincent Price.

SHIP REGISTRY ACT AND WAR RISK INSURANCE

By late July 1914, Representative Alexander, chairman of the Merchant Marine Committee, had already received telegrams from U.S. exporters requesting that the U.S. registry be opened freely to foreign-built vessels.[60] The reason was to make vessels available to shippers under a neutral (U.S.) flag given the impeding European war. As previously alluded to, the free ship provision in the Panama Canal Act had failed to attract a single foreign-built vessel to the U.S. registry.[61]

On July 31 President Wilson met with Representative Underwood and Senator John W. Kern (D-IN), the House and Senate majority leaders, and requested that they see what could be done to encourage vessels to reflag as American vessels.[62] On the same day, after receiving Chamberlain's drafting assistance, Alexander introduced legislation to eliminate the Panama Canal Act age restriction and to authorize the president to waive manning and other requirements for reflagged vessels.[63]

On Saturday, August 1, Chairman Alexander called a Merchant Marine committee meeting, but there was no quorum.[64] In Alexander's view, the international trade situation was an emergency because U.S. commerce "was threatened with paralysis." On Monday August 3, President Wilson held a press conference during which he said that getting U.S. commodities to Europe was a top administration priority.[65]

Objections were raised on August 3 that the vessel transfers would be ineffective in providing the transferred vessels neutrality protection. Representative Sereno Payne, for example, argued that permitting vessels to reflag and retain their foreign crews was "almost a subterfuge" and that if any of the reflagged vessels were seized, the United States might be drawn into the war.[66] Representative Albert Johnson (R-WA) put in the record an article from the *Baltimore Sun* with the sub-headings "Changing Flags Useless" and "Under American Registry the Vessels May Still Be Liable to Capture."[67]

Experts opined that the Declaration Concerning Laws on Naval War signed in London in 1909 effectively prevented the transfer of ownership of a vessel to a neutral flag if it occurred just before or after a war's outset.[68] The U.S. position was that bona fide transfers without any seller reservations should be honored. The mere fact that the motivation was to avoid capture and seizure should not be held against the purchaser.[69] The British/French view was that a transfer for the purpose of avoiding capture and seizure was inherently suspect.

Concerns were expressed in particular about vessels being registered in the United States by U.S. corporations owned by non-U.S. citizens.[70] Representative Charles F. Curry (R-CA) stated that reflagged vessels "will embroil us with European belligerents" and quoted a King Solomon proverb to the effect that "'he that passeth by, and meddleth with strife belonging not to him, is like one that taketh a dog by the ears.'"[71]

Underwood argued that other countries would have no basis for complaint since they generally permitted free vessel transfers. In his view, bona fide transfers should be respected under international law; furthermore, he noted that although several countries had signed the London Declaration, none had ratified it. To further advance the argument, Underwood put in the record a Chamberlain memorandum verifying that it was normal international practice for each country to have the discretion to determine its own vessel registry qualifications.[72] The president's request and Underwood's explanation were sufficient, and the bill passed the House on August 3 under suspension of the rules.[73]

The process in the Senate delayed the legislation. The Interoceanic Canals Committee reported a relatively straightforward modification of the House-passed bill on the same day. But then things got bogged down.[74] At one point the proceedings were delayed because Mrs. Ellen Louise Axson Wilson, the president's wife, died on August 6.[75]

The most controversial amendments offered would have permitted foreign-built vessels into the coastwise trade and would have required corporations to be substantially U.S. citizen-owned. Senator Jones offered a coastwise amendment on August 5 that would have given the president the emergency authority to authorize foreign-built vessels to participate in the trade between the West and East Coasts.[76] Jones was concerned that Washington State interests would be disadvantaged as vessels serving that trade left for the North Atlantic.

Senator Jacob Gallinger, who managed the legislation in the Senate, was opposed.[77] At that time and until August 1918, Gallinger was the chairman of the Senate Republican Conference, the functional equivalent of the "Minority Leader."[78] Gallinger strongly supported the ship registry bill but resisted inclusion of the coastwise trade, arguing that the Jones amendment would defeat the purpose of the legislation: to increase the size of the U.S.-flag fleet in the foreign trade. He believed it likely that reflagged vessels would gravitate to the coastwise trade if that was permitted.[79]

Several senators wanted to go further and make broader changes to the coastwise laws. Senator Borah, for example, argued that the coastwise trade was a "monopoly" and said, "What reason can be assigned for leaving this monopoly to stand untouched?"[80]

The Jones amendment was expanded to cover all the U.S. coastwise trade in addition to trade between the East and West Coasts by Senators John Sharp Williams and McCumber. They wanted to permit foreign-built vessels to participate in trade with the other coasts.[81]

Senator Willard Saulsbury Jr. (D-DE) offered an amendment to require that U.S. corporations owning U.S. registered vessels be wholly owned by U.S. citizens to prevent "disagreeable complications" with belligerent countries.[82] Senator James A. O'Gorman (D-NY) argued that the ownership amendment would prevent vessels from reflagging by disrupting existing ownership arrangements.[83] Saulsbury accepted a revision to make the ownership requirement two-thirds rather than wholly owned, but the amendment was handily defeated anyway.[84] The cause was taken up by Senator Albert R. Cummins (R-IA) who offered an amendment to require only majority U.S. citizen ownership. That amendment passed by one vote.[85]

Senator Newlands re-introduced his concept of having the U.S. Navy build auxiliary vessels that could also be used commercially.[86] His amendment, which Jones supported, failed.[87] The bill as modified by the coastwise and majority corporation ownership amendments passed the Senate by consent on August 11, 1914.[88]

A conference report included a provision that would have permitted foreign-built vessels to register in the United States for two years following enactment with full coastwise trading privileges.[89] No citizen ownership provision was included. Alexander, Underwood, and Borah—all free ship advocates—were among the seven conferees. The leading Senate negotiator was Senator O'Gorman. O'Gorman explained that the Cummins corporate ownership provision was stricken because it impaired "the beneficent results expected of the legislation."[90] O'Gorman defended the coastwise provision, arguing that "92 per cent of all the vessels in the American coastwise trade are either owned or under the control of the railroads of the country or of shipping combinations which are operated in disregard of the Sherman antitrust law."[91]

Gallinger countered that the emergency did not justify altering long-standing coastwise laws, as there was ample capacity in the coastwise trade available for charter.[92] He also painted a dire picture of how the provision would ruin U.S. shipyards and U.S. domestic ship owners.

Numerous telegrams were put in the record opposing foreign-built vessels being granted coastwise trading privileges. Among them was an August 13 telegram from William Matson of the Matson Navigation Company, stating that "it would be a positive crime to let foreign owners step in on an equal basis and earn the fruits of our labors."[93]

Jones produced telegrams from lumber interests complaining about the lack of vessels and argued that the repeal of the Panama Canal tolls exemption for U.S.-flag vessels had been the death knell of the U.S. intercoastal fleet.[94] Jones added that he thought Gallinger had exaggerated the potential harm from opening the coastwise trade to foreign-built vessels.

The sentiment of the Senate came to rest on simplifying the situation. The conference report with the coastwise trade permission was rejected on August 17.[95] The simple original House bill eliminating the five-year age restriction and granting the president authority to waive manning and other requirements was immediately adopted.[96]

When President Wilson signed the legislation on August 18, 1914, the *New York Times* likened the law to the one President Ulysses Grant proposed in 1870 to deal with the Franco-Prussian War.[97] Jones eventually got what he wanted although he had to wait until October 1917. Then, a law was enacted permitting re-registered vessels to engage in the coastwise trade for the duration of the war pursuant to Shipping Board permissions (excepting to and from Alaska).[98]

The Senate passed another bill introduced by Senator John W. Weeks (R-MA) on August 3 that played a part in the later consideration of the Ship Purchase Bill.[99] The "Weeks Bill" would have authorized the Navy to utilize its auxiliary vessels to establish mail lines so long as that could be done "without impairment to the paramount duties of the Navy."[100]

Recognizing that more needed to be done, McAdoo called a conference of business leaders which met on August 14 to discuss the shipping situation.[101] A leading participant was the National Foreign Trade Council organized in May 1914 by James A. Farrell, the president of the United States Steel Corporation.[102] A special council meeting on August 10 urged enactment of a program that included the ship registry bill and proposed U.S. Government-provided war risk insurance.[103]

The McAdoo conference adopted the council's recommendations and Congress swiftly passed without controversy the "War Risk Insurance Act" signed into law on September 2, 1914.[104] That Act authorized the creation of a Bureau of War Risk Insurance to issue policies and pay claims.[105] One of the first claims paid was for the sinking of the *William P. Frye*.[106]

The registration of foreign-built vessels in the United States began almost immediately after the Ship Registry Act was signed.[107] President Wilson issued a September 4 executive order permitting re-registered vessels to retain their foreign citizen officers for seven years, but U.S. citizens would have to fill open positions commencing two years after U.S. registration.[108]

Britain's Board of Trade had the legal right to refuse the transfer of vessels to U.S. flag but did not do so for the hundred or so vessels that came from Britain.[109] Chamberlain attributed this to the fact that most of the vessels were beneficially owned by Americans prior to the war.

For vessels coming from other registries, British officials made it clear they would abide by the London Declaration in the main and therefore the burden of proof that a sale was bona fide rested with the vessel purchaser.[110] Former German vessels were singled out by the British and French as being inherently suspect and so would be subject to seizure and adjudication in prize courts.[111]

Almost 150 vessels reflagged under the Ship Registry Act by June 30, 1915, comprising about 525,000 tons, more than triple the size of the pre-war foreign trading U.S. fleet. However, almost sixty of those vessels were owned by three companies: the Standard Oil Co., the United Fruit Co., and the United States Steel Products Co.[112] Most of the vessels were engaged in the Central American and South American trades—not in the North Atlantic.

About a dozen seizures by the belligerents of the U.S. reflagged vessels did in fact occur, as had been predicted by the reflagging naysayers. But most vessels were released because, in those cases, the vessels were beneficially owned by Americans prior to the war.[113]

The most prominent case of reflagging trouble was that of the *Dacia*, a former Hamburg-American Line vessel that had been purchased by Edward N. Breitung of Michigan in December 1914.[114] The avowed purpose was to ship cotton to Bremen, Germany.[115] Britain made it known immediately that it would not consider the *Dacia* a neutral vessel and she would be seized.[116] Britain considered that Breitung, a U.S. citizen but an ethnic German, was acting for Germany.[117]

The U.S. government argued that the sale was bona fide. It further argued that the vessel would submit to inspection to ensure that it was not carrying contraband (such as ammunition) and that the cotton shipper was an innocent party and should not be harmed in the process.[118] The United States requested that the British pass on this one shipment, while reserving rights.[119] The British countered that they would compensate the cotton cargo owner but that the vessel would be seized and the vessel transfer adjudicated.[120]

The vessel quickly became a cause célèbre in both British and American newspapers.[121] Behind the scenes, Britain informed the U.S. government that buying German vessels and putting them back into the pre-war trades would be viewed as a hostile act.[122] The *New York Times* editorialized that the *Dacia* was being used to manufacture "'indignity to the American flag'" to draw the U.S. into war.[123] The Treasury Department refused to provide war risk insurance for the vessel but did issue it for the cotton cargo.[124]

Both governments sought to defuse the situation and the episode ended anticlimactically when a French cruiser captured the *Dacia* on February 27, 1915. The British government may have quietly asked the French to make the capture to avoid a direct confrontation with the United States.[125] The U.S. government communicated to France that it would reserve its position but take no action until the French Prize Council rendered its decision regarding the vessel's neutrality.[126] The *Dacia* was ultimately forfeited and sold by the French Prize Council, only to be sunk by a U-boat in November 1915 under French flag.[127] The U.S. government distanced itself from the matter, insisting that Breitung exhaust local remedies first, which did not occur until November 30, 1916.[128]

President Wilson did not give up easily on the U.S. interpretation of neutral vessel transfers, despite efforts by his diplomats to avoid another collision with Britain.[129] His reasoning, promoted by McAdoo, was that the United States had to be free to acquire the interned German vessels since that was probably the only way to expand the fleet quickly.

SHIP PURCHASE BILL

McAdoo came away from the August 14 business conference with the view that more had to be done to alleviate ocean shipping problems. Lying in bed on the morning of August 16, McAdoo wrote the outline of a government ship purchase plan.[130] He proposed U.S. government ownership of the stock of a private corporation, which would in turn own and operate commercial vessels.[131] Wilson agreed to the plan even though both he and McAdoo knew it would be strongly opposed.[132] It is likely, however, that neither anticipated the political storm that the plan would precipitate or the ensuing two-year battle.

In his memoirs, McAdoo recalled the battle as a "fantastic nightmare of partisanship and politics."[133] The battle occurred in two distinct phases: (1) from late 1914 to the end of the Sixty-Third Congress on March 3, 1915 when the administration tried but failed to strong-arm the legislation's approval; and (2) from that failure to the eventual success in September 1916 as a result of compromise and the growing need for war preparedness.

Strong-Arm Phase.[134] Chairman Alexander introduced the first legislation on August 24 and immediately held hearings in the Merchant Marine Committee with McAdoo as the primary witness.[135] McAdoo made the case that the bill was responding to an emergency and was not a permanent measure (which later became a bone of contention), that it was necessary because private capital was unwilling or unable to fill the shipping capacity void, that the government had been successful with the steamships it owned via the Panama Canal Railroad Co., and that the primary focus was expanding the South American trade.

McAdoo evidenced no neutrality concerns about buying German vessels and declared that "there is no more punctilious citizen of the United States with respect to the neutrality of this country than the President of the United States." After Alexander pointed out that vessel owners had already increased their prices in anticipation of selling to the U.S. government, McAdoo responded that "no junk will be bought and no excessive prices will be paid." McAdoo may have radiated neutrality confidence, but both the British and the French governments were privately warning Wilson not to purchase the German interned vessels.[136]

The Merchant Marine Committee recommended the bill on September 8.[137] That turned out to be the highwater mark before Congress left for the November elections. The committee majority report emphasized opening trade to South America and the ability of the U.S. government to use the vessels it owned to control shipping freight rates.

In contrast, the minority led by Representative Greene argued that the legislation was too important to move hastily. They believed that the U.S. government should not compete with commercial lines, that there would not be any increase in tonnage, that the government would lose money, and that neutrality issues were being underestimated.[138] Ominously for the proposal, two Democrats on the committee joined the Republican minority report.

Opposition had surfaced even before the legislation was introduced.[139] By late August, it was reported that Washington, DC, "was alive with hostile lobbyists."[140] Within a week of the introduction of the bill, "opposition of the bitterest character developed" wherein a "swarm of lobbyists, representing shipping concerns, descended on both houses of Congress."[141]

On December 8, at the beginning of the third session of Congress, President Wilson said in his Annual Message to Congress that the "government must open these gates of trade and open them wide; open them before it is altogether profitable to open them or altogether reasonable to ask private capital to open them at a venture."[142] Moreover, "when the carriage has become sufficiently profitable to attract and engage private capital and engage it in abundance, the Government ought to withdraw." In the meantime, freight rates began to climb precipitously.[143]

The Democratic leadership called out the legislation from the Senate Commerce Committee, effectively bypassing Chairman James P. Clarke (D-AR). The supportive report dated December 16, 1914, was authored by Senator Duncan Fletcher, and parroted Alexander's report.[144] Five Republicans, led by Senator Theodore E. Burton (R-OH), dissented. They argued that higher freight rates were due to factors other than a lack of vessels, such as port congestion, which would not be remedied by the administration's bill. The minority also noted that the legislation was promoted as an emergency measure but had no express sunset date.

The fight to come became apparent on January 4, 1915, when the Senate bill was offered for discussion and Senator Lodge forced a vote just to take the bill up for consideration. Senator Gallinger complained about undue haste. Senator Jones complained that the Democrats were loudly proclaiming that they had the votes and would ram the bill through which inflamed partisanship.[145]

JOURNEY TO THE JONES ACT

Senator Elihu Root made the opposition argument at the outset of the bill's consideration.[146] Root was the former secretary of state under Roosevelt and secretary of war under McKinley (after the Spanish-American War), a 1912 Nobel Peace Prize winner and a pre-war expert on neutrality when he served as the President of the American Society of International Law. Root argued that the legislation would commit the federal government to an unbounded expense, that it would threaten America's neutrality and, most of all, it would put the U.S. government in the position of displacing private enterprise.

The Republican position was supported by many private business groups, including the National Foreign Trade Council. In its reports, the council argued that government ownership would deter private enterprise.[147] The council also argued that merchant marine policy should be de-politicized and given to a permanent shipping board to recommend law changes to Congress.[148]

Fletcher responded that the proposed government vessel ownership "is not a permanent business undertaking." Vessels owned by the government-owned corporation would be in a better position than private companies to avoid war risks because the government could guarantee strict compliance with neutrality obligations.[149] Fletcher also noted that the shipping crisis was an emergency and there were no alternatives to government ownership and operation because free ships, discriminating duties, and bounties were either already employed (Ship Registry Act), impractical because of commercial treaties (discriminating duties), or had been refused by the American people (subsidies/bounties).

The president appeared to have the votes at the beginning of 1915.[150] Democrats held fifty-three of the ninety-six Senate seats and a few Republicans appeared sympathetic. However, partisanship was going to play a big role in the debate.

On January 21, 1915, Senator Gallinger led the Republican senators in caucus. They determined to fight the bill with everything at their command, including an extended filibuster.[151]

A January 23 caucus of Senate Democrats counter-agreed to press the Ship Purchase Bill, to hold it "continuously before the Senate, and to refuse to let it give way even to the appropriation bills" to put pressure on the Republicans.[152] The die were cast for a head-on collision between the parties.

Chairman Alexander and President Wilson inflamed the situation with January 5 and 8 speeches. Alexander appeared before the Boston Chamber of Commerce where he lambasted vessel owners and newspapers. He accused them of simultaneously complaining about extraordinarily high freight rates because there were no available vessels while expressing opinions that no government intervention was necessary.[153]

Meanwhile, President Wilson delivered a Jackson Day address in Indianapolis in which he called out "extortionate charges for ocean carriage" and criticized Republicans for preventing an effective response to help American exporters.[154] He also said that they were using the rules of the Senate "to defy the nation."

A Republican filibuster commenced on Friday January 29 to prevent a vote on the Ship Purchase Bill; it lasted for three days over the weekend. The Senate was in continuous session for thirty-six hours until a truce was called.[155]

When the Senate resumed on Monday morning, Senator James Clarke dropped a bomb on the proceedings. In a surprise to most of the Democrats, he moved to recommit the legislation to committee.[156] Clarke had the support of six other Democrats—Senators John H. Bankhead (D-AL), Johnson N. Camden (D-KY), Thomas W. Hardwick (D-GA), Gilbert M. Hitchcock (D-NE), O'Gorman and James K. Vardaman (D-MS). In response, Senator William J. Stone (D-MO), who was one of the floor managers for the Democrats and chairman of the Foreign Relations Committee, laid into the "seven conspirators" two days later for "holding secret conclaves, whispering and conspiring together" and springing "a complete and cruel surprise on their colleagues on this side of the Chamber."[157]

JOURNEY TO THE JONES ACT

Stone pointed out that the Democratic caucus had made the Ship Purchase Bill a party line vote and the seven were violating caucus rules. At one point, Stone said, "I prefer the leadership of Woodrow Wilson to that of Elihu Root, Henry Cabot Lodge, Theodore Burton, William Edgar Borah, Jacob H. Gallinger, or that of any recreant alleged Democrat who goes about with a murderous dagger in his sleeve. [Laughter in the galleries.]." The situation remained bitter for the remainder of the session with both Stone and the "bolters," as they were called, trading barbs about loyalty and patriotism.[158]

The concept of "pairing" came into focus during this period of hyper-partisanship. Under that practice, senators with opposite viewpoints whose votes would cancel each other out agreed to "pair." Doing so allowed them to attend to business away from the Senate floor, which accounted for many non-votes. Pairs were broken for the filibuster as senators returned to Washington, DC.[159] The physical presence near the Senate floor was required at certain times during the debate, such as on February 8 and 9 when virtually every senator was answering quorum calls.

Senator Burton created a side show by offering a resolution to require an investigation into whether the administration had already pre-negotiated vessel purchases implying that money was going to be made by the administration's friends.[160] McAdoo wrote in his memoirs that this was "a striking example of a familiar, though contemptible, method that is frequently employed by crafty politicians to attack a beneficial measure through innuendo."[161] The Democrats amended the resolution to also investigate improper influence by the "ship trust lobby."[162] Both investigations were not completed until the fall of 1916 and were inconclusive.[163]

McAdoo tried to generate public support with speeches.[164] In them, McAdoo argued that Congress had willingly given private vessel owners the right to register foreign-built belligerent-flag vessels in the United States but now hesitated to grant the same right to the president. He railed against a proposal by vessel owners for the government to guarantee private corporation debt as a "dangerous experiment."[165]

Burton took the opposite position before the Chamber of Commerce, which voted overwhelmingly against the Ship Purchase Bill in a February 1915 referendum.[166] One of Burton's arguments, which was advanced throughout the deliberations, was that the administration was being unclear about when government ownership would end because it secretly wanted permanent ownership.[167] Senator Du Pont argued that the legislation was of "doubtful constitutionality" and "highly socialistic."[168]

The filibuster reappeared whenever there was a push by the Democrats to seek a vote on the administration's bill.[169] Senator Jones did his part by talking for almost fourteen hours straight on February 8-9.[170] Senator James A. Reed (D-MO) sarcastically characterized the predicament: "Senators have been arranged in relays, a part of them to retire to their downy couches of ease and to the embracing arms of sweet slumber, while one or two able-bodies and lung-experienced aerial athletes continue to pour forth a ceaseless flow of eloquence."[171]

Wilson's advisors attempted to convince him in mid-to-late January that government ownership had to have a sunset date to have a chance of being enacted. But the president would not budge, even though he had told Congress on January 8 that the government would eventually leave the market.[172]

There was a last gasp attempt at a potential compromise using the Weeks Bill, which had passed the Senate on August 3, 1914. With Wilson's tacit support, the House added a version of the Ship Purchase Bill to the Weeks legislation, introduced by Senator Thomas P. Gore (D-OK) (grandfather of Gore Vidal).[173]

The combined Weeks-Gore bill addressed the neutrality issue with a proviso that "during the continuance of the present European war no purchases shall be made in a way which will disturb the conditions of neutrality." The House also added a sunset provision to the legislation and handily passed the combined bills on February 16 although 19 Democrats defected.[174]

Representative Champ Clark (D-MO), the speaker of the House, had advised the president on February 11, 1915, that the only way to get the bill "through this Congress is for you & your Senatorial supporters to accept the amendment now proposed in the Senate which will bring in line the seven opposing Democrats."[175] Clark was presumably referring to the combined Weeks-Gore bill.

On February 18, Senate Democrats surrendered on their legislative agenda hostage strategy when they agreed to ask the House for a conference on the House-passed Weeks-Gore Bill and to permit other bills to be considered.[176] No conference agreement was reached prior to the end of the Sixty-Third Congress in March 1915.[177]

Views since then differ on President Wilson's strategy. Either he was unwilling to compromise with the "bolters" because he wanted to purchase German vessels and have permanent government ownership or the "seven" reneged on an arrangement for temporary ownership and added other demands which Wilson found unacceptable.[178] Secretary of the Navy Josephus Daniels recorded in his cabinet diaries that Wilson would not budge from his position on the U.S. right to purchase German vessels.[179] Indeed, in a February 2 press conference, Wilson said as much.[180] And after the fact, McAdoo issued a statement attacking Lodge who he said knew that the U.S. government could not relent on its neutral rights to purchase belligerent vessels.[181]

War Preparedness and Compromise Phase. There was a debate in the Wilson administration as to how to proceed following the defeat in early 1915. The focus was on the original Weeks Bill since it had passed the Senate. McAdoo realized that the administration's ownership idea could be tied to national security and military preparedness.[182]

It also fit with the war's direction. Britain and France were increasingly tightening their shipping restrictions on neutral nations and Germany was expanding the war zone. Those actions further hampered American trade and made it more difficult for the United States to avoid picking a side.

The most dramatic incident that affected merchant marine policy was the sinking of the *Lusitania* on May 7, 1915, near the coast of Ireland.[183] Among the 1,198 persons killed (there were about 1,900 on board including the crew of over 600) were 128 Americans. Alfred Gwynne Vanderbilt, Cornelius Vanderbilt's heir, was one of the Americans killed.[184]

The sinking began to turn public opinion in support of being prepared in the event the United States was drawn into the war. McAdoo and the administration noted the change in sentiment and sought to marshal it in favor of the Ship Purchase Bill.[185] McAdoo first laid the foundation by asking the Navy how many auxiliary vessels they would need in time of war.[186]

The Navy asserted that the auxiliaries it needed should come from a U.S. government-owned fleet rather than directly from the Navy.[187] The Navy's rationale for not requesting its own fleet of reserve auxiliaries was that it was far better for the U.S. government to build vessels to designs approved by the Navy which would be commercially active than for the Navy to own vessels kept idle.

The Navy also indicated that "experience has shown that if we rely upon buying or chartering naval auxiliaries after war has been declared, the Government does not secure suitable craft and those who man such auxiliaries lack the training needed for the best service of the Navy." The Navy added that the government had "paid extravagant prices" in the Spanish-American War for commercial vessels. It estimated that it needed four hundred merchant vessels, totaling about 1.2 million tons, to support the existing fleet of warships and that, at best, only 800,000 tons could come from the existing U.S.-flag commercial fleet.

JOURNEY TO THE JONES ACT

McAdoo also had to get the administration behind a modified Ship Purchase Bill.[188] To do so, he first convinced Wilson to again make it a priority. McAdoo also had to win over Secretary William Redfield who was skeptical because he thought it would once again split the Democratic party. McAdoo was persistent and Redfield came on board by October 1915.

In a further effort to drum up support for the bill, McAdoo went on a fall 1915 speaking tour to the West Coast.[189] McAdoo fully laid out his argument in Indianapolis in a speech entitled a "Naval Auxiliary Merchant Marine."[190] This speech is considered one of the most important speeches of the first term of the Wilson Administration.[191]

McAdoo made the case that waiting until a war starts is too late to buy auxiliary vessels, an argument solidly based on the Spanish-American War experience. Vessels might not be available at all or would be available at high prices and not be well suited to a war effort. He also made a populist anti-monopoly appeal, claiming that the shipping industry should come under U.S. government oversight because unregulated conferences and combinations were harming cargo shippers. And he pointed out that the Weeks Bill had passed the Senate and was supported by Republicans including Senator Gallinger. That bill had authorized Navy vessels to engage in commercial service, which arguably was more radical than general U.S. government ownership through a private corporation.

When the U.S. Chamber of Commerce held another referendum in June 1915, government ownership of vessels was again rejected.[192] But a government-owned corporation to guarantee private debt and assist private maritime companies was approved with a small majority. Large majorities were in favor of subsidizing private vessels to equalize costs, outlawing deferred rebates, and federal supervision of ocean rates.

President Wilson made the case one more time in his December 7, 1915, Annual Message to Congress.[193] Specifically, he declared that without such a fleet, "our independence is provincial, and is only on land and within our borders." He asserted, as McAdoo had done again and again, that the United States had to step in until private capital filled the need. "When the risk has passed and private capital begins to find its way in sufficient abundance into these new challenges," Wilson wrote, "the government may withdraw." He urged Congress to pass a Ship Purchase Bill which would be "similar to those made to the last Congress but modified in some essential particulars."

Chairman Alexander introduced the administration's new bill on January 31, 1916.[194] The proposed shipping board would no longer be governed solely by government officials. The board would have the authority to construct vessels in the United States or abroad and all such vessels would become "vessels of the United States" but without the privilege of operating in the U.S. coastwise trade, except to U.S. territories.

Chamberlain had complained after the start of the war that the United States should account for the possibility that vessels reflagged under the Ship Registry Act might leave the U.S. flag at any time because no authority existed to prevent such reregistration.[195] During 1915, most of the major ship registry countries in the world passed laws forbidding vessel transfers without government permission.[196] Chamberlain recommended that the United States do likewise, and general authority to deny vessel transfers was included in the proposed legislation.

The bill proposed to meet the needs of the commercial market and national defense somewhere in the middle. All vessels acquired would have to be "of a type, as far as the commercial requirements of the marine trade of the United States may permit suitable for use as naval auxiliaries and Army transports." For that purpose, the board would be given authority to issue $50 million in Panama Canal bonds. The board would also be given vague but expansive authority to regulate common carriers in U.S. commerce.

As in prior proposals, the bill authorized the board to form a corporation to construct, own, and operate vessels. Any vessels chartered by the corporation were required to be chartered to "U.S. citizens," which were not defined. The proposal did not suggest a remedy for the two primary criticisms of earlier legislation: the purchase of belligerent vessels by the U.S. government or a sunset provision.

Hearings were held in early 1915 in the House Merchant Marine Committee which produced an extensive record.[197] Rear Admiral William S. Benson, the first chief of naval operations, McAdoo, Redfield, and Secretary of Labor Wilson all testified.

One new development was having to consider potential foreign country prohibition on vessel transfers to the U.S. registry. This meant that the U.S. government would largely have to look for interned vessels, U.S.-owned vessels, or newly constructed vessels to acquire, which was noted by McAdoo in his testimony.[198] The other new development was the enactment of the Seamen's Act on March 4, 1915. Several witnesses, including Representative Humphrey, argued that the Seamen's Act was having the opposite effect intended by the Ship Purchase Bill since vessels were leaving the U.S.-flag blaming that Act for their decision.[199]

Alexander introduced a revised bill based on the hearing record that would largely become the Shipping Act, 1916. The Merchant Marine Committee recommended it on May 9, 1916.[200] The revised bill expanded the shipping board to five president-appointed commissioners, added a preference for constructing vessels in the U.S ("other things being equal"), limited the foreign vessel transfer authority, and added a citizenship definition.[201]

Under that citizenship definition, contained in section 2 of the bill, a corporation could only be considered a U.S. citizen if it was organized in the United States, its president and "managing directors" were U.S. citizens, and a "controlling interest" was owned by U.S. citizens. That citizenship definition has been modified over time, but the phrase "section 2 citizen" remains in wide use.[202]

Most importantly, the revised bill added a sunset provision of five years, although it did not contain any limitation on the acquisition of belligerent-owned vessels. The committee report stated that it expected the board to be able to increase the U.S. merchant marine by about 25 to 35 percent.[203]

The committee noted that British and French war losses up to January 22, 1916, had been about 2.1 million tons, and that about 630,000 tons of German vessels were interned in U.S. ports.[204] The committee also observed that there had been an explosion in U.S. shipyard activity. On July 1, 1914, 1915 and 1916, respectively, there were 24, 62, and 176 vessels under construction on the U.S. seaboard (excluding the Great Lakes).[205]

Representative Greene again led the minority report which noted that the board was to be charged with studying shipbuilding and operating costs and U.S. navigation laws to recommend changes. The minority argued that this means "it is proposed to attempt a cure at once in a given way and to ascertain the nature of the disease at leisure." The minority agreed that common carriers should be subject to government oversight, but it was not "necessary, expedient, or wise at this time to invest the board with the extraordinary and unusual powers as proposed" and, given that "two-thirds of the world's commerce is carried by tramp steamers," "it is unfair to burden the minor fraction of our carrying trade... with restrictions."

The legislation received a boost in the summer of 1916 from aggressive British and French moves to restrict U.S exports to Europe, as well as their announcement at a "Paris Economic Conference" of the intent to form a trading block using shipping as a trade control measure.[206] Senator Fletcher quoted British sources expressing alarm that the United States would grow its fleet and take British markets while Britain was crippled with war debt.[207] The National Foreign Trade Council started to think of the carrier regulatory powers in terms of retaliation against potential post-war discrimination against U.S.-flag vessels.[208]

The only amendment to the legislation that went to a vote was offered by Representative Frederick W. Rowe (R-NY); it would have pared back board authority.[209] That amendment failed.[210] Speaking to the whole of the legislation, Speaker Clark said on the House floor that "a man that is opposed to rehabilitating the American merchant marine ought to be turned over to a board of alienists to see what is the matter with his head. [Laughter.]." The bill handily passed the House on May 20, 1916.[211]

Senator Clarke distanced himself from the process by putting a subcommittee of the Senate Commerce Committee chaired by Senator Furnifold McL. Simmons (D-NC), a notorious segregationist and white supremacist, in charge of hearings. Senator Jones was an active participant as the ranking Republican on the subcommittee.

During the subcommittee's deliberations, Jones highlighted the testimony of B.S. Grosscup, a Tacoma, Washington attorney.[212] Grosscup, representing American shipping companies serving Alaska, complained that Canadian lines were taking passengers from Seattle to Prince Rupert on foreign vessels and then boarding other foreign vessels for Alaskan ports. The practice had been sanctioned by the U.S. government because when Congress added the words "any part of the voyage" to the coastwise merchandise statute in 1898 to close a loophole, those same words were not added to the passenger statute.

The July 19 Commerce Committee Report under Simmons's name recommended that the bill "should speedily be enacted into law" with several changes to the House bill. There was no minority report. The committee narrowed the regulatory authority of the board and restricted the corporation's rights. It was allowed to operate vessels in situations only where the "board shall be unable, after bona fide effort" to contract for private operation. Most dramatically, the Senate version completed the compromise initiated by the Wilson administration in early 1915 by limiting the board's authority to buy vessels "under the registry or flag of a country which is then engaged in war."

The Senate commenced active consideration of the bill on August 9, 1916, for what turned out to be a completely anti-climactic event after the political fireworks of early 1915. Senator Simmons stated plainly at the outset "that we have met the objections of the group of Democrats on this side and what I consider the fundamental objections of the Senators on the other side."[213] Jones remained adamant that the bill was a partisan bill and that its passage was a "prearranged theatrical performance" to give the president a triumph going into the 1916 election.[214]

Senator Bankhead, one of the original seven bolters, played his part by announcing on August 12 that he would vote for the bill. Bankhead could not help but also say the bill would have already been law had the changes been made in March 1915 and "that our position in this matter has been absolutely and speedily vindicated."[215] Jones offered his discriminating duties and Grosscup-related amendments, which were both rejected.[216] The coastwise amendment would be brought up again in 1920 in a modified form.

On August 18, the Senate handily passed the bill.[217] Four of the original Senate "bolters" voted for the bill; one was no longer in Congress and two were absent. Senator James Vardaman's original opposition purportedly contributed to his election loss in 1918 in Mississippi.[218] Borah, Gallinger, and Jones all voted against the bill; Lodge did not vote. The House concurred on August 30, and President Wilson signed the bill into law on September 7, 1916.[219]

McAdoo was disappointed. He was quoted in July 1916 saying that "of all the crass follies that was ever perpetrated on a nation the worst was blocking of our efforts."[220] To Wilson he wrote privately that the legislation had been "tremendously emasculated" by "shipping interests."[221] In his memoirs, he wrote that "the opportunity to buy merchant ships had gone" because the Germans were sinking vessels so fast that "every ship that remained afloat was held as one holds a jewel."[222] McAdoo also wrote that the subsequent huge war shipbuilding program cost was "the staggering price for the filibuster of the shipping bill in 1915 and the selfish obstruction which delayed its passage."[223] In public, McAdoo was upbeat and said that the

Shipping Act "will vindicate itself as thoroughly... as the Federal Reserve Act."[224]

The 1916 Shipping Act, despite the limitations decried by McAdoo, marked a substantial change in the relationship between the U.S. government and the U.S. merchant marine. It demarcated the end of a period of intervention limited to indirect support and the beginning of an era of direct intervention.

---

[1] J. Russell Smith, Influence of the Great War upon Shipping (New York: Oxford University Press, 1919), 26–29.
[2] U.S. Congress, Senate, Increased Ocean Transportation Rates, 63rd Cong., 3rd sess., 1914, S. Doc. 63-673, 4.
[3] Alexander D. Noyes, War Period in American Finance 1908-1925 (New York: G. P. Putnam's Sons, 1926), 64–65.
[4] Annual Report of the Secretary of the Treasury on the State of the Finances for the Fiscal Year Ended June 30, 1914 (Washington, DC: Government Printing Office, 1915), 4.
[5] Increased Ocean Transportation Rates, S. Doc. 63-673, part 1, 4.
[6] Annual Report of the Secretary of the Treasury on the State of the Finances for the Fiscal Year Ended June 30, 1914, 1–4, 11–18.
[7] First Annual Report of the Shipping Board, 19.
[8] Smith, Influence of the Great War Upon Shipping, 33–35.
[9] Increased Ocean Transportation Rates, S. Doc. 63-673, part 2, 15.
[10] "Eleanor Wilson Weds W. G. M'Adoo," New York Times, May 8, 1914, 1.
[11] Douglas B. Craig, Progressives at War: William G. McAdoo and Newton D. Baker, 1863–1941, Kindle ed. (Baltimore: Johns Hopkins Press, 2013); Philip M. Chase, William Gibbs McAdoo: The Last Progressive (1863–1914), PhD diss., University of Southern California (2008); John Broesamle, William Gibbs McAdoo, A Passion for Change: 1863-1917 (Port Washington, NY: Kennikat Press, 1973); William G. McAdoo, Crowded Years (Boston: Houghton-Mifflin, 1931); Mary Synon, McAdoo: The Man and His Times, a Panorama in Democracy (Indianapolis, IN: Bobbs-Merrill, 1924); Burton J. Hendrick, "McAdoo and the Subway," McClure's Magazine 36, no. 5 (March 1911): 485–500.
[12] James C. Bonner, "Sherman at Milledgeville in 1864," Journal of Southern History 22, no. 3 (August 1956): 273–91.
[13] "McAdoo Once Driven from Knoxville with Fire Hose," Knoxville-News-Sentinel, February 1, 1941, 1.
[14] Brian J. Cudahy, Rails under the Mighty Hudson (New York: Fordham University Press, 2002).

[15] "Trolley Tunnel Open to Jersey," New York Times, February 26, 1908, 1; Louis E. Van Norman, "The Achievement of the Hudson Tunnels," American Review of Reviews 37, no. 4 (April 1908): 425–32; George Chiasson, "Rails under the Hudson Revisited–The Hudson and Manhattan," Electric Railroaders' Association, Inc., Bulletin 58, no. 9 (July 2015): 2–3.

[16] "Hudson Tube Terminal Plans Announced—Largest Office Building in the World at the Manhattan End," New York Times, December 23, 1906, 27; Darius Sollohub, "The Twins before the Twin Towers: the Hudson Terminals and Their Bifurcated Form," 93rd ACSA Annual Meeting Proceedings (2005): 342—57; Bernard D'Orazio, "In 1874, a Daring Downtown Plan–Build a Train Tunnel under the Hudson," Tribeca Trib, April 23, 2018.

[17] For example, "Things in Store for Mr. M'Adoo," New York Times, February 27, 1908, 6 ("He is admired and praised as a doer and an achiever."); Hendrick, "McAdoo and the Subway," 485–500.

[18] Broesamle, William Gibbs McAdoo, 27.

[19] William G. McAdoo, "The Relations between Public Service Corporations and the Public," lecture delivered before the Graduate School of Business Administration of Harvard University (April 6, 1910) (New York: Alexander Hamilton Institute, 1910), 7.

[20] Broesamle, William Gibbs McAdoo, 32–33.

[21] Walter Lippman, Men of Destiny (New York: Macmillan, 1927), 116.

[22] "Letter from N. Baker to W. Lippman dated Oct. 25, 1923," quoted in Craig, Progressives at War, 276.

[23] "The New Road," Time Magazine (January 7, 1924), 1.

[24] McAdoo, Crowded Years, 109.

[25] Broesamle, Williams Gibbs McAdoo, 52–55.

[26] Broesamle, Williams Gibbs McAdoo, 74.

[27] Chase, William Gibbs McAdoo, 65.

[28] William L. Silber, When Washington Shut Down Wall Street (Princeton, NJ: Princeton University Press, 2007).

[29] "William G. M'Adoo Dies in the Capital of a Heart Attack," New York Times, February 2, 1941, 1.

[30] Craig, Progressives at War, 267.

[31] For example, "Prohibition Nullification and Lawlessness," Address of William Gibbs McAdoo on Nullification and Lawlessness Delivered at the Mid-Winter Meeting of the Ohio State Bar Association, Toledo, Ohio, January 28, 1927, https://books.google.com/books/about/Prohibition_Nullification_and_Lawlessnes.html?id=iHfmAAAAMAAJ.

[32] "M'Adoo Defies "'Enemies'–He Says Bootleggers, Big Business and Corrupt Press Fight Him," New York Times, June 30, 1924, 1.

[33] Broesamle, Williams Gibbs McAdoo, 158–65.

[34] Chase, William Gibbs McAdoo, 39, 144.

[35] Chase, William Gibbs McAdoo, 231–34.
[36] For example, "M'Adoo to Fight Anti-Klan Plank," New York Times, June 20, 1924, 2.; Chase, William Gibbs McAdoo, 231—34; "Battle Lines Are Formed–Hostile Forces Are Drawn Up for Fight on Repudiating the Klan," New York Times, June 23, 1924, 1.
[37] Chase, William Gibbs McAdoo, 149, 401.
[38] "Eleanor Wilson Weds W. G. M'Adoo," New York Times, May 8, 1914, 1.
[39] Craig, Progressives at War, 104.
[40] Craig, Progressives at War, 104.
[41] Chase, William Gibbs McAdoo, 149–50, 154–71, 354–55, 401–02; Craig, Progressives at War, chap. 13.
[42] "Eleanor Wilson Weds W. G. M'Adoo," New York Times, May 8, 1914, 1; "Eleanor Wilson McAdoo Divorces Senator at Five-Minute Hearing on Incompatibility," New York Times, July 18, 1934, 1.
[43] "M'Adoo Out of Cabinet–Tells Wilson He Must Retire to Increase His Personal Income," New York Times, November 23, 1918, 1; McAdoo, Crowded Years, 498–99 ("I was spending more than I earned, several times more, and my financial means were dwindling").
[44] "McAdoo Quits Law Firm Here; Will Move to California and Practice in Los Angeles," New York Times, March 2, 1922, 1.
[45] Craig, Progressives at War, 252.
[46] Broesamle, William Gibbs McAdoo, 34–35; "W. G. M'Adoo Hurt in an Auto Smash," New York Times, (May 19, 1911), 1.
[47] David H. Stratton, "Splattered with Oil: William G. McAdoo and the 1924 Democratic Presidential Nomination," Southwestern Social Science Quarterly 44, no. 1 (June 1963): 62–75; "Employed M'Adoo for His Prestige," New York Times, March 3, 1924, 1.
[48] J. Leonard Bates, "The Teapot Dome Scandal and the Election of 1924," American Historical Review 60, no. 2 (January 1955): 303–22.
[49] "McAdoo Quits Law Firm Here; Will Move to California and Practice in Los Angeles," New York Times, March 2, 1922; 1.
[50] "Editorial," Nation, 118, no. 3060 (February 27, 1924), 217.
[51] For example, "McAdoo and Underwood Lead for Democratic Nomination," New York Times, June 3, 1923, 152; James C. Prude, "William Gibbs McAdoo and the Democratic National Convention of 1924," Journal of Southern History 38, no. 4 (November 1972): 621–28.
[52] Robert K. Murray, The 103rd Ballot: Democrats and the Disaster in Madison Square Garden (New York: HarperCollins, 1976).
[53] Joseph C. Vance, "The William Gibbs McAdoo Papers," Quarterly Journal of Current Acquisitions 15, no. 3 (May 1958): 168–76, 175–76; "William G. M'Adoo Dies in the Capital of a Heart Attack," New York Times, February 2, 1941, 1 ("He Swung 1932 Nomination to Roosevelt").

54 "McAdoo Elected to Ship Post," New York Times, November 11, 1938, 51; "President Lines to Get 6 New Ships——Assignment is Reported Here After Senator McAdoo Has Parlay with Officials," New York Times, November 13, 1938, 57.

55 United States Maritime Commission Report to Congress for the Period Ended October 25, 1938 (Washington, DC: Government Printing Office, 1939), 10—11.

56 "McAdoo, 71, Will Wed Nurse, 26; Marriage Today Will be His Third" and "Her Mother Tells of Plans," New York Times, September 14, 1935, 16.

57 "End of a Great Career," New York Times, February 3, 1941, 16; "Wm. G. McAdoo Dies Suddenly of Heart Attack in His Hotel," Washington Evening Star, February 1, 1941, 1.

58 Olivia B. Waxman, "Jared Kushner Wouldn't Be the First Powerful Son-in-Law in Presidential History," Time Digital Magazine (January 11, 2017). https://time.com/4630730/donald-trump-jared-kushner-william-gibbs-mcadoo.

59 Thomas J. Knock, "'History with Lightning': The Forgotten Film Wilson," American Quarterly 28, no. 5 (Winter 1976): 523–43.

60 51 Cong. Rec. 13175 (August 3, 1914).

61 Annual Report of the Commissioner of Navigation to the Secretary of the Commerce and Labor (1912), 15-17.

62 "May Give Our Flag to Foreign Ships," New York Times, August 1, 1914, 5; "Washington Alert to Aid Situation–Congress Extending Privileges of Banks–American Registry for Foreign Ships," New York Times, August 1, 1914, 5.

63 51 Cong. Rec. 13183 (August 3, 1914); "Bill to Save Our Sea Trade–Wilson and Underwood Frame It to Bring Vessels under Our Flag," New York Times, August 2, 1914, 3.

64 51 Cong. Rec. 13175—76 (August 3, 1914).

65 "Press Conference of Wilson (August 3, 1914)," Papers of Woodrow Wilson, vol. 30, 331.

66 51 Cong. Rec. 13181.

67 51 Cong. Rec. 13182; "Proposed Ship Bill is Held Inadequate," Sun (New York), August 3, 1914, 8.

68 "Ship Transfers May Not be Respected–British Rule Demands That They Must Take Place Sixty Days before War," Sun, (New York), August 5, 1914, 6; U.S. Congress, Senate, Declaration of International Naval Conference, 63rd Cong., 2nd sess., 1914, S. Doc. 63-563, "Declaration Concerning the Law of Naval War, London, 26 February 1909," Articles 55 and 56.

69 Declaration of International Naval Conference, S. Doc. 63-563, "Opinion of the Solicitor of State Department, 'The Transfer of Merchant Ships of a Belligerent to a Neutral after the Outbreak of War (Aug. 7, 1914),'" 83–89.

70 U.S. Attorney General, "Registry and Enrollment of Vessels," Op. Atty. Gen. 29, no. 188 (July 11, 1911).

71 51 Cong. Rec. 13184–85 (August 3, 1914).

72 51 Cong. Rec. 13189–90.

[73] 51 Cong. Rec. 13190.
[74] U.S. Congress, Senate, Admission of Foreign-Built Ships to American Registry, 63rd Cong., 2nd sess., 1914, S. Rep. 63-719.
[75] 51 Cong. Rec. 13388 (August 6, 1914); "Delay Ship Registry Bill–Senate Ready to Vote When It Learns of Mrs. Wilson's Death," New York Times, August 7, 1914, 5.
[76] 51 Cong. Rec. 13293 (August 5, 1914).
[77] 51 Cong. Rec. 13383 (August 6, 1914); 51 Cong. Rec. 13499–500 (August 8, 1914).
[78] Congressional Research Service, Party Leaders in the United States Congress, 1789–2019, CRS Report no. RL 30567 (updated September 4, 2019).
[79] 51 Cong. Rec. 13526 (August 8, 1914); 51 Cong. Rec. 13599–600 (August 11, 1914).
[80] 51 Cong. Rec. 13597.
[81] 51 Cong. Rec. 13604–10.
[82] 51 Cong. Rec. 13577.
[83] 51 Cong. Rec. 13578, 13587.
[84] 51 Cong. Rec. 13586–87, 13592.
[85] 51 Cong. Rec. 13612–14.
[86] 51 Cong. Rec. 13610.
[87] 51 Cong. Rec. 13612.
[88] 51 Cong. Rec. 13614.
[89] U.S. Congress, Senate, Registry of Foreign-Built Vessels, 63rd Cong., 2nd sess., 1914, Sen. Doc. 63-564; U.S. Congress, House, Admission of Foreign-Built Ships to American Registry, 63rd Cong., 2nd sess., 1914, H. Rep. 63-1087.
[90] 51 Cong. Rec. 13708 (August 14, 1914).
[91] 51 Cong. Rec. 13708–10.
[92] 51 Cong. Rec. 13711, 13714–19.
[93] 51 Cong. Rec. 13707.
[94] 51 Cong. Rec. 13720–26.
[95] 51 Cong. Rec. 13839–40.
[96] 51 Cong. Rec. 13839–40; "Ship Registry Bill Passes the Senate," New York Times, August 18, 1914, 12.
[97] 38 Stat. 698 (August 18, 1914). Congress later enacted legislation to further the process of reflagging in terms of repealing discriminating duties against any vessel owned by a U.S. citizen that was not a "vessel of the United States" and to permit consular officials to issue provisional registry certificates. 38 Stat. 1193 (March 4, 1915); "Grant Saw Chance in '70," New York Times, August 18, 1914, 12.
[98] 55 Cong. Rec. 7812 (October 5, 1917); 40 Stat. 392 (October 6, 1917).
[99] 51 Cong. Rec. 13141 (August 3, 1914).
[100] 51 Cong. Rec. 6661–63 (April 14, 1914).
[101] "Federal Insurance Sought for Exports," New York Times, August 11, 1914, 4.
[102] National Foreign Trade Council, Its Purpose, Personnel and Accomplishments, India House, New York (November 1916), 3–6.

[103] National Foreign Trade Council, Its Purpose, Personnel and Accomplishments, 6.
[104] 38 Stat 711 (September 2, 1914).
[105] The U.S. government retains to this day the authority to issue war risk insurance. 46 U.S.C. § 53912.
[106] Annual Report of the Secretary of the Treasury on the State of the Finances for the Fiscal Year Ended June 30, 1915 (Washington, DC: Government Printing Office, 1916), 14.
[107] "Oceana Changes Flags–First Ship to Get American Registry under New Law," New York Times, August 23, 1914, 8.
[108] Woodrow Wilson, Executive Order no. 2039 (September 4, 1914) (regarding crewing of foreign vessels registered in the United States).
[109] Annual Report of the Commissioner of Navigation to the Secretary of Commerce (1915), 14.
[110] "Get British View of Ship Transfers," New York Times, August 26, 1914, 16.
[111] "Ships in Transfer Subject to Seizure," New York Times, September 1, 1914, 5.
[112] Annual Reports of the Secretary of Commerce (1915) (Washington, DC: Government Printing Office, 1915), 215.
[113] Annual Report of the Commissioner of Navigation to the Secretary of Commerce (1915), 13; for example, "Prize Court Must Rule on Ship Sales," New York Times, September 26, 1914, 6; "Transferred Oil Ship Seized off Sandy Hook," New York Times, October 19, 1914, 1; "America Files New Ship Protest–England Frees the Rockefeller–Prompt Demand for Release of the Brindilla," New York Times, October 23, 1914, 4. Chamberlain also refused to register certain vessels the department believed were not genuinely transferred. "Misled in Ship Deal—Richard Wagner Explains His Part in Purchase of Cargo Fleet," New York Times, June 18, 1915, 4.
[114] "Our Flag on German Ship," New York Times, December 28, 1914, 1.
[115] "Says E. N. Breitung Got Hamburg Liner," New York Times, December 29, 1914, 1; "The Dacia Obtains American Registry," New York Times, January 5, 1915, 1.
[116] "Memorandum from the British Embassy to the Department of State (January 2, 1915)" and "Letter from the British Ambassador (Spring Rice) to the Secretary of State (January 12, 1915)," Papers Relating to the Foreign Relations of the United States, 1915, Supplement, The World War, U.S. Department of State, Office of the Historian, Historical Documents, Documents 936 & 941; "British Conditions on Ship Purchases," New York Times, (January 7, 1915), 5; "Dacia is Barred from German Ports," New York Times, January 9, 1915, 1; "British Will Seize Dacia if She Sails," New York Times, January 12, 1915, 4; "Britain Formally Says Dacia Will Be Seized," Sun (New York), January 22, 1915, 1.
[117] "Telegram from the Ambassador in Great Britain (Page) to the Secretary of State (January 19, 1915)," Papers Relating to the Foreign Relations of the United States,1915, Supplement, The World War, Document 949.
[118] "Letter from the Secretary of State to the British Ambassador (Spring Rice) (January 13, 1915)," Papers Relating to the Foreign Relations of the United States,

1915, Supplement, The World War, Document 942; "May Shift Dacia to Holland Port," New York Times, January 14, 1915, 1.

[119] For example, "U.S. Offers Britain Plan to Avert Dacia Seizure," Sun (New York), January 14, 1915, 1.

[120] "Telegram from the Ambassador in Great Britain (Page) to the Secretary of State (January 15, 1915)," Papers Relating to the Foreign Relations of the United States, 1915, Supplement, The World War, Document 945.

[121] For example, "Urge Seizure of the Dacia—London Papers Say She Must Figure in a Test Case," New York Times, (January 16, 1915), 2; The Times Documentary History of the War— Naval–Part 3 (London: Printing House Square, 1918), vol. 7, 26–31.

[122] "Telegram from the Ambassador in Great Britain (Page) to the Secretary of State (Jan. 18, 1915)," Papers Relating to the Foreign Relations of the United States: 1915 Supplement, The World War, Document 948.

[123] "The Case of the Dacia," New York Times, January 21, 1915, 8.

[124] "May Let the Dacia Deliver Her Cargo," New York Times, January 15, 1915, 4; "Attitude of Great Britain toward the Dacia," Commercial & Financial Chronicle 100, no. 2587 January 23, 1915): 277.

[125] Ross Gregory, "A New Look at the Case of the Dacia," Journal of American History 55, no. 2 (September 1968): 292—96.

[126] "Telegram from the Secretary of State to the Ambassador in France (Sharp) (July 2, 1915)," Papers Relating to the Foreign Relations of the United States, 1915, Supplement, The World War, Document 662.

[127] "Test Ship Dacia Sunk by Submarine," New York Times, November 10, 1915, 2.

[128] "Telegram from the Secretary of State to Breitung and Company, Limited (August 31, 1915)," Papers Relating to the Foreign Relations of the United States, 1915, Supplement, The World War, Document 765 (and note 2).

[129] "Telegram from the Secretary of State to the Ambassador in Great Britain (Page) (January 23, 1915)," Papers Relating to the Foreign Relations of the United States, 1915, Supplement, The World War, Document 951.

[130] Broesamle, William Gibbs McAdoo, 217–18.

[131] Broesamle, William Gibbs McAdoo, 218.

[132] McAdoo, Crowded Years, 296.

[133] McAdoo, Crowded Years, 296.

[134] Lawrence C. Allin, "Ill-Timed Initiative—The Ship Purchase Bill of 1915," American Neptune 33, no. 3 (July 1973): 178–98.

[135] 51 Cong. Rec. 14193 (August 24, 1914); U.S. Congress, House, Merchant Marine and Fisheries Committee, Hearing before the House Merchant Marine and Fisheries Committee on H.R. 18518, 63rd Cong., 2nd sess., 1914.

[136] Link, Wilson: The Struggle for Neutrality, 1914–1915 (Princeton, NJ: Princeton University Press, 1960), 89—90; "Telegram from the Ambassador in Great Britain

(Page) to the Secretary of State (Jan. 18, 1915)," Papers Relating to the Foreign Relations of the United States, 1915 Supplement, the World War (Washington, DC: Government Printing Office, 1928), Document 948.

[137] H.R. 18666, 63rd Cong., 2nd sess., 51 Cong. Rec. 14759 (September 4, 1914); U.S. Congress, House, Government Ownership and Operation of Merchant Vessels in the Foreign Trade of the United States, 63rd Cong., 2nd sess., 1914, H. Rep. 63-1149.

[138] Government Ownership and Operation of Merchant Vessels in the Foreign Trade of the United States, H. Rep. 63-1149, part 2.

[139] McAdoo, Crowded Years, 305.

[140] Broesamle, William Gibbs McAdoo, 226.

[141] McAdoo, Crowded Years, 305.

[142] Woodrow Wilson, Second Annual Message, December 8, 1914, UC Santa Barbara, the American Presidency Project, https://www.presidency.ucsb.edu/documents/second-annual-message-19.

[143] U.S. Congress, Senate, Increased Ocean Transportation Rates, 63d Cong., 3d sess., 1914, S. Doc. 63-673.

[144] U.S. Congress, Senate, Promotion of Foreign Commerce of the United States by Providing Adequate Shipping Facilities, 63rd Cong., 3rd sess., 1914, S. Rep. 63-841.

[145] 52 Cong. Rec. 904–06 (January 4, 1915).

[146] 52 Cong. Rec. 908–09.

[147] National Foreign Trade Council, Official Report of the Second National Foreign Trade Convention, St. Louis (1915), 254.

[148] National Foreign Trade Council, Third National Foreign Trade Convention, New Orleans, LA (1916), 238–54.

[149] 52 Cong. Rec. 908–09 (January 4, 1915).

[150] "President Opposed to Extra Session—Is Sure That None Will Not Be Needed to Pass the Ship Purchase Bill," New York Times, January 6, 1915, 10.

[151] "Ship Bill Foes Unite," Washington Post, January 22, 1915, 1.

[152] "Democrats Bound by Ship Bill Pledge," New York Times, January 24, 1915, 1; "White House Happy over Shipping Bill," New York Times, January 25, 1915, 6.

[153] 52 Cong. Rec. appendix 112 (1915).

[154] "Woodrow Wilson Jackson Day Address in Indianapolis (January 8, 1915)," Papers of Woodrow Wilson, vol. 32, 29.

[155] "Truce on Ship Bill," Washington Post, January 31, 1915, 1.

[156] 52 Cong. Rec. 2786 (February 1, 1915); "Revolt Imperils Ship Purchase," New York Times, February 2, 1915, 1.

[157] 52 Cong. Rec. 2943–46 (February 3, 1915).

[158] For example, 52 Cong. Rec. 4009 (February 18, 1915).

[159] "Look to Marshall to Save Ship Bill," New York Times, February 5, 1915, 1.

[160] 52 Cong. Rec. 2852 (February 2, 1915); 52 Cong. Rec. 3088 (February 5, 1915); 52 Cong. Rec. 3700 (February 13, 1915).

[161] McAdoo, Crowded Years, 310.
[162] 52 Cong. Rec. 3777 (February 15, 1915).
[163] "Ship Bill Inquiry Ends," New York Times, April 8, 1915, 17.
[164] U.S. Congress, Senate, The Shipping Bill, 63rd Cong., 3rd sess., 1915, S. Doc. 63-713; U.S. Congress, Senate, The Administration and the Shipping Bill, 63rd Cong., 3rd sess., 1915, S. Doc. 63-950.
[165] Safford, Wilsonian Maritime Diplomacy, 43.
[166] "Order Referendum on Ship Purchase," New York Times, February 5, 1915, 4.
[167] 52 Cong. Rec. 3991 (February 18, 1915).
[168] 52 Cong. Rec. 3246 (February 8, 1915).
[169] "Filibuster on Again," Washington Post, February 9, 1915, 1.
[170] 52 Cong. Rec. 3282—312 (February 8, 1915); "Senators Keep Up Debate on the Ship Bill – Jones Speaks All Night Opposing Measure," San Antonio Light, February 9, 1915, 1; "All-Night Session in Ship Bill Fight," New York Times, February 9, 1915, 1.
[171] 52 Cong. Rec. 3321 (February 8, 1915).
[172] Safford, Wilsonian Maritime Diplomacy, 63.
[173] "Democrats Plan Ship Fight Coup," Washington Evening Star, February 10, 1915, 2.
[174] "House Vote on Ships," Washington Post, February 17, 1915, 1.
[175] "Letter from C. Clark to W. Wilson (February 11, 1915)," Papers of Woodrow Wilson, vol. 32, 221.
[176] 52 Cong. Rec. 4020 (February 18, 1915); "Shelve Ship Bill into Conference," New York Times, February 19, 1915, 1; "Ship Bill Scotched," Washington Post, February 19, 1915, 1.
[177] "Ship Bill is Shelved," New York Times, March 4, 1915, 4.
[178] Safford, Wilsonian Maritime Diplomacy, 63–65.
[179] "Entry for January 26, 1915," Josephus Daniels, The Cabinet Diaries of Josephus Daniels 1913–1921, E. David Cronon, ed. (Lincoln, NE: University of Nebraska Press, 1963), 93–94.
[180] "Press Conference of Wilson (February 2, 1915)," Papers of Woodrow Wilson, vol. 32, 171.
[181] "Ship Bill Attack on Lodge by M'Adoo," New York Times, March 9, 1915, 8.
[182] McAdoo, Crowded Years, 311–12.
[183] "Lusitania Sunk by a Submarine, Probably 1,000 Dead," New York Times, May 8, 1915, 1.
[184] "Vanderbilt Left His Wife at Home," New York Times, May 8, 1915, 4.
[185] McAdoo, Crowded Years, 312; Safford, Wilsonian Maritime Diplomacy, 71.
[186] Annual Report of the Secretary of the Treasury on the State of the Finances (Washington, DC: Government Printing Office, 1916), 92–93.
[187] Annual Reports of the Navy Department for Fiscal Year 1915 (Washington, DC: Government Printing Office, 1916): 36–38.

[188] Broesamle, William Gibbs McAdoo, 230–31.
[189] McAdoo, Crowded Years, 311–12.
[190] U.S. Congress, Senate, A Naval Auxiliary Merchant Marine, 64th Cong., 1st sess., 1915, S. Doc. 64-4. Senator Fletcher also defended the legislation before the Academy of Political Science in New York on November 12, 1915. U.S. Congress, Senate, What Congress Has Done to Build Up an American Mercantile Marine, 64th Cong., 1st sess., 1915, S. Doc. 64-10.
[191] Broesamle, William Gibbs McAdoo, 231.
[192] "Merchants Oppose Government Ships," New York Times, June 24, 1915, 14.
[193] Woodrow Wilson, Third Annual Message, December 7, 1915, UC Santa Barbara, the American Presidency Project, https://www.presidency.ucsb.edu/documents/third-annual-message-19.
[194] 53 Cong. Rec. 1929 (January 31, 1916) (text of H.R. 10500).
[195] Annual Report of the Commissioner of Navigation to the Secretary of the Commerce (1915), 13.
[196] U.S. Congress, House, Creating a Shipping Board, a Naval Auxiliary, a Merchant Marine, and Regulating Carriers by Water Engaged in the Foreign and Interstate Commerce of the United States, 64th Cong., 1st sess., 1916, H. Rep. 64-659, 68.
[197] U.S. Congress, House, Committee on Merchant Marine and Fisheries, Hearings before the House Committee on Merchant Marine and Fisheries on H.R. 10500, 64th Cong., 1st sess., 1916.
[198] Hearings before the House Committee on Merchant Marine and Fisheries on H.R. 10500, 274; Creating a Shipping Board, H. Rep. 64-659, 67–74.
[199] Hearings before the House Committee on Merchant Marine and Fisheries on H.R. 10500., 721–724.
[200] 53 Cong. Rec. 7618 (May 8, 1916).
[201] Hearings before the House Committee on Merchant Marine and Fisheries on H.R. 10500, 1–25.
[202] Currently at 46 U.S.C. § 50501.
[203] Creating a Shipping Board, a Naval Auxiliary, a Merchant Marine, and Regulating Carriers by Water Engaged in the Foreign and Interstate Commerce of the United States, H. Rep. 64-659, 74.
[204] A list of the German interned vessels was put in the record in 1915. 52 Cong. Rec. 1936 (January 20, 1915).
[205] 53 Cong Rec. 8332 (May 19, 1916) (letter from Chamberlain to Rep. James L. Slayden, April 20, 1916).
[206] Safford, Wilsonian Maritime Diplomacy, 90–91.
[207] 53 Cong. Rec. 12357–58 (August 9, 1916).
[208] National Foreign Trade Council, European Economic Alliances, India House, New York (1916), 12.
[209] 53 Cong. Rec. 8322 (May 19, 1916).
[210] 53 Cong. Rec. 8356.

[211] 53 Cong. Rec. 8374–75 (May 20, 1916).
[212] "B. S. Grosscup Dies in Tacoma," Seattle Daily Times, January 5, 1935, 1.
[213] 53 Cong. Rec. 12343 (August 9, 1916).
[214] 53 Cong. Rec. 12432 (August 11, 1916).
[215] 53 Cong. Rec. 12528—29 (August 12, 1916).
[216] 53 Cong. Rec. 8052–57 (May 16, 1916) (S. 5067); 53 Cong. Rec. 8055 (list of countries that would have to be notified if U.S. imposed discriminating duties). Jones also offered an amendment to study the marine insurance market which was added to section 12 of the legislation. 53 Cong. Rec. 12732 (August 16, 1916) and 12814 (August 18).
[217] 53 Cong. Rec. 12825 (August 18, 1916); "Ship Bill Passed by Senate, 38 to 21," New York Times, August 19, 1916, 1.
[218] Albert D. Kirwan, Revolt of the Rednecks, Mississippi Politics: 1876–1925 (Gloucester, MA.: Peter Smith, 1964), 285—86.
[219] 53 Cong. Rec. 13464 (August 20, 1916); 39 Stat. 728 (September 7, 1916).
[220] "Merchant Marine Urgent, Says M'Adoo," New York Times, July 22, 1916, 11.
[221] Quoted in William Gibbs McAdoo, 234.
[222] McAdoo, Crowded Years, 315.
[223] McAdoo, Crowded Years, 316.
[224] "President Approves the Shipping Bill," New York Times, September 8, 1916, 5.

Charles M. Schwab and Edward N. Hurley, circa 1918, Library of Congress

Chapter 19 — Shipping Board

The long and painful process to get the Shipping Board authorized was matched by the fits and starts to get the board operational. The board was consumed at first by a dispute between William Denman, the first board chairman, and Maj. Gen. George W. Goethals, the first general manager of the Emergency Fleet Corporation established by the board to construct vessels. The dispute was ostensibly over whether the corporation should order wooden vessels.

The Wooden Ship Controversy

On December 22, 1916, President Wilson nominated Bernard Baker, Theodore Brent, William Denman, John A. Donald, and John B. White for the new Shipping Board.[1] Baker, Denman and Donald were Democrats; Brent and White were Republicans. Only Baker and Donald had direct maritime experience since they were both founders of steamship lines. Baker had also materially assisted the government in the Spanish-American War and had advised McAdoo on shipping matters during consideration of the Ship Purchase Bill.[2]

Denman was an admiralty attorney from California who had also provided drafting assistance to McAdoo on the Ship Purchase Bill.[3] He claimed a range of maritime experience, including representation of Fred. Olsen & Co., a Norwegian company, for some of the first diesel-powered motor vessels operating between the United States and northern Europe. Denman indicated that this and other experiences led him to propose that the board prioritize diesel-powered vessels for construction.

Bad blood arose immediately between Denman and Baker, who expected to be chairman. Both were known to be stubborn and obstinate men.[4] An early disagreement was on how to deal with the British. Denman wanted to be tough on the British because of their aggressive neutrality view, which Baker thought was a mistake.[5]

McAdoo communicated with Baker that the administration preferred Denman to be chairman to balance out coastal interests since he was the only one from the West Coast.[6] Baker responded by resigning, and Denman was elected as chairman on January 30, 1917.[7]

The board immediately recommended that the president invoke the new foreign vessel transfer authority to prevent any U.S.-flag vessel from leaving the registry.[8] It did so out of fear of an exodus to neutral flags since war with Germany seemed imminent. In fact, on January 31 Count Johann von Bernstorff, Germany's ambassador to the United States, delivered Germany's announcement that it would sink any vessel in the war zone around Britain, without warning regardless of what flag was flown. In response, President Wilson issued the national emergency reflag proclamation on February 5.[9]

The board quickly determined that U.S. shipyards were already full of orders for steel cargo vessels. The board later reported to the Senate that as of May 1, 1917, 537 steel vessels aggregating more than two million tons were under construction.[10] The board was compelled to look for alternatives because the need was critical and U.S. shipyards were already at capacity.

One alternative was to seek authority to take over ongoing construction projects, which the board requested but Congress did not provide until June 1917.[11] Without those emergency powers, the only apparent alternative at the time was to order wooden vessels as a temporary expedient until steel vessel construction caught up with demand.

Denman meanwhile was antagonizing the White House. When he became chairman, he objected to British bunkering (vessel refueling) agreements, whereby vessel owners had to promise to boycott any country at war with Britain as a condition of receiving fuel. This apparently stemmed from an experience he had with a client who had been blacklisted by the British government for allegedly trading with Germany. Denman was suspicious that Britain was using trading restrictions to prevent U.S. inroads into foreign markets.[12]

Although the bunkering restrictions were the sort of British action the Wilson administration had previously complained about, March 1917 was no longer the time for strict neutrality. On March 16 Secretary of State Robert Lansing sent a letter to President Wilson, accusing Denman of "pro-German sympathies, or else anti-British feeling."[13] On the same day, Edward M. House (Wilson's close aid, known as "Colonel House") wrote Wilson that "the British are terribly upset" about Denman.[14]

The Wilson administration also had to replace Baker on the board and appointed Raymond B. Stevens, a progressive Democrat from New Hampshire who had served one term in the U.S. House of Representative and lost a 1914 Senate race against Gallinger.[15] Like Denman, he was a graduate of Harvard Law School. The shipping industry questioned why another commissioner without shipping experience had been appointed to the board. Stevens came from an agricultural background. A local newspaper headline read, "Farmer Gets Place on Shipping Board."[16]

Denman started formulating a plan to build eight hundred to one thousand steam-powered wooden vessels of 3,000 to 3,600 tons each in fourteen months' time (about sixty-five a month).[17] The idea came from Frederic A. Eustis, a wealthy thirty-nine-year-old yachtsman with a Harvard engineering degree who convinced Denman that a large fleet of modular wooden vessels could be built to supplement steel vessels.[18]

Eustis was assisted by F. Huntington Clark, a mining engineer who had been recommended by McAdoo and Wilson.[19] Clark boasted that the vessels would be the "Ford of the Seas" and the tonnage could be built "faster than Germany can sink it."[20] The entire plan was being pursued by a team without vessel construction experience. Chamberlain, for example, wrote that "the scheme was entirely impracticable" and there were many public criticisms.[21]

The plan nevertheless had its supporters. It was met with enthusiasm by the U.S. Chamber of Commerce when Denman presented it on April 5.[22] In that same speech, Denman suggested Maj. Gen. George Washington Goethals of Panama Canal fame had endorsed the wooden vessel construction program and would soon be taking it over. Moreover, the plan was not unprecedented—Britain had also ordered wooden vessels to supplement steel vessel construction during war-time for similar reasons.[23]

It was Eustis's idea to involve Goethals.[24] It was readily apparent that the wooden ship program would benefit from Goethals's endorsement since Goethals had built up a substantial public reputation as a builder and a doer.[25] However, when Eustis approached Goethals, the latter indicated only lukewarm support and had in fact turned down the job of supervising construction on April 4.[26]

On that same day, Wilson approved the board's wooden vessel construction plan upon the recommendation of the Council on National Defense.[27] On April 6, Wilson signed the joint resolution declaring war on Germany.[28]

U.S. Customs officials and U.S. Army units had been waiting for the moment and ninety-one German vessels were immediately seized.[29] Twenty-seven were seized in the New York area by the Twenty-Second Infantry Regiment, credited as undertaking the first U.S. act of war against Germany.[30]

In anticipation of the seizures, the German crews had attempted to sabotage the vessels, but the U.S. Navy did wonders repairing them for U.S. duty.[31] The first repaired vessel, the *DeKalb*, was carrying U.S. troops two months later and most of the repairs to the fleet were done in five months.

About twenty of the German vessels were passenger vessels, such as the *Vaterland* (renamed the *Leviathan*, one of the largest vessels in the world), and therefore ideal troop transports. These seized German vessels transported more than a quarter of the men sent to France.³² The *Leviathan* alone transported more than 175,000 of the total 2.1 million.³³

President Wilson informed Goethals by an April 11 letter that he had approved the board's wooden vessel construction plan, that he was pleased that Goethals had given the plan his "enthusiastic support," and that he was also happy to have "the use of your directing genius in the marshaling of the resources of the country for the rapid construction of the tonnage required."³⁴ The press started reporting the news about Goethals before he received the president's letter and, of course, he knew that he had not given such support.³⁵ Goethals apparently felt he had no choice but to accept the job. He was peeved about the way he had been maneuvered.³⁶

When Goethals attended his first board meeting on April 14, Commissioner Stevens reported that he "was the angriest-looking man I'd ever seen."³⁷ At that meeting, Goethals insinuated that Denman was a liar and tried to see the president immediately after without success. Goethals took the job, but only after telling Denman that he would do it on the condition of having full control—a request that was not fulfilled.³⁸

An enormous task lay before the board. British prime minister Lloyd-George told the American Luncheon Club in London on April 12 that "the road to victory, the absolute assurance of victory, has to be found in one word, 'ships,' and a second word, 'ships,' and a third word, 'ships.'"³⁹

The board formed a District of Columbia corporation on April 16, 1917, with capital stock of $50 million, as authorized by the 1916 Shipping Act, naming it the "United States Emergency Fleet Corporation."⁴⁰ The board delegated to the corporation the execution of its wooden vessel construction program. Denman was appointed the president of the corporation and a trustee. Goethals was general manager and a trustee. The by-laws of the corporation, written at President Wilson's behest (according to Denman), stated that only the president of the corporation could sign contracts.⁴¹ The general manager was to conduct the corporation's business.

Meanwhile, Eustis and Clark were commissioning wooden vessel designs and promising shipbuilders that they would get contracts. Many of those promises implied that Goethals would approve them.[42] It was reported that "the wooden ship idea had drawn a swarm of contract hunters to Washington."[43]

Goethals put an end to the scheming and proceeded with his plan for greatly expanding U.S. steel vessel construction through modular construction.[44] Such construction was attractive because it permitted a wide range of manufacturing facilities to participate in vessel construction and could alleviate the shipyard bottle neck.

He also investigated a significant expansion of U.S. shipyard capacity.[45] The largest project was to be at Hog Island, Philadelphia (discussed in the next chapter). The land purchase and construction contracts were in an advanced stage, but unsigned, at the time Goethals resigned.

On May 12, in closed door testimony before the Senate Appropriations Committee considering urgent deficiency legislation, Goethals testified that he was not in favor of an enormous wooden vessel construction program and that steel vessels would be cheaper to build than wooden vessels.[46] The board tried to tidy things up by issuing a "vigorous denial" on May 20 that there was any difference of opinion.[47] However, that denial also softened the board's position stating that the board "never wanted to build wooden ships, but has been driven to it by necessity." The board claimed that when it canvassed the steel shipbuilding industry, it determined that there was simply no additional capacity.

The first public split between Denman and Goethals occurred because of an impromptu speech Goethals made to the American Iron and Steel Institute on May 25 in New York. In that speech, Goethals announced the goal of building 3 million tons of vessels in eighteen months and said that the "original program of the Shipping Board to turn out wooden ships on an enormous scale was hopeless."[48] Goethals later argued that he was misquoted: he claimed that he said *his task* was hopeless.[49]

Goethals admitted he coined a phrase later oft-repeated that there was also no wood to build the enormous fleet because "the birds are now nesting in the trees that are going into those ships."[50] This phrase must have stung Denman because in a letter to the Senate Commerce Committee in 1918 he wrote, "I believed we would secure a large additional tonnage from wood despite the fact that the birds were singing in the trees from the timbers of which they were to be constructed.[51]

Goethals's remarks regarding the hopelessness of the wooden program were widely reported.[52] The board immediately issued a statement contradicting Goethals. It indicated that wooden vessels would be needed even if the eighteen-month steel program was completed and that "a public dinner with the head of the Steel Trust" was not a proper place to discuss national policy.[53]

The board had been aware of Goethals's position for some time. He had written a memorandum to the board on April 25 stating that the wooden ship program was impossible. He argued that what should be done is have the president sign an executive order putting private shipyards under board control with appropriations of $500 million for new steel vessel construction.[54] Wooden vessels would also be built, but in a much-reduced program.[55]

The Denman-Goethals feud played out in the congressional consideration of the Urgent Deficiencies Act. That Act was set to expand substantially the president's authority to requisition vessels under construction as well as shipyards and to provide a large, unprecedented, appropriation for that purpose.[56]

The House, siding with Denman and Wilson, left it up to the president to delegate the authority as he saw fit.[57] The Senate, siding with Goethals, would have provided the authority to the general manager of the Fleet Corporation or otherwise as the president saw fit.[58] As passed, the president received complete delegation discretion together with a shipbuilding appropriation of $250 million and an authorization of $500 million essentially as Goethals had requested.[59]

Goethals finally got to see the president on May 31.[60] President Wilson was apparently cagey in the meeting and made no commitments.

On June 6, Clark and Eustis met with Wilson through the intercession of Clark's father, John Bates Clark, Wilson's longtime friend and a professor of economics at Columbia University.[61] They argued that Goethals was making a big mistake to de-emphasize the wooden ship program. Wilson apparently urged them to go public with their views, which they did on June 7.[62]

In public they argued that Goethals was holding up the program by insisting on flat price contracts (versus cost-plus contracts) which U.S. shipyards would not accept. Only wooden vessels could fill the gap before there was enough steel ones available, they claimed.[63] Denman was caught flat-footed because he did not know about the Clark-Eustis-Wilson meeting.[64]

Goethals immediately fired Eustis and Clark for disloyalty and untruthfulness.[65] He pointed out that he had already let contracts totaling more than the corporation's authorized capitalization, that even the board agreed with his flat price contract approach, and that he had laid out his plan for a massive building program to proceed as soon as the authority and funds came from Congress.

Eustis held the title of assistant manager of the corporation, but he was also employed as a special agent by the board.[66] The board voted 3 to 2 to retain him. Stevens led the effort to oust Eustis and to grant Goethals the authority he wanted. He would later meet with Wilson on June 20 to argue in favor of putting all construction in the hands of a single person.[67]

On June 11, Goethals wrote a long memorandum to the president outlining his plan for a vessel construction program.[68] He wrote that he had already let contracts for 104 vessels with 18 of steel construction, 32 of composite steel and wood construction and 54 of wood construction for a cost of $80 million.

He continued to argue that an additional 1.7 million tons of steel vessels could be delivered within eighteen months, plus 1 million tons of wooden vessels if authority was given to commandeer shipyards.

Immediately after Wilson signed the Urgent Deficiencies Act, Goethals took the liberty of also sending Wilson a draft executive order that would vest all functions relating to vessel construction in the general manager, leaving functions relating to completed vessels in the board.[69] At about the same time, Goethals sent to Denman for signature a contract to build ten steel vessels at Downey Shipbuilding Company of Arlington, New York, which had a facility on Staten Island.[70] Like many other vessels that seemed so important at the time, these ten vessels were in fact constructed but none was delivered before the war was over.[71]

Denman refused to sign the contract and went public with his view that the steel price was excessive.[72] Goethals disagreed because he believed that the steel prices would be set separately by the government, and it was more important to get the project moving than worry about the price.[73] Denman's position was little different than the position Wilson later took when he warned "profiteers" to charge fair prices to the government.[74]

Goethals had not copied the board on any of his communications to the President.[75] Denman was also on his own private path to get Wilson's support. Denman met with Wilson on June 18, and on June 29 Denman sent his own draft executive order agreed to by a 3 to 2 vote of the board.

Denman had no choice but to also separately write to the president, which he did on June 21 writing that "I have not seen a copy of General Goethals' proposed scheme of commandeering" shipyards and warning that the rate of German sinkings was alarming and had to be addressed.[76] He continued to argue that "no matter how long it may take to build wooden ships, even if it were longer than steel, we must have them for supplements to the steel program."

The bickering only intensified after Wilson signed on July 11 the executive order sent to him by Denman.[77] Even though Denman had drafted the order, it was ambiguous as to whether it granted authority to the corporation president, the trustees, or the general manager. Denman interpreted the order to have given him full authority, and he wrote Goethals to that effect.[78]

Goethals took the opposite position and went public with his plan to take over shipyards and ongoing construction contracts in order to put pressure on the president to side with him.[79] This power play, however, ran into Denman's clear authority to sign contracts. Goethals claimed that the board was holding back shipbuilding in a national emergency by not signing contracts. Denman also went to the press, arguing that the board was simply being careful to avoid the government paying excessive amounts.[80]

On July 19, Wilson wrote to Goethals with the bad news that he had to "put yourself in the hands of the directors" of the corporation.[81] Denman immediately moved to implement the eight hundred wooden vessel program. Goethals resigned on July 20.

Denman's turn to face the president was next. In a cabinet meeting on July 7, Secretary Baker expressed the mood of Wilson's close advisers when he said that "Denman is impossible."[82] On July 24 the president wrote to Denman, urging him to "take the same disinterested and self-forgetting course that General Goethals has taken."[83] When Denman was denied a meeting with Wilson, he resigned. Commissioner White, who had been in ill health, resigned the same day as did Commissioner Brent both of whom had supported Denman.[84]

The *Scientific American* editorialized, "The American people are asking themselves why, in getting rid of that arch obstructionist, Denman, it was necessary to sacrifice the most distinguished military engineer in America."[85] The president "evidently... considered this the simplest way to cut the Gordian Knot."

Also on the same day, Wilson nominated Edward Nash Hurley and Bainbridge Colby to be commissioners.[86] The board elected Hurley to serve as chairman on July 27 and Stevens to serve as vice chairman. Hurley served in that position until July 31, 1919, and therefore was primarily responsible for the construction and management of the war-time fleet. Rear Adm. W. L. Capps, who was the chief constructor of the Navy, was made general manager, and he served until December 1917 when he left because of ill health.

Denman, who had gone back to private practice in California, defended his actions in subsequent congressional hearings. He argued that the wooden vessels had in fact been necessary and would have performed a valuable service if the war had lasted longer.[87] General Goethals did not go public with his version of events, although the controversy became a staple of subsequent congressional hearings on board matters.

President Franklin Roosevelt nominated Denman in 1935 to serve on the U.S. Court of Appeals for the Ninth Circuit. He was in active status on that court until 1957 and died at the age of eighty-six. Goethals was recalled to active service as the acting quartermaster general of the Army in December 1917 where he served until March 1919. His work in ensuring that the Army was supplied in Europe and elsewhere was exemplary and he received numerous awards from the U.S. and Allied governments for that service.[88] Goethals died in 1928 at the age of seventy.

In a 1918 article, Stevens claimed that the "so-called controversy between General Goethals and Mr. Denman, while it occupied a good deal of space in the public press, did not as a matter of fact interfere much with the construction of ships."[89] There was a lot of truth to that statement since the corporation had under contract at the time about 840,000 tons of wooden vessels, 200,000 tons of steel and wood composite vessels and 590,000 tons of steel vessels for a total of about 1.6 million tons.[90]

In his 1927 memoir, *The Bridge to France*, Hurley attributed the Denman-Goethals dispute to the "faulty scheme of organization" at the Corporation.[91] Hurley also argued that there was really no difference of opinion that steel vessels were preferred, and wooden vessels were only needed because of the emergency. In fact, at the last board meeting attended by Goethals in July 1917, the minutes reflect Goethals saying, "I advocated the use of steel and wood, going to as much of both as we could get."[92]

When Hurley became chairman, the corporation's bylaws were amended in late November 1917.[93] Complete power was given to the president of the corporation who could then delegate that authority to a general manager appointed by that president. This simple change was credited with improving the efficiency of the organization.[94]

In terms of aiding the war effort, the wooden vessel program was a failure.[95] The problems faced in securing workmen, suitable wood, and steam engines had been severely underestimated by the Denman team (and Goethals).[96] There were also a range of management problems, such as paying a disproportionate amount of the progress payments for the laying of a keel. This led to a host of incomplete vessels rather than concentrating resources on completing vessels.[97] The first wooden vessel was not delivered until May 1918. By November 1918, when the war ended, only about 100 had been delivered of 350,000 deadweight tons (a measurement of cargo carrying capacity abbreviated "DWT.")[98] Many of the wooden vessels performed almost no service at all and created substantial disposal issues (discussed in a subsequent chapter).

The Board Chairmen

Following the Denman-Goethals debacle, the Shipping Board needed a strong-willed chairman, with good organizational skills and solid political connections, and it got one in the form of Edward Nash Hurley. Hurley was succeeded by equally determined and connected men: John Barton Payne from August

5, 1919, until March 13, 1920, and William S. Benson from March 13, 1920, to June 30, 1921.

Hurley. Hurley was born in 1864 in Galesburg, Illinois the fifth of ten children of Irish immigrant parents.[99] He quit school at fifteen and by the age of seventeen he was a fireman of a rail switching engine. He worked engines on the railroads for three years until 1889, during which time he had joined the Brotherhood of Locomotive Engineers. This gave him some credibility when the Shipping Board encountered labor troubles.[100]

The story goes that while later working as a railroad supply salesman, Hurley chanced on an old friend in Chicago on Dearborn Street in 1896. The friend had invented a pneumatic air drill.[101] Hurley bought the invention rights and formed the Standard Pneumatic Tool Company, which originated and developed the pneumatic tool industry.[102] Hurley personally drove the first rivet on a vessel on the Clyde to demonstrate the technology in 1897.[103] The company was a fabulous success and the sale of the company in 1902 made Hurley rich.[104]

For a while, Hurley engaged in farming and raising livestock in Wheaton, Illinois, until he organized the Hurley Machine Company in 1908 to manufacture electric home appliances, including ironing machines and vacuum cleaners. Hurley's second company was as successful as the first and he introduced the first U.S. electric clothes washing machine (the "Thor Electric Washing Machine"), among other innovations.

Hurley became active in Democratic politics in Wheaton and provided financial support for Wilson's run for New Jersey governor and then for president.[105] In 1913 he declined an appointment as comptroller of the currency.[106] In 1915 he was selected to serve on the newly formed Federal Trade Commission and was eventually its chairman, a position he held until early 1917, when he resigned to return to his company.[107]

Hurley preached in favor of business cooperation to compete in the world market. He told the American Iron and Steel Institute in May 1916 that businesses should form trade associations and cooperate with the government.[108] As he said many times "cooperation is the watchword of the era upon which we are entering—cooperation between employer and employee, among business men, and between Government and business."[109]

Hurley was out of government for only a very short time before Wilson selected him to replace Denman. At the time, it was reported that he was a "'find' of the Wilson Administration," that he "attracted attention by his grasp of big affairs and his executive ability," and "that he is a close personal friend of President Wilson."[110] A business acquaintance from Chicago said that "probably no man in Washington, with the exception of Colonel House, is closer to the President or has more of his confidence."[111] When Hurley hesitated because he had no experience in shipbuilding, Joseph Tumulty stated on behalf of the president "'You tell Hurley this is personal.'"[112]

As chairman of the Shipping Board, Hurley threw himself into the enormous task of creating the fleet of vessels needed to prosecute the war and became a member of Wilson's war cabinet, which included the secretaries of treasury, war, and the Navy.[113] In a speech to the National Marine League of the U.S.A. on March 26, 1918, Hurley framed the problem the board faced: "Shipping is the essence of the struggle in which the world is now engaged—the central beam in the whole war structure. If that fails, all else fails. We are engaged in a race with the submarine."[114] The goal he set was to make the United States "the mecca of the shipbuilding trade of the world."[115]

He was called the "boss riveter," "Shipbuilder to Uncle Sam," and "Hurry-up Hurley."[116] When Hurley retired from the board in 1919, he was lauded by the *New York Times*, which wrote "there may have been other men who knew more about shipbuilding than he did, but none who could better impersonate Uncle Sam determined to see it through."[117]

Throughout, Hurley maintained his sense of humor. When Goethals persistently complained about a lack of vessels when he ran the Army supply operations, Hurley "jokingly" told Goethals to back off or he would name one of the Denman's wooden vessels "The General Goethals."[118] George Rublee, who served with Hurley on the Federal Trade Commission, wrote that Hurley was "good natured, hearty sort of fellow, amusing," but also "was as quick as a cat about any protection of himself."[119]

Hurley publicly expressed the hope that a prominent American merchant marine could exist after the war without displacing foreign nations in an ever-expanding international trade environment.[120] In April 1918 he stated, "We are building ships not alone for the war, but for the future of world trade."[121] He also believed the United States had a moral obligation to set an example and help connect the world without ruinous competition.[122]

Privately, Hurley expected a commercial "war after the war" and was wary of British policies and objectives.[123] He set out in March 1919 his ideas about private ownership of the fleet the U.S. government had built to meet the competition.[124] Those ideas, discussed in a subsequent chapter, keyed the 1920 Merchant Marine Act.

After leaving the board, Hurley continued to support the American merchant marine with speeches, articles, and the 1920 book *The New Merchant Marine* and the 1927 memoir of the war years entitled *The Bridge to France*.[125] In 1921 he pointed out that 90 percent of the vessels built by the Board burned oil for fuel instead of coal and so had a decided international cost advantage.[126] In 1928 he wrote an open letter to President Calvin Coolidge urging the government to end its vessel operations, which had continued since the war.[127] He also wrote about this business ideas in the 1919 book *The Awakening of Business*.[128]

After he left government, Hurley became a business consultant.[129] He served on various boards and organizations from 1919 to 1933 including as president of the American Manufacturers' Export Association starting in 1930.[130] In that same year, he gave a substantial gift to the University of Notre Dame to establish "The Edward N. Hurley College of Foreign and Domestic Commerce."[131] Hurley Hall still exists at the University. Hurley died in November 1933 in Chicago at the age of sixty-nine. He was remembered at that time as the head of war shipping.[132]

Payne. Payne was born in January 1855 in Pruntytown, which was then in Virginia and now in West Virginia.[133] His family moved in 1860 to the village of Orlean, about a dozen miles west of Warrenton in Fauquier County, Virginia, about fifty miles west of Washington, DC.[134] The village had been founded by Payne's great-grandfather and still contains "John Barton Payne Road." Like Hurley, Payne came from a large family, the eighth of ten children. Like McAdoo's, Payne's family suffered during the Civil War including enduring a Union army occupation.

He never forgot his roots. In 1912, he purchased a farm near Warrenton which he donated upon his death to the American Red Cross, the College of William and Mary and Washington & Lee University.[135] He helped fund the Warrenton Library (now the John Barton Payne Community Hall). He also had a monument placed at the Orlean cemetery honoring Payne family members who had served as soldiers. Twenty-eight of them died in the Civil War, including his oldest brother who was a Confederate lieutenant.[136]

Earning his first money as a twelve-year-old helping to drive a flock of turkeys to Washington, DC for sale, Payne spent the money on a shotgun. He later returned to Pruntytown and went to work for the clerk of the local circuit court where he "read the law" (by literally reading Blackstone's *Commentaries* from cover to cover) and passed the West Virginia bar exam in 1876 without any formal schooling.[137]

Payne started a law practice in Kingwood in Preston County, West Virginia at the age of twenty-one, soon was appointed chairman of the Preston County Democratic Committee in 1877 and served as a special judge of the Circuit Court of Tucker County and mayor of Kingwood. In 1882 he moved to Chicago and was admitted to the Illinois Bar in 1883 at the age of twenty-eight, joining as a partner the firm of Aldrich, Payne & Defrees. Charles H. Aldrich was later U.S. solicitor general under President Harrison.

From 1893 to 1898, Payne was one of the elected judges of the Superior Court of Cook County and was thereafter often referred to as "Judge Payne." His campaign literature stated that "Mr. Payne believes in the Methodist Church and the Democratic party."[138]

From 1903 to 1917, Payne was a name partner in the firm of Winston, Payne, Strawn & Shaw, a firm that exists today as Winston & Strawn LLP. He was very active in Chicago, including serving as the president of the Board of South Park Commissioners. In 1912 Payne and Hurley fought a fire in a bucket brigade at the Chicago Golf Club in Wheaton.[139]

In 1913 Payne turned down the position of U.S. solicitor general and in 1916 was mentioned as a possible candidate for secretary of war.[140] He was finally ready for service as Wilson's fireman when the United States entered the war. In relatively quick succession he went to the West Coast to aid in settling shipyard strikes in 1917, advised the commissioner of the revenue on implementation of the War Revenue Act, was counsel to the Shipping Board/Emergency Fleet Corporation, came up with the plan to nationalize America's railroads, and served under McAdoo as general counsel to the Railroad Administration.[141] In August 1919 he was confirmed as chairman of the Shipping Board and served until March 1920.

Almost immediately after he was confirmed, Payne announced plans for a permanent U.S.-flag fleet of up to two thousand vessels to include all the first-class large steel vessels built by the corporation and under construction.[142] In private February 1920 correspondence, Senator Jones indicated that "my experience with Judge Payne is that he is quite arbitrary although desiring to be fair."[143]

In the spring of 1920, Wilson asked Payne to serve as secretary of the interior. Payne only agreed because Wilson insisted and told the president "my heart is in the Shipping Board."[144] Payne also said that although "while of course gratified, as anybody would be, to go into the Cabinet, I felt a personal disappointment" leaving the board.[145]

It was reported that "Judge Payne has brought into the cabinet a new and very breezy element."[146] He was known to say, "Let's get this done, let's get it working!"[147] In 1921, Payne resigned from the Department of Interior and was appointed by President Harding as chairman of the American Red Cross which he served without salary until his death in 1935. He received numerous awards from countries all over the world for his service.[148]

In Washington, Payne lived at 1601 I Street NW, one block from Lafayette Square in a home built by Supreme Court Justice Horace Gray in 1874. The cover of the eleventh issue of *Time Magazine* featured him on May 12, 1923.[149] The cover story described him as "a man with a thoroughly American history—from Pruntytown (Va.) poverty to Chicago power, by way of labor and the law."

Payne became a major art collector. He acquired his first serious painting in 1895 as a means of collecting on a debt.[150] He had the help of Arthur Dawson, an English painter, who later painted Payne's portrait (still owned by the U.S. Department of Interior). Many of Payne's paintings came from Thomas Barbour Bryan, his father-in-law by his second marriage to Jennie Byrd Bryan in 1913. He made substantial donations from his collection over time, including forty paintings to the Commonwealth of Virginia while he was chairman of the Shipping Board.[151] That was the beginning of the collection held by the Virginia Museum of Fine Arts, the country's first state art museum.[152] In 1932, Payne donated $100,000 to construct a building for that museum.[153] Payne was also active in getting the museum located and built.[154]

When he died in 1935 just a two days shy of his eightieth birthday, the *New York Times* editorialized that Payne "had throughout the earlier periods of his life shown that interest which Pericles claimed for the Athenians—an 'interest at once in private and public affairs'" and that he "illustrated the finest type of citizenship."[155] Silas Strawn, his former law partner, was at his bedside when he died at the George Washington University Hospital, along with Dr. Cary T. Grayson, President Wilson's personal physician.[156] His funeral service was held one block from his home on I Street at St. John's Episcopal Church, which he had helped restore in memory of his second wife.[157]

Benson. Born in 1855 near Macon, Georgia, Benson was not as poor as McAdoo as a child, but like McAdoo he also felt the effects of General Sherman's march through Georgia.[158] While Benson's father and his oldest brother were away serving in the Confederate Army, Benson's family survived the Union Army occupation by driving cows into a nearby swamp and selling milk to Union soldiers. Many years later when Benson was a U.S. Navy admiral, he sat next to Gen. James H. Wilson at a dinner in Philadelphia and said to him, "I remember you, general, more distinctly than you remember me. After you captured Macon, in the spring of 1865, you established your headquarters in the building next to my grandfather's mansion. And there I called on you to get permission to sell milk to your soldiers."[159] Wilson was the Union officer who captured Confederate president Jefferson Davis.

Although Benson only had about two years of formal schooling, he decided to go to the U.S. Naval Academy at the age of seventeen. He found a congressional sponsor but then failed his mathematics entrance exam.[160] Reappointed, he passed his entrance exams but failed his first-year mathematics exams and was almost thrown out. He graduated in June 1877, forty-third out of a class of forty-six. At the academy he was known for his sense of honor and fair play, earning the nickname "Judge."[161]

Benson met his future wife, Mary Augusta Wyse, at the academy and they were married in 1879. Mary was Catholic and they were married in a Catholic church in Pikesville, Maryland. Benson later converted and was baptized in 1880, estranging him from his mother.[162] He wound up being the highest ranking Catholic in the U.S. military in World War I, which drew bigoted criticisms. In April 1920 he received a high papal award, which elicited further negative attention.[163] The *New York Times* reported in December 1922 that there were efforts to remove him from the Shipping Board because he was Catholic.[164]

Benson slowly but steadily advanced in the Navy, which was typical for the era. He was an ensign for seven years and was not promoted to lieutenant commander until July 1900. Despite multiple efforts, Benson did not manage to get a sea post during the Spanish-American War. He had several postings during his career to the U.S. Naval Academy, including as commandant of midshipmen in 1907. His last sea command was of the new dreadnought *U.S.S. Utah* from 1911 to June 1913 with the rank of captain. By that time, he was considered "one of the most qualified ship commanders in the navy."[165]

Benson was then put in command of the Philadelphia Navy Yard which meant, with the associated Navy districts, that he was in command of about five thousand Navy personnel by 1915. While at the yard, he developed a close relationship with Secretary of the Navy Daniels.

This was during a period when reform minded Navy officers publicly agitated to reorganize the Navy to make it more autonomous and coordinated to include a chief of staff like the Army. This public agitation rubbed Daniels and Wilson the wrong way, particularly the role played by Rear Admiral Bradley A. Fiske. Fiske, the secretary's aide for operations, often clashed with Daniels and went around Daniels to Congress.[166]

Congress authorized in March 1915 the chief of naval operations position "charged with the operations of the fleet and with the preparation and readiness of plans for its use in war."[167] Wilson and Daniels surprised the world by selecting Benson to be the first CNO announced on April 28, 1915.[168]

JOURNEY TO THE JONES ACT

Daniels passed over twenty-six rear admirals and five more senior captains to select Benson.[169] Benson, who was due to be promoted to rear admiral in November, was immediately made a rear admiral by virtue of his new position.

Benson was given only a few aides and a small office in the State, War, and Navy Building next to the White House (now the Eisenhower Executive Office Building).[170] He also had to find a way to work with Daniels when Benson in fact was as reform minded as many other Navy officers.

From the beginning of his service as CNO, Benson was focused on the peace after the war.[171] On the eve of the U.S. entry into the war, Benson wrote Daniels a long memorandum arguing that the United States should be prepared to assist the Allies but also anticipate their defeat by the Germans and be prepared for competing against Britain and Japan if Germany was defeated. That meant continuing the building program focused on battleships and battle cruisers authorized by the Naval Act of 1916.[172]

When the war started, Rear Adm. William S. Sims, who had been sent to London in March 1917 to serve as liaison with the Allies, took up the British point of view. He argued that the submarine was the main threat, and that the United States should divert destroyers to anti-submarine operations near Britain and warship production from battleships to destroyers. Both Benson and Daniels resisted that view, arguing that the United States had to maintain the ability to defend itself with a battle fleet, although they eventually agreed with Sims. Some of their hesitancy was due to their limited understanding early in the war of the ferocity of the German submarine campaign, which Britain had kept secret.

Benson developed good relationships with British naval officers during the war but was always first and foremost a nationalist. For example, he never agreed with Sims that U.S. and British interests were one and the same. Britain also insisted on having a fleet superior to the U.S.-fleet because of its worldwide commitments, which Benson would not accept. Daniels stated in his memoirs that "Wilson was fortunate in having so level-headed a Naval adviser in Paris as Benson, one whose Americanism was undiluted."[173] After the war, Daniels was to refer to this negotiation after the Armistice in 1918-1919 as "the Sea Battle of Paris."[174]

In early 1920, Sims precipitated a congressional investigation into Navy preparedness and the Navy's 1917 response to the submarine war which he alleged was dilatory and cost the Allies.[175] Daniels recorded in his diary that Sims "virtually indicted the whole Navy Department" and "particularly roasted Operations," meaning Benson's charge.[176]

Sims related that Benson told him before he left for Britain, "Don't let the British pull the wool over your eyes. It is none of our business pulling their chestnuts out of the fire. We would as soon fight the British as the Germans." This quote, which was widely publicized, fed Benson's general reputation of being anti-British, although nothing came of the hearings.[177]

Benson had already reached retirement age in September 1919. Once Payne was selected as secretary of interior in early 1920, Benson was selected to replace him as chairman of the Shipping Board.[178] Benson served until June 30, 1921, and then as commissioner until the end of his term in June 1928. As chairman, Benson was an active proponent of a merchant fleet sufficient to support the Navy and transport most of the country's commerce. The *New Republic*, a critic of maritime promotional programs, referred to Benson's policy as "nationalistic and belligerent," implying that "foreign ships trading at American ports must be treated with hostility, since they place our commerce under the domination of alien interests."[179]

Benson promoted the U.S. merchant marine and publicized its importance despite lagging interest during his commissioner years.[180] For example, he wrote a book about the history and need for a U.S. merchant marine in 1923 with the subtitle *A Necessity in Time of War; A Source of Independence and Strength in Time of Peace*.[181] He argued that "our only protection" in time of war was "to have an ample merchant marine under our own flag, subject to no call which has priority over our own."[182] In his recounting of the history of the merchant marine, he also noted the positive effect of the 1381 law of Richard II.[183]

Benson was seventy-three when he finally left the board and government service in 1928. He had been able to have built a comfortable home in the Embassy Row neighborhood of Washington, DC at 2420 Tracy Place NW only a few blocks from the house where President Wilson and Mrs. Wilson retired. There Benson spent his retirement enjoying visits from his children and grandchildren. Among his varied interests, he served as the president of the Army and Navy Country Club in Arlington, Virginia.

Benson died unexpectedly on May 20, 1932. It was reported at the time that the Sims controversy and his brushes with the British "served to emphasize an intense patriotism which was perhaps his outstanding characteristic."[184]

---

[1] "President Chooses the Shipping Board," New York Times, December 23, 1916, 4; L. W. Moffett, "Shipping Board Strips for Action," Marine Review 47, no. 2 (February 1917): 39–42.
[2] Moffett, "Shipping Board Strips for Action," 39; "Bernard Baker Pleased," New York Times, July 25, 1917, 2.
[3] Moffet, "Shipping Board Strips for Action," 39.
[4] Williams, Wilson Administration, 45, 54.
[5] Joseph Bucklin Bishop and Farnham Bishop, Goethals, Genius of the Panama Canal (New York: Harper & Brothers Publishers, 1930), 276 (quoting letter from Baker to President Wilson).
[6] "Quits Shipping Board," Marine Review 47, no. 3 (March 1917): 109.
[7] "B. N. Baker Quits Shipping Board," New York Times, January 28, 1917, 8; "Pick Denman as Chairman," New York Times, January 31, 1917, 10.
[8] U.S. Congress, Senate, Commerce Committee, Hearings before the Senate Commerce Comm. on the United States Shipping Board Emergency Fleet Corporation, 65th Cong., 2nd sess., vol. 1, 1918, 1105.
[9] 39 Stat. 1814 (February 5, 1917).
[10] U.S. Congress, Senate, Merchant Vessel Construction in American Shipyards, 65th Cong., 1st sess., 1917, S. Doc. 65-41.
[11] Darrell Hevenor Smith and Paul V. Betters, The United States Shipping Board, Its History, Activities and Organization (Washington, DC: Brookings Institution, 1931), 9; 40 Stat. 182, 182–85 (June 15, 1917).

[12] Williams, Wilson Administration, 68—69.
[13] "Letter from R. Lansing to W. Wilson (March 16, 1917)," Papers of Woodrow Wilson, vol. 41, 418.
[14] "Letter from E. House to W. Wilson (March 16, 1917)," Papers of Woodrow Wilson, vol. 41, 418.
[15] For example, "R.B. Stevens Named," Washington Evening Star, February 9, 1917, 7.
[16] "Farmer Gets Place on Shipping Board," Marine Review 47 (March 1917): 87.
[17] "Enlists Wooden Ships to Win War," Marine Review 47 (May 1917): 156; "Plan for Standard Ships of 3,600 Tons," New York Times, March 14, 1917, 6.
[18] "Submarine's Nemesis," New York Times, April 29, 1917, 54.
[19] Williams; "Ready to Launch Building of Fleet," New York Times, April 15, 1917, 1.
[20] "'Ford of the Seas' to Combat U-Boats," New York Times, March 9, 1917, 2.
[21] Williams, Wilson Administration, 60; Lincoln Colcord, "Landlubbers and Ships," Collier's, The National Weekly 59, no. 25 (September 8, 1917): 5-6, 27-28; Lincoln Colcord, "Shipping–The Neck of the Bottle," Collier's, The National Weekly 60, no. 12 (December 1, 1917), 4–7.
[22] "Tells the Chamber of Wood Ship Plans," New York Times, April 6, 1917, 9.
[23] U.S. Congress, House, Select Committee on U.S. Shipping Board Operations, Hearings before the House Select Committee on U.S. Shipping Board Operations, 66th Cong., 3d sess., part 13, 1920, part 13, 5114 (testimony of Edward Hurley).
[24] Hearings before the House Select Committee on U.S. Shipping Board Operations, part 8, 3188-3189 (testimony of William Denman); Bishop and Bishop, Goethals, 287 (quoting from Goethals' private papers).
[25] Hearings before the House Select Committee on U.S. Shipping Board Operations, part 8, 3188–89.
[26] Williams, Wilson Administration, 76.
[27] Williams, Wilson Administration, 76.
[28] 40 Stat. 1 (April. 6, 1917).
[29] "27 Ships Taken Here," New York Times, April 7, 1917, 1; "German Ships Seized by the Government," New York Times, April 7, 1917, 2.
[30] Benedict Crowell and Robert Forrest Wilson, The Road to France: The Transportation of Troops and Supplies, 1917-1918 (New Haven, CT: Yale University Press, 1921), vol. 2, 336. The author's grandfather–Constantinos A. Papavizas, an immigrant from Greece–enlisted in this regiment immediately after the war was declared and was honorably discharged as a sergeant at the end of the war.
[31] U.S. Navy Department, Annual Report of the Secretary of the Navy for the Fiscal Year 1918 (Washington, DC: Government Printing Office, 1918), 575–78.
[32] U.S. War Department, Annual Reports, 1919, "Report of the Chief of Transportation Service to the Secretary of War" (Washington, DC: Government Printing Office, 1920), 4865.
[33] Crowell and Wilson, Road to France, vol. 2, 346.

[34] "Letter from W. Wilson to G. Goethals (April 11, 1917)," Papers of Woodrow Wilson, vol. 42, 32; "Shipping Is Now Our Big Problem," New York Times, April 11, 1917, 1.

[35] "Goethals Ready to Serve," New York Times, April 13, 1917, 14; "Washington Rushes Plans to Get Ships," New York Times, April 14, 1917, 11.

[36] Williams, The Wilson Administration and the Shipbuilding Crisis of 1917, 78–79; "Goethals in the Right Place," Philadelphia Inquirer, April 14, 1917, 10.

[37] Bishop and Bishop, Goethals, 307.

[38] Williams, Wilson Administration, 79.

[39] "Allied Admirals Call on Daniels; Lloyd George Welcomes Us in War to Insure 'Real Peace' to World," New York Times, April 13, 1917, 1.

[40] First Annual Report of the Shipping Board, 7.

[41] Hearings before the House Select Committee on U.S. Shipping Board Operations, part 8, 3190.

[42] Williams, Wilson Administration, 96—97.

[43] W. C. Mattox, Building the Emergency Fleet (Cleveland: Penton Publishing, 1920), 18.

[44] Williams, Wilson Administration, 110.

[45] Mark H. Goldberg, The "Hog Islanders," The Story of 122 American Ships (Kings Point, NY: The American Merchant Marine Museum, 1991), 4–5.

[46] "Rush Shipbuilding, Is Senate Demand," New York Times, May 19, 1917, 16.

[47] "Ship Board Denies Clash with Goethals," New York Times, May 21, 1917, 18.

[48] "Goethals to Build Merchant Marine of Steel Vessels," New York Times, May 26, 1917, 1.

[49] Bishop and Bishop, Goethals, 323 (quoting from Goethals letter to his son); 55 Cong. Rec. 6054 (August 15, 1917) (Denman statement).

[50] "Goethals Says Wooden Ships Are Impossible," New York Daily Tribune, May 26, 1917, 1.

[51] Hearings before the Senate Commerce Committee on the United States Shipping Board Emergency Fleet Corporation, part 5, 54.

[52] For example, "Goethals to Build Merchant Marine of Steel Vessels," New York Times, May 26, 1917, 1.

[53] "Denman Rebukes Goethals for His Talk on Ships," New York Times, May 28, 1917, 1.

[54] Williams, Wilson Administration, 95; Bishop and Bishop, Goethals, 311–13.

[55] Williams, Wilson Administration, 108.

[56] 40 Stat. 182 (June 15, 1917).

[57] U.S. Congress, House, Urgent Deficiencies for Military and Naval Establishments, 65th Cong., 1st sess., 1917, H. Rep. 65-61.

[58] 55 Cong. Rec. 2531—32 (May 18, 1917).

[59] 40 Stat. 182 (June 15, 1917).

[60] Williams, Wilson Administration, 118.

61 Williams, Wilson Administration, 119–20.
62 Bishop and Bishop, Goethals, 329–30.
63 "Ship Dispute Renewed," Washington Post, June 8, 1917, 2; "Goethal's Aids Appeal to Public for Woodenships," New York Times, June 8, 1917, 1.
64 Goethal's Aids Appeal to Public for Woodenships," New York Times, June 8, 1917, 1.
65 "Goethals Ousts Aids," Washington Post, June 9, 1917, 2; "Goethals Drops Eustis and Clark from His Staff," New York Times, June 10, 1917, 1.
66 "Wooden Ships' Advocated Criticise Goethals," New York Times, June 10, 1917, 6-3.
67 Williams, Wilson Administration, 142–43.
68 "Letter from G. Goethals to W. Wilson (June 11, 1917)," Papers of Woodrow Wilson, vol. 42, 475.
69 "Letter from G. Goethals to W. Wilson (June 15, 1917)," Papers of Woodrow Wilson, vol. 42, 523.
70 Williams, Wilson Administration, 123–24.
71 Colton, "Shipbuilding History: Construction Records of U.S. and Canadian Shipbuilders and Boatbuilders," http://shipbuildinghistory.com/shipyards/emergencylarge/downey.htm.
72 "Denman Rejects Goethal's Prices," New York Times, June 18, 1917, 3.
73 Mattox, Building the Emergency Fleet, 24–25.
74 "President Denounces Profiteers; Says Fair Prices Must Prevail in War; Assails Ship Owners for High Rates," New York Times, July 12, 1917, 1.
75 Williams, Wilson Administration, 139, 148–50.
76 "Letter from W. Denman to W. Wilson (June 21, 1917)," Papers of Woodrow Wilson, vol. 42, 555.
77 Woodrow Wilson, Executive Order no. 2664 (July 11, 1917) (regarding delegation of authority to the United States Shipping Board Emergency Fleet Corporation).
78 Williams, Wilson Administration, 163.
79 "Gives Free Hand to Gen. Goethals," New York Times, July 13, 1917, 1.
80 "Denman Holds Up Goethals' Start of Ship Program," New York Times, July 17, 1917, 1.
81 "Goethals Resigns; Denman Dropped," New York Times, July 25, 1917, 1; "Letter from W. Wilson to G. Gocthals (July 19, 1917)," Papers of Woodrow Wilson, vol. 43, 211.
82 "Entry for July 7, 1917," Cabinet Diaries of Josephus Daniels, 174.
83 "President to End Ship Board Clash," New York Times, July 24, 1917; 55 CONG. REC. 6053 (August 15, 1917) (Denman statement).
84 Williams, Wilson Administration, 178–80.
85 "General Goethals a Great National Asset," Scientific American 117, no. 6 (August 11, 1917): 94.
86 First Annual Report of the Shipping Board, 5–6.

[87] For example, U.S. Congress, Senate, Commerce Committee, Hearings before the Senate Commerce Committee on the United States Shipping Board Emergency Fleet Corporation, 65th Cong., 2d sess., 1918, vol. 1, 1064–1118 and 65th Cong., 3rd sess., part 5, 1919, 53–55.
[88] For example, "Honors for U.S. Officers," New York Times, January 10, 1919, 7.
[89] R. B. Stevens, "Problems before the Shipping Board," Academy of Political Science Proceedings 7, no. 4 (February 1918): 749–55.
[90] Hearings before the Senate Commerce Committee on the United States Shipping Board Emergency Fleet Corporation, vol. 1, 25 (testimony of E. N. Hurley).
[91] Edward N. Hurley, The Bridge to France (Philadelphia: J. B. Lippincott, 1927), 28.
[92] Hearings before the House Select Committee on U.S. Shipping Board Operations, part 8, 3178.
[93] Hearings before the Senate Commerce Committee on the United States Shipping Board Emergency Fleet Corporation, vol. 1, 8–15 (a compare version of the bylaws is in the hearing record).
[94] For example, Report of Director General Charles Piez to the Board of Trustees of United States Shipping Board Emergency Fleet Corporation, Apr. 30, 1919 (Washington, DC: Government Printing Office, 1919), 7.
[95] William Joe Webb, "The United States Wooden Steamship Program during World War I," American Neptune 35, no. 4 (October 1975): 275–88.
[96] Third Annual Report of the Shipping Board, 69.
[97] S. M. Evans, A Discussion of Conditions Affecting Ship Production (Washington, DC: Government Printing Office, 1918), appendix 5 (this report on all vessel production was produced for the Shipping Board).
[98] Third Annual Report of the Shipping Board, 171.
[99] Edwin Wildman, "Edward N. Hurley–Shipbuilder to Uncle Sam," Forum 59 (April 1918): 411–23. "'Hurry Up' Hurley," World's Work 34, no. 6 (October 1917): 683–85; "The Illinois Boy Who Quit His Job and Made $1,257,000 in Five Years," St. Louis Post-Dispatch, August 19, 1917, 63.
[100] "America's Boss Riveter, Now Building Great Fleet of Ships for Uncle Sam, Was a Railroad Shop Employee at 15," Trenton Evening Times, November 4, 1917, 7.
[101] "Edward N. Hurley, Wilson Aide, Dead," New York Times, November 15, 1933, 21.
[102] James B. Morrow, "The Limelight Thrown on One of the President's Counselors," Times-Picayune, August 19, 1917, 1 (magazine section).
[103] Hearings before the Senate Commerce Committee on the United States Shipping Board and Emergency Fleet Corporation, 1917, 6 (testimony of Edward N. Hurley).
[104] "The Illinois Boy Who Quit His Job and Made $1,257,000 in Five Years," 63.
[105] Untitled, Chicago Eagle, June 28, 1913, 5; Hurley, Bridge to France, 1–15.
[106] "Edward N. Hurley," Chicago Eagle, November 1, 1913, 7.

[107] "Chairman Hurley Resigns—Says His Own Business Needs Him—Denies Friction," New York Times, January 5, 1917, 8.

[108] U.S. Congress, Senate, Cooperation and Efficiency in Developing Our Foreign Trade, 64th Cong., 1st sess., 1916, S. Doc. 64-459.

[109] Cooperation and Efficiency in Developing Our Foreign Trade, S. Doc. 64-459, 8.

[110] "Capps a Naval Inventor, Hurley a Manufacturer, and Colby a New York Lawyer," New York Times, July 25, 1917, 2.

[111] "Hurley and Capps, Who Must Provide the Ships," New York Times Magazine, July 29, 1917, 7.

[112] Hurley, Bridge to France, 18.

[113] A. Scott Berg, Wilson (New York: Berkley Books, 2013), 447.

[114] Speech Delivered by Edward N. Hurley, Chairman of the United States Shipping Board, at Delmonico's, New York, on the Evening of March 26, 1918, before the National Marine League of the U.S.A. www.ftc.gov/public-statements/1918/03/speech-edward-n-hurley-chairman-us-shipping-board; Edward N. Hurley, "Bridging the Atlantic with Ships," Scientific American 118, no. 14 (April 6, 1918): 304-305; U.S. Committee on Public Information, "Chairman Hurley, in Address to National Marine League, Tells of Work Accomplished by the U.S. Shipping Board," Official Bulletin 2, no. 268 (March 27, 1918), 12.

[115] Speech Delivered by Edward N. Hurley, Chairman of the United States Shipping Board, at Delmonico's, New York, 11.

[116] "America's Boss Riveter," Trenton Evening Times, November 4, 1917, 7; "'Hurry-Up' Hurley;" Wildman, "Edward N. Hurley–Shipbuilder to Uncle Sam," 411—23.

[117] "Chairman Hurley's Retirement," New York Times, July 12, 1919, 8.

[118] Hurley, Bridge to France, 55.

[119] Columbia University, Oral History Research Office, The Reminiscences of George Rublee (1972), 135.

[120] For example, Edward N. Hurley, "Business on the Seven Seas," System 34 (December 1918): 810–12.

[121] "Speech of April 24, 1918," quoted in Burton I. Kaufman, Efficiency and Expansion–Foreign Trade Organization in the Wilson Administration 1913—1921 (Westport, CT: Greenwood Press, 1974), 189.

[122] Safford, Wilsonian Maritime Diplomacy, 142–44.

[123] Safford, Wilsonian Maritime Diplomacy, 142–44.

[124] Edward N. Hurley, "Plan for the Operation of the New American Merchant Marine," address before the National Marine League, Commodore Hotel, New York (March 27, 1919), https://www.ftc.gov/news-events/news/speeches/plan-operation-new-american-merchant-marine.

[125] Edward N. Hurley, The New Merchant Marine (New York: Century, 1920).

[126] "Hurley Says Our Ships Can Give Good Service," New York Times, (October 31, 1921), 3.

[127] Edward N. Hurley in a letter to President Coolidge Outlines Further Reasons for Supporting the President's Plan for a Privately-Owned Merchant Marine (Chicago: Illinois Manufacturers' Association, 1928).

[128] Edward N. Hurley, The Awakening of Business (Garden City, NY: Doubleday, Page, 1920).

[129] "President Allows Hurley to Retire," New York Times, July 11, 1919, 12.

[130] "Hurley Heads Export Association," New York Times, January 28, 1930, 32.

[131] "Notre Dame Gets Gift of $200,000," New York Times, November 12, 1930, 9; Hurley also remembered Notre Dame in his will. "Will of Edward Hurley," New York Times, December 3, 1933, 2N.

[132] "Edward N. Hurley, Wilson Aide, Dead," New York Times, November 15, 1933, 21.

[133] John Toler, "The Greatest Volunteer to Humanity" and "John Barton Payne's Life of Public Service Part 2," Piedmont Lifestyle (July 1 and August 1, 2018); "An Ethic of Service and Success," Winston & Strawn, the First 150 Years (American Lawyer Media Custom Publishing, 2004), 61; "Payne's Gifts Sparked Museum," Richmond Times Dispatch, March 11, 1984, F-1; "John B. Payne Dies in Washington, 79," New York Times, January 24, 1935, 19; Thomas H. Uzzell, "Shipping Board's New Skipper," Nation's Business 7, no. 11 (November 1919): 19—20, 86; Frederic B. Crossley, Courts and Lawyers of Illinois (Chicago: American Historical Society, 1916), vol. 3, 1115.

[134] Also referred to as "Orleans" in many publications about Payne.

[135] "John Barton Payne Left $1,100,000 Estate," Chicago Daily News, January 29, 1935, 2.

[136] Brooke Payne, The Paynes of Virginia (Richmond, VA: William Byrd Press, 1937), 437.

[137] William Blackstone, Commentaries on the Laws of England (Oxford: Clarendon Press, 1765).

[138] "For the Bench," Chicago Eagle, November 4, 1893, 2.

[139] "Chicago Golf Club Fire," New York Times, August 25, 1912, C5.

[140] "Chicago Men for Cabinet?" New York Times, February 17, 1916, 9.

[141] "Advisers Named on War Tax Act," New York Times, November 29, 1917, 6.

[142] "Aims to Build Up Merchant Marine," New York Times, August 23, 1919, 18.

[143] "Letter from W. Jones to G. Kittinger (February 4, 1920)," Papers of Wesley Livsey Jones, box 183, folder 10.

[144] "Payne Succeeds Lane in Cabinet," San Francisco Chronicle, February 13, 1920, 1.

[145] Hearings before the Senate Commerce Committee on the Establishment of an American Merchant Marine, 1914.

[146] "John B. Payne, General Superintendent of the U.S.," Oregonian, July 4, 1920, 7.

[147] "John B. Payne, General Superintendent of the U.S.," 7.

[148] For example, "Belgium Honors John Barton Payne," New York Times, September 7, 1922, 3.

[149] "Foreign News: Two Lawyers," Time Magazine 1, no. 11 (May 12, 1923).
[150] "Payne's Gifts Sparked Museum," Richmond Times Dispatch, March 11, 1984, F3.
[151] "$1,000,000 Collection of Masterpieces to Virginia," Spokesman 36, no. 5 (May 1920): 143.
[152] "Payne Gift to Virginia—Shipping Board Chairman Presents 40 Paintings Worth a Million," New York Times, January 9, 1920, 16.
[153] Edwin Slipek Jr., "Open Indulgence," Richmond Style Weekly, (March 31, 2010); "Historic Mason Estate Presented to Virginia–Gov. Pollard Also Announces Gift of $100,000 for Art Museum from John Barton Payne," New York Times, February 27, 1932, 3.
[154] Elizabeth Geesey Holmes, "The Virginia Museum of Fine Arts: Its Founding, 1930—1936" (1993), MA diss., College of William and Mary (1993).
[155] "John Barton Payne," New York Times, January 25, 1935, 20.
[156] "John B. Payne Dies in Washington, 79," New York Times, January 24, 1935, 19.
[157] "Leaders of World Mourn J. B. Payne," New York Times, January 25, 1935, 21.
[158] Mary Klachko and David F. Trask, Admiral William Shepherd Benson, First Chief of Naval Operations (Annapolis, MD: U.S. Naval Institute Press, 1987).
[159] James B. Morrow, "Who Should Run Our Ships?" Nation's Business 8, no. 10 (October 1920): 15.
[160] "Became Distinguished Admiral Despite Early Flunk in Math," Evening Star, Washington, DC, October 24, 1922, 6.
[161] Klachko, Admiral William Shepherd Benson, 5.
[162] William J. Shepherd, "Faith and Freedom, Admiral William S. Benson," Potomac Catholic Heritage 24 (Summer 2013): 16–20, 16; Klachko, Admiral William Shepherd Benson, 7, 200.
[163] "Benson Given Papal Order–Admiral Decorated as a Knight of St. Gregory," Baltimore American, April 12, 1920, 12; "Admiral Benson with Cardinal Gibbons, Who Conferred Decoration on Him," Sunday Star (Washington, DC), April 25, 1920, 7.
[164] "Church Line Drawn in Fight on Benson," New York Times, December 2, 1922, 15.
[165] Klachko, Admiral William Shepherd Benson, 23.
[166] Thomas C. Hone and Curtis A. Utz, History of the Office of the Chief of Naval Operations 1915—2015 (Washington, DC: Naval History and Heritage Command, 2020), 13–17.
[167] 38 Stat. 928, 929 (March 3, 1915).
[168] "Names Capt. Benson as New Naval Chief–President Surprises Washington in Selection of First Incumbent of Powerful Office," New York Times, April 29, 1915, 6.
[169] Klachko, Admiral William Shepherd Benson, 30.
[170] Hone, History of the Office of the Chief of Naval Operations 1915–2015, 25–36.
[171] "Trouble after the War—Admiral Benson Thinks We Should Be Prepared for It Then," New York Times, June 6, 1915, 3.

[172] 39 Stat. 556 (August 29, 1916).

[173] Josephus Daniels, The Wilson Era, Years of War and after 1917—1923 (Chapel Hill: University of North Carolina Press, 1946), 370.

[174] Daniels, Wilson Era, ch. 35; Jerry W. Jones, "The Naval Battle of Paris," Naval War College Review 62, no. 2 (Spring 2009): 1–13.

[175] "Sims Attacks Daniels' Policies; Army Medal Inquiry by the House," Washington Post, January 14, 1920, 1.

[176] "Entry of January 14, 1920," Cabinet Diaries of Josephus Daniels, 484.

[177] For example, "Sims Says Benson Warned of British," New York Times, March 23, 1920, 18; "Benson Admits Cautioning Sims," New York Times, May 7, 1920, 17.

[178] "Entry of February 16, 1920," Cabinet Diaries of Josephus Daniels, 495.

[179] "Coddling Our Merchant Marine," New Republic 23, no. 299 (August 25, 1920): 352.

[180] For example, William S. Benson, "The Achievements of the Shipping Board," Pan-American Magazine 32, no. 3 (February 1921): 159–61.

[181] William S. Benson, The Merchant Marine (New York: MacMillan, 1923).

[182] Benson, Merchant Marine, 9.

[183] Benson, Merchant Marine, 8.

[184] W. S. Benson Dead; Retired Admiral," New York Times, (May 21, 1932), 15.

Launch of the SS Quistconck at Hog Island, August 5, 1918, National Archives

Chapter 20 – Shipping Board at War and in Peace

The Shipping Board and Fleet Corporation went through an enormous expansion from early 1917 to late 1918, then a period of substantial contraction that was both sudden (orders canceled) and gradual (vessels delivered for years that could not easily be canceled), and then finally were reconstituted for peace time. The enormous activity generated allegations of gross fraud, favoritism, and inefficiency which resulted in congressional investigations from 1917 to well into the 1920s.[1] But the result of the effort was undeniable. The board and corporation built a massive fleet of vessels and what to do with that fleet after the war became the overriding maritime policy question.

Mobilization

Hurley's first major step after becoming Board Chairman was to send telegrams on August 3, 1917, nine days after he was confirmed, to all U.S. shipyards requisitioning all useful vessels under construction.[2] A total of 431 vessels with a total tonnage of about 3 million DWT were initially affected.[3] Of this number, 255 were complete by October 1, 1918.[4] Hurley later wrote that "it was as if 431 bombshells... had exploded" resulting in "endless hearings" and "practically every shipyard and ship owner appeared and put up a desperate fight."[5]

The next steps were to order more vessels and to expand U.S. shipyard capacity. Before Hurley became chairman, 1.6 million tons of vessels, had already been ordered.[6] By December 1917, contracts were let for an additional 3.9 million tons. The board's goal was to deliver six million DWT of vessels in 1918 and to have the capacity to deliver between six and ten million DWT per year thereafter.[7]

There was also a massive Navy building program, which filled almost 70 percent of the capacity of the eighteen largest pre-war U.S. shipyards, including Bath Iron Works, Cramp & Sons, and Newport News Shipbuilding.[8] To expand the shipyard base, the Fleet Corporation lent funds to create or expand forty-one shipyards.[9]

As stated by the board in late 1917, "The Corporation is now engaged in what is probably the greatest construction task ever attempted by a single institution... It is controlling substantially all the shipbuilding of the country other than naval vessels, and its program calls for the completion in 1918 of eight times the tonnage delivered in 1916."[10]

Congress allocated huge sums for the effort. Ultimately, over $3.5 billion was spent by the corporation to construct and operate vessels.[11] For context, the entire federal government budget in fiscal year 1916 was about $700 million.[12]

Congress gave the board authority on October 6, 1917, to permit foreign-flag vessels and foreign-built vessels under U.S. flag to engage in the U.S. coastwise trade for the period of the war plus 120 days.[13] Alaska was excluded. The board had requested the authority to ensure that the coastwise trade was adequately served.[14] Most of the 370 permits granted were for single voyages.[15]

The corporation next requisitioned the use of all *existing* useful U.S.-flag vessels.[16] The requisition purpose was to ensure that cargoes were prioritized by a central authority and "that the nations at war with Germany may not be financially exhausted by extortionate transportation charges."[17] Approximately 500 vessels were affected, out of a total of 740 steamships in the U.S.-flag fleet as of August 1, 1917. The balance were vessels too small for effective ocean service.[18]

The corporation thereafter acted like a time charterer of the vessels where the private owners remained in physical control and employed the crew.[19] Vessels turned over to the Navy were bareboat chartered, meaning that the Navy then had to provide the crew and operate the vessels.

The corporation looked under every rock for vessels. For example, it ordered about forty vessels built of concrete.[20] It also mobilized a dozen large vessels from the Great Lakes by cutting them in half so that they could fit through the Canadian Welland Canal locks.[21] On November 15, 1917, the board looked abroad and authorized the purchase or charter of enemy vessels interned or seized in other countries such as Brazil, China, and Peru.[22]

There was more corporation tumult at the end of 1917. Admiral Capps resigned due to ill health and was replaced by Rear Admiral Frederic R. Harris who lasted only about a month before Hurley asked him to resign on December 18.[23] Senator Warren G. Harding (R-OH) took partisan advantage and advanced a Senate resolution to investigate the board.[24] Harding pointed out in support of his resolution that "judging from the press," there "is a conflict of authority and an interminable tangle of red tape."[25]

Hurley replaced Harris with Charles A. Piez, then a vice president of the corporation.[26] Piez was a mechanical engineer born in Mainz, Germany, to naturalized U.S. citizen parents. Like Hurley, he had no shipbuilding experience, having last been the president of an equipment company.

A substantial work force was needed to man and construct the corporation's fleet. The crews had to be recruited and trained at a time when every essential industry was short of personnel.[27] The International Seamen's Union membership more than doubled from about forty thousand members in July 1917 to about ninety thousand members in September 1919.[28] The corporation's training program for U.S. citizens serving as mariners had some success during the war, and U.S. citizen membership during that period increased from about 29 percent to 44 percent of the total.

A tremendous expansion of shipyard employment also occurred. There were about ninety thousand employed in U.S.

shipyards in 1917.[29] At the peak of the workforce in 1919, there were about 270,000 workers in shipyards constructing steel vessels and about 80,000 constructing wood and composite vessels which did not include another 375,000 in industrial plants manufacturing parts and components.[30] An extensive training program had to be devised and implemented for persons needed with special skills.[31]

Labor relations were often fractious.[32] Prices were rising everywhere, and wages did not always keep up. Add to that the enormous pressure to construct vessels as soon as possible with many inexperienced shipyard management teams and labor strife was inevitable. However, this danger was no worse in shipyards than in steel mills, railroads, ports etc.

To settle labor disputes, an agreement was entered into in August 1917 to establish a joint government-labor board called the "Shipbuilding Labor Adjustment Board."[33] Wilson appointed V. Everit Macy, a philanthropist active in the Westchester County, New York, to the Adjustment Board and he was elected the chairman.[34] Known as the "Macy Board," it operated until the end of March 1919.

Hurley at first insisted that the corporation should have the final say on Macy Board settlements. He eventually relented, and the Macy Board was given the authority to make binding decisions.[35] Although there were strikes, the Macy Board succeeded in providing a venue to settle disputes.[36]

Hurley blamed the high shipbuilding cost during the war, for which the board was later criticized, on the Macy Board.[37] In Hurley's view, the U.S. government paid too high a price to achieve industrial peace. Piez disagreed and wrote that "the Macy Board was the sole instrument that saved the shipyards from constantly increasing demands for wage increases and constant interruptions to the course of production."[38]

Public relations were important to the effort. Robert D. Heinl, a newspaper editor who became the head of the corporation publicity arm, used print media to publicize the building program.[39] One of the most successful publications was a pamphlet entitled "The Man of the House Is the Shipbuilder." It was meant to introduce ordinary mechanics, painters, and others to the idea that they could help to build vessels.[40] Heinl also arranged for John Philip Sousa to produce a march entitled "The Volunteers" which was played by shipyard bands.[41]

To garner further publicity, the corporation enlisted the "Four Minute Men," a national organization of volunteer speakers established by the U.S. government's Committee on Public Information.[42] This group of about twenty thousand members gave short speeches in movie theaters promoting the shipbuilding program in early 1918 prior to movie showings.

It also helped that shipyard workers had a deferral from the draft.[43] That deferral became even more important after the draft system was tightened on May 17, 1918, when a "Work or Fight" order was issued by the Army provost marshal general.[44]

The provost marshal determined that many draft eligible men were in "noneffective occupations" with respect to the war effort, such as working at hotels. These men should be required to work in a defense industry or join the U.S. armed forces.[45] This drove some professional baseball players to seek refuge by playing on shipyard teams.[46] For example, "Babe" Ruth toyed with the idea of playing for the Chester Shipyard (the former Roach shipyard) team in July 1918.[47] The provost marshal directed local draft boards to be vigilant and ensure that persons seeking deferments were genuinely employed doing defense work.[48]

Charles Dana Gibson, the American illustrator who created the "Gibson Girl," was chosen by the Committee on Public Information to enlist artists in the war effort and many created posters for the corporation.[49] His group was called the "Division of Pictorial Publicity" and they met most Fridays in New York and then adjourned to have dinner at Keen's English Chop House (still operating as "Keen's Steakhouse").[50]

By early 1918 it became obvious that there was a lack of war shipping coordination.[51] The War Department, the Navy, the

War Industries Board (charged with control and allocation of fundamental industrial materials) and other agencies and private interests each demanded vessels from the board without any central prioritization.

A shipping coordination body apparently came together when P. A. S. Franklin, then the president of IMM, arrived early for a regular Wednesday government shipping meeting in January 1918. He went to see Goethals. Hurley and Secretary Baker were already there.[52] They asked Franklin to address the shipping problem, and he "proceeded to outline a preconceived plan to pool and liquidize the entire ocean marine under a single management." The plan was accepted on the spot and Franklin was put in charge of it, paperwork to follow.[53]

Franklin returned to New York to establish an organization headquartered at 45 Broadway, the former offices of the Hamburg-American Line. He was joined by two New York admiralty lawyers, Cletus Keating, and J. Parker Kirlin, both of whom had done work for IMM.

The Shipping Control Committee was formally organized in February 1918. It comprised Franklin, Henry H. Raymond (president of the Clyde and Mallory Lines), and Sir Connor Guthrie, K. B. E., who acted as liaison to the British Ministry of Shipping.[54] Raymond was later the president of the American Steamship Owners' Association. In practice, Franklin became "the supreme dictator of American cargo tonnage of every sort."[55] As of September 30, 1918, the committee controlled a fleet of 1,356 vessels of 7.2 million DWT.[56]

The housing and local transportation situation near certain shipyards, such as in Philadelphia, became critical.[57] Hurley requested authority to build housing in the amount of $35 million.[58] The U.S. Congress authorized $50 million on March 1, 1918.[59] On April 22 Congress also authorized the takeover of local transportation systems.[60] The program made local transportation available for 125,000 shipyard workers and housing for almost 30,000 workers.[61]

JOURNEY TO THE JONES ACT

For more vessel tonnage, the Allied governments turned to the Dutch fleet. The Netherlands, surrounded by Germany and German-occupied Belgium, sought to preserve its neutrality in the face of German threats and was reluctant to make vessels available.[62] An agreement with Britain to hand over vessels voluntarily fell through by early on March 20, 1918.[63]

On that day, as soon as the final Dutch answer was received, President Wilson issued a proclamation, ordering the U.S. Navy to take over all Dutch vessels in U.S. territorial waters (87, of about 350,000 tons).[64] The takeover had been anticipated and many Dutch vessels were already without crews, which had shipped onto other vessels.[65] The U.S. government nevertheless had to repatriate nearly three thousand men. More than half went home on the liner *Nieuw Amsterdam* in late March.[66]

In contrast to the Dutch situation, the United States was able to obtain the voluntary use of vessels from several other countries, including reaching chartering agreements with Denmark, Norway, and Sweden.[67] The United States also reached an agreement with Japan in the spring of 1918 to charter vessels and to purchase vessels in exchange for one ton of steel for each deadweight ton purchased.[68] The steel sent to Japan was instrumental in expanding and rejuvenating Japan's shipyards.[69] Even with all these efforts, it took a "drastic restriction of nonessential imports" by the War Trade Board to free up the tonnage needed to sustain the war effort.[70]

It also became apparent in the spring of 1918 that the ship construction program was foundering.[71] The War Department added to the pressure by increasing the shipping requirement from 100,000 to 350,000 men per month.[72] A decision was made to bring in the best organizational talent the United States had to offer.[73]

Hurley wanted Henry Ford, but he declined.[74] At least Hurley got a camping trip out of it. In August 1918, Hurley joined Ford, Thomas Edison, Harvey Firestone, and John Burroughs on one of their annual camping trips.[75] They called themselves the "Vagabonds." Burroughs wrote about it in his 1921 book

Under the Maples.[76] He recalled that "the ship question was the acute question of the hour," and Hurley's information gave the campers "great comfort."[77]

With Ford's refusal, Hurley turned to Charles M. Schwab, the chairman of the board of the Bethlehem Steel Corporation, then the largest private shipbuilder in the world, with six U.S. shipyards.[78] Schwab, whose life embodied a rags to riches story, was as reluctant as Ford because Bethlehem was preoccupied with huge U.S. government contracts.[79] He was worried about the reception he would receive from President Wilson since he had been a noted supporter of Charles Evans Hughes in the 1916 presidential campaign. Schwab was also concerned that he would be subjected to criticisms concerning overlapping interests, since he would retain his Bethlehem ownership.[80] His concern was well-founded: he was later investigated for expense charges and for failing to oversee Bethlehem contracts profit limits.[81]

Hurley smoothed over the selection with President Wilson, but the deal was not sealed until Bainbridge Colby, then a Board commissioner, took Schwab to the White House on April 16, 1918.[82] As related by Colby, Wilson came out from a meeting to greet Schwab. Wilson apparently thought Schwab had already agreed to serve. The president "put out both hands to Mr. Schwab and spoke in acknowledgment of his sacrifices and his patriotism in a way that would have moved any man. It affected Mr. Schwab, and in that instant his doubts and hesitation were gone and he agreed to be drafted."[83]

Schwab was appointed to the newly created position of director general of the corporation.[84] Congratulations came from all over the world, including a telegram from Winston Churchill.[85] Piez remained vice president and general manager.[86] Hurley turned over the corporation's business entirely to Schwab, who served from early April 1918 until two weeks after the Armistice. All corporation matters concerning Bethlehem Steel were walled off from Schwab and handled by Piez.

JOURNEY TO THE JONES ACT

Schwab's first act was to move the corporation out of Washington, DC.[87] When the corporation was formed in April 1917, it had six employees.[88] By June 1918 it had twenty-four hundred in the home office spread out among twenty-three structures in Washington.[89] At its peak in the fall of 1918, the corporation had almost eight thousand employees.[90] Schwab moved the headquarters to 140 North Broad Street in Philadelphia.[91] As a result, the corporation moved closer to the center of East Coast shipyard activity and away from Washington interference.[92]

Schwab also made two other significant contributions. In May 1918, he began shifting vessel construction contracts from a cost-plus profit model, where the shipyard took no risk, to lump sum contracts, with cost escalators, where at least some of the risk was shifted to the yard.[93] And he took steps to boost employee morale.[94] For example, the corporation organized a July 4, 1918 simultaneous launching of ninety-four vessels around the country (including fifty-two wooden vessels). This comprised about 470,000 DWT, much more than British shipyards delivered in the entire month of July 1918 (about 210,000 DWT).[95]

The *San Francisco Chronicle* headlined the event as "Big Splash Is Death Blow to Autocracy."[96] In Philadelphia, "as each ship, freighter, transport or destroyer, splashed its way in the water, a miniature vessel sped on a glistening wire extended from the tower of City Hall to a window in the United Gas Improvement Company Building, Broad and Arch streets."[97]

In the fall of 1918, the Fleet Corporation had to deal with another problem: the outbreak of influenza known as the "Spanish flu."[98] One of the hardest hit cities in America was Chester, Pennsylvania. A special hospital was opened for the corporation's employees in Philadelphia and, because of that and other measures, the death rate was comparatively low for the corporation and its shipyards.[99]

The tonnage pressed into service was impressive, but so was the German submarine campaign. On the one hand, the United

States did not lose a single troopship going to France and back, and only lost a modest number of cargo vessels (33 out of 616) in Army service.[100] The board lost "only" 51 vessels during the war.[101]

On the other hand, the loss in aggregate Allied cargo capacity to sustain the war effort and to prevent starvation in Allied and neutral countries was acute. For the year ending June 30, 1918, the Allies and neutral nations lost about 7.5 million DWT.[102] Another 1.4 million DWT was lost from July to September 1918. By the end of 1917, the combined merchant fleets of Britain, France, and Italy had lost 25 percent of their vessels since the start the war.[103] Only about one-fourth of the losses were being replaced with new construction in those countries. It was not until August 1918 that monthly vessel deliveries exceeded monthly war-time losses.[104]

These losses gave the board the reason to set a goal of constructing 6 million DWT of vessels in 1918. Plans for a greatly increased presence in Europe formulated in the summer of 1918 nevertheless might have outrun the corporation's building schedule. General Pershing wrote to the War Department in August 1918 complaining about the lack of shipping for the 1919 war plans.[105] Consideration was given to increasing the Army in France from sixty divisions of about 2.5 million men to eighty divisions (3.4 million) and maybe even one hundred divisions (4.3 million).[106]

The needs could not be met out of existing shipyards and new green field yards were needed, both large "agency" shipyards, as they were known, like Hog Island in Philadelphia, and smaller private shipyards like the one built by the Virginia Shipbuilding Corporation in Alexandria, Virginia. These yards epitomized both the grandiosity of the vessel construction program and its many abuses, inefficiencies, and frauds.

JOURNEY TO THE JONES ACT

HOG ISLAND

Goethals laid the groundwork for a tremendous expansion of U.S. shipyard capacity before resigning from the Fleet Corporation. Just the three largest shipyards built from the ground up by the corporation in 1918 were slated to have the capacity to produce each year more vessels than the largest annual production of any country prior to 1918.[107]

Goethals led the planning for mass production of fabricated vessels, utilizing inland bridge, boiler, and tank manufacturing facilities.[108] Theodore E. Ferris designed the vessels for the corporation, both of wood and of steel.[109] When Ferris died in 1953, he was credited with directly or indirectly designing eighteen hundred vessels.[110]

Goethals involved three men from outside the corporation in his planning: Henry R. Sutphen of the Submarine Boat Corporation of Newark, New Jersey (a subsidiary of Electric Boat Company), George J. Baldwin of the American International Corporation or AIC (a 1915-formed investment trust with several subsidiaries, including Pacific Mail Steamship Company and the New York Shipbuilding Company), and W. Averell Harriman of the Merchant Shipbuilding Corporation.[111] The corporation eventually awarded a no-risk agency contract to each of these companies to build a shipyard for the corporation's account. This fueled later congressional oversight investigations.

When Goethals started on his fabrication path with these large industrial interests, Denman warned the Wilson administration that Goethals was being overly influenced by Wall Street financiers.[112] Malcolm McAdoo, Secretary McAdoo's brother, was friendly with Denman and warned Denman that the group around Goethals were a "gang of pirates."[113]

By the time Goethals resigned, draft contracts had been negotiated. The first concept was to pay a lump sum for the construction of new shipyards, including the delivery of a certain number of vessels.[114] The pricing that came back was astronomical. It had to account for the great many unknowns, so the corporation switched to an agency cost-plus model, with the profit negotiated down to about 6 percent on delivered vessels. The only check in the system to prevent price gouging on expenses that the government reimbursed would be corporation auditor review.

One of the other shipyard plans presented to Denman and Goethals came from Philip Manson, the president of the Pacific & Eastern Steamship Company.[115] That company was a paper entity formed as a joint venture with Chinese interests. Manson had been one of the few outspoken shipping proponents of the Ship Purchase Bill.[116] As shipyard plans were made, Manson recommended that the corporation build small shipyards around the country and operate them itself. Manson, who had precious little shipping experience and no shipyard experience, was politely shrugged off by Goethals and then by Admiral Capps.[117]

Manson also had a litigious history and was known to be an exaggerator and a self-promotor.[118] After his ideas were ignored by the corporation, he became an industry gadfly, criticizing the corporation's plan to build large privately managed shipyards as a huge waste of taxpayer dollars.[119]

It took a while for Hurley and Capps to pick up the pieces after Denman and Goethals resigned. Four agency yards were then authorized: AIC at Hog Island in Philadelphia; the Merchant Shipbuilding Corporation at Bristol, Pennsylvania (between Philadelphia and Trenton on the Delaware River); the Submarine Boat Corporation at Newark; and the Carolina Shipbuilding Co. at Wilmington, North Carolina.[120] The corporation estimated that when these four shipyards were operational, they would be able to deliver nearly five hundred vessels a year.[121]

By far the largest of the four would be at Hog Island, which would have fifty of the ninety-four "slipways" (meaning an inclined place where a vessel can be assembled and launched). Hog Island, purchased from a Native American tribe in 1681, was used for agricultural purposes for centuries and probably got its name from the fact that hogs roamed freely on the island.[122] Senator James Vardaman, a vocal critic of the agency shipyards, said in February 1918 that he could not miss a congressional hearing "where we are now considering Hog Island, with all that the name implies."[123]

The contract for Hog Island was signed in September 1917.[124] Fifty 7,500-DWT vessels capable of 11.5 knots speed were initially ordered, with the potential to also order 8,000 DWT combination troop/cargo vessels capable of 15 knots. AIC would purchase the property, but all the costs for constructing the shipyard would be for the corporation's account. AIC would receive a fee for each vessel delivered and rent on the real estate. The corporation had an option to purchase the real estate at cost, and if not purchased, AIC had the option to purchase the shipyard improvements at cost.

Work on the shipyard commenced on October 1, 1917. The land had become stable over time through diking and the dumping dredge spoils on the island. Even so, the corporation admitted that, in the fall of 1917 that "the Hog Island site was a low malarial swamp, infested with mosquitoes, practically uninhabited." A severe winter set back construction efforts, but the yard was nevertheless 50 percent complete by February 12, 1918, when the first keel was laid.[125]

As mentioned earlier, Senator Harding initiated Senate Commerce Committee hearings in December 1917 focused initially on Hog Island.[126] The House took up its own investigation via a Select Committee on Shipping Board Operations formed in July 1919 under the chairmanship of Joseph Walsh (R-MA). Known as the "Walsh Committee," that investigation concluded with a March 1921 report.[127] Hundreds of witnesses appeared, and a record of thousands of pages was created by the two committees (as well as other committees). The Shipping Board and corporation were some of the most congressionally scrutinized U.S. government entities in World War I.

Hog Island was the first object of congressional scrutiny because it was immediately obvious that the problems were substantial.[128] A serious congestion of rail cars in the winter of 1917/1918 caused ripple effects around the country, including residential winter coal shortages.[129] The yard became a haven for those avoiding the draft to the point that it came to be called a "resort for slackers."[130] One whistle-blower wrote that "men urinated from barracks windows; often stool anywhere on grounds" and "if more restrictions are not made, when spring comes there will be so much sickness at island no progress will be made at all."[131]

Piez wrote a forthright January 1918 report on the condition of the shipyard.[132] Arguing that vessel deliveries be made the priority by capping the yard at thirty-two slipways (which was not done), Piez concluded that:

> Hog Island was laid out on too grand a scale; that the site, considering cost, speedy completion, and accessibility, was badly chosen; that the yard should have been devoted to the construction of but a single type of vessel instead of imposing upon a new organization the task of completing two radically different types of vessel, and that the construction work should have been concentrated on a quarter of the completed plant so that this quarter might have been immediately available for the construction of vessels, thus affording an opportunity of training up an organization, which could have been effectively expanded as the remaining portions of the yard were completed.

These observations (akin to those made by Manson and rejected) were repeated as criticisms of the Hog Island shipyard throughout the congressional investigations.

The hearings also concentrated on what value AIC provided since the U.S. government paid for everything, including the salaries of AIC employees working on the project. Representative Irvine Lenroot (R-WI) said that "the only 'know how' that they [AIC] have furnished the Government is knowing how to loot the Treasury, and they have been exceedingly successful in that."[133] Vardaman commented that Hog Island "was conceived in the greed for gain, brought forth in a gush of mock patriotism, and swaddled in the American flag."[134]

These criticisms were leveled even though AIC was associated with Stone & Webster, a large, prominent, and well-regarded engineering concern.[135] In a December 1918 Department of Justice investigation report, "the strong engineering organization of Stone & Webster" was cited as one of the attributes AIC brought to the table. The report also noted AIC's ability to spend its own money as necessary without relying on the U.S. government's reimbursement (which was notoriously late).[136]

Other criticisms were leveled at the price paid for the real estate, the fact that the suppliers who provided materials at exorbitant prices were represented on AIC's Board of Directors, and that the AIC payroll was padded.[137] Probably the most serious problem was that the shipyard was behind schedule. Senator Hiram W. Johnson (R-CA) summarized the view of many senators: "The extravagance at Hog Island we could forgive if we got the ships, but when we do not get the ships and we have the extravagance too, that is the particular place where I feel we have a right to have some little irritation."[138]

The corporation reacted to the disorganization by appointing Adm. Francis T. Bowles on February 1, 1918, to assume control of the shipyard. Hurley instructed Bowles to be on alert for irregularities and to call for investigations if needed.[139] Piez praised his work in "'taking the slack out of everything'" in his first few weeks.[140] President Wilson followed with a February 12 request that led to the Justice Department report just mentioned.[141]

AIC's management was unapologetic. George Baldwin blamed the loss of two and a half months on the Denman/Goethals controversy.[142] Baldwin insisted that AIC had performed well, despite being asked to do a five-year job in twenty-two months under war-time conditions. Charles A. Stone, AIC's chairman, invited the fullest inquiry in connection with the referral to the Justice Department.[143]

AIC also launched a public relations campaign. The company invited a *New York Times* reporter to the yard in February 1918 who parroted the company's public relations messages.[144] Then the general press was let into the shipyard for the first time for a flag-raising event on Washington's Birthday, on February 22, 1918.[145] A subsequent critic of the Hog Island project wrote that "the day's exposure was an utter masterpiece of public relations expertness."[146] The *New York Times*, for example, was won over, concluding that, despite the expense which would probably be found excessive, "there is no doubt of the magnitude and success of the undertaking."[147]

AIC engaged Commander Stevenson Taylor, the president of the American Bureau of Shipping (the leading U.S. vessel classification society), to review project progress.[148] Taylor defended the scope of the program saying that "there is only one thing that will win this war, and that is the building of ships, ships and more ships, ships and more ships; and anything that stops that program is criminal, in my estimation."

AIC also invited the Commerce Committee to Hog Island and five senators, including Senators Harding, Vardaman, and Johnson, attended.[149] They started by eating the 30¢ meal at the shipyard cafeteria. Harding was impressed, calling it "infinitely better than any 30-cent meal I was ever able to get." He was also satisfied with the yard's progress. Vardaman continued to criticize "a number of indefensible, unwise and extravagant things," accusing AIC of pursuing the work "for the money there was in it, and to make every penny they can."

It was not until August 5, 1918, that the yard was finally able to launch a vessel. Mrs. Wilson (the president's second wife), a descendant of Pocahontas, was accorded the privilege of naming the Hog Island vessels. She selected *Quistconck* for the first vessel, "the ancient Indian name of the island."[150]

JOURNEY TO THE JONES ACT

The *Philadelphia Inquirer* estimated that there were one hundred thousand in attendance at the launching and four hundred collapsed from the heat as the temperature reached 105 degrees Fahrenheit.[151] The first lady christened the vessel at the event which cost $38,000.[152] "Mrs. Wilson was wearing a dress of lavender-gray chiffon voile, with black velvet trimmings" and "the President, 'the coolest-looking man in sight,' as some remarked, was in natty white flannels." Intense planning resulted in a flawless event, despite rumors that the vessel would sink upon launching.[153] These rumors persisted for months, claiming the vessel was unseaworthy and had to be immediately drydocked. Both claims were false.[154]

Later it was determined that the vessel was only about 65 percent complete when launched, and she was not in fact delivered until December 3, 1918. This received unfavorable congressional attention.[155] Questions were even raised about the necessity of the U.S. government spending $38,000 on a party.[156] The much-maligned *Quistconck* changed owners several times, but she was a stout vessel and was not scrapped until 1953.[157]

The Justice Department issued its report in response to the president's request on September 12, 1918.[158] The Wilson administration did not make it public until December 20, 1918, inviting accusations that it was being suppressed.[159] Justice concluded "that the facts do not justify criminal process." The report, however, called out many instances of waste and mismanagement. Most damning was a comparison of Hog Island to the Bristol and Newark shipyards, constructed contemporaneously and with the same conditions. Justice determined that the cost at Hog Island per slipway was two to three times as expensive as the other agency yards.

The Justice Department excoriated AIC for not implementing a system of ensuring what was being paid for things. The department found that the condition of the yard prior to February when Admiral Bowles took over was "an 'organized riot,' 'tangled mess,' or 'state of chaos'" and recommended that AIC be taken to arbitration to determine if money should be recovered from AIC. This never occurred.

Hog Island did, eventually, hit its stride. The largest shipyard in the world encompassed 250 buildings (including a hospital, YMCA, hotel, cafeteria, and trade school), 80 miles of standard rail track utilized by 20 locomotives, and a water frontage of 20,000 feet. Fifty vessels could be assembled at one time with berths for another twenty-eight to be outfitted. At its peak, the yard employed about thirty-four thousand men.[160]

Hog Island launched sixty-two cargo vessels (referred to as "Type A") and four combination cargo/transports (referred to as "Type B") in 1919. By the time the last vessel was delivered in January 1921, 110 Type As had been delivered along with 12 Type Bs.[161] The balance of the initial orders was canceled.

The vessels that came to be known as "Hog Islanders" were generally regarded as the ugly ducklings of the sea. They had a vertical bow and were squared off in so many ways to facilitate assembly construction. From a distance, it was difficult to determine which was the bow and which was the stern. Joseph P. Cotton, effectively the general counsel to the corporation during Goethal's tenure and McAdoo's eventual law partner, said in congressional testimony that "this fabricated ship looks like a skyscraper lying down on its side."[162]

The Hog Islanders were practical vessels and there was no shortage of buyers for them after the war, although the U.S. government did not recover its costs.[163] One of the leading commercial owners was Lykes Bros. Steamship Company which purchased seventeen. Six Type A vessels were transferred to the Navy—all of them survived World War II.[164] Many of the other Hog Islanders saw service in World War II and were lost in action. Seven of the Type Bs became commercial passenger/cargo vessels. The last surviving Hog Islander, originally named the *Scantic* and delivered in June 1919, was scrapped in 1971.[165]

Hog Island continued to be criticized for years after the war was over. P. A. S. Franklin argued that "it would have been a great mistake for the E.F.C. [Emergency Fleet Corporation] not to have provided a shipyard like Hog Island in the serious emergency that existed in shipping" and the shipyard "was of great value in helping to win the war, both in giving moral assistance to our allies and in alarming our enemies."[166]

Hurley, Piez, and Schwab settled on similar themes. Hurley argued in his memoirs that the corporation would not have been able to meet the needs of a hundred-division or even an eighty-division Army in France—even with all the agency shipyards at full production.[167] In his memoirs, Hurley wrote that "the one-hundred-division program would have swamped us hopelessly!" and "we never could have caught up with the arrears of 1918 and 1919."[168] Privately, Hurley laid the blame for the troubles at Hog Island to the selection of the site "by another administration," meaning Denman/Goethals.[169]

Piez argued that criticisms were "uninformed" and that "as a war undertaking, with the vast possibilities of production and the moral effect secured from the magnitude of the undertaking, this gigantic enterprise is not subject to criticism." Schwab may have summarized Hog Island's place in the war effort best when he said that "Hog Island suffered from the same cause that harmed other war industries—the fact that the war ended before it had an opportunity to prove its real value."[170]

On February 14, 1920, the Shipping Board purchased the land from AIC for $1.7 million and paid $2 million for canceled contracts.[171] No productive use could be found for the yard in the 1920s, and it was finally sold to the City of Philadelphia in 1930 for $3 million.[172]

Hog Island eventually became the site of the Philadelphia International Airport. The most enduring legacy of the shipyard may be the term "hoagie," since the submarine meat sandwiches brought by immigrants to the shipyard may have acquired that Philadelphia name through association with the island.[173]

Charlie Papavizas

Virginia Shipbuilding Corporation

Hog Island was not the only shipyard to create controversy. Congressional investigations of war profiteering during and after the war targeted shipyards all over the country. One of those yards stood out: the Virginia Shipbuilding Corporation shipyard in Alexandria, Virginia started by the financial scoundrel Charles W. Morse.

Morse was born in 1856 into a prominent Bath, Maine shipping and shipbuilding family.[174] He was the first Morse to attend college, graduating from Bowdoin College in 1877. In college, Morse negotiated ice trades, earning him a tidy sum by the time he graduated. After graduating, he formed his own firm and went to New York in 1880. At the time, ice blocks were an essential commodity for the summer and the principal sources for New York and New England were upstate New York and Maine.

Morse figured out how to form companies, sell shares with just IOUs in return, and then use the stock proceeds as collateral to finance the companies with bank debt. He started rolling up New York ice handling/storage companies in exchange for stock and married the operation to New York City political interests.[175] He took control of the city ice businesses one by one, and his political allies restricted access to New York from other ice sources. In that way, he doubled the prices in 1900 and quickly became known as the "Ice King."[176] There was a public uproar, Morse backed off and was later forced out of the American Ice Company—but only after he had made millions.

Morse's new wealth permitted him to live in a four-story brownstone at 724 Fifth Avenue in Manhattan between Fifty-Sixth and Fifty-Seventh Streets on what was known as "Vanderbilt Row."[177] In 1911, Morse sold the house, which was replaced in 1923 by a twelve-story office building. It still exists across the street from the Trump Tower.[178]

Morse used the same worthless stock methods to amalgamate coastal/river passenger vessel lines from 1901 to 1907. His lines served the East Coast, Albany to New York City, and

JOURNEY TO THE JONES ACT

Puerto Rico in the "Hudson Navigation Company," adding the titles "Steamship King" and "Admiral of the Atlantic Coast" to his name.[179]

Morse then moved on to banking. By 1907 he had bought stock in thirty-one banks.[180] His pyramid of interlocking banks, all propped up with paper assets or depositor's accounts, collapsed in October 1907 when a drop in copper prices triggered a run on the banks. Morse had a lot to do with the nationwide "Financial Panic of 1907" and was prosecuted by Henry L. Stimson, the assistant attorney general for the Southern District of New York, in 1908 for bank fraud (Stimson was secretary of war from 1911 to 1913 and again from 1940 to 1945 and secretary of state from 1929 to 1933). Morse was found guilty and sentenced to federal prison in Georgia for fifteen years.

During this time, Morse was front-page news with headlines such as "Meteoric Career of Ice King Morse is Unparalleled."[181] Morse blamed New York governor Teddy Roosevelt for singling him out for prosecution and argued that he did not do anything different than many other New York bankers.[182] Morse felt that Roosevelt needed a scapegoat for the "Panic."[183]

While in prison, Morse never stopped working the angles. In addition to conducting a multi-pronged public relations campaign to put pressure on President Howard Taft to pardon him, he found a way to engage in financial speculation, and mentoring fellow prisoner Carlo "Charles" Ponzi.[184]

After two years in prison, Morse appeared to become seriously ill; several doctors who examined him reported that he was near death. Morse may have poisoned himself with soap or other chemicals so as to mimic kidney failure.[185] President Taft, who had resisted prior efforts to pardon Morse, relented and signed a pardon on January 18, 1912.[186] The pardon process was helped along by two attorneys, Thomas B. Felder from Georgia and Henry M. Daugherty, a former two-term congressman from Ohio who was instrumental in getting Taft the 1908 Republican party presidential nomination (and later Harding the 1920 nomination).[187]

Felder and Daugherty were promised a substantial success fee if Morse was pardoned. After being pardoned, Morse had a "miraculous" recovery and immediately went on a long trip to Europe.[188] Taft was "chagrined" and later wrote about the Morse pardon (which was issued in tandem with another mercy pardon), "Well, one of them kept his contract and died, but the other seems to be one of the healthiest men in the community today."[189]

Morse did not pay the promised success fee.[190] Much later, Daugherty got his revenge as the U.S. attorney general in the Harding administration, when he brought an indictment against Morse in 1922 for war profiteering.[191]

Morse slowly reestablished himself after he was pardoned.[192] Morse again took over Hudson Navigation and opened a Wall Street office "to begin what was termed a campaign of reprisal against his business enemies."[193] One of those opportunities was buying thirteen vessels in 1916 when the Interstate Commerce Commission ordered railroads to divest vessels on the Great Lakes.[194]

Morse also rode the shipbuilding gravy train. He purchased in 1916 the Noank Shipyard near New London, Connecticut, with three wooden slipways and a farm near Groton. There, he intended to build six slipways which he combined in a company called Groton Iron Works. Groton signed its first contract with the Fleet Corporation on June 15, 1917 ("Contract no. 15"), to construct twelve Ferris-design wooden hulls. He signed his second contract on August 11 to construct six steel vessels of 8,800 DWT each.[195]

On December 7, 1917, Groton Iron Works obtained another contract to construct twelve steel 9,400-DWT vessels at a shipyard site in Alexandria, Virginia. Groton Iron Works was responsible for providing whatever funds were necessary to construct the shipyard, a commitment Morse would not keep.

It is unclear how Morse, given his notorious history, managed to get government shipbuilding contracts.[196] Representative Charles C. Carlin (D-VA), the local Alexandria congressman and the manager of the 1924 Underwood presidential campaign, appears to have been instrumental with the Virginia contract.[197]

Carlin had proposed to the Fleet Corporation that "Battery Cove" in Alexandria, Virginia be investigated as a possible shipyard location. Carlin also suggested that Morse consider the location to build steel vessels and interceded with the Fleet Corporation on Morse's behalf.[198] The award of contracts to Groton Iron Works was reportedly opposed by Piez and Admiral Bowles.[199] Morse claimed that he was asked by the "Shipping Board, or some of the then officers of it" to build the Connecticut and Virginia shipyards.[200] It was also alleged in a subsequent fraud case that McAdoo had a hand in obtaining the contracts for Morse.[201]

On January 2, 1918, the Virginia contract was assigned to another Morse company with a new name: Virginia Shipbuilding Corporation (VSC).[202] On February 7, 1918, VSC acquired forty-seven acres of infill land at "Jones Point" on the Potomac River to build a shipyard with four slipways.[203] The site is now a park underneath one end of the Interstate 95 Woodrow Wilson Memorial Bridge across the Potomac River. Almost nothing is left of the shipyard. The vessels to be constructed there were to be the first large steel vessels ever constructed on the Potomac.[204]

In the spring VSC announced a local contest to give the Alexandria shipyard a motto to inspire production. The winning slogan, suggested by Mrs. Isabel F. Fornshill of Queen Street, was "More Tons, Less Huns." It was displayed in an 18 x 20 foot red, white, and blue illuminated sign at the yard's entrance.[205] Mrs. Fornshill's winning slogan beat out "O U Boats!" and "Each Boat We Float Gets Wilhelm's Goat."[206] The prize was $10.

The first slipway was completed in eighty-five working days.[207] VSC claimed that was a world record.[208] By April 1918, there were eleven hundred men working at the yard, a number that eventually rose to thirty-five hundred. On May 30, 1918, President Wilson came to dedicate the shipyard, with Representative Carlin playing the role of master of ceremonies. Wilson drove the first rivet at the event, which was attended by more than one thousand onlookers.[209] The first vessel was named by Mrs. Wilson the *Gunston Hall*, after the home of George Mason located south of the yard on the Potomac River.

Of the ten vessels eventually launched, none was delivered before the Armistice. The first vessel, which was supposed to be delivered by early October 1918, was delivered in June 1919. The second to last vessel, named the *Colin H. Livingstone*, was not delivered until October 1920.[210] Livingstone was the president of VSC, formerly Senator Elkins's private secretary, and then also the president of the Great Falls and Old Dominion Railroad (later the Washington and Old Dominion Railroad) running from Washington, DC to Great Falls, Virginia. The very last vessel, the *Georgie M. Morse*, was launched on November 20, 1920—more than two years after the end of the war.[211] She was never delivered.[212]

The vessels constructed by VSC proved unlucky, although the Fleet Corporation was satisfied with the workmanship.[213] Four of the vessels constructed in 1919 wound up being owned by the corporation because of VSC's financial troubles and were scrapped in 1930.[214] Four of the remaining five were sold to third parties and served in World War II commercial service but were lost in hostile action by 1943. The *Livingstone*, for example, then under the name *Empire Moose*, fell behind the convoy it was supposed to be a part of on August 29, 1940. It was torpedoed and sank northwest of Ireland.[215] The crew arrived safely in Killybegs County, Donegal.

The Alexandria shipyard was thinly capitalized from the beginning. A senior corporation employee wrote in October 1919, "from the time I first became connected with the Fleet Corporation, the Morses were in need of finances and therefore their problems were being constantly discussed."[216] Charlie Morse was the chairman of the board of VSC, and the two vice presidents were one of Morse's sons and a cousin.

VSC was aided for a while by Schwab, who appears to have been acquainted with Morse.[217] Schwab helped push through an April 1918 Fleet Corporation loan to VSC to construct the shipyard, secured by a mortgage on the yard.[218] VSC had run out of funds by then because of its thin capitalization.[219]

Then the Fleet Corporation staff withheld progress payments. Under the letter of the contract, the government funds spent exceeded the physical state of vessel construction.[220] Schwab directed the release of progress payments, which continued until the end of the war.[221] VSC later complained that it was unjustifiably denied progress payments despite allegedly meeting construction milestones.[222]

VSC, like many shipyards built on green fields, was beset from the beginning by a housing shortage. A separate Morse entity purchased a large part of the Rosemont section of Alexandria in June 1918 to build houses to sell and rent to VSC employees.[223] The problem was that the money for housing came from money provided by the government meant for vessels.

The corporation started an investigation regarding the misuse of funds in November 1918.[224] Investigators concentrated on J. H. Phillip Reinhardt, one of the two corporation auditors at the yard. The investigators determined that Reinhardt and a fellow auditor "were extremely loose, to put it mildly, in their methods of handling the vouchers" for government reimbursement.[225] The investigation also revealed that Reinhardt was accepting regular payments and trips from VSC to approve all vouchers, and that he knew he had approved vouchers for shipyard expenditures, which went to the Rosemont project, as well as a boat and car for Morse's son (among other things).[226]

VSC refused to cooperate with the investigation, and the corporation again stopped making progress payments.[227] The corporation commenced an audit in July 1919, determining that the diversion of funds for Rosemont was not against the letter of the contract but had left the yard with insufficient funds.[228] This came to public light in the Walsh Committee hearings in the spring of 1920.[229] The results of the Fleet Corporation's investigation were turned over to the Justice Department in October 1919. The corporation refused a second loan to VSC unless additional security could be provided, and Morse offered additional security based on a convoluted vessel sale scheme.[230]

In September 1919 a contract settlement was negotiated on behalf of VSC by McAdoo and Cotton, then in private practice, which cleared the air for a short time.[231] Things did not work out as agreed, and McAdoo received backlash for years for representing a known swindler wasting government funds.[232] In a June 1922 letter to President Wilson, McAdoo wrote that he never represented Morse personally and there was nothing untoward about representing VSC.[233]

Another contract settlement occurred in July 1920.[234] The last vessel was launched in November 1920 and relations again became acrimonious. VSC sued the board in December, seeking to recover funds VSC claimed were due and unpaid.[235] Although VSC had moderate success in court, claims by its creditors caught up with the company and VSC filed for bankruptcy in April 1921.[236]

Not long after, the board commenced a new investigation of Morse, made public on November 30, 1921.[237] On December 1, alerted that a fraud indictment was coming from a grand jury in Washington, DC, Morse made his way anonymously onto a French vessel bound for Le Havre.[238] His escape, however, was foiled as he was met in Le Havre by French police and avoided arrest only by agreeing to sail back to New York as soon as possible.[239]

Morse, his three sons, and four others were indicted at the end of February 1922 (with Daugherty as the U.S. attorney general).[240] This was a period when the Justice Department was aggressively pursuing war-time contractors for profiteering and fraud.[241] Numerous Fleet Corporation related officials testified including Goethals, McAdoo, and Schwab.[242]

While pointedly looking at Morse's three sons, Schwab joked in his testimony that sons should not be hired in a family business and remarked that "he had rarely met Charles W. Morse when he was not looking for a loan."[243] Morse's attorney argued that Fleet Corporation should be on trial, not Morse, at which point Morse "wept copiously."[244] The trial lasted fifteen weeks. The jury was out almost twenty hours before finding all the defendants not guilty. Morse's counsel said that Daugherty was "responsible for this indignity to Mr. Morse."[245]

Still, the U.S. government had the last symbolic laugh, winning a civil suit against VSC in 1925 with a judgment of $11.5 million.[246] Morse was also indicted for mail fraud in connection with stock transactions involving VSC-related business entities.[247] Morse's wife died in July 1926; soon thereafter Morse suffered what is likely a series of strokes and was placed under guardianship by his sons.[248] The other defendants were acquitted in December 1926.[249]

Morse lived his last years in his sister's home in Bath, Maine, and died in January 1933 at the age of seventy-seven with only a small estate.[250] According to his obituary, "he appeared in the financial sky like a meteor, often leaving a searing path."

In February 1935 Parker Brothers released the board game *Monopoly*. The likeness on the "Community Chest" and "Chance" cards (of a man with a mustache and top hat) has been said to bear "a strong resemblance to Charlie Morse."[251]

Demobilization and the Paris Peace Talks

The sudden end of hostilities with the signing of the Armistice in November 1918 caught the Shipping Board flat-footed. Hurley had enunciated a vision of using the war-time fleet as a means of supporting U.S. peacetime commerce and of remaining a world shipbuilding power.[252] But now that the war was over, the board had no plan, much less a political consensus to accomplish that. That void was ultimately filled by the 1920 Merchant Marine Act. In the meantime, the board had to deal with the tremendous near-term demands for vessels and the need to adjust shipyard capacity to the new peacetime reality. Simultaneously, the board followed Wilson's lead to use a U.S. government fleet as a peace agreement bargaining chip.

The first order of business was getting the U.S. Army (including the war dead) home. A sizable fleet was still needed for that purpose well into 1920.[253] On November 11, 1918, the Shipping Board controlled a fleet of about twelve hundred vessels, of which about six hundred were in direct Army or Navy service.[254] The Army transported home the last large group during the first part of 1920 bringing back about 500,000 men, equipment, and supplies utilizing almost 170 vessels.[255] By the end of that time, all but twenty-five vessels directly controlled by the Army had been turned over to the board.

Although repatriation of the Army had priority, there was also substantial pressure to release vessels for commercial service. International trade was needed to sustain U.S. employment as defense industries were winding down.[256] This conflicted with an informal administration policy not to unduly antagonize Britain by aggressively pursuing markets. As put by Secretary of Commerce William Redfield, the administration planned to "go after trade in a normal way" and not "play the hog with our feet in the trough and our eyes on the ground."[257]

Substantial friction had arisen during the war between the United States and Britain over vessel access, leading to open mutual distrust.[258] The bad feelings had started with neutrality disputes going back to the *Dacia*. There had also been numerous flash points after the United States entered the war, including the board's refusal to turn over control of its vessels for Allied operation.

The situation was not improved with a Hurley publicity campaign in 1918 to develop U.S. enthusiasm for a substantial merchant marine after the war. For example, Hurley wrote an August 1918 article for the *Saturday Evening Post* entitled "Why Our Ships Will Now Stay on the Ocean."[259] The U.S. press openly speculated as to "Who Shall Be Mistress of the Sea" after the war.[260] Even the Germans were attuned to the friction and dropped leaflets warning British troops that "what is the use of winning the war at the expense of our commerce, and so that Americans collar it?"[261]

To respond to commercial demands, and in accord with its pre-war commitment, the Shipping Board on January 6, 1919, released requisitioned vessels not over 4,000 DWT to their private U.S. owners.[262] Vessels were still subject to board approval of rates and routes. By June 30, 1919, 457 vessels had been returned to the control of the owners. The Scandinavian and Dutch vessels were all redelivered by November 1919.

The need for famine relief increased the pressure on the fleet needed for Army repatriation and U.S. commercial needs. Herbert C. Hoover, who had served as chairman of the Commission for Relief in Belgium (a private organization) and the head of the federal Food Administration during the war, was also appointed director of the American Relief Administration formed on February 24, 1919, to provide famine assistance in Europe.[263]

Hoover and Hurley, who had sailed together to Europe on November 16, 1918, often clashed about shipping priorities.[264] While Hoover kept demanding more vessels, Hurley sought to balance commercial needs with famine relief. This was, in part, to forestall U.S. unemployment and U.S. social unrest by keeping up demand for U.S. exports.[265] Hoover did not credit these considerations and wrote that Hurley "could not resist the great pressure from American exporters for ships."[266]

Hoover pressed his case with President Wilson, who sent a March 22, 1919, telegram to Hurley and Secretary of War Newton Baker ordering an all-out effort to get food to northern Europe. Wilson pointed out that "the human, political and military issues that revolve upon any failure of delivery of this program are incalculable."[267] On March 27, Hoover wrote to Wilson that "every country that we have under relief is rumbling with social explosion."[268] The famine relief effort reached its peak in May 1919. About 260 vessels were dispatched and were successful in stabilizing the food situation despite Hoover's criticisms.[269]

Another pressing issue was what to do with the corporation's construction program. The first step was to suspend construction to determine whether it was more economical to abandon a vessel or finish it for potential sale.[270] This was easier said than done. The corporation had to adjudicate twenty-two hundred vessel cancellation claims involving $850 million in contracts after the war ended.[271]

On December 12, 1918, the prohibition against transfer of wooden vessels to foreign registry was removed, but the restriction on steel vessels remained. On December 16 Senator Jones offered a resolution to require a report from the board on the construction of vessels for foreign account.[272] The board responded without elaboration that the foreign order ban remained "in force temporarily by direction of the President."[273]

Jones complained that permission for the sale of wooden vessels had come too late and that Washington State had lost substantial orders to Canada.[274] He was also upset that no reason was being given for not selling steel vessels to foreign buyers. Seeking to break the impasse, Jones introduced legislation in January 1919 to freely permit foreign sales, which passed the Senate by consent on February 28, 1919.[275]

The unstated reason for not permitting foreign sales was that Wilson wanted to use U.S. economic might as leverage in achieving U.S. peace aims.[276] This would include U.S. ship construction capacity and a substantial U.S. government-owned merchant marine. As recorded by Secretary of the Navy Josephus Daniels just before the Armistice, Wilson said, "'I wish no ships & nothing done till peace. I intend to carry as many weapons to the peace table as I can conceal on my person... I will be cold & firm. GB [Great Britain] selfish.'"[277]

JOURNEY TO THE JONES ACT

The strategy fed into the fears of the other Allies. As Hurley wrote to Wilson on December 12, 1918:

> In all the conferences I have had on this side, I have been impressed with the fact that it is not the League of Nations, nor an International Court, nor even Freedom of the Seas that is feared by Lloyd-George, Clemenceau, Orlando [leaders of Britain, France, and Italy] or their associates. What they are thinking about, as you are probably already aware, is the increased power of our shipping, commerce and finance.[278]

The strategy nevertheless could only work for a limited time. Not only was there U.S. domestic political pressure to sell vessels abroad, but Britain also was hitting its vessel construction stride.[279]

The White House announced on November 18, 1918, that the president would go in person to attend the peace negotiations in Paris.[280] Wilson had already sent Hurley to get access to German vessels still blockaded in Germany by the British for purposes of the famine relief effort.

The U.S. Senate changed hands in the November 5, 1918, election, which is how Wesley Jones became chairman of the Commerce Committee in 1919. Knowing that Republicans would control Congress in the spring put additional pressure on Wilson to get a peace deal as soon as possible. It also worked against his aims since the Allies were aware of his timing problem.

Wilson amped up the pressure by increasing the power of the Shipping Board on December 3, 1918, to raise and lower freight and terminal charges to meet foreign competition.[281] Hurley announced plans on December 26 to establish shipping offices around the world to support a national fleet. Other announcements followed, including one concerning the establishment of a fleet of 15 million DWT.[282] The implication was that the U.S. government would be willing to use its vessels and rates to capture trade lanes at will.[283]

Board decisions had devolved to John H. Rosseter, corporation director of operations, with Hurley and Wilson in France and Stevens (the board vice chairman) in London.[284] Rosseter had been the long-serving Pacific Mail Steamship Company vice president and general manager before he joined the corporation.[285] When he was appointed, it was reported that one of Rosseter's "greatest ambitions is to make the United States a maritime power of the first magnitude."[286]

Rosseter took direction from Wilson and Hurley to meet Allied maritime competition by getting vessels into commercial service as soon as possible.[287] He also drastically cut freight rates to meet British competition. This was a policy opposed within the administration by Secretary of Commerce Redfield and others, including Commissioner Stevens.[288] Stevens argued that cutthroat shipping competition between the United States and Britain would cause economic instability and harm other countries.

One episode illustrates the commercial rivalry that had developed between the United States and Britain. Over the winter of 1918-1919, there was a severe coal shortage in many countries such as Italy, which had been a traditional market for German coal.[289] The U.S. government offered to ship American coal in U.S.-flag vessels to Italy in part to avoid social unrest in U.S. coal fields.[290] But in early 1919, apparently fearing the snatching of a potential market from British coal producers, Britain threatened to stop its deliveries of coal to the U.S. Army in Europe if the U.S. plan proceeded.[291]

The International Mercantile Marine Company served as another flash point.[292] The British government had requisitioned vessels owned by IMM at the outset of the war. After the signing of the Armistice, Britain put pressure on the British management of IMM to sell those eighty-five vessels to a British syndicate.[293] It was only at that time that the U.S. government discovered the full extent of the agreement J. P. Morgan had entered into with Britain.[294] U.S. policy makers, including McAdoo, Hurley, and Colby, were outraged and advised Wilson to buy the vessels.[295]

JOURNEY TO THE JONES ACT

This issue became mixed up with the fate of the German fleet seized by the United States and the vessels interned in Germany during the war. On December 1, 1918, Wilson informed the Allies that the 2.6 million tons of German and Austrian vessels in belligerent ports should all be turned over for famine relief.[296] The president was also adamant that the vessels seized in the United States would not be divided among the Allies particularly given how much effort the country had put into repairing and refurbishing the vessels.[297]

An agreement was reached on March 17, 1919, known as the "Wilson-Lloyd-George Agreement" at Brussels.[298] The Allies conceded the U.S. position on the seized vessels (although the United States had to pay into the reparations fund an amount approximating the vessel's value) and the United States temporarily obtained an additional eight German liners to use to return American troops. The balance of the German vessels was slated initially for German famine relief and then later to be divided among the Allies.[299] The U.S. government subsequently quietly abandoned its plan to purchase the IMM vessels.[300]

Meanwhile, in spring 1919, the pressure to provide relief for U.S. shipyards was building. In the first June Senate Commerce Committee hearing on merchant marine policy with Jones as chairman, the main theme was when the administration would permit the construction of vessels in the United States for foreign owners (discussed in the next chapter).[301] Piez had criticized the cancellation policy at his retirement dinner on April 30, 1919, arguing that it would have been better to finish the vessels and lay them up than cancel the program.[302] A parade was also organized in Philadelphia of about seventy thousand shipyard workers on May 18 to urge support for a continued shipbuilding program. Hurley was allowed to lead the parade because of his membership in the Brotherhood of Locomotive Engineers.[303]

The United States also attempted to get international agreement to abide by the 1915 Seamen's Act standards.[304] Hurley was one of two U.S. representatives to the Commission on International Labor Legislation that met in Paris in early 1919. He recommended all nations abide by the Seamen's Act standards and adopt "international uniformity of freight rates."[305] The Allies viewed the whole effort as an attempt by the United States to increase everyone else's labor rates, and unsurprisingly the U.S. effort ran into stiff resistance.[306]

Furuseth predicted that "the effort at the coming Peace Conference will be to nullify this law and thus shut out a very serious competitor on the ocean."[307] He was right. The Labor Commission report to the Paris Peace Conference presented on April 11, 1919, refused to outlaw imprisonment of seamen for leaving vessels.[308] Other questions relating to the treatment of seamen were put off for another meeting.[309] The only solace the United States obtained was being able to retain the Seamen's Act protections via a protocol.[310]

The U.S delegation returned disappointed in the maritime results of the Paris peace talks.[311] There was some success with the disposition of the German vessels, but the effort to get agreement on seamen's rights or to rationalize shipping in any way utterly failed. The other negotiators were wary of U.S. shipping objectives just as they were wary of other more general peace objectives. The world viewed the Wilson administration's moralism cynically and as a cover for a U.S. attempt to dominate global commerce.

Lurking in the background was a competition between the United States and Britain over oil.[312] Oil was obviously becoming essential to world shipping as most vessels by the end of the war were being constructed to run on oil and diesel engines were installed in many of them. In his last report to Wilson, on July 31, 1919, Hurley emphasized the necessity for the United States to secure overseas sources of oil for U.S. Navy and merchant marine use to prevent the U.S. fleet from being "at the mercy of foreign bunkering stations for fuel oil."[313] Subsequent annual reports from the Shipping Board detailed the difficulties encountered in ensuring that fuel would be available to U.S.-flag vessels around the world.[314]

JOURNEY TO THE JONES ACT

As he prepared to leave the board, Hurley remained optimistic about future U.S. maritime prospects despite the peace negotiation disappointment. In a March 1, 1919, public report to the board, Hurley wrote that "in America, you have heard much about British competition. In Great Britain I heard a great deal about American competition."[315]

GHOST FLEET AT MALLOWS BAY[316]

While the new merchant marine was being created, the Shipping Board had to deal with the emergency vessels constructed that had no place in the commercial trades. The most notorious example of the disposal process occurred on the Potomac River, first in Alexandria at the Virginia Shipbuilding Corporation facility and then to the final resting place known as the "Ghost Fleet at Mallows Bay" (Maryland).

As soon as the war ended, Senator Harding pounced on the continuing vessel construction program, which he claimed was from four to six times normal cost.[317] Senator William M. Calder (R-NY) severely criticized the wooden vessel program as a complete waste and questioned whether any of the wooden vessels had performed any valuable service.[318] Piez responded that mistakes were made but that they were due to the "tremendous pressure to which the technical department of the Fleet Corporation was subjected" and that wooden vessels had nevertheless been successfully delivered.[319] Piez reported that 731 wooden vessels had been ordered during the war and that 134 vessels were complete by October 31, 1918. The corporation ultimately finished 296 wooden and 26 composite vessels.[320]

Over two hundred of these vessels carried cargoes in 1919 including to Europe.[321] However, the freight market collapsed in 1920 and wooden and composite vessels as well as the smaller steel vessels lost what little commercial utility they had in the first place. As a result, the corporation had to lay up almost six hundred vessels by early 1921.[322] Many of them were moved to the James River in Virginia north of the Jamestown settlement near the village of Claremont. There floated over three hundred wooden and composite vessels which required regular pumping to avoid sinking.

Some vessels were sold, but the majority remained in the James River when they were offered for sale in the fall of 1922. Of those, a total of 218 wooden vessels, nine composite and several other vessels were sold in September 1922 to George D. Perry and William F. Humphrey, two California lawyers.[323] Perry and Humphrey, who were affiliated with IMM, paid $750,000 for vessels constructed by the Fleet Corporation at a cost of $300 million.[324] Western Marine and Salvage Company, controlled by the purchasers, leased the former VSC shipyard in Alexandria from the receiver later that year and announced plans to salvage most of the vessels to take about three years at the rate of two a week.[325]

One of the first two vessels to arrive in Alexandria for salvage was the *SS Alanthus*, which had played a critical role in saving the crew of the submarine *U.S.S. S-5*.[326] That submarine was undergoing full power trials mid-day on September 1, 1920, about fifty miles from the Delaware coast when she sank bow forward practicing a crash dive and her bow became stuck in the seabed. When the crew discovered that the stern was above the water line, they managed to drill a small hole through which they "thrust a pole, a sailor's white undershirt tied to it, and wigwagged signals of distress."[327] The signal was noticed by the *Alanthus* twenty-seven hours after the submarine sank.

The *Alanthus* did not have a wireless operator but managed to get the attention of the passing *SS General George W. Goethals*, which did. The *Alanthus* jury-rigged air and water pumps to bring fresh air and water into the submarine while the *Goethals* crew worked feverishly to create a larger opening by drilling fifty-six holes in a circle and working with a sledgehammer. The "jagged circular steel plate that resembles a large saw blade" they removed is housed in the Navy Memorial Museum in the Washington Navy Yard.[328] The entire crew managed to get through the hole by about 3 a.m. on September 3.[329]

JOURNEY TO THE JONES ACT

Western Marine did not get a chance to scrap the *Alanthus* in an orderly way because she caught fire on or about October 25, 1922, while in Alexandria.[330] The fire spread to the shore and other vessels, but the main salvage continued once the fire was out although it took four months to repair damage to the facilities.[331]

The first anchorage Western Marine secured was on the Potomac River at Widewater, Virginia south of the Marine Corps Base Quantico. In April 1923 a fire started aboard one of the vessels anchored there which quickly spread to four others with an additional five threatened as they were all tied together.[332] A small group of Marines arrived from the base and assisted the watchmen in cutting the cables tying the vessels together, preventing more vessels from being burned.[333] Army engineers nevertheless approved Widewater as an anchorage for about two hundred vessels, but with conditions Western Marine found onerous.[334]

After vessels were stripped in Alexandria, they were towed back to Widewater to be burned to the water line with the intention of beaching them and letting the elements take care of the rest.[335] However, local fishermen argued that the whole operation interfered with an important wildlife area and Western Marine was forced to look for alternatives.

Western Marine purchased a six-hundred-acre farm across the Potomac in Maryland near Marlow's Creek in April 1924. It was not until July 1925 that the Army granted a permit for further recovery of metals and the burning of the vessels at that site. The name given to the areas in the permit was "Mallows Bay."

Over the course of the next few years, vessels were taken to Mallows Bay in groups, eventually numbering 169 vessels to be picked over for any scrap metal that could be salvaged.[336] Thirty-one vessels were burnt together on November 7, 1925, and it was reported that "as the torch was applied to the doomed vessels, a horde of squealing rats plunged into the water."[337]

Charlie Papavizas

Scrap prices declined in the Great Depression and Western Marine abandoned the project in March 1931. Locals continued picking at the vessel carcasses for years until World War II, when Bethlehem Steel was awarded a contract to recover what metals remained, which continued until 1945.[338]

The vessel graveyard consisting of over two hundred hulks (not all them being corporation-ordered wooden vessels) was abandoned and forgotten until plans were drawn in the 1960's to either finally remove the wrecks to land and burn them or permanently entomb then in the water by filling them with stones.[339] The Potomac Electric Power Company entered the fray with a plan to build a nearby power plant and refused to stabilize the wrecks in place, which led to years of legal disputes until the wrecks were abandoned in the 1980s. Meanwhile, they became miniature islands with vegetation and trees growing on them, and the bay became a thriving wildlife habitat.

In large part because of the writings of local maritime historian Donald G. Shomette, an effort was started to preserve the Mallows Bay site for national historical purposes.[340] The State of Maryland nominated the bay for designation as a national marine sanctuary, which occurred on September 3, 2019.[341] And so ended, finally, the Denman-Eustis-Clark wooden vessel dream.

---

[1] For example, U.S. Congress, Senate, Appearance of Ex-Government Officials before Shipping Board or Emergency Fleet Corporation, 68th Cong., 1st sess., 1924, S. Doc. 68-101.

[2] United States-Norway Arbitration under the Special Agreement of June 30, 1921, Case of the United States of America, Permanent Court of Arbitration at the Hague (Washington, DC: Government Printing Office, 1922), 212 (example of one of the telegrams sent and the follow-up letter mailed the same day). The Emergency Fleet Corporation had been given this authority in July 1917. Woodrow Wilson, Executive Order no. 2664 (July 11, 1917).

[3] Second Annual Report of the Shipping Board, 33, 116–17.

[4] Second Annual Report of the Shipping Board, 117.

[5] Hurley, Bridge to France, 32.

[6] Hearings before the Senate Commerce Committee on the United States Shipping Board Emergency Fleet Corporation, vol. 1, 1918, 25-27 (testimony of E. Hurley).

[7] Second Annual Report of the Shipping Board, 129.
[8] Second Annual Report of the Shipping Board, 120.
[9] Second Annual Report of the Shipping Board, 123.
[10] First Annual Report of the Shipping Board, 7.
[11] Hearings before the Senate Commerce Committee on the Establishment of an American Merchant Marine, 1840 (testimony of J. Payne); Fourth Annual Shipping Board Report, June 30, 1920, 111–12; U.S. Congress, Senate, Report of U.S. Shipping Board, 67th Cong., 1st sess., 1921, S Doc. 67-38, 6 (shows the appropriations to February 28, 1921, for the Shipping Board and Fleet Corporation to total about $3.3 billion).
[12] The White House, Office of Management and Budget, Historical Tables, Table 1.1 – Summary of Receipts, Outlays, and Surpluses or Deficits: 1789-2028, https://www.whitehouse.gov/omb/budget/historical-tables.
[13] 40 Stat. 392 (October 6, 1917).
[14] Second Annual Report of the Shipping Board, 40.
[15] Second Annual Report of the Shipping Board, 40; 58 CONG. REC. 3517 (August 1, 1919).
[16] "Takes Over All American Ships above 2,500 Tons," New York Times, October 13, 1917, 1; "Government Seizes 500 Ocean Steamers," New York Times, October 16, 1917, 2; Salvatore R. Mercogliano, "The Shipping Act of 1916 and Emergency Fleet Corporation: America Builds, Requisitions, and Seizes a Merchant Fleet Second to None," Northern Mariner 26, no. 4 (October 2016): 407—24.
[17] First Annual Report of the Shipping Board, 14.
[18] Third Annual Report of the Shipping Board, 36. That number was 444 of almost 3 million DWT as of November 12, 1918. Second Annual Report of the United States Shipping Board, Dec. 1, 1918, 35–36.
[19] Second Annual Report of the Shipping Board, 34.
[20] Second Annual Report of the Shipping Board, 142–43. Hurley indicated in his memoirs that the concrete vessel idea came from Congress, and the Shipping Board and Fleet Corporation were not in favor. Hurley, Bridge to France, 56–57.
[21] Hurley, Bridge to France, 44–45.
[22] Second Annual Report of the Shipping Board, 45.
[23] Hurley, Bridge to France, 53-55; Hearings before the Senate Commerce Committee on the United States Shipping Board Emergency Fleet Corporation, vol. 2, 1918, 1526–52 (Harris testimony).
[24] 56 CONG. REC. 480–85 (December 18, 1917).
[25] Harding referred to the following story: George Rothwell Brown, "Piez Succeeds Harris," Washington Post, December 18, 1917, 1.
[26] Hurley, Bridge to France, 57–59.
[27] For example, "Labor Shortage Becoming Acute," New York Times June 28, 1918, 17; Edward Hungerford, "Merchant Mariners," Collier's, The National Weekly 63, no. 1 (January 4, 1919): 7–8, 42.

[28] Hearings before the Senate Commerce Committee on the Establishment of an American Merchant Marine, 1657.

[29] P. H. Douglas and F. E. Wolfe, "Labor Administration in the Shipbuilding Industry during War Time," Journal of Political Economy 27, no. 3 (March 1919): 145–87.

[30] Third Annual Report of the Shipping Board, 73; Mattox, Building the Emergency Fleet, 70.

[31] The Training of Shipyard Workers, Report on the Work to the United States Shipping Board Emergency Fleet Corporation Industrial Relations Division Education and Training Section (Philadelphia: U.S. Shipping Board, 1919), 19.

[32] For example, "Wilson Will Try to Adjust Strike of Ship Workers," New York Times, February 17, 1918, 1; Hurley, Bridge to France, chap. 20; Willard E. Hotchkiss and Henry R. Seager, History of the Shipbuilding Labor Adjustment Board 1917 to 1919 (Washington, DC: Government Printing Office, 1921).

[33] Hotchkiss and Seager, History of the Shipbuilding Labor Adjustment Board, 7–9.

[34] "Everit Macy Dies in Arizona Hotel," New York Times, March 22, 1930, 14.

[35] Hotchkiss and Seager, History of the Shipbuilding Labor Adjustment Board, 12–13.

[36] Report of Director General Charles Piez to the Board of Trustees of United States Shipping Board Emergency Fleet Corporation (Washington, DC: Government Printing Office, 1919), 16.

[37] Hurley, Bridge to France, 187–89.

[38] Report of Director General Charles Piez to the Board of Trustees of United States Shipping Board Emergency Fleet Corporation, 16.

[39] Mattox, Building the Emergency Fleet, 71–76.

[40] Connecticut State Library, State Library Collections, State Publications, The Man of the House is the Shipbuilder, https://collections.ctdigitalarchive.org/islandora/object/30002%3A5333903.

[41] U.S. Committee on Public Information, "U.S. Should Produce 1,600 New Ships, from 130 Yards, This Year, Says Chairman Hurley," Official U.S. Bulletin, vol. 2, no. 253 (March 9, 1918), 3.

[42] U.S. Committee on Public Information, "Talks to Four-Minute Men on Ship-Building Program," Official Bulletin 2, no. 220 (January 29, 1918), 2; Committee on Public Information, Purpose and Plan of the Four Minute Men (Washington, DC: Government Printing Office, 1918), General Bulletin no. 7A; "Need Labor in Shipyards—Four Minute Men Hear of Demand That Must Be Met," New York Times, January 29, 1918, 24. The process was not without its hiccups. For example, "Charge Apathy in Shipyard Drive," New York Times, February 7, 1918, 1.

[43] 40 Stat. 76, 79 (May 12, 1917) (merchant mariners were also exempt); Second Report of the Provost Marshal General to the Secretary of War on the Operations of the Selective Service System to December 20, 1918 (Washington, DC: Government Printing Office, 1919), 62–74.

[44] Second Report of the Provost Marshal General to the Secretary of War on the Operations of the Selective Service System, 75.
[45] Second Report of the Provost Marshal General to the Secretary of War on the Operations of the Selective Service System, 75.
[46] "Crowder Explains Edict—Work-or-Fight Order Affects Only Men of Draft Age," New York Times, July 3, 1918, 13; Frank Fitzpatrick, "For Baseball, World War I Was an Unwinnable Battle," Philadelphia Inquirer, April 21, 2017, https://www.inquirer.com/philly/sports/20170423_For_baseball__World_War_I_was_an_unwinnable_battle.html.
[47] "Ruth Is Missing from the Red Sox," Philadelphia Inquirer, July 4, 1918, 6.
[48] "Major Leaguers Seek Ship Berths," Evening Public Ledger (Philadelphia), July 10, 1918, 13.
[49] Eric Van Schaack, "The Division of Pictorial Publicity in World War I," Design Issues 22, no.1 (Winter 2006): 32–45, 33; Hurley, Bridge to France, 159–60; United States Shipping Board, Emergency Fleet Corporation, Official Posters (Philadelphia: Publications Section, 1918).
[50] "C. D. Gibson's Committee for Patriotic Posters," New York Times Magazine, January 20, 1918, 11.
[51] For example, "One-Man Control for War Purchases," New York Times, January 18, 1918, 8.
[52] Crowell and Wilson, Road to France, vol. 2, chap. 26.
[53] Goethals recollection of what occurred was different. He testified in a 1921 congressional hearing that he sent a letter to the secretary of war about February 1 that there were insufficient supply vessels available to keep up with the rate of men being sent to France. U.S. Congress, House, Select Committee on Expenditures in the War Department, Hearings before the Select Committee on Expenditures in the War Department on War Expenditures, 66th Cong., 1st sess., 1921, serial 1, parts 1—13, 532. He further testified that because of that letter there was a conference among Major Gen. John Biddle, the acting Army chief of staff, Hurley and Franklin and the decision was made to form a central shipping control body to coordinate all U.S. government shipping.
[54] "Leave Shipping Control," New York Times, December 14, 1918, 18; United States Shipping Board Operations, H. Rep. 66-1399, 32 (Shipping Board Shipping Control Committee resolution); "H. H. Raymond Made Shipping Controller," New York Times, January 29, 1918, 2; "Connop Guthrie, War Shipping Aide," New York Times, October 3, 1945, 19.
[55] Crowell and Wilson, Road to France, vol. 2, 378; Hurley, Bridge to France, 101–09.
[56] Second Annual Report of the Shipping Board, 65.

57 Hearings before the Senate Commerce Committee on the United States Shipping Board Emergency Fleet Corporation, vol. 2, 1918; U.S. Congress, House, Merchant Marine and Fisheries Committee, Hearings before the House Merchant Marine and Fisheries Committee on Housing for Employees of Shipyards Building Ships for the United States Shipping Board Emergency Fleet Corporation, 65th Cong., 2nd sess., 1918.

58 William J. Williams, "Accommodating American Shipyard Workers, 1917-1918: The Pacific Coast and the Federal Government's First Public Housing and Transit Programs," Pacific Northwest Quarterly 84, no. 2 (April 1993): 51–59.

59 40 Stat. 438 (March 1, 1918).

60 40 Stat. 535 (April 22, 1918).

61 Report of Director General Charles Piez to the Board of Trustees of United States Shipping Board Emergency Fleet Corporation, 193–94. A complete list of housing and transit projects was provided to the Senate Commerce Committee by Chairman Payne in March 1920. Hearings before the Senate Commerce Committee on the Establishment of an American Merchant Marine, 1862.

62 "Germany Threatens Holland if She Yields Ships to Us," New York Times, March 19,1918 1.

63 "Dutch Refuse Ship Transfer on Allied Terms," New York Times, March 19, 1918, 1; "Grant Brief Delay in Seizing Ships," New York Times, March 20, 1918, 1.

64 For a list of the vessels see Annual Report of the Commissioner of Navigation to the Secretary of Commerce (1918), appendix N.

65 "Navy Officers Here Get Seizure Order," New York Times, March 21, 1918, 2.

66 "First Dutch Ship Put in Commission," New York Times, March 24, 1918, 21; Second Annual Report of the Shipping Board, 47–52.

67 Second Annual Report of the Shipping Board, 52–53.

68 Second Annual Report of the Shipping Board, 53.

69 Laurence Dunn, Merchant Ships of the World 1910-1929 (New York: Macmillan, 1973), 152.

70 War Department Annual Reports, 1918, vol. 1, 33.

71 For example, "Letter from E. Hurley to W. Wilson (April 3, 1918)," Papers of Woodrow Wilson, vol. 47, 233.

72 Hearings before the Select House Committee on U.S. Shipping Board Operations, 4134 (Piez testimony).

73 Hearings before the Select House Committee on U.S. Shipping Board Operations, 4134—36; Robert Hessen, "Charles Schwab and the Shipbuilding Crisis of 1918," Pennsylvania History: A Journal of Mid-Atlantic Studies 38, no. 4 (October 1971): 389–99, 391.

74 Hurley, Bridge to France, 135.

75 Hurley, Bridge to France, chap. 26.

76 John Burroughs, Under the Maples (Boston: Houghton Mifflin, 1921).

77 Burroughs, Under the Maples, 113.

78 Colton, "Shipbuilding History: Construction Records of U.S. and Canadian Shipbuilders and Boatbuilders," http://shipbuildinghistory.com/merchantships/1atlantic.htm.

79 Robert Hessen, Steel Titan, The Life of Charles M. Schwab (New York: Oxford University Press, 1975).

80 Hearings before the House Select Committee on U.S. Shipping Board Operations, part 11, 3968–69.

81 U.S. Congress, House, United States Shipping Board Operations, 66th Cong., 3rd sess., 1921, H. Rep. 66-1399, 20–22; "War Controversy Taken to Court," Iron Age 115, no. 17 (April 23, 1925): 1189–91.

82 For example, "Letter from A. Shaw to W. Wilson (April 20, 1918)," Papers of Woodrow Wilson, vol. 47, 385.

83 "Ex-Secretary of State Colby Adds Important Chapter to the History of the Great War," Iron Age 115, no. 17 (April 23, 1925): 1191, 1245 (reprinting statement of Bainbridge Colby).

84 "Schwab Placed in Full Control of Shipbuilding," New York Times, April 17, 1918, 1; "Schwab Centres on Ship Task," New York Times, April 19, 1918, 5.

85 U.S. Committee on Public Information, Official Bulletin 2, no. 291 (April 23, 1918), 4.

86 Hearings before the Select Committee on U.S. Shipping Board Operations, part 11, 4134–35.

87 "Schwab's Appointment an Epoch in War Making," New York Times, April 21, 1918, 5.

88 Report of Director General Charles Piez to the Board of Trustees of United States Shipping Board Emergency Fleet Corporation, 12.

89 Report of Director General Charles Piez to the Board of Trustees of United States Shipping Board Emergency Fleet Corporation, 12; Second Annual Report of the Shipping Board, 96; Hurley, Bridge to France, 47.

90 Report of the President of the United States Shipping Board Emergency Fleet Corporation to the Board of Trustees (Washington, DC: Government Printing Office, 1919), 9.

91 Mattox, Building the Emergency Fleet, chap. 12.

92 Mattox, Building the Emergency Fleet, 187–88.

93 Hessen, "Charles Schwab and the Shipbuilding Crisis of 1918," 396–97.

94 Mattox, Building the Emergency Fleet, 257-261; Charles M. Schwab, "Doing the Impossible," Collier's, The National Weekly 61, no. 26 (September 7, 1918): 9.

95 "Now Plan to Launch 100 Ships on July 4," New York Times, July 1, 1918, 7; "List of 94 Steel and Wooden Ships That Will Be Launched in America Today," New York Times, July 4, 1918, 11; "Nearly 100 Ships in Nation's Splash," New York Times, July 5, 1918, 1; Donald G. Shomette, "Tidal Wave: The Greatest Ship Launch in History," Sea History 158 (Spring 2017): 28–32; Annual Report of the Commissioner of Navigation to the Secretary of Commerce (1918), 16.

[96] "U.S. Launches 100 Ships on 4th" and "Big Splash is Death Blow to Autocracy," San Francisco Chronicle, July 5, 1918, 1 (the one hundred number also included six Navy destroyers).

[97] "Total of 95 Cargo Ships Left Ways," Evening Public Ledger (Philadelphia), July 5, 1918, 1; "City's 'Fourth' a World Pledge," Evening Public Ledger (Philadelphia), July 3, 1918, 4.

[98] Mattox, Building the Emergency Fleet, 167.

[99] "Successful Spanish Influenza Treatment by Shipping Board," Shipping– A Weekly Record of Maritime Transportation 5, no. 1 (October 5, 1918): 12.

[100] Report of Chief of Transportation Service, War Department Annual Reports, 1919 (Washington, DC: Government Printing Office, 1920), vol. 1, part 4, 4867.

[101] Hearings before the Senate Commerce Committee on the Establishment of an American Merchant Marine, 1883.

[102] Annual Report of the Commissioner of Navigation to the Secretary of Commerce (1918), 24.

[103] Hurley, Bridge to France, 60.

[104] U.S. Shipping Board, Shipping Facts (Washington, DC: Government Printing Office, 1918), 1—2.

[105] "Letter from J. Pershing to N. Baker (August 17, 1918)," John J. Pershing, My Experiences in the World War (New York: Frederick A. Stokes, 1931), 550–51.

[106] Hurley, Bridge to France, 74.

[107] Second Annual Report of the Shipping Board, 120.

[108] Bishop and Bishop, Goethals, 342–46 (quoting July 25, 1917, memorandum of Joseph P. Cotton).

[109] For example, Theodore E. Ferris, Douglas Fir Ship, Specifications for the Construction of a Standard Wood Steamship (Washington, DC: Government Printing Office, 1917). The wooden design was criticized because it required large-size, not easily available, timbers. "Union Suggests Way to Rush Ships," New York Times, March 1, 1918, 3.

[110] "Theodore Ferris, Naval Architect," New York Times, June 1, 1953, 23.

[111] Williams, The Wilson Administration and the Shipbuilding Crisis of 1917, 100.

[112] "Letter W. Denman to W. Wilson (July 18, 1917)," Papers of Woodrow Wilson, vol. 43, 204.

[113] Williams, Wilson Administration and the Shipbuilding Crisis of 1917, 172.

[114] Hearings before the Senate Commerce Committee on U.S. Shipping Board Emergency Fleet Corporation, 1918, vol. 2, 1456.

[115] Hearings before the Senate Commerce Committee on U.S. Shipping Board Emergency Fleet Corporation, 1918, vol. 2, 1923—42. Paul M. Zeiss, a prominent maritime policy historian, used the Manson plan to bludgeon the Shipping Board and Emergency Fleet Corporation for gross mismanagement missing many of the signs that Manson was not credible. Zeis, American Shipping Policy, 100–05. For

example, Zeiss cites (100n20) a letter written by Representative Alexander as "endorsing" Manson when in fact the letter appears carefully written merely to indicate that Manson supported the Ship Purchase Bill and not to endorse any of Manson's positions. U.S. Congress, House and Senate, Joint Hearings before the Senate Commerce Committee and the House Merchant Marine and Fisheries Committee to Amend Merchant Marine Act of 1920, 67th Cong., 2nd sess., 1922, vol. 2, 1625.

[116] For example, "Government-Owned Ships," New York Times, September 11, 1914, 8 (Manson letter to the editor); "Ships for Foreign Trade," New York Times, August 5, 1916, 8.

[117] Hearings before the Senate Commerce Committee on the U.S. Shipping Board Emergency Fleet Corporation, 1918, vol. 2, 1925–27.

[118] For example, "Steamship Oceana Held by Receiver," New York Times, June 9, 1912) 12 (in connection with the receivership of the Bermuda-Atlantic Steamship Company, another former Manson company); Noel H. Pugach, "American Shipping Promoters and the Shipping Crisis of 1914–1916: The Pacific & Eastern Steamship Company," American Neptune 35, no. 3 (July 1975): 166–82, 173.

[119] For example, "Attacks Shipping Plan—Philip Manson Wants the Government to Take Over Yards," New York Times, February 23, 1918, 13; "Manson Hits Ship Board," New York Times, February 3, 1920, 10.

[120] Second Annual Report of the Shipping Board, 120.

[121] Second Annual Report of the Shipping Board, 132.

[122] John W. Lawrence, "Hog Island," The Encyclopedia of Greater Philadelphia, https://philadelphiaencyclopedia.org/archive/hog-island.

[123] 56 CONG. REC. 1853 (February 8, 1918).

[124] Hearings before the Senate Commerce Committee on the U.S. Shipping Board Emergency Fleet Corporation, 1918, vol. 2, 260–71.

[125] Second Annual Report of the Shipping Board, 130.

[126] "Shipping Investigation Forecasts Profiteers' Exposure," Evening Bulletin (Philadelphia), January 3, 1918, 3; "Hog Island Yard Late, Says U.S. Ship Constructor," New York Daily Tribune, January 4, 1918, 6; Hearings before the Senate Commerce Committee on the U.S. Shipping Board Emergency Fleet Corporation, 1919, part 8.

[127] United States Shipping Board Operations, H. Rep. 66-1399.

[128] U.S. Committee on Public Information, "Full Text of Report on Hog Island Shipyard Inquiry; No Fraud Disclosed but Accounts in Chaotic Condition and Plant Cost is Held to be Above 'Reasonable Need,'" Official U.S. Bulletin 2, no. 495 (December 23, 1918): 9–14, 10.

[129] For example, "While U.S. Demands Coal Freight Cars Await Unloading," Philadelphia Inquirer, January 18, 1918, 1; Hearings before the Senate Commerce Committee on the U.S. Shipping Board Emergency Fleet Corporation, 1918, vol. 1, 553.

[130] "Draftees Do Not Need a Notary," Evening Public Ledger (Philadelphia), January 15, 1918, 3; Hearings before the Senate Commerce Committee on the U.S. Shipping Board Emergency Fleet Corporation, 1918, vol. 2, 1262 (Letter S. Felton to E. Hurley [January 18, 1918]).

[131] Hearings before the Senate Commerce Committee on the U.S. Shipping Board Emergency Fleet Corporation, 1918, vol. 2, 1430–33.
[132] Hearings before the Senate Commerce Committee on the U.S. Shipping Board Emergency Fleet Corporation, 1918, vol. 2, 1259–62.
[133] 56 CONG. REC. 1979 (February 11, 1918).
[134] 57 CONG. REC. 4852 (March 3, 1919).
[135] Hearings before the Senate Commerce Committee on the U.S. Shipping Board Emergency Fleet Corporation, 1918, vol. 2, 1756–60.
[136] "Full Text of Report on Hog Island Shipyard Inquiry," Official U.S. Bulletin, vol. 2, no. 495 (December 23, 1918): 9–14.
[137] For example, "President Probing Hog Island Payroll; Reports of Padding," Philadelphia Inquirer, February 19, 1918, 1.
[138] Hearings before the Senate Commerce Committee on the U.S. Shipping Board Emergency Fleet Corporation, 1918, vol. 2, 1463.
[139] U.S. Committee on Public Information, "Letter from E. Hurley to F. Bowles (February 12, 1918)," Official U.S. Bulletin, vol. 2, no. 235 (February 15, 1918), 1.
[140] "Finds No Hog Island Graft—Bowles' Changes Commended by Piez After Inspection," New York Times, (February 18, 1918), 2.
[141] U.S. Committee on Public Information, "Letter from W. Wilson to T. Gregory (February 13, 1918)," Official U.S. Bulletin 2, no. 235 (February 15, 1918): 1.
[142] Hearings before the Senate Commerce Committee on the U.S. Shipping Board Emergency Fleet Corporation, 1918, vol. 2, 1716–17; "Ascribes Delay to Goethals Row," New York Times, February 13, 1918, 1.
[143] For example, "Fullest Inquiry Invited by Corporation Head," Evening Star (Washington, DC), February 16, 1918, 15.
[144] "Hog Island's Shipyard—What Visitor Saw in Day's Travels through the Great Plant Where Expenses Are Now Being Investigated," New York Times, February 17, 1918, 43.
[145] "Reveal Hog Island Achievements for the First Time," New York Times, February 23, 1918, 1.
[146] James J. Martin, The Saga of Hog Island (Colorado Springs: Ralph Myles, 1977), 19.
[147] "Conditions at Hog Island," New York Times, February 24, 1918, E-2.
[148] Hearings before the Senate Commerce Committee on the U.S. Shipping Board Emergency Fleet Corporation, 1918, vol. 2, 2385–92.
[149] "Senate Committee Visits Hog Island," New York Times, February 26, 1918, 5.
[150] "Launch First Ship at Hog Island," New York Times, August 6, 1918, 9; "Mrs. Wilson at Launching of Quistconck," Evening Public Ledger (Philadelphia), August 5, 1918, 1.
[151] "Mrs. Wilson Sends Quistconck on Way with Flow of Wine," Philadelphia Inquirer, August 6, 1918, 1; "High U.S. Officials to See Launching," Philadelphia Inquirer, August 5, 1918, 13.

[152] "Letter from W. Wilson to J. Tumulty (August 2, 1918)," Papers of Woodrow Wilson, vol. 49, 164.

[153] "Treasonable Rumor Affects Quistconck," Evening Public Ledger (Philadelphia), August 5, 1918, 3.

[154] Hearings before the Senate Commerce Committee on the U.S. Shipping Board Emergency Fleet Corporation, 1919, part 8, 357, 392, 398–401.

[155] Martin, Saga of Hog Island, 21.

[156] Hearings before the Senate Commerce Committee on the U.S. Shipping Board Emergency Fleet Corporation, 1919, 79–80.

[157] Colton, "Shipbuilding History: Construction Records of U.S. and Canadian Shipbuilders and Boatbuilders," www.shipbuildinghistory.com/history/shipyards/4emergencylarge/wwone/aisc.htm.

[158] Full Text of Report on Hog Island Shipyard Inquiry," Official U.S. Bulletin.

[159] "Letter J. Tumulty to W. Wilson (December 12, 1918)," Papers of Woodrow Wilson, vol. 53, 371; "Found No Graft at Hog Island," New York Times, December 21, 1918, 5.

[160] Second Annual Report of the Shipping Board, 132.

[161] Fourth Annual Report of the Shipping Board, 103–04.

[162] Hearings before the Senate Commerce Committee on the U.S. Shipping Board Emergency Fleet Corporation, 1918, vol. 2, 1459.

[163] Mark H. Goldberg, The "Hog Islanders," The Story of 122 American Ships (Kings Point, NY: American Merchant Marine Museum, 1991), 36–125.

[164] Goldberg, Hog Islanders, 255–60.

[165] Colton, "Shipbuilding History: Construction Records of U.S. and Canadian Shipbuilders and Boatbuilders," shipbuildinghistory.com/shipyards/emergencylarge/aisc.htm.

[166] Hearings before the Senate Commerce Committee on the United States Shipping Board Emergency Fleet Corporation, part 8, 254–57.

[167] Hurley, Bridge to France, 129–34.

[168] Hurley, Bridge to France, 131.

[169] "Letter H. Hurley to W. Wilson (January 28, 1918)," Papers of Woodrow Wilson, vol. 46, 123.

[170] Mattox, Building the Emergency Fleet (Schwab preface, 14).

[171] Fourth Annual Report of the Shipping Board, 104.

[172] "Plan Terminal on Hog Island," Evening Star (Washington, DC), April 10, 1930, 16.

[173] Sandy Hingston, "Seven Theories You Might Not Know about Where the Word 'Hoagie' Comes From," Philadelphia, May 5, 2016, https://www.phillymag.com/foobooz/2016/05/05/the-word-hoagie-origin.

[174] Philip H. Woods, Charlie Morse: Ice King & Wall Street Scoundrel (Charleston, SC: History Press, 2011).

[175] "Mayor Admits Big Ice Stock Holdings," New York Times, June 10, 1900, 1.

[176] "One Hundred Per Cent, Rise in Ice," New York Times, May 6, 1900, 18.
[177] M. G. van Rensselaer, "Recent Architecture in America–V–City Dwellings," Century Magazine 31, no. 4 (February 1886): 548—58.
[178] "Record Price for Fifth Avenue Plot," New York Times, February 7, 1920, 17.
[179] For example, "Morse Buys Sound Lines from the New Haven," New York Times, February 7, 1907, 1; Woods, Charlie Morse, 62–66.
[180] New England Historical Society, "The Panic of 1907 and the Maine Man Who Caused It," (updated 2021), www.newenglandhistoricalsociety.com/the-panic-of-1907-and-the-maine-man-who-caused-it.
[181] "Meteoric Career of Ice King Morse Is Unparalleled," Washington Times, October 17, 1909 1.
[182] For example, "Former 'Ice King' Seeks Congressional Inquiry," Evening Star (Washington, DC), January 8, 1914, 4.
[183] "Morse Nearly Even," Sunday Star (Washington, DC), October 3, 1909, 12.
[184] Henry F. Pringle, The Life and Times of William Howard Taft (Newtown, CT: American Political Biography Press, 1939), vol. 2, chap. 33; "Morse Speculated from the Prison," Norwich Bulletin (Connecticut), January 3, 1912, 1; Doug Cook, "Whispering Pines: Charlie Morse's Second Act and Denouement," Bowdoin Daily Sun, July 15, 2015; Eric Burns, 1920, The Year That Made the Decade Roar (New York: Pegasus Books, 2015), 112.
[185] 62 Cong. Rec. 7380 (May 22, 1922) (Letter from Thomas B. Felder to Leon O. Bailey [October 12, 1917]).
[186] "Morse Pardoned in Death's Shadow," New York Times, January 19, 1912, 1. The whole health saga is laid out in Pringle, Life and Times of William Howard Taft, vol. 2, chap. 33.
[187] "Thomas B. Felder Dies in Savannah," New York Times, March 13, 1926, 17; James N. Giglio, "Lawyer as Lobbyist: Harry M. Daugherty and the Charles W. Morse Case, 1911–1922," Ohio History Journal 79, nos. 3 & 4 (Summer-Autumn 1970): 152–77.
[188] "Morse Fooled the Army Examiners," New York Times, September 6, 1911, 11.
[189] "Taft Is Chagrined over Morse Pardon," New York Times, November 16, 1913, 5; William Howard Taft, Ethics in Service (New Haven, CT: Yale University Press, 1915), 60.
[190] 62 Cong. Rec. 7380 (May 22, 1922) (Letter T. Felder to L. Bailey [October 12, 1917]).
[191] "Morse, with 3 Sons, 8 Others, Indicted," New York Times, February 28, 1922, 1.
[192] Woods, Charlie Morse, 103.
[193] "Morse's Year Almost Up," New York Times, January 11, 1913, 3.
[194] Woods, Charlie Morse, 104–06.
[195] Hearings before the Select U.S. Shipping Board Operations Committee on Shipping Board Operations, part 2, 1050–63.

[196] Hearings before the Senate Commerce Committee on the Establishment of an American Merchant Marine, 982.
[197] U.S. Congress, Senate, Appearance of Ex-Government Officials before Shipping Board or Emergency Fleet Corporation, 68th Cong., 1st sess., 1924, S. Doc. 68-101.
[198] Appearance of Ex-Government Officials before Shipping Board or Emergency Fleet Corporation, S. Doc. 68-101; T. Michael Miller, "Jones Point: Haven of History," Yearbook: The Historical Society of Fairfax County, Virginia 21 (1986-1988): 15–73, 58.
[199] U.S. Congress, House, Select Committee on U.S. Shipping Board Operations, Hearings before the Select Committee on U.S. Shipping Board Operations on C. W. Morse Contracts, 66th Cong., 2nd sess. (1920), part 3, 315.
[200] Hearings before the Senate Commerce Committee on the Establishment of an American Merchant Marine, 982.
[201] "Bowles Denies Effort to Influence M'Adoo," New York Times, May 30, 1923, 2.
[202] "Makes Name Change," Alexandria Gazette, January 19, 1918 1.
[203] "Sale of Jones's Point," Alexandria Gazette, February 7, 1918, 1.
[204] "Potomac's First Big Ship since Days of Washington Soon to Ride Ways to Sea," Washington Times, January 14, 1919, 8.
[205] Lila Spitz, "'More Tons, Less Huns': World War I Shipbuilding in Alexandria," Boundary Stones, WETA, December 23, 2016, https://boundarystones.weta.org/about.
[206] "'More Tons, Less Huns,'" Alexandria Gazette, April 4, 1918, 1.
[207] Woods, Charlie Morse, 109–10.
[208] "Potomac's First Big Ship Since Days of Washington Soon to Ride Ways to Sea," Washington Times, January 14, 1919, 8.
[209] "Keel of the First Ship to Be Laid Tomorrow," Alexandria Gazette, May 29, 1918, 1; "President Wilson Becomes Ship Builder in Alexandria Yesterday Afternoon," Alexandria Gazette, May 31, 1918, 1.
[210] "Launch Freighter at Alexandra, VA—Colin H. Livingstone 9,400 Tons, Is Christened by Builder's Daughter," Washington Post, June 27, 192), 2.
[211] "Georgie W. Morse," Alexandria Gazette, November 15, 1920, 1; "Georgie M. Morse Glides from Ways," Alexandria Gazette, November 20, 1920, 1.
[212] Sixth Annual Report of the Shipping Board, 161; "Wooden Ship File Burns All Night, Evening Star (Washington, DC), October 25, 1922, 4; "Big Iron Ship is Towed to Claremont, VA," Alexandria Gazette, October. 30, 1922, 1.
[213] Hearings before the Select Committee on U.S. Shipping Board Operations on C. W. Morse Contracts, part 3, 364.
[214] Colton, "Shipbuilding History: Construction Records of U.S. and Canadian Shipbuilders and Boatbuilders," http://shipbuildinghistory.com/shipyards/emergencylarge/virginia.htm.
[215] "Empire Moose," uboat.net, https://uboat.net/allies/merchants/ship/497.html.
[216] Hearings before the Select Committee on U.S. Shipping Board Operations on C. W. Morse Contracts, part 3, 45.

[217] Woods, Charlie Morse, 109–10.
[218] Hearings before the Select Committee on U.S. Shipping Board Operations on C. W. Morse Contracts, part 3, 316, part 2, 1102–05 (contract).
[219] Hearings before the Select Committee on U.S. Shipping Board Operations on C. W. Morse Contracts, exec. sess., 65.
[220] Hearings before the Select Committee on U.S. Shipping Board Operations on C. W. Morse Contracts, exec. sess., 53–54.
[221] Hearings before the Select Committee on U.S. Shipping Board Operations on C. W. Morse Contracts, part 3, 316, part 2, 1102–05 (contract).
[222] Hearings before the Select Committee on U.S. Shipping Board Operations on C. W. Morse Contracts, part 3, 309–25.
[223] "Area in Alexandria Bought for Building," Washington Herald, June 15, 1918, 9.
[224] Hearings before the Select Committee on U.S. Shipping Board Operations on C. W. Morse Contracts, exec. sess., 11.
[225] Hearings before the Select Committee on U.S. Shipping Board Operations on C. W. Morse Contracts, exec. sess., 12.
[226] Hearings before the Select Committee on U.S. Shipping Board Operations on C. W. Morse Contracts, exec. sess., 33.
[227] Hearings before the Select Committee on U.S. Shipping Board Operations on C. W. Morse Contracts, exec. sess., 35, 53.
[228] Hearings before the Select Committee on U.S. Shipping Board Operations on C. W. Morse Contracts, exec. sess., 49, 51, 56.
[229] "House Will Probe Morse Contracts," Washington Times, April 24, 1920, 2; "Says Morse Company Misused Building Fund," New York Times, May 6, 1920, 15.
[230] Hearings before the Select Committee on U.S. Shipping Board Operations on C. W. Morse Contracts, part 3. [231] Hearings before the Select Committee on U.S. Shipping Board Operations on C. W. Morse Contracts, part 2, 1115–18, 1208–09, 1239–40.
[232] For example, "M'Adoo Is Drawn into Ship Inquiry as Morse Lawyer," New York Times, November 13, 1920, 1; "Witness Names M'Adoo in Ship Waste Inquiry," Washington Herald, November 14, 1920, 2; "Reed Links M'Adoo to Morse's Affairs," New York Times, February 26, 1924, 3.
[233] "Letter from W. McAdoo to W. Wilson (June 2, 1922)," Papers of Woodrow Wilson, vol. 68, 72.
[234] Virginia Shipbuilding Corporation v. U.S. Shipping Board Emergency Fleet Corporation, 292 F. 440, 447 (E.D. Va. 1923), 11 F.2d 156 (E.D. Va. 1925).
[235] "VA Ship Company Sues U.S. Board," Alexandria Gazette, December 14, 1920, 1 (in state court); "Seek to Enjoin U.S. Shipping Board," Alexandria Gazette, January 20, 1921, 1; "Restrains U.S.B. From Interfering," Alexandria Gazette, February 7, 1921, 1.
[236] Frederick Tilp, This Was Potomac River (Alexandria, VA: privately published, 1978), 81.

237 "To Ask Indictment of Charles W. Morse," New York Times, November 30, 1921, 3.
238 "C.W. Morse Sails for France, Foiling Inquiry; Left Last Friday on the Paris as 'C. Morris,'" New York Times, December 1, 1921, 1.
239 "Morse, to Escape Arrest at Havre, Agrees to Return," New York Times, December 3, 1921, 1.
240 "Morse Indicted for Fraud," Norfolk Post, February 27, 1922, 1; "Charles W. Morse and 11 Others Are Indicted," Alexandria Gazette, February 27, 1922, 1.
241 For example, "War Fraud Suits Yield $3,198,385," New York Times, June 2, 1923, 12; Annual Report of the Attorney General of the United States for Fiscal Year 1923 (Washington, DC: Government Printing Office, 1923), 4–11.
242 "Goethals in Morse Case," New York Times, April 30, 1923, 3; "M'Adoo Says Morse Paid $83,000 in Fees," New York Times, July 18, 1923, 17.
243 "C. M. Schwab Enlivens Trial of the Morses; Opposed Employing Sons; Hit Father's Loans," New York Times, July 25, 1923, 1.
244 "Morse Weeps in Court When Called Victim," New York Times, July 7, 1923, 3.
245 "Morse and 3 Sons Acquitted by Jury," New York Times, August 5, 1923, 1.
246 Virginia Shipbuilding Corporation v. U.S., 22 F.2d 38 (4th Cir. 1927).
247 U.S. v. Morse, 24 F.2d 1001 (S.D. NY 1926).
248 "C.W. Morse Has Stroke," Oregonian, August 3, 1926, 2; "Guardian Named for C. W. Morse," Evening Star (Washington, DC), September 8, 1926, 13.
249 "Court Discharges Morse Fraud Jury," Evening Star (Washington, DC), December 6, 1926, 16.
250 "C. W. Morse Dead; Former Financier," New York Times, January 13, 1933, 15.
251 Cook, "Whispering Pines."
252 For example, Speech Delivered by Edward N. Hurley, Chairman of the United States Shipping Board, at Delmonico's, New York, on the Evening of March 26, 1918, before the National Marine League of the U.S.A.
253 "Need Ten Months for Army's Return," New York Times, November 30, 1918, 1.
254 Fourth Annual Report of the Shipping Board, 54.
255 War Department Annual Reports, 1920 (Washington, DC: Government Printing Office, 1921), vol. 1, 1505–06.
256 "Ask Ships for Trade with Latin America," New York Times, November 18, 1918, 9.
257 "Denies Plan to Bar Trade Expansion," New York Times, November 23, 1918, 1; "Call on Redfield for His Trade Plans," New York Times, December 2, 1918, 6.
258 Safford, Wilsonian Maritime Diplomacy, chap. 7.
259 Edward N. Hurley, "Why Our Ships Will Now Stay on the Ocean," Saturday Evening Post 191, no. 6 (August 10, 1918): 14.
260 Mark Sullivan, "Who Shall Be Mistress of the Sea?" Collier's, The National Weekly 62, no. 39 (December 14, 1918): 5–6. 25–27.
261 Hurley, Bridge to France, 128–29.

[262] Third Annual Report of the Shipping Board, 18–19.
[263] "All Relief Work Put under Hoover," New York Times, January 4, 1919, 1.
[264] "Hoover and Hurley Sail on Olympic," New York Times, November 17, 1918, 9.
[265] For example, Herbert Hoover, An American Epic (Chicago: Henry Regnery Company, 1960), vol. 2, 397–401.
[266] Hoover, American Epic, vol. 2, 398, 399.
[267] "Telegram W. Wilson to E. Hurley and N. Baker (March 22, 1919)," Papers of Woodrow Wilson, vol. 56, 190.
[268] "Letter H. Hoover to W. Wilson (March 27, 1919)," Papers of Woodrow Wilson, vol. 56, 339.
[269] Fourth Annual Report of the Shipping Board, 54.
[270] Third Annual Report of the Shipping Board, 9–10.
[271] Third Annual Report of the Shipping Board, 81.
[272] 57 CONG. REC. 490 (December 16, 1918).
[273] U.S. Congress, Senate, Construction of Ships in American Yards for Foreign Account, 65th Cong., 3rd sess., 1919, S. Doc. 65-334.
[274] U.S. Congress, Senate, Ship Construction for Foreign Account, 65th Cong., 3rd sess., 1919, S. Rep. 65-680.
[275] 57 CONG. REC. 1080 (January 7, 1919); 57 CONG. REC. 4538 (February 28, 1919).
[276] For example, "America and the League of Nations," New Republic 17, no. 213 (November 30, 1918): 116—20.
[277] "Entry for October 17, 1918," and "Entry for November 6, 1918," Cabinet Diaries of Josephus Daniels, 342 and 347.
[278] "Letter E. Hurley to W. Wilson (Dec. 12, 1918)," Papers Relating to the Foreign Relations of the United States, The Paris Peace Conference, 1919, U.S. Department of State, Office of the Historian, Historical Documents, vol. 2, document no. 545.
[279] Fourth Annual Report of the Shipping Board, 90.
[280] "Text of the Official Announcement of the President's Plan to Go to Europe," New York Times, November 19, 1918, 1.
[281] Woodrow Wilson, "Delegating to the United States Shipping Board and to the United States Shipping Board Emergency Fleet Corporation, respectively, powers granted to the President by Acts of Congress relative to the Emergency Shipping Fund and approved on or prior to November 4, 1918," Executive Order no. 3018 (December 3, 1918).
[282] "Trade Fleet Offices to Dot the Globe," New York Times, December 27, 1918, 9; Charles Piez, "Merchant Marine of 15,000,000 Tons," New York Times, January 19, 1918, Sec. 20, 11.
[283] For example, "Will Meet All Rate Cuts," New York Times, February 15, 1919, 13.
[284] "Letter H. Robinson to W. Wilson (April 30, 1919)," Papers of Woodrow Wilson, vol. 58, 269.
[285] "John H. Rosseter, Marine Head, Dies," New York Times, April 30, 1936, 19.

286 "Who's Who in the Trade," Tea & Coffee Trade Journal 34, no. 6 (June 1918): 543–44.
287 "American Ships for Foreign Trade in 30 Days, J. H. Rosseter Promises," New York Times, April 27, 1919, sec. 2, 1.
288 Safford, Wilsonian Maritime Diplomacy, 173.
289 William Notz, "The World's Coal Situation during the War: I," Journal of Political Economy 26, no. 6 (June 1918): 567–611, 602.
290 "Letter H. Garfield to W. Wilson (March 1, 1919)," Papers of Woodrow Wilson, vol. 55, 362; Safford, Wilsonian Maritime Diplomacy, 188–91.
291 "Letter H. Garfield to W. Wilson (March 3, 1919)," Papers of Woodrow Wilson, vol. 55, 397.
292 Safford, Wilsonian Maritime Diplomacy, 165.
293 "America Offers to Buy Fleet of Marine Company," New York Times, November 27, 1918, 1.
294 "Letter from E. Hurley to W. Wilson (January 20, 1919)," Papers of Woodrow Wilson, vol. 54, 171.
295 For example, "Letter W. McAdoo to W. Wilson (November 16, 1918)," Papers of Woodrow Wilson, vol. 53, 112; "Letter J. Daniels to W. Wilson (November 18, 1918)," Papers of Woodrow Wilson, vol. 53, 110; "Letter W. Wilson to B. Colby (November 18, 1918)," Papers of Woodrow Wilson, vol. 53, 111.
296 For example, "Letter E. House to A. Balfour (December 1, 1918)," Papers Relating to the Foreign Relations of the United States, The Paris Peace Conference, 1919, U.S. Department of State, Office of the Historian, Historical Documents, vol. 2, no. 840.48/2606.
297 "The Council of Four: Minutes of the Meetings March 20 to May 24, 1919," Papers Relating to the Foreign Relations of the United States, The Paris Peace Conference, 1919, U.S. Department of State, Office of the Historian, Historical Documents, vol. 5, 161—63.
298 "Henry Robinson, Coast Financier," New York Times, November 4, 1937, 25.
299 "Letter H. Robinson to W. Wilson (April 19, 1919)," Papers of Woodrow Wilson, vol. 57, 498; "Bulk of German Shipping to be for American and British Use," New York Times, March 16, 1919, 1; "Germany to Deposit $90,000,000 for Food," New York Times, March 19, 1919, 3.
300 Jeffrey J. Safford, "Edward Hurley and American Shipping Policy: An Elaboration on Wilsonian Diplomacy, 1918-1919," Historian 35, no. 4 (August 1973): 568–86, 584.
301 Hearings before the Senate Committee on Commerce on the Establishment of an American Merchant Marine, 1–36.
302 For example, "Piez Raps Hurley Shipping Policy," Trenton Evening Times, May 1, 1919, 10.
303 Hurley, Bridge to France, 253.
304 "Seeks World Compact on Seamen's Wages," New York Times, November 19, 1918, 7.

[305] "Letter E. Hurley to W. Wilson (November 9, 1918)," Papers of Woodrow Wilson, vol. 53, 9.
[306] Safford, "Edward Hurley," 576.
[307] "Letter A. Furuseth to W. Wilson (November 16, 1918)," Papers of Woodrow Wilson, vol. 53, 107.
[308] "Preliminary Peace Conference, Protocol No. 4, Plenary Session of April 11, 1919," Papers Relating to the Foreign Relations of the United States, The Paris Peace Conference, 1919, U.S. Department of State, Office of the Historian, Historical Documents, vol. III, no 180.0201/4.
[309] "Preliminary Peace Conference, Protocol No. 4, Plenary Session of April 11, 1919," Papers Relating to the Foreign Relations of the United States, The Paris Peace Conference, 1919, annex 1, part 1, chap. 4, 268.
[310] "Preliminary Peace Conference, Protocol No. 4, Plenary Session of April 11, 1919," Papers Relating to the Foreign Relations of the United States, The Paris Peace Conference, 1919, annex II, "Protocol to Article 19," 282; "Letter H. Robinson to W. Wilson (March 24, 1919)," Papers of Woodrow Wilson, vol. 56, 236; "Letter A. Furuseth to W. Wilson (March 26, 1919)," Papers of Woodrow Wilson, vol. 56, 308.
[311] Safford, Wilsonian Maritime Diplomacy, 194–95.
[312] Safford, Wilsonian Maritime Diplomacy, 200–01.
[313] "Letter E. Hurley to W. Wilson (July 31, 1919)," Papers of Woodrow Wilson, vol. 62, 77.
[314] For example, Fourth Annual Report of the Shipping Board, 15–16.
[315] Edward N. Hurley, World Shipping Data, Report on European Mission (Washington, DC, Mar. 1, 1919),1.
[316] Donald G. Shomette, Ghost Fleet of Mallows Bay and Other Tales of the Lost Chesapeake (Centreville, MD: Tidewater Publishers, 1996).
[317] 56 CONG. REC. 11610 (November 21, 1918) S. Res. 343, 65th Cong., 2nd sess. (1918).
[318] "Letter W. Calder to E. Hurley (November 21, 1918)," U.S. Congress, Senate, Cost of Ship Construction. 65th Cong., 3rd sess., 1918, S. Doc. 65-315, 8–9.
[319] U.S. Congress, Senate, Cost of Ship Construction, S. Doc. 65-315, 5–8.
[320] Shomette, Ghost Fleet of Mallows Bay, 233.
[321] Webb, "The United States Wooden Steamship Program during World War I," 275–88, 285.
[322] Fifth Annual Report of the Shipping Board, 201.
[323] Seventh Annual Report of the Shipping Board, 147, 151, 247.
[324] U.S. Congress, House, Merchant Marine and Fisheries Committee, Hearings before the House Merchant Marine, Radio, and Fisheries Committee on Merchant Marine Investigation, 72nd Cong., 1st sess., 1932, appendix, 985; "United States Lines Sold to East-West Pool; Policies Continue, Leviathan Stays on Run," New York Times, October 31, 1931, 1.

325 "Lease for Ship Plant Signed Today," Alexandria Gazette, October 10, 1922, 1; "Salvaging Ships to Be Done Here," Alexandria Gazette, October 13, 1922, 1; "Shipyard to Open Monday Says J. N. Barde," Alexandria Gazette, October 18, 1922, 1.

326 "Salvaging Ships to Be Done Here," Alexandria Gazette, October 13, 1922, 1.

327 "Submarine S-5 Flooded by Failure of Air Valve," Evening Star (Washington, DC), September 4, 1920, 1.

328 Frederick N. Rasmussen, "The Sub Went Down, Crew Survived," Baltimore Sun, December, 7, 2002.

329 "Rescue of 37 from S-5 Due to Engineer" and "Story of Rescue Told by Radiograms," Baltimore Sun, September 4, 1920, 1; "Engineer Hero of S-5 Rescue," Washington Times, September 4, 1920, 1.

330 "Firemen Battle Fire All Night," Alexandria Gazette, October 25, 1922, 1.

331 "Two More Ships Arrive to be Dismantled," Alexandria Gazette, November 6, 1922, 1.

332 "10 of Ship Board Wooden Vessels Afire in Potomac," Evening Gazette (Worcester, MA), April 18, 1923, 1.

333 "Five Ships Burned in Potomac River," Evening Star (Washington, DC), April 19, 1923, 5.

334 Shomette, Ghost Fleet at Mallows Bay, 239–46.

335 Shomette, Ghost Fleet at Mallows Bay, 243–58.

336 U.S. Congress, House, Protecting America's Estuaries: The Potomac, 91st Cong., 2nd sess., 1970, H. Rep. 91-1761, 4; "75 Wooden Ships Await Wreckers," Evening Star (Washington, DC), July 28, 1929, 11; "40 War-Time Ships Left to Be Burned," Evening Star (Washington, DC), December 4, 1929, 25.

337 "31 Wooden Ships, Built during War, Are Burned in Bay," Washington Post, November 8, 1925, 3.

338 U.S. Congress, House, Protecting America's Estuaries: The Potomac. 91st Cong., 2nd sess., 1970, 4; Shomette, Ghost Fleet at Mallows Bay, 271–75.

339 Protecting America's Estuaries: The Potomac, H. Rep. 91-1761, 4–12.

340 For example, Shomette, Ghost Fleet of Mallow's Bay; Donald G. Shomette, Maritime Alexandria, the Rise and Fall of an American Entrepôt (Westminster, MD: Heritage Books, 2008); Donald G. Shomette, "The Ghost Fleet of Mallows Bay," Invention & Technology Magazine 14, no. 3 (Winter 1999): 12–23.

341 85 Fed. Reg. 50,736 (September 26, 2019).

Secretary of the Navy Josephus Daniels and Admiral William S. Benson, USN, outside the Ritz Hotel, Paris, circa late 1918, early 1919, U.S. Naval Historical Center Photograph

Chapter 21—Framing the 1920 Merchant Marine Act

The Fleet Corporation's final construction program consisted of 3,256 vessels of about 18 million DWT.[1] Of these, 1,820 were delivered by March 1920.[2] The United States had a fleet of 15.7 million DWT in the foreign trade in 1920, about four times the size of the 1917 fleet and about thirteen times that of the 1910 fleet.[3] It was reported that "during this period it [Fleet Corporation] owned and operated more vessels than had any other organization or government in the history of world shipping."[4]

The corporation built many commercially valuable vessels, although it also controlled hundreds of the wrong kinds of vessels, such as wooden and concrete vessels.[5] The fleet was also a long way from fully adopting oil burning internal combustion diesel engines.[6] The vessels constructed were therefore a war achievement, but a peace problem.[7] As it was put in *Colliers* magazine, "Our merchant marine of to-day is a bounty poured into our lap by war. Will we be able to keep our flag on the seas?"[8]

A maritime peace plan was needed. Everything was on the table including continued government vessel ownership and operation, private ownership and operation, or some hybrid of these options. Choices had to be made whether to sell the vessels all at once and let the market sort things out or sell the vessels over time. Many of the previous ideas for promoting a U.S. merchant marine were considered together with new ideas such as preferential domestic rail rates. There was also tidying up to do since issues had developed with the Shipping Board structure and authority, the ability of the board to enforce international shipping regulation contained in the 1916 Shipping Act, and the 1913 loophole in the coastwise laws revealed by the Wickersham opinion.

Charlie Papavizas

The 1920 Merchant Marine Act was that peace plan, and it started with Shipping Board proposals that were considered and amended by the two congressional committees of jurisdiction under Republican control—the House Merchant Marine Committee chaired by Representative William Greene and the Senate Commerce Committee chaired by Senator Wesley Jones.

SHIPPING BOARD PROPOSALS

Jones kicked off the process with a December 1918 Senate resolution requesting that the Shipping Board recommend what legislation the Congress should enact to promote the U.S. merchant marine.[9] At the time, the board was publicly supporting the president's plan to use the fleet as leverage in Paris. Board representatives were talking publicly about dumping the fleet at low prices and competing head-to-head with Britain. On January 16, 1919, for example, Hurley announced a trial balloon that the U.S. government was willing to write-off $1 billion to get vessels into American owner's hands at a favorable cost.[10] He later softened his view indicating that study was needed before selling the fleet, although he was confident the United States could compete.[11]

The *New York Times* editorial page captured in February 1919 the dilemma the United States faced, "One thing is certain," the op-ed read, "Unless private enterprise is permitted to take over the ships on reasonable terms the alternative is government ownership, with the prospect that it will increase the burden of taxation intolerably, and in the end fail, because of inefficient methods, to hold the seas against competition."[12]

Bainbridge Colby, who had served with Hurley on the Shipping Board since 1917, sent the president his own proposal in February 1919 when he resigned.[13] Colby argued that a privatized U.S merchant marine would not be able to hold its "own against the concentrated national competition of greater maritime nations." He recommended the formation of a company "owned and managed by private interests but financially backed and supervised by the government" to own the government vessels. Colby argued against selling the vessels to private interests because such sales would involve "unnecessary sacrifice of government investments."

Hurley sent Wilson privately his plan on March 15, 1919, after conferring with Representative Alexander, the Merchant Marine Committee ranking member.[14] Hurley set forth six options, ranging from government ownership and operation to private ownership and operation, and recommended the vessels be sold to American citizens at the current world market price rather than the government war-time cost. He also recommended easy payment terms—25 percent down and the rest to be paid in installments over ten years. The government would take back a mortgage for the unpaid balance. A portion of the interest earned by the government from the installment loans and other earnings would be paid into a "merchant marine development fund." Each vessel-owning company would have a government-appointed director on its board of directors.

Also, according to Hurley's plan, some vessels would be sold to serve on routes the Shipping Board determined essential. Vessel owners losing money on such routes would be compensated from the development fund. If vessels earned a profit on such routes above debt service, half of that profit would be paid into the same fund. The board would have the authority to foreclose on mortgages if it determined that losses were due to owner mismanagement. All vessels would be owned and operated by the government until sold.

Hurley concluded that he was recommending "a policy which I believe can be criticised [sic] only by selfish shipping interests anxious to keep out smaller companies." He optimistically expected the write-off from the government cost of building the vessels to be no more than 20 percent (in other words, far less than the $1 billion he had floated publicly). Hurley did not deal in his initial plan with whether vessels should be sold all at once or over time and how that would work.

Hurley was contemporaneously on a merchant marine propaganda tour that took him across the country making speeches.[15] On March 31, 1919 shortly after making a speech to a group in Washington, DC, he suffered an attack of dizziness and nausea.[16] His physician prescribed rest and he spent about ten days in Tampa before resuming his travel schedule.[17] It was Hurley's first vacation since his camping trip with the "Vagabonds."

Upon returning to work, Hurley organized a conference of business interests in Washington, DC, in May 1919 to discuss various alternatives.[18] The positions taken in subsequent 1919-20 congressional hearings were all previewed. The Farmers' National Council argued, for example, that the fleet should remain government-owned and be operated "for the benefit of the people as a whole." The American Manufacturers' and Exporters' Association argued for selling the vessels "at the earliest possible moment."

On June 11, Hurley sent a Shipping Board plan to Representative William Greene endorsed by Commissioner Donald.[19] At the time, there were only three commissioners. Raymond Stevens, the third commissioner, sent separate overlapping recommendations. On August 5 Judge Payne was confirmed as board chairman, and on August 22 he wrote a memorandum to President Wilson concurring with the prior board recommendations.[20]

The board's proposal repeated Hurley's private proposal with a few additions. Regarding the government ordering more commercial vessels beyond the war construction program, the board recommended that there should be no more orders other than as "needed to balance the fleet."

Furthermore, the board believed that "only flagrant mismanagement in the distribution of ships by the Government would be likely to cause overberthing in any trade route," despite continued government ownership. It also recommended new legislation granting recorded vessel mortgages priority to provide effective security and proposed that the United States should "discard the mail subvention or bonus principle" and simply pay for mail services rendered.

Stevens approved of putting the vessels into private hands over time but was pessimistic about the ability of the market to absorb the enormous fleet. He noted that the fleet in foreign trade was roughly 2 million DWT prior to the war and the private fleet after the war was about 3 million DWT, with the government still owning about 13 million DWT.[21] He observed that:

> American shipping organizations are not yet sufficiently developed. The ability of American ships to compete in the world's market is not yet demonstrated. American capital is not yet accustomed to shipping investments. For all these reasons I believe that the absorption of this great tonnage will be slow.

Stevens's fears were realized, as the Shipping Board wound up owning vessels for many years after the war. Stevens also criticized Hurley's "merchant marine development fund" as being too open-ended, likening it to a "form of Government subsidy" to which "there are grave social and economic objections." He concluded that the market was too much in flux to determine whether any subsidy was appropriate, and that issue should be revisited in two or three years (and in fact it was by President Harding in 1922).

Chairman Payne later put his gloss on the Shipping Board's recommendations in a December 1919 speech.[22] He remarked that "the question is not between public and private ownership, but between American and foreign ownership." The aim was to create a viable U.S. merchant marine: "Ships alone will not do this. Indeed, unless we have men, money, and brains in the shipping business, ships may become a liability rather than an asset." Payne rejected the notion that creation of a merchant marine could be done quickly, declaring that "many seem to think the Shipping Board can do this by reducing the price of ships, and instantly shipping men will spring up and all our ships will be bought by private owners, and, presto! a merchant marine is a fact. This is a serious error." He continued, "Ships can not [sic] be sold in large numbers until the country is prepared to buy them. It is not now prepared."

Charlie Papavizas

1919 Senate Hearings and Jones's Proposals

Senator Jones made it obvious from the beginning that he was serious about developing a comprehensive plan.[23] He conducted extensive hearings from 1919 to 1920 with the express subject being "Establishment of an American Merchant Marine."[24] Jones believed that the opportunity presented to the United States was the same as that presented to Britain after the Civil War because now it was the United States with a virtually untouched fleet and Britain that had suffered during the war.[25]

In the summer of 1919, the Commerce Committee mainly heard from Shipping Board witnesses, starting with Hurley focusing on winding down the construction program.[26] The committee pressed Hurley hard as to why U.S. shipyards, which were staring into the abyss of vastly reduced government orders, could not take orders from foreign customers. In fact, on February 28, 1919, the Senate had passed legislation to take away the board's authority to prevent foreign sales.[27] Jones reintroduced the legislation on June 2, 1919, in the Sixty-Sixth Congress.[28]

At the Commerce Committee hearing on June 10, Hurley explained that the board wanted to negotiate in each instance the possibility of salvaging corporation-purchased items for such vessels. Senator Walter E. Edge (R-NJ) captured the committee's sentiment when he said that the government "is playing in what I would rather consider a small business" expressing his disapproval of the board holding up shipyards to get its needs met first.[29] (Edge was governor of New Jersey during World War I and part of World War II and achieved contemporary fame when he was portrayed in the period crime drama *Boardwalk Empire*).

As the hearing progressed, Hurley also explained that it was imperative for the future of the U.S. merchant marine that the fleet be "re-balanced."[30] Larger, faster, better built vessels were required. Hurley also bluntly told the committee that there were twice as many U.S. shipyards as were needed.[31] He explained that the Shipping Board resisted foreign orders because it was concerned that foreign customers would order large vessels from U.S. yards thereby making that capacity unavailable to the U.S. government to balance the fleet.

Rosseter echoed Hurley's view that the wrong vessels were still being delivered. He pleaded with the committee to support the building of larger and faster vessels with internal combustion (diesel) engines. He acknowledged that the political inclination was not to order new vessels while large losses were looming for vessels still being delivered.[32]

Rosseter also emphasized that the establishment of defined vessel routes should be a paramount objective, although the lack of U.S. import cargoes would hamper that goal. At the time, U.S. trade was heavily weighted toward exports whereas Britain had a more balanced trade, making it easier for British vessels to travel both out bound and in bound with cargoes. U.S.-flag vessels often returned to the United States in ballast without cargo, which put them at a substantial commercial disadvantage.

Hurley worked with the Commerce Committee overnight and on June 11 made public a letter addressing the issue. In the letter, the Shipping Board permitted foreign sales but encouraged interaction to determine if the Fleet Corporation had materials usable in new construction projects (such as boilers, engines, winches, or chains).[33]

At the time the hearings started, there was worldwide excess demand for vessels since vessels repatriating armies and used in famine relief were not yet fully released for commercial service and war-time losses had not yet been fully made up. But that was expected to change. Stevens emphasized in the hearings that vessel supply was almost assuredly going to exceed demand with the world fleet anticipated to be substantially larger in 1921 than it was in 1914.[34] Hurley nevertheless argued that the government should try and take advantage of the current high demand by only selling vessels at or near war-time cost in order to "stabilize the whole situation through the selling of the ships and the building of ships.[35]

Jones carefully considered the Shipping Board's proposal and initial hearings, and, after as he said, "consulting with men of experience," developed two alternative overlapping bills which he introduced on November 3, 1919.[36] Jones declared the legislative object:

> We do not desire, and it is not our purpose, to drive other nations off the sea, but we do want to do, and we ought to do, at least our proportionate part of our own and the world's carrying trade, so that our commerce shall have a fair chance in the world's markets, and that we may be hereafter fully prepared for any emergency that may confront us.[37]

Much of the rest of Jones's legislative introduction coincided with Hurley's views such as that "the fleet should be properly balanced," and the vessels cannot be "given away" since "the people will not stand for that."

Rather, the guiding principle should be that the government should get out of the shipping business, but only "without unnecessary sacrifice and just as a private individual would get rid of property, he did not desire to keep but that he did not have to dispose of at a sacrifice." This reasonable sounding phraseology, virtually impossible to implement in practice, was to be at the core of the upcoming policy debate.

The bill Jones discussed on the Senate floor was future-oriented.[38] It started with a declaration of national policy, implicit in the 1916 Shipping Act preamble, that it was "necessary for the national defense and for the proper growth of our foreign commerce that the United States shall have an American merchant marine." The main vessel-building, selling, and operating work of the Shipping Board and Fleet Corporation would be turned over to a new corporation, which would be charged with achieving the declared national purpose. Reflecting the policy confusion about what to prioritize, the new corporation was to dispose of vessels "upon the best terms possible... to secure the greatest possible return to the Government" and "without interfering with the primary purposes of the Act."

The other bill would dissolve the Fleet Corporation and transfer all property and authority to the Shipping Board for the purposes of orderly liquidation of the fleet. In that instance, the board was directed to dispose of vessels "as soon as practicable after this Act becomes law." Even in this privatization, the establishment of shipping lines with government-owned vessels was authorized which implicitly acknowledged that the vessels could not be sold immediately to private parties.

Both bills would repeal emergency authorities granted to the Shipping Board, such as the right to set charter rates.[39] They would repeal the 1914 Foreign Registry Act permission for foreign-built vessels to be U.S. registered. The bills would also repeal the October 6, 1917, Act's permission for foreign-built vessels to engage in the U.S. coastwise trade. Both bills would extend the coastwise laws to U.S. territories with direction for the Board/Corporation to establish steamship lines service to those islands as necessary. Finally, both bills addressed Jones's favorite merchant marine policy subject—discriminating duties—by directing the president to abrogate treaty provisions limiting the right of the United States to impose duties discriminating in favor of U.S. vessels.

THE GREENE BILL

Chairman Greene introduced on October 9, 1919, his own bill to deal with the peace transition. The proposed legislation would repeal emergency authorities, concentrate all authority in the Shipping Board (vs. authority granted to the president and delegated to the board), and leave the original 1916 Shipping Act authorities largely intact.[40] The bill contained neither a plan for the future of the merchant marine nor an outside date for when the vessels would have to be sold. The committee expected to supplement the bill with later legislation.

P. A. S. Franklin spoke for several vessel owners at the House hearings held in October 1919 in favor of immediate sale of the fleet.[41] At the time, he noted that the United States had an opportunity with the departure of the German commercial fleet that "should not be lost to the citizens of the United States." Franklin concluded that the only thing holding the merchant marine back was the lack of a definitive government policy and that "no man will invest a large volume of money in shipping if he has to compete with the United States Government."[42]

At the opposite extreme was the Farmers' National Council, represented by Benjamin C. Marsh. (Marsh, born in Bulgaria to American missionaries, served a series of social welfare causes for fifty years.)[43] Marsh argued that farmers's organizations were adamantly in favor of permanent U.S. government ownership of the fleet.[44]

Marsh complained that the Shipping Board was engaged in insider capitalism with half of the vessels allocated by the board for operation going to companies connected with Fleet Corporation personnel, such as to Pacific Mail Steamship Co., where Rosseter had worked. In his 1953 autobiography, Marsh argued that the war-built vessels "were a major prize, which 'private enterprise' buccaneers were eager to grab" and that oceanic trade was an "additional source of paytriotism [sic]."[45]

Marsh also complained that Schwab and others had solicited public funds from farmers and laborers to buy Liberty Bonds during the war to construct vessels with Schwab saying that "undoubtedly, after the war is over, the ships that are building now will pay for themselves many times over."[46] Now the war had ended, and industry professionals were arguing that the vessels had to be written down if they were put in private hands.

Indeed, U.S. shipyards argued that vessels "should not be sold for a song." For example, the Baltimore *Sun* published a series of interviews in November 1919 with Holden A. Evans, head of Baltimore Dry Docks and Shipbuilding Company, who argued that dumping the vessels would knock down the shipbuilding market.[47] Board/Fleet Corporation witnesses such as

Robert A. Dean, general counsel to the board, and who generally provided technical testimony, also opposed any requirement to sell vessels immediately.[48]

Ultimately, the committee approved a "skinny" bill with only thirteen sections focused on winding down the shipbuilding program.[49] The Greene Bill contained its own formulation of merchant marine policy in section 3, including authorizing the Shipping Board "to sell, *as soon as practicable*, to citizens of the United States... all government-owned vessels.[50] Only vessels the board deemed "unnecessary to the promotion and maintenance of an efficient American merchant marine" could be sold to non-U.S. citizens.[51] In addition, the board was authorized to consider the "prevailing domestic and foreign market price of and demand for vessels."

The difference between the Greene and Jones approaches was summarized in the *Pacific Marine Review*: "the main difference between the two bills is that in one [Greene] the government proposes to get out of the shipping business with a jolt, and let nature takes its course. With the other [Jones] it is proposed that the government back out gradually, and as it is doing so, it proposes to nurse along and develop a new crop of shipping men and set private ownership and operation going gradually without any rude jolting."[52]

Greene introduced his bill on the House floor on November 8, 1919, declaring that there was "no opposition in the committee of any nature" and that the "Shipping Board are agreeable to the bill."[53] He also praised ranking minority member Representative Alexander "in the highest terms" for his bipartisan approach and George W. Edmonds (R-PA) for taking the lead on the legislation The floor debate was a love fest.

The Merchant Marine Committee had already reported on October 4, 1919, legislation known as the "Rowe Bill" to make it easier for U.S. citizen mariners to qualify as "able-bodied seamen" (ABs).[54] The Seaman's Act required that either an AB or an officer man every lifeboat, a requirement that had elicited complaints from vessel owners. The Rowe Bill shortened the time before a U.S. citizen seaman could become an AB when combined with formal training with the purpose of encouraging citizens to go to sea. The International Seamen's Union opposed the bill because it would "lower the seamen's calling by overcrowding it with inexperienced men."[55] The Rowe Bill nevertheless passed the House by consent.[56]

Representative Edmonds pointed out that "as long as the Government continued the policy of trying to get the war price," no private interest would purchase vessels from the government because it was cheaper to order new. Alexander pointed out that "the vessels must be operated in competition with the merchant marine of the world, whether under Government or private ownership." He also declared, to applause, that "it should be our fixed purpose and determination to build up and maintain a merchant marine that will be adequate to carry at least 50 percent of our commerce in the foreign trade."

Rowe expressed the committee view that "the real meat of this bill is in section 3." He also summarized the committee's consideration:

> We had before us all classes of men, with various ideas. Some would not sell a ship, but want the Nation to operate the last one. Some thought we ought to dispose of every ship within a year. We can not [sic] take either extreme. We must give to somebody a chance to sell and dispose of these ships, and nobody is better qualified than the Shipping Board to do this, and to work them into the commerce of the Nation under the American flag. [Applause.][57]

Representative Joe Cannon, then seventy-three years old and no longer speaker of the House, used his floor time to reminisce about the Collins Line and early subsidy scandals and how the country turned away from the sea when the continental United States opened to development.[58] Cannon pointed out that at the outset of the war, "we would not have had any merchant marine, in my judgment, if it had not been that we monopolized the coastwise trade of the United States, and a wonderful trade it was," and criticized the opening of that trade to foreign vessels during the war under the October 6, 1917 Act. The House handily passed the bill, generally known as the "Greene Bill," on November 8, 1919.[59]

1920 SENATE HEARINGS

The Commerce Committee resumed hearings on January 21, 1920, lasting until March 13 focusing on the future of the merchant marine. Jones was active throughout. The examination of the issues in 1920 was intense, with hearings held on thirty-eight days over seven weeks including six Saturdays taking testimony from over one hundred witnesses encompassing over two thousand pages of testimony.

Despite the intensity, it was alleged after the 1920 Merchant Marine Act that the Act was the handiwork of only a few Senators.[60] Most Commerce Committee hearings were in fact attended by about eight senators out of the nineteen on the committee.

The government and every sector of the private shipping industry were represented in the hearings. Both Hurley and Payne testified, and Benson provided additional recommendations after the hearings ended. Many familiar characters like Chamberlain, Franklin, and Furuseth testified. Others like Denman and Marvin wrote letters or submitted reports. In the process, Jones had to deal with a "four-cornered fight" among U.S. vessel owners, U.S. shipyards, companies operating vessels for the Shipping Board, and the board itself, and so arranged to hear from every interest in the 1920 hearings.[61]

Hanging over the hearings was the question of how to compete with Britain. On the second day, Jones introduced into the record a November 12, 1919, article entitled "The Lookout Man" from the British *Fairplay* magazine.[62] The article quoted Jones's floor statement about seeking "our part of the world's carrying trade" and stated a typical British response:

> When it comes to survival of the fittest, we have invariably done our level best to crush or mold opposition, and, as regard America's new mercantile marine, we shall go on doing it, and expect her to do the same to us.

Reportedly, Jones thereafter "carried this article with him constantly, pulling it out and playing it to its hilt when the occasion warranted."[63]

Emil P. Albrecht, president of the Philadelphia Bourse, summed up the U.S. vessel owners' view: "Sell it. Sell it quickly. Sell it at practically any price. But sell it under restrictions and on such terms as will insure [sic] its remaining under our flag."[64]

On the other side, the committee also heard from Benjamin Marsh that the farmers wanted the vessels to remain government-owned and from the gadfly Manson that "there is also much grafting and crookedness by many of these private operators" and the vessels should not be sold until the government established profitable lines.[65]

Admiral Robert E. Coontz, the chief of naval operations, who had succeeded Benson, stated that "the Navy is vitally interested in the establishment of an American merchant marine." The reasons were that "it is an indispensable arm of service in time of war," "it enables the United States to take her proper place in diplomatic and trade relations with the world, and "it is the nursery of seamen."[66] He also said that "the war would have been lost to the Allies and to the United States" but for the U.S. merchant marine, and that "in any future war a merchant marine is just as essential a part of our fighting forces as the regular Navy."

Coontz argued that the war-time fleet should remain government-owned: "It would be practically impossible to sell our ships to private corporations at a price acceptable to them and at the same time acceptable to public opinion." Moreover, in his view, all merchant mariners should be naval reservists and the government should subsidize their pay which would be cheaper than separately having an inactive naval reserve.

The Army's main issue related to how fast the port facilities would be turned over to the Shipping Board particularly the piers in Hoboken, New Jersey, owned before the war by the Hamburg-American Line and North German Lloyd Line. The U.S. government seized these facilities together with the interned German vessels in April 1917.[67] Hoboken had so many German residents before the war that it was known as "Little Bremen."[68] The German population was driven out when the U.S. entered the war.[69] The War Department made Hoboken one of the main ports of embarkation to France with 80 percent of troops shipping from there.[70] The town became famous through a phrase attributed to General Pershing, who is reported to have promised in the summer of 1918 to the troops that they would be in "Heaven or Hoboken before Christmas" or more commonly "Heaven, Hell or Hoboken by Christmas."[71]

Vessel manning costs came up in the committee hearings. Senator William Calder and others put figures in the record that U.S. manning costs were twice as high as British costs and various complaints were made against the Seaman's Act.[72] Nevertheless, both Senator Jones and Senator Duncan Fletcher, the ranking Democrat on the Commerce Committee, committed early in the legislative process to keeping the Seaman's Act.[73]

Furuseth argued that the Seaman's Act had been misrepresented by the newspapers responding to British shipping lines, which were their major advertisers. Jones agreed.[74] Furuseth also repeated the argument he had made many times leading up the Seaman's Act that there was no difference between U.S. seaman and foreign seaman costs when skill level and port of embarkation were considered.

Furuseth took the opportunity to talk about what made an effective merchant marine. In his view, "sea power is made up of men and ships; not ships and men" and "if you want sea power, you must be willing to pay the price in men." Furuseth urged perseverance in enforcing the Seaman's Act as written.

Application of the Act to foreign vessels when in U.S. ports, he believed, would eventually force an equalization of wages and standards.

Captain William A. Wescott, president of the Masters, Mates, and Pilots of the Pacific Coast, testified against continued use of non-citizens as officers aboard U.S.-flag vessels. The citizen requirement was suspended in 1914 in connection with the Ship Registry Act.[75] Wescott was particularly opposed to the executive orders of September 1, 1916, and February 7, 1920, which sought to induce serving non-citizen officers to become U.S. citizens because, he claimed, there was no shortage of existing U.S. citizen officers to serve.[76]

Senator Jones and Eugene Chamberlain engaged in a wide-ranging discussion regarding maritime policy. Jones asked if changes were needed to the U.S. "navigation laws." Chamberlain recounted how he had been asked repeatedly by Congress to identify "antiquated navigation laws," a phrase he attributed to David A. Wells. He pointed out that the primary navigation law that was the focus for decades was the U.S-build requirement, which the committee intended to retain for the U.S. coastwise trade.

Chamberlain argued there should still be some date set by which the vessels would have to be sold. Jones disagreed, stating that fixing a date "would be the worst way" because "that would give people who want to buy the ships just exactly the thing they want."[77] Jones said virtually the exact same words on May 21, in seeking to close Senate debate (the proposed amendment "would simply play into the hands of those who want to buy ships").[78]

The committee also considered requiring U.S. railroads to offer preferential rates to U.S.-flag vessels engaged in carrying exports. That idea was supported by N. Sutton Myrick from the U.S. Chamber of Commerce.[79] The chamber's suggestion was later echoed by other witnesses and Benson on behalf of the Shipping Board.[80]

Testimony was also taken about Shipping Board proposals adopted by the House Merchant Marine Committee to Americanize marine insurance, bolster U.S. vessel classification services, and improve the status of vessel mortgages and other measures—all essential components of a functioning national merchant marine. Professor Solomon Huebner (later known as the "father of insurance education") testified on marine insurance.[81] Huebner worked closely with Edmonds, who introduced two bills addressing the insurance issues Huebner identified.[82] The professor asserted that marine insurance could be used "as a powerful weapon for acquiring and controlling important channels of foreign trade."[83] U.S. marine insurance, he said, was hindered by U.S. antitrust laws and state regulations.[84]

N. Sutton Myrick added that "we should go as far as we can in encouragement of our American classification society... because classification and insurance go hand in hand." Congress had heard as early as 1870—in connection with the Lynch Committee hearings—that Lloyd's Register, the British national vessel classification society, was disadvantaging U.S.-built vessels.[85]

The American Bureau of Shipping (ABS) was one of Lloyd's U.S. competitors (eventually, its sole U.S competitor). ABS, founded in New York in 1862 as the American Shipmasters' Association, adopted the ABS name in 1898.[86] The Fleet Corporation had preferred using ABS for its vessels, but not exclusively at first.[87] Commander Stevenson Taylor, head of ABS, wrote in November 1919 that as a permanent U.S. merchant marine was established the fleet "ought not to be entrusted to supervision of the subjects of any foreign government, however friendly they may be."[88]

Jones introduced legislation in 1920 to address the issue.[89] That bill became, in almost identical language, section 25 of the 1920 Act. The legislation made ABS the government's official classification society by requiring all agencies to "recognize the American Bureau of Shipping as their agency."

Another focus was to provide effective vessel financial security to the U.S. government and private lenders. As already seen from Chairman Hurley's proposals for post-war policy, Hurley anticipated selling vessels on easy credit terms with the U.S. government being secured by a vessel mortgage.

The problem was that vessel mortgages were not then favored under U.S. law. They are technically not "maritime contracts" and so were not enforceable in federal courts sitting as "admiralty courts." The concept of "admiralty courts" was borrowed from English experience, where special courts dealt with maritime contract disputes and maritime torts (accidents).[90] The U.S. Constitution in article 3, section 2, expressly grants to federal civil courts this separate jurisdiction over "cases of admiralty and maritime jurisdiction." Without federal jurisdiction, vessel mortgages had to be enforced in state courts, with widely varying results. This undermined confidence in vessel mortgages as effective financial security.

Even worse, the general view was that vessel mortgages were inferior in priority to all maritime liens. Under long-standing judge-made common law, a "maritime lien" arises as a matter of law as soon as a service is provided to a vessel (such as repairs or fuel) until it is paid without the need to record or otherwise provide notice of the lien. Liens also arose when the vessel was involved in an accident such as colliding with a pier and followed the vessel wherever it went. Since such liens are commonplace, "silent," and followed the vessel, a person lending to a vessel owner taking a vessel mortgage was at substantial risk of having no priority at all. Most third parties would have superior maritime liens.

Ira A. Campbell, an attorney working for the Shipping Board, drafted federal mortgage legislation. The proposal placed jurisdiction of vessel mortgages in federal courts sitting in admiralty, clarified the foreclosure process, and gave recorded mortgages priority over all maritime liens arising by contract after the recording of the mortgage, with certain exceptions, such as for crew wages. The House Merchant Marine Committee

JOURNEY TO THE JONES ACT

held several separate hearings on the subject starting on August 27, 1919.[91] There was substantial opposition, particularly from repair shipyards.[92]

The committee also heard from discriminating duty adherents. Homer L. Ferguson, president of Newport News Ship Building & Dry Dock Co. during both World War I and II, argued that countries should be permitted to discriminate in their carrying trade to the disadvantage of countries carrying goods between two countries other than their own (i.e., the indirect trade).[93] (Ferguson, who had graduated first from the Naval Academy, was vice president of Newport News Ship Building when Alfred L. Hopkins, the president, died on the *Lusitania*.)

When Jones asked about whether commercial treaties would be an impediment, Ferguson responded, "That is the usual bugaboo" and distinguished U.S. commitments in direct bilateral trade from discrimination that could be applied to the indirect trade. Ferguson offered legislation seeking to ensure that discriminating duties could be re-introduced without violating the 1815 U.S.-Britain commercial treaty and similar agreements. Jones admitted that his "personal views" were in accord with re-introduction of discriminating duties but that "what the committee will do I do not know."[94]

Fields S. Pendleton, a New York vessel owner, related the history of the Maine maritime greats—Lynch, Blaine, Dingley, and Frye—and claimed that the Ocean Mail Act of 1891 "was so mutilated by Joseph G. Cannon and 16 Representatives from the middle northwest that the effect was slight and few lines were established."[95] He was referring to the convoluted final actions of the House of Representatives in watering down and then passing the Ocean Mail Act. He also complemented Jones for his 1913 "great speech" on discriminating duties.

In the last days of the hearings, the committee mainly heard from Shipping Board witnesses starting with Payne and ending with Rosseter. Payne was adamant that the fleet should be sold to private interests and the board should stop ordering new vessels: "A good deal can be said, and a good deal has been said, in favor of a balanced fleet. It is my conviction, however, that private persons should build the ships that are necessary, and that the Government should go out of the shipping business as rapidly as it can." Further, he stated, "I do not believe it is possible to establish a permanent merchant marine owned and operated by the Government; that its ownership and operation by private persons is a sine qua non to the successful establishment of a merchant marine."[96]

Payne explained that it was not "possible for the government to operate this fleet at a profit."[97] He reasoned that it would be impossible for one person or board to successfully oversee the operation of two thousand vessels in a worldwide business. Payne did not believe that the U.S. government needed to own a fleet to be able to regulate the trade or as a naval auxiliary. The U.S. Navy was in accord when it stated in 1919 that it did not recommend "the general construction of specially designed fleet auxiliaries, believing that for present needs merchant vessels will have to be acquired and adapted for naval uses."[98]

Payne was not sanguine about selling all the vessels quickly even if the Shipping Board price was reduced from the war cost to the present building cost.[99] He believed there was not enough expertise, experience, or capital in the U.S.-flag industry to absorb so many vessels in a short time. Specifically, he felt that even if the war price was cut in half, "the shipping concerns are not in a position to do it. They have not got the money. They cannot finance it."[100]

Payne was equally adamant that the board should not be subject to a time limit to sell the fleet.[101] On how fast the sale process would be, Jones and Payne had the following colloquy:

> Jones — In connection with your suggestion, as I understand you, you do not believe that the Shipping Board, in a proper business way, can dispose of these ships within a year or so?
>
> Payne —Impossible, Senator.

Jones — You do not agree with those shipping men who think we can do it within two years at the outside?

Payne — You can not [sic] do it in five years to save your life.

Jones — Your opinion is very much in accord with my own.[102]

To develop that expertise and experience, Payne argued that the government should put vessels in the hands of private companies pursuant to operating agreements.[103] Given time, Payne thought that U.S. vessel owners could succeed and downplayed the difference in crew wages, arguing that other factors, such as port turn-around time, were more important than the crew bill.[104]

Both Commissioners Thomas A. Scott and Stevens echoed Payne's points about the necessity to sell vessels at current replacement cost rather than substantially greater war cost.[105] Scott also emphasized that the Shipping Board was in the process of reforming its vessel operating agreements. Early agreements were straight cost-plus agreements, which provided no incentive to the operator working as agent for the U.S. government to make a profit. The new agreements gave to the private operator a percentage of profits and a percentage of any savings on expected repairs.[106]

At Jones's request, Rosseter had responded to questions in January 1920 and had been asked to address specific provisions in the Greene Bill and the Jones proposals.[107] In his letter, Rosseter defended the government setting high prices for vessels in 1919 because "immediate revenues justified a very high valuation." But that period was ending, and low British capital costs had to be met to establish a permanent American merchant marine.

At the hearing, Rosseter again emphasized that the fleet was unbalanced, that all the wooden vessels and many of the smaller steel vessels should be sold as soon as possible, and that the board should order large, speedy vessels.[108] Senator Knute Nelson called everything below 5,000 DWT "rubbish."[109]

Rosseter agreed with Payne that private interests could not take over the fleet all at once: "The line, so to speak, of Americans experienced in operation and with facilities in foreign countries is altogether too thin," he declared.[110] Rosseter believed strongly that vessels should be sold or operated on condition that they be put in certain routes. This, he argued, could be "done without prejudice or injury to existing American lines."[111]

Rosseter was confident that the U.S. merchant marine could compete effectively but not if impeded by the U.S. government or if the U.S. government failed to match foreign support for their ocean carriers. In his view, "the shipowner has to face world conditions in competition, and he should not be asked to do more than his competitors are required to do."[112] Rosseter also argued for other industry supports—vessel sale prices had to be reduced to replacement value, there needed to be reasonable compensation for the carriage of U.S. mail, and there had to be "safeguarding American shipping against the menace of conference rules." He concluded that "without encouraging legislation we will fail."[113]

Jones and Rosseter agreed that British competition would be cutthroat. Jones for his part pointed out that U.S. shippers were being threatened by British carriers such that they would receive no service if the shipper utilized a U.S. carrier. Rosseter responded that U.S. carriers needed better enforcement of the anti-competitive practices addressed in the 1916 Shipping Act, such as deferred rebating—which in fact was added to the 1920 Act.[114]

Origin of the "Jones Act"

The Senate Commerce Committee held separate hearings on Alaskan water transportation in March 1920. The issue was whether to grant the Alaska Territorial Shipping Board federal authority to oversee territorial water trade.[115] Although the legislation went nowhere, the hearings on the Territorial Board nevertheless highlighted related Alaska coastwise trade issues addressed in the 1920 Act.[116]

The committee heard from Territorial Governor Thomas Riggs, Jr., as well two advisers to the Territorial Board.[117] They argued that two Canadian shipping lines, both subsidized by the Canadian government and with other cost and rail advantages, dominated shipping to Alaska.[118]

There was a "spirited tilt" in the hearing when the advisers accused James Wickersham, Alaska delegate to Congress, of representing Canadian interests.[119] Recall that Wickersham had chortled with Representative Underwood in 1913 when Representative Humphrey alleged that Canadian shipping interests needed to be restrained. The scene was described by a local reporter after the accusation was made:

> Governor Riggs, an advocate of the bill, edged over toward the committee table. W. L. Clark, representing the Pacific Steamship Company, hastily threw his cigar away and R. W. Jelsey, committee clerk, ceased gazing out of the window at the couple of pigeons that were arranging their spring housekeeping on a corner of the building. It was a tense moment. The prospects for trouble looked good but Senator Wesley L. Jones, who has the physical ruggedness of a tank going into action, headed off hostilities by pounding heavily on the table with the palm of his hand, and announcing in a loud voice that the committee would remain in charge of the hearing.[120]

Wickersham flatly denied the charges. The main innuendo arose from a statement he had made that "in view of the ability of the Canadian lines to handle the business cheaper than the American lines, he was in favor of turning the entire traffic over to the Grand Trunk Pacific and the Canadian Pacific Railroad Cos."[121] Jones did not find that persuasive, noting that many

Americans "opposed any special efforts to the upbuilding of the American merchant marine on the ground that if the British can do it cheaper."[122]

The action shifted to the general Commerce Committee hearings on maritime policy, where W. L. Clark outlined long-standing efforts by foreign interests to undermine U.S. coastwise laws.[123] He reiterated what he had said in previous congressional hearings, namely that foreigners already owned U.S.-flag vessels via "dummy corporations." Here, he was referring to corporations "the securities of which are entirely owned by other Governments or citizens of other countries."[124]

Clark recounted the congressional colloquy in 1898 which gave rise to the Wickersham opinion.[125] This Wickersham loophole became particularly significant when the Canadian Grand Trunk Pacific Railway was completed to Prince Rupert in British Colombia in 1915. That permitted U.S. freight and passengers to travel by Canadian rail to Prince Rupert and then by Canadian vessels to Skagway, Alaska.[126]

Clark offered statutory language to address dummy corporations and the Wickersham loophole. Specifically, he would outlaw the sale of any ticket in the United States for mixed coastwise/foreign travel, include the words "by land and water" in the law, and restrict the U.S. coastwise trade to corporations owned at least 75 percent by U.S. citizens. While the first suggestion did not become law, the latter two did in the 1920 Act. Clark explained that his proposal would change the law so that it "can not [sic] be interpreted so that a short rail carriage shall vitiate our coastwise laws and permit foreign carriers to engage in our coastwise trades."

Further, Clark suggested that the coastwise laws be extended to the Philippines and other U.S. territories with one year's notice to ensure adequate American service. Jones expressed a concern that U.S. service might be inadequate, but Clark assured Jones that it was "beyond any question" that including the Philippines "would transform the Pacific trades.[127]

JOURNEY TO THE JONES ACT

Jones had reason to be concerned about providing adequate service to outlying U.S. possessions. Specifically, there had been complaints about the lack of passenger service to Hawaii since at least the summer of 1907, when the Oceanic Steamship Co. (known as the "Spreckels Line") showed signs of financial failure and withdrew three steamships that had served Hawaii as an intermediate stop to Australia/New Zealand.[128]

Renewal of the service depended on the Gallinger mail subsidy legislation which failed, and so the service was not renewed.[129] Chamberlain noted in his annual report at the time that the loss of the Spreckels Line service had resulted in "serious inconvenience" to Hawaii residents.[130] Hawaiian business interests agitated for coastwise law relief. The situation was so acute that President Roosevelt in his December 1907 annual message to Congress requested that "the coastwise shipping laws should be so far relaxed to prevent Hawaii suffering as it is now suffering."[131]

Delegate Jonah Kūhiō Kalaniana'ole (R-HI) introduced legislation in early 1908 to permit foreign vessels to transport passengers between Hawaii and the U.S. mainland until a new U.S.-flag service was put in place.[132] (Kalaniana'ole was the first native Hawaiian to serve in the U.S. House of Representatives starting as a delegate in 1903 and was also a member of the Hawaiian royal family. He was often referred to in Congress as "Prince.")[133] The legislation he proposed passed the House on May 28, 1908, but was not considered in the Senate, apparently because Matson Navigation Co. assured Hawaii that it would put a new vessel in the trade.[134]

During 1908, the Hawaiian Chamber of Commerce, which originally requested the legislation, flip-flopped several times on whether to seek permission for foreign vessels to serve Hawaii. The chamber appeared to be trying to get more U.S.-flag service while not antagonizing Matson, the main provider of existing U.S.-flag transportation service.[135] When the chamber renewed its support in December 1908, Matson reacted negatively.[136] No

Hawaii coastwise relief legislation was enacted, although Kalaniana'ole again introduced similar legislation in the next two Congresses.[137]

The service issues were exacerbated by World War I, during which vessels moved from the Pacific to the Atlantic. The 1917 legislation granting the president authority to issue coastwise permits alleviated the situation—but that authority was set to expire 120 days after the end of the war.

Hearings were held in the House in 1919 where Kalaniana'ole and other Hawaiian witnesses pleaded for an extension because of poor passenger service.[138] Charles J. McCarthy, governor of Hawaii, testified before the Commerce Committee that "we want American ships if we can get them" "but it does not stand to reason that when there are no American ships to do the business we should be forbidden to travel on foreign ships which touch at our ports."[139]

Kalaniana'ole introduced a House Joint Resolution in June 1919 to extend the time for the waiver authority just for Hawaii.[140] Representative Frank D. Scott (R-MI) (later chairman of the Merchant Marine Committee from 1925-1927) introduced companion legislation that would have extended the waiver authority to July 1, 1920 and thereafter have permitted foreign vessels to carry passengers between the U.S. mainland and Hawaii by paying a fee to the U.S. government of $40 per passenger.[141] The favorable House report indicated that "virtually no portion" of the vessels that shifted from the Pacific to the Atlantic had returned, with the result that for Hawaii "the passenger tonnage is grossly inadequate."[142]

Representative Rufus Hardy (D-TX), carrying the water of the old free ships policy, argued that the United States build requirement should be repealed entirely since U.S. shipyards had nothing to fear while they were leading the world. He claimed that maintaining the reservation would mean that U.S. shipyards would build to the reserved coastwise price. That, he believed, would eventually ruin U.S.-flag vessels in the foreign trade, which would have to pay the high U.S. construction price: "This is a critical period in the life of our merchant marine; if we yield to the demand of the shipbuilders we may as well bid farewell to any hope of success in the carrying trade of the world." Despite support for the Hardy bill, it was not until the 1920 Act that relief was provided to Hawaii.

COMMERCE COMMITTEE BILL

The Commerce Committee hearings ended on Saturday March 13, 1920. Admiral Benson's appointment as chairman of the Shipping Board became effective on the same day. Secretary of the Navy Daniels wrote in his diary for February 16 that Mrs. Wilson had asked Benson to be chairman, and that Daniels told Benson that it was "a gratifying appointment & the best that could be made."[143]

Benson immediately made it known that he believed that the United States was in a commercial maritime struggle with Britain. For example, Secretary of War Baker wrote President Wilson on May 12, 1920, that "in the Admiral's view, the present problem is one of fierce and final competition between the British mercantile marine and the American mercantile marine."[144]

To meet the challenge, Benson sought immediate transfer of all vessels and land-side marine facilities from the War and Navy Departments to the Shipping Board. Benson believed the Army services interfered with "the establishment of profitable and attractive commercial lines." He also made it clear that he was concerned about U.S. maritime worldwide access to fuel and to secure communications because Britain was appropriating sources of oil around the world and many international telegraph lines were British controlled.[145] Moreover, the admiral complained about foreign propaganda against the U.S. merchant marine.[146]

To address those issues and more, Senator Jones formed an informal subcommittee of nine senators to draft legislation based on the Greene Bill and the recommendations offered in the hearings.[147] All the subcommittee members were from coastal states. Jones later said that this group "worked day and night in preparation" of the legislation "in an entirely non-partisan spirit."[148]

According to Jones, speaking after the fact in August 1920, he prepared the initial draft of the legislation by adding provisions to the Greene Bill.[149] He knew that many of those provisions had been controversial in the past. As he said, "I had several provisions that five years ago would have been opposed by practically every Democrat in the Senate and House, and by a good many Republicans." Therefore, he claimed that he did not want to include a preferential rail provision because he "did not want to load the bill down too much" and looked to the Shipping Board to get their views.

The Shipping Board made its support of the rail preference clear in two April 1920 letters from Benson and Dean who also rejected direct subsidies and focused on strengthening U.S. coastwise laws. Dean advocated tightening U.S. citizenship laws to deal with what Clark had termed "dummy corporations." Benson asserted that "unless our coasting fleet be wholly and unequivocally owned by loyal United States citizens, it can not [sic]be rated a dependable unit in time of national emergency."

As to rail rates, Dean asserted that "no nation ever grew to maritime prominence without artificial protection" and that this could be "successfully accomplished for the American merchant marine without subsidy." Both Benson and Dean pointed to Germany and Japan, which had grown their merchant fleets with state aids as examples of where preferential rail rates could be successful. There was substantial public criticism from the private sector about this plan including accusations that the board was deceiving Congress as to the efficacy of such a policy.[150]

On May 4 the Commerce Committee favorably reported the Greene Bill with a potpourri of amendments worked out by Jones's informal subcommittee.[151] The committee report reads like a Jones speech noting that "nations are not free that depend on foreign fleets to carry their products and bring to them their supplies" and "We do not seek to dominate ocean trade.

But we do seek to do a just and proper part of it, and especially or our own." The report also indicated that "a large tonnage" "does not make a permanent merchant marine" and that commercial agencies, business facilities, efficient and different types of vessels, and equality of operating costs were all needed.

The first thing the reported legislation did was take the purpose from Jones's 1919 legislative proposals and graft it as section 1 to the Greene Bill. Thus, the legislation would cement into law a vision of a privately owned U.S. merchant marine, which was always implied and would now be express. That purpose is: "That it is necessary for the national defense and for the proper growth of its foreign and domestic commerce that the United States shall have a merchant marine... to carry the greater portion of its commerce and serve as a naval or military auxiliary in time of war or national emergency, ultimately to be owned and operated privately by citizens of the United States."

On vessel sales, the committee kept the phrase "as soon as practicable" from the Greene Bill but added "consistent with good business methods and the objects and purposes to be attained by this Act." The proposed legislation also benchmarked the sale price against the prevailing U.S. shipyard price after deducting depreciation as a floor below which vessels would not be sold.

The committee adopted the Hurley/Rosseter view that the fleet would have to be re-balanced over time (but within fiscal constraints), establishing a $50 million construction fund to be funded from board profits. The fund could be used by the Shipping Board to construct vessels or provide aid up to two-thirds of the cost for the purpose of establishing and maintaining "steamship lines deemed desirable and necessary by the board."

Furthermore, the committee compromised on the transfer of docks, piers etc. to the Shipping Board by making such transfer immediate upon enactment but giving the president the authority to suspend such transfer to support War and Navy Department operations. It also accepted the board's citizenship recommendations and proposed language to tighten both vessel transfer and citizenship requirements for the U.S. coastwise trade to require 100 percent U.S. citizen beneficial ownership of corporations.

The committee accepted Clark's amendments to close the Wickersham loophole and to prohibit the U.S. sale of tickets for mixed foreign and domestic voyages almost word-for-word. There was, however, one significant addition. The committee added to the Clark language, and for the first time to the U.S. coastwise laws, the phrase "vessel built in" the United States as a qualification requirement. Previously, the U.S. build requirement arose by virtue of it being a U.S. registry requirement. The new phrase was probably added to inhibit any further indirect relaxations of the U.S.-build requirement as had occurred, for example, with the 1914 Foreign Registry Act.[152]

Clark's suggestion to extend the coastwise laws to the "island Territories and possessions of the United States" after a one-year delay was also accepted. Every encompassed place, including Hawaii, was further accommodated by requiring the Shipping Board to establish adequate U.S.-flag steamship service where it did not exist. In other words, the same chicken and egg problem of which goes first, requirement or service, complicated application of the coastwise laws to territories and possessions in 1920 as it had with the Philippines from 1898 to 1908.

The committee even addressed Clark's point that the Shipping Board needed legal authority to create rules expeditiously. Their report provided that "far-reaching power is placed in the Shipping Board to make and control rules and regulations affecting shipping, and to meet foreign competition."

The House Merchant Marine Committee's ancillary bills regarding marine insurance, vessel classification, and vessel mortgages were all included. The committee noted that "mortgage security on ships is now practically worthless," and that "we hope to develop and build up an American Bureau of Shipping that will be an American Lloyds and eventually have the standing in the world's shipping that the great English agency has to-day." The committee legislation also beefed up the authority of the board to combat deferred rebates, discriminatory contracts, and unjust trade practices by giving the board authority to bar foreign vessels from the U.S. market if found in violation.

To stimulate the U.S. merchant marine in the foreign trade, the committee included the requirement, requested by the Shipping Board, that U.S. railroads provide their best rates to U.S.-flag vessels engaged in the foreign trade. It also included proposals that all U.S. mail be carried on U.S.-flag vessels "if practicable," and that U.S. owners in the foreign trade be exempt from the special profits taxes enacted during the war. Adjustments were proposed in the Seaman's Act to make it easier to enforce against foreign vessels and to improve the remedies available to injured seamen.

Perhaps most important to Senator Jones, the proposed legislation "authorized and directed" the president to terminate any commercial treaty which restricted the right of the United States to impose discriminatory duties in favor of U.S-flag vessels, again as Jones had proposed in 1919 and before.

Finally, whoever wrote the proposed statutory language had an eye for detail. The Greene Bill referred to the 1916 Shipping Act as the "Shipping Act of 1916" which the Commerce Committee corrected to "Shipping Act, 1916" as indeed it was written in the original law. That author was equally precise about the 1920 Merchant Marine Act. The last section of the law indicates it should be cited as the "Merchant Marine Act, 1920" not "Merchant Marine Act of 1920."

---

[1] Hearings before the Senate Commerce Committee on the Establishment of an American Merchant Marine, 1819.
[2] Hearings before the Senate Commerce Committee on the Establishment of an American Merchant Marine, 1819.
[3] Fourth Annual Report of the Shipping Board, 52.
[4] Smith and Betters, The United States Shipping Board, 33.
[5] For example, Hearings before the Senate Commerce Committee on the Establishment of an American Merchant Marine, 158, 189–92, 197–98.

[6] Hearings before the Senate Commerce Committee on the Establishment of an American Merchant Marine, 333–34 (Letter of W. Lisle, editor Motorship, to Senate Commerce Committee [January 9, 1920]).
[7] Edmund E. Day, "The American Merchant Fleet: A War Achievement, a Peace Problem," The Quarterly Journal of Economics 34 (August 1920): 567–606.
[8] Frederick Palmer, "It's All Yours, America," Collier's, The National Weekly 66, no. 3 (July 17, 1920): 8.
[9] S. Res. 368, 65th Cong., 3rd sess. (1918).
[10] "Outlines Policy to Gain Sea Trade," New York Times, January 17, 1919, 6.
[11] "Hurley Discussed Shipping Outlook," New York Times, January 29, 1919, 13; "Can Hold Own on Seas, Says Hurley," New York Times, February 12, 1919, 20.
[12] "The Merchant Marine," New York Times, February 13, 1919, 14.
[13] "Letter B. Colby to W. Wilson (January 30, 1919)," Papers of Woodrow Wilson, vol. 54, 394; "Letter W. Wilson to B. Colby (February 27, 1919,)" Papers of Woodrow Wilson, vol. 55, 302.
[14] "Tumulty's Summary of Message from E. Hurley to W. Wilson (March 15, 1919)," Papers of Woodrow Wilson, vol. 55, 532–33.
[15] For example, "Hurley Tells How New Merchant Marine Aids Farm and Stockman," New Orleans Item, March 9, 1919, 37; "U.S. Merchant Fleet for Benefit of People," Philadelphia Inquirer, March 28, 1919, 1; Edward N. Hurley, "Hurley Tells of Merchant Marine," Plain Dealer (Cleveland), April 5, 1919, 19.
[16] "Shipping Board Chairman on Verge of Breakdown," Washington Herald, April 1, 1919, 1; "Hurley Goes to Florida for Rest," Washington Times, April 1, 1919, 4.
[17] "Letter from H. Robinson to W. Wilson (April 30, 1919)," Papers of Woodrow Wilson, vol. 58, 269; "Visit of Edward N. Hurley is Prevented by Sickness," Times-Picayune, April 2, 1919, 5.
[18] Report of Conference Held in Washington, D.C. on May 22, 23, 1919 between the United States Shipping Board Emergency Fleet Corporation and Representatives of Shipowners, Manufacturers, Bankers, and Farmers Associations (Washington, DC: Government Printing Office, 1919).
[19] The Establishment and Development of an Adequate Merchant Marine as Suggested by the United States Shipping Board, A Communication to Hon. Wm. S. Greene (Washington, DC: Government Printing Office, 1919).
[20] "Memorandum from J. Payne to W. Wilson (August 22, 1919)," Papers of Woodrow Wilson, vol. 62, 465.
[21] Hearings before the Senate Commerce Committee on the Establishment of an American Merchant Marine, 184—85.
[22] Hearings before the Senate Commerce Committee on the Establishment of an American Merchant Marine, 465—67; 59 CONG. REC. 561–62 (December 15, 1919); John Barton Payne, "The Valley and Merchant Marine," Mississippi Valley Magazine 2 (March 1920): 11, 36.

[23] For example, "Ship Policy Up to New Congress," Marine Review 49, no. 11 (November 1919): 531–32; "New Ship Bills before Congress," Marine Review 49, no. 12 (December 1919): 579–81.

[24] Hearings before the Senate Commerce Committee on the Establishment of an American Merchant Marine.

[25] L. W. Moffett, "What Congress Plans for U.S. Shipping," Marine Review 49, no. 2 (February 1919): 51–55, 53.

[26] For example, "American Merchant Marine," Traffic World 25, no. 5 (January 31, 1920): 202–04.

[27] 57 Cong. Rec. 4538 (February 28, 1919).

[28] 58 Cong. Rec. 498 (June 2, 1919). Reported by the Senate Commerce Committee on June 5. U.S. Congress, Senate, Construction of Ships for Foreign Account, 66th Cong., 1st sess., 1919, S. Rep. 66-8.

[29] Hearings before the Senate Commerce Committee on the Establishment of an American Merchant Marine, 15.

[30] Hearings before the Senate Commerce Committee on the Establishment of an American Merchant Marine, 158.

[31] Hearings before the Senate Commerce Committee on the Establishment of an American Merchant Marine, 17.

[32] Hearings before the Senate Commerce Committee on the Establishment of an American Merchant Marine, 189–90, 309.

[33] Hearings before the Senate Commerce Committee on the Establishment of an American Merchant Marine, 37; "Foreign Contract Lid Is Off, Says Hurley in Senate," Oregon Daily Journal, June 11, 1919, 5.

[34] Hearings before the Senate Commerce Committee on the Establishment of an American Merchant Marine, 184–85.

[35] U.S. Congress, House, Committee on Merchant Marine and Fisheries, Hearings before the House Merchant Marine Committee on Shipbuilding for Domestic and Foreign Account, 66th Cong., 1st sess., 1919, 19.

[36] 58 Cong. Rec. 7869 (November 3, 1919); "Senator Jones Seeks Advice from Seattle," Seattle Daily Times, July 7, 1919, 16; S. 3355, 66th Cong., 1st sess., 1919; S. 3356, 66th Cong., 1st sess., 1919; "Plans for Encouraging Our Merchant Marine," Nautical Gazette 98, no. 5 (January 31, 1920): 164.

[37] 58 Cong. Rec. 7869 (November 3, 1919).

[38] For example, "Jones Proposes Maritime Policy," Seattle Daily Times, November 3, 1919, 1.

[39] 40 Stat. 913 (July 18, 1918); 40 Stat. 438 (March 1, 1918).

[40] 58 Cong. Rec. 6659 (October 9, 1919) (H.R. 9823); "Plan New Policy for Our Shipping," New York Times, October 13, 1919, 21.

[41] U.S. Congress, House, Hearings before the House Committee on Merchant Marine and Fisheries on Providing for the Disposition, Regulation, or Use of the Property Built or Acquired by the United States, 66th Cong., 1st sess., 1919, 217–37.

42 "Owners Outline Proposed Ship Policy," Marine Review 49, no. 2 (February 1919): 55–56.
43 "B. C. Marsh Dead; Welfare Leader," New York Times, (January 1, 1953), 23.
44 Hearings before the House Merchant Marine and Fisheries Committee on Providing for the Disposition, Regulation, or Use of the Property Built or Acquired by the United States, 67–110.
45 Benjamin C. Marsh, Lobbyist for the People, a Record of Fifty Years (Washington, DC: Public Affairs Press, 1953), 67.
46 Marsh, Lobbyist for the People, 104.
47 "Life or Death of Our Shipping Depends on Action of Congress," Baltimore Sun, November 25, 1919, 9; "Proper Solution of Ship Problem Vital to Interest of Local Port," Baltimore Sun, November 26, 1919, 9; "Time and Settled Policy Deemed Salvation of U.S. Ship Industry," Baltimore Sun, November 27, 1919, 9.
48 Hearings before the House Merchant Marine and Fisheries Committee on Providing for the Disposition, Regulation, or Use of the Property Built or Acquired by the United States, 18–42, 56–65.
49 U.S. Congress, House, Promotion and Maintenance of the American Merchant Marine, 66th Cong., 1st sess., 1919, H. Rep. 66-443.
50 H.R. 10378, 66th Cong., 1st sess., 1919, § 3 (emphasis supplied).
51 H.R. 10378, 66th Cong., 1st sess., 1919, § 4.
52 "'Americus,'" "Notes from the Eastern Front," Pacific Marine Review 17 (January 1920): 60–61.
53 58 CONG. REC. 8142 (November 8, 1919).
54 U.S. Congress, House, Amending Section 13 of the Seamen's Act, 66th Cong., 1st sess., 1919, H. Rep. 66-353.
55 "A Telling Protest," Seamen's Journal 23, no. 10 (November 12, 1919): 11.
56 58 CONG. REC. 6562–75 (October 8, 1919).
57 58 CONG. REC. 8152 (November 8, 1919).
58 58 CONG. REC., 8165.
59 58 CONG. REC. 8173.
60 "How Jones Bill Was Rushed through Congress," Nautical Gazette 99, no. 14 (October 2, 1920): 424.
61 "Outline Policy in New Senate Bill," Marine Review 50, no. 5 (May 1920): 273–74.
62 Hearings before the Senate Commerce Committee on the Establishment of an American Merchant Marine, 397. The Fairplay article is also quoted in the Senate Commerce Committee report on H.R. 10378. U.S. Congress, Senate, Promotion and Maintenance of the American Merchant Marine, 66th Cong., 2d sess., 1920, S. Rep. 66-573, 2.
63 Safford, Wilsonian Maritime Diplomacy, 223.
64 Hearings before the Senate Commerce Committee on the Establishment of an American Merchant Marine, 895.

[65] Hearings before the Senate Commerce Committee on the Establishment of an American Merchant Marine, 808, 2028—29 (letter from the Farmers' National Council against sale of the vessels).

[66] Hearings before the Senate Commerce Committee on the Establishment of an American Merchant Marine 1011—29.

[67] "Army Put in Charge of Piers in Hoboken," New York Times, April 20, 1917, 1.

[68] Jonathan Lurie, "'Heaven, Hell or Hoboken:' Anti-German Sentiment in Hoboken, 1917–1918, Some Examples," New Jersey Studies: An Interdisciplinary Journal 4, no. 1 (2018): 12–23.

[69] For example, "Waterfront Closed to Enemy Aliens," New York Times, July 11, 1917, 5.

[70] Annual Reports for the War Department for the Year 1918 (Washington, DC: Government Printing Office, 1918), vol. 1, 30.

[71] For example, "It's Heaven, Hell or Hoboken by Christmas," Chattanooga News, August 9, 1918, 6; "Lieutenant Bullitt Is among U.S. Heroes Killed in Action," Evening Public Ledger (Philadelphia), August 16, 1918, 5; "Heaven, Hell or Hoboken by Xmas Pershing Slogan," Evening News (San Jose, California), August 26, 1918, 6; "Soldiers' Letters," New Ulm Review (Minnesota), August 29, 1918, 9; "'Heaven or Hoboken before Christmas' Is New Pershing Slogan," Plain Dealer (Cleveland), August 30, 1918, 8; and "Providence Man Quotes Pershing as Optimistic," Evening Bulletin (Providence,) August 30, 1918, 8.

[72] Hearings before the Senate Commerce Committee on the Establishment of an American Merchant Marine, 430, 468–74, 481–91.

[73] L. W. Moffett, "What Congress Plans for U.S. Shipping," Marine Review 49, no. 2 (February 1919): 51—55.

[74] Hearings before the Senate Commerce Committee on the Establishment of an American Merchant Marine, 1634—35.

[75] Woodrow Wilson, Executive Order no. 2039 (September 4, 1914).

[76] Woodrow Wilson, Executive Order no. 2448 (September 1, 1916); Woodrow Wilson, Executive Order no. 3224 (February 7, 1920).

[77] Hearings before the Senate Commerce Committee on the Establishment of an American Merchant Marine, 1815.

[78] 59 Cong. Rec. 7419 (May 21, 1920).

[79] Hearings before the Senate Commerce Committee on the Establishment of an American Merchant Marine, 580, 789–90.

[80] Promotion and Maintenance of the American Merchant Marine, S. Rep. 66-573, 6–9; Hearings before the Senate Commerce Committee on the Establishment of an American Merchant Marine, 1462.

[81] S. S. Huebner, Report on the Status of Marine Insurance in the United States (Washington, DC.: Government Printing Office, 1920); "Suggestion of Relief for Marine Insurance," Evening Star (Washington, DC), (February 23, 1920), 19; "New Laws Asked for Ship Risks," Washington Times, February 24, 1920, 2.

[82] 59 CONG. REC. 1602 (January 15, 1920) (H.R. 11772) and 59 CONG. REC. 6441 (May 1, 1920) (H.R. 13889).
[83] Hearings before the Senate Commerce Committee on the Establishment of an American Merchant Marine, 1335.
[84] Hearings before the Senate Commerce Committee on the Establishment of an American Merchant Marine, 1355–56.
[85] For example, Causes of the Reduction of American Tonnage, H.R. Rep. 41-28, 30–31, 82.
[86] The History of the American Bureau of Shipping 150th Anniversary (Houston: American Bureau of Shipping, 2013).
[87] Hearings before the Senate Commerce Committee on the Establishment of an American Merchant Marine, 1878.
[88] "Stevenson Taylor, Ship Leader, Dead," New York Times, May 20, 1926, 25; Stevenson Taylor, "American Bureau of Shipping," Nautical Gazette 97, no. 8 (November 22, 1919): 200—201.
[89] 59 CONG. REC. 3704 (March 1, 1920).
[90] Charles S. Cumming, "The English High Court of Admiralty," Tulane Maritime Law Journal 17 (Spring 1993): 209–55.
[91] Hearings before the House Merchant Marine Comm. on Recording of Mortgages on Vessels and Subordinating Maritime Liens upon Vessels for Necessaries to the Liens of Mortgages, 66th Cong., 1st Sess. (1919).
[92] Hearings before the Senate Commerce Committee on the Establishment of an American Merchant Marine, 980.
[93] Hearings before the Senate Commerce Committee on the Establishment of an American Merchant Marine, 1192–94.
[94] Hearings before the Senate Commerce Committee on the Establishment of an American Merchant Marine, 1237–68.
[95] Hearings before the Senate Commerce Committee on the Establishment of an American Merchant Marine, 1276–78.
[96] Hearings before the Senate Commerce Committee on the Establishment of an American Merchant Marine, 1874, 1903.
[97] Hearings before the Senate Commerce Committee on the Establishment of an American Merchant Marine., 1888.
[98] Hearings before the Senate Commerce Committee on the Establishment of an American Merchant Marine, appendix A, "General Board," 151.
[99] Hearings before the Senate Commerce Committee on the Establishment of an American Merchant Marine, 1888.
[100] Hearings before the Senate Commerce Committee on the Establishment of an American Merchant Marine, 1913.
[101] Hearings before the Senate Commerce Committee on the Establishment of an American Merchant Marine, 1901.

[102] Hearings before the Senate Commerce Committee on the Establishment of an American Merchant Marine, 1912.
[103] Hearings before the Senate Commerce Committee on the Establishment of an American Merchant Marine, 1883.
[104] Hearings before the Senate Commerce Committee on the Establishment of an American Merchant Marine, 1889, 1895–6.
[105] Hearings before the Senate Commerce Committee on the Establishment of an American Merchant Marine, 1928–48.
[106] Hearings before the Senate Commerce Committee on the Establishment of an American Merchant Marine, 1934–39.
[107] Hearings before the Senate Commerce Committee on the Establishment of an American Merchant Marine, 1215–22.
[108] Hearings before the Senate Commerce Committee on the Establishment of an American Merchant Marine, 1949–54.
[109] Hearings before the Senate Commerce Committee on the Establishment of an American Merchant Marine, 1959.
[110] Hearings before the Senate Commerce Committee on the Establishment of an American Merchant Marine, 1966.
[111] Hearings before the Senate Commerce Committee on the Establishment of an American Merchant Marine, 1975.
[112] Hearings before the Senate Commerce Committee on the Establishment of an American Merchant Marine, 1982.
[113] Hearings before the Senate Commerce Committee on the Establishment of an American Merchant Marine, 1994.
[114] Hearings before the Senate Commerce Committee on the Establishment of an American Merchant Marine, 1990.
[115] U.S. Congress, Senate, Commerce Committee, Hearings before the Senate Commerce Committee on Alaska Water Transportation, 66th Cong., 2nd sess., 1920.
[116] "Congress' Refusal to Grant Government Line of Vessels to Alaska Foreseen by Board," Alaska Daily Empire, June 5, 1920, 3.
[117] "Maurice D. Leehey–Attorney Was Founder of the Seattle Mining Club," New York Times, May 5, 1932, 19; "Maurice Leehey, Veteran Seattle Attorney, Dead," Seattle Daily Times, May 4, 1932, 3.
[118] For example, "Governor Riggs in Washington Working on Legislation Vital to Territorial Shipping Board," Anchorage Daily Times, March 3, 1920, 1; "Gov. Riggs and Semmes Tell of Transportation," Alaska Daily Empire, March 25, 1920, 1.
[119] "Spirited Tilt before Senate Committee," Evening Star (Washington, DC), March 30, 1920, 2; "Fight Words but No Fight at Hearings," Alaska Daily Empire, April 1, 1920, 1; "Semmes Calls Wickersham Lobbyist for Canadian Steamship Concerns," Alaska Daily Empire, March 27, 1920, 1.
[120] J. J. Underwood, "Lively Tilt at Alaskan Hearing," Seattle Daily Times, March 28, 1920, 11.

[121] Hearings before the Senate Commerce Committee on Alaska Water Transportation, 66th Cong., 2nd Sess. (1920), 93.
[122] Hearings before the Senate Commerce Committee on Alaska Water Transportation, 93.
[123] H.R. 10164, 55th Cong., 2nd sess., 1898; H. Rep. no. 1621, 55th Cong., 2nd sess., 1898 ("Had it not been for this immunity from foreign competition our merchant marine would have been driven from the ocean years ago."); "Foreign Lobbies Try to Destroy U.S. Merchant Marine, Witness Says," Washington Times, February 21, 1920, 2.
[124] Hearings before the Senate Commerce Committee on the Establishment of an American Merchant Marine, 1920, 1438.
[125] Hearings before the Senate Commerce Committee on the Establishment of an American Merchant Marine, 1439.
[126] Hearings before the Senate Commerce Committee on the Establishment of an American Merchant Marine, 1442–43.
[127] Hearings before the Senate Commerce Committee on the Establishment of an American Merchant Marine, 1457.
[128] Foreclosure Suit Mark End of Oceanic," Evening Bulletin (Honolulu), June 7, 1907, 3; "Oceanic Company to Go to the Wall," Hawaiian Star, June 10, 1907, 2; "Oceanic Company Will Disappear in Complete Wreck," Evening Bulletin (Honolulu), June 21, 1907, 4.
[129] "To Run Vessels to Australia," San Francisco Chronicle, August 20, 1907, 13.
[130] Annual Report of the Commissioner of Navigation to the Secretary of the Commerce and Labor (1907), 19–20.
[131] Theodore Roosevelt, Seventh Annual Message, December 3, 1907, UC Santa Barbara, the American Presidency Project, https://www.presidency.ucsb.edu/documents/seventh-annual-message-4.
[132] 42 CONG. REC. 666 (January 13, 1908); U.S. Congress, House, Passenger Transportation Between Hawaii and the Mainland, 60th Cong., 1st sess., 1908, H. Rep. 60-965; U.S. Congress, Senate, Passenger Transportation Between Ports of Hawaii and Other Ports of United States, 60th Cong., 1st sess., 1909, S. Rep. 60-661.
[133] For example, U.S. Congress, House, Merchant Marine and Fisheries, Hearings before the House Merchant Marine Committee on Extending Relief to the Territory of Hawaii by Providing Additional Shipping Facilities between the Territory of Hawaii and the Mainland, 66th Cong., 1st sess., 1919, part 2.
[134] 42 CONG. REC. 7142 (May 28, 1908); Passenger Transportation Between Hawaii and the Mainland, H. Rep. 60-965; 58 CONG. REC. 3519 (August 1, 1920).
[135] "The Coastwise Law Is Again under Fire," Hawaiian Gazette, December 1, 1908, 6; "Matson Steamer Plans Approved," Hawaiian Gazette, December 4, 1908, 8; "Chamber of Commerce Reverses Its Action," Hawaiian Star, December 10, 1908, 7; "Matson May Cut Out New Travel Boat," Hawaiian Star, December 12, 1908, 1.

[136] "Suspension of Coastwise Laws Again Asked For," Pacific Commercial Advertiser, December 10, 1908, 1; "Matson May Cut Out New Travel Boat," Hawaiian Star, December 12, 1908, 1.

[137] H.R. 7539, 61st Cong., 1st sess., 1909; H.R. 11618, 62nd Cong., 1st sess., 1911.

[138] U.S. Congress, House, Merchant Marine and Fisheries Committee, Hearings before the House Merchant Marine Committee on Extending Relief to the Territory of Hawaii by Providing Additional Shipping Facilities between the Territory of Hawaii and the Mainland, 66th Cong., 1st sess., 1919.

[139] Hearings before the Senate Commerce Committee on the Establishment of an American Merchant Marine, 1328–29.

[140] 58 CONG. REC. 1538 (June 21, 1919).

[141] 58 CONG. REC. 3517 (August 1, 1919).

[142] U.S. Congress, House, Protection of United States Coastwise Trade, 66th Cong., 1st sess., 1919, H. Rep. 66-135.

[143] "Entry for February 16, 1920," Cabinet Diaries of Josephus Daniels, 495; "Benson to Succeed Payne," New York Times, February 18, 1920, 3.

[144] "Letter N. Baker to W. Wilson (May 12, 1920)," Woodrow Wilson Papers, vol. 65, 277.

[145] "Pleas for Shipping Open Marine Week," New York Times, April 13, 1920, 20.

[146] "Finds Propaganda to Harm U.S. Ships," New York Times, April 14, 1920, 22.

[147] "Merchant Marine Bill," Traffic World 25, no. 13 (March 27, 1920): 570–71.

[148] Tacoma Commercial Club and Chamber of Commerce. Transcript of Conference with Senator Wesley L. Jones on Section 28, 'Merchant Marine Act, 1920,' August 10, 1920, 13.

[149] Transcript of Conference with Senator Wesley L. Jones on Section 28, "Merchant Marine Act, 1920," 14–16.

[150] "Shipping Board Accused of Misrepresentation," Nautical Gazette 98, no. 21 (May 22, 1920): 771–72; "Shipping Board Misinforms the Senate," Nautical Gazette 98, no. 21 (May 22, 1920): 789.

[151] Promotion and Maintenance of the American Merchant Marine, S. Rep. 66-573.

[152] Mark D. Aspinwall, "Coastwise Trade Policy in the United States: Does It Make Sense Today?" Journal of Maritime Law and Commerce 18, no. 2 (April 1987): 243–62, 248.

Albert Lasker, circa 1920s, Library of Congress

Chapter 22—1920 Merchant Marine Act Enactment

Senate Consideration

Jones wasted no time once the Commerce Committee issued its May 4 report bringing the bill up for Senate floor consideration on May 10.[1] Over the next ten days, he marched through the Commerce Committee amendments to the Greene bill one at a time—explaining, cajoling, and compromising where necessary. Virtually everything was agreed to by consensus except for two recorded votes, both on tax provisions. On May 21 the Senate agreed to the bill without a recorded vote. It was a stunning achievement given the breadth and ambition of the bill and the decades of contentious partisan disagreement on maritime policy that preceded it.

The first section was the declaration of national purpose. Although maritime historians have pointed to the declaration as a groundbreaking definition of maritime policy goals, it was added by consent without debate.[2] Jones defended the declaration soon after enactment and later as "the chart to guide in the interpretation and application of every other section of the act as a Bible to direct those who must administer it."[3]

Serious questions were raised concerning extending the coastwise laws to the Philippines. Senator Knute Nelson argued that such an extension "would be a death blow to the commerce and trade of the Philippine Islands."[4] In response, Jones looked to history and said that Britain had built up her merchant marine by restricting its colonial trade under its Navigation Acts and that the United States should do the same. He indicated that "we should make out Manila the great distributing point in the Orient for the products of this country." The Philippines would be protected, Jones continued, because the Shipping Board was directed to ensure that there was adequate U.S.-flag vessel service.

Senator Nelson also asked whether the bill expanded the scope of the coastwise laws. He focused on the prohibition of the purchase of through passenger tickets in the United States between two U.S. places via foreign conveyance (Clark's proposal).[5] Nelson argued that the provision was "unduly and unjustly restrictive" even though he was "aware of the antipathy on the Pacific coast against" Canadian rail lines. Jones responded that "the only provisions contained in this bill with reference to that feature of the coastwise law is a provision which prevents its evasion." He continued, "Whether the coastwise law should be repealed is another question, but so long as we apply the coastwise policy to our ports it seems to me, we should not permit a foreign country to evade the law."

In support of his position, Jones described a situation in which the Canadian Steamship Co. had a ticket office in Seattle where it sold two tickets. The first ticket was for transportation from Seattle to Vancouver and the second from Vancouver to Skagway, Alaska. Jones described this as a "clear evasion of the law" and demanded that the Senate "should not keep [the laws] on our statute books and permit them to be nullified by alien competitors."

Senator Charles S. Thomas (D-CO) argued against the need to tighten the coastwise laws by saying the United States should follow Britain's example and abandon its navigation restrictions.[6] As previously noted in chapter 9, Britain repealed its coastwise trade restrictions in 1854.[7] Thomas also noted that one of the complaints in the Declaration of Independence was "the destruction of our trade... due to the discriminations placed by Acts of Parliament upon the carrying resources of the American colonies." Thomas did not see how coastwise evasions could be entirely prevented since anyone could buy a ticket to Vancouver and then separately buy a ticket to Skagway in Canada. Jones insisted that a change was needed anyway to "prevent a palpable evasion of our law."

Thomas also objected to including the Philippines within U.S. coastwise laws.[8] He eerily predicted that "if, in the providence of God, there is stored away in the events of the future a collision between the United States and Japan, it is unfortunate to think that the outposts of this great Republic have been extended 10,000 miles across the sea and have planted themselves in the Philippine Islands, only about two days' sail from Japan."

Senator William H. King (D-UT) asked Thomas whether he had any evidence that U.S-flag vessels engaged in the coastwise trade "have been charging extortionate or, at least, unfair rates."[9] Thomas replied that "the operation of every enterprise… which is protected by ironclad legislation… will not be particularly modest nor particularly conscientious in fixing of its charges." In response, King asked Jones if the Commerce Committee had any evidence of coastwise monopoly profits, to which Jones answered there was none.

Senator King also asked if the coastwise laws were being expanded in the bill. Jones replied, "There is nothing in this bill that deals with the coastwise laws or coastwise shipping except the provision extending the application of the coastwise laws to the Philippine Islands, or to the island possessions of the United States." He also said that the provision to prevent the evasion of the coastwise laws" was focused on "the situation between Seattle and Skagway, Alaska." Jones flatly stated that "we do not deal in general in this bill with the coastwise laws" and that "so long as the coastwise laws remain on the statute books as they are we ought to see that they are observed." Finally, Jones emphasized that "the bill deals primarily with our foreign ocean-going shipping in the foreign trade."

In response to the possibility of foreign retaliation if the United States reserved its trade to the Philippines, Jones scoffed and said that all those countries needed United States more than it needed them. On the possibility of the Philippine Islands gaining independence, Jones declared that "they are ours now" and "there is some trade that we can get, and if we do not get it there will be nobody to blame except ourselves."

The provision in the bill granting the Shipping Board broad authority to make rules and regulations like the British Board of Trade was also agreed to.[10] There were, however, gripes about giving the board too much authority. For example, Senator James A. Reed (D-MO) argued that "I have not seen anything about the Shipping Board's performances up to date to lead me to the conclusion that we ought to confer any more powers upon that board."[11]

A further concern was raised about the new board power to exclude any foreign vessel found to violate the 1916 Shipping Act.[12] Senators objected to the lack of due process whereby the board would be the "judge and the jury, the complainant and everything else." They also cited the possibility of foreign retaliation. Jones accommodated the objection by adding "after due opportunity to be heard" to the relevant section.

With respect to the grandfather permission to be granted to foreign-built vessels to continue to participate in the coastwise trade, there was no controversy. Jones explained that only a few foreign vessels qualified under the provision because it required that the vessels be wholly owned by U.S. citizens; the Senate accepted this explanation.[13]

Some of the ancient rivalry between the political parties resurfaced with the mail contract provision raised by Senator Nelson.[14] Underwood (who was first elected to the Senate in 1914 and was the Senate minority leader in 1920) recounted the history of U.S. discriminating duties, the era of reciprocity, and argued for a return to discriminating duties as he had tried to do in 1913.

The cost of the Ocean Mail Act of 1891 was brought up. Despite historic Democratic antipathy to subsidies, Underwood supported the mail rate provision. He analogized the vague mail subsidy provision included in the proposed legislation to the establishment of rural mail routes where discretion had to be given to the postmaster until such time as there was enough information to establish fixed rates.[15] Similarly, Senator James A. Reed (D-MO) noted that maybe it was time for the Democratic party to "abandon its longtime policy of refusing to vote subventions or subsidies."

Senator Irvine L. Lenroot (R-WI) argued that the bill gave the Shipping Board and the postmaster general too much leeway to determine rates with the only limit being that U.S.-flag vessels should be utilized "if practicable." He suggested that the bill be amended to include "within the limits of appropriations," and Jones accepted the change on the spot.[16] Jones also later amended the bill to provide that the rates paid be "just and reasonable."[17]

There was confusion about the classification society provision.[18] Senator King asked why private owners were being forced to use a particular classification society. Jones corrected him by pointing out that the section only required that U.S. government vessels utilize the American Bureau of Shipping and that it was hoped that government use "will develop confidence in private shipbuilders and private owners."

Edge gave a long speech about how it was a mistake to hamstring the sales process with a large unwieldy board and conflicting sale requirements. He noted that at the same time the operation of vessels was preferred, since the board was being given very broad powers to operate vessels. Holding the board in selling vessels "to an impracticable and inconsistent hard-and-fast rule... will compel them to remain in business at the expense of the American people," and "it is not going to be an efficient merchant marine if the captain is instructed to furl the mainmast at six bells, regardless of conditions, or to reef the flying jib at three bells even though the weather is calm."[19]

Edge also criticized the proposed amendment in the pending legislation to the U.S. citizenship test in the 1916 Shipping Act.[20] Congress had tightened the citizenship requirement in 1918 relating to citizens owning a corporate controlling interest to prevent "every possible device by which foreign interests could obtain control in law or fact over corporations formed under American law."[21] The bill as reported at Chairman Benson's behest took this admonition to heart and required U.S. corporations to be 100 percent U.S. citizen-owned to register a "vessel of the United States." Edge argued that non-citizens could buy stock of public companies at any time which would make "our corporations innocent lawbreakers" and that "100 percent American ownership in a corporation is absolutely impossible of enforcement." This 100 percent requirement was altered later in conference.

One of the most controversial provisions in the bill after enactment—granting preferential rail rates to U.S.-flag vessels—was adopted without discussion.[22] The *Baltimore Sun* nevertheless noted that this was "a powerful indirect subsidy for American shipping."[23]

Another provision permitting insurance companies to form associations for marine re-insurance purposes was just as non-controversial. Similarly, the "Ship Mortgage Act of 1920," included as a single section of the bill, was not substantially debated.[24]

The changes to the Seaman's Act were further agreed to without fanfare.[25] The Rowe Bill was amended to permit U.S. citizens to become AB's with only one year at sea upon examination, but fast-tracked U.S. citizens could not comprise more than one-fourth of the number of AB's required.

Furuseth got a tightening of the prohibition against advance wages and allotments even if those were agreed to outside the United States and a reversal of the *Luckenbach* Supreme Court decision which limited seamen's injury recovery rights.[26] "Seamen" were granted an express cause of action for any "personal injury" suffered "in the course of employment" on the same basis as provided "to railway employees."[27]

The most controversial sections in the bill on the Senate floor were the tax provisions. The Revenue Act of 1918 imposed war-profits and excess-profits taxes on U.S. businesses.[28] The bill alleviated some of these by granting relief to U.S. vessel owners engaged in the foreign trade when constructing new vessels in the United States.[29] It also included a provision authorizing the Shipping Board to adjust depreciation rates as Rosseter had suggested. Motions to strike the two provisions both failed on recorded votes, although the depreciation provision was dropped in conference anyway.[30]

Having settled this issue, the Senate returned to Clark's proposed change to prohibit the sale of through tickets. Senators McCumber and Nelson argued that the provision would serve as an "immense inconvenience to the travelling public."[31] Jones pointed out that "there would be many more American boats" in Seattle to carry passengers to Alaska "if we could free ourselves from the clutch of the Canadian Pacific." Eventually Jones dropped the ticket sale provision because, as he said, Nelson's devotion to Alaska "makes it hard for me to press the amendment."

The next discussion, which was mainly between Senator Lodge and Jones, concerned the discriminating duties section related at the beginning of this book.[32] Both Senators Lodge and Thomas referred admiringly to Senator Frye and his work in favor of the U.S. merchant marine. Jones also added that abrogation of the treaties will be a "club in our hands" to meet Britain's attempt to monopolize worldwide oil resources. Jones had already shown an interest in this topic by writing to the Department of State on March 9, 1920, requesting information on what State was doing to support U.S. oil companies abroad.[33]

Senator King made a last-ditch effort to prevent the Shipping Board from constructing more vessels and to re-insert the original five-year limit on the government authority to own vessels.[34] Jones had to once again argue that the bill balanced losses from quick sales against potential losses from continued operation and favored the latter to gradually help make the merchant marine self-sustaining. Lodge captured the view of many senators who stated that while if he had his way, he "would stop the whole Shipping Board business now," the bill afforded the country "the greatest opportunity to preserve to the taxpayers of the country what can be preserved from the huge expenditure which has been made."

To this, King responded that "I do not care who may constitute the Shipping Board, there will be waste and extravagance and inefficiency." Moreover, the failure to set a time limit would "put the Government of the United States into the shipping business forever, and I make the prediction that if this bill shall pass in this form the Government of the United States will be out more than $3,000,000,000 during the next 10 years." King nevertheless conceded saying that "it is so manifest that the Senate is committed to this bill, with all of its features, good, bad, and indifferent, that any further attack upon it would be futile." The Senate passed the Commerce Committee bill on May 21 by consent.[35]

END GAME

A conference committee was appointed to resolve the differences between the Greene Bill and the Senate-approved bill. Representative Alexander had been confirmed as secretary of commerce on December 16, 1919, and so played no direct role in the conference.

The committee produced three reports between June 2 and June 4 in quick succession.[36] On June 1 the conference committee pulled an all-nighter.[37] All the managers signed the final report except Representative Hardy. Almost 150 amendments were considered (although most were minor or ministerial, such as changing section numbers). Virtually all the provisions Greene, Jones, and the Shipping Board had proposed were included in the main in the final legislation although the board was not given the direct power to construct new vessels (versus utilizing the construction fund to help finance such construction).

The conference committee made several significant coastwise trade changes. The House accepted the Jones/Clark amendment to the 1898 coastwise law but requested a proviso, stating that the new "by land and water" formulation would not "apply to transportation between points within the continental United States, *excluding Alaska*" over certain through routes on Canadian railroads.[38] This was essentially what Senator Nelson sought on the Senate floor. Transportation on the Yukon River was also excluded until such time as the board determined that service provided by U.S. citizens was adequate.

Alaska resented the exclusion at the time and long after.[39] George B. Grigsby, then delegate from Alaska to Congress, declared that several provisions in the legislation would be "disastrous" for Alaska. In particular, he complained that the coastwise provision "was drawn by representatives of private steamship companies to preserve the monopoly now enjoyed by private concerns in the Alaskan trade."[40] George Wickersham wrote a letter to Secretary of State Colby on June 19 "denouncing" the 1920 Act because it excluded Canadian rail lines in Alaskan transportation.[41] James Michener in his novel *Alaska* has a quote from an Anchorage grocer that reflected wide spread Alaskan feelings about the Act: "'That damned Jones Act is strangling us.'"[42]

The Alaska Fifth Territorial Legislature adopted a resolution in April 1921 stating that the Alaska exclusion "is a vicious discrimination against and a great injustice and injury to our people."[43] The resolution instructed the territorial attorney general to sue the United States claiming a violation of article 1, section 9 of the U.S. Constitution, which prohibits port preferences (the "Port Preference Clause"). The Supreme Court ruled against Alaska on the basis that the clause expressly protects "States" and Alaska was not at the time a "State."[44]

Alaska continued to remonstrate, without success.[45] According to one estimate, the 1920 Act more than tripled the cost of Alaska-bound cargoes versus Hawaii-bound cargoes from the continental United States. It was not until Alaska became a state in 1958 that the word "excluding" was changed to "including."[46]

With respect to the citizenship objection raised by Senator Edge, the House requested that the 100 percent U.S. citizen ownership requirement for the domestic trade be changed to 75 percent.[47] The House also requested that the U.S. citizen "controlling interest" standard for the foreign trade be retained, and both changes became law.

On June 3 the Seattle Chamber of Commerce sent Jones a telegram opposing the rail preference provision, arguing it would divert cargoes away from the Pacific Northwest.[48] A. F. Haines, the vice president and general manager of the Pacific Steamship Company (which Clark represented) argued against the chamber position. He said (insinuating that opposition to the rail provision stemmed from foreign agitation) that "'I am only an American and will let the foreigners do the rest of the talking." Jones was to feel substantial local political heat because of the adoption of that provision (section 28), as discussed in the next section.

The Senate took up the final conference report on June 4. Several Democratic Senators re-debated the core policy issue of when to sell vessels just before the vote.[49] The Senate vote in favor of the legislation was 45 to 14. The vote was bipartisan with twenty-two Democratic senators among the forty-five in favor, including Underwood, the minority leader, and Senator Gerry, the minority whip. Ten of the fourteen nays were Democrats, joined by Borah and three other Republicans.

The Republican leadership all voted aye. Senator Miles Poindexter, Jones's fellow Republican Washington senator and the National Senatorial Committee chair, did not vote. Future President Warren Harding was among the ayes.

La Follette did not vote and played no part in the Senate deliberations because of health troubles starting in early 1920. He was in Rochester, Minnesota scheduled to have a gall bladder operation in early June 1920.[50] The Washington State labor press, which criticized Jones for selling out the public interest to private vessel owners, lamented La Follette's absence, writing that he "would probably have been the most efficient opponent of the steal."[51]

House consideration of the conference report on June 4 was messier than in the Senate.[52] Greene threw down the gauntlet when describing the vessel classification provision: "I propose to classify the man who objects to this bill and who votes against its enactment into law as an affiliated agent of the British Lloyd's, and to put those who vote for the bill as valuable agents of the American Bureau of Shipping. [Applause.]." He also called the legislation a "purely American bill" and a "perfect bill."

Representative Tom D. McKeown (D-OK) took offense pointing out that "we passed a bill of eight pages through this House [the Greene Bill], and the Senate amends the bill and conferees come in now and bring back a hodgepodge, and in a bill 56 pages long, and... the conferees bring it in here and say to the Congress, 'If you object to it, you are the agents of the English Lloyds'... I say it is not a fair way to legislate." McKeown went on, "I am opposed to disposing of this matter at this late hour without everybody having a fair chance to know the contents of the bill [Applause]."

Representative Ewin L. Davis (D-TN) was even more adamant in his opposition. Davis, a House freshman and later chairman of the House Merchant Marine Committee from 1931 to 1933, said that the conference report contained "vicious and un-American provisions" "adopted at the instance of and for the benefit of certain private shipping and railroad interests, and was written by their representatives." He argued that the construction fund, the rail rate preference, the war-profits tax leniency, and other provisions all amounted to subsidies. He was particularly unhappy about the declaration of purpose in the bill because under it we "definitely commit ourselves to a policy that we are going 'to do whatever may be necessary to encourage and develop a merchant marine' owned by private citizens."

Representative Bankhead tried to calm the waters among Democrats by pointing out that Alexander had been in favor of the original Greene Bill. Another Democrat chimed in, claiming, "I just talked with Secretary Alexander," who apparently said, "that if he were here, he would vote for it."

The rushed process was evident. Questions flew back and forth. At one point, Representative Richard Yates (R-IL) said, "Mr. Speaker, it is a joke and a farce to try to discuss the bill with everybody talking at once." One colloquy between Representative Thomas L. Blanton (D-TX) and Representative Edmonds illustrated the confusion. Blanton asked why there was an Alaska rail exclusion in the coastwise law added in conference. Edmonds mixed up the issue with the Yukon exception, thereby missing the point and asserted that the proviso "leaves the Yukon free to American and English ships alike" which had little to do with the Alaska Canadian rail exclusion.

The debate concluded with a statement by former House Speaker Cannon who said he would vote for an imperfect bill because "if we get a merchant marine, we have to contrive some means to make up the difference between what it costs the world to sail on the world's highway and what it costs us." He continued, "I do not see, after listening to all that has been said, how we can make the condition any worse than it is now." Cannon concluded with, "One thing there is with this bill, and that is it protects the coastwise trade of the United States. [Applause.] And we would have been in purgatory if we had not had the coastwise trade prior to the war, because we did have some ships in the coastwise trade and some shipbuilding establishments on the coasts of the United States."[53]

The final vote in favor of the legislation on June 4 was 145 to 120, with 158 not voting.[54] At the time, there were 240 Republicans and 192 Democrats in the House. The *Washington Times* headlined, "Jones Bill, Jammed through Houses, Goes to President Today."[55]

The merchant marine legislation was one of almost twenty bills sent to Wilson at the end of the session of Congress.[56] The legislation was described in the press as having had a "tempestuous voyage."[57]

Whether Wilson would sign the bill was apparently decided at a cabinet meeting held on June 1.[58] As recorded by Secretary of the Navy Daniels in his diary, Albert S. Burleson, the postmaster general, and David F. Houston, the treasury secretary, opposed "certain provisions" in the merchant marine act. At the time, the cabinet contained two former Shipping Board members, Secretaries Payne (interior) and Colby (state). Daniels also recorded that the "president said he favored freedom of the seas but wished the American flag to float there & was strong for merchant shipping." At the same meeting, Wilson reiterated his view about Britain: "'Daniels and I know the feeling of the British & their selfishness. We were up against that in Paris.'"

In a June 4 message to railroad unions on unrelated issues, Wilson wrote about "the problem of the Government-owned merchant marine and other similar urgent matters" and that the legislation the president received was "so unsatisfactory that I could accept it, if at all, only because I despaired of anything better."[59] Wilson nevertheless signed the Merchant Marine Act, 1920 into law on June 5. According to Dr. Grayson, Wilson's personal physician, that day the president "was in better spirits than any day since he was taken ill last September."[60] Eleven measures were pocket vetoed because they were allegedly received too late for review.[61]

In the immediate aftermath, Senator Jones was upset because he was also identified with another signature achievement: the Federal Water Power Act of 1920. That bill went unsigned on June 5.[62] Jones was among many who thought that the bill had been pocket vetoed, which he called a "national calamity."[63]

Jones continued to work the issue and cut a deal with Secretary of the Interior Payne to remove an administration objection relating to national parks. He and Senator Underwood promised to introduce legislation in the next session of Congress to provide a special permitting process for park water projects.[64] The *New York Times* reported that the president signed the water bill after also being assured by the U.S. attorney general that it was constitutional to sign after adjournment.[65] Ultimately, local Washington State press gave Jones credit for both the Water Power Act and the Merchant Marine Act.[66]

Aftermath

West Coast interests immediately put Jones on the defensive.[67] They worried that the rail preference provision would drive business to East Coast ports because of the lack of U.S.-flag West Coast service. In response to those concerns, Jones announced on June 17 that he would seek repeal of that section if it worked the way the ports feared it would. On June 27 he urged U.S. businessmen not to be "'stampeded by foreign propaganda'" before he had a chance to meet with them in person.[68] Meanwhile, Chairman Benson responded to the pressure by announcing on July 1 that "'the Shipping Board will allocate American ships to move the business" as necessary.[69] Jones also issued a statement to the effect that the Act gave the board ample authority to remedy cargo diversions.[70]

The Tacoma Chamber of Commerce invited Jones to a conference to be held on August 10.[71] Over one hundred people attended including senior management of Pacific Steamship Co., representatives of all the major West Coast ports, and the press. Cornelius Vanderbilt Jr. (great grandson of Cornelius Vanderbilt, also known as Cornelius Vanderbilt IV) was there on behalf of the *New York Times*.[72]

Jones gave a long speech about the legislation and section 28. He was emphatic that only negative experience would cause him to seek changes in the legislation and that nothing else could persuade him. As to the details of section 28, Jones left the meeting and turned over the discussion to W. L. Clark, the private attorney who had substantially influenced the 1920 Act. Dean was supposed to take questions on behalf of the Shipping Board, but he had not yet arrived by the time Jones left.

What ensued—based on the transcript and the stories written including Vanderbilt's special to the *New York Times*—was an acrimonious four-hour exchange.[73] Clark was combative throughout. Vanderbilt wrote that "at times the scene resembled almost a riot," and "business men in their shirt sleeves, because of the great heat which is unusual on this coast, rose in anger at statements which Mr. Clarke made."

JOURNEY TO THE JONES ACT

S. J. Wettrick of the Seattle Chamber of Commerce was upset that Jones did not stay the day, saying that "our purpose is not to convince Mr. Clarke that he is wrong about it—it is to convince Senator Jones that he is wrong about it (Applause)." Wettrick also implied that both Jones and Benson did not really understand section 28. Clark closed the proceedings saying that the public had had ample time to express their views in the legislative process and that if there is anybody that knows what section 28 means "those people are Admiral Benson and the general counsel of the shipping board [meaning Dean]."

Dean finally made it to Seattle after the meeting and came to section 28's defense.[74] He went on a charm offensive up and down the West Coast culminating in a meeting on September 1 with the Seattle Chamber of Commerce in the Rainier Club where the chamber assured him that Seattle would "cooperate heartily in making the act workable."[75]

Jones and Clark repeatedly defended section 28 publicly in the face of continued protests.[76] Jones asserted, for example, in early 1921 that "the sole purpose and effect of Section 28 is to provide that if American shipping is available then preferential freight rates shall not be given to imports or exports carried over American railroads unless such exports or imports are carried in American ships."[77] He also blamed criticisms on foreign interests: "A large part of this criticism, though honestly made by our people, I am convinced has its origin in alien interests."

The Shipping Board (meaning Benson and Donald) nevertheless suspended the operation of section 28 almost immediately upon enactment on June 9.[78] The board did not reverse that suspension until February 1923. Shipper opposition, however, remained substantial, and the board re-suspended section 28 in February 1924. Subsequently, the provision never became permanently effective.[79]

Section 34, Jones's discriminating duty provision, also faced stiff opposition.[80] Foreign diplomats immediately warned of retaliation and asserted that section 34 could bring into force the 1913 Underwood 5 percent discriminating duty.[81] Jones issued a statement on June 21 defending the provision saying that it "was one of the most important laws ever passed by Congress" and "we are entering no brotherly love Sunday school picnic in seeking our part of the world's carrying trade."[82]

In connection with the enactment of the 1920 Act, Secretary of Commerce Alexander prepared an abstract of the Act for the president, delivered on June 25, drawing his attention to the need to appoint members to the new board and to comply with the abrogation notice aspect of section 34, which required the president to act within ninety days after the law was signed.[83]

Chamberlain argued that section 34 "should be repealed before inevitable injury to our shipping and foreign trade results from it."[84] As recounted earlier, he wrote that

> the policy is mediæval rather than merely "antiquated" originating in the fourteenth century. Its best-known application resulted in three years of naval warfare of 1651-1654 between England and Holland... Our early resort to it was in retaliation for discriminations by other Governments, notably the British, and it ceased with the end of the Napoleonic wars when foreign Governments began to stop those discriminations against us through treaties.

At an August 24 cabinet meeting, Daniels wrote in his diary that other nations had protested the section, complaining "that a treaty is not a scrap of paper & cannot be abrogated except by mutual consent."[85] For his part, Colby indicated that Wilson "must act or defy Congress." Wilson "was for declaring Congress could not change a treaty," but Alexander argued that by signing the legislation, President Wilson had approved the notification process. Daniels concluded that the "best thought seemed that Colby should notify countries of the law & ask them to consent. If they refused then to take matter up with Congress which would shortly thereafter be in session. But troublesome question."

On August 30, Payne made public a letter he wrote the U.S. Chamber of Commerce warning that if section 34 were followed, "the country will find itself very greatly embarrassed."[86] On September 18 Colby asked Wilson for direction recommending Wilson issue a statement stating that Congress did not have the constitutional right to abrogate treaties.[87] Colby even drafted a notification to countries of U.S. intentions, but Wilson backed him off.[88] On September 20, Wilson wrote to Colby that while "it is hardly necessary to volunteer a public statement about my decision to observe the obligations of our treaties of commerce," a public statement would still be a good idea.[89]

Colby sent the president the draft statement on September 23, which Wilson issued to the press the next day.[90] The statement indicated that section 34 was unconstitutional and would result in the breach of thirty-two commercial treaties which "would be wholly irreconcilable with the historical respect the United States has shown for its international engagements." The statement concluded,

> The Merchant Marine act was approved June 5, in the final rush of the session's close, with no opportunity to suggest, much less secure, its revision in any particular. To have vetoed the act would have sacrificed the great number of sound and enlightened provisions which it undoubtedly contains. Furthermore, the fact that one section of the law involves elements of illegality rendering the section inoperative need not affect the validity and operation of the act as a whole.

Colby explained to the press about a week later that the president supported and wanted to promote the U.S. merchant marine.[91] At the same time, Wilson believed that section 34 invited retaliation which would do more harm than good.

The Wilson administration thus decided to back off finally the commercial confrontation that had epitomized the Paris peace negotiations.[92] William S. Culbertson, who worked with Hurley at the Federal Trade Commission and allegedly ghost-wrote Hurley's 1920 memoir *The New Merchant Marine*, wrote that section 34 was "the keystone" of the 1920 Act and that "our national leaders were unwilling to destroy the entire structure of our international commercial relations for the purpose of establishing a shipping policy whose desirability was by no means assured."[93]

Jones went public saying that the president's decision was "'another example of Mr. Wilson's autocratic disposition and his disregard of such laws as do not suit him, even though he may have signed the measure."[94] Jones also pointed out that he believed Congress could have abrogated the treaties directly but that section 34 "directed the president to proceed in a dignified, courteous way to have them abrogated" through a notice process. He concluded that "this act of the president will bring rejoicing to the marine interests of our rivals for world trade."

Wilson's position gave rise to muted questions of impeachment for defying Congress which apparently only amused the president.[95] He did not change his mind, and President Harding followed suit. In his first annual message to Congress in December 1921, Harding agreed not to implement section 34 saying that implementation "would involve us in a chaos of trade relationships and add indescribably to the confusion of the already disordered commercial world."[96] In February 1922, in another message to Congress he softened the criticism writing that "there was no doubt about the high purpose of Congress to apply this proven practice to the upbuilding of the merchant marine."

In the face of these setbacks, Jones tried to rally support for the Act and its discriminatory provisions, speaking in its defense to various groups, including the Washington State Bar Association on September 30.[97] On December 17, 1920, he appeared at an Academy of Political Science meeting in New York together with several maritime experts—former Shipping Board Commissioner Stevens, private attorney J. Parker Kirlin, J. W. Powell (vice president of Bethlehem Shipbuilding), Winthrop Marvin, and Frederick R. Coudert of Coudert Bros.[98] He did not, however, receive much support from this group. Stevens, Kirlin, and Coudert condemned the discriminatory features of the Act as counter-productive. Coudert opined on whether Congress was authorized to direct the president to abrogate treaties.[99] Kirlin also recounted how the Gallinger Commission had rejected discriminatory duties in 1905.[100] None of the speakers mentioned either section 27 (coastwise trade) or section 33 (seamen's injury rights) in their papers.

Powell argued that "it is incorrect to say that the Jones Act was hastily passed. No statute received more hours of study by better minds than the piece of legislation which is under discussion today." A similar view expressed in the trade press was that the legislation must have been "backed up by an almost unanimous public opinion" because of "the way in which the measure was put through at the eleventh hour in a belated session of the Senate just prior to a presidential primary."[101]

Another controversial provision was the extension of the coastwise laws to the Philippines.[102] Notably, Secretary of War Baker had written a letter to the conference committee in opposition. The Philippines government argued after enactment that the "benefits alleged are conjectural, while the damage will be of stupendous proportions" and that the law was "passed against the will and over the protest of the Philippine Government."[103] The coastwise laws were not, in fact, ever extended to the Philippines because of this opposition.

The news of the day focused on the preferential rail, discriminating duty, and Philippines sections of the 1920 Act. There was little contemporary publicity about the two sections—sections 27 and 33—most people today consider the "Jones Act." In contrast, the "Ship Mortgage Act, 1920" contained as a section in the Merchant Marine Act was the subject of substantial public interest.[104] And so was the section providing for an American classification society.[105]

About the only people who observed the enactment of section 27 were Alaskans, as noted before. No one mentioned the section at the August 1920 Tacoma conference. Jones took political heat in Washington state because of section 28, the railroad provision, not section 27.[106] Moreover, neither the Shipping Board nor Chamberlain mentioned it in their annual reports at the time.

The International Seamen's Union was at first skeptical that section 33 regarding seaman's injuries would achieve much, although the Union was generally happy with the Act.[107] The Union wrote that the 1920 Act was "frankly and decisively speaking a piece of home made, brass bound, and copper fastened, double riveted anti-crimping, anti-fouling America First legislation as applied to the Merchant Marine."[108] Furuseth enthusiastically endorsed Jones in the November 1920 election although supporting a Republican was not typical for his union. He wrote that it would "be a misfortune for the workers in Washington if Jones was not re-elected."[109]

American vessel owners were also pleased with the 1920 Act. The American Steamship Owners' Association issued a statement calling the Act "the greatest legislative step in behalf of an American merchant marine that has been taken in the past century."[110] Henry Raymond, president of the association and who had served on the war-time Shipping Control Committee, also said he was not surprised about the rumors that foreign owners had put together a fund to attack Jones and the Act.

Progressives praised the 1920 Act for avoiding a fire sale of the fleet. The *New Republic* indicated that "the bill is a complete victory for those who have resisted the cry (popular among business men and Republican politicians) for the immediate sale of the government's merchant fleet."[111] And the journal observed "that the new merchant marine bill has steered clear of this dangerous policy of forced sale is due mainly to the wisdom and persistence of Senator Jones... to whom the best parts of the new law owe their authorship."

At the same time, the *New Republic* was totally against the promotional parts of the 1920 Act claiming that the Act was "the old policy of maritime protection and subsidy dressed in new clothes."[112] Moreover, it "rests upon the humiliating assumption that American shipowners... must be coddled and pampered by a paternalistic government."

Criticisms aside, Jones received favorable publicity for his work on the 1920 Act and the Water Power Act in the *Literary Digest*, which claimed that the laws "generally ranked by the press of the country as the two most important bills enacted into law during the recent session of Congress."[113] Other periodicals described Jones as a "forceful politician" and noted that he was "more than a match for the Senators in debate, and brushed the opposition aside with a wave of his hand."[114]

Jones's friends were not above generating favorable publicity for the senator. His papers at the University of Washington contain a hand-written puff piece extolling Jones's involvement with both Acts written to be distributed just before the September 7 Republican Senate primary. The effort succeeded. One September 6 headline read, "Jones, Real Senate Leader, Grinds Out Two Important Bills while Others Debate."[115]

Both political parties took credit for the 1920 Act.[116] The June 8, 1920, Republican platform claimed, "We stopped the flood of public treasure, recklessly poured into the lap of an inept shipping board." Moreover, "we endorse the sound legislation recently enacted by the Republican Congress that will insure [sic] the promotion and maintenance of the American Merchant Marine." The June 28 Democratic platform provided that "we desire to congratulate the American people upon the rebirth of our Merchant Marine... It was under a democratic administration that this was accomplished."

Meanwhile, on the side of the opposition, full page ads were placed in the Washington State newspapers in early September against Jones relating to the legislation. His Republican nomination opponents claimed that section 28 would mean commercial disaster for the Pacific Northwest.[117] British and Japanese interests were blamed for the ads, and the Justice Department conducted an inquiry.[118]

Jones's supporters protested against foreign money being spent to defeat him in the November 1920 election.[119] Haines, vice president of the Pacific Steamship Company, was quoted as saying, "'I am satisfied that foreign money is being spent to defeat Senator Wesley Jones upon the theory that by defeating him they will discredit the merchant marine act, and by discrediting the marine act they will probably get it repealed.'"

In the end, Jones won the Republican primary and then the general election with just over 56 percent of the vote with Democrat and Farmer-Labor candidates splitting the balance. Winthrop Marvin wrote that "foreign interests and short-sighted local interests that combined for a time to oppose his renomination were beaten and repudiated in the primaries and are now again confounded at the polls."[120]

Jones remained a staunch supporter of the 1920 Act.[121] As was noted at the time, "the Senator is sturdily defending his measure and appears to be not in the least worried over the agitation against it."[122] In 1921 he defended the Act as "an earnest effort to lay the foundation of a policy that will build up and maintain an adequate American merchant marine in competition with the shipping of the world."[123]

In early 1921 Jones complained about how British interests and the U.S. Chamber of Commerce were undermining the 1920 Act.[124] He called out by name on the Senate floor a Shipping Board employee who he said denied vessels to a U.S. carrier because it might hurt British carriers. The chamber's magazine published in December 1920 a story entitled "Flying the Flag on a Deficit" which charged that the board was losing a staggering amount of money through inefficiency.[125]

At that time, as vessels were released from Army/Navy service and famine relief, the board placed them on routes all over world. The U.S. merchant marine appeared to be going in the right direction. There were over two hundred routes by June 1920, served by about thirteen hundred steel vessels totaling about 8.2 million DWT.[126] U.S.-flag vessels carried the highest percentage of U.S. foreign trade in 1920 since the Civil War, at about 43 percent.[127] In 1921 it began to decline, to slightly less than 40 percent, and continued to drop to 34 percent by 1928.[128]

The Shipping Board overextended itself by appointing over 150 managing agents of U.S. government-owned vessels, making it difficult for the board to monitor efficiency and prevent fraud.[129] Also, the mere establishment of routes did not fill vessels with cargo. Many of the vessels sailed with only part cargoes, and trade routes overlapped, resulting in U.S.-flag vessels competing with each other despite the early assurances in the legislative process that this would not occur. The board cut the number of managing agents in half over the next year as vessels were laid up due to the worldwide shipping recession. The board deficits were nevertheless substantial.[130]

The reasonable sounding compromise in the 1920 Act to sell vessels judiciously over time and to nurture a substantial privately owned U.S. merchant marine foundered on the rocks of the worldwide shipping recession. The board wrote that during 1920 "the demand for steel cargo vessels declined sharply, due to depression in the shipping business."[131] Many American vessel owners were at a severe cost disadvantage, having bought vessels from the board at high 1919 prices. Because vessels were bought mainly on credit, defaults led to the board having to repossess vessels and again put them on the market further depressing vessel prices.

The board indicated that "in November 1920, the depression in shipping began to give indications of becoming very serious, involving the lay up of a large number of vessels."[132] At the peak, the board laid up 750 vessels of about five million DWT. The number laid up declined modestly in 1921 to 690 vessels.[133] Even in April 1921, the board had more vessels laid up than were active.[134]

Another problem was transitioning the 1916 Act board into the 1920 Act board. The 1920 Act provided that existing board members would continue until the president appointed a new board of seven. On June 5 there were only two commissioners,

Benson and Donald.[135] On November 10, 1920, Wilson finally made recess appointments of seven commissioners including Benson and Donald.[136] Jones held up the nominees to give President Harding a free hand to nominate his own slate and called the nominees "nondescript."[137]

On March 4, 1921, when Harding was inaugurated, those existing appointments lapsed, and Harding appointed Benson effectively as *the board* on March 11, 1921, until a full board could be nominated and confirmed. This hobbled the board not only because Benson was reluctant to make critical decisions while the president was considering his nominations, but because it made it impossible to sell vessels to non-citizens without conditions because five commissioners had to approve such sales.[138] It did not help matters that the board was dealing with a labor dispute between vessel owners and seamen stemming from the board trying to reduce costs.[139]

There was reason for optimism that Harding would make wise appointments to the Shipping Board. He had been an active member of the Commerce Committee during the Merchant Marine Act hearings in 1920 and was a U.S. merchant marine supporter, a position that stemmed from his admiration of Senator Mark Hanna of Ohio.[140] Harding nominated seven board members in early June 1921, including Benson (but not as chairman) and Donald, and they were all confirmed by June 30, 1921. It was the first time the board was fully constituted since March 1919.[141]

Harding appointed Albert D. Lasker from Chicago as chairman.[142] Lasker was a pioneering advertising executive who had helped design Harding's election advertising campaign but was without shipping experience. He was an ardent baseball fan and the owner of the Chicago Cubs until he sold the team to minority owner William Wrigley, Jr. in 1925. Lasker was not Harding's first choice and was reluctant to take the job. However, Harding pressed him, and Lasker agreed although he promised to stay only for two years (which he did, leaving in June 1923). (While in Washington, DC, Lasker lived with his family in a 1912-built house at 1706 18th Street, NW which still exists and is now the U.S. home of the Russian News & Information Agency.)

Part of the problem in identifying someone to take charge was the continuing negative publicity encountered by the Shipping Board due to the ongoing Walsh Committee investigation.[143] The committee reached a crescendo in January 1921 when Schwab wept on the witness stand denying a charge that he had diverted government money to his private account.[144] The March 1921 Walsh Committee report exonerated Schwab.[145] That report also pointed out the board's accounting deficiencies, which Lassiter emphasized in his public statements.

Lasker lowered expectations for the new board by making it clear from the outset that he was stepping into a mess. On June 24, 1921, he announced that the board was facing "'the most colossal commercial wreck the world ever knew.'"[146] In July he went public with allegations that the board was squandering public funds at an enormous rate.[147] He also testified before Congress that "the books are in deplorable condition" and "as I look into the details, I find them worse than my worst expectations."[148] Harding informed Congress in early 1922 that the board was losing $16 million a month.[149]

The reconstituted board decided to hire three persons to oversee its main functions much like the earlier board did with Piez, Schwab, and Rosseter.[150] The board wanted to pay such personnel more than double the salaries paid to the commissioner's themselves, which was heavily criticized.[151] This prompted Harding to write to Jones on August 20, 1921, defending Lasker for "making a very heavy sacrifice to give his time and talents."[152]

Lasker also appeared to back track on the premise of the 1920 Act by advocating for continued government ownership and operation of vessels. Here again Lasker wrote Jones a letter saying that the goal would always be private ownership but that poor worldwide market conditions did not yet permit this outcome.[153]

To reduce costs, the board took an ax to the number of board and corporation employees and expenditures and seized vessels it believed were being mismanaged.[154] Unsurprisingly, Lasker was criticized from all sides and his tenure was described as tumultuous and unsettled.[155]

Eventually, Harding and the board came to the view that the only way to stop the government hemorrhaging funds was private vessel operation with direct subsidies.[156] This was effectively an acknowledgment that the 1920 Act mechanisms to support the U.S. merchant marine in the foreign trade had failed.

Harding proposed a subsidy program in February 1922 whereby a portion of overall import duties collected would go into a fund to pay bounties almost in the exact same formulation as earlier bounty schemes.[157] A bill passed the House in November 1922, but it never passed the Senate.[158] Senator Jones was active in picking up the pieces and in getting Congress to enact the Merchant Marine Act, 1928. That law, fittingly known as the "Jones-White Act," started the journey from the 1920 Merchant Marine Act.[159]

---

[1] 59 CONG. REC. 6803 (May 10, 1920). Jones kept his constituents appraised of his work by providing a summary of the bill to the Seattle Daily Times. J. J. Underwood, "U.S. Shipping Bill Explained by Jones," Seattle Daily Times, May 5, 1920, 15.
[2] For example, Zeis, American Shipping Policy, 117; Samuel A. Lawrence, United States Merchant Shipping Policies and Politics (Washington, DC: Brookings Institution, 1966), 41, 369; Andrew Gibson and Arthur Donovan, The Abandoned Ocean: A History of United States Maritime Policy (Columbia: University of South Carolina Press, 2000), 119; 59 CONG. REC. 6805 (May 10, 1920).
[3] "Senator Defends His Marine Bill," Washington Times, June 21, 1920, 13; Wesley L. Jones, The Merchant Marine Act of 1920, Proceedings of the Academy of Political Science 9, no. 2 (February 1921): 89–98, 89.
[4] 59 CONG. REC. 6810–13 (May 10, 1920).
[5] 59 CONG. REC. 6810–6811.
[6] 59 CONG. REC. 6860–61.
[7] 17 & 18 Vict. c. 5 (March 23, 1854).

[8] 59 Cong. Rec. 6861–62 (May 10, 1920).
[9] 59 Cong. Rec. 6862.
[10] 59 Cong. Rec. 6858–59.
[11] 59 Cong. Rec. 6869.
[12] 59 Cong. Rec. 6859–60.
[13] 59 Cong. Rec. 6864–65,
[14] 59 Cong. Rec. 6865, 6867.
[15] 59 Cong. Rec. 6868 (May 11, 1920).
[16] 59 Cong. Rec. 6865.
[17] 59 Cong. Rec. 7345 (May 20, 1920).
[18] 59 Cong. Rec. 6984–85 (May 13, 1920).
[19] 59 Cong. Rec. 6986, 6990.
[20] 59 Cong. Rec. 6989–90.
[21] 40 Stat. 900 (July 15, 1918); U.S. Congress, House, Increasing the Powers of the United States Shipping Board, 65th Cong., 2nd sess., 1918, H. Rep. 65-658, 4.
[22] 59 Cong. Rec. 6990 (May 13, 1920).
[23] "The New Shipping Bill," Baltimore Sun, May 22, 1920, 6.
[24] 59 Cong. Rec. 6992–94 (May 13, 1920).
[25] 59 Cong. Rec. 7043–44.
[26] 247 U.S. 372 (1918).
[27] 45 U.S.C. § 51 et seq.
[28] 40 Stat. 1057 (February 24, 1919).
[29] 41 Stat. 988, 997 (June 5, 1920). In addition, the proceeds of the sale of any U.S.-flag vessels constructed prior to January 1, 1914, would be exempt from income tax if invested in building new vessels in the United States.
[30] 59 Cong. Rec. 7341 and 7345 (May 20, 1920).
[31] 59 Cong. Rec. 7347–50; "Senator Walsh Says Measure Discriminates against New England," New York Times, May 30, 1920, 6.
[32] 59 Cong. Rec. 7350–53 (May 20, 1920).
[33] "Letter from B. Colby to W. Jones (April 15, 1920)," Papers Relating to the Foreign Relations of the United States, 1920, U.S. Department of State, Office of the Historian, Historical Documents, vol. 1, no. 811.6363/8.
[34] 59 Cong. Rec. 7415–420 (May 21, 1920).
[35] 59 Cong. Rec. 7420.
[36] 59 Cong. Rec. 8163–8171 (June 2, 1920); U.S. Congress, House, American Merchant Marine, 66th Cong., 2nd sess., 1920, H. Rep. 66-1093; 59 Cong. Rec. 8398–53 (June 3, 1920); 59 Cong. Rec. 8493–00 (June 4, 1920); U.S. Congress, House, American Merchant Marine, 66th Cong., 2nd sess., 1920, H. Rep. 66-1102; 59 Cong. Rec. 8589–99 (June 4, 1920).
[37] "Conferees Support Merchant Marine," New York Times, June 3, 1920, 32.
[38] American Merchant Marine, H. Rep. 66-1102, 33.
[39] For example, "Battle Looms on Shipping Policy," Seattle Daily Times, May 1, 1920, 2.

40 "Grigsby Fights Marine Measure," Seattle Daily Times, May 28, 1920, 24; "Against Extending Coastwise Laws to Philippines," Nautical Gazette 98, no. 23 (June 5, 1920: 847.
41 Diary of James Wickersham, June 19, 1920, https://vilda.alaska.edu/digital/collection/cdmg21/id/8299/rec/34.
42 Michener, Alaska, 819.
43 Territory of Alaska, Session Laws, Resolutions and Memorials 1921 (Juneau, AK: Alaska Daily Empire Print, 1921), 162—63.
44 Territory of Alaska v. Troy, 258 U.S. 101 (1922).
45 Earnest Gruening, The State of Alaska (New York: Random House, 1954), 243.
46 72 Stat. 339, 351 (July 7, 1958).
47 59 CONG. REC. 8599 (June 4, 1920).
48 "Chamber Opposed to Rate Discrimination," Seattle Daily Times, June 3, 1920, 24; "Seven to Act on Jones Bill," Seattle Star, (May 29, 1920), 1; "Oppose Clause in Shipping Bill," Seattle Daily Times, May 28, 1920, 24.
49 59 CONG. REC. 8465–70 (June 4, 1920).
50 "La Follette to Undergo Operation," New York Times, June 7, 1920, 5.
51 "Wesley L. Jones, Candidate for Re-Election," Labor Journal (Everett, Washington), June 25, 1920, 2.
52 59 CONG. REC. 8589–09 (June 4, 1920).
53 59 CONG. REC. 8607.
54 59 CONG. REC. 8608–09.
55 "Ship Sacrifice Up to Wilson," Washington Times, June 5, 1920, 2.
56 59 CONG. REC. 8678 (June 5, 1920).
57 "Pass Merchant Fleet Bill," New York Times, June 5, 1920, 16.
58 "Entry for June 1, 1920," Cabinet Diaries of Josephus Daniels.
59 "Wilson Denounces Congress Record," New York Times, June 6, 1920, 1.
60 "Wilson Passes a Busy Day, in Fine Trim, Says Grayson," New York Times, June 6, 1920, 1.
61 "President Kills Eleven Measures by 'Pocket Veto,'" Evening Star (Washington, DC), June 6, 1920, 1.
62 Jerome G. Kerwin, "Federal Water-Power Legislation," (PhD diss., Columbia University, 1926), 261-263.
63 "Denounces Pocket Veto," New York Times, June 8, 1920, 4; "Veto of Water Power Bill Is a Calamity," Cordova Daily Times, June 8, 1920, 2.
64 "Water Power Bill Saved by Senator," Denver Rocky Mountain News, June 20, 1920, 5; "Water Bill Signed by Ingenuity of 2," Oregonian, June 19, 1920, 8.
65 "President Signs Water Power Bill," New York Times, June 19, 1920, 20.
66 "Priest Rapids Will Be First Big Power Site," Seattle Daily Times, June 20, 1920, 7; "President Signs Ship Board Bill," Seattle Daily Times, June 6, 1920, 1 ("Work of Senator Jones").

[67] For example, "The Disastrous Effects of Section 28 of the Merchant Marine Act Sponsored by Senator Jones... of Washington...," Seattle Star, June 28, 1920, 8.
[68] "Jones Says Act Will Not Harm," Seattle Daily Times, June 17, 1920, 24; "Jones to Explain New Marine Law," Oregonian, June 27, 1920, 22.
[69] "Benson Replies to Trade Threats," New York Times, July 2, 1920, 32.
[70] "Pacific Coast Trade Will Be Safeguarded," Nautical Gazette 99, no. 3 (July 17, 1920): 67–68.
[71] Transcript of Conference with Senator Wesley L. Jones on Section 28.
[72] "Cornelius Vanderbilt Jr., Newsman, Author, Dead," New York Times, July 8, 1974, 32.
[73] "Declares Ship Law Is Here to Stay," New York Times, August 12, 1920, 15; "Shipping Board Asked to Save Coast's Trade," Seattle Daily Times, August 11, 1920, 1; "Senator Jones Defends His Bill at Takoma," Nautical Gazette 99, no. 8 August 21, 1920: 228.
[74] "Says Section 28 Will Benefit U.S.," Seattle Daily Times, August 12, 1920, 18.
[75] "Jones Marine Act Not to be Feared, Says Attorney," San Francisco Chronicle, August 25, 1920, 14; "Shipping Board Plans Explained by Counsel," Seattle Daily Times, September 2, 1920, 21.
[76] "By the Mark and by the Deep—Making a Fetich [sic] of the Jones Law," Nautical Gazette 99, no. 8 (August 21, 1920): 243; "Talks on Ship Board," Seattle Sunday Times, November 14, 1920, 25; David S. Kennedy, "New Shipping Board Begins Enforcement of the Merchant Marine Act," Nautical Gazette 99, no. 24 (December 11, 1920): 5, 19; "In Re Section 28," Pacific Marine Review 18 (February 1921): 118–19.
[77] Jones, "The Merchant Marine Act of 1920," 95.
[78] Fifth Annual Report of the Shipping Board, 27–28.
[79] Eighth Annual Report of the Shipping Board, 15–16; E. S. Gregg, "The Failure of Merchant Marine Act of 1920," American Economic Review 11, no. 4 (December 1921): 601–15, 606.
[80] For example, "More Arguments Against Section 34 of the Jones Law," Nautical Gazette 99, no. 26 (December 25, 1920): 16.
[81] "Telegram from the Ambassador in Great Britain to the Secretary of State (August 11, 1920)," Papers Relating to the Foreign Relations of the United States, 1920, U.S. Department of State, Office of the Historian, Historical Documents, vol. 2, no. 800.6363/163.
"May Levy Preferential Duty," New York Times, July 10, 1920, 4.
[82] "Urges US to Fight for American Ships," New York Times, June 21, 1920, 12.
[83] "Letter from J. Alexander to W. Wilson (June 25, 1920)," Papers of Woodrow Wilson, vol. 65, 467.
[84] Annual Report of the Commissioner of Navigation to Secretary of Commerce (1920), 31–32.
[85] "Entry for August 24, 1920," Cabinet Diaries of Josephus Daniels.

[86] "See Trade Lost by Shipping Act," New York Times, August 31, 1920, 13; "Shipping Law May Lead U.S. into Trade War," Seattle Daily Times, September 2, 1920, 1.

[87] "Letter from B. Colby to W. Wilson (September 18, 1920)," Papers of Woodrow Wilson, vol. 66, 125.

[88] Bainbridge Colby, The Close of Woodrow Wilson's Administration and the Final Years (New York: Publishers Printing, 1930), 20.

[89] "Letter from W. Wilson to B. Colby (September 20, 1920), Papers of Woodrow Wilson, vol. 66, 128.

[90] "Letter from B. Colby to W. Wilson (September 23, 1920), Papers of Woodrow Wilson, vol. 66, 136; "President Won't Denounce Treaties; Defies Congress," New York Times, September 25, 1920, 1.

[91] "Says Wilson Wants Shipping Built Up," New York Times, September 30, 1920, 20.

[92] Safford, Wilsonian Maritime Diplomacy, 237.

[93] Safford, Wilsonian Maritime Diplomacy, 238n45; William Smith Culbertson, International Economic Policies, A Survey of the Economics of Diplomacy (New York: D. Appleton, 1925), 444; J. Richard Snyder, "William S. Culbertson and the Formation of Modern American Commercial Policy, 1917—1925," Kansas Historical Quarterly 35, no. 4 (Winter 1969): 396–410.

[94] "Jones' Shipping Law Author Raps Wilson," Oregonian, (September 26, 1920), 1.

[95] "Wilson View of Jones Marine Act Roils Congress' Members; Impeachment Cry Is Heard," San Francisco Chronicle, September 27, 1920, 4; Colby, Close of Woodrow Wilson's Administration, 20.

[96] Warren G. Harding, First Annual Message, December 6, 1921, UC Santa Barbara, the American Presidency Project, www.presidency.ucsb.edu/documents/first-annual-message-19; Warrant G. Harding, Address to Congress on Assistance to the Merchant Marine, February 28, 1922, UC Santa Barbara, the American Presidency Project, www.presidency.ucsb.edu/documents/address-congress-assistance-the-merchant-marine.

[97] "Jones Explains Ship Measure to Lawyers," Seattle Daily Times, September 30, 1920, 14.

[98] "Experts Discuss Merchant Marine Act at Political Science Academy Meeting," Nautical Gazette 99, no. 25 (December 18, 1920): 3–4, 19; "Urge Support of Government to Aid Shipping," New York Daily Tribune, December 11, 1920, 17; Raymond B. Stevens, "International Aspects of American Maritime Policies," Proceedings of the Academy of Political Science 9, no. 2 (February 1921): 99–103; J. Parker Kirlin, "The Operating Problems of the American Merchant Marine," Proceedings of the Academy of Political Science 9, no. 2 (February 1921): 104–15; Frederic R. Coudert, "Comments on the Merchant Marine Act of 1920," Proceedings of the Academy of Political Science 9, no. 2 (February 1921: 116–28; J. W. Powell, "Current Problems in American Ship Building," Proceedings of the Academy of Political

Science 9, no. 2 (February 1921): 129–32; Winthrop L. Marvin, "Merchant Marine Policies," Proceedings of the Academy of Political Science 9, no. 2 (February 1921): 139–43.

[99] Coudert, "Comments on the Merchant Marine Act of 1920," 116–28; Reeves, "The Jones Act and the Denunciation of Treaties,"15; Howard Thayer Kingsbury, "The Refusal of the President to Give Notice of Termination of Certain Treaty Provisions under the Jones Act," American Journal of International Law 15 (January 1921): 39–41.

[100] Kirlin, "The Operating Problems of the American Merchant Marine," Proceedings of the Academy of Political Science, 114–15.

[101] "All Aboard," Pacific Marine Review 17 (July 1920): 64–65.

[102] "Against Extending Coastwise Laws to Philippines," Nautical Gazette 98, no. 23 (June 5, 1920): 847.

[103] "Filipinos' Ship Protest," New York Times, August 25, 1920, 8.

[104] For example, Philip Adler, "Current Legislation–The Ship Mortgage Act, 1920," Columbia Law Review 20, no. 7 (November 1920): 788–91.

[105] "American Bureau of Shipping—New Marine Act Strengthens Its Position and Makes It a Potential Rival of Lloyd's," Nautical Gazette 99, no. 1 (July 2, 1920): 21–22.

[106] For example, "Why Seattle Desires Light on Ship Bill," Seattle Daily Times, September 2, 1920, 1; "Expect Benson to Enforce Rail Preferentials," New York Daily Tribune, November 18, 1920, 23.

[107] "H.R. 10378," Seamen's Journal 33, no. 38 (May 26, 1920): 6; "Maritime Compensation," Seamen's Journal 33, no. 43 (June 30, 1920): 6; U.S. Department of Labor, Workmen's Compensation and the Protection of Seamen, Bulletin no. 869, (Washington, DC.: Government Printing Office, 1946), 52—53.

[108] "Safe So Far!" Seamen's Journal 33, no. 43 (June 30, 1920): 8; "Protests against Jones Act," Seamen's Journal 34, no. 2 (September 15, 1920): 6.

[109] "Ship Men Indorse Jones," Oregonian, September 3, 1920, 13; George Perry Morris, "In the Limelight," Washington Herald, September 9, 1920, 4. As a result of an interview with Senator Jones' son in 1959, William Forth indicates as follows regarding the labor changes made in the 1920 Act: "Mr. Jones stated that his father was 'very fond' of Furuseth. He felt that Jones's [sic] desire to improve the lot of seamen was as important a motive in the Act of 1920 as was the improvement of the merchant marine generally." Forth, Wesley L. Jones, 503 n 44.

[110] "Steamship Men Oppose Foreign Shipping Attacks," New York Daily Tribune, September 14, 1920, 22.

[111] "The New Merchant Marine Act," New Republic 23, no. 289 (June 16, 1920): 76–77.

[112] "Coddling Our Merchant Marine," 352–353.

[113] "Dawn of a New Water-Power Era," Literary Digest 66, no. 2 (July 10, 1920): 18–19.

[114] "How Jones Bill Was Rushed through Congress," Nautical Gazette 99, no. 14 (October 2, 1920): 424.
[115] "Jones, Real Senate Leader, Grinds Out Two Important Bills while Others Debate," Post-Intelligencer (Seattle), September 6, 1920, 1.
[116] 1920 Democratic Party Platform, June 28, 1920, UC Santa Barbara, the American Presidency Project, Democratic Party Platforms, https://www.presidency.ucsb.edu/documents/1920-democratic-party-platform; Republican Party Platform of 1920, June 8, 1920, UC Santa Barbara, The American Presidency Project, Republican Party Platforms, https://www.presidency.ucsb.edu/documents/republican-party-platform-1920.
[117] "Says Jones Bill Means Disaster," Seattle Daily Times, September 4, 1920, 3.
[118] "Alien Attacks on Jones Bill to be Probed," New York Daily Tribune, September 13, 1920, 18.
[119] "Says Foreign Money Spent Against Jones," Cordova Daily Times, September 29, 1920, 7.
[120] Winthrop L. Marvin, "President-Elect and His Chief Lieutenants Strongly for the American Merchant Marine," Marine Journal 43, no. 6 (November 13, 1920): 7.
[121] For example, "Shipping Needs Nation's Aid, Says Senator Jones," New York Daily Tribune, September 22, 1920, 21.
[122] "Wesley L. Jones," Nautical Gazette 99, no. 10 (September 4, 1920): 306.
[123] Jones, "The Merchant Marine Act of 1920," 89.
[124] "Jones Sees Plot of British to Kill New U.S. Marine," Evening Star (Washington, DC), January 20, 1921, 1.
[125] James B. Morrow, "Flying the Flag on a Deficit," Nation's Business 8, no. 12 (December 1920): 11–12.
[126] Fourth Annual Report of the Shipping Board, 57.
[127] Fifth Annual Report of the Shipping Board, 50.
[128] U.S. Congress, House, Hearings before the House Merchant Marine Committee on the Merchant Marine, 70th Cong., 1st sess., 1928, 4.
[129] Fourth Annual Report of the Shipping Board, 257–59.
[130] Sixth Annual Report of the Shipping Board, 99.
[131] Fifth Annual Report of the Shipping Board, 64.
[132] Fifth Annual Report of the Shipping Board, 145.
[133] Sixth Annual Report of the Shipping Board, 136.
[134] Fifth Annual Report of the Shipping Board, 200.
[135] Fifth Annual Report of the Shipping Board, 13.
[136] "Picks New Shipping Board," New York Times, November 7, 1920, 9.
[137] "Senate Not to Confirm Wilson's Shipping Board," New York Daily Tribune, November 24, 1920, 17; "Jones Will Oppose New Shipping Board," Philadelphia Inquirer, November 24, 1920, 22.

[138] "Shipping Board Out as Harding Goes In," New York Times, March 5, 1921, 22; "Shipping Board in Doubt," New York Times, March 9, 1921, 22; 41 Stat. 988, 991 (June 5, 1920); "Ships Will be Sold at Once," Washington Times, June 13, 1920, 1.
[139] "Agrees to Lower Wages for Seamen," New York Times, April 2, 1921, 7; "Ship Board Grants Workers a Hearing," New York Times, April 3, 1921, 20; "Ship Strike at End; Sign Peace Today," New York Times, June 14, 192), 32.
[140] John Gunther, Taken at the Flood, The Story of Albert D. Lasker (New York: Harper & Brothers, 1960),128—29; "President-Elect Harding's Message to Shipping Men of America," Nautical Gazette 99, no. 19 (November 6, 1920): 3—4.
[141] Third Annual Report of the Shipping Board, 13.
[142] "Albert D. Lasker, Chicago Business Man, Chosen by President as Chairman of Shipping Board," New York Times, June 7, 1921, 1; Gunther, Taken at the Flood, chap. 9.
[143] For example, "The Shipping Board Scandal," New York Times, November 13, 1920, 10; "Shipping Board Bookkeeping," New York Times, November 19, 1920, 14; "Walsh Committee Agents Charge Graft in Shipping Board," Nautical Gazette 99, no. 20 (November 13, 1920): 5—6.
[144] Hearings before the House Select Committee on U.S. Shipping Board Operations, part 11, 4568; "Schwab on Stand Weeps as He Tells of Meeting Morse," New York Times, January 26, 1921, 1.
[145] United States Shipping Board Operations, H. Rep. 66-1399, 20–22.
[146] "Ship Board Faces 'Colossal Wreck,'" New York Times, June 25, 1921, 1.
[147] "Laster Finds Fleet Squandering Money in Morass of Debt," New York Times, July 19, 1921, 1; "Lasker Shocks Dawes," Seattle Daily Times, July 25, 1921, 2.
[148] 61 Cong. Rec. 5331–33 (August 20, 1921) (Statement of July 18, 1921).
[149] 62 Cong. Rec. 3134–36 (February 28, 1922).
[150] "Lasker to 'Draft' Shipping Experts," New York Times, June 26, 1921, 15; "Picks Three Men to Put Our Fleet on Paying Basis," New York Times, July 12, 1921, 1.
[151] For example, 61 Cong. Rec. 5324–26 (August 20, 1921).
[152] 61 Cong. Rec. 5333 (August 20, 1921).
[153] 61 Cong. Rec. 5326.
[154] For example, "Laster Starts War on Pier Profiteering," New York Times, October. 22, 1921, 8; "Ship Board to Sell the Towns It Built," New York Times, November 2, 192), 9.
[155] "Harding Impatient at Lasker Critics," New York Times, August 31, 1921, 15; "Lasker Belittles Senate Criticism," New York Times, October 22, 1921, 8; William Hard, "Lasker Record is Lesson to America," Washington Times, June 16, 1923, 2; David Lawrence, "Lasker Soon Out of Shipping Board," Evening Star (Washington, DC.), June 8, 1923, 3.
[156] For example, "Statement of Albert D. Lasker, 'What Are We to Do with Our Government Owned Ships;'" "U.S. Must Run Marine, Says President," Washington Times, June 16, 1923, 2.

[157] 62 Cong. Rec. 3134–36 (February 28, 1922).
[158] 63 Cong. Rec. 429 (November 29, 1922).
[159] "New Ship Law Fails to Reach Eye of Public," Seattle Daily Times, August 7, 1928, 3.

Chapter 23—Conclusion

The United States had an internationally competitive merchant marine when it was founded because of the prowess of its people in the construction and operation of wooden sailing vessels. The main challenge at the time was foreign trade barriers. The U.S. government made it the main U.S. maritime policy to eliminate those barriers by imposing retaliatory discriminating duties and negotiating free trade agreements. The government succeeded, and the U.S. merchant marine prospered.

Once the commercial advantages disappeared, which was clearly the case by the end of the Civil War, the United States had a choice. The country could abandon private vessel ownership in the foreign trade, maintain a government-owned fleet, and accept likely operating losses into the foreseeable future as necessary to sustain a fleet under U.S. control. Or the United States could let the international market do its will by prioritizing cheap ocean transportation, which would almost certainly have meant the eventual end of U.S.-flag international commercial shipping. Or the United States could attempt to offset the cost disadvantages by re-adopting discriminations or direct and indirect aids.

No one seriously suggested government ownership in 1865 or really at any time until 1915 when Secretary McAdoo and President Wilson proposed it. As between the other two choices—*laissez faire* or support of a private merchant marine—the country was divided in 1865 as it had been from the beginning at the Constitutional Convention. There was always a contingent prioritizing cheap transportation versus a contingent willing to pay a national price for maintaining a U.S. presence on the world's oceans. The two positions, as this book relates, mostly canceled each other out from the Civil War to World War I. The United States neither abandoned the foreign trading fleet nor supported it sufficiently to sustain a substantial international presence.

This stalemate was unbroken by the experiences of the Spanish-American War, the Boer War, and the voyage of the Great White Fleet, all of which demonstrated that the U.S. was vulnerable commercially and militarily without a U.S.-flag foreign trading fleet. Nothing, it seemed, could overcome the country's love for cheap international ocean transportation and its dislike for paying taxes to support a privately-owned fleet or paying the indirect costs associated with trade discrimination.

World War I appeared, but only appeared, to change the country's maritime policy trajectory. The United States spent an enormous sum and built and manned a large fleet of vessels, which put the nation back on the global merchant marine map—but it was not a permanent maritime policy. The Shipping Board and Fleet Corporation built vessels as fast as possible for war-time needs without regard to commercial utility. Not enough attention was paid to expanding everything else that goes into a private merchant marine including vessel classification, insurance, shore-side expertise, foreign shipping agents, etc. Moreover, the war ended in the middle of that shipbuilding program, which meant that commercially inappropriate vessels would continue to be built and delivered after the war ended.

The building program succeeded not because it was efficient, but because enough money and talent were thrown at it to get the job done. As it was, the prolonged debate on the 1916 Shipping Act and the slow creation of an effective Shipping Board and Fleet Corporation hampered the effort. The idea of direct government intervention in the U.S. merchant marine birthed in 1915 did not become fully effective until early 1918, with the Hurley-Schwab-Piez-Franklin team.

The government vessel policy choices were limited after the war—sell the fleet immediately and get the U.S. government out of the business or keep the government permanently in that business. Both were political non-starters. Congress plotted a middle, reasonable-sounding, course of empowering the board to sell vessels judiciously over time to get the U.S. merchant marine gradually into private hands.

It turned out to be the worst of the three choices. The board was given the almost impossible task of running a government fleet side by side with an independent privately-owned fleet. The result was that the government fleet remained bloated and unwieldy and a financial drain on the Treasury with no clear path to private ownership.

The urgent sale of as many vessels as possible at greatly reduced prices with the laying up and scrapping of much if not most of the fleet may have worked better. It stood a chance of balancing the fleet for market conditions and concentrating limited U.S. shipping expertise both in government and in the private sector on a small but substantial fleet containing the most commercially viable vessels.

In terms of supporting a privately-owned fleet, the policy choices after the war were also limited. Substantial direct subsidies were never in the cards in 1919-1920. The merchant marine did not on the surface appear to need or merit subsidies. Subsidies were also anathema at the time, and it is highly unlikely that the public would have gone along with directly subsidizing privately-owned vessels the government had bought at a high price and then sold at a low price.

That left either leaving it up to the privately-owned fleet to find a way to compete without government support or providing indirect assistance to such a fleet. The Greene Bill would have done the former. The Congress, with Jones leading the way, chose the latter. The primary means of indirect support chosen, such as preferential rail rates, however, were neutered and cast aside after the law was enacted. The other improvements in the 1920 Act were insufficient on their own to overcome cost, market, and other international commercial obstacles.

As a result, the long-standing maritime policy conversation re-started in the early 1920s as if the war had not occurred and the 1920 Act had not been enacted. The Harding administration proposed direct subsidies in a formulation that easily could have been advanced by any Republican administration from 1865 to 1914. What occurred after is a tale for another book.

What the 1920 Act did accomplish was to cement into law the necessity for having a foreign trading merchant marine and the principle that it should be privately owned. That has been an enduring legacy, and it remains official U.S. policy today.

Despite Alaskan lamentations, the 1920 Act did not fundamentally change U.S. coastwise laws going back to 1789/1817. Those laws, pre-dating the 1920 Act, sustained a large U.S. maritime industry important to the U.S. World War I effort when everything else had largely failed to sustain a substantial U.S. merchant marine.

As Jones said, and as contemporaneous history supports, the 1920 Act was not a watershed moment in U.S. coastwise policy. The "Jones Act" was about foreign trade, not domestic trade. Senator Jones surely would be chagrined to know that his ideas to sustain the war-built fleet on the world's oceans would be ignored over time in favor of provisions regarding coastwise trade and seamen's injuries that were incremental and not contemporaneously noteworthy.

Jones probably would not be amused, however, by the many mischaracterizations that have taken hold, including that the United States reserved its domestic trade to U.S.-flag vessels in the "Jones Act." What would probably be the most distressing is that every domestic maritime policy dispute is now associated with his name. Jones's contributions deserve better. Hopefully, this book can do something to correct the record and give Jones the proper maritime policy credit he merits and not lay at his feet every dispute about the reservation of U.S. domestic trade to U.S.-flag vessels.

Acknowledgments

This book is partly the result of the COVID-19 pandemic, probably like many books written since 2020. The pandemic freed up time, making it possible to write the book I had already decided I would write—but probably not until after I retired from the active practice of law.

The current state of digitization also made the research from home possible meaning that the shutdowns did not interfere with the research process. There are now public or semi-public sources for books, periodicals, correspondence, government publications and everything in between going back hundreds of years. And where something has not been digitized, it can usually be obtained easily at low cost from an on-line book seller, making most trips to the library unnecessary.

Still, some sources have not been digitized making in person review necessary. The papers of Senator Wesley Jones at the University of Washington archives are the most prominent example of that for purposes of this book. In that endeavor I had the very able assistance of Ross A. Coen, a University of Washington graduate student who searched the papers and copied what (little, it turned out) could be gleaned about Jones and the U.S. merchant marine.

Just because things are on-line does not, of course, mean they are easy to find. When I exhausted my search abilities, I could always turn to Mikhail Koulikov, a research librarian at Winston & Strawn LLP, who without exaggeration could find *anything* that had appeared at one time in print.

Before I went too far with the manuscript, I thought it would be useful to see if I was on the right track, so I contacted Christopher J. McMahon who had retired as the Maritime Administration Emory S. Land Chair of Merchant Marine Affairs at the

Naval War College and is a widely published author on merchant marine subjects. Chris was generous with his time and kind enough to provide encouragement. Further encouragement was provided by friends in the maritime industry, including William P. Doyle, R. Christian Johnsen, Brian W. Schoeneman, and Augustin ("Augie") Tellez. I am also grateful to my former law partner John A. Waits, who first introduced me to Secretary Ray Mabus, his lifelong friend, and to Ray for writing the foreword.

Finding a publisher was no easy task for a work of this kind and Frederick M. Haden Jr., Taylor Baldwin Kiland, and C. W. Goodyear were very helpful. Taylor also helped whip the book into shape together with Irina du Quenoy who is a terrific editor. Finally, I would like to thank Dennis Lowery of Adducent who agreed to publish the book and take a chance on it finding an audience.

APPENDIX

WORLD WAR II LIBERTY SHIPS NAMED FOR DRAMATIS PERSONAE

The United States reprised the World War I crash cargo shipbuilding program in World War II based in part on the Hog Island experience. Eighteen U.S. shipyards constructed 2,710 vessels of a standard modular design provided initially by Great Britain. Like the "Hog Islanders," these vessels were thought of as the "ugly ducklings" of the seas but became famously known as the "Liberty" ships. The U.S. Maritime Commission (successor to the U.S. Shipping Board) determined not to name any vessel after a living person and many of the vessels were named after prominent deceased Americans (including Confederates like Jefferson Davis). Other than that, there were no naming rules *per se*, and with so many vessels they wound up with a wide range of names of people from all walks of life, many of which were chosen by clubs or local communities. Among the vessels were the following named for persons listed in the Dramatis Personae at the outset of this book:

Name	U.S. Maritime Commission Hull Number
Alexander, Joshua W.	1004
Baker, Bernard N.	0966
Baker, Newton D.	1520
Blaine, James G.	0333
Chamberlain, Eugene Tyler	2368
Collins, Edward K.	2315
Dewey, George	1202
Dingley, Nelson	0810
Donald, John A.	1005
Elkins, Stephen B.	0618
Fletcher, Duncan U.	1529
Frye, William Pierce	0212
Furuseth, Andrew	0491
Gallatin, Albert	0277

Gallinger, Jacob H.	0794
Goethals, George W.	0599
Hale, Eugene	0791
Hanna, Mark	0573
Hurley, Edward N.	0963
La Follette, Robert M.	1024
Maguire, James G.	2183
Marvin, Winthrop L.	3069
McAdoo, William G.	0443
Nelson, Knute	0731
Payne, John Barton	1535
Piez, Charles	0965
Roach, John	2267
Root, Elihu	1524
Rosseter, John H.	1580
Schwab, Charles M.	0964
Stevens, Raymond B.	3016
Underwood, Oscar	2238
Wilson, William B.	1537

Notably, Wesley L. Jones is not among the names used for Liberty ships. Nor is P. A. S. Franklin, John Farquhar, William Greene, Clement Griscom, Henry Cabot Lodge, or John Lynch. The Board chairmen William Denman and Albert Lasker were both still alive during World War II. Chairman/CNO Benson had a class of destroyers and a class of war transports named after him. One of the transports was named after Admiral R. E. Coontz.

Sources: John Henshaw, *Liberty's Provenance* (Barnsley, United Kingdom: 2019); Greg H. Williams, *The Liberty Ships of World War II* (Jefferson, NC: McFarland, 2014); and L. A. Sawyer and W. H. Mitchell, *The Liberty Ships, The History of the "Emergency" Type Cargo Ships Constructed in the United States during World War II* (Cambridge, MD: Cornell Maritime Press, 1970).

Charlie Papavizas

Timeline of Significant U.S. Merchant Marine Legislation 1789–1920

Date	Citation	Name of Act	Summary
07/04/1789	1 Stat. 24	An Act for laying a duty on goods, wares, and merchandises imported into the United States	Preferred U.S.-built/U.S.-owned vessels for the carriage of tea through a duty discount and other merchandise from China or India through a duty surcharge; and generally provided a 10 percent discount for U.S.-built/U.S. owned carriage
07/20/1789	1 Stat. 27	An Act imposing duties on tonnage	Imposed tonnage duty with lowest rate for U.S-built/U.S.-owned vessels; higher rate for U.S.-built/foreign owned; highest rate for all others. U.S.-built/U.S.-owned in coastwise trade to only pay once a year.
09/01/1789	1 Stat. 55	An Act for registering and clearing vessels, regulating the coasting trade	First U.S. vessel registration law: vessels had to be U.S.-built, master a U.S. citizen, and wholly owned by U.S. citizens without provision for corporate ownership; U.S. citizens residing abroad did not qualify.
07/20/1790	1 Stat. 131	An Act for the government and regulation of seamen in the merchants service	First U.S merchant mariner law

Date	Citation	Title	Description
07/20/1790	1 Stat. 135	An Act imposing duties on the tonnage of ships or vessels	Repealed July 20, 1789, tonnage duty law and re-imposed rates taking into account vessel registration law
02/16/1792	1 Stat. 229	An Act concerning certain fisheries of the United States, and for the regulation and government of fishermen employed therein	Provided fishing vessel subsidies repealed in 1866
12/31/1792	1 Stat. 287	An Act concerning the registering and recording of ships or vessels	Repealed 1789 vessel registration law and substituted a law patterned on the law of Great Britain including the requirement that all vessels "of the United States" had to be U.S.-built
02/18/1793	1 Stat. 305	An Act for enrolling and licensing of ships in the coasting and fishing trade, and for regulating the same	Established enrollment and licensing system for vessels in the coastwise trade
06/27/1797	1 Stat. 523	An Act in addition to an act, entitled "An act concerning the registering and recording of ships and vessels"	Prohibited the re-registration of vessels of the United States that become foreign owned
02/25/1804	2 Stat. 259	An Act relating to the recording, registering and enrolling of ships or vessels in the district of Orleans	Permitted vessels owned by Louisiana territory residents to be U.S. registered
03/27/1804	2 Stat. 296	An Act to amend the act intituled [sic] "An	Prohibited naturalized U.S. citizens from owning

		Act supplementary to the act	U.S.-flag vessels if they lived abroad
03/27/1804	2 Stat. 299	An Act for imposing more specific duties on the important of certain articles; and also, for levying and collecting light money on foreign ships or vessels	Imposed an additional tonnage duty on foreign vessels denominated as "light money"
03/03/1813	2 Stat. 809	An Act for the regulation of seamen on board the public and private vessels of the United States	Required full U.S. citizen crew on vessels of the United States except for citizens of any foreign nation that did not prohibit the employment of U.S. citizens on the vessels of that nation
03/03/1815	3 Stat. 224	An Act to repeal so much of the several acts imposing duties on the tonnage of ships and vessel, and on goods, wares and merchandise, imported into the United States, as imposes a discriminating duty on tonnage, between foreign vessels and vessels of the United States	Authorized the president to waive discriminating duties in favor of U.S.-flag vessels in the direct trade with any nation if reciprocated
03/01/1817	3 Stat. 351	An Act concerning the navigation of the United States	American Charta Maritima Restricted direct trade to vessels of the trading country or U.S.-flag vessels if a foreign country had adopted the same re-

				striction; restricted coastwise trade to U.S.-owned vessels; provided a tonnage duty preference to U.S.-flag vessels on coastwise and foreign voyages where U.S. citizens were employed
03/03/1817	3 Stat. 369		An Act to continue in force the second section of the act, entitled "An act supplementary to an act to regulate the duties on imports and tonnage"	Imposed a punitive duty on any vessel from a country where U.S.-flag vessels could not trade
04/18/1818	3 Stat. 432		An Act concerning navigation	Closed U.S. ports to British vessels arriving from ports where U.S.-flag vessels were excluded
03/03/1825	4 Stat. 129		An Act to authorize the register or enrollment and license to be issued in the name of the president or secretary of any incorporated company owning a steamboat or vessel	Permitted corporations to own U.S.-flag vessels provided no stock was owned by non-citizens
05/24/1828	4 Stat. 308		An Act in addition to an act, entitled "An act concerning discriminating duties of tonnage and impost"	Authorized the president to waive discriminating duties in favor of U.S.-flag vessels in the direct and indirect trade with any nation if reciprocated
05/29/1830	4 Stat. 419		An Act to amend the acts regulating the commercial intercourse between the United	Repealed 1818 Act and authorized the president to grant full opening to

		States and certain colonies of Great Britain	Britain upon full reciprocity
07/07/1838	5 Stat. 304	An Act to provide for the better security of the lives of passengers on board vessels propelled in whole or in part by steam	Required steamboats to be enrolled and take out new licenses after government inspection of boilers and machinery, effectively requiring passenger vessels in domestic trade to be U.S. registered
03/03/1845	5 Stat. 732	An Act to reduce the rates of postage, to limit the use and correct the abuse of the franking privilege etc.	Authorized for the first time international mail carriage contracts but rate to be paid no more than average rate
03/03/1847	9 Stat. 187	An Act providing for the Building and Equipment of four naval Steamships	Authorized Collins Line/Pacific Mail Steamship contracts
05/27/1848	9 Stat. 232	An Act extending Privileges to American Vessels engaged in a certain mentioned Trade	Authorized U.S.-flag vessels to touch at a foreign port while on a coastwise voyage subject to certain conditions; implied that only U.S. registered vessels could engage in the U.S. coastwise trade
12/23/1852	10 Stat. 149	An Act authorizing the Secretary of the Treasury to issue Registers to Vessels in certain cases	First U.S. wrecked-vessel act
06/11/1858	11 Stat. 313	An Act to Repeal the fifth Section of an Act entitled "An Act to authority the Register or	Repealed the 1825 requirement that corporations could not have non-citizen stockholders

			Enrollment and License etc."	
06/28/1864	13 Stat. 201		An Act repealing certain provisions of law concerning seamen on board public and private vessels of the United States	Repealed all prior U.S. citizen manning laws provided all officers had to be U.S. citizens
02/20/1866	14 Stat. 3		An Act to regulate the Registering of Vessels	Prohibited any U.S.-flag vessel from returning to the U.S. registry once registered abroad even if it remained U.S. citizen-owned
07/18/1866	14 Stat. 178		An Act further to prevent Smuggling	Tightened Act of March 3, 1817, prohibiting transshipment of cargo in Canada during a U.S. coastwise voyage; required the use of U.S.-flag steam tugboats towing U.S.-flag vessels
07/28/1866	14 Stat. 328		An Act to protect the Revenue	Repealed fishing bounties originally enacted in 1792
02/25/1867	14 Stat. 410		An Act to amend the twenty-first Section of an Act entitled "An Act further to prevent Smuggling"	Restricted the 1866 towing law so as not to apply to towing in whole or in part in foreign waters
07/27/1868	15 Stat. 240		An Act to extend the Laws of the United States relating to Customs, Commerce, and Navigation over the	Extended coastwise laws to Alaska and permitted vessels owned by Alaskan residents to be U.S. registered

				Territory ceded to the United States by Russia
06/06/1872		17 Stat. 230	An Act to reduce Duties on Imports, and to reduce Internal Taxes	Permitted shipbuilding inputs such and iron and steel rods to be imported duty-free provided that any vessel built with such items would not be able to engage in the U.S. coastwise trade
07/07/1872		17 Stat. 262	An Act to authorize the Appointment of Shipping-Commissioners by the several Circuit Courts of the United States	Shipping Commissioners Act of 1872
06/09/1874		18 Stat. 64	An Act in reference to the operations of the shipping commissioners' act	Exempted domestic voyages from Shipping Commissioners Act
03/03/1875		18 Stat. 340	An Act making appropriations for the service of the Post Office Department etc.	Repealed Pacific Mail Steamship contract authority
08/02/1882		22 Stat. 186	An Act to regulate the carriage of passengers by sea	Mandated improvements to passenger vessels focused on emigrants
06/26/1884		23 Stat. 53	An Act to remove certain burdens on the American merchant marine	1884 Dingley Act: required all officers to be U.S. citizens; restricted seamen's wage advances and allotments and included other seamen's reforms

Date	Statute	Title	Description
07/05/1884	23 Stat. 118	An Act to constitute a Bureau of Navigation in the Treasury Department	Created Bureau of Navigation
06/19/1886	24 Stat. 79	An Act to abolish certain fees for official services to American vessels and to amend the laws relating to shipping commissioners	Reversed many Dingley Act seamen's reforms; Passenger Vessel Services Act
08/19/1890	26 Stat. 320	An Act to amend the laws relative to shipping commissioners	Re-introduced desertion penalties for seamen signing articles before a shipping commissioner
03/03/1891	26 Stat. 830	An Act to provide for ocean mail service between the United States and foreign ports	1891 Ocean Mail Act
02/18/1895	28 Stat. 667	An Act to amend an Act entitled "An Act to amend the laws relative to shipping commissioners"	Maguire Act of 1895, reversing 1886 and 1890 seamen's laws
05/28/1896	29 Stat. 188	An Act to amend section forty-one hundred and thirty-one of the Revised Statutes of the United States	Manning requirement changed to officers manning watch had to be U.S. citizens
03/03/1897	29 Stat. 687	An Act to amend the laws relating to navigation	Relaxed the post-Civil War restriction on U.S.-flag vessels seeking to return to the U.S.-flag

02/17/1898	30 Stat. 248	An Act to amend the laws relating to navigation	Added "for any part of the voyage" to coastwise trading law; increased passenger act penalty
12/21/1898	30 Stat. 755	An Act to amend the laws relating to American seamen, for the protection of such seamen, and to promote commerce	White Act of 1898
04/12/1900	31 Stat. 77	An Act temporarily to provide revenues and a civil government for Porto Rico	Extended coastwise laws to Puerto Rico and permitted vessels owned by Puerto Rico residents to be U.S. registered
04/30/1900	31 Stat. 141	An Act to provide a government for the Territory of Hawaii	Extended coastwise laws to Hawaii and permitted vessels owned by Hawaiian residents to be U.S. registered
04/28/1904	33 Stat. 518	An Act to require the employment of vessels of the United States for public purposes	Cargo Preference Act of 1904
02/22/1906	34 Stat. 17	An Act to repeal section forty-one hundred and thirty-six of the Revised Statutes relating to the admission to registry of repaired foreign vessels	Repealed first wrecked-vessel Act
05/28/1906	34 Stat. 204	An Act concerning foreign-built dredges	Dredging Act of 1906
08/24/1912	37 Stat. 560	An Act to provide for the opening, maintenance, protection, and	Panama Canal Act of 1912; required president and managing directors of

		operation of the Panama Canal	corporations owning U.S. vessels to be U.S. citizens
10/03/1913	38 Stat. 114	An Act to reduce tariff duties and to provide revenue for the government	Underwood Tariff Act of 1913: included 5 percent discriminating duty favoring U.S.-flag vessels
08/18/1914	38 Stat. 698	An Act to provide for the admission of foreign-built ships to American registry for the foreign trade	Ship Registry Act of 1914
09/02/1914	38 Stat. 711	An Act to authorize the establishment of Bureau of War Risk Insurance in the Treasury Department	War Risk Insurance Act of 1914
02/24/1915	38 Stat. 812	An Act to provide for the register and enrollment of vessels built in foreign countries when such vessels have been wrecked on the coasts of the United States	Wrecked-Vessel Act
03/04/1915	38 Stat. 1164	An Act to promote the welfare of American seamen in the merchant marine of the United States	Seamen's Act of 1915
09/07/1916	39 Stat. 728	An Act to establish a U.S. Shipping Board for the purpose of encouraging, developing, and creating a naval auxiliary and naval reserve and a merchant marine	Shipping Act, 1916

			to meet the requirements of the commerce of the United States	
06/15/1917	40 Stat. 182		An Act making appropriations to supply urgent deficiencies in appropriations for the military and naval establishments on account of war expenses	Created Emergency Shipping Fund and expanded the president's emergency shipping authorities
10/06/1917	40 Stat. 392		An Act giving the U.S. Shipping Board power to suspend present provisions of law and permit vessels of foreign registry and foreign-built... to engage in the coastwise trade during the present war	Permitted foreign vessels to engage in the U.S. coastwise trade if permitted by the Shipping Board with Alaska excluded
07/15/1918	40 Stat. 900		An Act to amend the Act approved September seventh, nineteen and sixteen	Tightened U.S. vessel citizenship requirements
06/05/1920	41 Stat. 988		An Act to provide for the promotion and maintenance of the American merchant marine, to repeal certain emergency legislation, and provide for the disposition, regulation, and use of property acquired hereunder	Merchant Marine Act, 1920

SELECTED BIBLIOGRAPHY

ORIGINAL SOURCES AND GOVERNMENT PUBLICATIONS

Adams, Charles Francis. *The Works of John Adams*. Boston: Charles C. Little and James Brown, 1851.

Adams, Henry, ed. *The Writings of Albert Gallatin*. Philadelphia: J. B. Lippincott, 1879.

Adams Papers—Digital Edition. Massachusetts Historical Society. https://www.masshist.org/publications/adams-papers.

Albrecht, Arthur E. "International Seamen's Union of America: A Study of Its History and Problems." *Bulletin of the United States Bureau of Labor Statistics*, no. 342. Washington, DC: Government Printing Office, 1923.

American State Papers: Documents, Legislative and Executive, of the Congress of the United States, from the First Session of the First to the Third Session of the Thirteenth Congress. Library of Congress, American Memory, Lawmaking Home. https://memory.loc.gov/ammem/amlaw/lwsplink.html.

Annals of Congress, Debates and Proceedings in the Congress of the United States. Library of Congress, American Memory, Lawmaking Home. https://memory.loc.gov/ammem/amlaw/lwac.html.

Bureau of Insular Affairs. War Department. *Fourth Annual Report of the Philippine Commission, 1903*. Washington, DC: Government Printing Office, 1904.

California Bureau of Labor Statistics. *Investigation into Condition of Men Working on the Waterfront and on Board Pacific Coast Vessels, San Francisco, June 29–July 10, 1887*. Sacramento, CA: 1887.

Cobbett, William. *The Parliamentary History of England from the Earliest Period to the Year 1803*. Vol. 23. London: T. C. Hansard, 1814.

Congressional Globe, The. Library of Congress, American Memory, Lawmaking Home. https://memory.loc.gov/ammem/amlaw/lwcg.html.

JOURNEY TO THE JONES ACT

Daniels, Josephus. *The Cabinet Diaries of Josephus Daniels, 1913–1921*. Edited by E. David Cronon. Lincoln: University of Nebraska Press, 1963.

Deane Papers, The. New York Historical Society. New York: Publication Fund Series, 1887–91.

Diary of James Wickersham. Alaska State Library, Historical Collections, Alaska Digital Archives. https://vilda.alaska.edu/digital/collection/cdmg21/id/6113/rec/26.

Elliot, Jonathan, ed. *Debates in the Several State Conventions, on the adoption of the Federal Constitution, as Recommended by the General Convention at Philadelphia in 1787*. Library of Congress, Digital Collections, A Century of Lawmaking for a New Nation: U.S. Congressional Documents and Debates 1774 to 1875. https://www.loc.gov/item/17007172/.

Farrand, Max, ed. *The Records of the Federal Convention of 1787*. Library of Congress, Digital Collections, A Century of Lawmaking for a New Nation: U.S. Congressional Documents and Debates 1774 to 1875. https://www.loc.gov/item/11005506/.

Federalist Papers, The. Library of Congress Research Guides Main Reading Room. https://guides.loc.gov/federalist-papers/full-text.

Firth, C. H., and R. S. Rait, eds. *Acts and Ordinances of the Interregnum, 1642–1660*. London: His Majesty's Stationery Office, 1911.

Founders Online: Correspondence and Other Writings of Seven Major Shapers of the United States: George Washington, Benjamin Franklin, John Adams (and family), Thomas Jefferson, Alexander Hamilton, John Jay and James Madison. National Archives. https://founders.archives.gov.

Gage, Lyman, ed. *Circular Instructions of the Treasury Department Relative to the Tariff, Navigation, and Other Laws for the Year Ending December 31, 1898*. Washington, DC: Government Printing Office, 1898.

Hamilton, Stanislaus Murray, ed. *The Writings of James Monroe*. Vol. 1. New York: G. P. Putnam's Sons, 1898.

Hotchkiss, Willard E., and Henry R. Seager. *History of the Shipbuilding Labor Adjustment Board 1917 to 1919*. Washington, DC: Government Printing Office, 1921.

Journals of the Continental Congress 1774–1789. Library of Congress, Digital Collections, A Century of Lawmaking for a New Nation: U.S. Congressional Documents and Debates 1774 to 1875. https://www.loc.gov/item/05000059/.

Link, Arthur, ed. *The Papers of Woodrow Wilson Digital Edition*. Charlottesville: University of Virginia Press, 2017.

Maclay, Edgar S. *Journal of William Maclay, United States Senator from Pennsylvania 1789–1791*. Library of Congress, Digital Collections, A Century of Lawmaking for a New Nation: U.S. Congressional Documents and Debates 1774 to 1875. https://www.loc.gov/item/09026607/.

Memorial Services Held in the House of Representatives of the United States, Together with Remarks Presented in Eulogy of Wesley L. Jones. Washington, DC: Government Printing Office, 1933.

Papers of Wesley Livsey Jones. University of Washington University Libraries. Pacific Northwest Historical Documents Collection.

Papers Relating to the Foreign Relations of the United States. U.S. Department of State, Office of the Historian, Historical Documents. https://history.state.gov/historicaldocuments.

Report of Director General Charles Piez to the Board of Trustees of United States Shipping Board Emergency Fleet Corporation, April 30, 1919. Washington, DC: Government Printing Office, 1919.

Reports of the Decisions Rendered by the Supreme Court of the Hawaiian Islands. Honolulu: Hawaiian Gazette Company, 1899.

Royal Commission on Shipping Rings. *Report of the Royal Commission on Shipping Rings with Minutes of Evidence and Appendices*. London: Darling & Son, 1909.

Saugstad, Jesse E. *Shipping and Shipbuilding Subsidies: A Study of State Aid to the Shipping and Shipbuilding Industries in Various Countries of the World*. U.S. Department of Commerce, Trade Promotions Series, no. 129, 1932.

Second Report of the Provost Marshal General to the Secretary of War on the Operations of the Selective Service System to December 20, 1918. Washington, DC: Government Printing Office, 1919.

Short, Lloyd M. *The Bureau of Navigation: Its History, Activities and Organization*. Institute for Government Research, Service Monographs of the United States Government, no. 15, 1923.

Sparks, Jared, ed. *The Diplomatic Correspondence of the American Revolution*. Boston: Nathan Hale and Gray & Bowen, 1829–30.

Speech Delivered by Edward N. Hurley, Chairman of the United States Shipping Board, at Delmonico's, New York, on the Evening of March 26, 1918, before the National Marine League of the U.S.A. www.ftc.gov/public-statements/1918/03/speech-edward-n-hurley-chairman-us-shipping-board.

Taylor, Robert J., ed. *Papers of John Adams*. Cambridge, MA: Belknap Press of Harvard University Press, 1979.

UC Santa Barbara. American Presidency Project. Presidential Messages and Party Platforms. https://www.presidency.ucsb.edu/.

United Nations. "Alabama Claims of the United States of America against Great Britain (May 8, 1871)." *Reports of International Arbitral Awards*. Vol. 29. 2012.

U.S. Attorney General. "Wrecked Vessel: Issue of Register." *Op. Att'y Gen.* 15, no. 402 (December 5, 1877).

———. "Dingley Tariff Act: Discriminating Duty." *Op. Att'y Gen.* 21, no. 597 (September 20, 1897).

———. "American Registry." *Op. Att'y Gen.* 22, no. 566 (August 11, 1899).

———. "Coal for Navy: Transportation in Foreign Vessels." *Op. Att'y Gen.* 26, no. 415 (October 3, 1907).

——— "Registry and Enrollment of Vessels." *Op. Att'y Gen.* 29, no. 188 (July 11, 1911).

———. "Transportation of Merchandise from Seattle to Fairbanks." *Op. Att'y Gen.* 30, no. 3 (January 4, 1913).

U.S. Commissioner of Navigation. *Annual Reports*. Washington, DC: Government Printing Office, 1884–1920.

U.S. Committee on Public Information. "Full Text of Report on Hog Island Shipyard Inquiry; No Fraud Disclosed but Accounts in Chaotic Condition and Plant Cost Is

Held to Be above 'Reasonable Need.'" *Official U.S. Bulletin* 2, no. 495 (December 23, 1918).

U.S. Congress. House. *Mercantile Marine: Letter from the Secretary of Treasury*, 39th Cong., 1st sess., 1866, H. Ex. Doc. 39-25.

———. House. *Causes of the Reduction of American Tonnage*. 41st Cong., 2nd sess., 1870, H. Rep. 41-28.

———. House. *American Shipping*. 47th Cong., 2nd sess., 1882, H. Rep. 47-1827.

———. House. *American Merchant Marine in the Foreign Trade*. 51st Cong., 1st sess., 1890, H. Rep. 51-1210.

———. House. Committee on Merchant Marine and Fisheries. *Hearings before the House Merchant Marine Comm. on H.R. Bill no. 4663, Known as the "Tonnage Bill."* 51st Cong., 1st sess., 1890.

———. House. *Ocean Mail Service*. 51st Cong., 1st sess., 1890, H. R. Rep. 51-2889.

———. House. *Hearings before the Committee on Merchant Marine and Fisheries on Sundry Bills Relating to the American Merchant Marine, Known as the "Maguire" Bills*. 53rd Cong., 2nd sess., 1894, H. Misc. Doc. 53206.

———. Senate. *Preservation of American Coastwise Shipping Trade*. 55th Cong., 2nd sess., 1898, S. Rep. 55-1129.

———. Senate. *Hawaiian Commission*. 55th Cong., 3d sess., 1898, S. Doc. 55-16.

———. Senate. *Promotion of Commerce and Increase of Foreign Trade, Etc.*, 55th Cong., 3rd sess., 1899, S. Doc. 55-60.

———. Senate. *Revival of the Merchant Marine*. 56th Cong., 1st sess., 1900, S. Doc. 56-149.

———. House. *Employment of Vessels of the United States for Public Purposes*, 58th Cong., 2nd sess., 1904, H. Rep. no. 58-1893.

———. Senate. *Employment of United States Vessels for Public Purposes*. 58th Cong., 2nd sess., 1904, S. Rep. 58-182.

———. Senate. *Report of the Merchant Marine Commission.* 58th Cong., 3rd sess., 1905, S. Rep. 58-2755.

———. House. Committee on Merchant Marine and Fisheries. *Hearings before the House Merchant Marine Comm. on the Development of the American Merchant Marine and American Commerce,* 59th Cong., 1st sess., 1906.

———. House. *Development of the American Merchant Marine and American Commerce.* 59th Cong., 1st sess., 1906, H. Doc. 59-564.

———. House. *Purchase of Material and Equipment for Use in Construction of the Panama Canal.* 59th Cong., 1st sess., 1906, H. Rep. 59-4878.

———. Senate. *Foreign-Built Dredges,* 59th Cong., 1st sess., 1906, S. Rep. 59-2384.

———. House. *Development of the American Merchant Marine and American Commerce.* 59th Cong., 2nd sess., 1907, H. Rep. 59-6442.

———. House. Merchant Marine and Fisheries Committee. *American Merchant Marine in Foreign Trade and the National Defense.* 61st Cong., 2nd sess., 1910, H. Rep. 61-502.

———. House. *Report and Hearings of the Select Committee Appointed to Investigate Certain Charges Under House Resolution 543.* 61st Cong., 3rd sess., 1911.

———. House. *Amending Laws Relating to Navigation,* 62nd Cong., 2nd sess., 1912, H. Rep. 62-653.

———. House. *American Registries for Certain Seagoing Vessels.* 62nd Cong., 2nd sess., 1912, H. Rep. 62-405.

———. Senate. *Desertion of Seamen from United States Vessels.* 62nd Cong., 2nd sess., 1912, S. Rep. 62-482.

———. House. Committee on Merchant Marine and Fisheries. *Proceedings of the Committee on the Merchant Marine and Fisheries in the Investigation of Shipping Combinations under House Resolution 587.* Washington, DC: Government Printing Office, 1913.

———. House. Committee on Merchant Marine and Fisheries. *Hearings before the House Merchant Marine and Fisheries Committee on S. 136.* 63rd Cong., 2nd sess., part 1, 1913.

———. House. Tariff Schedules: Hearings before the Committee on Ways and Means. 62nd Cong., 3rd sess., 1913, H. Doc. 62-1447.

———. Senate. William Pierce Frye: Memorial Addresses Delivered in the Senate and the House of Representatives of the United States. 62nd Cong., 3rd sess., 1913, S. Doc. 62-1145.

———. Senate. *Declaration of International Naval Conference*. 63rd Cong., 2nd sess., 1914, S. Doc. 63-563.

———. Senate. *Increased Ocean Transportation Rates*. 63rd Cong., 3rd sess., 1914, S. Doc. 63-673.

———. House. Committee on Merchant Marine and Fisheries, *Hearings before the House Committee on Merchant Marine and Fisheries on H.R. 10500*. 64th Cong., 1st sess., 1916.

———. House. Creating a Shipping Board, a Naval Auxiliary, a Merchant Marine, and Regulating Carriers by Water Engaged in the Foreign and Interstate Commerce of the United States. 64th Cong., 1st sess., 1916, H. Rep. 64-659.

———. Senate. Commerce Committee. Hearings before the Senate Commerce Committee on the United States Shipping Board Emergency Fleet Corporation. 65th Cong., 2nd-3rd sess., 1917–19.

———. Senate. *Cost of Ship Construction*. 65th Cong., 3rd sess., 1918, S. Doc. 65-315.

———. House. Hearings before the House Committee on Merchant Marine and Fisheries on Providing for the Disposition, Regulation, or Use of the Property Built or Acquired by the United States. 66th Cong., 1st sess., 1919.

———. House. Select Committee on U.S. Shipping Board Operations, Hearings before the House Select Committee on U.S. Shipping Board Operations on C. W. Morse Contracts. 66th Cong., 2nd sess., 1920.

———. Senate. Commerce Committee. Hearings before the Senate Commerce Committee on the Establishment of an American Merchant Marine. 66th Cong., 2nd sess., 1920.

———. House. Select Committee on U.S. Shipping Board Operations, *Hearings before the House Select Committee on U.S. Shipping Board Operations*. 66th Cong., 2nd-3rd sess., 1920–21.

———. House. *American Merchant Marine*. 66th Cong., 2nd sess., 1920, H. Rep. 66-1102.

———. House. *United States Shipping Board Operations*. 66th Cong., 3rd sess., 1921, H. Rep. 66-1399.

———. House. *Protecting America's Estuaries: The Potomac*. 91st Cong., 2nd sess., 1970, H. Rep. 91-1761.

U.S. Department of State. *Papers Relating to the Foreign Relations of the United States: 1915 Supplement, The World War*. Washington, DC: Government Printing Office, 1928.

———. *Papers Relating to the Foreign Relations of the United States, 1920*. Edited by Joseph V. Fuller. Washington, DC: U.S. Government Printing Office, 1936, vol. 1.

———. Papers Relating to the Foreign Relations of the United States, The Paris Peace Conference, 1919. Edited by Joseph V. Fuller. Washington, DC: Government Printing Office, 1942.

U.S. Navy Department. *Annual Reports*. Washington, DC: Government Printing Office, 1897, 1898, 1908, 1915, and 1918.

U.S. Secretary of the Treasury. *Annual Report of the Secretary of the Treasury on the State of the Finances for the Fiscal Year Ended June 30, 1914*. Washington, DC: Government Printing Office, 1915.

U.S. Shipping Board. *Annual Reports*. Washington, DC: Government Printing Office, 1917–24.

———. *Report on the History of Shipping Discriminations and on Various Forms of Government Aid to Shipping*. Washington, DC: Government Printing Office, 1922.

U.S. War Department. *Annual Reports*. Washington, DC: Government Printing Office, 1898, 1899, 1911, 1918, and 1920.

Willcox, William B., Douglas M. Arnold, Dorothy W. Bridgwater, Jonathan R. Dull, Claude A. Lopez, and Catherine M. Prelinger, eds. *The Papers of Benjamin Franklin*. New Haven, CT: Yale University Press, 1982.

Wilson, Woodrow. *Executive Order no. 2039*. September 4, 1914. (Regarding admission of foreign-built ships).

———. *Executive Order no. 2664*. July 11, 1917. (Regarding powers of the U.S. Shipping Board Emergency Fleet Corporation).

BOOKS, DISSERTATIONS, AND AUTHORED WEB SITES

American Bureau of Shipping. *The History of the American Bureau of Shipping, 1962–2006*. Houston: American Bureau of Shipping, 2006.

Axtell, Silas B. *A Symposium on Andrew Furuseth*. New Bedford, MA: Darwin Press, 1948.

Banks, Ronald F. "The Senatorial Career of William P. Frye." MA diss., University of Maine, 1958.

William W. *American Navigation: The Political History of Its Rise and Ruin and the Proper Means for Its Encouragement*. Boston: Houghton, Mifflin, 1902.

Benson, William S. *The Merchant Marine*. New York: MacMillan, 1923.

Broesamle, John J. *William Gibbs McAdoo: A Passion for Change 1863–1917*. Port Washington, NY: Kennikat Press, 1973.

Clark, Norman H. *The Dry Years: Prohibition and Social Change in Washington*. Rev. ed. Seattle: University of Washington Press, 1988.

Colby, Bainbridge. *The Close of Woodrow Wilson's Administration and the Final Years*. New York: Publishers Printing, 1930.

Colton, Tim. "Shipbuilding History: Construction Records of U.S. and Canadian Shipbuilders and Boatbuilders." https://shipbuildinghistory.com.

Craig, Douglas B. *Progressives at War: William G. McAdoo and Newton D. Baker, 1863–1941*. Baltimore: Johns Hopkins University Press, 2013. Kindle ed.

Crowell, Benedict, and Robert Forrest Wilson. *The Road to France: The Transportation of Troops and Supplies, 1917–1918*. New Haven, CT: Yale University Press, 1921.

JOURNEY TO THE JONES ACT

Crowley, John E. *The Privileges of Independence: Neomercantilism and the American Revolution*. Baltimore: Johns Hopkins University Press, 1993.

Cudahy, Brian J. *Rails under the Mighty Hudson*. New York: Fordham University Press, 2002.

Dalzell, George W. *The Flight from the Flag: The Continuing Effect of the Civil War upon the American Carrying Trade*. Chapel Hill: University of North Carolina Press, 1940.

Daniels, Josephus. *The Wilson Era: Years of War and after 1917–1923*. Chapel Hill: University of North Carolina Press, 1946.

deKay, James Tertius. *The Rebel Raiders: The Astonishing History of the Confederacy's Secret Navy*. New York: Ballantine Books, 2002.

De La Pedraja, René. *A Historical Dictionary of the U.S. Merchant Marine and Shipping Industry: Since the Introduction of Steam*. Westport, CT: Greenwood Press, 1994.

Dewey, George. *Autobiography of George Dewey Admiral of the Navy*. New York: Charles Scribner's Sons, 1913.

Dickerson, Oliver M. *The Navigation Acts and the American Revolution*. 1951; repr., New York: Octagon Books, 1974.

Dunmore, Walter T. *Ship Subsidies: An Economic Study of the Policy of Subsidizing Merchant Marines*. Boston: Houghton-Mifflin, 1907.

Edge, Frederick Milnes, *The Destruction of the American Carrying Trade: A Letter to Earl Russell*. London: William Ridgeway, 1863.

Elleman, Bruce A., and S. C. M. Paine, eds. *Commerce Raiding: Historical Case Studies, 1755–2009*. Newport, RI: Naval War College Press, 2013.

Forth, William Stuart. "Wesley L. Jones: A Political Biography." PhD diss., University of Washington, 1962.

Gibson, Andrew, and Arthur Donovan. *The Abandoned Ocean: A History of United States Maritime Policy*. Columbia: University of South Carolina Press, 2000.

Gill, Peter B. "The Sailor's Union of the Pacific from 1885–1929." University of Washington. University Libraries. Pacific Northwest Historical Monographs.

https://digitalcollections.lib.washington.edu/digital/collection/pnwhm/id/1030/rec/4.

Goldberg, Mark H. *The "Hog Islanders": The Story of 122 American Ships*. Kings Point, NY: American Merchant Marine Museum, 1991.

Goode, W. A. M. *With Sampson through the War*. New York: Doubleday & McClure, 1899.

Griscom, Lloyd Carpenter. *Diplomatically Speaking*. New York: Literary Guild of America, 1940.

Grose, Howard. *John Roach: Born December 25, 1813. Died January 10, 1887*. New York: Atlantic Publishing and Engraving, 1887.

Gunther, John. *Taken at the Flood, The Story of Albert D. Lasker*. New York: Harper & Brothers, 1960.

Hall, Henry. *American Navigation with Some Account of the Causes of Its Recent Decay, and of the Means by Which Its Prosperity May Be Restored*. New York: D. Appleton, 1880.

Hancock, David. *Oceans of Wine, Madeira and Emergence of American Trade and Taste*. New Haven, CT: Yale University Press, 2009.

Harlow, Vincent T. *The Founding of the Second British Empire*. Vol. 1. London: Longmans, 1964.

Harper, Lawrence A. *The English Navigation Laws*. New York: Octagon Books, 1973.

Hart, Robert A. *The Great White Fleet: Its Voyage around the World 1907–1909*. Boston: Little, Brown, 1965.

Harvard College Class of 1878 Fiftieth Anniversary Report 1878–1928. Cambridge, MA: Riverside Press, 1928.

Hill, Charles S. *History of American Shipping, Its Prestige, Decline, and Prospect*. New York: American News, 1883.

Hone, Thomas C., and Curtis A. Utz. *History of the Office of the Chief of Naval Operations 1915–2015*. Washington, DC: Naval History and Heritage Command, 2020.

JOURNEY TO THE JONES ACT

Hurley, Edward N. *The Bridge to France*. Philadelphia: J. B. Lippincott, 1927.

———. *The New Merchant Marine*. New York: Century, 1920.

Hutchins, John G. B. *The American Maritime Industries and Public Policy, 1789-1914*. Cambridge, MA: Harvard University Press, 1941.

James, Coy Hilton. *Silas Deane: Patriot or Traitor?* Lansing: Michigan State University Press, 1975.

Jantscher, Gerald R. *Bread upon the Waters: Federal Aids to the Maritime Industries*. Washington, DC: Brookings Institution, 1975.

Kilmarx, Robert A., ed. *America's Maritime Legacy: A History of the U.S. Merchant Marine and Shipbuilding Industry since Colonial Times*. Boulder, CO: Westview Press, 1979.

Klachko, Mary, and David F. Trask. *Admiral William Shepherd Benson, First Chief of Naval Operations*. Annapolis, MD: U.S. Naval Institute Press, 1987.

La Follette, Belle Case, and Fola La Follette. *Robert M. Follette, June 14, 1855–June 18, 1925*. New York: Macmillan, 1953.

Lawrence, Samuel A. *United States Merchant Shipping Policies and Politics*. Washington, DC: Brookings Institution, 1966.

Long, John D. *The New American Navy*. New York: Outlook, 1903.

Mahan, Alfred Thayer. *The Influence of Sea Power upon History, 1660–1783*. Boston: Little, Brown, 1890.

Martin, James J. *The Saga of Hog Island*. Colorado Springs, CO: Ralph Myles, 1977.

Marvin, Winthrop L. *The American Merchant Marine: Its History and Romance from 1620 to 1902*. New York: Charles Scribner's Sons, 1910.

Marx, Daniel, Jr. *International Shipping Cartels*. Princeton, NJ: Princeton University Press, 1953.

Mattox, W. C. *Building the Emergency Fleet*. Cleveland: Penton Publishing, 1920.

Maxwell, Lloyd W. *Discriminating Duties and the American Merchant Marine*. New York: H. W. Wilson, 1926.

McAdoo, William G. *Crowded Years: The Reminiscences of William G. McAdoo*. Boston: Houghton Mifflin, 1931.

Michener, James A. *Alaska: A Novel*. New York: Random House, 1988, Dial Press Trade Paperbacks Edition, 2014.

Miller, Edward S. *War Plan Orange: The U.S. Strategy to Defeat Japan, 1897–1945*. Annapolis, MD: U.S. Naval Institute Press, 1991.

Mussey, Henry Raymond, and William L. Ransom, eds. *Proceedings of the Academy of Political Science in the City of New York: The American Mercantile Marine*. Vol. 6.1915–1916. New York: Academy of Political Science, 1916.

Paullin, Charles Oscar. *Paullin's History of Naval Administration, 1775–1911*. Annapolis, MD: U.S. Naval Institute Press, 2012. Reprint.

Pickelhaupt, Bill. *Shanghaied in San Francisco*. 1996. Repr., Mystic, CT: Mystic Seaport, 2007.

Pringle, Henry F. *The Life and Times of William Howard Taft*. Vol. 2. Repr. Newtown, CT: American Political Biography Press, 1967.

Rienow, Robert. *The Test of the Nationality of a Merchant Vessel*. New York: Columbia University Press, 1937.

Roach, John. *The American Carrying Trade*. New York: H. B. Grose, 1880.

Roland, Alex, Jeffrey W. Bolster, and Alexander Keyssar. *The Way of the Ship: America's Maritime History Reenvisioned, 1600–2000*. New Jersey: John Wiley & Sons, 2008.

Safford, Jeffrey J. *Wilsonian Maritime Diplomacy 1913–1921*. New Brunswick, NJ: Rutgers University Press, 1978.

Schwartz, Stephen. *Brotherhood of the Sea: A History of the Sailor's Union of the Pacific 1885–1985*. 1986; Reprint., London: Routledge, 2019.

Setser, Vernon G. *The Commercial Reciprocity Policy of the United States 1774–1829*. 1936. Reprint, New York: DA Capo Press, 1969.

Sheffield, John Lord. *Observations on the Commerce of the American States*. London: J. Debrett, 1784.

Shomette, Donald G. *Ghost Fleet of Mallows Bay, and Other Tales of the Lost Chesapeake*. Centreville, MD: Tidewater Publishers, 1996.

Smith, Darrell Hevenor, and Paul V. Betters. *The United States Shipping Board: Its History, Activities and Organization*. Washington, DC: Brookings Institution, 1931.

Smith, J. Russell. *Influence of the Great War upon Shipping*. New York: Oxford University Press, 1919.

Stevens, John Austin. *Albert Gallatin*. Boston: Houghton, Mifflin, 1899.

Swann Jr., Leonard Alexander. *John Roach: Maritime Entrepreneur*. Annapolis, MD: U.S. Naval Institute Press, 1965.

Tacoma Commercial Club and Chamber of Commerce. *Transcript of Conference with Senator Wesley L. Jones on Section 28, "Merchant Marine Act, 1920,"* August 10, 1920.

Taylor, Paul S. *The Sailors' Union of the Pacific*. New York: Ronald Press, 1923.

Tyler, David B. *The American Clyde: A History of Iron and Steel Shipbuilding on the Delaware from 1840 to World War I*. New York: University of Delaware Press, 1958.

Vale, Vivian. *The American Peril: Challenge to Britain on the North Atlantic 1901–1904*. Manchester, UK: Manchester University Press, 1984.

Van Vlack, Milton C. *Silas Deane, Revolutionary War Diplomat and Politician*. Jefferson, NC: McFarland, 2013.

Walters, Raymond, Jr. *Albert Gallatin: Jeffersonian Financier and Diplomat*. New York: Macmillan, 1957.

Warren, Charles. *The Making of the Constitution*. Boston: Little, Brown, 1928.

Weintraub, Hyman. *Andrew Furuseth, Emancipator of the Seamen*. Berkeley: University of California Press, 1959.

Wells, David A. *Our Merchant Marine: How It Rose, Increased, Became Great, Declined and Decayed*. New York: G. P. Putnam's Sons, 1883.

Whitehurst, Clinton H., Jr. *The U.S. Merchant Marine: In Search of an Enduring Maritime Policy*. Annapolis, MD: U.S. Naval Institute Press, 1983.

Williams, William J. *The Wilson Administration and the Shipbuilding Crisis of 1917: Steel Ships and Wooden Steamers*. Lewiston, NY: Edwin Mellen Press, 1992.

Woods, Philip H. Bath. *Maine's Charlie Morse: Ice King and Wall Street Scoundrel*. Charleston: History Press, 2011.

Zeiss, Paul Maxwell. *American Shipping Policy*. Princeton, NJ: Princeton University Press, 1938.

PERIODICALS AND JOURNALS

Anderson, Dennis Kent, and Godfrey Tryggve Anderson. "The Death of Silas Deane: Another Opinion." *New England Quarterly* 57, no. 1 (March 1984): 98–105.

"Andrew Furuseth and His Fifteen-Year Siege of Congress." *Current Opinion* 49, no. 1 (July 1915): 18–19.

Aspinwall, Mark D. "Coastwise Trade Policy in the United States: Does It Make Sense Today." *Journal of Maritime Law and Commerce* 18, no. 2 (April 1987): 243–62.

Benns, F. Lee. "The American Struggle for the British West India Carrying-Trade, 1815–1830." *Indiana University Studies* 10, no. 56 (March 1923): 6–207.

Boyd, Julian P. "Silas Deane: Death by a Kindly Teacher of Treason?" *William and Mary Quarterly* 16, no. 2 (April 1959), no. 3 (July 1959), and no. 4 (October 1959): 165–87, 319–42, and 515–50.

Carlisle, Rodney. "Flagging-Out in the American Civil War," *Northern Mariner/le marin du nord* 22, no. 1 (January 2012): 53–65.

Chadwick, F. E. "Our Merchant Marine: The Causes of Its Decline, and the Means to Be Taken for Its Revival." *U.S. Naval Institute Proceedings* 8, no. 1 (January 1882): 75–120.

Chamberlain, Eugene Tyler. "A Present Chance for American Shipping." *North American Review* 158, no. 448 (March 1894): 277–82.

"Coddling Our Merchant Marine." *New Republic* 23, no. 299 (August 25, 1920): 352.

Coker, William S. "The Panama Canal Tolls Controversy: A Different Perspective." *Journal of American History* 55, no. 3 (December 1968): 555–64.

Conrad, Agnes C. "Hawaiian Registered Vessels." *Hawaiian Journal of History* 3 (1969): 31–41.

Cook, Doug. "Whispering Pines: Charlie Morse's Second Act and Denouement." *Bowdoin Daily Sun*, July 15, 2015.

Coudert, Frederic R. "Comments on the Merchant Marine Act of 1920." *Proceedings of the Academy of Political Science* 9, no. 2 (February 1921): 116–28.

Dickerson, Oliver M. "John Hancock: Notorious Smuggler or Near Victim of British Revenue Racketeers." *Mississippi Valley Historical Review* 32, no. 4 (March 1946): 517–40.

Dorwart, Jeffery Michael. "A Mongrel Fleet: America Buys a Navy to Fight Spain. 1898." *Warship International* 17, no. 2 (1980): 128–55.

Furuseth, Andrew. "The Dawn of Another Day." *American Federationist* 22, no. 9 (September 1915): 717–21.

Goldstein, Kalman. "Silas Deane: Preparation for Rascality." *Historian* 43, no. 1 (November 1980): 75–97.

Hendrick, Burton J. "McAdoo and the Subway." *McClure's Magazine* 36, no. 5 (March 1911): 485–500.

Hessen, Robert. "Charles Schwab and the Shipbuilding Crisis of 1918." *Pennsylvania History: A Journal of Mid-Atlantic Studies* 38, no. 4 (October 1971): 389–99.

"In Memory of the Emancipator of Seamen—Andrew Furuseth, 150th Anniversary." *West Coast Sailors*, March 12, 2004.

Irwin, Douglas A. *Revenue or Reciprocity? Founding Feuds over Early U.S. Trade Policy*. National Bureau of Economic Research, NBER Working Paper Series, Working Paper 15144 (July 2009).

Jones, Wesley L. "The Merchant Marine Act of 1920." *Proceedings of the Academy of Political Science* 9, no. 2 (February 1921): 89—98.

Kirlin, J. Parker. "The Operating Problems of the American Merchant Marine." *Proceedings of the Academy of Political Science* 9, no. 2 (February 1921): 104—15.

La Follette, Robert M. "Andrew Furuseth and His Great Work." *La Follette's Magazine* 7, no. 4 (April 1915): 2.

Lint, Gregg L. "John Adams on the Drafting of the Treaty Plan of 1776." *Diplomatic History* 2, no. 3 (Summer 1978): 313—20.

Marshall, Dexter. "Clement Acton Griscom." *Cosmopolitan* 35, no. 1 (May 1903): 57—59.

Marvin, Winthrop L. "The Great Ship Combine." *American Monthly Review of Reviews* 26, no. 6 (December 1902): 679—88.

Mathews, John L. "The Coming Ashore of Andrew Furuseth." *Everybody's Magazine* 25, no. 1 (July 1911): 60—71.

McGee, John S. "Ocean Freight Rate Conferences and the American Merchant Marine." *University of Chicago Law Review* 27, no. 2 (Winter 1960): 191–314.

"Men We Are Watching: Eugene Tyler Chamberlain." *Independent, A Weekly Magazine* 72, no. 3324 (August 15, 1912): 364–65.

Minchinton, Walter E. "Silas Deane and Lord Sheffield's 'Observations on American Commerce.'" *Revista da Universidade de Coimbra* 28 (1980): 83–98.

Navin, Thomas R., and Marian V. Sears. "A Study in Merger: Formation of the International Mercantile Company." *Business History Review* 28, no. 4 (December 1954): 291–328.

Perry, Lawrence. "The Head of the International Shipping Corporation." *World's Work* 5, no. 2 (December 1902): 2857–60.

Reeves, Jesse S. "The Jones Act and the Denunciation of Treaties." *American Journal of International Law* 15, no. 1 (January 1921): 33–38.

Roberts, Daniel. "A Navy of Foreigners, Mercenaries, and Amateurs: Naval Enlistment in the Spanish-American War." *International Journal of Naval History* 13, no. 1 (April 2016).

Safford, Jeffrey J. "Edward Hurley and American Shipping Policy: An Elaboration on Wilsonian Diplomacy, 1918–1919." *Historian* 35, no. 4 (August 1973): 568–86.

Sandburg, Carl. "The Face of Andy Furuseth." *La Follette's Magazine* 5, no. 4 (July 12, 1913): 8.

Shaw, Barton C. "The Hobson Craze." *U.S. Naval Institute Proceedings* 102, no. 876 (February 1976): 54–60.

Sheldon, George Willliam. "Old Shipping Merchants of New York." *Harper's New Monthly Magazine* 84, no. 501 (February 1892): 457–71.

Sherman, Constance D. "An Account of the Scuttling of His Majesty's Sloop Liberty." *American Neptune* 20, no. 4 (October 1960): 243–49.

Sloan, Edward W. "Collins versus Cunard: The Realities of a North Atlantic Steamship Rivalry, 1850–1858," *International Journal of Maritime History* 4, no.1 (June 1992): 83–100.

———. "The *Baltic* Goes to Washington: Lobbying for a Congressional Steamship Subsidy, 1852." *Northern Mariner* 5, no. 1 (January 1995): 19–32.

Taylor, Paul S. "Eight Years of the Seamen's Act." *American Labor Legislative Review* 15, no. 1 (March 1925): 52–63.

Tucker, Ray T. "Jones of Washington: A Portrait of the Author of the 'Five-and-Ten' Law." *Outlook and Independent* 152, no. 7 (June 12, 1929): 247–49, 273.

Webb, William Joe. "The United States Wooden Steamship Program during World War I." *American Neptune* 35, no. 4 (October 1975): 275–88.

Whitney, Ralph. "The Unlucky Collins Line." *American Heritage* 7, no. 2 (February 1957): 48–53.

Wildman, Edwin. "Edward N. Hurley: Shipbuilder to Uncle Sam." *Forum* 59, (April 1918): 411–23.

Wolkins, George G. "The Seizure of John Hancock's Sloop 'Liberty.'" Massachusetts Historical Society. *Proceedings: October,1921–June, 1922.* 44 (1923): 239–84.

Wright, Edward Needles. "The Story of Peter Wright & Sons Philadelphia Quaker Shipping Firm 1818–1911." *Quaker History* 56, no. 2 (Autumn 1967): 67–89.

INDEX

Adams, Charles Francis, 97, 101, 102
Adams, John, 1, 17, 29, 31–34, 36, 39, 50, 55, 97
Adams, John Quincy, 68, 97
Adams, Samuel, 38
admiralty courts, 484
Adriatic, SS, 86
Alabama, CSS, 95–99
Alabama Claims Tribunal, 97, 100–101, 268
Alanthus, SS, 445–446
Alaska (Michener), 322, 514
Alaska, coastwise laws and, 6, 152, 158–159, 211–213, 218, 225–226, 348, 364, 411, 487–489, 507–508, 512–514, 517, 543
Alaska Territorial Shipping Board, 487–488
Albany Argus (periodical), 149–150
Albrecht, Emil P., 479
Alden, Philura Deane, 40
Aldrich, Charles H., 394
Alexander, Joshua W., vii, 248–249, 250, 271, 273, 300–302, 344, 352, 361–362, 468, 476–477, 513, 516, 521
Alexander Committee, 270–273
alien exclusion laws, 296–297
Allison, William B., 156–157
American Bureau of Shipping (ABS), 425, 482, 495–496, 510, 516
American Federation of Labor (AFL), 290, 298
American Intercourse Bill (1783), 38
American International Corporation (AIC), 420–428
American Iron and Steel Institute, 383, 390–391
American Line, 138, 184, 262
American Manufacturers' and Exporters' Association, 469
The American Merchant Marine (Marvin), 194
American President Lines, 343
American Relief Administration, 438
American Revolution, 26, 30, 48
American Ship and Commerce Corporation, 185

American Shipping and Industrial League, 134, 189
American Steamship Association, 195
American Steamship Company, 184, 261–262
American Steamship Owners' Association, 525
An American Transport in the Crimean War (Codman), 114
Anti-Saloon League, 223, 326
Arago, SS, 295–296
Arctic, SS, 82, 84–85
Argyle (brig), 114
Arlington Hotel, 113, 116
armed neutrality, 325
Army War College, 198
Arnold, Benedict, 33, 34, 36, 38
Arthur, Chester, 125, 133, 186
Articles of Confederation, 32, 48–50
Asiatic Squadron, 171, 172–174
Aspinwall, William H., 87–90, 97
Atlanta, USS, 187
Atlantic, SS, 82
Atlantic Coast International Seamen's Union, 298
Atlantic Transport Line, 168, 263, 266
The Awakening of Business (Hurley), 392
Bacon, Augustus O., 215
Baker, Bernard N., vii, 168, 263–264, 378–379
Baker, Newton D., vii, 340, 387, 492, 524
Baldwin, George J., 420, 424
Baltic, SS, 82, 83
Baltimore Dry Docks and Shipbuilding Company, 475
Bancroft, Edward, 33, 37, 40
Bankhead, John H., 355, 365, 516
bareboat chartering, 412
Barker, Samuel L., 247
Bates, William B., 136, 139
Bath Iron Works, 411
battleships, 184, 239, 240, 243–244, 251, 398
Benson, William S., vii, 362, 390, 396–400, 478, 481, 492–493, 519–520, 529
Bernard, Francis, 27
Bernstorff, Johann von, 379
Bethlehem Steel Corporation, 417, 447

Bingham, Henry H., 295
Blaine, James G., vii, 124–126, 128
Blanton, Thomas L., 517
Board of Trade, 270, 349
Boer War, 7, 236–237, 541
Borah, William E., 250, 320, 346, 365, 515
Borland, Solon, 83
Boston, USS, 187, 217
Boston Herald (periodical), 195, 261
bounties and bounty bills, 5, 115, 123, 126, 137–138, 188–194
Bowles, Francis T., 424, 426, 432
Brady, John R., 186
Breitung, Edward N., 350–351
Brent, Theodore, 378, 387
The Bridge to France (Hurley), 389, 392
Britain
   Board of Trade, 270, 349
   Boer War, 7, 236–237, 541
   bunkering restrictions, 379–380
   Civil War neutrality violations, 97, 99–101
   commercial treaties, 16, 67–70
   discriminating duties against, 5–6, 15–17, 55–59, 68
   fleet size, 3–4, 95, 236
   Hay-Pauncefote Treaty (1901), 246–247, 249
   Morgan's deal with, 265–266
   Napoleonic Wars, 67
   navigation acts repealed, 131, 507
   neutrality, 97, 99–100, 110, 168, 172–173, 378, 380, 437
   Royal Commission on Shipping Rings, 268–270
   World War I, 398–399
Britannic, HMHS, 266
Brown, Arthur Morgan, 220
Brown, James, 82, 84
Brown, Vernon C., 295
Brown, William, 84
Brown Brothers & Co., 82, 268
Bryan, Jennie Byrd, 395
Bryan, William Jennings, 303, 320
Bulloch, James Dunwoody, 95–99

Bulloch, Martha, 96
Bureau of Navigation, 126, 128, 148, 170
Bureau of War Risk Insurance, 349
Burleson, Albert S., 517
Burroughs, John, 416–417
Burton, Theodore E., 299–300, 353, 356–357
Butler, Benjamin F., 116
Butler v. McClellan, 282
Calcutta Conference, 268
Calder, William M., 444, 480
California, SS, 88
California gold rush, 88, 90, 109
Camden, Johnson N., 355
Campbell, Ira A., vii, 484
Canada, coastwise laws and, 6, 10, 156, 211, 213, 225–227, 364, 412, 488–489, 507, 513–514
Canadian Pacific Railroad, 155–157, 488–489
Cannon, Joe, 477–478
Cannon, Joseph G., 137, 199, 484, 517
Capps, W.L., 388, 412, 421
Captain Ringbolt. see Codman, John
cargo preference
   Cargo Preference Act (1904), 6–7, 237–239, 241, 244, 319
   Panama Canal, 245–246
Carlin, Charles C., 432–433
Carmack, Edward W., 238
Carolina Shipbuilding Co., 421
"Causes of the Reduction of American Tonnage" report, 110–112
Cavalier Parliament, 21
Cervera y Topete, Pascual, 223
Chalmers, George, 38
Chamberlain, Eugene Tyler, vii, 170, 173, 189–194
   birth and early years, 148
   bounty advocacy, 189–190, 193–194
   as Bureau of Navigation commissioner, 20, 139–140, 214–215, 217, 221, 224–225, 305, 344, 349, 361, 380, 490
   and Cleveland, 149–150
   Commerce Committee hearings, 478, 481, 521
   death, 153

discriminating duties opposition, 152
education, 148–149
on Frye, 126
International Convention on Safety of Life at Sea, 301
press career, 149
tolls controversy, 247, 248
Chamberlain, Joshua Lawrence, 148
Chandler, William E., 187
Charles I, 19, 20
Charles II, 20
Charta Maritima, 19
Chelentis v. Luckenbach S.S. Co., 305–306, 511
Chester Shipyard, 414
Chicago, USS, 187
Child, Josiah, 21–22, 58
China, SS, 218–219
China Mail Service investigation, 89
Chinese Exclusion Act (1882), 171
Churchill, Winston, 417
citizenship definition of corporations, 362, 510–511
City of New York, SS, 134, 168, 262
City of Paris, SS, 134, 168, 262
City of Peking, SS, 168, 185
City of Tokyo, SS, 185
Civil War
  British neutrality violations during, 97, 99–101
  effects on U.S.-flag commercial fleet, 4, 95–96, 109–110, 540
  tariffs adopted during, 109
Clark, Champ, 358, 364, 383, 385
Clark, F. Huntington, 380
Clark, John Bates, 385
Clark, William L., vii, 489, 495, 512, 519–520
Clarke, James P., viii, 353, 355, 364
classification of vessels, 109, 482, 510, 515–516
Clay, Alexander S., 193
Clay, Lucius D., 193
Clay, William, 68
Cleveland, Frances, 140
Cleveland, Grover, 123, 133, 138–140, 149–150
Clinton, Bill, 217

Clyde, William P., 136
Clyde River (Scotland), 112–114, 182
Clymer, George, 53
coal shortage, 441
Coast Seamen's Journal (periodical), 289
Coast Seamen's Union, 289–290
coastwise laws
  Alaska and, 6, 152, 158–159, 211–213, 218, 225–226, 348, 364, 411, 487–489, 507–508, 512–514, 517, 543
  Canada and, 6, 10, 156, 211, 213, 225–227, 364, 412, 488–489, 507, 513–514
  Dingley tariff, 155–157
  domestic reservation, 73–75, 211
  foreign-built vessel privileges, 346–348, 411, 474, 491–492, 509
  Hawaii and, 217–221, 490–492
  Jones amendment, 346–348
  Merchant Marine Act provisions, 508–509, 513–514
  Philippines and, 213–217, 489, 506–508, 524
  Ship Purchase Bill amendment, 364–365
  territories and, 167, 474, 495
  tolls controversy, 246–250
  tonnage duties, 2, 3, 59
  U.S.-build requirement, 495
  Wickersham loophole, 158–159, 226–227, 466, 488–489, 495, 512
Cobden, Richard, 97
Coburn, John, 117
Codman, John, viii, 112–116, 118, 128, 132, 135, 136, 183, 186–187, 189–190
Codman, Robert, 113
Cohen, Arthur, 268
Colby, Bainbridge, viii, 388, 417, 467–468, 521–522
Coleridge, Samuel Taylor, 243
Colin H. Livingstone, USS, 433
Colliers (periodical), 466
colliers, use of foreign, 241–242, 244
Collins, Edward Knight, viii, 81–87
Collins Act (1847), 82, 87
Collins Line, 4, 80–87, 123, 268, 477

Commerce Committee, 190, 193, 222, 246, 299–300, 353, 384, 422, 425, 442, 471, 478, 489
commerce raiders, 95–102
Commercial Convention (1815), 16, 67–70
Commission on International Labor Legislation, 442–443
Commissioners of Customs Act (1767), 27
Committee of Detail, 51
Committee on Public Information, 414
concrete vessels, 412, 466
conferences, 7, 260–261, 268–270, 271–273
Congress of the Confederation, 49–54
Constitutional Convention, 50–54, 540
Continental Congress, 30–33
   Committee for Secret Correspondence, 34, 35
   Committee of Secrecy, 34
   Committee on Foreign Affairs, 35–36
Convention Parliament, 20–21
Coolidge, Calvin, 392
Coontz, Robert E., 479–480
corporations
   citizenship definition of, 362, 510–511
   dummy, 489, 493
   social responsibility of, 339–340
Cotopaxi, SS, 114
Cotton, Joseph P., 427, 435
cotton trade, 95
Coudert, Frederick R., 523–524
Council on National Defense, 381
Cox, Samuel S., 129–132, 186–187
Cramp & Sons, 134, 182–185, 194, 263, 411
Cramp, Charles Henry, viii, 118, 136, 182–183, 187, 189
Cramp, Edwin S., 183–184
Cramp, William, 182
Crimean War, 95, 114
crimping system, 284–288
Cromwell, Oliver, 19, 20, 159
Cross, Doris Isabel, 343
Cuba, 213
Culbertson, William S., 522–523
Cummins, Albert R., 347

Cunard, Samuel, 80
Cunard Line, 4, 80, 82–84, 262, 265–266, 268
Curry, Charles F., 345
Cushman, Francis W., 321
Dacia, SMR, 350–351, 437
Dana, Richard Henry, 282–283, 284
Daniels, Josephus, 358, 397–399, 439, 492, 517–518, 521
Daugherty, Henry M., 430–431
Davis, Ewin L., 516
Davis, Jefferson, 86, 396
Dawson, Arthur, 395
De Armond, David A., 224–225
De Kalb, Johann von Robais, 127–128
De Kalb, USS, 127, 381
Dean, Robert Augustus, viii, 476, 493, 520
Deane, Silas, viii, 32, 33–40, 127
Death Valley Days (television series), 130, 287
Declaration Concerning Laws on Naval War (1909), 101, 345, 349
Declaration of Independence, 26, 35
deferred rebate system, 268
Delaware River, shipbuilding industry, 182–188
Delaware River Iron Shipbuilding and Engine Works, 185
Delmonico's, 186
Democratic Party
  credit claimed for Merchant Marine Act, 526
  discriminating duties supported by, 147
  free ships support by, 5, 123
  subsidies opposed by, 5, 123
  tariffs opposed by, 5, 123
  tolls controversy, 249–250
Denman, William, viii, 378–389, 391–392, 420–421
Dewey, George, viii, 170, 171–174, 198, 219, 239, 242
Dickinson, John, 31
Dill, Clarence C., 324
Dingley, Nelson, Jr., viii, 124, 125, 128–133, 136, 156, 159
Dingley Act (1884), 130–133, 295, 299
Dingley Committee, 129–130, 186–187
Dingley Tariff Act (1897), 128, 155–157
discipline, on ships, 282–284

discriminating duties, 5–6, 15–17, 55–59, 68, 147–148, 152, 305, 474, 484, 512, 520–523, 540
"Division of Pictorial Publicity," 414
Dodsworth, A. W., 200–201
Dodsworth, John W., 200–201
Doheny, Edward L., 342
Dollar Steamship Company, 343
Dolphin, USS, 187–188
Dominion Line, 264
Donald, John A., viii, 378, 469, 529
Donlevy, Brian, 284
Doremus, Frank E., 247–249
Downey Shipbuilding Company, 386
Dramatic Line, 81
dredges, 212–213
Drydock Company, 184
Du Pont, Henry A., 323, 357
East India Company, 18, 21
East Indies, trade with, 67–68
economic nationalism, 17
Edge, Frederick Milnes, 99–100
Edge, Walter E., 471, 510, 514
Edison, Thomas, 416
Edmonds, George W., 476–477, 482, 517
Edmunds, George F., 189–194
Edward, 17
Elizabeth I, 1, 18
Elkins, Stephen B., ix, 155–156, 159, 189, 222, 433
Ellsworth, Oliver, 52
Emergency Fleet Corporation, 9–11, 378, 382, 384–389, 410, 431–436, 466, 473–474, 541
Empire Moose, USS, 433
Enricu (ship), 96
entrepôt trade, 19–20, 26
equestrianopathy, 115
Eustis, Frederic A., ix, 380, 383, 385
Evans, Holden A., 475
Fairplay (periodical), 478–479
Falls of Clyde (ship), 220–221
famine relief program, 438–439, 442, 527

Farmers' National Council, 469, 475
Farquhar, John M., ix, 136
Farrell, James A., 349
Federal Reserve Act (1913), 341, 366
Federal Water Power Act (1920), 518, 526
Federalist Paper no. 11, 56–57
Federalist Paper no. 12, 57
Felder, Thomas B., 430–431
Ferguson, Homer L., 484
Ferris, Theodore E., 420
fighting ships, 272–273
Fillmore, Millard, 84
Finker, Edward, 29
Finland, SS, 184, 194
Firestone, Harvey, 416
First Anglo-Dutch War (1652-1654), 20
Fiske, Bradley A., 397
Fithian, George W., ix, 136–137, 138–139
Fitzsimons, Thomas, 59
Five Percent Discount cases, 160
Five-and-Ten Law, 327–328
Fleming, Sarah Hazelhurst, 338
Fletcher, Duncan U., ix, 225, 342, 353–354, 363, 480
flogging, 282–283
Food Administration, 438
Ford, Henry, 416–417
Foreign Commerce Commission, 242–243
Foreign Enlistment Act (1819), 97
Foreign Registry Act (1914), 474, 495
Foreign Relations Committee, 100
foreign-built vessels
   coastwise trading privileges, 346–348, 411, 474, 491–492, 509
   free ships policy, 116–117, 140, 181, 344
   government use of, 237
   reflagging of, 118, 173, 181, 349–350, 378–379
   reliance on, 131
   Ship Purchase Bill, 352–358
   subsidies to, 193, 251, 264
   tonnage tax applied to, 59

U.S. registry of, 111, 132, 135, 169, 173, 190, 192, 194, 218, 250–251, 263, 347, 349
   wrecked vessel exemption, 222
foreign-registered vessels, 3, 8, 73, 101–103
Fornshill, Isabel F., 432
Forsyth, John, 71–72
Fort Ticonderoga, 34
Fortrey, Samuel, 21
"Four Minute Men," 414
France
   Deane Affair, 34–40
   Napoleonic Wars, 67
   Treaty of Alliance with, 32–33, 35
Franco-Prussian War, 118–119, 348
Franklin, Benjamin, 31, 32, 33, 35, 39
Franklin, Philip Albright Small, ix, 266–267, 415, 427–428, 474–475, 478
Fred. Olsen & Co., 378
free ships
   Democrat support for, 5, 123
   foreign-built vessels permitted as, 346–347
   legislation, 138–140
   Maine's opposition to, 124–130
   opposition to by shipyards and owners, 181–182
   Panama Canal Act (1912), 8–9, 250–252
   vs. subsidies, 115–119, 123–124
free trade, 2, 38, 57, 540
   vs. protected trade, 5
   reciprocity, 67–75
French Prize Council, 351
Frye (ship), 127
Frye, William P., ix, 169, 218, 512
   bounty bills, 126, 188–194
   cargo preference legislation, 238
   death, 201
   Dingley Act (1884), 131–132
   legislation to repeal wrecked vessel exemption, 224
   merchant marine committee, 263
   Ocean Mail Act (1891), 134, 137–138
   Panama Canal cargo preference, 245

Senate career, 124–128
  subsidies support, 151, 181
  tariff legislation, 154–155, 159
  tolls controversy, 246–247
Fugitive Slave Act (1793), 281
Furuseth, Andrew, ix, 151, 288–294, 297–298, 300–306, 443, 478, 480, 511, 525
Gaelic Storm (band), 287
Gaines, John W., 222
Gallatin, Abraham Alfonse Albert, ix, 67–69, 72, 74, 199–200
Gallinger, Jacob H., ix, 194–195, 198, 252, 346–348, 353–354, 365
Gallinger Commission. see Merchant Marine Commission (1905)
Galveston (dredge), 213
Garfield, James, 125, 186
General George W. Goethals, SS, 445
George III, 134
Georgie M. Morse, USS, 433
Gérard de Rayneval, Conrad Alexandre, 36
Germany, 10, 82, 134, 238, 325, 350, 359, 379–382, 411, 418, 442
Gerry, Elbridge, 52
Ghost Fleet at Mallows Bay, 444–447
Gibbon, Edward, 39
Gibson, Charles Dana, 414
Globe (ship), 113
Goethals, George Washington, x, 246, 378–389, 391–392, 420–421, 436
Gompers, Samuel, 290
Gore, Thomas P., 357
Grace Line, 87, 90
Graham, William, 86
Grand Trunk Pacific Railway, 488–489
Grant, Ulysses S., 89, 101, 118, 348
Gray, Horace, 395
Grayson, Cary T., 396, 518
Great Lakes Carriers' Association, 304
Great Northern, SS, 184
Great Western, SS, 81

Great White Fleet, 8, 239–244, 541
Greene, William S., x, 250–251, 299, 352, 363, 467, 469, 474–478, 515–516
Greene Bill, 542
Grigsby, George B., 514
Griscom, Clement A., x, 134, 149, 189, 193, 261–267
Grosscup, B.S., 364
Grosvenor, Charles H., 199, 216, 222, 225
Groton Iron Works, 431–432
Guam, 166, 173, 213, 250
Gunston Hall, USS, 433
Guthrie, Connor, 415
Hague Convention (1907), 101
Haines, A. F., 515
Hale, Eugene, x, 116, 238, 243
Hamburg-American Line, 264, 270, 350, 480
Hamilton, Alexander, 15, 51, 56–57
Hancock, John, 26, 27–29
Hancock, Winfield Scott, 186
Hanna, Marcus A., x, 188–194, 263, 529
Harding, Warren G., 150, 395, 412, 422, 425, 430–431, 444, 470, 513, 515, 523, 529–531, 542
Hardwick, Thomas W., 355
Hardy, Rufus, 491–492
Harlan & Wolff, 264
Harlan, John Marshall, 296
Harriman, W. Averell, 185, 187, 420
Harris, Frederic R., 412
Harrison, Benjamin, 31, 123, 125, 133, 138
Harvard University, 148–149, 339, 380
Havermeyer, William F., 186
Hawaii, coastwise laws and, 213, 217–221, 490–492
Hawaiian Chamber of Commerce, 490–491
Hayes, Rutherford, 126
Hay-Pauncefote Treaty (1901), 246–247, 249
Heinl, Robert D., 413–414
Herbert, Hilary A., 136
Hill, David Bennett, 149–150
Hitchcock, Gilbert M., 355
Hobson, Richmond Pearson, 223–224

Hog Island, 383, 419, 420–428
Holm (dredge), 212
Holmes, Oliver Wendell, Sr., 113
Hoover, Herbert, 329, 438–439
Hopkins, Alfred L., 484
House, Edward M., 380
Houston, David F., 517
Howland, John, 87
Hudson & Manhattan Railroad Company (H&M), 339
Hudson Navigation, 431
Huebner, Solomon S., 271–272, 482
Hughes, Charles Evans, 417
Humphrey, William E., x, 158–159, 227, 236, 251, 271, 299, 330, 445, 488
Hurley, Edward Nash, x, 394
   Commerce Committee hearings, 471–473, 478
   merchant marine proposals, 436, 467–470, 484
   The New Merchant Marine, 392, 523
   Shipping Board chairmanship, 388, 389–393, 410–413, 416–417, 428, 440–444
Hutchinson, Thomas, 28
Huus v. New York & Porto Rico Steamship Company, 214, 216
Hyde, Jonathan, 266
Increased Penalties Act (1929), 319, 327–328
Indiana, USS, 184
Industrial Workers of the World (IWW), 293
The Influence of Sea Power upon History (Mahan), 197–198
influenza outbreak, 418
Inman Line, 134, 262
The Innocents Abroad (Twain), 114
Insular Cases, 214
insurance
   associations, 511
   rating of vessels for, 109
   Shipping Board proposals, 482
   war risk, 337, 349
International Convention on Safety of Life at Sea, 153, 301, 321
International Marine Conference, 149, 263
International Mercantile Marine Company (IMM), 7, 90, 184,

193–194, 261, 264, 266–267, 441–442
International Navigation Company (INC), 134, 138, 168, 184, 261–263
International Seamen's Union of America (ISU), 290, 294, 412, 477, 525
Interoceanic Canals Committee, 346
Interregnum, 20–21
Interstate Commerce Commission (ICC), 270–273, 431
Iowa, USS, 184
iron vessels, 4, 84, 95, 96, 109, 110, 182–183, 185
Ismay, J. Bruce, 266–267
Ismay, Thomas H., 264, 266
Isthmian Canal Commission, 245–246
Jackson, Andrew, 69, 75
Japan, 239–240, 242, 416
Jay, John, 39, 50, 55
Jefferson, Thomas, 17, 57, 60–61, 67, 74, 159
John D. Spreckels Bros. Company, 220
Johnson, Albert, 345
Johnson, Andrew, 100
Johnson, Hiram W., 424, 425
Jones, Wesley Livsey, v, x
  and Anti-Saloon League, 223, 326
  birth and early years, 319–320
  "Blacksmith Senator" nickname, 322
  on British shipping dominance, 265
  cargo preference legislation, 6–7, 237–238, 319
  character, 321–323
  coastwise amendment, 346–348
  Commerce Committee bill, 492–496
  Commerce Committee chairmanship, 440, 442, 467, 471, 478, 485–487
  death, 329 330
  debate with Lewis, 321
  defense of Merchant Marine Act, 527
  discriminating duties advocacy, 5–6, 15–17, 147, 159–160, 474, 484, 521–524
  Federal Water Power Act credit, 518, 526
  Five-and-Ten Law sponsorship, 327–328
  foreign sales legislation, 439

free ships support, 250, 252
  government shipping intervention opposition, 9
  legal practice, 320
  legislative career, 319, 322, 324, 329
  marriage and family life, 320
  Merchant Marine Act credit, 518, 526, 543
  merchant marine proposals, 473–474
  neutrality position, 324–325
  Panama Canal toll exemption support, 8
  on Payne, 394
  political philosophies, 323–324
  Prohibition support, 319, 324, 325–329
  reciprocity opposition, 75
  Ship Purchase Bill opposition, 353, 357, 364–365
  state legislative career, 320–321
  subsidy legislation support, 201
  toll exemption support, 250
  war effort support, 325
  "Yakima Jones" nickname, 320
Jones, William A., 215
Jones, William C., 321
Jones Act
  legacy of, 13
  origin of, 487–492
  section 27 of Merchant Marine Act, 6, 75, 524
  section 33 of Merchant Marine Act, 280, 305, 524
  use of term, iv–v
Jones-White Act (1928), 531
"jumping ship," 285–286, 295–296
Kalākaua, 218
Kalaniana'ole, Jonah Kūhiō, 490–491
Kasagi, 184
Kearsarge, USS, 98
Keating, Cletus, 415
Keen's English Chop House, 414
Kelly, James, 287–288
Kennedy, John F., 158
Kern, John W., 303, 344
Keystone Line, 261
King, William H., 508, 510, 512–513

Kirlin, J. Parker, x, 415, 523
Knoxville Street Railroad Company, 338–339
Kroonland, SS, 184, 194
Ku Klux Klan, 157–158, 341
La Follette, Robert M., x, 149, 151–152, 291–292, 298–304, 325, 515
Ladd, Alan, 284
Laird Brothers, 96
Laird Rams project, 97
Lamont, Daniel S., 149
Lansing, Robert, 303, 380
Lasker, Albert D., xi, 529–531
Laurence, John, 57–60
Lee, Arthur, 32, 35–36
Lee, Richard Henry, 30–31, 38, 51
Lee Resolution, 31, 32
Lenroot, Irvine, 423–424, 510
Leviathan, USS, 381–382
Lewis, J. Hamilton, 320–321
Leyland Line, 263–264
Liberty, HMS, 26–30
Liberty Loans program, 341, 475
Life (periodical), 153
Lili'uokalani, 217
Lippman, Walter, 340
Livernash, Edward J., 298
Livingstone, Colin H., 433
Lloyd-George, David, 382
Lloyd's Register, 109, 482
Lockwood, LeGrand, 89
Lodge, Henry Cabot, xi, 15–16, 195, 215–216, 248, 353, 358, 512
London Daily News (periodical), 265
London Declaration (1909), 101, 345, 349
Long, John D., xi, 167, 169, 171–172, 223
"The Lookout Man," 478–479
Louisiana Purchase, 213
Lowndes, William, 72–73
Luce, James F., 84–85
Luce, Stephen B., 197, 198

Lusitania, RMS, 266, 324, 359, 484
Lykes Bros. Steamship Company, 427
Lynch, John, xi, 103, 110, 112, 114, 115–118, 124
Lynch Committee, 110–112, 115–119, 183, 243, 482
Macfarlane, George W., 218–219
Maclay, William, 59–60
Macy, V. Everit, 413
Madeira wine trade, 26–29
Madison, James, 2, 3, 39, 48, 49, 51, 52, 55–56, 57–60, 68, 69, 70–71, 74
Maguire, James G., xi, 291, 294–296
Maguire Act (1895), 295
Mahan, Alfred Thayer, 197–198, 240
mail carriage contracts
    Collins Line, 81–87
    Pacific Mail Steamship Company, 87–90
    subsidies for, 81–90, 123, 125
Maine, shipbuilding industry, 124
Mallory, Stephen, II, 215–216
Mallows Bay Ghost Fleet, 444–447
Malolo, SS, 184
Manila Prize Cases, 174–175
Manson, Philip, 421, 479
Marine Society of New York, 134
Marine Workers' Industrial Union, 294
maritime labor reform movement, 281, 288–294, 297–298. *see also* Seamen's Act (1915)
maritime liens, 484
maritime trade
    British regulation of, 1, 3, 17–22, 26
    discrimination against non-treaty countries, 55–59
    domestic U.S., 2
    effects of war on, 236
    foreign free trade reciprocity, 67–75
    integration between colonies and England, 22
    reciprocal national treatment, 16, 31–33, 38
    tonnage duties, 2, 3, 55–59
    World War I effects on, 337–338, 359
Marsh, Benjamin C., 475, 479
Martin, John A., 152–153, 247

Marvin, Winthrop Lippit, xi, 194–195, 197, 243, 248, 267, 523
Mason, George, 52–53, 433
Massachusetts, USS, 184
Matson, William, 220, 221, 348
Matson Line, 184
Matson Navigation Company, 220, 348, 490
Matsonia, USS, 184
Mauretania, RMS, 266
McAdoo, Cotton & Franklin, 342
McAdoo, Malcolm, 420
McAdoo, Williams Gibbs, Jr., xi, 158, 169, 338–344, 349, 351–352, 356–361, 365, 378–379, 432, 435–436
McCarthy, Charles J., 491
McCumber, Porter J., 238, 346, 512
McKenna, Joseph, 156–157
McKeown, Tom D., 516
McKinley, William, 123, 147, 150, 156–158, 168, 190, 214, 218, 220, 224
McMillin, Benton, 128
Melville, Herman, 114, 284
mercantilism, 17–18, 19, 57
merchant marine (U.S.)
  Benson's promotion of, 399–400
  British competition, 3–4
  Civil War effects on, 4, 109–110
  commerce raiders effect on, 102
  decline of, 4–5
  dominance of, 3
  expansion of, 61
  fleet ownership proposals, 467–470, 541–542
  fleet size, 3, 95, 466
  government subsidies, 4, 5, 7, 80
  government-owned fleet, 9–12
  Hurley's support for, 437–438
  Jefferson's report on importance of, 61
  purpose of, 494
  routes, 527–528
  Spanish-American War effects on, 166–167, 197
  vessels, 3, 6
Merchant Marine Act (1920)

accomplishments of, 543
  aftermath of, 518–531
  changes enacted by, 12–13
  citizenship provision, 514–515
  coastwise provisions, 75, 227, 508–509, 513–514
  Commerce Committee bill, 492–496
  declaration of national purpose, 506
  discriminating duty provision, 160, 512, 520–523
  Greene Bill, 474–478, 492–494
  impetus for, 11
  Jones Act used to refer to, iv–v
  Jones's proposals, 473–474
  mail subsidies, 201
  passage of, 513–518
  as a peace plan, 467
  rail preference provision, 493, 496, 511, 515
  rail preference provision (section 28), 519–520
  seamen injury provisions, 280, 305, 496, 511, 524, 525, 543
  section 25, 482
  section 27, 6, 75, 524–525
  section 28, 519–520, 525, 526
  section 33, 280, 305, 524
  section 34, 520–523
  Senate consideration, 506–513
  Senate hearings (1919), 471–474
  Senate hearings (1920), 478–487
  Shipping Board proposals, 467–470
  vessel classification provision, 482, 510, 515–516
Merchant Marine Act (1928), 319, 329, 531
Merchant Marine Act (1936), 81, 201–202, 283
Merchant Marine Commission (1905), 15, 61, 80, 147, 181, 183, 194–202, 236–238
Merchant Marine Committee, 136–137, 139, 190, 194, 199, 212, 238, 250–251, 271, 299, 301–302, 344, 352, 362, 467–468, 482–484
Merchant Marine League, 200, 242
Merchant Shipbuilding Corporation, 420–421
Merrimac, USS, 169, 221–225
Michener, James, 322, 514

militias, 170
Millerand, Alexandre, 153
Mitchell, John H., 215
Monitor, USS, 183
Monopoly (game), 436
Monroe, James, 17, 49–50, 68
Moody, William H., 226
Morgan, J. Pierpont, xi, 7, 193, 260–261, 263–267, 441
Morgan Iron Works, 185, 187
Morris, Gouverneur, 52
Morris, Robert, 31, 34, 37, 53
Morse, Charles W., xi, 342, 429–436
mortgage legislation, 483–484, 511
Morton, Oliver H.P.T., 88
most favored nation status, 32
Moyers, Bill, 126–127
Mun, Thomas, 18–19
Myrick, N. Sutton, 481–482
Nanshan, SS, 170, 171–175, 222
Napier, Robert, 80
Napoleon Bonaparte, 67
Nation (periodical), 343
National Foreign Trade Council, 349, 363
National Marine League, 391
National Prohibition Act (1919), 326–327
Native American tribes, 34
Naval Affairs Committee, 82
"Naval Auxiliary Merchant Marine" (McAdoo), 360
Naval War College, 168
Navigation Act (March 1, 1817), 3, 6, 19, 48, 69–75
   coastwise reservation, 73–75
   Committee of Detail recommendations, 51–52
   concerns of Southern states, 50–51
   indirect trade prohibition, 71–73
   non-intercourse bill, 72–73
   passenger loophole, 211–212
   port-to-port evasion loopholes, 225–227
   wrecked vessel exemption, 221–225
Navigation Acts (1651/1660), 1, 3, 19–22, 26, 31, 39, 52–53, 58, 70–71, 74, 159

Navy Memorial Museum, 445
Negley, James S., 113, 118
Nelson, Knute, xi, 300, 487, 506–507, 509, 512
Nelson, Minda, 320
Netherlands, 416
neutrality
  armed, 325
  British, 97, 99–100, 110, 172–173, 378, 380, 437
  of *Dacia*, 351, 437
  Dutch, 416
  obligations, 8–9, 127, 324, 354
  purchase of German vessels and, 352, 357–358
  of transferred vessels, 102, 192, 345
Neutrality Proclamation (1861), 97, 99
New Ironsides, USS, 183
The New Merchant Marine (Hurley), 392, 523
New Republic (periodical), 288, 399, 525–526
New York & Cuba Mail Co., 138
New York Herald (periodical), 134, 187
New York Maritime Association, 295
New York Port Authority, 339
New York Shipbuilding Corporation, 184, 420
New York Times (periodical)
  on the *Alabama* sinking, 98
  on Alexander Committee report, 272, 273
  on the *Arctic* sinking, 85
  on Benson, 397
  on Chamberlain, 149
  on Codman, 115, 116, 118, 189
  on the *Dacia*, 350
  on Dingley Tariff, 156
  on Furuseth, 294
  on Goethals, 246
  on Hog Island project, 425
  on Hurley, 391
  on Jones, 327, 329
  on McAdoo, 343–344
  on merchant marine fleet ownership, 191, 467
  on Morgan's British deal, 265
  on Payne, 396

on reflagging law, 140
  on Roach, 186, 188
  on tolls controversy, 249
Newberry, Truman H., 242
Newlands, Francis G., 219, 242–243, 347
Newlands Resolution, 219, 220
Newport News Shipbuilding, 184, 411, 484
Nieuw Amsterdam, SS, 416
Noank Shipyard, 431
North German Lloyd Line, 264, 270, 480
Northern Pacific, SS, 184
Observations on the Commerce of the American States, 38–39
Ocean Mail Act (1891), 6, 123, 124, 126, 133–138, 166, 251, 484, 509
Ocean Steam Navigation Company, 82
Oceanic Steamship Company, 169, 218, 490
O'Gorman, James A., 347, 355
oil supply, 443, 492, 512
Olympia, USS, 172
Order in Council (1783), 39, 49
Oregon, SS, 88
Organic Act (1900), 220–221
Outhwaite, Joseph H., 137
Outlook (periodical), 127
Pacific & Eastern Steamship Company, 421
Pacific, SS, 82, 86
Pacific Mail Steamship Company, 4, 87–90, 123, 138, 168, 185–186, 297, 304, 420–421, 441, 475
Pacific Marine Review (periodical), 476
Pacific Steamship Company, 515, 519
Packwood, Joseph, 29–30
Paine, Thomas, 36
Panama, SS, 88
Panama Canal, 8, 244
Panama Canal Act (1912)
  cargo preference, 245–246
  free ships initiative, 123, 132, 140, 151, 250–252
  rail preference and, 8–9, 90, 273
  tolls controversy, 246–250
Panama Canal Railway, 87–88

Paris Economic Conference, 363
Paris Peace Conference, 440–444
Passenger Vessel Services Act (PVSA), 212
Payne, John Barton, xii, 389–390, 393–396, 399, 469–470, 478, 484–486, 518, 522
Payne, Sereno E., xii, 188–194, 226, 345
Pendleton, Fields S., 484
Pennsylvania Railroad Company, 184, 261
Perry, George D., 445
Pershing, John, 480
Persia, SS, 86
Peter Wright & Sons, 261–262, 270–271
Pettigrew, Richard F., 221
Petty, William, 37–38
Philadelphia Inquirer (periodical), 140, 426
Philadelphia Packet (periodical), 36
Philippine Autonomy Act (1916), 215
Philippine Commission, 216–217
Philippine Organic Act (1902), 215, 216
Philippines
   coastwise laws and, 213–217, 489, 506–508, 524
   U.S. maritime laws and, 15
   as a U.S. territory, 6–7
Phillips, David Graham, 126–127
Pierce, Franklin, 85
Piez, Charles A., xii, 412, 417, 423, 428, 432, 442, 444
Pinckney, Charles Cotesworth, 53
"Plan of Treaties" (1776), 1
Poindexter, Miles, 515
Ponzi, Carlo, 430
Port Authority Trans-Hudson (PATH), 339
port-to-port evasions, 225–227
Post Office Appropriation Act (1885), 124, 133
Post Office Committee, 83
Potomac Electric Power Company, 447
Powell, J. W., 523
Price, Vincent, 344
Prinz Eitel Friedrich, SS, 127
Profiles in Courage (Kennedy), 158
Profiles in Courage (television show), 157–158

Prohibition, 319, 324, 325–328, 341
Puerto Rico, 213
Quaker City, USS, 114
Queen Frederica, SS, 184
Quistconck, SS, 425–426
rail preference, 493, 496, 511, 515, 519–520, 542
Randolph, Edmund, 39, 49, 53
rate wars, 260–261, 267. *see also* conferences
Raymond, Henry H., 415, 525
Reagan, Ronald, 130
reciprocal national treatment, 16, 31–33, 38
Reciprocity Act (1817), 74
Red "D" Line, 138
Red Star Line, 194, 262
Redfield, William C., xii, 300, 360, 437, 441
Reed, James A., 357, 509
reflagging prohibition, 102–103, 251
Reid, William, 29
Reinhardt, J. H. Phillip, 434
Republican Party
   credit claimed for Merchant Marine Act, 526–527
   discriminating duties supported by, 147
   subsidies supported by, 123–124
   tariffs supported by, 5
The Resolution for Independence, 31
Reventlow, Ernst von, 242
Revenue Act (1864), 111
Revenue Act (1913), 128, 157–160
Revenue Act (1918), 511
Ricardo, David, 19
Ricardo, Osman, 19
Richard II, 17, 400
Richards, John K., 156
Riggs, Thomas, Jr., 488
The Rime of the Ancient Mariner (Coleridge), 243
Rivington Royal Gazette (periodical), 37
Roach & Sons, 185–188
Roach, John, xii, 123, 125, 133, 185–188
Roach, John Baker, 187
Romney, HMS, 27–28

Roosevelt, Franklin D., 201, 343, 388
Roosevelt, Theodore, 8, 95, 123, 148–149, 150, 167, 171, 190, 194, 199, 325, 430, 490
  and the Great White Fleet, 239–244
  Panama Canal cargo preference, 245–246
Root, Elihu, xii, 198–199, 238, 252, 354
Rosseter, John H., xii, 441, 454, 472, 475, 486–487, 511
Rowe, Frederick W., 363
Rowe Bill, 476–477, 511
Royal Commission on Shipping Rings, 268–270
Rublee, George, 392
Rump Parliament, 19
Russell, Earl, 99, 102
Ruth, Babe, 414
Rutledge, John, 53, 54
S-5, USS, 445
Sailor's Life and Sailor's Yarns (Codman), 114
Sailor's Union of the Pacific (SUP), 290–291, 293–294, 296, 304
Sally (sloop), 29–30
Sampson (tug), 182
Sampson, William T., 149, 223
San Francisco Chronicle (periodical), 418
Sandburg, Carl, 293
Saratoga, Battle of, 35
Saulsbury, Willard, Jr., 347
Schenck, Robert C., 118
Schley, Winfield Scott, 223
Schwab, Charles M., xii, 417–418, 428, 434, 436, 475, 530
Scientific American (periodical), 243–244, 387
Scott, Frank D., 491
Scott, Thomas A., 486
Sea Magna Charta, 19
seamen
  Chinese, 296–297
  crimping system and, 284–288
  injury provisions in Merchant Marine Act, 280, 305, 496, 511, 524, 525, 543
  labor reform movement, 288–294, 297–298
  legal treatment of, 280

special status of, 280–284
  union organization by, 7, 288, 290
Seamen's Act (1915), 7, 11–12, 90, 282–283, 293–306, 323–324, 362, 442–443, 476–477, 480–481, 511
Seamen's Journal (periodical), 289
Search, Theodore C., 189
Seattle Chamber of Commerce, 520
segregation, 323, 341
Selective Service Act (1917), 325
Semmes, Raphael, 98–99
Seven Years' War, 27, 31
Seward, Charles, 84
Shakespeare (ship), 81
"Shanghai Kelly" (song), 287–288
"shanghaiing," 284, 287–288
Sheffield, John Baker Holroyd, 38–39
Sherman, John, 88–89, 201
Sherman, Roger, 53
Sherman Anti-Trust Act, 271, 347
Ship Mortgage Act (1920), 511, 524
Ship Purchase Bill, 338, 351–352, 421. *see also* Shipping Act (1916)
  strong-arm phase, 352–358
  war preparedness and compromise phase, 358–366
Ship Registry Act (1914), 8–9, 10, 123, 341, 344–351, 481
shipbuilding industry
  Britain, 182
  Clyde River (Scotland), 112–114, 182
  Delaware River, 182–188
  Emergency Fleet Corporation mobilization of, 410–419
  free materials legislation, 250, 252
  Hog Island, 383, 419, 420–428
  labor force, 412–415
  Maine, 124
  wooden vessel controversy, 378–389
  during World War I, 363
Shipbuilding Labor Adjustment Board, 413
Shipping Act (1916), 7, 9, 15, 112, 365–366, 473, 510–511. *see also* Ship Purchase Bill
shipping articles agreements, 280–281

Shipping Commissioners Act (1872), 290
Shipping Control Committee, 415
Shomette, Donald G., 447
Silas Deane Highway, 33
Silas Deane Middle School, 33
Simmons, Furnifold McL., 364–365
Sims, William S., 398–399
sinking ships
  Alabama, 98–99
  Arctic, 84–85
  by Germans, 365, 386
  Lusitania, 324, 359
  Merrimac, 224
  Pacific, 86
  Titanic, 7, 266
  William P. Frye, 127, 349
Sirius, SS, 81
slavery, 2, 52–53
Slayden, James L., 237–238
Slocum, Henry Warner, 131–133
Smith, Adam, 22
Smith, Samuel, 72
Smith, William, 59
Snow, Ambrose, 134, 136
Société Anonyme de Navigation Belgo-Américaine, 261
Society of Naval Architects and Marine Engineers (SNAME), 262
Solveig (ship), 222
Sousa, John Philip, 414
South Carolina, USS, 184
Southern Pacific Railroad, 90
Spanish-American War, 6, 134, 138, 166–171, 184, 189, 197, 213, 236, 359, 541
Sperry, Charles S., 242
Spight, Thomas, 199, 298–299
Spreckels, Claus, 169, 218
Spreckels Line, 490
Springer, William M., 138
St. Louis, SS, 134, 139–140, 168, 184, 190, 263
St. Paul, SS, 134, 140, 168, 184, 190, 263

Standard Oil Co., 350
Steamship Sailor's Union, 290
steamships, 81–83, 86, 96–97, 110
Steenerson, Halvor, 200
Stevens, Raymond B., xii, 380, 382, 385, 388, 441, 469–470, 486, 523
Stimson, Henry L., 430
Stone & Webster, 424
Stone, Charles A., 425
Stone, William J., 250, 355–356
Strawn, Silas, 396
Submarine Boat Corporation, 420
subsidies
   bounties, 5, 115, 126, 137–138, 188–194
   bribery accusations during legislative consideration of, 200–201
   compared to socialism, 137, 192
   Democrat opposition to, 5, 123
   vs. free ships, 115–119, 123–124
   historically, 80
   Lynch Committee report on, 110–112
   mail carriage contracts, 81–90, 123, 125
   Merchant Marine Commission, 194–202
   Republican support for, 5, 123–124
   subventions as, 196–197
   support for by shipyards and owners, 181–182
subventions, 5, 196–197
Sugar Act (1764), 27, 29
Sumner, Charles, 100
Sutphen, Henry R., 420
Tacoma Chamber of Commerce, 519
Taft, William H., 123, 150, 199–200, 216, 245–246, 249, 300, 430
Tariff Act (1883), 154
Tariff Act (1890), 154
Tariff Act (1894), 154–155
tariffs, 5, 60, 109, 123, 154
taxes
   British enforcement of, 27–30
   colonial evasion of, 27

export, 52
import duties, 5–6, 15–17, 49, 55
on importation of slaves, 52
Revenue Act (1864), 111
tonnage duties, 2, 3, 55–59
Taylor, Robert, 287
Taylor, Stevenson, 425, 482
Ten Months in Brazil (Codman), 114
territories
coastwise laws and, 474, 495
as domestic trade, 6, 152
shipping services to, 167
Texas (dredge), 212
Thomas, Charles S., 507–508
Thorne v. White, 282
Time Magazine, 395
Titanic (film), 287
Titanic, RMS, 7, 153, 266–267, 300
tolls, 246–250
tonnage bills, 134–137
tonnage duties, 2, 3, 55–59
Toombs, Robert A., 86
tramp carriers, 183, 204, 260, 269, 363
The Treason of the Senate series (Phillips), 126–127
Treaty of Alliance (1778), 32, 35, 36
Treaty of Ghent (1814), 16, 67
Treaty of Paris (1898), 214, 216
Treaty of Washington (1871), 100–101, 225
Treaty of Westminster (1654), 20
Trumbull, John, 34
Tumulty, Joseph P., 304, 391
Turner, George, 192–193
Twain, Mark, 114
Twenty Years of Congress (Blaine), 125–126
Two Years before the Mast (Dana), 282, 286
Two Years before the Mast (film), 284
Under the Maples (Burroughs), 417
Underwood, Oscar W., xii, 147, 157–160, 227, 340–341, 344–345, 488, 509, 518
Underwood Tariff Act (1913), 5–6, 227

unions, 7, 288, 290, 293
United Fruit Co., 350
United States Lines Co., 267
University of Notre Dame, 392–393
Urgent Deficiencies Act, 384, 386
U.S. Army, 169, 170, 414, 436–437, 480
U.S. Bureau of Navigation, 20
U.S. Chamber of Commerce, 236, 357, 360, 381, 481, 527
U.S. Coast Guard, iv
U.S. Congress, first convening of, 2, 54–55
U.S. Constitution
  adoption of, 2
  article VI, 55
  commerce power, 52, 55–56
  Eighteenth Amendment, 326–327, 341
  federal admiralty court jurisdiction, 484
  Thirteenth Amendment, 296
U.S. Customs, 226
U.S. Department of Commerce, 304–305
U.S. Department of Justice, 424–427, 435
U.S. Department of State, 512
U.S. Department of the Treasury, 12, 95, 102–103, 337
U.S. House of Representatives
  first convening of, 55
  Merchant Marine Committee, 136–137, 139, 190, 194, 199, 212, 238, 250–251, 271, 299, 301–302, 344, 352, 362, 467–468, 482–484
  Post Office Committee, 83
  Ways and Means Committee, 89
U.S. Maritime Commission, 343
U.S. Navy, 87, 414
  Auxiliary Naval Force, 168–170, 348, 359
  Bureau of Equipment, 241
  Bureau of Navigation, 126, 128, 148, 170
  foreign citizens in, 170–171, 481
  interest in establishment of merchant marine, 479–480
  Spanish-American War planning, 167–171
U.S. Senate
  Commerce Committee, 190, 193, 222, 246, 299–300, 353, 384, 422, 425, 442, 471, 478, 489

consideration of Merchant Marine Act, 506–513
first convening of, 55
Foreign Relations Committee, 100
Merchant Marine Act hearings (1919), 471–474
Merchant Marine Act hearings (1920), 478–487
pairing of votes in, 356
Philippines Committee, 15
U.S. Shipping Board
  congressional scrutiny of, 412, 422–425, 512–513
  demobilization, 436–444
  Department of Justice investigation, 424–427
  Emergency Fleet Corporation, 9–11, 378, 382, 384–389, 410, 431–432, 433–436, 466, 473–474, 541
  establishment of, 9–11
  and Ghost Fleet at Mallows Bay, 444–447
  Harding's Board nominations, 529–531
  insurance proposals, 482
  Jones's proposals, 473–474
  merchant marine proposals, 467–470
  mobilization, 184, 410–419, 541
  on Navigation Act (March 1, 1817), 69–70
  reasons for lack of post-Civil War recovery for U.S.-flag fleet, 109–110
  sale of vessels, 494, 528–529
  shipyards authorized by, 420–428
  vessel acquisition authorization, 361–363
  Virginia Shipbuilding Corporation investigation, 342, 429–436
  Wilson's Board nominations, 378, 388, 391
  wooden vessel controversy, 378–389, 444–445
U.S. Steel Corporation, 349
U.S. Steel Products Co., 350
U.S. Supreme Court
  Arago case, 295–296
  Chelentis v. Luckenbach S.S. Co., 305–306, 511
  on connection between crew and vessel's master, 280
  Five Percent Discount cases, 160
  Huus v. New York & Porto Rico Steamship Company, 214, 216
  Insular Cases, 214

Manila Prize Cases, 174–175
Osceola case, 305
rate coordination antitrust case, 267
Utah, USS, 397
Vance, Zebulon B., 132–133
Vanderbilt, Aaron, 189
Vanderbilt, Alfred Gwynne, 359
Vanderbilt, Cornelius, 359, 519
Vanderbilt, Cornelius, Jr., 519
Vardaman, James K., 355, 365, 422, 425
Vaterland, SS, 381
vessel transfers, 344–351, 361, 379
vessels
  classification of, 109, 482, 510, 515–516
  iron, 4, 84, 95, 96, 109, 110, 182–183, 185
  mortgages, 483–484, 511
  sales legislation, 494
  steamships, 81–83, 86, 96–97, 110
  U.S. dependence on foreign, 7–8
  U.S.-flag, iv, vi, 236, 411–412
  wooden, 3–4, 10–11, 80–88, 95, 99, 109, 124, 182–183, 378–389, 444–445, 466, 540
Vest, George G., xiii, 53, 124, 129–130, 135–136, 151, 189, 192–194
Vesta, SS, 84
Victoria, 97, 99, 113
Vilas, William F., 133
Virginia Shipbuilding Corporation (VSC), 342, 419, 429–436
Volstead Act, 326–327, 341
Walsh, Joseph, xiii, 422
Walsh Committee, 422, 435, 530
War Department, 169, 170, 215–216, 237, 414, 416, 480
War Industries Board, 415
War of 1812, 2, 16, 67, 283
war risk insurance, 337, 349
War Risk Insurance Act (1914), 349
War Trade Board, 416
Washington, Booker T., 323
Washington, George, 26–27, 35, 55, 57, 59, 60, 134
Washington Naval Treaty (1922), 184

Ways and Means Committee, 89
Webb-Dean-Stevens Museum, 33
Weeks, John W., 348
Weeks-Gore bill, 357–358
Welles, Gideon, 97
Wells, David A., 54, 481
Wells, Erastus, 115–116
Wells, Ida B., 289
Wescott, William A., 481
West Indies, trade with, 1, 2, 38–39, 53, 68–69, 70
Western Marine and Salvage Company, 445–446
Wettrick, S. J., 520
Wheaton, Henry, 72
Wheeler, Joseph, 136–137
White, John B., 378, 387
White, Stephen M., 296
White Act (1898), 296
White Star Line, 7, 262, 264, 266
whitewashed tramps, 183, 224
Wickersham, George W., 158, 226–227, 488, 514
Wickersham, James, xiii, 159
Wilhelm II, 99
William P. Frye, SS, 127, 349
William Penn, SS, 114
Williams, John S., 251–252, 346
Wilson (film), 344
Wilson, Edith, 425–426, 433, 492
Wilson, Eleanor, 342, 343
Wilson, Ellen Louise Axson, 346
Wilson, James, 52
Wilson, James H., 396
Wilson, William B., xiii, 298–300
Wilson, Woodrow, 150, 323, 325, 417, 433
   famine relief program, 438–439, 442
   foreign sales opposition, 439–440
   and McAdoo, 340–342
   Merchant Marine Act signing, 517–518, 521–522
   naming of *De Kalb*, 127–128
   Paris Peace Conference, 440–444
   Seamen's Act signing, 300–304

Ship Purchase Bill, 15, 353–361
Ship Registry Act, 344, 348, 351
Shipping Act (1916), 365–366
tolls controversy, 249–250
Underwood Tariff Act signing, 157
U.S. Shipping Board, 378–389, 391
Wilson administration, 9, 11, 123
Wilson-Lloyd-George Agreement, 442
Winter Sketches from the Saddle (Codman), 115
women's suffrage, 323
Wood, Fernando, 116
wooden vessels, 3–4, 10–11, 80–88, 95, 99, 109, 124, 182–183, 378–389, 444–445, 466, 540
World War I, 8–10, 61, 101, 127, 138, 170, 184, 236, 244, 265, 337–338, 359, 363, 398–399, 418–419, 436–437, 541–542
World War II, 127, 184
wrecked vessels, 221–225
Wright, James A., 261
Wright, Peter, 261
Wrigley, William, Jr., 529
Wyse, Mary Augusta, 396–397
Yamamoto, Gomel, 239–240
Yates, Richard, 516–517
Zafiro, SS, 171–175
Zanuck, Darryl F., 344
Zealandia (ship), 169

www.ingramcontent.com/pod-product-compliance
Lightning Source LLC
Chambersburg PA
CBHW060350190426
43201CB00044B/1914